Linux+ Guide to Linux Certification

Kathryn Evans

Linux+ Guide to Linux Certification
Third Edition

Jason W. Eckert

COURSE TECHNOLOGY
CENGAGE Learning

Australia • Brazil • Japan • Korea • Mexico • Singapore • Spain • United Kingdom • United States

COURSE TECHNOLOGY
CENGAGE Learning™

**Linux+ Guide to Linux Certification,
Third Edition**
Jason W. Eckert

Vice President, Editorial, Career Education &
Training Solutions: Dave Garza

Director of Learning Solutions: Matthew Kane

Acquisitions Editor: Nick Lombardi

Managing Editor: Marah Bellegarde

Product Manager: Natalie Pashoukos

Developmental Editors: Ann Shaffer,
Kent Williams

Editorial Assistant: Sarah Pickering

Vice President, Marketing, Career Education &
Training Solutions: Jennifer Ann Baker

Marketing Director: Deborah S. Yarnell

Senior Marketing Manager: Erin Coffin

Associate Marketing Manager: Shanna Gibbs

Production Manager: Andrew Crouth

Content Project Manager: Brooke Greenhouse

Senior Art Director: Jack Pendleton

Manufacturing Coordinator: Amy Rogers

Technical Edit/Quality Assurance: Green Pen
Quality Assurance, LLC

Compositor: PreMediaGlobal

Library of Congress Control Number: 2010941575

ISBN-13: 978-1-4188-3721-1

ISBN-10: 1-4188-3721-0

Course Technology
20 Channel Center
Boston, MA 02210
USA

Cengage Learning is a leading provider of customized learning solutions with office locations around the globe, including Singapore, the United Kingdom, Australia, Mexico, Brazil, and Japan. Locate your local office at **international.cengage.com/region**.

Cengage Learning products are represented in Canada by Nelson Education, Ltd.

For your lifelong learning solutions, visit **course.cengage.com**.

Purchase any of our products at your local college store or at our preferred online store **www.cengagebrain.com**.

Printed in the United States of America
3 4 5 6 7 15 14 13

Brief Table of Contents

Table of Contents

Introduction

"In a future that includes competition from open source, we can expect that the eventual destiny of any software technology will be to either die or become part of the open infrastructure itself."

Eric S. Raymond, *The Cathedral and the Bazaar*

As Eric S. Raymond reminds us, Open Source Software will continue to shape the dynamics of the computer software industry for the next long while, just as it has for the last decade. Coined and perpetuated by hackers, the term "Open Source Software" refers to software in which the source code is freely available to anyone who wants to improve it (usually through collaboration). And, of course, at the heart of the Open Source Software movement lies Linux, an operating system whose rapid growth has shocked the world by demonstrating the nature and power of the open source model.

However, as Linux continues to grow, so must the number of Linux-educated users, administrators, developers, and advocates. Thus, we find ourselves at a time when Linux education is of great importance to the information technology industry. Key to demonstrating one's Linux ability is the certification process. This book, *Linux+ Guide to Linux Certification,* uses carefully constructed examples, questions, and practical exercises to give readers the necessary information to achieve Linux+ (Powered by LPI) certification from CompTIA. Whatever your ultimate goal, you can be assured that reading this book in combination with study, creativity, and practice will make the open source world come alive for you, as it has for many others.

The Intended Audience

Simply put, this book is intended for those who want to learn the Linux operating system and master the Linux+ certification exam from CompTIA (Powered by LPI). It does not assume any prior knowledge of Linux. Also, the topics introduced in this book and the certification exam are geared toward systems administration, yet they are also well suited for those who will use or develop programs for Linux systems.

Chapter Descriptions

Chapter 1, "Introduction to Linux," introduces operating systems as well as the features, benefits, and uses of the Linux operating system. This chapter also discusses the history and development of Linux and Open Source Software.

Chapter 2, "Linux Installation and Usage," outlines the procedures necessary for the preparation and installation of Linux on a typical computer system. This chapter also describes how to interact with a Linux system via a terminal and enter basic commands into a Linux shell, such as those commands used to obtain help and properly shut down the system.

Chapter 3, "Exploring Linux Filesystems," outlines the Linux filesystem structure and the types of files that can be found within it. This chapter also discusses commands that can be used to view and edit the content of those files.

Chapter 4, "Linux Filesystem Management," covers the commands you can use to locate and manage files and directories on a Linux filesystem. This chapter also outlines the different methods used to link files as well as how to interpret and set file and directory permissions.

Chapter 5, "Linux Filesystem Administration," discusses how to create, mount, and manage filesystems in Linux. This chapter also discusses the various filesystems available for Linux systems and the device files that are used to refer to the devices that may contain these filesystems.

Chapter 6, "Advanced Installation," introduces advanced storage concepts and configurations that may prove useful when installing Linux. This chapter also discusses alternative methods for installing Linux, common problems that may occur during installation, and the System Rescue feature of the Linux installation media.

Chapter 7, "Working with the BASH Shell," covers the major features of the BASH shell, including redirection, piping, variables, aliases, and environment files. This chapter also details the syntax of basic shell scripts.

Chapter 8, "System Initialization and X Windows," covers the different boot loaders that may be used to start the Linux kernel and dual boot the Linux operating system with other operating systems, such as Windows. This chapter also discusses how daemons are started during system initialization as well as how to start and stop them afterward. Finally, this chapter discusses the structure of Linux graphical user interfaces as well as their configuration and management.

Chapter 9, "Managing Linux Processes," covers the different types of processes as well as how to view their attributes, change their priority, and kill them. This chapter also discusses how to schedule processes to occur in the future using various utilities.

Chapter 10, "Common Administrative Tasks," details three important areas of system administration: printer administration, log file administration, and user administration.

Chapter 11, "Compression, System Backup, and Software Installation," describes utilities that are commonly used to compress and back up files on a Linux filesystem. This chapter also discusses how to install software from source code as well as how to use the Red Hat Package Manager (RPM).

Chapter 12, "Network Configuration," introduces networks, network utilities, and TCP/IP as well as how to configure TCP/IP on a NIC or PPP interface. This chapter also details the configuration of name resolution and common networking services and discusses the technologies you can use to administer Linux servers remotely.

Chapter 13, "Configuring Network Services," explores the detailed configuration of key infrastructure, Web, file sharing, e-mail, and database network services. More specifically, this chapter examines the structure and configuration of DHCP, DNS, NTP, NIS, FTP, NFS, Samba, Apache Web server, Sendmail, Postfix, and PostgreSQL services.

Chapter 14, "Troubleshooting, Performance, and Security," discusses the system maintenance cycle as well as good troubleshooting procedures for solving hardware and software problems. This chapter also describes utilities you can use to monitor and pinpoint the cause of performance problems, as well as utilities and procedures you can use to secure the Linux system against unauthorized access.

Additional information is contained in the appendices at the end of the book. **Appendix A** discusses the certification process, with emphasis on the Linux+ (Powered by LPI) certification. It also explains how the objective list for the Linux+ (Powered by LPI) certification matches each chapter in the textbook. **Appendix B** provides a copy of the GNU General Public License. **Appendix C** explains how to find Linux resources on the Internet and lists some common resources by category.

Features

To ensure a successful learning experience, this book includes the following pedagogical features:

- *Chapter objectives*—Each chapter begins with a detailed list of the concepts to be mastered within that chapter. This list provides you with a quick reference to the contents of the chapter as well as a useful study aid.

- *Illustrations and tables*—There are numerous illustrations of server screens and components that aid you in the visualization of common setup steps, theories, and concepts. In addition, there are many tables that provide details and comparisons of both practical and theoretical information and that can be used for a quick review of topics.

- *End-of-chapter material*—The end of each chapter includes the following features to reinforce the material covered in the chapter:

  - **Chapter Summary:** A bulleted list that gives a brief but complete summary of the chapter

  - **Key Terms list:** A list of all new terms and their definitions

  - **Review Questions:** A list of review questions that test your knowledge of the most important concepts covered in the chapter

  - **Hands-On Projects:** Projects that help you apply the knowledge gained in the chapter

  - **Discovery Exercises:** Additional projects that guide you through real-world scenarios and advanced topics

New to This Edition

This edition has been updated to include the concepts and procedures tested on the latest CompTIA Linux+ (Powered by LPI) certification. More specifically, this edition contains the following:

- Updated information pertinent to the latest Linux distributions

- Coverage of new storage technologies, such as LVM and ext4

- New and expanded material on key job-related networking services, including FTP, NFS, Samba, Apache, DNS, DHCP, NTP, Sendmail, Postfix, X, SSH, VNC, and SQL

- New and expanded material on security practices and technologies

Text and Graphic Conventions

Wherever appropriate, additional information and exercises have been added to help you better understand what is being discussed in the chapter. Icons throughout the text alert you to additional materials. The icons in this textbook are used as follows:

The Note icon indicates additional helpful material related to the subject being described.

Each Activity in this book is preceded by the Hands-On icon.

CertBlaster Test Preparation

Linux+ Guide to Linux Certification includes CertBlaster test preparation questions that mirror the look and feel of the CompTIA Linux+ (Powered by LPI) certification exam. For additional information on the CertBlaster test preparation questions, go to *http://www.dtipublishing.com*. To log in and access the CertBlaster test preparation questions for CompTIA's Linux+ (Powered by LPI) Certification exam, please visit *ftp://ftp.certblaster.com/1/Course/c_linux+09.exe*.

Please follow these directions to install and launch your CertBlaster application:

1. Click the title of the CertBlaster you want to download.
2. Save the program (.EXE) file to a folder on your C: drive. (Warning: If you skip this step, your CertBlaster will not install correctly.)
3. Click Start and choose Run.
4. Click Browse and then navigate to the folder that contains the .EXE file. Select the .EXE file and click Open.
5. Click OK and then follow the on-screen instructions. To complete the installation, you will need the CertBlaster access code. The access code can be found inside the card located in the back of your textbook.
6. When the installation is complete, click Finish.
7. Click Start, choose All Programs, and click CertBlaster.

Fedora 13 DVD

The DVD that accompanies this textbook is a 32-bit copy of the Fedora 13 operating system. You can use this DVD to install the Linux operating system on your PC so that you can complete the exercises within each chapter.

Student Resources

To access additional materials (including CourseMate, described in the next section), please visit *www.cengagebrain.com*. At the *CengageBrain.com* home page, search for the ISBN of your title (from the back cover of your book) using the search box at the top of the page. This will take you to the product page for your book, where you will be able to access these resources.

CourseMate

The CourseMate that accompanies *Linux+ Guide to Linux Certification* helps you make the grade. It includes the following:

- An interactive eBook, with highlighting, note taking, and search capabilities
- Interactive learning tools, including:
  - Quizzes
  - Flash cards
  - PowerPoint slides
  - Glossary
  - And more!

- CourseMate Printed Access Code (ISBN 1-1115-4163-9)
- CourseMate Instant Access Code (ISBN 1-1115-4162-0)

Companion Lab Manual

The Lab Manual provides you with the hands-on instruction necessary to prepare for the certification exam. Designed for classroom-led or self-paced study, labs complement main text content and offer a unique, practical approach to learning that is a key component to the exams. The Lab Manual includes lab activities, objectives, materials lists, step-by-step procedures, illustrations, and review questions.

- Lab Manual (ISBN 1-1115-4155-8)

Web-Based Labs

Web-Based Labs provide an actual real-life Linux lab environment over the Internet. With step-by-step labs based on the hands-on projects in the main text, you can log on anywhere, anytime via a Web browser to gain essential hands-on experience with the actual Linux operating system.

- Web-Based Labs (ISBN 1-1115-4156-6)

Course Notes

This six-panel quick reference card reinforces the critical knowledge related to Linux+ and the CompTIA Linux+ (Powered by LPI) certification exam in a visual and user-friendly format. Course Notes will serve as a great reference tool during the course and afterward.

- Course Notes (ISBN 1-1115-4157-4)

Instructor's Materials

A wide array of instructor's materials is provided with this book.

Instructor Resources CD

The Instructor Resources CD includes the following materials (also available online at *www.cengage.com*):

- *Electronic instructor's manual*—This manual contains additional material to assist in class preparation, including suggestions for classroom activities, discussion topics, and additional activities.
- *Solutions*—You are provided with solutions to all the end-of-chapter material, including review questions, hands-on projects, and discovery exercises.
- *PowerPoint presentations*—Microsoft PowerPoint slides are provided for each chapter. They're included as a teaching aid for classroom presentation and can be made available to students on the network, for chapter review, or printed out for classroom distribution. Instructors, feel free to add your own slides for additional topics you introduce to the class.

- *ExamView®*—ExamView®, the ultimate tool for objective-based testing needs, is a powerful test generator that enables instructors to create paper-, LAN-, or Web-based tests from test banks designed specifically for their Cengage Course Technology text. Instructors can utilize the ultraefficient QuickTest Wizard to create tests in less than five minutes by taking advantage of Cengage Course Technology's question banks, or they can create their own exams from scratch.

- *Figure files*—All figures and tables in the book are reproduced on the Instructor Resources CD in bitmap format. Similar to the PowerPoint presentations, these are included as a teaching aid for classroom presentation and can be made available to students for review or printed out for classroom distribution.

  o Instructor Resources CD (ISBN 1-1115-4158-2)

Blackboard and WebCT WebTutor

WebTutor for Blackboard and WebCT is a content-rich, Web-based teaching and learning aid that reinforces and clarifies complex concepts while integrating into your Blackboard or WebCT course. The WebTutor platform also provides rich communication tools for instructors and students, making it much more than an online study guide. Features include PowerPoint presentations, practice quizzes, and more, organized by chapter and topic.

- Blackboard WebTutor (ISBN 1-1115-4159-0)
- WebCT WebTutor (ISBN 1-1115-4160-4)

dtiMetrics

dtiMetrics is an online testing system that automatically grades students and keeps class and student records. dtiMetrics tests against Cengage's textbook as well as against the CompTIA Linux+ (Powered by LPI) certification exam, including a quiz for each chapter in the book along with a mid term and final exam. dtiMetrics is managed by the classroom instructor, who has 100 percent of the control, 100 percent of the time. It is hosted and maintained by dtiPublishing.

- dtiMetrics (ISBN 1-1115-4164-7)

LabConnection

LabConnection provides powerful computer-based exercises, simulations, and demonstrations for hands-on, skills courses such as this. It can be used as both a virtual lab and as a homework assignment tool, and it provides automatic grading and student record maintenance. LabConnection maps directly to the textbook and provides remediation to the text and to the CompTIA Linux+ (Powered by LPI) certification exam. It includes the following features:

- *Enhanced comprehension*—Through the LabConnection labs and guidance, while in the virtual lab environment, the student develops skills that are accurate and consistently effective.

- *Exercises*—Lab Connection includes dozens of exercises that assess and prepare the learner for the virtual labs, establishing and solidifying the skills and knowledge required to complete the lab.

- *Virtual labs*—Labs consist of end-to-end procedures performed in a simulated environment where the student can practice the skills required of professionals.

- *Guided learning*—LabConnection allows learners to make mistakes but alerts them to errors made before they can move on to the next step, sometimes offering demonstrations as well.
- *Video demonstrations*—Instructor-led video demonstrations guide the learners step-by-step through the labs while providing additional insights to solidify the concepts.
- *SCORM compliant grading and record keeping*—LabConnection will grade the exercises and record the completion status of the lab portion, easily porting to, and compatible with, distance learning platforms.

  - LabConnection online (ISBN 1-1115-4367-4)
  - LabConnection on DVD (ISBN 1-1115-4366-6)

CourseMate

Linux+ Guide to Linux Certification includes CourseMate, a complement to your textbook. CourseMate includes the following:

- An interactive eBook, with highlighting, note taking, and search capabilities
- Interactive learning tools, including:
  - Quizzes
  - Flash cards
  - PowerPoint slides
  - Glossary
  - And more!
- Engagement Tracker, a first-of-its-kind tool that monitors student engagement in the course

Go to *login.cengage.com* to access these resources.

CourseMate

- Printed Access Code (ISBN 1-1115-4163-9)
- Instant Access Code (ISBN 1-1115-4162-0)

Author Biography

Jason W. Eckert is a geek, technical trainer, consultant, and best-selling author in the information technology (IT) industry. With over 20 IT certifications, 20 years of IT experience, and 18 published textbooks covering topics such as UNIX, Linux, Apache, MySQL, Windows Server, Security, Microsoft Exchange, and BlackBerry Enterprise Server, Jason brings his expertise to every class that he teaches at triOS College (*www.trios.com*). Jason is also the Technology Faculty Head at triOS College, where he continues to refine and improve the college's technology programs.

Acknowledgments

First, I would like to thank the staff at Cengage for an overall enjoyable experience writing a textbook on Linux that takes a fundamentally different approach than traditional textbooks. Additionally, I want to thank Ann Shaffer and Kent Williams for working extremely hard to pull everything together and ensure that the book provides a magnificent Linux experience. Finally, I want to thank Frank Gerencser of triOS College for freeing me up to write this book, Starbucks for keeping me on schedule, and my daughter Mackenzie for continually reminding me that Linux is still cool.

Readers are encouraged to e-mail comments, questions, and suggestions regarding *Linux+ Guide to Linux Certification* to Jason W. Eckert: jason.eckert@trios.com.

Before You Begin

Linux can be a large and intimidating topic if studied in a haphazard way. So, as you begin your study of Linux, keep in mind that each chapter in this book builds on the preceding one. To ensure that you gain a solid understanding of core Linux concepts, read the chapters in consecutive order. You should also participate in a local Linux Users Group (LUG) and explore the Internet for Web sites, FAQs, HOWTOs, and newsgroups that will expand your knowledge of Linux.

Lab Requirements

The following hardware is required for the hands-on projects at the end of each chapter and should be listed on the Hardware Compatibility List available at *http://fedoraproject.org/wiki/HCL*:

- Pentium 4 or higher CPU
- 1GB of RAM
- 60GB hard disk
- DVD drive
- 3.5″ floppy diskette drive
- Network interface card
- Internet connection

Similarly, the following lists the software required for the hands-on projects at the end of each chapter:

- Fedrora 13 installation DVD

## chapter 1

Introduction to Linux

After completing this chapter, you will be able to:

- Understand the purpose of an operating system
- Outline the key features of the Linux operating system
- Describe the origins of the Linux operating system
- Identify the characteristics of various Linux distributions and where to find them
- Explain the common uses of Linux in industry

Linux technical expertise is becoming essential in today's computer workplace as more and more companies switch to Linux to meet their computing needs. Thus, it is important to understand how Linux can be used, what benefits Linux offers to a company, and how Linux has developed and continues to develop. In the first half of this chapter, you learn about operating system terminology and features of the Linux operating system, as well as the history and development of Linux. Later in this chapter, you learn about the various types of Linux and about the situations in which Linux is used.

Operating Systems

Every computer has two fundamental types of components: hardware and software. You are probably familiar with these terms, but it's helpful to review their meanings so you can more easily understand how Linux helps them work together. **Hardware** consists of the physical components inside a computer that are electrical in nature; they contain a series of circuits that are used to manipulate the flow of information. A computer can contain many different pieces of hardware, including the following:

- A processor (also known as the central processing unit or CPU), which computes information
- Physical memory (also known as random access memory or RAM), which stores information needed by the processor
- Hard disk drives, which store most of the information that you use
- Removable flash media drives, which store information on flash memory devices
- CD/DVD drives, which can read and write to CD and DVD discs
- Sound cards, which provide sound to external speakers
- Video cards, which display results to the computer monitor
- Circuit boards (also known as mainboards or motherboards), which hold and provide electrical connections between various hardware components

Software, on the other hand, refers to the sets of instructions or **programs** that allow the various hardware components to manipulate data (or files). When a bank teller types information into the computer behind the counter at a bank, for example, that bank teller is using a program that understands what to do with your bank records. Programs and data are usually stored on hardware media, such as CD-ROMs, DVDs, hard disks, or USB flash drives, although they can also be stored on other media or even embedded in computer chips. These programs are loaded into various parts of your computer hardware (such as your computer's memory and processor) when you first turn on your computer and when you start additional software, such as word processors or Internet browsers. Once a program has begun executing on your computer's hardware, that program is referred to as a **process**. In other words, a program is a file stored on your computer, whereas a process is that file in action, performing a certain task.

There are two types of programs. The first type, **applications**, includes those programs designed for a specific use and with which you commonly interact, such as word processors, computer games, graphical manipulation programs, and computer system utilities. The second type, **operating system (OS)** software, consists of a series of software components used to control the

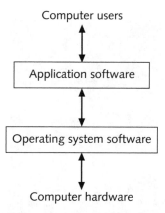

Figure 1-1 The role of operating system software

Source: Course Technology/Cengage Learning

hardware of your computer. Without an operating system, you would not be able to use your computer. Turning on a computer loads the operating system into computer hardware, which then loads and centrally controls all other application software in the background. At this point, the **user** (the person using the computer) is free to interact with the applications, perhaps by typing on the keyboard or clicking a mouse. Applications then take the information supplied by the user and relay it to the operating system. The operating system then uses the computer hardware to carry out the requests. The relationship among users, application software, operating system software, and computer hardware is illustrated in Figure 1-1.

The operating system carries out many different tasks by interacting with many different types of computer hardware. For the operating system to accomplish this, it must contain the appropriate device driver software for every hardware device in your computer. Each **device driver** tells the operating system how to use that specific device. The operating system also provides a **user interface**, which is a program that accepts user input indicating what is to be done, forwards this input to the operating system for completion, and, after it is completed, gives the results back to the user. The user interface can be a command-line prompt, in which the user types commands, or it can be a **graphical user interface (GUI)**, which consists of menus, dialog boxes, and symbols (known as icons) that the user can interact with via the keyboard or the mouse. A typical Linux GUI is shown in Figure 1-2.

Finally, operating systems offer **system services**, which are applications that handle system-related tasks, such as printing, scheduling programs, and managing network access. These system services determine most of the functionality that is seen in an operating system. Different operating systems offer different system services, and many operating systems allow users to customize the services they offer.

The Linux Operating System

Linux (pronounced "Lih-nucks") is an operating system that is used today to run a variety of applications on a variety of hardware. Similar to other operating systems, the Linux operating system loads into computer memory when you first power on your computer and initializes

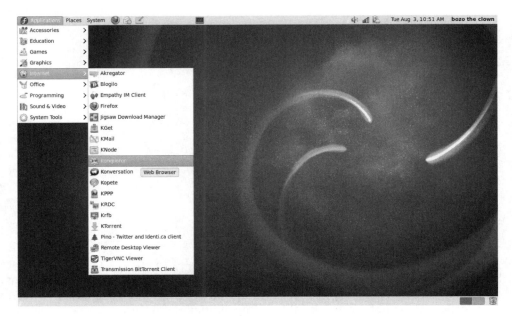

Figure 1-2 A Linux graphical user interface

Source: Course Technology/Cengage Learning

(or activates) all of the hardware components. Next, it loads the programs that display the interface. From within the interface, you can execute commands that tell the operating system and other applications to perform specific tasks. The operating system then uses the computer hardware to perform the tasks required by the applications.

Linux has the ability to manage thousands of tasks at the same time, including allowing multiple users to access the system simultaneously. Hence, Linux is referred to as a **multiuser** and **multitasking** operating system.

Versions of the Linux Operating System

The core component of the Linux operating system is called the Linux **kernel**. The Linux kernel and supporting software (called function libraries) are written almost entirely in the C programming language, which is one of the most common languages that software developers use when creating programs.

Although a variety of software can be used to modify the appearance of Linux, the underlying kernel is common to all versions of Linux. The Linux kernel is developed continuously, and, thus, it is important to understand the different version numbers of the Linux kernel to decide which kernel version is appropriate for your needs. Because the Linux kernel is directly responsible for controlling the computer's hardware (via device drivers), you might sometimes need to upgrade the Linux kernel after installing Linux to take advantage of new technologies or to fix problems (also known as bugs) related to your computer's hardware. Consequently, a good understanding of your system's hardware is important in deciding which kernel to use.

A complete list of kernels and kernel versions, along with a list of their improvements, can be found on the Internet at *www.kernel.org*.

In some cases, updates in the form of a kernel module or a kernel patch can be used to provide or fix hardware supported by the kernel. Kernel modules and kernel patches are discussed later in this book.

Identifying Kernel Versions

Linux kernel versions are made up of the following three components:

- Major number
- Minor number
- Revision number

Let's look at a sample Linux kernel version, 2.5.9. In this example, the **major number** is the number 2, which indicates the major revision to the Linux kernel. The **minor number**, represented by the number 5, indicates the minor revision and stability of the Linux kernel. An odd minor number indicates a developmental kernel, whereas an even minor number indicates a production kernel. **Developmental kernels** are not fully tested and imply instability; they are tested for vulnerabilities by people who develop Linux software. **Production kernels** are developmental kernels that have been thoroughly tested by several Linux developers and are declared to be stable. In the previous example, the kernel has a major number of 2 and a minor number of 5. Because the minor number is odd, you know that this is a developmental kernel. This kernel will eventually be improved by Linux developers, tested, and declared stable. When this happens, the version of this kernel will change to 2.6 (indicating a production kernel).

Changes to the Linux kernel occur frequently. Those changes that are very minor are represented by a **revision number** indicating the most current changes to the version of the particular kernel that is being released. For example, a 2.6.12 kernel has a major number of 2, a minor number of 6, and a revision number of 12. This kernel is the 12th release of the 2.6 kernel. Some kernels might have over 100 different revisions as a result of developers making constant improvements to the kernel code.

When choosing a kernel for a mission-critical computer such as an e-mail server, ensure that the minor number is even. This reduces the chance that you will encounter a bug in the kernel and, hence, saves you the time needed to change kernels.

Table 1-1 shows the latest revisions of each major and minor kernel released since the initial release of Linux.

Licensing Linux

Companies often choose Linux as their operating system because of the rules governing Linux licensing. Unlike most other operating systems, Linux is freely developed and continuously improved by a large community of software developers. For this reason, it is referred to as **Open Source Software (OSS)**.

Kernel Version	Date Released	Type
0.01	September 1991	First Linux kernel
0.12	January 1992	Production (stable)
0.95	March 1992	Developmental
0.98.6	December 1992	Production (stable)
0.99.15	March 1994	Developmental
1.0.8	April 1994	Production (stable)
1.1.95	March 1995	Developmental
1.2.12	July 1995	Production (stable)
1.3.100	May 1996	Developmental
2.0.36	November 1998	Production (stable)
2.1.132	December 1998	Developmental
2.2.26	February 2004 (latest release; was developed concurrently with newer kernels)	Production (stable)
2.3.99	May 2000	Developmental
2.4.17	December 2001	Production (stable)
2.5.75	July 2003	Developmental
2.6.35	August 2010	Production (stable)

Table 1-1 Latest revisions of common Linux kernels

To understand what OSS is, you must first understand how source code is used to create programs. **Source code** refers to the list of instructions that a software developer writes to make up a program; an example of source code is depicted in Figure 1-3.

After the software developer finishes writing the instructions, the source code is compiled into a format (called machine language) that only your computer's processor can understand and execute. To edit an existing program, the software developer must edit the source code and then recompile it.

```
#define MODULE
#include <linux/module.h>
int init_module(void){
        printk("My module has been activated.\n");
        return 0;
}
void cleanup_module(void){
        printk("My module has been deactivated.");
}
```

Figure 1-3 Source code

Source: Course Technology/Cengage Learning

The format and structure of source code follow certain rules defined by the **programming language** in which it was written. Programmers write Linux source code in many different programming languages. After being compiled into machine language, all programs look the same to the computer operating system, regardless of the programming language in which they were written. As a result, software developers choose a programming language to create source code based on ease of use, functionality, and comfort level.

The fact that Linux is an OSS operating system means that software developers can read other developers' source code, modify that source code to make the software better, and redistribute that source code to other developers who might improve it further. Like all OSS, Linux source code must be distributed free of charge, regardless of the number of modifications made to it. People who develop OSS commonly use the Internet to share their source code, manage software projects, and submit comments and fixes for bugs (flaws). In this way, the Internet acts as the glue that binds together Linux developers in particular and OSS developers in general.

 The complete open source definition can be found on the Internet at *www.opensource.org*.

Some implications of the OSS way of developing software are as follows:

- Software is developed very rapidly through widespread collaboration.
- Software bugs (errors) are noted and promptly fixed.
- Software features evolve very quickly based on users' needs.
- The perceived value of the software increases because it is based on usefulness and not on price.

The OSS process of software development was never intended to generate revenue directly. Its goal was to help people design better software by eliminating many of the problems associated with traditional software development, which is typically driven by predefined corporate plans and rigid schedules. By contrast, OSS development assumes that software creation is an art in which a particular problem can be solved in many different ways. One software developer might create a program that measures widgets using four pages of source code, while another developer might create a program that does the same task in one page of source code. You might think that this openness to multiple ways of solving a problem would result in a haphazard software development process, but the sharing of ideas, which is the heart of OSS development, keeps developers focused on the best possible solutions. Also, while OSS developers contribute their strengths to a project, they learn new techniques from other developers at the same time.

As you can imagine, the ability to share ideas and source code is beneficial to software developers. However, a company's business model changes drastically when OSS enters the picture. The main issue is this: How can a product that is distributed freely generate revenue? After all, without revenue any company will go out of business.

Because the selling of software for profit discourages the free sharing of source code, OSS generates revenue indirectly. Companies usually make money by selling computer hardware that runs OSS, by selling customer support for OSS, or by creating **closed source software** programs that run on open source products such as Linux.

Type	Description
Open source	Software in which the source code and software can be obtained free of charge and can be modified
Closed source	Software in which the source code is not available; although this type of software might be distributed free of charge, it is usually quite costly
Freeware	Closed source software that is given out free of charge
Shareware	Closed source software that is initially given out free of charge, but that requires payment after a certain period of use

Table 1-2   **Software types**

The OSS development process is, of course, not the only way to develop and license software. Table 1-2 summarizes the types of software you are likely to encounter. The following sections explain these types in more detail.

Types of Open Source Licenses
Linux adheres to the **GNU General Public License (GPL)**, which was developed by the **Free Software Foundation (FSF)**. The GPL stipulates that the source code of any software published under its license must be freely available. If someone modifies that source code, that person must also redistribute that source code freely, thereby keeping the source code free forever.

GNU stands for "GNU's not UNIX."

The GPL is freely available on the Internet at *www.gnu.org* and in Appendix B, "GNU General Public License," of this book.

Another type of open source license is the **artistic license,** which ensures that the source code of the program is freely available, yet allows the original author of the source code some control over the changes made to it. Thus, if one developer obtains and improves the source code of a program, the original author has the right to reject those improvements. As a result of this restriction, artistic licenses are rarely used because many developers do not want to work on potentially futile projects.

In addition to the two different open source licenses mentioned, many types of open source licenses are available that differ only slightly from one another. Those licenses must adhere to the open source definition but might contain extra conditions that the open source definition does not.

A list of approved open source licenses can be found on the Internet at *www.opensource.org*.

Types of Closed Source Licenses Closed source software can be distributed for free or for a cost; either way, the source code for the software is unavailable from the original developers. The majority of closed source software is sold commercially and bears the label of its manufacturer. Each of these software packages can contain a separate license that restricts free distribution of the program and its source code in many different ways.

Examples of closed source software are software created by companies such as Microsoft, Apple, or Electronic Arts.

Another type of closed source software is **freeware**, in which the software program is distributed free of charge, yet the source code is unavailable. Freeware might also contain licenses that restrict the distribution of source code. Another approach to this style of closed source licensing is **shareware**, which is distributed free of charge, but which users have to pay for after using it for a certain number of hours, or in order to gain access to certain features of the program. Although both freeware and shareware do not commonly distribute their source code under an open source license, some people incorrectly refer to freeware as OSS, assuming that the source code is free as well.

Linux Advantages

Many operating systems are in use today; the main ones include Linux, Microsoft Windows, UNIX, and Mac OS X. Notably, Linux is the fastest growing operating system released to date. Though Linux was only created in 1991, the number of Linux users estimated by Red Hat in 1998 was 7.5 million, and the number of Linux users estimated by Google in 2010 was over 40 million (including the number of Linux-based Android smartphone and device users). Since 1998, many large companies, including IBM, Hewlett-Packard, Intel, and Dell, have announced support for Linux and OSS. In the year 2000, IBM announced plans to spend one billion dollars on Linux and Linux development alone.

There are a multitude of reasons so many people have begun using Linux. The following advantages are examined in the sections that follow:

- Risk reduction
- Meeting business needs
- Stability and security
- Flexibility for different hardware platforms
- Ease of customization
- Ease of obtaining support
- Cost reduction

Risk Reduction Companies need software to perform mission-critical tasks, such as database tracking, Internet business (e-commerce), and data manipulation. However, changing customer needs and market competition can cause a company to change software frequently. This can be very costly and time consuming but is a risk that companies must take. Imagine that a fictitious company, ABC Inc., buys a piece of software from a fictitious software vendor, ACME Inc., to integrate their sales and accounting information with customers via the Internet. What would happen if ACME goes out of business or stops supporting the software due to lack of sales? In either case, ABC would be using a product that has no software support, and any problems that ABC has with the software after that time would go unsolved and could result in lost revenue. In addition, all closed source software is eventually retired after it is purchased, forcing companies to buy new software every so often to obtain new features and maintain software support.

Instead, if ABC chooses to use an OSS product and the original developers become unavailable to maintain it, then ABC is free to take the source code, add features to it, and maintain it themselves, provided the source code is redistributed free of charge. Also, most OSS does not retire after a short period of time because collaborative open source development results in constant software improvement geared to the needs of the users.

Meeting Business Needs Recall that Linux is merely one product of open source development. Many thousands of OSS programs are in existence, and new ones are created daily by software developers worldwide. Most open source Internet tools have been developed for quite some time now, and the focus in the Linux community in the past few years has been on developing application software for Linux, such as databases and office productivity suites. Almost all of this software is open source and freely available, compared with other operating systems, in which most software is closed source and costly.

OSS is easy to locate on the Web at sites such as SourceForge at *www.sourceforge.net*, FreshMeat at *www.freshmeat.net*, and GNU Savannah at *http://savannah.gnu.org*. New software is published to these sites daily. SourceForge alone hosts over 230,000 different software developments.

Common software available for Linux includes, but is not limited to, the following:

- Scientific and engineering software
- Software emulators
- Web servers, Web browsers, and e-commerce suites
- Desktop productivity software (for example, word processors, presentation software, spreadsheets)
- Graphics manipulation software
- Database software
- Security software

In addition, companies that run the UNIX operating system might find it easy to migrate to Linux. For those companies, Linux supports most UNIX commands and standards, which makes transitioning to Linux very easy because the company likely would not need to purchase additional software or retrain staff. For example, suppose a company that tests scientific products has spent much time and energy developing custom software that ran on the UNIX operating system. If this company transitions to another operating system, staff would need to be retrained or hired, and much of the custom software would need to be rewritten and retested, which could result in a loss of customer confidence. If, however, that company transitions to Linux, staff would require little retraining, and little of the custom software would need to be rewritten and retested, hence saving money and minimizing impact on consumer confidence.

For companies that need to train staff on Linux usage and administration, several educational resources and certification exams exist for various Linux skill levels. Certification benefits and the CompTIA Linux+ certification are discussed at the end of this book, in Appendix A, "Certification."

In addition, for companies that require a certain development environment or need to support custom software developed in the past, Linux provides support for most programming languages.

Stability and Security OSS is developed by those people who have a use for it. This collaboration between several developers with a common need speeds up software creation, and when bugs in the software are found by these users, bug fixes are created very quickly. Often, the users who identify the bugs can fix the problem because they have the source code, or they can provide detailed descriptions of their problems so that other developers can fix them.

By contrast, customers using closed source operating systems must rely on the operating system vendor to fix any bugs. Users of closed source operating systems must report the bug to the manufacturer and wait for the manufacturer to develop, test, and release a solution to the problem, known as a **hot fix**. This process might take weeks or even months to occur. For most companies and individuals, this process is slow and costly. The thorough and collaborative open source approach to testing software and fixing software bugs increases the stability of Linux; it is not uncommon to find a Linux system that has been running continuously for months or even years without being turned off.

Security, a vital concern for most companies and individuals, is another Linux strength. Because Linux source code is freely available and publicly scrutinized, security loopholes are quickly identified and fixed, usually by several different developers. In contrast, the source code for closed source operating systems is not released to the public for scrutiny, which means customers must rely on the vendor of that closed source operating system to provide security. A security breach unnoticed by the vendor can easily be exploited by the wrong person. Every day, new computer viruses (destructive programs that exploit security loopholes) are unleashed on the Internet, with the goal of infiltrating closed source operating systems, such as Windows. By contrast, the number of viruses that can affect Linux is exceedingly low. As of April 2008, Linux had fewer than 100 known viruses, whereas Windows had more than 1,000,000 known viruses. Most Linux systems today that run antivirus software do so because they host files that may be shared with Windows computers.

A list of recent computer viruses can be found on the Internet at *www.securelist.com*.

Flexibility for Different Hardware Platforms Another important feature of Linux is that it can run on a variety of different computer **hardware platforms** frequently found in different companies. Although Linux is most commonly installed on the Intel x86/x64 platforms, Linux can also be installed on other types of hardware, such as the Alpha. This means that companies can run Linux on very large and expensive hardware for big tasks, such as graphics rendering or chemical molecular modeling, as well as on older hardware, such as an old Sun UltraSPARC computer, to extend its lifetime in a company. Few other operating systems run on more than two different hardware platforms, making Linux the ideal choice for companies that use a variety of different or specialized hardware.

Following is a partial list of hardware platforms on which Linux can run:

- Intel x86/x64
- Itanium
- Mainframe (S/390)
- ARM
- Alpha
- MIPS
- M68K
- PA-RISC
- SPARC
- UltraSPARC
- PowerPC

In addition to the platforms in the preceding list, Linux can be customized to work on most hardware. Thousands of high-tech companies rely on embedded operating system technology to drive their systems. NASA space shuttles, Motorola cell phones, Google Android smartphones, Amazon Kindle eBook readers, TomTom GPS navigation systems, Nokia Maemo Internet tablets, and Linksys wireless routers all run Linux. This focus on mobile and embedded devices will become more important in the future as the need for new functionality increases. The rich set of OSS developers at work today makes Linux an attractive choice for manufacturers of mobile and embedded devices.

Ease of Customization   The ease with which you can control the inner workings of Linux is another attractive feature, particularly for companies that need their operating system to perform specialized functions. If you desire to use Linux as an Internet Web server, you can simply recompile the Linux kernel to include only the support needed to be an Internet Web server. This results in a much smaller and faster kernel.

A small kernel performs faster than a large kernel because it contains less code for the processor to analyze. Generally, you should remove any unnecessary features from the kernel to improve performance.

Today, customizing and recompiling the Linux kernel is a well-documented and easy process; however, it is not the only way to customize Linux. Only software packages necessary to perform certain tasks need to be installed; thus, each Linux system can have a unique configuration and set of applications available to the user. Linux also supports the Shell and PERL programming languages, which you can use to automate tasks or create custom tasks.

Consider a company that needs an application that copies a database file from one computer to another computer yet also needs to manipulate the database file (perhaps by checking for duplicate records), summarize the file, and then finally print it as a report.

This might seem like a task that would require expensive software; however, in Linux, you can simply write a short PERL script that uses common Linux commands and programs together to perform these tasks in a few minutes. This type of customization is invaluable to companies because it allows them to combine several existing applications to perform a certain task, which might be specific only to that company and, hence, not previously developed by another free software developer. Most Linux configurations present hundreds of small utilities, which, when combined with Shell or PERL programming, can quickly and easily make new programs that meet many business needs.

Ease of Obtaining Support For those who are new to Linux, the Internet offers a world of Linux documentation. **Frequently asked questions (FAQs)** and easy-to-read instructions known as **HOWTO** documents are arranged by topic and are available to anyone. HOWTO documents are maintained by their authors yet are centrally collected by the **Linux Documentation Project (LDP)**, which has over 250 Web sites worldwide that allow you to search or download HOWTO documents.

A search of the word *HOWTO* on a typical Internet **search engine** such as *www.google.com* displays thousands of results, or you can download the worldwide collection of HOWTO documents at *www.tldp.org*.

In addition, several Internet newsgroups allow Linux users to post messages and reply to previously posted messages. If someone has a specific problem with Linux, that person can simply post the problem on an Internet newsgroup and receive help from those who know the solution to the problem. Linux newsgroups are posted to often; thus, you can usually expect a solution to a problem within hours. A list of common Linux newsgroups can be found on the Internet at *http://groups.google.com*.

Appendix C, "Finding Linux Resources on the Internet," describes how to navigate Internet resources and lists some common resources useful throughout this book.

Although online support is the most common method of getting help, other methods are available. Most Linux distributions provide professional telephone support services for a modest fee, and many organizations exist to give free support to those who ask. The most common of these groups are referred to as **Linux User Groups (LUGs)**, and most large cities across the globe have at least one. LUGs are groups of Linux users who meet regularly to discuss Linux-related issues and problems. An average LUG meeting consists of several new Linux users (also known as Linux newbies), administrators, developers, and experts (also known as Linux Gurus). LUG meetings are a place to solve problems as well as learn about the local Linux community. Most LUGs host Internet Web sites that contain a multitude of Linux resources, including summaries of past meetings and discussions. One common activity seen at a LUG meeting is referred to as an Installfest; several members bring in their computer equipment to install Linux and other Linux-related software. This approach to transferring knowledge is very valuable to LUG members because concepts can be demonstrated and the solutions to problems can be modeled by more experienced Linux users.

 To find a list of available LUGs in your region, search for the words *LUG cityname* on an Internet search engine such as *www. google.com* (substituting your city's name for "cityname"). When searching for a LUG, also keep in mind that a LUG is named for its region; for example, the LUG in Hamilton, Ontario, Canada, is known as HLUG (Hamilton Linux Users Group).

Cost Reduction Linux is less expensive than other operating systems, such as Windows, because there is no cost associated with acquiring the software. In addition, a wealth of OSS can run on a variety of hardware platforms running Linux, and a large community of developers is available to diagnose and fix bugs in a short period of time for free. However, although Linux and the Linux source code are distributed freely, implementing Linux is not cost free. Costs include purchasing the computer hardware necessary for the computers hosting Linux, hiring people to install and maintain Linux, and training users of Linux software.

The largest costs associated with Linux are the costs of hiring people to maintain the Linux system. However, closed source operating systems have this cost in addition to the cost of the operating system itself. The overall cost of using a particular operating system is known as the **total cost of ownership (TCO)**. Table 1-3 shows an example of the factors involved in calculating the TCO for operating systems.

The History of Linux

Linux is based on the UNIX operating system developed by Ken Thompson and Dennis Ritchie of AT&T Bell Laboratories in 1969, and it was developed through the efforts of many people as a result of the hacker culture that formed in the 1980s. Therefore, to understand how and why Linux emerged on the operating system market, you must first understand UNIX and the hacker culture. Figure 1-4 illustrates a timeline representing the history of the UNIX and Linux operating systems.

UNIX

The UNIX operating system has roots running back to 1965, when the Massachusetts Institute of Technology (MIT), General Electric, and Bell Labs began development of an operating system called **Multiplexed Information and Computing Service (MULTICS)**. MULTICS was a test project intended to reveal better ways of developing time-sharing operating

Operating System	Linux	Closed Source Operating System
Operating system cost	$0	Greater than $0
Cost of administration	Low: Stability is high, and bugs are fixed quickly by open source developers	Moderate/High: Bug fixes are created by the vendor of the operating system, which could result in costly downtime
Cost of additional software	Low/None: Most software available for Linux is also open source	High: Most software available for closed source operating systems is also closed source
Cost of software upgrades	Low/None	Moderate/High: Closed source software is eventually retired, and companies must buy upgrades or new products to gain functionality and stay competitive

Table 1-3 Calculating the total cost of ownership

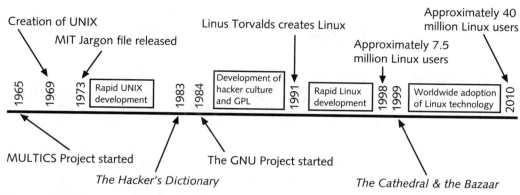

Figure 1-4 Timeline of UNIX and Linux development

Source: Course Technology/Cengage Learning

systems, in which the operating system regulates the amount of time each process has to use the processor. However, the project was abandoned in 1969.

Ken Thompson, who had worked on the MULTICS operating system, continued to experiment with operating systems after the project was abandoned and developed an operating system called **UNIX** in 1969 that ran on the DEC (Digital Equipment Corporation) PDP-7 computer. Shortly thereafter, Dennis Ritchie invented the C programming language that was used on Ken Thompson's UNIX operating system. The C programming language was a revolutionary language. Most programs at the time needed to be written specifically for the hardware of the computer, which involved referencing volumes of information regarding the hardware to write a simple program. However, the C programming language was much easier to use to write programs, and it was possible to run a program on several different machines without having to rewrite the code. The UNIX operating system was rewritten in the C programming language, and by the late 1970s the UNIX operating system ran on different hardware platforms, something that the computing world had never seen until that time. Hence, people called UNIX a portable operating system.

Unfortunately, the company that Ken Thompson and Dennis Ritchie worked for (AT&T Bell Laboratories) was restricted by a federal court order from marketing UNIX. In an attempt to keep UNIX viable, AT&T sold the UNIX source code to several different companies, encouraging them to agree to standards among them. Each of these companies developed its own variety, or **flavor**, of UNIX yet adhered to standards agreed upon by all. AT&T also gave away free copies of the UNIX source code to certain universities to promote widespread development of UNIX. The University of California at Berkeley **BSD (Berkeley Software Distribution)** UNIX, which entered the computing scene in the early 1980s, is one result of this. In 1982, one of the companies to whom AT&T sold UNIX source code (Sun Microsystems) marketed UNIX on relatively cheaper hardware and sold thousands of UNIX-running computers to various companies and universities.

Throughout the 1980s, UNIX found its place primarily in large corporations that had enough money to purchase the expensive computing equipment needed to run UNIX (usually a DEC PDP-11, VAX, or Sun Microsystems computer). A typical UNIX system in the 1980s could cost over $100,000, yet it performed thousands of tasks for client computers (also known as dumb terminals). Today, UNIX still functions in that environment; most large companies employ different flavors of UNIX for their heavy-duty, mission-critical tasks, such as e-commerce and database hosting. Common flavors of UNIX today include Sun Microsystems' **Solaris** UNIX, Hewlett-Packard's **HP-UX**, and IBM's **AIX** UNIX.

The Hacker Culture

The term **hacker** refers to a person who attempts to expand his knowledge of computing through experimentation. It should not be confused with the term **cracker,** which refers to someone who illegally uses computers for personal benefit or to cause damage.

Most hackers in the early days of UNIX came from engineering or scientific backgrounds because those were the fields in which most UNIX development occurred. Fundamental to hacking was the idea of sharing knowledge. A famous hacker, Richard Stallman, promoted the free sharing of ideas while he worked at the Artificial Intelligence Lab at MIT. He believed that free sharing of all knowledge in the computing industry would promote development. In the mid-1980s, Stallman formed the Free Software Foundation (FSF) to encourage free software development. This movement was quickly accepted by the academic community in universities around the world, and many university students and other hackers participated in making free software, most of which ran on UNIX. As a result, the hacker culture was commonly associated with the UNIX operating system.

Unfortunately, UNIX was not free software, and by the mid-1980s some of the collaboration seen earlier by different UNIX vendors diminished and UNIX development fragmented into different streams. As a result, UNIX did not represent the ideals of the FSF, so Stallman founded the **GNU Project** in 1984 to promote free development for a free operating system that was not UNIX.

A description of the FSF and GNU can be found on the Internet at *www.gnu.org.*

This development eventually led to the publication of the GNU Public License (GPL), which legalized free distribution of source code and encouraged collaborative development. Any software published under this license must be freely available with its source code; any modifications made to the source code must then be redistributed free as well, keeping the software development free forever.

As more and more hackers worked together developing software, a hacker culture developed with its own implied rules and conventions. Most developers worked together without ever meeting each other; they communicated primarily via newsgroups and e-mail. *The Hacker's Dictionary,* published in 1983 by MIT, detailed the terminology collected since the mid-1970s regarding computing and computing culture. The FSF, GNU, GPL, and *The Hacker's Dictionary* all served to codify the goals and ideals of the hacker culture, but it wasn't until the publication of *The Cathedral and the Bazaar,* in 1999, that the larger world was introduced to this thriving culture. In this important book, hacker Eric S. Raymond described several aspects of the hacker culture:

- Software users are treated as codevelopers.
- Software is developed primarily for peer recognition and not for money.

- The original author of a piece of software is regarded as the owner of that software and coordinates the cooperative software development.

- The use of a particular piece of software determines its value, not its cost.

- Attacking the author of source code is never done. Instead, bug fixes are either made or recommended.

- Developers must understand the implied rules of the hacker culture before being accepted into it.

This hacker culture proved to be very productive, with several thousand free tools and applications created in the 1980s, including the famous Emacs editor, which is a common tool used in Linux today. During this time period, many programming function libraries and UNIX-like commands also appeared as a result of the work on the GNU Project. Hackers became accustomed to working together via newsgroup and e-mail correspondence. In short, this hacker culture, which supported free sharing of source code and collaborative development, set the stage for Linux.

Linux

Although Richard Stallman started the GNU Project to make a free operating system, the GNU operating system never took off. Much of the experience gained by hackers developing the GNU Project was later pooled into Linux. A Finnish student named **Linus Torvalds** first developed Linux in 1991 when he was experimenting with improving **MINIX** (Mini-UNIX, a small educational version of UNIX developed by Andrew Tannenbaum) for the Intel x86 platform. The Intel x86 platform was fast becoming standard in homes and businesses across the world and was a good choice for any free development at the time. The key feature of the Linux operating system that attracted the development efforts of the hacker culture was the fact that Torvalds had published Linux under the GNU Public License.

Since 1991, when the source code for Linux was released, the number of software developers dedicated to improving Linux increased each year. The Linux kernel was developed collaboratively and was centrally managed. However, many Linux add-on packages were developed freely worldwide by those members of the hacker culture who were interested in their release. Linux was a convenient focal point for free software developers. During the early- and mid-1990s, Linux development proceeded at full speed, with hackers contributing large amounts of their time to what turned into a large-scale development project. All of this effort resulted in several distributions of Linux. A **distribution** of Linux is a collection, or bundle, of software containing the commonly developed Linux operating system kernel and libraries, combined with add-on software specific to a certain use. Well-known distributions of Linux include **Red Hat**, Mandrake, and **SuSE**.

This branding of Linux was not the result of the kind of fragmentation that UNIX experienced in the late-1980s. All distributions of Linux shared a common kernel and utilities; the fact that they contained different add-on packages simply made them look different on the surface. Linux still derived its usefulness from collaborative development.

Linux development continued to expand throughout the late-1990s as more and more developers grew familiar with the form of collaborative software development advocated by the hacker culture. By 1998, when the term OSS first came into use, there were already many thousands of OSS developers worldwide. Many small companies that offered Linux solutions for business were formed. People invested in these companies by buying stock in them.

Unfortunately, this trend was short-lived. By the year 2000, most of these companies had vanished. At the same time, the OSS movement caught the attention and support of many large companies (such as IBM, Compaq, Dell, and Hewlett-Packard), and there was a shift in Linux development to support the larger computing environments and mobile devices.

It is important to note that Linux is a by-product of OSS development. Recall that the OSS developers are still members of the hacker culture and, as such, are intrinsically motivated to develop software that has an important use. Thus, OSS development has changed over time; in the 1980s, the hacker culture concentrated on developing Internet and programming tools, whereas in the 1990s, the hacker culture focused on Linux operating system development. Since the year 2000, there has been great interest in embedded Linux (Linux operating systems that run on smaller hardware devices) and in developing application programs for use on the Linux operating system. Graphics programs, games, and custom business tools are only some of the popular developments that OSS developers have released in the past couple of years. Because Linux is currently very well developed, more application development can be expected from the OSS community in the next decade.

Linux Distributions

It is time consuming and inefficient to obtain Linux by first downloading and installing the Linux kernel and then adding desired OSS packages. Instead, it's more common to download a distribution of Linux containing the Linux kernel, common function libraries, and a series of OSS packages.

 Remember that though different Linux distributions appear different on the surface, they run the same kernel and contain many of the same packages.

Despite the fact that various distributions of Linux are essentially the same under the surface, they do have important differences. Different distributions might support different hardware platforms. Also, Linux distributions include predefined sets of software; some Linux distributions include a large number of server-related tools, such as Web servers and database servers, whereas others include numerous workstation and development software applications. Still others might include a complete set of open source tools that you can use to customize a Linux system to perform specific functions. In that case, you simply choose the open source tools you want to install. For example, you might choose to install a database server.

Linux distributions that include many specialized tools might not contain a GUI; an example of this is a Linux distribution that fits on a floppy and can be used as a **router**. Most distributions, however, do include a GUI that can be further customized to suit the needs of the user.

The core component of the GUI in Linux is referred to as **X Windows**. There are two implementations of X Windows: XFree86 and X.org. XFree86 is the traditional implementation of X Windows, and X.org is the latest implementation of X Windows based on the original MIT X Windows project that was released as OSS in 2004. In addition to X Windows, several Linux window managers and desktop environments are available, which together affect the look and feel of the Linux GUI. X Windows in combination with a window manager and desktop environment is referred to as a **GUI environment**. The two main competing GUI environments available in Linux are the **GNU Network Object Model Environment (GNOME)** and the **K desktop environment (KDE)**. Both of these GUI environments are more or less comparable in functionality, although users might have a personal preference for one desktop over the other. This is often the case when a company wants to do a great deal of software development in the GUI environment; the GNOME desktop written in the C programming language uses the widely available gtk toolkit, whereas the KDE desktop written in the C++ programming language uses the qt toolkit. Which language and toolkit best fits the need will be the one preferred at that time. Most common Linux distributions ship with both GNOME and KDE GUI environments, whereas others offer support for both so that either GUI environment can be easily downloaded and installed. A comparison of these two GUI environments can be seen in Figures 1-5 and 1-6.

In addition to GNOME and KDE, there are several other desktop environments available to Linux systems. One example is XFCE, which is a lightweight desktop environment designed for Linux systems with few CPU and RAM resources.

Another difference between Linux distributions is language support, with some distributions offering more support for certain languages than others. Two examples are SuSE Linux, which has increased support for the German language, and TurboLinux, which has increased support for Japanese and Chinese. As a result, these two distributions of Linux are most popular in countries with populations that primarily speak those languages. Many Linux distributions are specialized for different languages, and most Linux documentation, such as HOWTO documents, is available in many different languages.

Figure 1-5 The GNOME desktop

Source: Course Technology/Cengage Learning

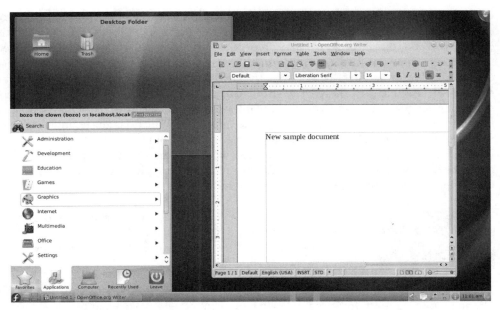

Figure 1-6 The KDE desktop

Source: Course Technology/Cengage Learning

Although these differences between Linux distributions can help narrow the choice of which Linux distribution to install, one of the most profound reasons that companies choose one distribution over another is support for package managers. A **package manager** is a software system that installs and maintains software. It keeps track of installed software, requires a standard format and documentation, and can manage and remove software from a system by recording all relevant software information in a central software database on your computer.

   A package manager in Linux is similar to the Add/Remove Programs or Programs and Features applet within the Windows Control Panel.

The most widely supported package manager is the Red Hat Package Manager (RPM). Most Linux software is available in RPM format, and the Red Hat Package Manager is standard on many Linux distributions. The Debian Package Manager offers the same advantages as the Red Hat Package Manager, yet few distributions offer it. In addition to obtaining software in package manager format, you can also download software in tarball format. A **tarball** is merely a compressed archive of files, like WinZip or RAR. A tarball usually contains scripts that install the software contents to the correct location on the system, or source code that can be compiled into a working program and copied to the system. Unfortunately, tarballs do not update a central software database and, as a result, are very difficult to manage, upgrade, or remove from the system. Traditionally, most Linux software was available in tarball format, but more and more people are using package managers to install software.

A complete list of Linux distributions can be found on the Internet at *www.linux.org*. You can search this list by hardware platform, software category, or language.

Anyone can create a Linux distribution by packaging OSS with the Linux kernel. As a result, over 200 publicly registered Linux distributions exist. Many of these are small, specialized distributions designed to fulfill certain functions, but some are mainstream Linux distributions used widely throughout the computing world. Typically, a distribution is associated with a Web site from which the distribution can be downloaded for free. In addition, most Linux distributions can be obtained from several different Web sites, such as *http://iso.linuxquestions. org*. Many distributions of Linux are also available on DVDs for a small fee from various computer stores and Web sites; however, downloading from the Internet is the most common method of obtaining Linux.

Table 1-4 briefly lists some mainstream Linux distributions, their features, and where to find them on the Internet.

Common Uses of Linux

As discussed earlier, an important feature of Linux is its versatility. Linux can provide services meeting the needs of differing companies in a variety of situations. Furthermore, configuring these services is straightforward, given the wide range of documentation freely available on the Internet; you can simply choose the services that are required and then customize Linux to provide those services. These services can be used on a local computer **workstation**, or you can configure a service to allow other computers to connect to it across a network. Services that are used on the local computer are referred to as **workstation services**, whereas services that are made available for other computers across a network are known as **server services**.

A computer that hosts a server service is commonly referred to as a **server**.

Although thousands of different server and workstation services are available that you can use to customize Linux, configurations of Linux that are commonly used today include the following:

- Internet servers
- File and print servers
- Application servers
- Supercomputers
- Scientific workstations
- Office/personal workstations

Distribution	Features	Platforms	Location
Red Hat Linux	The most common Linux distribution used today, Red Hat Linux offers tools useful in any Linux environment. Two distributions of Red Hat are available: the Enterprise distribution, geared for enterprise environments, and the Fedora distribution, geared for all environments (servers, desktops, netbooks, etc.). Both editions ship with GNOME, KDE, and RPM.	x86/x64 Itanium Alpha UltraSPARC PPC Mainframe M68K MIPS ARM	www.redhat.com http://fedoraproject.org
SuSE Linux	The most common Linux distribution in Europe and the second most common Linux distribution in North America, SuSE offers software packages for almost any business need. Novell purchased SuSE Linux to replace its NetWare OS and distributes enterprise versions of SuSE packaged with Novell software. SuSE Linux ships with GNOME, KDE, and RPM.	x86/x64 Itanium AMD64 Alpha PPC UltraSPARC Mainframe	www.opensuse.org www.novell.com/linux/
Slackware Linux	A distribution with many features similar to UNIX, Slackware Linux is commonly used in multiprocessor environments due to its enhanced multiprocessor support. It ships with GNOME and KDE.	x86/x64 Alpha UltraSPARC	www.slackware.com
Debian Linux	The Linux distribution that offers the largest number of packages, Debian Linux contains software packages for any use and ships with GNOME, KDE, the Debian Package Manager, and RPM.	x86/x64 Itanium Alpha UltraSPARC M68K PPC MIPS ARM	www.debian.org
Ubuntu Linux	A Debian-based distribution that caters largely to new Linux users, Ubuntu Linux is designed to be easy to use and supports nearly all hardware, including netbooks. It typically ships with GNOME and the Debian Package Manager.	x86/x64 Itanium Alpha UltraSPARC M68K PPC MIPS ARM	www.ubuntu.com
TurboLinux	The most common distribution of Linux in Asia, TurboLinux is famous for its clustering abilities. It ships with GNOME, KDE, and RPM.	x86/x64 Itanium Alpha Mainframe	www.turbolinux.com

Table 1-4 Common Linux distributions

Internet Servers

Linux hosts a wide range of Internet services, and it was from these services that Linux gained much popularity in the 1990s. All of these services are available free of charge, and like all OSS they undergo constant improvement, which makes Linux an attractive choice when planning for the use of Internet services in a company. Companies that use services on a computer to serve client computers are said to have an Internet server. Linux provides hundreds of network services that provide the framework for an Internet server; the most common of these services include the following:

- Mail services
- Routing
- FTP services
- Firewalls and proxy services
- Web services
- News services
- DNS services

Many of these applications are discussed in more detail later in this book.

Mail Services In the 1980s and early 1990s, e-mail was a service found primarily in universities. Today, almost every Internet user has an e-mail account and uses e-mail on a regular basis. E-mail addresses are easy to acquire and can be obtained free of charge.

E-mail is distributed via a network of e-mail servers, also known as **mail transfer agents** (**MTAs**). Many MTAs are freely available for Linux, including sendmail, postfix, smail, and qmail. Before the user can access her e-mail, it must be downloaded from an MTA; the service that provides this is known as a **mail delivery agent** (**MDA**). Linux also provides several of these services; procmail and fetchmail are two of the most common. Finally, the user views her e-mail using a program known as a **mail user agent** (**MUA**). Common MUAs available for Linux include mutt, pine, printmail, elm, mail, Thunderbird, Evolution and Eudora.

Routing Routing is a core service that is necessary for the Internet to function. The Internet is merely a large network of interconnected networks; in other words, it connects company networks, home networks, and institutional networks so that they can communicate with one another. A router is a computer or special hardware device that provides this interconnection. It contains information regarding the structure of the Internet and sends information from one network to another. Companies can use routers to connect their internal networks to the Internet as well as to connect their networks together inside the company. Linux is a good choice for this as it provides support for routing and is easily customizable. Many Linux distributions, each of which can fit on a single floppy disk, provide routing capabilities.

FTP Services The most common and efficient method for transferring files over the Internet is by using the File Transfer Protocol (FTP). In addition, FTP is commonplace when transferring files on an internal company network because it is very quick and robust. A user simply starts the FTP service on her computer (now known as an FTP server) and allows users to connect; users on other computers then connect to this server using an FTP client program and download any desired files. Most FTP servers available on the Internet allow any user to connect and are, hence, called anonymous FTP servers. Furthermore, most operating systems, such as Linux, UNIX, Microsoft Windows, and Macintosh, are distributed with an FTP client program, making it easy for users to connect to these FTP servers.

Although several FTP service software programs are available for Linux, the most commonly used is the Very Secure FTP Server, which can be downloaded from the Internet at *http://vsftpd.beasts.org*.

Firewalls and Proxy Services   The term "firewall" describes the structures that prevent a fire from spreading. In the automobile industry, a firewall protects the passengers in a car if a fire breaks out in the engine compartment. Just as an automobile firewall protects passengers, a computer firewall protects companies from outside intruders on the Internet. Most firewalls are computers that are placed between the company network and the company's connection to the Internet; all traffic must then pass through this firewall, allowing the company to control traffic at this firewall, based on a complex set of rules. Linux has firewall support built directly into the kernel. Utilities such as ipchains and netfilter/iptables, which are included with most distributions, can be used to configure the rules necessary to make a system a firewall.

You can find out more about using netfilter/iptables to configure Linux firewalls on the Internet at *www.netfilter.org/*.

Because firewalls are usually located between a company's internal network and the Internet, they often provide other services that allow computers inside the company easy access to the Internet. The most common of these services are known as proxy services. A **proxy server** requests Internet resources, such as Web sites and FTP sites, on behalf of the computer inside the company. In other words, a workstation computer inside the company simply sends a request to the proxy server connected to the Internet. The proxy server then obtains and returns the requested information to the workstation computer. One proxy server can allow thousands of company workstation computers access to the Internet simultaneously without lengthy configuration of the workstation computers. Proxy servers keep track of the information passed to each client by maintaining a Network Address Translation (NAT) table. Although both ipchains and netfilter/iptables can perform some proxy server functions, the most common proxy server used on Linux is Squid. Squid retains a copy of any requested Internet resources (via a process known as caching) so that it can respond more quickly to future requests for the same resources.

To obtain or find information regarding the Squid proxy server on the Internet, visit *www.squid-cache.org*.

Web Services Although many Internet tools and services are available, the most popular is the Internet browser, which can connect client computers to servers worldwide, hosting information of many types: text, pictures, music, binary data, video, and much more. The community of servers that hosts this information is known as the World Wide Web (WWW), and a server hosting information is known as a Web server. On a basic level, a Web server is just a server using Hypertext Transfer Protocol (HTTP) to provide information to requesting Web browsers running on client computers. However, Web servers can also process programs known as Common Gateway Interface (CGI) scripts and provide secure connections such as Secure Sockets Layer (SSL). A CGI is a program that runs on the Web server and enables connection to a resource running on another server on the network not connected to the Internet, such as a database. This is very useful, as not all information provided over the Internet needs to reside on Web servers. CGIs can be written in several programming languages, including C and C++, making them readily compatible with Linux. SSL is a secure method of communicating with a Web server in which the information passing between the client computer and the Web server is encrypted to keep it secure. This form of transmission is widely used any time confidentiality is required, such as in Internet banking or in transferring a client's credit card information in e-commerce. You can tell SSL is in use when the http:// in the browser's address bar changes to https://.

To better understand how SSL works, obtain an e-mail address from *www.gmail.com/* and note the change in the browser's address bar immediately after providing your username and password when you log in to check your e-mail account.

Many open source Web server software packages are available for Linux. The most widely used is the Apache Web Server, comprising more than 55 percent of all Web servers in the world during 2009.

For more information about the Apache Web Server on the Internet, visit *http://httpd.apache.org*.

News Services Web servers host valuable information, but most do not provide any means for users to communicate with each other. This functionality is provided by a news server, which allows users to post messages in forums called **newsgroups** and allows other users to read and reply to those messages. Newsgroups are sometimes referred to as computer bulletin boards and are similar to bulletin boards seen around a school campus and in other public places; persons having or requiring information or services post a notice that others see and respond to. Newsgroup forums are grouped according to topic. Posting to a newsgroup is often a very quick way to find the solution to a problem because people who read the posting are likely to have had the same problem and found the solution. In addition, newsgroup forums can be moderated, in which a person or group responsible for the forum edits messages before they are posted to ensure they fit the forum's theme. This ensures proper newsgroup etiquette, which dictates that before posting a question you search previous postings to ensure that the question has not already been asked and answered and that only messages relevant to the newsgroup's topic are posted. Many OSS developers use newsgroups to exchange information and coordinate software creation. As with e-mails, a special program called a newsreader is necessary to access newsgroups and read postings hosted on news servers. Common Linux newsreaders include Gnews, PAN, Gnus, Thunderbird, and pine. The most popular open source news server software available for Linux is called InterNetNews (INN); it is included with most common Linux distributions and is maintained by an open source organization called the Internet Systems Consortium, which continually develops and improves several open source Internet technologies.

For more information from the Internet on how to subscribe to newsgroups, visit *http://groups.google.com/*.

DNS Services   Each computer on a network needs a unique way to identify itself and to refer to other computers. This is accomplished by assigning each computer a number called an **Internet Protocol (IP) address**. An IP address is a long string of numbers that would be very hard for the typical person to remember. Thus, IP addresses are often associated with more user-friendly names. In particular, servers are identified by names like *www.linux.org*, which are known as **fully qualified domain names (FQDNs)**. When you use a Web browser such as Microsoft Internet Explorer or Netscape Navigator to request information from a Web server, you typically type the Web server's FQDN into your browser's address bar. However, FQDNs exist only for the convenience of the human beings who use computer networks. The computers themselves rely on IP addresses. Thus, before your browser can retrieve the requested information from the Web server, it needs to know the IP address associated with the FQDN you typed into the address bar. Your browser gets this information by contacting a server hosting the Domain Naming Service (DNS). The DNS server maintains a list of the proper FQDN to IP mappings and quickly returns the requested IP address to your browser. Your browser can then use this IP address to connect to the target Web site.

For companies wanting to create a DNS server, Linux is an inexpensive solution, as many distributions of Linux ship with a DNS known as BIND (Berkeley Internet Name Daemon).

Each computer participating on the Internet must have an IP address.

Names for computers such as *www.linux.org* are also known as fully qualified domain names (FQDNs).

You can find the latest version of BIND on the Internet at the Internet Systems Consortium Web site, *www.isc.org*.

File and Print Servers

Networks were created to share resources, primarily printers and information. In business, it is not cost effective to purchase and install a printer on the computer of every user who needs to print. It is far easier and cheaper to install one central printer on a server and let multiple users print to it across the computer network. Often, information must also be commonly available to users to allow them to collaborate on projects or perform their daily jobs. Duplicating data on every user machine would consume too much hard drive space, and coordinating changes to this data would be nearly impossible. By employing a network, this information can be made available to all who need it and can be easily kept up to date. Another benefit to this central storage of information is that a user can access data regardless of the computer that he logs in to. Central storage also allows a company to safeguard its information by using devices to back up or make copies of stored data on a regular basis in the event a computer failure occurs. Most companies perform backups of data at least every week to ensure that if data is lost on the central server it can be restored from a backup copy quickly.

Linux is well suited to the task of centrally sharing resources. It is inherently a fast, light operating system, and a distribution suited to the task can be installed on the central server. Linux is not only able to share information with other Linux and UNIX machines using services such as Network File System (NFS), it is also able to share resources with computers running other operating systems, such as Microsoft Windows or Mac OS X. Client computers are able to access a shared resource on a server running Linux provided that server has the appropriate service available. The most common service used to allow clients to connect to shared information and printers on a Linux server is Samba, which makes a Linux server appear as a Windows server to Windows clients.

Samba can be found on the Internet at *www.samba.org.*

Application Servers

An application server is a computer running a program that acts as an intermediary between a client computer and the information, normally stored in a database, that the client computer needs.

A **database** is an organized collection of data that is arranged into tables of related information. The client requests that some data be changed or displayed, and the application server interacts with the database to manipulate and retrieve the required information. This is often described as a front-end/back-end relationship. The front end runs on the client computer and is the interface the user sees and interacts with to request data. The front end takes this request, formulates it so that the server can understand it, and passes the request along to the back-end application running on the server. This back-end application then interacts with the database and returns the results to the front-end application on the client computer, which then puts it into a user-friendly format and displays it to the user. With the rapid development of the Internet in the 1990s, many companies centralized their key software elements on Internet application servers, making it possible to serve client computers worldwide. This approach saves both time and money when changes need to be made to the software. It also means only one central database needs to be maintained. A **database management system (DBMS)** is a collection of programs and tools designed to allow for the creation, modification, manipulation, maintenance, and access of information from databases.

Several free open source DBMS programs and tools facilitate the creation, management, and retrieval of data from a database as well as interaction with a variety of closed source databases, including those from Microsoft and Oracle.

For a list of open source DBMS software available for Linux on the Internet, visit *http://sourceforge.net* and navigate to Database, Database Engines/Servers.

The two most popular and widely used DBMSs available for Linux today are PostgreSQL and MySQL (My Structured Query Language). Both are powerful, fast, and light and can interact with other databases, such as Oracle. They can also be integrated with most Web servers via CGI scripts for use as an application server on the Internet. Most other open source technology has support for both PostgreSQL and MySQL.

To learn more about PostgreSQL on the Internet, visit *www.postgresql.org*. To learn more about MySQL on the Internet, visit *www.mysql.com*.

Application servers need not only be used for interaction with databases but can provide management functionality as well, allowing access and administration from anywhere in the world via the Internet. Management interfaces have taken advantage of the comprehensive development surrounding client Web browsers and Internet technologies and now offer a full range of computer management capabilities from the comfortable and standard interface of the client Web browser. One common open source management interface for Linux is Webmin, which is a customizable application server that gives users the ability to manage almost all services available in Linux from anywhere on the Internet.

Webmin can be found on the Internet at *www.webmin.com*.

Supercomputers

Many companies and institutions use computers to perform extraordinarily large calculations for which most computers would be unsuitable. To accomplish these tasks, companies either buy computers with multiple processors or use specialized services to combine several smaller computers in a way that allows them to function as one large supercomputer. Combining several smaller computers is called **clustering**. Companies and individuals requiring this type of computing make up the supercomputing community, a community that is growing quickly today as technology advances in new directions.

Although it might seem logical to purchase computers that have a large number of processors, the performance of a computer relative to the number of processors decreases as you add processors to a computer. In other words, a computer with 64 processors does not handle 64 times as much work as a computer with one processor, given the physical limitations within the computer hardware itself; a computer with 64 processors might only perform 50 times as much work as a computer with a single processor. The ability for a computer to increase workload as the number of processors increases is known as **scalability**, and most computers, regardless of the operating system used, do not scale well when there are more than 32 processors. As a result of this limitation, many people in the supercomputing community **cluster** several smaller computers together to work as one large computer. This approach results in much better scalability; 64 computers with one processor each working toward a common goal can handle close to 64 times as much as a single processor.

Most of the supercomputing community has focused on Linux when developing clustering technology. The most common method of Linux clustering is known as **Beowulf clustering**, which is easy to configure and well documented. Although there are many different ways to implement a Beowulf cluster, the most common method is to have one master computer send instructions to several slave computers, which compute parts of the calculation concurrently and send their results back to the master computer. This type of supercomputing breaks tasks down into smaller units of execution and executes them in parallel on many machines at once; thus, it is commonly referred to as parallel supercomputing, and many free programs are available that are written to run on parallelized computers. Beowulf parallel supercomputer technology has been aggressively developed since the mid-1990s and has been tested in various environments. Currently, thousands of Beowulf clusters exist worldwide in various institutions, companies, and universities.

You can find more information about Beowulf clusters on the Internet at *www.beowulf.org*.

Scientific/Engineering Workstation

Many of the developers from Richard Stallman's Free Software Foundation came from the scientific and engineering community, which needed to develop many programs to run analyses. In the 1980s and early-1990s, this scientific and engineering community largely developed software for the UNIX operating system that was common in universities around the world. However, today, this community is focusing on developing software for Linux. Any software previously made for UNIX can be ported to Linux easily. Scientists and engineers often use parallel supercomputers to compute large tasks, and OSS developers, with a background in scientific computing, have done much of the development on Beowulf technology. One example of this is SHARCnet (Shared Hierarchical Academic Research Computing Network) in Ontario, Canada, in which several universities have developed and tested supercomputing technology and parallel programs for use in the scientific and engineering fields.

You can find more information about SHARCnet on the Internet at *www.sharcnet.ca*.

Often, the programs that are required by the scientific and engineering community must be custom developed to suit the needs of the people involved. However, many OSS programs, which you can use or modify, are freely available in many different scientific and engineering fields, including, but not limited to, the following list:

- Physics, Astrophysics, and Biophysics
- Fluid Dynamics and Geophysics
- Biocomputation
- Materials and Polymer Chemistry
- General Mathematics and Optimization
- Data Mining
- Number Theory
- Computer/Linear/Array Algebra
- Mathematical Visualization and Modeling
- Statistics and Regression Analysis
- Data Plotting and Processing
- Computer Graphics Generation
- Computer Modeling
- Paleontology
- Molecular Modeling
- Electrical Engineering
- Artificial Intelligence
- Geographic Modeling and Earth Sciences
- Oceanography

Office/Personal Workstation

Server services for Linux were the primary focus of OSS development for Linux in the 1990s, but recently this focus has been expanded to many other types of software, including workstation software designed to be of benefit to end users in the office and home environments. By definition, a workstation is a single-user computer, more powerful than a typical home system; however, people commonly call any single-user computer that is not a server a workstation. It is where users work and interact, running programs and connecting to servers. Today, you will find Linux on desktops, laptops, and netbooks running many different OSS packages that provide the ability to create, organize, and manipulate office documents and graphic art, including, but not limited to, the following:

- Graphic editing software (such as Gimp)
- Desktop publishing software (such as Scribus)
- Media software (such as VLC)
- Financial software (such as Gnucash)

- Office productivity suites (such as OpenOffice.org)
- Bittorrent clients (such as qBitTorrent)

Chapter Summary

- Linux is an operating system whose kernel and associated software packages are freely developed and improved upon by a large community of software developers in collaboration. It is based on the UNIX operating system and has roots in the hacker culture perpetuated by the Free Software Foundation.

- Because Linux is published under the GNU Public License, it is referred to as OSS. Most additional software that is run on Linux is also OSS.

- Companies find Linux a stable, low-risk, and flexible alternative to other operating systems. It can be installed on several different hardware platforms to meet business needs and results in a lower TCO.

- Linux is available in different distributions, all of which have a common kernel, but which are packaged with different OSS applications.

- A wide variety of documentation and resources for Linux exists in the form of Internet Web sites, HOWTOs, FAQs, newsgroups, and LUGs.

- Linux is an extremely versatile operating system that can provide a wide range of workstation and server services to meet most computing needs of companies and individuals.

Key Terms

AIX   A version of UNIX developed by IBM.

application   The software that runs on an operating system and provides the user with specific functionality (such as word processing or financial calculation).

artistic license   An open source license that allows source code to be distributed freely but changed only at the discretion of the original author.

Beowulf clustering   A popular and widespread method of clustering computers together to perform useful tasks using Linux.

BSD (Berkeley Software Distribution)   A version of UNIX developed out of the original UNIX source code and given free to the University of California at Berkeley by AT&T.

closed source software   The software whose source code is not freely available from the original author; Windows 7, for example.

cluster   A grouping of several smaller computers that function as one large supercomputer.

clustering   The act of making a cluster; *see also* cluster.

cracker   A person who uses computer software maliciously for personal profit.

database   An organized set of data.

database management system (DBMS)   Software that manages databases.

developmental kernel   A Linux kernel whose minor number is odd and has been recently developed yet not thoroughly tested.

device driver   A piece of software containing instructions that the kernel of an operating system uses to control and interact with a specific type of computer hardware.

distribution   A complete set of operating system software, including the Linux kernel, supporting function libraries and a variety of OSS packages that can be downloaded from the Internet free of charge. These OSS packages are what differentiate the various distributions of Linux.

flavor   A specific type of UNIX operating system. For example, Solaris and BSD are two flavors of UNIX.

Free Software Foundation (FSF)   An organization, started by Richard Stallman, that promotes and encourages the collaboration of software developers worldwide to allow the free sharing of source code and software programs.

freeware   Software distributed by the developer at no cost to the user.

frequently asked questions (FAQs)   An area on a Web site where answers to commonly posed questions can be found.

fully qualified domain name (FQDN)   A string of words identifying a server on the Internet.

GNU   An acronym that stands for "GNU's not UNIX."

GNU General Public License (GPL)   A software license ensuring that the source code for any OSS will remain freely available to anyone who wants to examine, build on, or improve upon it.

GNU Network Object Model Environment (GNOME)   One of the two competing graphical user interface (GUI) environments for Linux.

GNU Project   A free operating system project started by Richard Stallman.

graphical user interface (GUI)   The component of an operating system that provides a user-friendly interface comprising graphics or icons to represent desired tasks. Users can point and click to execute a command rather than having to know and use proper command-line syntax.

GUI environment   A GUI core component such as X Windows, combined with a window manager and desktop environment that provides the look and feel of the GUI. Although functionality might be similar among GUI environments, users might prefer one environment to another due to its ease of use.

hacker   A person who explores computer science to gain knowledge. It should not be confused with the term *cracker*.

hardware   The tangible parts of a computer, such as the network boards, video card, hard disk drives, printers, and keyboards.

hardware platform   A particular configuration and grouping of computer hardware, normally centered on and determined by processor type and architecture.

hot fix   A solution made by a closed source vendor that fixes a software bug.

HOWTO   A task-specific instruction guide to performing any of a wide variety of tasks; freely available from the Linux Documentation Project at *http://tldp.org/*.

HP-UX   A version of UNIX developed by Hewlett-Packard.

Internet Protocol (IP) address   A unique string of numbers assigned to a computer to uniquely identify it on the Internet.

K desktop environment (KDE)   One of the two competing graphical user interfaces (GUI) available for Linux.

kernel   The central, core program of the operating system. The shared commonality of the kernel is what defines Linux; the differing OSS applications that can interact with the common kernel are what differentiate Linux distributions.

Linus Torvalds   A Finnish graduate student who coded and created the first version of Linux and subsequently distributed it under the GNU Public License.

Linux   A software operating system originated by Linus Torvalds. The common core, or kernel, continues to evolve and be revised. Differing OSS bundled with the Linux kernel is what defines the wide variety of distributions now available.

Linux Documentation Project (LDP)   A large collection of Linux resources, information, and help files supplied free of charge and maintained by the Linux community.

Linux User Group (LUG)   An open forum of Linux users who discuss and assist each other in using and modifying the Linux operating system and the OSS run on it. There are LUGs worldwide.

mail delivery agent (MDA)   The service that downloads e-mail from a mail transfer agent.

mail transfer agent (MTA)   An e-mail server.

mail user agent (MUA)   A program that allows e-mail to be read by a user.

major number   The number preceding the first dot in the number used to identify a Linux kernel version. It is used to denote a major change or modification.

MINIX   Mini-UNIX created by Andrew Tannenbaum. Instructions on how to code the kernel for this version of the UNIX operating system were publicly available. Using this as a starting point, Linus Torvalds improved this version of UNIX for the Intel platform and created the first version of Linux.

minor number   The number following the first dot in the number used to identify a Linux kernel version, denoting a minor modification. If odd, it is a version under development and not yet fully tested. *See also* developmental kernel and production kernel.

Multiplexed Information and Computing Service (MULTICS)   A prototype time-sharing operating system that was developed in the late-1960s by AT&T Bell Laboratories.

multitasking   A type of operating system that has the capability to manage multiple tasks simultaneously.

multiuser   A type of operating system that has the capability to provide access to multiple users simultaneously.

newsgroup   An Internet protocol service accessed via an application program called a newsreader. This service allows access to postings (e-mails in a central place accessible by all newsgroup users) normally organized along specific themes. Users with questions on specific topics can post messages, which can be answered by other users.

Open Source Software (OSS)   The programs distributed and licensed so that the source code making up the program is freely available to anyone who wants to examine, utilize, or improve upon it.

operating system (OS)   The software used to control and directly interact with the computer hardware components.

package manager   The software used to install, maintain, and remove other software programs by storing all relevant software information in a central software database on the computer.

process   A program loaded into memory and running on the processor, performing a specific task.

production kernel   A Linux kernel whose minor number (the number after the dot in the version number) is even and which is, therefore, deemed stable for use after widespread testing.

program   A set of instructions that knows how to interact with the operating system and computer hardware to perform a specific task; stored as a file on some media (for example, a hard disk drive).

programming language   The syntax used for developing a program. Different programming languages use different syntaxes.

proxy server   A server or hardware device that requests Internet resources on behalf of other computers.

Red Hat   One of the most popular and prevalent distributions of Linux in North America, distributed and supported by Red Hat Inc. Fedora is a Red Hat-based Linux distribution.

revision number   The number after the second dot in the version number of a Linux kernel, which identifies the certain release number of a kernel.

router   A computer running routing software, or a special-function hardware device providing interconnection between networks; it contains information regarding the structure of the networks and sends information from one component network to another.

scalability   The capability of computers to increase workload as the number of processors increases.

search engine   An Internet Web site, such as *www.google.com*, where you simply enter a phrase representing your search item and receive a list of Web sites that contain relevant material.

server   A computer configured to allow other computers to connect to it from across a network.

server services   The services that are made available for other computers across a network.

shareware   The programs developed and provided at minimal cost to the end user. These programs are initially free but require payment after a period of time or a certain amount of usage.

software   The programs stored on a storage device in a computer that provide a certain function when executed.

Solaris   A version of UNIX developed by Sun Microsystems from AT&T source code.

source code   The sets of organized instructions on how to function and perform tasks that define or constitute a program.

SuSE   One of the most popular and prevalent distributions of Linux in Europe.

system service   The additional functionality provided by a program that has been incorporated into and started as part of the operating system.

tarball   A compressed archive of files containing scripts that install Linux software to the correct locations on a computer system.

total cost of ownership (TCO)   The full sum of all accumulated costs, over and above the simple purchase price of utilizing a product. Includes training, maintenance, additional hardware, and downtime.

UNIX   The first true multitasking, multiuser operating system, developed by Ken Thompson and Dennis Ritchie, from which Linux was originated.

user   A person who uses a computer.

user interface   The interface the user sees and uses to interact with the operating system and application programs.

workstation   A computer used to connect to services on a server.

workstation services   The services that are used to access shared resources on a network server.

X Windows   The core component of the GUI in Linux.

Review Questions

1. Every computer consists of physical components and nonphysical components. The nonphysical components of a computer that understand how to work with the physical components are referred to as:

   a. hardware

   b. records

   c. software

   d. processors

2. The operating system software is necessary for a computer to function. True or False?

3. Linux is a _____ and _____ operating system.

   a. production, stable

   b. multiuser, multitasking

   c. processing, operating

   d. large, useful

4. The core component of the Linux operating system is the Linux kernel. If you were a Linux systems administrator for a company, when would you need to upgrade your Linux kernel? (Choose all that apply.)

   a. when you need to have support in Linux for new hardware

   b. when you need another user interface

   c. when you need to increase the stability of Linux

   d. when you need to use kernel modules

5. Which of the following kernels are developmental kernels? (Choose all that apply.)

   a. 2.3.4

   b. 2.5.5

   c. 2.2.7

   d. 2.4.4

6. A production kernel refers to a kernel whose:

   a. revision number is even

   b. minor number is odd

    c.   major number is odd

    d.   minor number is even

7. Many types of software are available today. Which type of software does Linux represent?

    a.   Open Source Software (OSS)

    b.   closed source software

    c.   freeware

    d.   shareware

8. Which of the following are characteristics of OSS? (Choose all that apply.)

    a.   The value of the software is directly related to its price.

    b.   The software is developed collaboratively.

    c.   The source code for software is available for a small fee.

    d.   Any bugs are fixed quickly.

9. To which license does Linux adhere?

    a.   open license

    b.   artistic license

    c.   GNU General Public License

    d.   free source license

10. What are some good reasons for using Linux in a corporate environment? (Choose all that apply.)

    a.   Linux software is unlikely to be abandoned by its developers.

    b.   Linux is secure and has a lower total cost of ownership than other operating systems.

    c.   Linux is widely available for many platforms and supports many programming languages.

    d.   Most Linux software is closed source.

11. Which of the following are common methods for gaining support for Linux?

    a.   HOWTO documents at *http://tldp.org/*

    b.   a local Linux User Group

    c.   Internet newsgroups

    d.   all of the above

12. Which two people are credited with creating the UNIX operating system? (Choose two answers.)

    a.   Dennis Ritchie

    b.   Richard Stallman

    c.   Linus Torvalds

    d.   Ken Thompson

13. Who formed the Free Software Foundation to promote open development?

    a. Dennis Ritchie

    b. Richard Stallman

    c. Linus Torvalds

    d. Ken Thompson

14. Which culture embraced the term GNU (GNU's not UNIX) and laid the free software groundwork for Linux?

    a. the hacker culture

    b. the MIT culture

    c. the cracker culture

    d. the Artificial Intelligence culture

15. Linux was developed by _____ to resemble the _____ operating system.

    a. Linus Torvalds, MINIX

    b. Linus Torvalds, GNU

    c. Richard Stallman, GNU

    d. Richard Stallman, MINIX

16. When the core components of the Linux operating system are packaged together with other OSS, it is called a:

    a. new kernel

    b. new platform

    c. Linux distribution

    d. GNU Project

17. Which common GUI environments are available in most Linux distributions? (Choose all that apply.)

    a. GNOME

    b. CDE

    c. KDE

    d. RPM

18. Which of the following are factors that determine which Linux distribution a user will use? (Choose all that apply.)

    a. package manager support

    b. hardware platform

    c. kernel features

    d. language support

19. What is the most common open source Web server available for Linux?

    a. Samba

    b. Apache

    c. Quid

    d. pine

20. Which of the following can be used on Linux to provide file and print services?

    a. Samba

    b. Apache

    c. Quid

    d. pine

Discovery Exercises

1. You work for a large manufacturing company, which is considering Linux as a solution for some or all servers in its IT Department. The company hosts an Oracle database on UNIX, and the UNIX servers that host this database contain several small programs that were custom made. Furthermore, Windows 7 is currently used on desktops throughout the company, and users store their data on Windows Server 2008 file servers. What considerations must you keep in mind before migrating your company's servers to Linux? Which distribution(s) and OSS would you choose to accomplish this? If you need to create a report detailing the benefits of moving to an open source solution using Linux, what benefits would you list in the report to persuade others in the company that Linux lowers the total cost of ownership?

2. At a local Linux User Group (LUG) meeting, some people who are unfamiliar with Linux ask you to explain what the GPL is and how it relates to OSS. These people also don't understand how OSS generates profit, and they're under the impression that the quality of OSS is poor compared with commercial software. They suggest that the potential for OSS in the future might be limited. How do you reply? Include examples to demonstrate your points. To which Web sites can you direct them for further information?

3. As a software developer working for a large clothing store chain, you are responsible for creating software used to connect retail store computers to a central database at the head office. Recently, some friends of yours suggested that you publish your software under the GPL. What are some direct benefits to publishing your software under the GPL? To publish software made for a company under the GPL, you need the company's permission because the company owns any software that it pays developers to create. When you approach people in your company regarding OSS and explain how companies benefit from releasing software as open source, you are asked what benefits the company will receive from funding an open source project over time. Your company also wants to know what the procedure is for releasing and maintaining OSS. What benefits will you present to them? Where could you send them to gain more information on procedures involved in the open source community?

4. You are a network administrator who is in charge of a medium-sized Linux network. The company you work for asks you to implement routing in the network, a topic with which you are unfamiliar. Where could you go to learn what you must obtain to enable routing on your Linux network? Provided that you have a functional Web browser and an Internet connection, explore this topic on the Internet and list the Web sites that you used to obtain the information required. This information might range from broad descriptions of what you need to do to accomplish a certain task to detailed guides and instructions on putting your plan into action. From these sources of information, devise a report outlining the major steps necessary to implement routing on your network.

5. At a company function, a top executive corners you and complains that your department is wasting too much money. The executive demands to know why the company must spend so much money on computers and software, especially operating systems and related licenses (for closed source programs and operating systems). Write a report that defends your department by explaining the nature of hardware, software, and operating systems. In the report, be certain to explain how OSS and the Linux operating system can be used to reduce these costs in the long term.

6. You are contacted by a project organizer for a university computer science fair. The project organizer asks you to hold a forum that discusses the origins of the Linux operating system, including how it has evolved and continues to develop. The main focus of this forum is to encourage university students toward participating in the open source community and, as a result, should also detail the philosophy, major features, and methods of the hacker culture. Prepare a bulleted list of the major topics that you will discuss, and write down some sample questions that you anticipate from the participants as well as your responses.

7. Research three different distributions of Linux on the Internet. Record where you went to obtain your information. Compare and contrast the different distributions with regard to their strengths and the packages available for each. After you finish, locate and visit two Linux newsgroups. How did you locate them and where did you obtain the information? What are the topics specific to each? In each newsgroup, find two questions posted by a user in need of a solution to a problem, and follow the thread of responses suggested by others to solve that problem.

## chapter 2

Linux Installation and Usage

After completing this chapter, you will be able to:

- Prepare for and install Fedora Linux using good practices
- Outline the structure of the Linux interface
- Enter basic shell commands and find command documentation
- Properly shut down the Linux operating system

This chapter explores the concepts and procedures needed to install a Fedora Linux system. The latter half of the chapter explains the various components you will use when interacting with the operating system as well as how to enter basic shell commands, obtain help, and properly shut down the Linux system.

Installing Linux

The installation of Linux requires careful planning, the selection of an installation method, and the configuration of various parts of the Linux operating system via an installation program.

Preparing for Installation

An operating system is merely a set of software programs that interact with and control the computer hardware. Thus, all operating systems require a certain minimum set of computer hardware components to function properly. Although most up-to-date hardware is sufficient to run the Linux operating system, it is nonetheless important to ensure that a computer meets the minimum hardware requirements before performing an installation.

These minimum installation requirements can be obtained from several different sources. If you obtained the operating system on DVD, a printed manual or a file on the DVD might specify these requirements. You can also find the minimum hardware requirements for most operating systems on the vendor's Web site. For the Fedora 13 Linux operating system, you can find the minimum hardware requirements at *http://docs.fedoraproject.org* or in Table 2-1.

Furthermore, each operating system supports only particular types of hardware components. Although some operating systems such as Linux support a wider variety of hardware components than other operating systems, each individual hardware component in your computer should be checked against the **Hardware Compatibility List (HCL)** readily found on the vendor's Web site.

Type of Hardware	Requirement
Central processing unit (CPU)	Minimum: Pentium Pro class – 200MHz Recommended: Pentium Pro class – 400MHz
Random access memory (RAM)	Minimum for text-mode: 256MB Minimum for graphical: 384MB Recommended for graphical: 512MB
Free disk space (hard disk drive)	Minimum: 90MB free space (for a minimal installation) Full Installation: 10GB free space Recommended: 20GB free space Additional free space for file storage or other software you plan to install
Additional drives	DVD drive (for DVD-based installation)
Peripheral devices	Fedora-compliant peripheral devices (for example, video cards, sound cards, network cards)

Table 2-1 Fedora 13 hardware requirements

For Fedora Linux, the HCL can be found on the Internet at *http://fedoraproject.org/wiki/HCL.*

In addition to identifying hardware components to ensure that they are supported by the Linux operating system and meet minimum requirements, you should also identify the software components that will be used in the Linux operating system. These components include the computer's host name, Internet or network configuration parameters, and the specific software packages that you plan to install. Each of these is discussed in depth later in this chapter.

Because you need to document so many pieces of hardware and software information, you should create a preinstallation checklist that contains all important installation information as well as hardware information that can be confirmed on the HCL and verified following installation to ensure that all hardware was detected properly by the Linux OS. At minimum, a preinstallation checklist should look something like Table 2-2. Don't be concerned if you don't understand all of the terms included in this checklist. You will learn about many of these topics in subsequent chapters.

Hardware or Software Item	Description
CPU (Type and MHz)	Intel Core 2 Duo (1.86GHz)
RAM (MB)	1024MB
Keyboard model and layout	101-key keyboard connected to USB port
Mouse model and device	Two-button Microsoft Intellimouse connected to USB port
Hard disk size (MB)	80GB
Host name	localhost.localdomain
Network Card Internet Protocol Configuration (IP address, Netmask, Gateway, DNS servers, DHCP)	DHCP: not used IP address: 192.168.6.188 Netmask: 255.255.255.0 Gateway: 192.168.6.1 DNS servers: 200.10.2.1, 200.10.82.79
Packages to install	GNOME desktop Samba Squid Apache GIMP Emacs
Video card make and model	Nvidia GeForce 6100
Video card RAM (MB)	128MB
Monitor make and model	Samsung Syncmaster 551s
Monitor VSync and HSync Ranges	HSync: 30–55KHz VSync: 50–120Hz

Table 2-2   **Sample preinstallation checklist**

Installation Methods

Before performing a Linux installation, you must choose the source of the Linux packages and the installation program itself. Although installing from DVD media that contain the appropriate packages is the most common method, many different Linux installation methods are available. You can also install from the following locations:

- An FTP server across the network
- An HTTP Web server across the network
- An NFS server across the network
- An SMB server across the network
- Packages located on the hard disk
- CD-ROM media

The DVD installation method is discussed in this chapter; other methods are discussed in Chapter 6. To install from DVD, you simply place the Linux DVD in the DVD drive and turn on the computer. Most computers automatically search for a startup program on the DVD immediately after being turned on; the computer can then use the DVD to start the Linux installation. Alternatively, most modern computers allow you to manually select the boot device using a special manufacturer-specific key during the startup sequence, such as F12.

Turning on a computer to load an operating system is commonly referred to as booting a computer. Because the Linux installation program on DVD can be loaded when you first turn on the computer, it is referred to as a bootable DVD.

Performing the Installation

Installing the Linux operating system involves interacting with an installation program, which prompts the user for information regarding the nature of the Linux system being installed. This installation program also allows a user to identify or change hardware components that are detected automatically by the installation program. More specifically, the installation procedure for Fedora 13 Linux involves the following stages:

- Starting the installation
- Choosing the language, keyboard, and storage type
- Selecting a host name, time zone, and root password
- Configuring storage devices
- Configuring the boot loader
- Selecting and installing packages
- Completing the firstboot wizard

Starting the Installation   As mentioned earlier, to perform a DVD-based installation of Fedora Linux, or to upgrade your current installation of Linux, you simply place the Fedora Linux DVD in the DVD drive and boot the computer from the DVD. An initial welcome screen indicates that the installation program has loaded, as shown in Figure 2-1.

Figure 2-1 Beginning a Fedora installation

Source: Course Technology/Cengage Learning

Pressing the Enter key at this screen selects the first option and performs a default graphical installation or upgrade that automatically detects hardware and suits most hardware configurations included on the HCL. This chapter assumes you are using this first option in the welcome screen. However, if your video card cannot display the remainder of the installation screens after selecting this option, you can return to this screen (by shutting down your PC and booting your Fedora Linux DVD again) and select Install system with basic video driver instead.

The Linux installation program itself is a small Linux distribution called SYSLINUX. SYSLINUX does not have a full range of hardware support. As a result, if your hardware is not detected by SYSLINUX **NOTE** during the installation process, it will usually be detected by Fedora Linux on the first boot following installation.

The third option in the welcome screen, Rescue installed system, boots a small RAM-based Linux system from your installation DVD. This feature, called **System Rescue**, can be used to repair a Linux system that cannot be started. You will learn more about System Rescue in Chapter 6.

If you accidentally leave your DVD in the DVD drive of your installed Linux system and the system boots from the DVD instead of the hard disk, you can choose Boot from local drive at the welcome screen to boot the Linux system on your hard disk.

Alternatively, if you suspect that areas of your RAM have errors that will prevent the installation from completing, you can select Memory test at the welcome screen to run the **memtest86** utility. This utility tests your RAM for errors, as shown in Figure 2-2.

Checking the Media for Errors Assuming you choose the default selection in the welcome screen (Install a new system or upgrade an existing system), you are asked to check the installation media for errors prior to installation, as shown in Figure 2-3. Although it is an optional installation step, it is good practice to test DVDs that have not

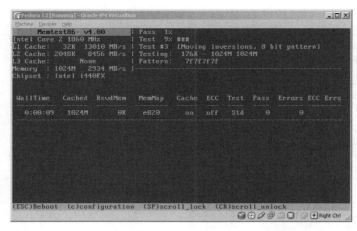

Figure 2-2 The memtest86 utility

Source: Course Technology/Cengage Learning

Figure 2-3 Testing DVD media

Source: Course Technology/Cengage Learning

been used to install Linux in the past to ensure that media errors will not cause the installation to abort later on.

Choosing the Language, Keyboard, and Storage Type
After the media have been tested, the graphical interface portion of the installation starts and you see another welcome screen. Next, you are prompted to answer a series of questions to complete the installation. The first screen allows you to choose the installation language, as shown in Figure 2-4.

After the language selection screen, you are asked to choose the keyboard configuration, as shown in Figure 2-5. The default model and layout of your keyboard are automatically detected, and as a result it is seldom necessary to change this setting. It is good practice, however, to verify that the information on the screen is correct before continuing. When in doubt, choose a U.S. English layout, because that is likely to work in most situations.

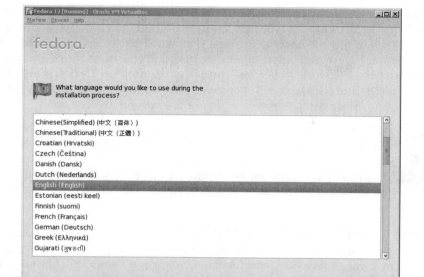

Figure 2-4 Selecting an installation language

Source: Course Technology/Cengage Learning

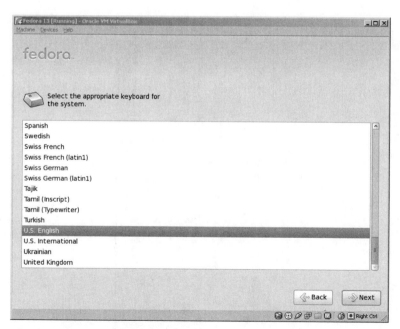

Figure 2-5 Verifying keyboard configuration

Source: Course Technology/Cengage Learning

After you choose your keyboard configuration, the installation program prompts you to select the type of storage devices that will be used to host the Linux OS. See Figure 2-6. If you want to install Linux on an internal or locally attached hard disk drive, the default selection of Basic Storage Devices is appropriate. However, if you want to install Linux on an external Storage Area Network (SAN) or Direct Access Storage Device (DASD), you need to select Specialized Storage Devices. If you select that option, the installation program will then prompt you for their configuration and load the appropriate drivers.

If you are installing Linux on a brand-new hard disk, you will be prompted to initialize the drive at this point during the installation process. Alternatively, if your hard disk already has a previous version of Fedora Linux, you will be prompted to either upgrade this system to Fedora 13 or perform a new installation.

Selecting a Host Name, Time Zone, and Root Password
Next, the installation prompts you to supply a host name that will identify your system on the network. By default, Fedora 13 uses a host name of localhost.localdomain, as shown in Figure 2-7, but you should change this in a production environment to reflect the format hostname.domainname. For example, server1.class.com refers to the host called server1 in the class.com domain.

Most network and system services on a Linux system that interact with other components rely on timestamps for correct operation. As a result, it is important to select the correct time zone for your local system, as shown in Figure 2-8.

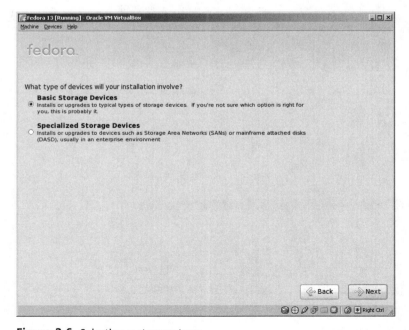

Figure 2-6 Selecting a storage type

Source: Course Technology/Cengage Learning

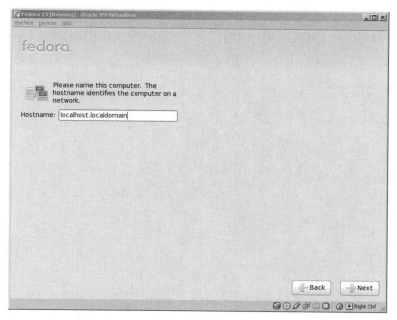

Figure 2-7 Selecting a host name

Source: Course Technology/Cengage Learning

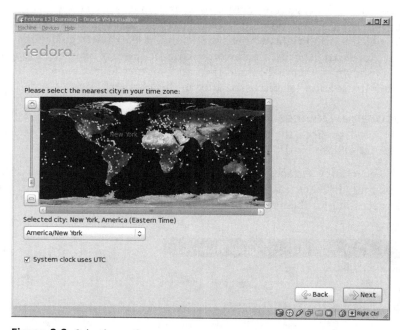

Figure 2-8 Selecting a time zone

Source: Course Technology/Cengage Learning

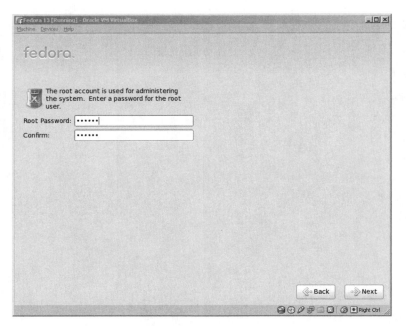

Figure 2-9 Setting a root password

Source: Course Technology/Cengage Learning

All Linux systems require secure access, which means that each user must log in with a valid user name and password before gaining access to a user interface. This process is called **authentication**. During installation, you need to configure two user accounts: the administrator account (root), which has full rights to the system, and at least one regular user account. To accomplish this, you should specify a password that is at least six characters long for the root user account, as shown in Figure 2-9, and then add another user account to the system on the first boot after installation (as discussed later in this chapter).

Configuring Storage Devices Next, you need to specify the location of storage devices that will be used to store the Linux OS. The most common storage devices used today to host the Linux OS are hard disks.

Parallel Advanced Technology Attachment (PATA) hard disks physically connect to your computer in one of four different configurations. As shown in Table 2-3, Linux refers to each of these disks according to their configuration on your computer.

Description	Linux Name
Primary master PATA hard disk	had
Primary slave PATA hard disk	hdb
Secondary master PATA hard disk	hdc
Secondary slave PATA hard disk	hdd

Table 2-3 PATA hard disk configurations

PATA hard disks were referred to as **Integrated Drive Electronics (IDE)** or **Advanced Technology Attachment (ATA)** hard disks in the past.

You can verify your PATA hard disk configuration by accessing your computer's **Basic Input/Output System (BIOS)** configuration. You can access your BIOS configuration by pressing the appropriate manufacturer-specific key during system startup, such as F10.

Newer server systems typically use **Serial Advanced Technology Attachment (SATA)** or **Small Computer Systems Interface (SCSI)** hard disks. Unlike PATA, you can have more than four SATA and SCSI hard disks within a system. The first SATA/SCSI hard disk is referred to as sda, the second SATA/SCSI hard disk is referred to as sdb, and so on.

Regardless of type, each hard disk is divided into small sections called **partitions**. Before you can store files in a partition, you must format it with a filesystem. A **filesystem** is a structure that specifies how data should reside on the hard disk itself.

In the Windows operating system, each drive letter (for example, C:, D:, E:) can correspond to a separate filesystem that resides on a partition on the hard disk.

There are limits to the number and type of partitions into which a hard disk can be divided. Hard disks can contain a maximum of four major partitions (called **primary partitions**). To overcome this limitation, you can optionally label one of these primary partitions as "extended"; this **extended partition** can then contain an unlimited number of smaller partitions called **logical drives**. Each logical drive within the extended partition and all other primary partitions can contain a filesystem and be used to store data. The table of all partition information for a certain hard disk is stored in the first readable sector outside all partitions, and it is called the **Master Boot Record (MBR)**.

The MBR is limited to hard disks that are less than 2TB in size. Hard disks larger than 2TB use a **GUID Partition Table (GPT)** instead of an MBR. The MBR and GPT are functionally equivalent.

Recall that a primary master PATA hard disk is referred to as hda in Linux; the first primary partition on this drive is labeled hda1, the second hda2, and so on. Because there are only four primary partitions allowed on a hard disk, logical drives inside the extended partition are labeled hda5, hda6, and so on. An example of this partition strategy is listed in Table 2-4.

For SATA and SCSI disks, simply replace hda with sda in Table 2-4.

Description	Linux Name	Windows Name
First primary partition on the primary master PATA hard disk	hda1	C:
Second primary partition on the primary master PATA hard disk	hda2	D:
Third primary partition on the primary master PATA hard disk	hda3	E:
Fourth primary partition on the primary master PATA hard disk (EXTENDED)	hda4	F:
First logical drive in the extended partition on the primary master PATA hard disk	hda5	G:
Second logical drive in the extended partition on the primary master PATA hard disk	hda6	H:
Third logical drive in the extended partition on the primary master PATA hard disk	hda7	I:

Table 2-4   Example of a partitioning scheme for a primary master IDE hard disk

Partitioning divides a hard disk into adjacent sections, each of which can contain a separate filesystem used to store data. Each of these filesystems can then be accessed by Linux if it is attached (or mounted) to a certain directory. When data is stored in that particular directory, it is physically stored on the respective filesystem on the hard disk. The Fedora installation program can automatically create partitions based on common configurations. However, it is generally good practice to manually partition to suit the needs of the specific Linux system.

At minimum, Linux typically requires only two partitions to be created: a partition that is mounted to the root directory in Linux (/) and that can contain all of the files used by the operating system, applications, and users, and a partition used for **virtual memory** (also known as **swap memory**). Virtual memory consists of an area on the hard disk that, when the physical memory (RAM) is being used excessively, can be used to store information that would normally reside in physical memory. When programs are executed that require a great deal of resources on the computer, information is continuously swapped from physical memory to virtual memory on the hard disk, and vice versa. Traditionally, Linux swap partitions were made to be at least the size of the physical RAM in the computer; however, Linux kernels of version 2.4 or later require much more space. In general, the swap partition for 2.4 kernels should be at least twice the size of the physical RAM. However, it can be much larger if the Linux system is intended to run large applications. A swap partition does not contain a filesystem and is never mounted to a directory because the Linux operating system is ultimately responsible for swapping information.

Although you might choose to create only root and swap partitions, extra partitions make Linux more robust against filesystem errors. For example, if the filesystem on one partition encounters an error, only data on one part of the system is affected and not the entire system (other filesystems). Because there are some common directories in Linux that are used vigorously and as a result are more prone to failure, it is good practice to mount these directories to their own filesystems. Table 2-5 lists directories that are commonly mounted to separate partitions, and also lists their recommended sizes.

Each of these filesystems might be of different types. The most common types used today are the **ext2, ext3, ext4, VFAT,** and **REISER** filesystems, although Linux can support upward of 50 different filesystems. Each filesystem essentially performs the same function, which is to

Directory	Description	Recommended Size
/	Contains all directories not present on other filesystems	Depends on the size and number of other filesystems present, but is typically 10GB or more
/boot	Contains the Linux kernel and boot files	200MB
/home	Default location for user home directories	200MB per user
/usr	System commands and utilities	Depends on the packages installed—typically 20GB or more
/usr/local	Location for most additional programs	Depends on the packages installed—typically 20GB or more
/opt	An alternate location for additional programs	Depends on the packages installed—typically 20GB or more
/var	Contains log files and spools	Depends on whether the Linux system is used as a print server (which contains a large spool). For print servers, 10GB or more is typical. For other systems, 2GB or more is usually sufficient.
/tmp	Holds temporary files created by programs	500MB

Table 2-5 Common Linux filesystems and sizes

store files on a partition. However, each filesystem offers different features and is specialized for different uses. The ext2 filesystem is the traditional filesystem still used on most Linux computers, and the Virtual File Allocation Table (VFAT) filesystem is compatible with the FAT and FAT32 filesystems in Windows. The ext3, ext4, and REISER filesystems, however, are much more robust than the ext2 and VFAT filesystems, as they perform a function called journaling. A **journaling** filesystem keeps track of the information written to the hard disk in a journal. If you copy a file on the hard disk from one directory to another, that file must pass into physical memory and then be written to the new location on the hard disk. If the power to the computer is turned off during this process, information might not be transmitted as expected and data might be lost or corrupted. With a journaling filesystem, each step required to copy the file to the new location is first written to a journal; this means the system can retrace the steps the system took prior to a power outage and complete the file copy. Both of these filesystems also host a variety of additional improvements compared with ext2 and VFAT, including faster data transfer and indexing, and as a result are common choices for Linux servers today.

After selecting a root password, the Fedora 13 installation process automatically detects the hard disks within your system and allows you to select your partition strategy, as shown in Figure 2-10. You can choose to:

- Allow the installation program to use all of the space on your hard disks to automatically create partitions

- Replace any existing Linux partitions on your hard disks with automatically created Linux partitions

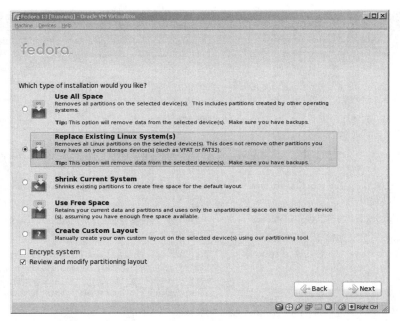

Figure 2-10 Selecting a partition strategy

Source: Course Technology/Cengage Learning

- Shrink all existing partitions (Windows and Linux) on your hard disks that have excess free space to make room for automatically created Linux partitions
- Use only free space that has not been partitioned on your hard disks for automatically created Linux partitions
- Manually create partitions
- Encrypt the data on partitions
- Review the partitions that were automatically created by the Linux installation program

It is best to manually create partitions that reflect the use of your system by selecting Create Custom Layout within Figure 2-10. Alternatively, you could choose to automatically create partitions and select Review and modify partitioning layout to make any necessary changes.

Figure 2-11 shows two manually created partitions on the first SATA hard disk. The first partition (sda1) is 30,000MB in size, contains the ext4 filesystem, and will be mounted to the root (/) directory on the Linux system. The second partition (sda2) is 4,000MB in size and used for swap only. The checkmark in the format column indicates that these new partitions will be formatted with a filesystem or prepared for use as virtual/swap memory. There is also 28,606MB of free space that can be partitioned at a later time.

If you choose the Create button shown in Figure 2-11, you are first prompted to choose a partition technology, as shown in Figure 2-12.

In addition to the standard partitions that we have discussed already, you can instead choose to create logical volumes using the **Logical Volume Manager** (**LVM**) or create a

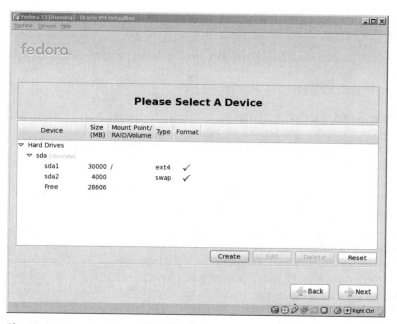

Figure 2-11 A sample partition layout

Source: Course Technology/Cengage Learning

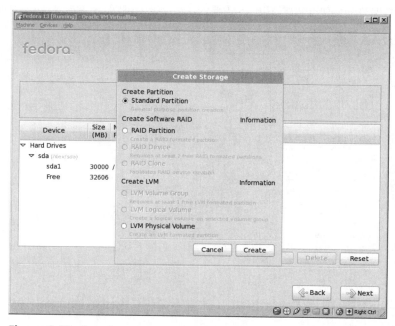

Figure 2-12 Choosing a partition technology

Source: Course Technology/Cengage Learning

software-based **Redundant Array of Inexpensive Disks (RAID)** volume that spans multiple disks. LVM and RAID are discussed in Chapter 5.

If you choose to create a standard disk partition, you will be prompted to supply information regarding its size, filesystem type, encryption options, and the directory that it will be mounted to (mount point), as shown in Figure 2-13.

Configuring the Boot Loader After you specify partitions and filesystems, you are prompted to configure the boot loader, as shown in Figure 2-14. A **boot loader** is a program, started by the BIOS at system startup, which loads the Linux kernel into memory from a hard disk partition inside the computer, yet can also be used to boot (start) other operating systems, such as Windows, if they exist on the hard disk. The boot loader that you can configure during Fedora 13 Linux installation is **GRand Unified Bootloader (GRUB)**. GRUB is discussed in more depth in Chapter 8.

Fedora Linux automatically detects Windows operating systems that reside on the hard disk and sets the boot loader to display a screen that allows you to choose the operating system to boot upon system startup; this entire process is called **dual booting**. If multiple OSs are listed within the screen shown in Figure 2-14, you can select which OS will be booted to by default if you do not choose an OS at the boot loader screen during system startup. You can also change the location of the boot loader (in Figure 2-14, it is installed on the MBR of sda) or set a boot loader password that must be entered before the Linux OS can be booted during system startup.

Selecting and Installing Packages Next, the Fedora installer prompts you to select the general role that your computer will perform. You also need to specify any software

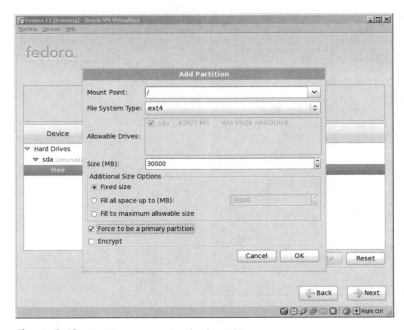

Figure 2-13 Creating a new standard partition

Source: Course Technology/Cengage Learning

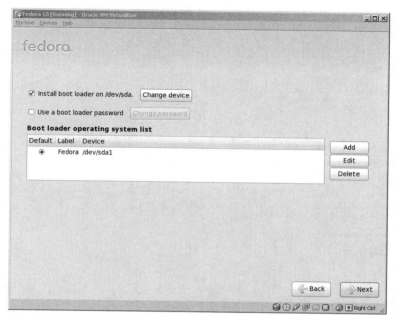

Figure 2-14 Configuring a boot loader

Source: Course Technology/Cengage Learning

repositories on the Internet from which you want to obtain software. The Graphical Desktop option, selected in Figure 2-15, is the default option, which indicates that you want to install the GNOME desktop environment as well as productivity applications suitable for a workstation. You can select additional software packages by selecting Customize now and choosing the individual packages, as shown in Figure 2-16.

It is important to consider available hard disk space when selecting packages. A full installation of Fedora 13 will place over 9GB of data on the hard disk. If you are installing a large number of packages, ensure that you have enough free space on the hard disk for Linux, swap, future applications, user data, log files, and working space for the packages installed and Linux OS. In general, you should have at least twice as much hard disk space as you initially expect to use.

After the packages have been selected, the Fedora installation program will start installing the packages to the filesystems that you have created for the Linux OS. This process could take several hours, depending on the packages selected and the speed of your computer system. After the package installation is finished, the Fedora installation program prompts you to reboot your system and eject your DVD.

Completing the Firstboot Wizard   On the first boot after installation, an interactive utility called the **firstboot wizard** appears before the login prompt, as shown in Figure 2-17. After this utility has been completed, it no longer appears when the computer is booted.

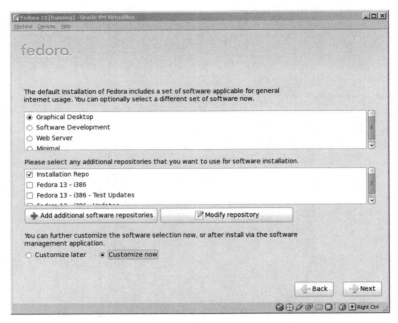

Figure 2-15 Selecting system role and software repositories

Source: Course Technology/Cengage Learning

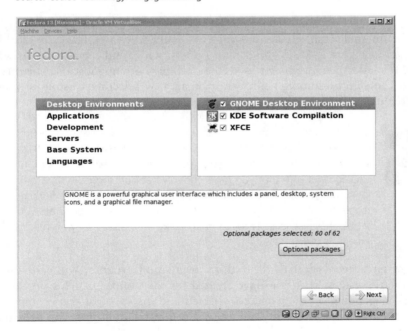

Figure 2-16 Selecting individual packages

Source: Course Technology/Cengage Learning

After you click the Forward button shown in Figure 2-17, you are required to accept a license agreement. Next, you are prompted to create a regular user account, as shown in

Figure 2-17 The firstboot wizard

Source: Course Technology/Cengage Learning

Figure 2-18. For daily user tasks, you should avoid logging in as the root user to minimize the chance that you will inadvertently change system configuration settings.

Linux users are authenticated by a password database on the local computer by default. If you click the Use Network Login button shown in Figure 2-18, you can instead choose to authenticate users based on a database that resides on another server on the network, as shown in Figure 2-19. **Network Information Service (NIS)** shares password databases among Linux systems, whereas **Lightweight Directory Access Protocol (LDAP)**, **Free Identity, Policy, and Audit (FreeIPA)**, and **Winbind** represent types of authentication and user information services that might be present on other servers on the network. If you select the Advanced Options tab shown in Figure 2-19, you can also configure other authentication options, as shown in Figure 2-20, including smart card and fingerprint reader support as well as the hashing algorithm that is used to encode passwords that are stored on the system.

After a user account and authentication have been configured, the installation program prompts you to set the date and time or choose to acquire this information from a reliable time server on the Internet using **Network Time Protocol (NTP)**, as shown in Figure 2-21.

Next, the installation program displays a full list of the hardware detected on your system, as shown in Figure 2-22. You should verify that the hardware on this list matches the hardware on your preinstallation checklist to ensure that Linux has all of the drivers for your hardware. Additionally, you can choose to send this hardware information across the Internet to the Fedora project to help Fedora developers plan driver development.

When you click the Finish button shown in Figure 2-22, your system completes the installation and proceeds to load the Linux OS.

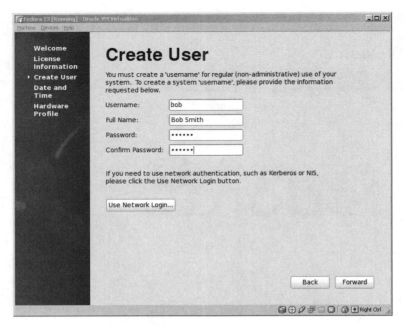

Figure 2-18 Creating a regular user account

Source: Course Technology/Cengage Learning

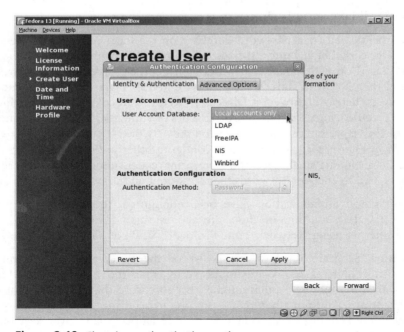

Figure 2-19 Choosing authentication options

Source: Course Technology/Cengage Learning

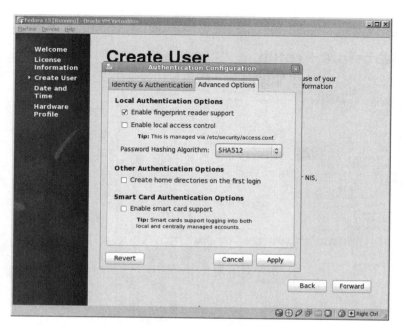

Figure 2-20 Advanced authentication options

Source: Course Technology/Cengage Learning

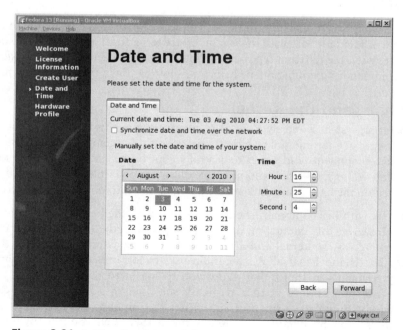

Figure 2-21 Setting the date and time

Source: Course Technology/Cengage Learning

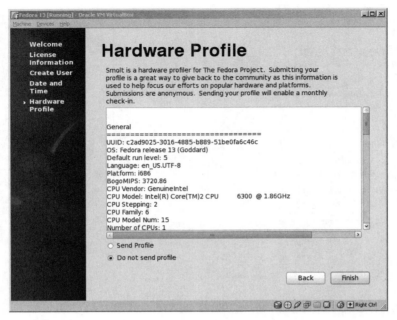

Figure 2-22 Viewing your hardware profile

Source: Course Technology/Cengage Learning

Basic Linux Usage

After the Linux operating system has been installed, you must log in to the system with a valid user name and password and interact with the user interface to perform useful tasks. To do this, it is essential to understand the different types of user interfaces that exist, as well as basic tasks, such as executing commands, obtaining online help, and shutting down the Linux system.

Shells, Terminals, and the Kernel

Recall that an operating system is merely a set of software components that allows you to use your computer hardware in a meaningful fashion. Every operating system has a core component, which loads all other components and serves to centrally control the activities of the computer. This component is known as the kernel, and in Linux this is simply a file, usually called "vmlinuz," which is located on the hard disk and loaded when you first turn on your computer.

When a user interacts with her computer, she is interacting with the kernel of the computer's operating system. However, this interaction does not happen directly; it must have a channel through which it can access the kernel and a user interface that passes user input to the kernel for processing. The channel that allows a certain user to log in is called a **terminal**, and there can be many terminals in Linux that allow you to log in to the computer locally or across a network. After a user logs in to a terminal, she receives a user interface called a **shell**, which then accepts input from the user and passes this input to the kernel for processing. The shell that is used by default in Linux is the **BASH shell** (**Bourne Again Shell**), which is an improved version of the Bourne shell from AT&T and the shell that is used throughout this book. The whole process looks similar to Figure 2-23.

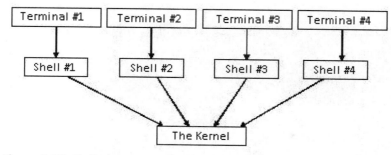

Figure 2-23 Shells, terminals, and the kernel

Source: Course Technology/Cengage Learning

As mentioned earlier, Linux is a multiuser and multitasking operating system; as such, it can allow for thousands of terminals. Each terminal could represent a separate logged-in user that has its own shell. The four different "channels" shown in Figure 2-23 could be different users logged in to the same Linux computer. Two users could be logged in locally to the server (seated at the server itself), and the other two could be logged in across a network, such as the Internet.

By default, when you log in to a terminal, you receive a command-line shell (BASH shell), which prompts you to type in commands to tell the Linux kernel what to do. However, in this computing age, most people prefer to use a graphical interface in which they can use a computer mouse to navigate and start tasks. In this case, you can simply choose to start a GUI environment on top of your BASH shell after you are logged in to a command-line terminal, or you can switch to a graphical terminal, which allows users to log in and immediately receive a GUI environment. A typical command-line terminal login prompt looks like the following:

```
Fedora release 13 (Goddard)
Kernel 2.6.33.3-85.fc13.i686.PAE on an i686 (tty2)

server1 login:
```

A typical graphical terminal login for Fedora Linux (called the GNOME Display Manager or gdm) is depicted in Figure 2-24.

To access a terminal device at the local server, you can press a combination of keys, such as Ctrl+Alt+F2, to change to a separate terminal. If you are logging in across the network, you can use a variety of programs that connect to a terminal on the Linux computer. A list of local Linux terminals, along with their names and types, is shown in Table 2-6.

After you are logged in to a command-line terminal, you receive a prompt where you can enter commands. The following example shows the user logging in as the root (administrator) user. As you can see in this example, after you log in as the root user, you see a # prompt:

```
Fedora release 13 (Goddard)
Kernel 2.6.33.3-85.fc13.i686.PAE on an i686 (tty2)

server1 login: root
Password:
```

Figure 2-24 The GNOME Display Manager (gdm)

Source: Course Technology/Cengage Learning

Terminal Name	Key Combination	Login Type
tty1 (:0)	Ctrl + Alt + F1	graphical
tty2	Ctrl + Alt + F2	command-line
tty3	Ctrl + Alt + F3	command-line
tty4	Ctrl + Alt + F4	command-line
tty5	Ctrl + Alt + F5	command-line

```
Last login: Mon Aug 16 09:45:42 from tty2
[root@server1 ~]#_
```

However, if you log in as a regular user to a command-line terminal (for example, user1), you see a $ prompt, as follows:

```
Fedora release 13 (Goddard)
Kernel 2.6.33.3-85.fc13.i686.PAE on an i686 (tty2)

server1 login: user1
Password:
Last login: Mon Aug 16 09:45:42 from tty2
[user1@server1 ~]$_
```

When you log in to a graphical terminal, the GUI environment of your choice is started; the default GUI environment in Fedora Linux is GNOME. After the GUI environment starts, you can access a command-line terminal window by navigating to the Applications menu, System Tools, Terminal, as shown in Figure 2-25.

 By default, the root user is not allowed to log in to a GUI environment. This helps ensure the security of your Linux system. Instead, you should log in to a GUI environment as a regular user. When you run a graphical administrative utility as a regular user, the GUI environment prompts you for the root user password to continue.

Basic Shell Commands

When using a command-line terminal, the shell ultimately interprets all information the user enters at the command line. This information includes the command itself, as well as options and arguments. **Commands** indicate the name of the program to execute and are case sensitive. **Options** are specific letters that start with a dash (that is, the hyphen character on your keyboard, -) and appear after the command name to alter the way the command works. Options are specific to the command in question; the persons who developed the command determined which options to allow for that command.

 Some options start with two dashes (- -); these options are referred to as POSIX options and are usually composed of a whole word, not just a letter.

Arguments also appear after the command name, yet do not start with a dash. They specify the specific parameters that tailor the command to your particular needs. Suppose, for example, that you want to list all of the files in the /etc/ntp directory on the hard disk. You could use the ls

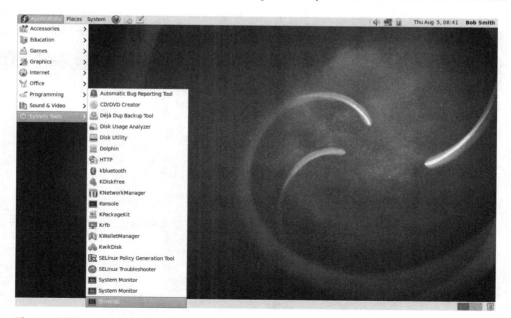

Figure 2-25 Accessing a command-line terminal in a GUI environment

Source: Course Technology/Cengage Learning

command with the −a option (which tells the `ls` command to list all files) and the `/etc/ntp` argument (which tells `ls` to look in the /etc/ntp directory), as shown in the following example:

```
[root@server1 root]# ls -a /etc/ntp
. .. crypto keys step-tickers
[root@server1 root]#_
```

After you type the command and press Enter in the preceding output, the `ls` command shows us that there are three files in the /etc/ntp directory. The command prompt then reappears, so that you can enter another command.

Commands, options, and arguments are case sensitive; an uppercase letter (A, for instance) is treated differently than a lowercase letter (a).

Always put a space between the command name, options, and arguments; otherwise, the shell does not understand that they are separate, and your command might not work as expected.

Although you can pass options and arguments to commands, not all commands need to have arguments or options supplied on the command line to work properly. The `date` command is one example; it simply prints the current date and time:

```
[root@server1 root]# date
Sun Aug 19 08:46:57 EDT 2012
[root@server1 root]#_
```

Table 2-7 lists some common commands that you can use without specifying any options or arguments.

If the output of a certain command is too large to fit on the terminal screen, simply use the Shift and Page Up keys simultaneously to view previous screens of information.

Command	Description
clear	Clears the terminal screen
reset	Resets your terminal to use default terminal settings
finger	Displays information on system users
who	Displays currently logged-in users
w	Displays currently logged-in users and their tasks
whoami	Displays your login name
id	Displays the numbers associated with your user account name and group names; these are commonly referred to as User IDs (UIDs) and Group IDs (GIDs)
date	Displays the current date and time
cal	Displays the calendar for the current month
exit	Exits out of your current shell

Table 2-7   Some common Linux commands

Also, Shift and Page Down can be used to navigate in the opposite direction, when pressed simultaneously.

You can recall commands previously entered in the BASH shell using the keyboard cursor keys (the up, down, right, and left arrow keys). Thus, if you want to enter the same command again, simply cycle through the list of available commands with the keyboard cursor keys and press Enter to reexecute that command.

Shell Metacharacters

Another important feature of the shell are shell **metacharacters,** which are keyboard characters that have special meaning. One of the most commonly used metacharacters is the $ character, which tells the shell that the following text refers to a variable. A variable is simply a piece of information that is stored in memory; variable names are typically uppercase words, and most variables are set by the Linux system automatically when you log in. An example of how you might use the $ metacharacter to refer to a variable is by using the echo command (which prints text to the terminal screen):

```
[root@server1 root]# echo Hi There!
Hi There!
[root@server1 root]# echo My shell is $SHELL
My Shell is /bin/bash
[root@server1 root]#_
```

Notice from the preceding output that $SHELL was translated into its appropriate value from memory (/bin/bash, the BASH shell). The shell recognized SHELL as a variable because it was prefixed by the $ metacharacter. Table 2-8 presents a list of common BASH shell metacharacters that are discussed throughout this book.

It is good practice to avoid metacharacters when typing commands unless you need to take advantage of their special functionality, as the shell readily interprets them, which might lead to unexpected results.

Metacharacter(s)	Description
$	Shell variable
~	Special home directory variable
&	Background command execution
;	Command termination
< << > >>	Input/Output redirection
|	Command piping
* ? [ ]	Shell wildcards
' " \	Metacharacter quotes
`	Command substitution
( ) { }	Command grouping

Table 2-8 Common BASH shell metacharacters

 If you accidentally use one of these characters and your shell does not return you to the normal prompt, simply press the Ctrl and c keys in combination and your current command is canceled.

There are some circumstances in which you might need to use a metacharacter in a command and prevent the shell from interpreting its special meaning. To do this, simply enclose the metacharacters in single quotation marks ' '. Single quotation marks protect those metacharacters from being interpreted specially by the shell (that is, a $ is interpreted as a $ character and not a variable identifier). You can use double quotation marks " " to perform the same task; however, double quotation marks do not protect $, \, and ` characters. If only one character needs to be protected from shell interpretation, you can precede that character with a \ rather than enclosing it within quotation marks. An example of this type of quoting is:

```
[root@server1 root]# echo My Shell is $SHELL
My Shell is /bin/bash
[root@server1 root]# echo 'My Shell is $SHELL'
My Shell is $SHELL
[root@server1 root]# echo "My Shell is $SHELL"
My Shell is /bin/bash
[root@server1 root]# echo My Shell is \$SHELL
My Shell is $SHELL
[root@server1 root]#_
```

As shown in Table 2-8, not all quote characters protect characters from the shell. The back quote characters ` ` can be used to perform command substitution; anything between back quotes is treated as another command by the shell, and its output is substituted in place of the back quotes. Take the expression `date` as an example:

```
[root@server1 root]# echo Today is `date`
Today is Tue Mar 29 09:28:11 EST 2005
[root@server1 root]#_
```

Getting Command Help

Most distributions of Linux contain more than 1,000 different Linux commands in their standard configuration, and, thus, it is impractical to memorize the syntax and use of each command. Fortunately, Linux stores documentation for each command in central locations so that it can be accessed easily. The most common form of documentation for Linux commands is **manual pages** (commonly referred to as **man pages**). Simply type the man command followed by a command name, and extensive information about that Linux command is displayed page-by-page on the terminal screen. This information includes a description of the command and its syntax as well as available options, related files, and commands. For example, to receive information on the format and usage of the whoami command, you can use the following command:

```
[root@server1 root]# man whoami
```

The manual page is then displayed page-by-page on the terminal screen. You can use the cursor (arrow) keys on the keyboard to scroll though the information or press q to quit. The manual page for whoami is similar to the following:

```
WHOAMI(1)          User Commands          WHOAMI(1)


NAME
whoami - print effective userid

SYNOPSIS
whoami [OPTION]...

DESCRIPTION
Print the user name associated with the current effective
user id. Same as id -un.

       --help    display this help and exit

       --version
          output version information and exit

AUTHOR
       Written by Richard Mlynarik.

REPORTING BUGS
       Report bugs to <bug-coreutils@gnu.org>.
       GNU coreutils home page:<http://www.gnu.org/software/coreutils/>
       General help using GNU software: <http://www.gnu.org/gethelp/>
       Report whoami translation bugs to <http://translationproject.org/>

COPYRIGHT
       Copyright©2010 Free Software Foundation, Inc. License GPLv3+: GNU
       GPL version 3 or later <http://gnu.org/licenses/gpl.html>.
       This is free software: you are free to change and redistribute it.
       There is NO WARRANTY, to the extent permitted by law.

SEE ALSO
       The full documentation is maintained as a Texinfo manual.
       If the info and whoami programs are installed at your site,
       the command

          info coreutils 'whoami invocation'

       should give you access to the complete manual.

GNU coreutils 8.4     April 2010        WHOAMI(1)
[root@server1 root]#_
```

Notice that the whoami command is displayed as WHOAMI(1) at the top of the preceding manual page output. The (1) denotes a section of the manual pages; section (1) means that whoami is a command that can be executed by any user. All manual pages contain certain section numbers that describe the category of the command in the manual page database; you can find a list of the different manual-page section numbers in Table 2-9.

Sometimes, there is more than one command, library routine, or file that has the same name. If you run the man command with that name as an argument, Linux returns the manual page with the lowest section number. For example, if there is a file called whoami as well as a command named whoami and you type man whoami, the manual page for the whoami command (section 1 of the manual pages) is displayed. To display the manual page for the whoami file format instead, you simply type man 5 whoami to display the whoami file format (section 5 of the manual pages).

Recall that many commands are available to the Linux user; thus, it might be cumbersome to find the command that you need to perform a certain task without using a Linux command dictionary. Fortunately, you have the ability to search the manual pages by keyword. To find all of the commands that have the word *usb* in their name or description, type the following:

[root@server1 root] # **man –k usb**

This command produces the following output:

```
aiptek             (4) - Aiptek USB Digital Tablet Input Driver for Linux
fxload             (8) - Firmware download to EZ-USB devices
lsusb              (8) - list USB devices
sane-canon630u     (5) - SANE backend for the Canon 630u USB scanner
sane-cardscan      (5) - SANE backend for Corex CardScan 800c usb scanner
sane-epjitsu       (5) - SANE backend for Epson-based Fujitsu scanners
sane-find-scanner  (1) - find SCSI and USB scanners and their device
sane-genesys       (5) - SANE backend for GL646 based USB scanners
sane-gt68xx        (5) - SANE backend for GT-68XX based flatbed scanners
sane-ma1509        (5) - SANE backend for Mustek BearPaw 1200F scanner
sane-mustek_usb2   (5) - SANE backend for SQ113 based flatbed scanners
sane-mustek_usb    (5) - SANE backend for Mustek USB flatbed scanners
sane-plustek       (5) - SANE backend for LM983 based flatbed scanners
sane-sm3600        (5) - SANE backend for Microtek scanners with M011
```

Manual Page Section	Description
1	Commands that any user can execute
2	Linux system calls
3	Library routines
4	Special device files
5	File formats
6	Games
7	Miscellaneous
8	Commands that only the root user can execute
9	Linux kernel routines
n	New commands not categorized yet

Table 2-9   Manual page section numbers

```
sane-sm3840        (5) - SANE backend for Microtek scanners with SCAN08
sane-u12           (5) - SANE backend for Plustek USB flatbed scanners
sane-usb           (5) - USB configuration tips for SANE
sisusb             (4) - SiS USB video driver
usb-devices        (1) - print USB device details
[root@server1 root]#_
```

After you find the command needed, you can simply run the `man` command on that command without the `-k` option to find out detailed information about the command.

You can also use the `apropos usb` command to perform the same function as the `man -k usb` command. Both commands yield the exact same output on the terminal screen.

If you do not see any output from the `man -k` or `apropos` commands following a Linux installation, you might need to run the `makewhatis` command to index the manual page database.

Another utility, originally intended to replace the `man` command in Linux, is the GNU **info pages.** You can access this utility by typing the `info` command followed by the name of the command in question. The `info` command returns an easy-to-read description of each command and also contains links to other information pages (called hyperlinks). Today however, both the info pages and the manual pages are used to find documentation because manual pages have been utilized in Linux since its conception and for over two decades in the UNIX operating system. An example of using the `info` command to find information about the `whoami` command follows:

```
[root@server1 root]# info whoami
```

The info page is then displayed interactively:

```
lsusb              (8) - list USB devices
File: coreutils.info, Node:whoami invocation, Next:groups invocation,
: logname invocation, Up: User information


20.3 'whoami': Print effective user ID
========================================


'whoami' prints the user name associated with the current effective
user ID. It is equivalent to the command 'id -un'.

   The only options are '--help' and '--version'. *Note Common
options::.


   An exit status of zero indicates success, and a nonzero value
indicates failure.


—zz-Info: (coreutils.info.gz)whoami invocation, 15 lines --All------
[root@server1 root]#_
```

 While in the info utility, press the ? key or Ctrl+h key combination to display a help screen that describes the usage of info. As with the man command, you can use the q key to quit.

Some commands do not have manual pages or info pages. These commands are usually functions that are built into the BASH shell itself. To find help on these commands, you must use the help command, as shown here:

```
[root@server1 root]# help echo
echo: echo [-neE] [arg …]
    Write arguments to the standard output.

    Display the ARGs on the standard output followed by a newline.

    Options:
      -n    do not append a newline
      -e    enable interpretation of the following backslash escapes
      -E    explicitly suppress interpretation of backslash escapes

    'echo' interprets the following backslash-escaped characters:
      \a    alert (bell)
      \b    backspace
      \c    suppress further output
      \e    escape character
      \f    form feed
      \n    new line
      \r    carriage return
      \t    horizontal tab
      \v    vertical tab
      \\    backslash
      \0nnn the character whose ASCII code is NNN (octal). NNN can be
      0 to 3 octal digits
      \xHH the eight-bit character whose value is HH (hexadecimal). HH
      can be one or two hex digits

    Exit Status:
    Returns success unless a write error occurs.
[root@server1 root]#_
```

Shutting Down the Linux System

Because the operating system handles writing data from computer memory to the disk drives in a computer, simply turning off the power to the computer might result in damaged user and system files. Thus, it is important to prepare the operating system for shutdown before turning off the power to the hardware components of the computer. To do this, you can issue the shutdown command, which can halt or reboot (restart) your computer after a certain period of time. To halt your system in 15 minutes, for example, you could type:

Command	Description
shutdown -h +4	Halts your system in four minutes
shutdown -r +4	Reboots your system in four minutes
shutdown -h now	Halts your system immediately
shutdown -r now	Reboots your system immediately
shutdown -c	Cancels a scheduled shutdown
halt	Halts your system immediately
poweroff	Halts your system immediately and powers down the computer
reboot	Reboots your system immediately

Table 2-10 Commands to halt and reboot the Linux operating system

[root@server1 root] # **shutdown -h +15**

This produces output similar to the following:

Broadcast message from root@server1.class.com
        (tty2) at 9:23 …

The system is going down for system halt in 15 minutes!

Notice from the preceding output that you do not receive the command prompt back again after the shutdown command has started. Thus, to stop the shutdown, simply press the Ctrl and c keys in combination to cancel the command. Alternatively, you can log in to another terminal and issue the command shutdown -c to cancel the shutdown.

To halt your system now, you could type:

[root@server1 root] # **shutdown -h now**

This command produces output similar to the following:

Broadcast message from root@server1.class.com
        (tty2) at 9:23 …

The system is going down for system halt NOW!

Other examples of the shutdown command and their descriptions are shown in Table 2-10.

Chapter Summary

- Prior to installation, you should verify hardware requirements using the HCL. Also, you should create a preinstallation checklist that contains key information required during the installation.

- Although there are many methods for installing Linux, a DVD-based installation is the easiest and most common method.

- A typical Linux installation prompts the user for information such as language, host name, date, time zone, keyboard layout, user account configuration, storage configuration, boot loader configuration, and the packages that need to be installed.

- Users must log in to a terminal and receive a shell before they are able to interact with the Linux system and kernel. A single user can log in to several different terminals simultaneously locally or across a network.

- Regardless of the type of terminal that you use (graphical or command-line), you are able to enter commands, options, and arguments at a shell prompt to perform system tasks, obtain command help, or shut down the Linux system. The shell is case sensitive and understands a variety of special characters called shell metacharacters, which should be protected if their special meaning is not required.

Key Terms

Advanced Technology Attachment (ATA)   *See also* Parallel Advanced Technology Attachment.

arguments   The text that appears after a command name, does not start with a dash "-" character, and specifies information the command requires to work properly.

authentication   The process whereby each user must log in with a valid user name and password before gaining access to the user interface of a system.

BASH shell   The Bourne Again Shell; it is the default command-line interface in Linux.

BIOS (Basic Input/Output System)   The part of a computer system that contains the programs used to initialize hardware components at boot time.

boot loader   A small program started by BIOS that executes the Linux kernel in memory.

command   A program that exists on the hard disk and is executed when typed on the command line.

dual booting   The process of installing more than one operating system on a computer. The user can then choose the operating system to load at system startup.

ext2   A nonjournaling Linux filesystem.

ext3   A journaling Linux filesystem.

ext4   An improved version of the ext3 filesystem with an extended feature set and better performance.

extended partition   A partition on a hard disk that can be further subdivided into components called logical drives.

filesystem   The way in which a hard disk partition is formatted to allow data to reside on the physical media; common Linux filesystems include ext2, ext3, ext4, REISER, and VFAT.

firstboot wizard   A configuration utility that is run at system startup immediately following a Fedora Linux installation.

Free Identity, Policy, and Audit (FreeIPA)   A set of security software that provides secure authentication across a network using several technologies that work together, including LDAP, Kerberos, NTP, and DNS.

GRand Unified Bootloader (GRUB)   A common boot loader used in Linux.

GUID Partition Table (GPT)   The area of a large hard disk (> 2TB) outside a partition that stores partition information and boot loaders.

Hardware Compatibility List (HCL)   A list of hardware components that have been tested and deemed compatible with a given operating system.

info pages   A set of local, easy-to-read command syntax documentation available by typing the info command.

Integrated Drive Electronics (IDE)   *See also* Parallel Advanced Technology Attachment.

journaling   A filesystem function that keeps a journal of the information that needs to be written to the hard disk; common Linux journaling filesystems include ext3, ext4, and REISER.

Lightweight Directory Access Protocol (LDAP)   A protocol that is used by services to query directory databases for purposes of authentication.

logical drives   The smaller partitions contained within an extended partition on a hard disk.

Logical Volume Manager (LVM)   A set of services that is used to manage logical volumes stored on one or more hard disks.

man pages   *See* manual pages.

manual pages   The most common set of local command syntax documentation, available by typing the man command. Also known as man pages.

Master Boot Record (MBR)   The area of a typical hard disk (< 2TB) outside a partition that stores partition information and boot loaders.

memtest86   A common RAM-checking utility.

metacharacters   The key combinations that have special meaning in the Linux operating system.

Network Information Service (NIS)   A set of services that is used to standardize the configuration and centralize the authentication of UNIX and Linux-based systems across a network.

Network Time Protocol (NTP)   A protocol that is used to synchronize the time on a computer from across a network such as the Internet.

options   The specific letters that start with a dash "-" or two and appear after the command name to alter the way the command works.

Parallel Advanced Technology Attachment (PATA)   A legacy hard disk technology that uses ribbon cables to typically attach up to four hard disk devices to a single computer.

partitions   A small section of an entire hard disk created to make the hard disk easier to use. Partitions can be primary or extended.

primary partitions   The separate divisions into which a hard disk can be divided (up to four are allowed per hard disk).

Redundant Array of Inexpensive Disks (RAID)   A type of storage that can be used to combine hard disks together for performance and/or fault tolerance.

REISER   A journaling filesystem used in Linux.

Serial Advanced Technology Attachment (SATA)   A hard disk technology that allows for fast data transfer along a serial cable. It is commonly used in newer workstation and server-class computers.

shell   A user interface that accepts input from the user and passes the input to the kernel for processing.

Small Computer Systems Interface (SCSI)   A high-performance hard disk technology that is commonly used in server-class computers.

swap memory   *See also* virtual memory.

System Rescue   A feature that allows you to boot a small Linux system from DVD to repair a Linux system that resides on the hard disk.

terminal   The channel that allows a certain user to log in and communicate with the kernel via a user interface.

VFAT (Virtual File Allocation Table)   A nonjournaling filesystem that might be used in Linux.

virtual memory   An area on a hard disk, known as a swap partition, that can be used to store information that normally resides in physical memory (RAM), if the physical memory is being used excessively.

Winbind   A set of software components that allows Linux computers to authenticate against a Microsoft Active Directory database.

Review Questions

1. What is the default shell in Linux called?

   a.   SH

   b.   BSH

   c.   CSH

   d.   BASH

2. What equivalent to the man command generally provides an easier-to-read description of the queried command and also contains links to other related information?

   a.   who

   b.   man help

   c.   man -descriptive

   d.   info

3. What command can you use to safely shut down the Linux system immediately?

   a.   shutdown -c

   b.   shutdown -r

   c.   down

   d.   halt

4. What command is equivalent to the man –k *keyword* command?

   a.   find *keyword*

   b.   man *keyword*

   c.   apropos *keyword*

   d.   appaloosa *keyword*

5. Which of the following is not a piece of information that the Fedora installation program prompts you for?

   a. time zone

   b. package selection

   c. firewall settings

   d. host name

   e. keyboard layout

6. Linux commands entered via the command line are not case sensitive. True or False?

7. Which command blanks the terminal screen, erasing previously displayed output?

   a. `erase`

   b. `clean`

   c. `blank`

   d. `clear`

8. When sitting at a computer running Linux, what key combination is pressed to open the graphical terminal?

   a. Ctrl+Alt+G

   b. Ctrl+Alt+F4

   c. Ctrl+Alt+F1

   d. Ctrl+7

9. After you log in to a terminal, you receive a user interface called a _____.

   a. GUID

   b. shell

   c. text box

   d. command screen

10. Users enter commands directly to the kernel of the Linux operating system. True or False?

11. How can you protect a metacharacter (such as the $ character) from shell interpretation?

   a. Precede it with a /.

   b. Follow it with a \.

   c. Precede it with a $.

   d. It cannot be done because metacharacters are essential.

   e. Precede it with a \.

12. You know a Linux command will perform a desired function for you, but you cannot remember the full name of the command. You do remember it will flush a variable from

your system. Which command typed at a command prompt displays a list of commands that would likely contain the command you desire?

   a.   man –k flush

   b.   man –k find all

   c.   man flush

   d.   man –key flush

13. Which command displays the users who are currently logged in to the Linux system?

   a.   finger

   b.   who

   c.   id

   d.   date

14. Which of the following packages can be used to standardize configuration files across Linux systems?

   a.   Samba

   b.   Apache

   c.   NIS

   d.   NFS

15. Which prompt does the root user receive when logged in to the system?

   a. $

   b.   @

   c.   #

   d.   !

16. Which prompt do regular users receive when logged in to the system?

   a. $

   b.   @

   c.   #

   d.   !

17. Which of the following refers to the third primary partition on the second SCSI hard disk within Linux?

   a.   hdb2

   b.   sda3

   c.   hdb3

   d.   sdb3

18. Which two partitions do you typically create at minimum during a Fedora Linux installation? (Choose two answers.)

   a. /

   b. /boot

   c. swap

   d. /home

19. You are planning to install 7GB of packages during the installation of your Linux server. Your Linux server has 2GB of RAM. How much free space should you have on your hard disk at minimum?

   a. 7GB

   b. 9GB

   c. 14GB

   d. 22GB

20. Which boot loader is available to choose from during the installation of Fedora Linux?

   a. LILO

   b. ABOOT

   c. GRUB

   d. TeX

Hands-On Projects

These projects should be completed in the order given and should take a total of three hours to complete. The software and hardware requirements for these projects include the following:

- A Fedora 13 DVD

- A Pentium 4 class or greater computer with at least 1GB of RAM, a 60GB hard disk, and a DVD drive.

- A Web browser and an Internet connection

Project 2-1

In this hands-on project, you fill in a preinstallation checklist.

1. Fill in the preinstallation checklist in Table 2-11 by supplying the appropriate information.

2. For any hardware components listed in the preceding preinstallation checklist, ensure that the hardware is listed on the HCL available on the Internet at *http://fedoraproject.org/wiki/HCL*.

Hardware or Software Item	Description
CPU (Type and MHz)	
RAM (GB)	
Language support	English
Keyboard model and layout	
Mouse model and device	
Hard disk type (PATA, SATA, eSATA, SCSI, iSCSI)	
Hard disk size (GB)	
Space required for swap partition (GB) *This should be equal to twice the amount of RAM!	
Space available for filesystems (GB) *This should be equal to the hard disk size less the amount swap	
Boot loader	GRUB
Host name	server1.class.com
Time zone	
Root password	secret
Additional user account name	user1
Additional user account password	secret
Packages to install	All packages except virtualization and additional language support
Video card make and model	
Video card RAM (MB)	
Monitor make and model	
Monitor VSync and HSync Ranges	

Table 2-11   Preinstallation checklist for Project 2-1

Project 2-2

In this hands-on project, you install Fedora 13 Linux on a computer.

1. Ensure that your DVD is bootable in your computer's BIOS.
2. Boot your computer using the Fedora 13 DVD.
3. Press **Enter** at the Welcome to Fedora 13 screen, accept the default installation option, and start the installation.
4. At the Disc Found screen, select **Skip** and press **Enter**. It is recommended that you skip disc checking unless you suspect errors on the disc media itself.
5. Click **Next** at the Fedora welcome screen.
6. Click **Next** at the language selection screen to accept the default installation language, English.

7. Click **Next** at the keyboard configuration screen to accept the default configuration, U.S. English.

8. Ensure that **Basic Storage Devices** is selected and click **Next**.

9. Type **server1.class.com** in the host name text box and click **Next**.

10. At the time zone selection screen, choose the correct time zone for your region and click **Next**.

11. When prompted to select a password for the root user, enter the password **secret** in both dialog boxes and click **Next**. When prompted to use the password even though it is based on a dictionary word, click **Use Anyway**.

12. When prompted to choose a type of partitioning (in other words, choose a partitioning scheme), select **Create Custom Layout** and click **Next**.

13. When you are asked to select a device, delete any existing partitions, and create the following two standard partitions:

    Partition 1:   Mount Point = /   Type = ext3   Size (Fixed) = 30000MB
    Partition 2:   Type = swap   Size (Fixed) = 4000MB

    ave all remaining space on your hard disk for future exercises.

13. Click **Next** when finished and then click **Write changes to disk** to partition your hard disk as well as prepare the root filesystem and swap.

14. Click **Next** at the boot loader configuration screen to install the GRUB bootloader on the MBR (or GPT) of your first hard disk.

15. When prompted to select installation packages, ensure that **Graphical Desktop** and the **Installation Repo** repository are selected. Choose **Customize Now** and click **Next**.

16. At the software selection screen, ensure that the following packages are selected:

    • Desktop Environments: Ensure that all desktop environments are selected.

    • Applications: Ensure that all packages are selected.

    • Development: Ensure that all packages are selected.

    • Servers: Ensure that all packages are selected.

    • Base System: Ensure that all packages are selected except Virtualization.

    • Languages: The default of English is appropriate; no additional selections are necessary.

18. Click **Next** when finished. Your system will analyze your selections for dependencies and install the operating system. This may take several minutes.

19. When the installation has completed, click **Reboot** and remove your DVD.

20. After your system has booted, click **Forward** at the Welcome screen of the firstboot wizard.

21. At the License Agreement screen, click **Forward**.

22. At the Create User screen, enter the following information:
    Username: user1
    Full Name: sample user one
    Password: secret

23. When finished, click **Forward**. When prompted to use the password even though it is based on a dictionary word, click **Yes**.

24. At the Date and Time screen, confirm the local date and time and click **Forward**.

25. At the Hardware Profile screen, ensure that **Do not send profile** is selected and click **Finish**. Click **No, do not send** when prompted to reconsider sending your hardware profile.

Project 2-3

In this hands-on project, you explore some command-line terminals on a Linux system and enter some basic commands into the BASH shell.

1. After your Linux system has been loaded, you are placed at a graphical terminal (tty1). Instead of logging in to this graphical terminal, press **Ctrl+Alt+F2** to switch to a command-line terminal (tty2) and then log in to the terminal using the user name **root** and the password **secret**. Which prompt did you receive and why? *because now I'm Superuser*

2. At the command prompt, type **date** and press **Enter** to view the current date and time. Now type **Date** and press **Enter**. Why did you receive an error message? Can you tell which shell gave you the error message? *BsH* *caps don't work in linux*

3. Switch to a different command-line terminal (tty5) by pressing **Ctrl+Alt+F5** and log in to the terminal using the user name **user1** and the password **secret**. Which prompt did you receive and why? *$ normal user*

4. At the command prompt, type **who** and press **Enter** to view the users logged in to the system. Who is logged in and on which terminal? *User-1 → tty5, Root → tty2, user1 → tty1*

5. Switch back to the terminal tty2 by pressing **Ctrl+Alt+F2**. Did you need to log in? Are the outputs from the date and Date commands still visible? *No* *Yes*

6. Try typing in each command listed in Table 2-7 in order (pressing **Enter** after each) and observe the output. What did the last command (exit) do? *logged off from the shell*

7. Switch to the terminal tty5 by pressing **Ctrl+Alt+F5** and type **exit** to log out of your shell.

Project 2-4

In this hands-on project, you log in to a graphical terminal in Fedora Linux and interact with the GNOME and KDE desktops.

1. Switch to the graphical terminal (tty1) by pressing **Ctrl+Alt+F1**, click **sample user one**, supply the password **secret**, and press **Enter**. Which desktop is started and why? *GNOME*

2. Observe the GNOME desktop. Use your mouse to select the **Applications** menu in the upper-left corner of your screen, select **System Tools**, and then select **Terminal** to open a BASH shell prompt. What prompt do you receive and why? *$ normal user*

3. At the command prompt, type **who** and press **Enter** to view the users logged in to the system. Note that tty1 is listed as running on port 0 (:0) and your Terminal application is running as a pseudo terminal session (pts/0) within your GUI environment.

4. Select the **System** menu, select **Log Out user1**, and then click **Log Out** to confirm the action.

5. At the graphical login screen, click **sample user one** and then choose **KDE** from the Sessions selection box at the bottom of the screen. Next, supply the password **secret** and press **Enter** to log in to the KDE desktop.

6. Observe the KDE desktop. Select the **Fedora** icon in the lower-left section of your screen and navigate to **Applications, System, Terminal** to open a BASH shell prompt. What prompt do you receive and why? *$, As user is normal user*

7. At the command prompt, type **echo $SHELL** and press **Enter** to view your current shell. Is this shell the same shell used for command-line terminals? *Yes*

8. Click the **Fedora** icon again. From this menu, select **Leave** and then **Logout**. Click **Logout** to confirm the action.

Project 2-5

In this hands-on project, you use and protect shell metacharacters.

1. Switch to a command-line terminal (tty2) by pressing **Ctrl+Alt+F2** and log in to the terminal using the user name **root** and the password **secret**.

2. At the command prompt, type **date;who** and press **Enter** to run the date command immediately followed by the who command. Use the information in Table 2-8 to describe the purpose of the ; metacharacter.

3. At the command prompt, type **echo This is OK** and press **Enter** to display a message on the terminal screen.

4. At the command prompt, type **echo Don't do this** and press **Enter**. Which character needs to be protected in the previous command? Press the **Ctrl** and **c** keys together to cancel your command and return to a BASH shell prompt. *Metacharacter ' .*

5. At the command prompt, type **echo "Don't do this"** and press **Enter**. What is displayed on the terminal screen?

6. At the command prompt, type **echo Don\'t do this** and press **Enter**. What is displayed on the terminal screen? *Don't do this*

7. At the command prompt, type **echo $SHELL** and press **Enter** to view the expansion of *bin/bash* a variable using a shell metacharacter. What is displayed on the terminal screen? Next, *which is current shell* type **echo $TEST** and press **Enter** to find out what happens when a variable that does not exist is used in a command. What is displayed? *empty blank response.*

8. At the command prompt, type **echo You have $4.50** and press **Enter**. What is displayed? Why? Which character needs to be protected in the previous command? *$* What are two different ways that you can protect this character from interpretation by the shell? *because it dont find any value variable (4) after $ prompt.*
You have .50
You have $4.50 (or)
You have $4.50

9. At the command prompt, type **echo 'You have $4.50'** and press **Enter**. What is displayed on the terminal screen? Did the single quotation marks protect this metacharacter from shell interpretation? *You have $4.50* → *Yes*

10. At the command prompt, type **echo "You have $4.50"** and press **Enter**. What is displayed on the terminal screen? Did the double quotation marks protect this metacharacter from shell interpretation? *You have $.50* → *NO*

11. At the command prompt, type **echo You have \\$4.50** and press **Enter**. What is displayed on the terminal screen? Did the backslash protect this metacharacter from shell interpretation? *yes*   *↓ You have $4.50*

12. At the command prompt, type **echo My name is `whoami`** and press **Enter**. What function do back quotes perform?   *eliminates any variables/commands*

13. Type **exit** and press **Enter** to log out of your shell.

Project 2-6

In this hands-on project, you find information about commands using online help utilities, and you log out of your shell.

1. Press **Ctrl+Alt+F2** to switch to a command-line terminal (tty2), and then log in to the terminal using the user name **root** and the password **secret**.

2. At the command prompt, type man –k cron and press **Enter** to view a list of manual pages that have the word "cron" in the name or description. Use Table 2-9 to determine what type of manual pages is displayed. How many manual pages are there for the crontab command? Are they different types of manual pages? *(9)*   *yes*

If you do not see any output from the man –k command, run the makewhatis command to index the manual pages.

3. At the command prompt, type **man crontab** and press **Enter** to view the manual page for the crontab command. Observe the syntax of the crontab command and press **q** when finished to quit the manual page and return to your command prompt.

4. At the command prompt, type **man 5 crontab** and press **Enter** to view the manual page for the crontab file format. Observe the syntax of the crontab file format and press **q** when finished to quit the manual page and return to your command prompt.

5. At the command prompt, type **info** and press **Enter** to view a list of available GNU info pages. When finished, press **q** to quit the info utility.

6. At the command prompt, type **info date** and press **Enter** to view syntax information regarding the date command, and press **q** to quit the info utility when finished.

7. At the command prompt, type **help** to view a list of BASH shell functions that have documentation. Because the list is too long for your terminal, press the **Shift** and **Page Up** keys simultaneously to shift one page up to view the top of the list. Then press the **Shift** and **Page Down** keys simultaneously to shift one page down to view your command prompt again.

8. At the command prompt, type **help exit** to view information on the exit command, a function of your BASH shell.

9. Type **exit** and press **Enter** to log out of your shell.

Project 2-7

In this hands-on project, you finalize your Linux installation by configuring your network interface and disabling your firewall and SELinux configuration. (You will learn more about configuring Firewalls and SELinux in Chapter 15.) Finally, you will properly shut down your Linux system.

1. Log in to the GNOME desktop as **sample user one**.

2. Open the **System** menu and navigate to **Administration, Network** and supply the root user password of **secret** when prompted. Next, use the Network utility to configure the network interface on your system to obtain Internet access. The configuration parameters to gain Internet access on your campus network will be provided by your instructor. Close the Network Configuration utility when finished.

3. Open the **System** menu again and navigate to **Administration, Firewall.** Supply the root user password of **secret** if prompted. Click **Disable**, click **Apply**, and then click **Yes** to disable your firewall. Close the Firewall Configuration utility when finished.

4. Open the **System** menu again and navigate to **Administration, SELinux Management**. Supply the root user password of **secret** if prompted. Change the **System Default Enforcing Mode** to **Disabled** and close the SELinux Administration utility.

5. Press **Ctrl+Alt+F2** to switch to a command-line terminal (tty2), and then log in to the terminal using the user name **root** and the password **secret**.

6. At the command prompt, type **shutdown –h now** to halt your system immediately. Which commands from Table 2-10 perform the same function as shutdown –h now?

halt

Discovery Exercises

1. You are the network administrator for Slimjim, a peripheral device company. The network uses Linux and you need information on some commands to perform your job. Open the manual pages and find all the commands that have the word "copy" in their name or description. What command did you use to accomplish this task? Are there any commands in this list that only a root user can execute? How are they indicated? Select any two of them and compare their info and manual pages. Access and read the manual pages on three other commands that interest you, either by using the command name or by searching for them with a related keyword (try using apropos).

2. Identify the errors with the following commands and indicate possible solutions. (*Hint:* Try typing them at a shell prompt to view the error message.)

```
Echo "This command does not work properly"
date -z
apropos man -k
help date
finger route
shutdown -c now
echo "I would like lots of $$$"
man 8 date
```

## chapter 3

Exploring Linux Filesystems

After completing this chapter, you will be able to:

- Understand and navigate the Linux directory structure using relative and absolute pathnames
- Describe the various types of Linux files
- View filenames and file types
- Use shell wildcards to specify multiple filenames
- Display the contents of text files and binary files
- Search text files for regular expressions using grep
- Use the vi editor to manipulate text files
- Identify common alternatives to the vi editor used today

An understanding of the structure and commands surrounding the Linux filesystem is essential for effectively using Linux to manipulate data. In the first part of this chapter, you explore the Linux filesystem hierarchy by changing your position in the filesystem tree and listing filenames of various types. Next, you examine the shell wildcard metacharacters used to specify multiple filenames as well as view the contents of files using standard Linux commands. You then learn about the regular expression metacharacters used when searching for text within files, and are introduced to the vi editor and its equivalents.

The Linux Directory Structure

Fundamental to using the Linux operating system is an understanding of how Linux stores files on the hard drive. Typical Linux systems could have thousands of data and program files on the hard drive; thus, a structure that organizes those files is necessary to make it easier to find and manipulate data and run programs. Recall from the previous chapter that Linux uses a logical directory tree to organize files into different directories (also known as folders). When a user stores files in a certain **directory**, they are physically stored in the filesystem of a certain partition on a hard disk inside the computer. Most people are familiar with the Windows operating system directory tree structure as depicted in Figure 3-1. Each filesystem on a hard drive partition is referred to by a drive letter (such as C: or D:) and has a root directory (indicated by the \ character) containing subdirectories that together form a hierarchical tree.

It is important to describe directories in the directory tree properly; the **absolute pathname** to a file or directory is the full pathname of a certain file or directory starting from the root directory. In Figure 3-1, the absolute pathname for the color directory is C:\windows\color, and the absolute pathname for the sue directory is D:\home\sue. In other words, we refer to C:\windows\color as the color directory below the windows directory below the root of the C drive. Similarly, we refer to D:\home\sue as the sue directory below the home directory below the root of the D drive.

Linux uses a similar directory structure, but with no drive letters. The structure contains a single root (referred to using the / character), with different filesystems on hard drive partitions mounted (or attached) to different directories on this directory tree. The directories that each filesystem is mounted to are transparent to the user. An example of a sample Linux directory tree equivalent to the Windows sample directory tree shown in Figure 3-1 is depicted in Figure 3-2. Note that the subdirectory named "root" in Figure 3-2 is different from the root (/) directory. You'll learn more about the root subdirectory in the next section.

In Figure 3-2, the absolute pathname for the color directory is /windows/color, and the absolute pathname for the sue directory is /home/sue. In other words, we refer to the /windows/

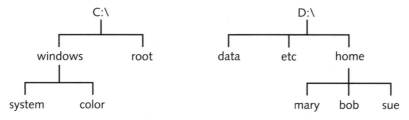

Figure 3-1 The Windows filesystem structure

Source: Course Technology/Cengage Learning

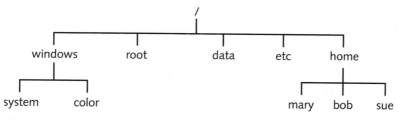

Figure 3-2 The Linux filesystem structure

Source: Course Technology/Cengage Learning

color directory as the color directory below the windows directory below the root of the system (the / character). Similarly, we refer to the /home/sue directory as the sue directory below the home directory below the root of the system.

Changing Directories

When you log in to a Linux system, you are placed in your **home directory**, which is a place unique to your user account for storing personal files. Regular users usually have a home directory named after their user account under the /home directory, as in /home/sue. The root user, however, has a home directory called root under the root directory of the system (/root), as shown in Figure 3-2. Regardless of your user name, you can always refer to your own home directory using the ~ **metacharacter**.

To confirm the system directory that you are currently in, simply observe the name at the end of the shell prompt or run the **pwd (print working directory) command** at a command-line prompt. If you are logged in as the root user, the following output is displayed on the terminal screen:

```
[root@server1 ~]# pwd
/root
[root@server1 ~]#_
```

However, if you are logged in as the user sue, you see the following output:

```
[sue@server1 ~]$ pwd
/home/sue
[sue@server1 ~]$_
```

To change directories, you can issue the **cd (change directory) command** with an argument specifying the destination directory. If you do not specify a destination directory, the cd command returns you to your home directory:

```
[root@server1 ~]# cd /home/mary
[root@server1 mary]# pwd
/home/mary
[root@server1 mary]# cd /etc
[root@server1 etc]# pwd
/etc
[root@server1 etc]# cd
[root@server1 ~]# pwd
/root
[root@server1 ~]#_
```

You can also use the ~ metacharacter to refer to another user's home directory by appending a user name at the end:

```
[root@server1 ~]# cd ~mary
[root@server1 mary]# pwd
/home/mary
[root@server1 mary]# cd ~
[root@server1 ~]# pwd
/root
[root@server1 ~]#_
```

In many of the examples discussed earlier, the argument specified after the cd command is an absolute pathname to a directory, meaning that the system has all the information it needs to find the destination directory because the pathname starts from the root (/) of the system. However, in most Linux commands, you can also use a relative pathname in place of an absolute pathname to reduce typing. A **relative pathname** is the pathname of a target file or directory relative to your current directory in the tree. To specify a directory underneath your current directory, simply refer to that directory by name (do not start the pathname with a / character). To refer to a directory one step closer to the root of the tree (also known as a **parent directory**), simply use two dots (..). An example of using relative pathnames to move around the directory tree is shown next:

```
[root@server1 ~]# cd /home/mary
[root@server1 mary]# pwd
/home/mary
[root@server1 mary]# cd ..
[root@server1 home]# pwd
/home
[root@server1 home]# cd mary
[root@server1 mary]# pwd
/home/mary
[root@server1 mary]#_
```

In the preceding example, we used ".." to move up one parent directory and then used the word "mary" to specify the mary **subdirectory** relative to our current location in the tree; however, you can also move more than one level up or down the directory tree:

```
[root@server1 ~]# cd /home/mary
[root@server1 mary]# pwd
/home/mary
[root@server1 mary]# cd ../..
[root@server1 /]# pwd
/
[root@server1 /]# cd home/mary
[root@server1 mary]# pwd
/home/mary
[root@server1 mary]#_
```

 You can also use one dot (.) to refer to the current directory. Although this is not useful when using the cd command, you do use one dot later in this book.

Although absolute pathnames are straightforward to use as arguments to commands when specifying the location of a certain file or directory, relative pathnames can save you a great deal of typing and reduce the potential for error if your current directory is far away from the root directory. Suppose, for example, that the current directory is /home/sue/projects/acme/plans and you need to change to the /home/sue/projects/acme directory. Using an absolute pathname, you would type `cd /home/sue/projects/acme`. However, using a relative pathname, you only need to type `cd ..` to perform the same task because the /home/sue/projects/acme directory is one parent directory above the current location in the directory tree.

An alternate method for saving time when typing pathnames as arguments to commands is to use the **Tab-completion feature** of the BASH shell. To do this, type enough unique letters of a directory and press Tab to allow the BASH shell to find the intended file or directory being specified and fill in the appropriate information. If there is more than one possible match, the Tab-completion feature alerts you with a beep; pressing Tab again after this beep presents you with a list of possible files or directories.

Observe the directory structure in Figure 3-2. To use the Tab-completion feature to change the current directory to /home/sue, you simply type `cd /h` and then press Tab. This changes the previous characters on the terminal screen to display cd /home/ (the BASH shell was able to fill in the appropriate information because the /home directory is the only directory underneath the / directory that starts with the letter "h"). Then, you could add an s character to the command so that the command line displays `cd /home/s`, then press Tab once again to allow the shell to fill in the remaining letters. This results in the command `cd /home/sue/` being displayed on the terminal screen (the sue directory is the only directory that begins with the s character underneath the /home directory). At this point, you can press Enter to execute the command and change the current directory to /home/sue.

In addition to directories, the Tab-completion feature of the BASH shell can also be used to specify the pathname to files and executable programs.

Viewing Files and Directories

The point of a directory structure is to organize files into an easy-to-use format. To locate the file you need to execute, view, or edit, you need to be able to display a list of the contents of a particular directory. You'll learn how to do that shortly, but first, you need to learn about the various types of files and filenames, as well as the different commands used to select filenames for viewing.

File Types

Fundamental to viewing files and directories is a solid understanding of the various types of files present on most Linux systems. Several different types of files can exist on a Linux system. The most common include the following:

- Text files
- Binary data files
- Executable program files

- Directory files
- Linked files
- Special device files
- Named pipes and sockets

Most files on a Linux system that contain configuration information are **text files**. Another type of file are programs that exist on the hard drive before they are executed in memory to become processes. A program is typically associated with several supporting **binary data files** that store information such as common functions and graphics. In addition, directories themselves are actually files; they are special files that serve as placeholders to organize other files. When you create a directory, a file is placed on the hard drive to represent that directory.

Linked files are files that have an association with one another; they can represent the same data or they can point to another file (in which case the linked file is also known as a shortcut file). **Special device files** are less common than the other file types that have been mentioned, yet they are important for systems administrators because they represent different devices on the system, such as hard disks and serial ports. These device files are used in conjunction with commands that manipulate devices on the system; special device files are typically found only in the /dev directory and are discussed in later chapters of this book. As with special device files, **named pipe files** are uncommon and used primarily by administrators. Named pipes identify a channel that passes information from one process in memory to another, and in some cases they can be mediated by files on the hard drive. Writes to the file are processed while another process reads from it to achieve this passing of information. Another variant of a named pipe file is a **socket file**, which allows a process on another computer to write to a file on the local computer while another process reads from that file.

Filenames

Files are recognized by their **filenames**, which can include up to 255 characters yet are rarely longer than 20 characters on most Linux systems. Filenames are typically composed of alphanumeric characters, the underscore (_) character, the dash (—) character, and the dot, or period (.), character.

It is important to avoid using the shell metacharacters discussed in the previous chapter when naming files. Using a filename that contains a shell metacharacter as an argument to a Linux command might produce unexpected results.

Filenames that start with a period (.) are referred to as hidden files. You need to use a special command to display them in a file list. This command is discussed later in this chapter.

Filenames used by the Windows operating system typically end with a period and three characters that identify the file type—for example, document.txt (a text file) and server.exe (an **executable program** file). However, most files on the hard drive of a Linux system do not follow this pattern, although some files on the Linux filesystem do contain characters at the end of the filename that indicate the file type. These characters are commonly referred to as

Filename Extensions	Description
.c	C programming language source code files
.cc .cpp	C++ programming language source code files
.html .htm	HTML (Hypertext Markup Language) files
.ps	Files formatted for printing with postscript
.txt	Text files
.tar	Archived files (contain other files within)
.gz .bz2 .Z	Compressed files
.tar.gz .tgz .tar.bz2 .tar.Z	Compressed archived files
.conf .cfg	Configuration files (contain text)
.so	Shared object (programming library) files
.o	Compiled object files
.pl	PERL (Practical Extraction and Report Language) programs
.tcl	Tcl (Tool Command Language) programs
.jpg .jpeg .png .tiff .xpm .gif	Binary files that contain graphical images
.sh	Shell scripts (contain text that is executed by the shell)

Table 3-1 Common filename extensions

filename extensions. Table 3-1 lists common examples of filename extensions and their associated file types.

Listing Files

Linux hosts a variety of commands that can be used to display files and their types in various directories on hard drive partitions. By far, the most common method for displaying files is to use the **ls command.** Following is an example of a file listing in the root user's home directory:

```
[root@server1 ~]# pwd
/root
[root@server1 ~]# ls
current myprogram project project12 project2 project4
Desktop myscript project1 project13 project3 project5
[root@server1 ~]#_
```

The files listed previously and discussed throughout this chapter are for example purposes only. The Hands-On Projects use different files.

The ls command displays all the files in the current directory in columnar format. However, you can also pass an argument to the ls command indicating the directory to be listed if the current directory listing is not required. In the following example, the files are listed underneath the /home/bob directory without changing the current directory:

```
[root@server1 ~]# pwd
/root
[root@server1 ~]# ls /home/bob
assignment1 file1 letter letter2 project1
[root@server1 ~]#_
```

When running the ls command, notice that files of different types are often represented as different colors. However, the specific colors used to represent files of certain types might vary from terminal to terminal and distribution to distribution. As a result, do not assume color alone indicates the file type.

Windows uses the dir command to list files and directories. To simplify the learning of Linux for Windows users, there is a dir command in Linux, which is simply a pointer or shortcut to the ls command.

Recall from the previous chapter that you can use switches to alter the behavior of commands. To view a list of files and their types, use the –F switch to the ls command:

```
[root@server1 ~]# pwd
/root
[root@server1 ~]# ls -F
current@ myprogram*  project    project12  project2  project4
Desktop/ myscript*   project1   project13  project3  project5
[root@server1 ~]#_
```

The ls –F command appends a special character at the end of each filename displayed to indicate the type of file. In the preceding output, note that the filenames current, Desktop, myprogram, and myscript have special characters appended to their names. The @ symbol indicates a linked file, the * symbol indicates an executable file, the / indicates a subdirectory, the = character indicates a socket, and the | character indicates a named pipe. All other file types do not have a special character appended to them and could be text files, binary data files, or special device files.

It is common convention to name directories starting with an upper-case letter, such as the D in the Desktop directory shown in the preceding output. This ensures that directories are listed at the beginning of the ls command output and allows you to quickly determine which names refer to directories when running the ls command without any options that specify file type.

Although the ls –F command is a quick way of getting file type information in an easy-to-read format, at times you need to obtain more detailed information about each file. The ls –l command can be used to provide a long listing for each file in a certain directory.

```
[root@server1 ~]# pwd
/root
[root@server1 ~]# ls -l
total 548
```

```
lrwxrwxrwx   1 root    root          9 Apr   7   09:56   current -> project12
drwx------   3 root    root       4096 Mar  29   10:01   Desktop
-rwxr-xr-x   1 root    root     519964 Apr   7   09:59   myprogram
-rwxr-xr-x   1 root    root         20 Apr   7   09:58   myscript
-rw-r--r--   1 root    root         71 Apr   7   09:58   project
-rw-r--r--   1 root    root         71 Apr   7   09:59   project1
-rw-r--r--   1 root    root         71 Apr   7   09:59   project12
-rw-r--r--   1 root    root          0 Apr   7   09:56   project13
-rw-r--r--   1 root    root         71 Apr   7   09:59   project2
-rw-r--r--   1 root    root         90 Apr   7   10:01   project3
-rw-r--r--   1 root    root         99 Apr   7   10:01   project4
-rw-r--r--   1 root    root        108 Apr   7   10:01   project5
[root@server1 ~]#_
```

Each file listed in the preceding example has eight components of information listed in columns from left to right:

1. A file type character
   - The d character represents a directory.
   - The l character represents a symbolically linked file (discussed in Chapter 5).
   - The b and c characters represent special device files (discussed in Chapter 6).
   - The n character represents a named pipe.
   - The s character represents a socket.
   - The – character represents all other file types (text files, binary data files).
2. A list of permissions on the file (also called the mode of the file)
3. A hard link count (discussed in Chapter 5)
4. The owner of the file (discussed in Chapter 5)
5. The group owner of the file (discussed in Chapter 5)
6. The file size
7. The most recent modification time of the file
8. The filename (Some files are shortcuts or pointers to other files and indicated with an arrow ->, as with the file called "current" in the preceding output; these are known as symbolic links and are discussed in Chapter 5.)

For the file named project in the previous example, you can see that this file is a regular file because the long listing of it begins with a – character, the permissions on the file are rw-r--r--, the hard link count is 1, the owner of the file is the root user, the group owner of the file is the root group, the size of the file is 71 bytes, and the file was modified last on April 7th at 9:58 a.m.

NOTE   On most Linux systems, a shortcut to the ls command can be used to display the same columns of information as the ls -l command. Some users prefer to use this shortcut, commonly known as an alias, which is invoked when a user types ll at a command prompt. This is known as the ll command.

The ls -F and ls -l commands are valuable to a user who wants to display file types; however, neither of these commands can display all file types using special characters. To display the file type of any file, you can use the **file command**; simply give the file command an argument specifying what file to analyze. You can also pass multiple files as arguments or use the * metacharacter to refer to all files in the current directory. An example of using the file command in the root user's home directory is:

```
[root@server1 ~]# pwd
/root
[root@server1 ~]# ls
current  myprogram  project   project12  project2  project4
Desktop  myscript   project1  project13  project3  project5
[root@server1 ~]# file Desktop
Desktop:  directory
[root@server1 ~]# file project Desktop
project:  ASCII text
Desktop:  directory
[root@server1 ~]# file *
Desktop:   directory
current:   symbolic link to project12
myprogram: ELF 32-bit LSB executable, Intel 80386, version 1, dynamically
linked (uses shared libs), stripped
myscript:  Bourne-Again shell script text executable
project:   ASCII text
project1:  ASCII text
project12: ASCII text
project13: empty
project2:  ASCII text
project3:  ASCII text
project4:  ASCII text
project5:  ASCII text
[root@server1 ~]#_
```

As shown in the preceding example, the file command can also identify the differences between types of executable files. The myscript file is a text file that contains executable commands (also known as a shell script), whereas the myprogram file is a 32-bit executable compiled program. The file command also identifies empty files, such as project13 in the previous example.

Some filenames inside each user's home directory represent important configuration files or program directories. Because these files are rarely edited by the user and can clutter up the listing of files, they are normally hidden from view when using the ls and file commands. Recall that filenames for hidden files start with a period character (.). To view them, simply pass the -a option to the ls command. Some hidden files that are commonly seen in the root user's home directory are shown next:

```
[root@server1 ~]# ls
current  myprogram  project   project12  project2  project4
Desktop  myscript   project1  project13  project3  project5
[root@server1 ~]# ls -a
```

```
.                        .gimp-1.2            project
..                       .gnome              project1
.bash_history            .gnome-desktop      project12
.bash_logout             .gnome_private      project13
.bash_profile            .gtkrc              project2
.bashrc                  .ICEauthority       project3
.cshrc                   .kde                project4
current                  .mcop               project5
.DCOPserver_server1_0    .MCOP-random-seed   .sane
Desktop                  .mcoprc             .sawfish
.first_start_kde         .mozilla            .tcshrc
.galeon                  myprogram           .Xauthority
.gconf                   myscript            .Xresources
.gconfd                  .nautilus           .xsession-errors
[root@server1 ~]#_
```

As discussed earlier, the period character (.) refers to the current working directory and the double-period character (..) refers to the parent directory relative to your current location in the directory tree. Each of these pointers is seen as a special (or fictitious) file when using the ls –a command, as each starts with a period.

You can also specify several options simultaneously for most commands on the command line and receive the combined functionality of all the options. For example, to view all hidden files and their file types, you could type:

```
[root@server1 ~]# ls -aF
./                       .gimp-1.2/           project
../                      .gnome/              project1
.bash_history            .gnome-desktop/      project12
.bash_logout             .gnome_private/      project13
.bash_profile            .gtkrc               project2
.bashrc                  .ICEauthority        project3
.cshrc                   .kde/                project4
current@                 .mcop/               project5
.DCOPserver_server1_0@   .MCOP-random-seed .sane/
Desktop/                 .mcoprc              .sawfish/
.first_start_kde         .mozilla/            .tcshrc
.galeon/                 myprogram            .Xauthority
.gconf/                  myscript             .Xresources
.gconfd/                 .nautilus/           .xsession-errors
[root@server1 ~]#_
```

The aforementioned options to the ls command (–l, –F, –a) are the most common options you would use when navigating the Linux directory tree; however, many options are available in the ls command that alter the listing of files on the filesystem. Table 3-2 depicts the most common of these options and their descriptions.

Wildcard Metacharacters

In the previous section, you saw that the * metacharacter stands for all the files in the current directory, much like a wildcard stands for, or matches, certain cards in a card game.

Option	Description	
-a --all	Lists all filenames	
-A --almost-all	Lists most filenames (excludes the . and .. special files)	
-C	Lists filenames in column format	
--color=n	Lists filenames without color	
-d --directory	Lists directory names instead of their contents	
-f	Lists all filenames without sorting	
-F --classify	Lists filenames classified by file type	
--full-time	Lists filenames in long format and displays the full modification time	
-l	Lists filenames in long format	
-lh -l --human-readable	Lists filenames in long format with human-readable (easy-to-read) file sizes	
-lG -l --no-group -o	Lists filenames in long format but omits the group information	
-r --reverse	Lists filenames reverse sorted	
-R --recursive	Lists filenames in the specified directory and all subdirectories	
-s	Lists filenames and their associated size in kilobytes (KB)	
-S	Lists filenames sorted by file size	
-t	Lists filenames sorted by modification time	
-U	Lists filenames without sorting	
-x	Lists filenames in rows rather than in columns	

Table 3-2 Common options to the `ls` command

As a result, the * metacharacter is called a **wildcard metacharacter**. Wildcard metacharacters can simplify commands that specify more than one filename on the command line, as you saw with the `file` command earlier. They match certain portions of filenames or the entire filename itself. Because they are interpreted by the shell, they can be used with most common Linux filesystem commands, including a few that have already been mentioned (`ls`, `file`, and `cd`). Table 3-3 displays a list of wildcard metacharacters and their descriptions.

Metacharacter	Description
*	Matches 0 or more characters in a filename
?	Matches 1 character in a filename
[aegh]	Matches 1 character in a filename—provided this character is either an a, e, g, or h
[a-e]	Matches 1 character in a filename—provided this character is either an a, b, c, d, or e
[!a-e]	Matches 1 character in a filename—provided this character is *not* an a, b, c, d, or e

Table 3-3 Wildcard metacharacters

Wildcards can be demonstrated using the `ls` command. Examples of using wildcard metacharacters to narrow the listing produced by the `ls` command are shown next:

```
[root@server1 ~]# ls
current   myprogram  project   project12  project2  project4
Desktop   myscript   project1  project13  project3  project5
[root@server1 ~]# ls project*
project  project1  project12  project13  project2  project3  project4
   project5
[root@server1 ~]# ls project?
project1  project2  project3  project4  project5
[root@server1 ~]# ls project??
project12  project13
[root@server1 ~]# ls project[135]
project1  project3  project5
[root@server1 ~]# ls project[!135]
project2  project4
[root@server1 ~]# _
```

Displaying the Contents of Text Files

So far, this chapter has discussed commands that can be used to navigate the Linux directory structure and view filenames and file types. You also need to know how to display the contents of these files. By far, the most common file type that users display is text files. These files are usually small and contain configuration information or instructions (called a shell script) that the shell interprets, but they can also contain other forms of text, as in e-mail messages. To display an entire text file on the terminal screen (a process known as **concatenation**), you can use the **cat command**. The following is an example of using the `cat` command to display the contents of an e-mail message (in the fictitious file project4):

```
[root@server1 ~]# ls
current   myprogram  project   project12  project2  project4
Desktop   myscript   project1  project13  project3  project5
[root@server1 ~]# cat project4
```

```
Hi there, I hope this day finds you well.

Unfortunately we were not able to make it to your dining
room this year while vacationing in Algonquin Park - I
especially wished to see the model of the Highland Inn
and the train station in the dining room.

I have been reading on the history of Algonquin Park but
no where could I find a description of where the Highland
Inn was originally located on Cache lake.

If it is no trouble, could you kindly let me know such that
I need not wait until next year when I visit your lodge?

Regards,
Mackenzie Elizabeth
[root@server1 ~]#_
```

You can also use the `cat` command to display the line number of each line in the file (in addition to the contents) by passing the –n option to the `cat` command. In the following example, the line numbers in the project4 file are displayed:

```
[root@server1 ~]# cat -n project4
     1  Hi there, I hope this day finds you well.
     2
     3  Unfortunately we were not able to make it to your dining
     4  room this year while vacationing in Algonquin Park - I
     5  especially wished to see the model of the Highland Inn
     6  and the train station in the dining room.
     7
     8  I have been reading on the history of Algonquin Park but
     9  no where could I find a description of where the Highland
    10  Inn was originally located on Cache lake.
    11
    12  If it is no trouble, could you kindly let me know such that
    13  I need not wait until next year when I visit your lodge?
    14
    15  Regards,
    16  Mackenzie Elizabeth
[root@server1 ~]#_
```

In some cases, you might want to display the contents of a certain text file in reverse order, which is useful when displaying files that have text appended to them continuously by system services. These files, also known as **log files**, contain the most recent entries at the bottom of the file. To display a file in reverse order, use the **tac command** (tac is cat spelled backwards), as shown next with the file project4:

```
[root@server1 ~]# tac project4
Mackenzie Elizabeth
Regards,

I need not wait until next year when I visit your lodge?
If it is no trouble, could you kindly let me know such that

Inn was originally located on Cache lake.
no where could I find a description of where the Highland
I have been reading on the history of Algonquin Park but

and the train station in the dining room.
especially wished to see the model of the Highland Inn
room this year while vacationing in Algonquin Park - I
Unfortunately we were not able to make it to your dining

Hi there, I hope this day finds you well.
[root@server1 ~]#_
```

If the file displayed is very large and you only want to view the first few lines of it, you can use the **head command.** The head command displays the first 10 lines (including blank lines) of a text file to the terminal screen, but can also take a numeric option specifying a different number of lines to display. The following shows an example of using the head command to view the top of the project4 file:

```
[root@server1 ~]# head project4
Hi there, I hope this day finds you well.

Unfortunately we were not able to make it to your dining
room this year while vacationing in Algonquin Park - I
especially wished to see the model of the Highland Inn
and the train station in the dining room.

I have been reading on the history of Algonquin Park but
no where could I find a description of where the Highland
Inn was originally located on Cache lake.
[root@server1 ~]# head -3 project4
Hi there, I hope this day finds you well.

Unfortunately we were not able to make it to your dining
[root@server1 ~]#_
```

Just as the head command displays the beginning of text files, the **tail command** can be used to display the end of text files. By default, the tail command displays the final 10 lines of a file, but it can also take a numeric option specifying the number of lines to display on the terminal screen, as shown in the following example with the project4 file:

```
[root@server1 ~]# tail project4

I have been reading on the history of Algonquin Park but
no where could I find a description of where the Highland
Inn was originally located on Cache lake.
```

If it is no trouble, could you kindly let me know such that
I need not wait until next year when I visit your lodge?

Regards,
Mackenzie Elizabeth
[root@server1 ~]# **tail -2 project4**

Regards,
Mackenzie Elizabeth
[root@server1 ~]#_

Although some text files are small enough to be displayed completely on the terminal screen, you might encounter text files that are too large to fit in a single screen. In this case, the cat command sends the entire file contents to the terminal screen; however, the screen only displays as much of the text as it has room for. To display a large text file in a page-by-page fashion, you need to use the more and less commands.

The **more command** gets its name from the pg command once used on UNIX systems. The pg command displayed a text file page-by-page on the terminal screen, starting at the beginning of the file; pressing the Spacebar or Enter key displayed the next page, and so on. The more command does more than pg did because it displays the next complete page of a text file if you press the Spacebar, but displays only the next line of a text file if you press Enter. In that way, you can browse the contents of a text file page-by-page or line-by-line. The fictitious file project5, an excerpt from Shakespeare's tragedy *Macbeth*, is too large to be displayed fully on the terminal screen using the cat command. Using the more command to view its contents results in the following output:

[root@server1 ~]# **more project5**
Go bid thy mistress, when my drink is ready,
She strike upon the bell. Get thee to bed.
Is this a dagger which I see before me,
The handle toward my hand? Come, let me clutch thee.
I have thee not, and yet I see thee still.
Art thou not, fatal vision, sensible
To feeling as to sight? or art thou but
A dagger of the mind, a false creation,
Proceeding from the heat-oppressed brain?
I see thee yet, in form as palpable
As this which now I draw.
Thou marshall'st me the way that I was going;
And such an instrument I was to use.
Mine eyes are made the fools o' the other senses,
Or else worth all the rest; I see thee still,
And on thy blade and dudgeon gouts of blood,
Which was not so before. There's no such thing:
It is the bloody business which informs
Thus to mine eyes. Now o'er the one halfworld
Nature seems dead, and wicked dreams abuse
The curtain'd sleep; witchcraft celebrates

```
Pale Hecate's offerings, and wither'd murder,
Alarum'd by his sentinel, the wolf,
--More--(71%)
```

As you can see in the preceding output, the more command displays the first page without returning you to the shell prompt. Instead, the more command displays a prompt at the bottom of the terminal screen that indicates how much of the file is displayed on the screen as a percentage of the total file size. In the preceding example, 71 percent of the project5 file is displayed. At this prompt, you can press the Spacebar to advance one whole page, or you can press Enter to advance to the next line. In addition, the more command allows other user interaction at this prompt. Pressing the h character at the prompt displays a Help screen as shown in the following output, and pressing the q character quits the more command completely without viewing the remainder of the file.

```
--More--(71%)
Most commands optionally preceded by integer argument k. Defaults in
brackets. Star (*) indicates argument becomes new default.
-------------------------------------------------------------------------
<space>                 Display next k lines of text [current screen size]
z                       Display next k lines of text [current screen size]
<return>                Display next k lines of text [1]
d or ctrl-D             Scroll k lines [current scroll size, initially 11]
q or Q or <interrupt>   Exit from more
s                       Skip forward k lines of text [1]
f                       Skip forward k screenfuls of text [1]
b or ctrl-B             Skip backward k screenfuls of text [1]
'                       Go to place where previous search started
=                       Display current line number
/<regular expression>   Search for kth occurrence of regular expression [1]
n                       Search for kth occurrence of last r.e [1]
!<cmd> or :!<cmd>       Execute <cmd> in a subshell
v                       Start up /usr/bin/vi at current line
ctrl-L                  Redraw screen
:n                      Go to kth next file [1]
:p                      Go to kth previous file [1]
:f                      Display current filename and line number
.                       Repeat previous command
-------------------------------------------------------------------------
--More-(71%)
```

Just as the more command was named as a result of allowing more user functionality, the **less command** is named similarly, as it can do more than the more command (remember that "less is more," more or less). Like the more command, the less command can browse the contents of a text file page-by-page by pressing the Spacebar or browse them line-by-line by pressing Enter. However, you can also use the cursor keys (that is, the arrow keys) on the keyboard to scroll up and down the contents of the file. The output of the less command when used to view the project5 file is as follows:

```
[root@server1 ~]# less project5
Go bid thy mistress, when my drink is ready,
```

She strike upon the bell. Get thee to bed.
Is this a dagger which I see before me,
The handle toward my hand? Come, let me clutch thee.
I have thee not, and yet I see thee still.
Art thou not, fatal vision, sensible
To feeling as to sight? or art thou but
A dagger of the mind, a false creation,
Proceeding from the heat-oppressed brain?
I see thee yet, in form as palpable
As this which now I draw.
Thou marshall'st me the way that I was going;
And such an instrument I was to use.
Mine eyes are made the fools o' the other senses,
Or else worth all the rest; I see thee still,
And on thy blade and dudgeon gouts of blood,
Which was not so before. There's no such thing:
It is the bloody business which informs
Thus to mine eyes. Now o'er the one halfworld
Nature seems dead, and wicked dreams abuse
The curtain'd sleep; witchcraft celebrates
Pale Hecate's offerings, and wither'd murder,
Alarum'd by his sentinel, the wolf,
Whose howl's his watch, thus with his stealthy pace.
project5

Like the more command, the less command displays a prompt at the bottom of the file using the : character or the filename of the file being viewed (project5 in our example), yet the less command contains more keyboard shortcuts for searching out text within files. At the prompt, you can press the h key to obtain a Help screen or the q key to quit. The first Help screen for the less command is shown next:

```
                      SUMMARY OF LESS COMMANDS

      Commands marked with * may be preceded by a number, N.
      Notes in parentheses indicate the behavior if N is given.


  h  H               Display this help.
  q  :q  Q  :Q  ZZ   Exit.
  ---------------------------------------------------------------------


                            MOVING


  e  ^E  j  ^N  CR   *  Forward  one line (or N lines).
  y  ^Y  k  ^K  ^P   *  Backward one line (or N lines).
  f  ^F  ^V  SPACE   *  Forward  one window (or N lines).
  b  ^B  ESC-v       *  Backward one window (or N lines).
  z                  *  Forward  one window (and set window to N).
  w                  *  Backward one window (and set window to N).
  ESC-SPACE          *  Forward  one window, but don't stop at end-of-file.
```

```
d  ^D        *    Forward one half-window(and set half-window to N)
u  ^U        *    Backward one half-window(and set half window to N)
ESC-(  RightArrow *  Left 8 character positions (or N positions).
ESC-)  LeftArrow  *  Right 8 character positions (or N positions).
F                    Forward forever; like "tail -f".

HELP -- Press RETURN for more, or q when done
```

The more and less commands can also be used in conjunction with the output of commands if that output is too large to fit on the terminal screen. To do this, simply use the | metacharacter after the command, followed by either the more or less command, as follows:

```
[root@server1 ~]# cd /etc
[root@server1 etc]# ls -l | more
total 3688
-rw-r--r--  1 root    root    15276 Mar 22 12:20 a2ps.cfg
-rw-r--r--  1 root    root     2562 Mar 22 12:20 a2ps-site.cfg
drwxr-xr-x  4 root    root     4096 Jun 11 08:45 acpi
-rw-r--r--  1 root    root       46 Jun 16 16:42 adjtime
drwxr-xr-x  2 root    root     4096 Jun 11 08:47 aep
-rw-r--r--  1 root    root      688 Feb 17 00:35 aep.conf
-rw-r--r--  1 root    root      703 Feb 17 00:35 aeplog.conf
drwxr-xr-x  4 root    root     4096 Jun 11 08:47 alchemist
-rw-r--r--  1 root    root     1419 Jan 26 10:14 aliases
-rw-r-----  1 root    smmsp   12288 Jun 17 13:17 aliases.db
drwxr-xr-x  2 root    root     4096 Jun 11 11:11 alternatives
drwxr-xr-x  3 amanda  disk     4096 Jun 11 10:16 amanda
-rw-r--r--  1 amanda  disk        0 Mar 22 12:28 amandates
-rw-------  1 root    root      688 Mar  4 22:34 amd.conf
-rw-r-----  1 root    root      105 Mar  4 22:34 amd.net
-rw-r--r--  1 root    root      317 Feb 15 14:33 anacrontab
-rw-r--r--  1 root    root      331 May  5 08:07 ant.conf
-rw-r--r--  1 root    root     6200 Jun 16 16:42 asound.state
drwxr-xr-x  3 root    root     4096 Jun 11 10:37 atalk
-rw-------  1 root    root        1 May  5 13:39 at.deny
-rw-r--r--  1 root    root      325 Apr 14 13:39 auto.master
-rw-r--r--  1 root    root      581 Apr 14 13:39 auto.misc
--More--
```

In the preceding example, the output of the ls -l command was redirected to the more command, which displays the first page of output on the terminal. You can then advance through the output page-by-page or line-by-line. This type of redirection is discussed in Chapter 7.

Displaying the Contents of Binary Files

It is important to employ text file commands, such as cat, tac, head, tail, more, and less, only on files that contain text; otherwise, you might find yourself with random output on the terminal screen or even a dysfunctional terminal. To view the contents of binary files, you typically use the program that was used to create the file. However, some commands can be used to safely display the contents of most binary files. The **strings command** searches for text characters in a binary file and outputs them to the screen. In many cases, these text characters might indicate what the binary file is used for. For example, to find the text characters inside the /bin/echo binary executable program page-by-page, you could use the following command:

```
[root@server1 ~]# strings /bin/echo | more
/lib/ld-linux.so.2
PTRh|
<nt7<e
|[^_]
[^_]
[^_]
Try '%s --help' for more information.
Usage: %s [OPTION]... [STRING]...
Echo the STRING(s) to standard output.
  -n             do not output the trailing newline
  -e             enable interpretation of the backslash-escaped characters
                    listed below
  -E             disable interpretation of those sequences in STRINGs
    --help       display this help and exit
    --version    output version information and exit
Without -E, the following sequences are recognized and interpolated:
  \NNN    the character whose ASCII code is NNN (octal)
  \\      backslash
  \a      alert (BEL)
  \b      backspace
  \c      suppress trailing newline
  \f      form feed
  \n      new line
--More--
```

Although this output might not be easy to read, it does contain portions of text that can point a user in the right direction to find out more about the /bin/echo command. Another command that is safe to use on binary files and text files is the **od command**, which displays the contents of the file in octal format (numeric base 8 format). An example of using the od command to display the first five lines of the file project4 is shown in the following example:

```
[root@server1 ~]# od project4 | head -5
0000000   064510   072040   062550   062562   020054   020111   067550   062560
0000020   072040   064550   020163   060544   020171   064546   062156   020163
0000040   067571   020165   062567   066154   006456   006412   052412   063156
0000060   071157   072564   060556   062564   074554   073440   020145   062567
0000100   062562   067040   072157   060440   066142   020145   067564   066440
[root@server1 ~]#_
```

You can use the −x option to the od command to display a file in hexadecimal format (numeric base 16 format).

Searching for Text Within Files

Recall that Linux was modeled after the UNIX operating system. The UNIX operating system is often referred to as the "grandfather" of all operating systems because it is over 40 years old and has formed the basis for most advances in computing technology. The major use of the UNIX operating system in the past 40 years involved simplifying business and scientific management through database applications. As a result, many commands (referred to as **text tools**) were developed for the UNIX operating system that could search for and manipulate text, such as database information, in many different and advantageous ways. A set of text wildcards was also developed to ease the searching of specific text information. These text wildcards are called **regular expressions (regexp)** and are recognized by several text tools and programming languages, including, but not limited to, the following:

- grep
- awk
- sed
- vi
- Emacs
- ex
- ed
- C++
- PERL
- Tcl

Because Linux is a close relative of the UNIX operating system, these text tools and regular expressions are available to Linux as well. By combining text tools (as you will see later), a typical Linux system can search for and manipulate data in almost every way possible. As a result, regular expressions and the text tools that use them are commonly used in business today.

Regular Expressions

As mentioned earlier, regular expressions allow you to specify a certain pattern of text within a text document. They work similarly to wildcard metacharacters in that they are used to match characters, yet there are many differences:

- Wildcard metacharacters are interpreted by the shell, whereas regular expressions are interpreted by a text tool program.
- Wildcard metacharacters match characters in filenames (or directory names) on a Linux filesystem, whereas regular expressions match characters *within* text files on a Linux filesystem.
- Wildcard metacharacters typically have different definitions than regular expression metacharacters.
- More regular expression metacharacters are available than wildcard metacharacters.

Regular Expression	Description	Example	Type
*	Matches 0 or more occurrences of the previous character	letter* matches lette, letter, letterr, letterrrr, letterrrrr, and so on	Common
?	Matches 0 or 1 occurrences of the previous character	letter? matches lette, letter	Extended
+	Matches 1 or more occurrences of the previous character	letter+ matches letter, letterr, letterrrr, letterrrrr, and so on	Extended
. (period)	Matches 1 character of any type	letter. matches lettera, letterb, letterc, letter1, letter2, letter3, and so on	Common
[...]	Matches one character from the range specified within the braces	letter[1238] matches letter1, letter2, letter3, letter8 letter[a-c] matches lettera, letterb, and letterc	Common
[^...]	Matches one character *not* from the range specified within the braces	letter[^1238] matches letter4, letter5, letter6, lettera, letterb, and so on (any character except 1, 2, 3, or 8)	Common
{ }	Matches a specific number or range of the previous character	letter{3} matches letterrr, whereas letter{2,4} matches letterr, letterrr, and letterrrr	Extended
^	Matches the following characters if they are the first characters on the line	^letter matches letter if letter is the first set of characters in the line	Common
$	Matches the previous characters if they are the last characters on the line	letter$ matches letter if letter is the last set of characters in the line	Common
(...|...)	Matches either of two sets of characters	(mother|father) matches the word "mother" or "father"	Extended

Table 3-4   Regular expressions

In addition, regular expression metacharacters are divided into two different categories: common regular expressions and extended regular expressions. Common regular expressions are available to most text tools; however, extended regular expressions are less common and available in only certain text tools. Table 3-4 shows definitions and examples of some common and extended regular expressions.

The grep Command

The most common way to search for information using regular expressions is the grep command. The **grep command** (the command name is short for **global regular expression print**) is used to display lines in a text file that match a certain common regular expression. To display lines of text that match extended regular expressions, you must use the **egrep command** (or the -E option to the grep command). In addition, the **fgrep command** (or the -F option to the grep command) does not interpret any regular expressions and consequently returns results much faster. Take, for example, the project4 file shown earlier:

```
[root@server1 ~]# cat project4
Hi there, I hope this day finds you well.

Unfortunately we were not able to make it to your dining
room this year while vacationing in Algonquin Park - I
especially wished to see the model of the Highland Inn
and the train station in the dining room.

I have been reading on the history of Algonquin Park but
no where could I find a description of where the Highland
Inn was originally located on Cache lake.

If it is no trouble, could you kindly let me know such that
I need not wait until next year when I visit your lodge?

Regards,
Mackenzie Elizabeth
[root@server1 ~]#_
```

The grep command requires two arguments at minimum; the first argument specifies which text to search for, and the remaining arguments specify the files to search. If a pattern of text is matched, the grep command displays the entire line on the terminal screen. For example, to list only those lines in the file project4 that contain the words "Algonquin Park," enter the following command:

```
[root@server1 ~]# grep "Algonquin Park" project4
room this year while vacationing in Algonquin Park - I
I have been reading on the history of Algonquin Park but
[root@server1 ~]#_
```

To return the lines that do not contain the text "Algonquin Park," you can use the –v option of the grep command to reverse the meaning of the previous command:

```
[root@server1 ~]# grep -v "Algonquin Park" project4
Hi there, I hope this day finds you well.

Unfortunately we were not able to make it to your dining
especially wished to see the model of the Highland Inn
and the train station in the dining room.

no where could I find a description of where the Highland
Inn was originally located on Cache lake.

If it is no trouble, could you kindly let me know such that
I need not wait until next year when I visit your lodge?

Regards,
Mackenzie Elizabeth
[root@server1 ~]#_
```

Keep in mind that the text being searched is case sensitive; to perform a search that is not case sensitive, use the −i option to the grep command:

```
[root@server1 ~]# grep "algonquin park" project4
[root@server1 ~]#_
[root@server1 ~]# grep -i "algonquin park" project4
room this year while vacationing in Algonquin Park - I
I have been reading on the history of Algonquin Park but
[root@server1 ~]#_
```

Another important note to keep in mind regarding text tools such as grep is that they match only patterns of text; they are unable to discern words or phrases unless they are specified. For example, if you want to search for the lines that contain the word "we," you can use the following grep command:

```
[root@server1 ~]# grep "we" project4
Hi there, I hope this day finds you well.
Unfortunately we were not able to make it to your dining
[root@server1 ~]#_
```

However, notice from the preceding output that the first line displayed does not contain the word "we"; the word "well" contains the text pattern "we" and is displayed as a result. To display only lines that contain the word "we," you can type the following to match the letters "we" surrounded by space characters:

```
[root@server1 ~]# grep " we " project4
Unfortunately we were not able to make it to your dining
[root@server1 ~]#_
```

All of the previous grep examples did not use regular expression metacharacters to search for text in the project4 file. Some examples of using regular expressions (see Table 3-4) when searching this file are shown throughout the remainder of this section.

To view lines that contain the word "toe" or "the" or "tie," you can enter the following command:

```
[root@server1 ~]# grep " t.e " project4
especially wished to see the model of the Highland Inn
and the train station in the dining room.
I have been reading on the history of Algonquin Park but
no where could I find a description of where the Highland
[root@server1 ~]#_
```

To view lines that start with the word "I," you can enter the following command:

```
[root@server1 ~]# grep "^I " project4
I have been reading on the history of Algonquin Park but
I need not wait until next year when I visit your lodge?
[root@server1 ~]#_
```

To view lines that contain the text "lodge" or "lake," you need to use an extended regular expression and the egrep command, as follows:

```
[root@server1 ~]# egrep "(lodge|lake)" project4
Inn was originally located on Cache lake.
I need not wait until next year when I visit your lodge?
[root@server1 ~]#_
```

Editing Text Files

Recall that text files are the most common type of file modified by Linux users and administrators. Most system configuration is stored in text files, as is commonly accessed information such as e-mail and program source code. Consequently, most Linux distributions come with an assortment of text editors, and many more are available for Linux systems via the Internet. Text editors come in two varieties: editors that can be used on the command line, including vi (vim), nano, and Emacs, and editors that must be used in a GUI environment, including Emacs-x and gedit.

The vi Editor

The **vi editor** (pronounced "vee eye") is one of the oldest and most popular visual text editors available for UNIX operating systems. Its Linux equivalent (known as vim, which is short for "vi improved") is, therefore, standard on almost every Linux distribution. Although the vi editor is not the easiest of the editors to use when editing text files, it has the advantage of portability. A Fedora Linux user who is proficient in using the vi editor will find editing files on all other UNIX and Linux systems easy because the interface and features of the vi editor are nearly identical across Linux and UNIX systems. In addition, the vi editor supports regular expressions and can perform over 1,000 different functions for the user.

To open an existing text file for editing, you can type vi filename (or vim filename) where *filename* specifies the file to be edited. To open a new file for editing, simply type vi or vim at the command line:

```
[root@server1 ~]# vi
```

The vi editor then runs interactively and replaces the command-line interface with the following output:

```
~
~
~
~
~
~                       VIM - Vi IMproved
~
~                       version 7.2.411
~                     by Bram Moolenaar et al.
~               Modified by <bugzilla@redhat.com>
~           Vim is open source and freely distributable
```

```
~
~                        Become a registered Vim user!
~              type   :help register<Enter>      for information
~
~              type   :q<Enter>                  to exit
~              type   :help<Enter>  or  <F1>  for on-line help
~              type   :help version7<Enter>      for version info
~
~
~
~
~
~
~                              0,0-1          All
```

The tilde (~) characters on the left indicate the end of the file; they are pushed further down the screen as you enter text. The vi editor is called a bimodal editor because it functions in one of two modes: **command mode** and **insert mode**. The vi editor opens command mode, in which you must use the keyboard to perform functions, such as deleting text, copying text, saving changes to a file, and exiting the vi editor. To insert text into the document, you must enter insert mode by typing one of the characters listed in Table 3-5. One such method to enter insert mode is to type the i key on the keyboard while in command mode; the vi editor then displays --INSERT-- at the bottom of the screen and allows the user to enter a sentence such as the following:

```
This is a sample sentence.
~
~
~
~
~
~
~
~
~
-- INSERT --
```

Key	Description
i	Changes to insert mode and places the cursor before the current character for entering text
a	Changes to insert mode and places the cursor after the current character for entering text
o	Changes to insert mode and opens a new line underneath the current line for entering text
I	Changes to insert mode and places the cursor at the beginning of the current line for entering text
A	Changes to insert mode and places the cursor at the end of the current line for entering text
O	Changes to insert mode and opens a new line above the current line for entering text
Esc	Changes back to command mode while in insert mode

Table 3-5 Common keyboard keys used to change to and from insert mode

When in insert mode, you can use the keyboard to type text as required, but when finished you must press the Esc key to return to command mode to perform other functions via keys on the keyboard. Table 3-6 provides a list of keys useful in command mode and their associated functions. After you are in command mode, to save the text in a file called samplefile in the current directory, you need to press the : character (by pressing the Shift and ; keys simultaneously) to reach a : prompt, where you can enter a command to save the contents of the current document to a file, as shown in the following example and in Table 3-7.

```
This is a sample sentence.
~
~
~
~
~
~
~
~
~
:w samplefile
```

As shown in Table 3-7, you can quit the vi editor by pressing the : character and entering q!, which then returns the user to the shell prompt:

```
This is a sample sentence.
~
~
~
~
~
~
~
~
~
:q!
[root@server1 ~]# _
```

The vi editor also offers some advanced features to Linux users, as explained in Table 3-7. Examples of some of these features are discussed next, using the project4 file shown earlier in this chapter. To edit the project4 file, simply type vi project4 and view the following screen:

```
Hi there, I hope this day finds you well.

Unfortunately we were not able to make it to your dining
room this year while vacationing in Algonquin Park - I
especially wished to see the model of the Highland Inn
and the train station in the dining room.

I have been reading on the history of Algonquin Park but
no where could I find a description of where the Highland
Inn was originally located on Cache lake.
```

Key	Description
w, W, e, E	Moves the cursor forward one word to the beginning or end of the next word, respectively
b, B	Moves the cursor backward one word
53G	Moves the cursor to line 53
G	Moves the cursor to the last line in the document
0, ^	Moves the cursor to the beginning of the line
$	Moves the cursor to the end of the line
x	Deletes the character the cursor is on
3x	Deletes three characters starting from the character the cursor is on
dw	Deletes one word starting from the character the cursor is on
d3w, 3dw	Deletes three words starting from the character the cursor is on
dd	Deletes one whole line starting from the line the cursor is on
d3d, 3dd	Deletes three whole lines starting from the line the cursor is on
d$	Deletes from cursor character to the end of the current line
d^, d0	Deletes from cursor character to the beginning of the current line
yw	Copies one word (starting from the character the cursor is on) into a temporary buffer in memory for later use
y3w, 3yw	Copies three words (starting from the character the cursor is on) into a temporary buffer in memory for later use
yy	Copies the current line into a temporary buffer in memory for later use
y3y, 3yy	Copies three lines (starting from the current line) into a temporary buffer in memory for later use
y$	Copies the current line from the cursor to the end of the line into a temporary buffer in memory for later use
y^, y0	Copies the current line from the cursor to the beginning of the line into a temporary buffer in memory for later use
p	Pastes the contents of the temporary memory buffer underneath the current line or after the current word
P	Pastes the contents of the temporary memory buffer above the current line or after the current word
J	Joins the line underneath the current line to the current line
Ctrl+g	Displays current line statistics
u	Undoes the last function (undo)
.	Repeats the last function (repeat)
/pattern	Searches for the first occurrence of pattern in the forward direction
?pattern	Searches for the first occurrence of pattern in the reverse direction
n	Repeats the previous search in the forward direction
N	Repeats the previous search in the reverse direction

Table 3-6 Key combinations commonly used in command mode

Function	Description
:q	Quits from the vi editor if no changes were made
:q!	Quits from the vi editor and does not save any changes
:wq	Saves any changes to the file and quits from the vi editor
:w filename	Saves the current document to a file called filename
:!date	Executes the date command using a BASH shell
:r !date	Reads the output of the date command into the document under the current line
:r filename	Reads the contents of the text file called filename into the document under the current line
:set all	Displays all vi environment settings
:set	Sets a vi environment setting to a certain value
:s/the/THE/g	Searches for the regular expression "the" and replaces each occurrence globally throughout the current line with the word "THE"
:1,$ s/the/THE/g	Searches for the regular expression "the" and replaces each occurrence globally from line 1 to the end of the document with the word "THE"

Table 3-7 Key combinations commonly used at the command mode : prompt

```
If it is no trouble, could you kindly let me know such that
I need not wait until next year when I visit your lodge?

Regards,
Mackenzie Elizabeth
~
~
~
~
~
~
~
"project4" 17L, 583C
```

Note that the name of the file as well as the number of lines and characters in total are displayed at the bottom of the screen (project4 has 17 lines and 583 characters in this example). To insert the current date and time at the bottom of the file, you can simply move the cursor to the final line in the file and, at the command prompt, type the bold text shown in the following output while in command mode:

```
Hi there, I hope this day finds you well.

Unfortunately we were not able to make it to your dining
room this year while vacationing in Algonquin Park - I
especially wished to see the model of the Highland Inn
and the train station in the dining room.

I have been reading on the history of Algonquin Park but
no where could I find a description of where the Highland
```

Inn was originally located on Cache lake.

If it is no trouble, could you kindly let me know such that
I need not wait until next year when I visit your lodge?

Regards,
Mackenzie Elizabeth
~
~
~
~
~
~
~
~

:r !date

When you press Enter, the output of the date command is inserted below the current line:

Hi there, I hope this day finds you well.

Unfortunately we were not able to make it to your dining
room this year while vacationing in Algonquin Park - I
especially wished to see the model of the Highland Inn
and the train station in the dining room.

I have been reading on the history of Algonquin Park but
no where could I find a description of where the Highland
Inn was originally located on Cache lake.

If it is no trouble, could you kindly let me know such that
I need not wait until next year when I visit your lodge?

Regards,
Mackenzie Elizabeth
Sat Aug 7 18:33:10 EDT 2010
~
~
~
~
~
~

To change all occurrences of the word "Algonquin" to "ALGONQUIN," you can, at the command prompt, type the bold text shown in the following output while in command mode:

Hi there, I hope this day finds you well.

Unfortunately we were not able to make it to your dining
room this year while vacationing in Algonquin Park - I

especially wished to see the model of the Highland Inn
and the train station in the dining room.

I have been reading on the history of Algonquin Park but
no where could I find a description of where the Highland
Inn was originally located on Cache lake.

If it is no trouble, could you kindly let me know such that
I need not wait until next year when I visit your lodge?

Regards,
Mackenzie Elizabeth
Sat Aug 7 18:33:10 EDT 2010
~
~
~
~
~
~

:1,$ s/Algonquin/ALGONQUIN/g

The output changes to the following:

Hi there, I hope this day finds you well.

Unfortunately we were not able to make it to your dining
room this year while vacationing in ALGONQUIN Park - I
especially wished to see the model of the Highland Inn
and the train station in the dining room.

I have been reading on the history of ALGONQUIN Park but
no where could I find a description of where the Highland
Inn was originally located on Cache lake.

If it is no trouble, could you kindly let me know such that
I need not wait until next year when I visit your lodge?

Regards,
Mackenzie Elizabeth
Sat Aug 7 18:33:10 EDT 2010
~
~
~
~
~
~
~

Another attractive feature of the vi editor is its ability to customize the user environment through settings that can be altered at the : prompt while in command mode. Simply type `set all` at this prompt to observe the list of available settings and their current values:

```
:set all
--- Options ---
  aleph=224             fileencoding=        menuitems=25        swapsync=fsync
noarabic                fileformat=unix      modeline            switchbuf=
  arabicshape           filetype=            modelines=5         syntax=
noallowrevins         nofkmap                modifiable          tabstop=8
noaltkeymap             foldclose=           modified            tagbsearch
  ambiwidth=single      foldcolumn=0         more                taglength=0
noautoindent            foldenable           mouse=              tagrelative
noautoread              foldexpr=0           mousemodel=         tagstack
                                               extend
noautowrite             foldignore=#         mousetime=500       term=xterm
noautowriteall          foldlevel=0        nonumber             notermbidi
  background=light      foldlevelstart=-1  nopaste                termencoding=
  backspace=2           foldmethod=manual    pastetoggle=      noterse
nobackup                foldminlines=1       patchexpr=           textauto
  backupcopy=auto       foldnestmax=20       patchmode=         notextmode
  backupext=~           formatoptions=tcq nopreserveindent     textwidth=0
  backupskip=/tmp/*   formatprg=             previewheight=12   thesaurus=
nobinary              nogdefault           nopreviewwindow    notildeop
nobomb                  helpheight=20        printdevice=         timeout
  bufhidden=            helplang=en          printencoding=       timeoutlen=
                                                                     1000
  buflisted           nohidden               printfont=         notitle
                                               courier
  buftype=              history=50           printoptions=        titlelen=85
-- More --
```

Note in the preceding output that most settings are set to either on or off; those that are turned off are prefixed with a "no." In the preceding example, line numbering is turned off (nonumber in the preceding output); however, you can turn it on by typing `set number` at the : prompt while in command mode. This results in the following output in vi:

```
1 Hi there, I hope this day finds you well.
2
3 Unfortunately we were not able to make it to your dining
4 room this year while vacationing in ALGONQUIN Park - I
5 especially wished to see the model of the Highland Inn
6 and the train station in the dining room.
7
```

```
 8 I have been reading on the history of ALGONQUIN Park but
 9 no where could I find a description of where the Highland
10 Inn was originally located on Cache lake.
11
12 If it is no trouble, could you kindly let me know such that
13 I need not wait until next year when I visit your lodge?
14
15 Regards,
16 Mackenzie Elizabeth
17 Sat Aug 7 18:33:10 EDT 2010
18
~
~
~
~
~
~
:set number
```

Conversely, to turn off line numbering, you could simply type set nonumber at the : prompt while in command mode.

Other Common Text Editors

Although the vi editor is the most common text editor used on Linux and UNIX systems, other text editors that are easier to use exist.

An alternative to the vi editor that offers an equal set of functionality is the GNU **Emacs (Editor MACroS) editor.** Emacs is not installed by default in Fedora 13. To install it, you can run the command yum install emacs at a command prompt to obtain Emacs from a free software repository on the Internet. Next, to open the project4 file in the Emacs editor, simply type emacs project4, and the following is displayed on the terminal screen:

```
File Edit Options Buffers Tools Help
Hi there, I hope this day finds you well.

Unfortunately we were not able to make it to your dining
room this year while vacationing in Algonquin Park - I
especially wished to see the model of the Highland Inn
and the train station in the dining room.

I have been reading on the history of Algonquin Park but
no where could I find a description of where the Highland
Inn was originally located on Cache lake.
```

If it is no trouble, could you kindly let me know such that
I need not wait until next year when I visit your lodge?

Regards,
Mackenzie Elizabeth


```
-UUU:----F1 project4   All L1  (Text)--------------------------------
For information about the GNU Emacs and the GNU system, type C-h C-a.
```

The Emacs editor uses the Ctrl key in combination with certain letters to perform special functions, can be used with the LISP (LISt Processing) artificial intelligence programming language, and supports hundreds of keyboard functions such as the vi editor. Table 3-8 shows a list of some common keyboard functions used in the Emacs editor.

Unfortunately, the Emacs editor is not an easy-to-use editor because the user must memorize several key combinations to work effectively or use advanced features. If you run Emacs within a GUI environment, a graphical version of the Emacs editor is started. The graphical Emacs editor is much easier to use because the command-line key combinations are replaced by graphical icons, menus, and optional sidebars for many features. If you type emacs project4 within a GUI environment, you will start a graphical Emacs session, as shown in Figure 3-3.

Another text editor that uses Ctrl key combinations for performing functions is the **nano editor** (based on the pine UNIX editor). Unlike vi or Emacs, nano is a very basic and easy-to-use editor that many Linux administrators use to quickly modify configuration files if they don't need advanced functionality. If you type nano project4, you will see the following displayed on the terminal screen:

```
GNU nano 2.2.4                 File: project4.txt
Hi there, I hope this day finds you well.
```

Unfortunately we were not able to make it to your dining
room this year while vacationing in Algonquin Park - I
especially wished to see the model of the Highland Inn
and the train station in the dining room.

I have been reading on the history of Algonquin Park but
no where could I find a description of where the Highland
Inn was originally located on Cache lake.

If it is no trouble, could you kindly let me know such that
I need not wait until next year when I visit your lodge?

Regards,
Mackenzie Elizabeth

Key	Description
Ctrl+a	Moves the cursor to the beginning of the line
Ctrl+e	Moves the cursor to the end of the line
Ctrl+h	Displays Emacs documentation
Ctrl+d	Deletes the current character
Ctrl+k	Deletes all characters between the cursor and the end of the line
Esc+d	Deletes the current word
Ctrl+x + Ctrl+c	Exits the Emacs editor
Ctrl+x + Ctrl+s	Saves the current document
Ctrl+x + Ctrl+w	Saves the current document as a new filename
Ctrl+x + u	Undoes the last change

Table 3-8 Keyboard functions commonly used in the GNU Emacs editor

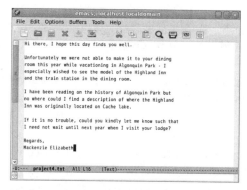

Figure 3-3 A graphical Emacs session

Source: Course Technology/Cengage Learning

```
                          [ Read 16 lines ]
^G Get Help  ^O WriteOut  ^R Read File  ^Y Prev Page  ^K Cut Text   ^C CurPos
^X Exit      ^J Justify   ^W Where Is   ^V Next Page  ^U UnCut Txt  ^T Spell
```

The bottom of the screen lists all the Ctrl key combinations. The ^ symbol represents the Ctrl key. This means that, to exit nano, you can press Ctrl+X (^X = Ctrl+X).

If you are using a GUI environment, you can instead use the **gedit editor** to quickly edit text files. Although the gedit editor does not have the advanced functionality that vi or Emacs has, it is the easiest editor to use as it is functionally analogous to the Windows Wordpad and Notepad editors. If you type gedit project4 in a GUI environment, you will see the screen shown in Figure 3-4.

Figure 3-4 The gedit text editor

Source: Course Technology/Cengage Learning

Chapter Summary

- The Linux filesystem is arranged hierarchically using a series of directories to store files. The location of these directories and files can be described using absolute or relative pathnames.

- The Linux filesystem can contain many types of files, such as text files, binary data, executable programs, directories, linked files, and special device files.

- The `ls` command can be used to view filenames and offers a wide range of options to modify this view.

- Wildcard metacharacters are special keyboard characters. They can be used to simplify the selection of several files when using common Linux file commands.

- Text files are the most common file type whose contents can be viewed by several commands, such as `head`, `tail`, `cat`, `tac`, `more`, and `less`.

- Regular expression metacharacters can be used to specify certain patterns of text when used with certain programming languages and text tool commands such as `grep`.

- Although many command-line and graphical text editors exist, vi (vim) is a powerful, bimodal text editor that is standard on most UNIX and Linux systems.

Key Terms

~ metacharacter   A metacharacter used to represent a user's home directory.

absolute pathname   The full pathname to a certain file or directory, starting from the root directory.

binary data file   A file that contains machine language (binary 1s and 0s) and stores information (such as common functions and graphics) used by binary compiled programs.

cat command   A Linux command used to display (or concatenate) the entire contents of a text file to the screen.

cd (change directory) command   A Linux command used to change the current directory in the directory tree.

command mode   One of the two modes in vi; it allows a user to perform any available text editing task that is not related to inserting text into the document.

concatenation   The joining of text to make one larger whole. In Linux, words and strings of text are joined together to form a displayed file.

directory   A special file on the filesystem used to organize other files into a logical tree structure.

egrep command   A variant of the grep command, used to search files for patterns using extended regular expressions.

Emacs (Editor MACroS) editor   A popular and widespread text editor more conducive to word processing than vi. It was originally developed by Richard Stallman.

executable program   A file that can be executed by the Linux operating system to run in memory as a process and perform a useful function.

fgrep command   A variant of the grep command that does not allow the use of regular expressions.

file command   A Linux command that displays the file type of a specified filename.

filename   The user-friendly identifier given to a file.

filename extension   At the end of a filename, a dot followed by a series of identifiers that denotes the file type; the filename extension .txt denotes a text file.

gedit editor   A common text editor used within GUI environments.

grep command   A Linux command that searches files for patterns of characters using regular expression metacharacters. The command name is short for "global regular expression print."

head command   A Linux command that displays the first set of lines of a text file; by default, the head command displays the first 10 lines.

home directory   A directory on the filesystem set aside for users to store personal files and information.

insert mode   One of the two modes in vi; it allows the user to insert text into the document but does not allow any other functionality.

less command   A Linux command used to display a text file page-by-page on the terminal screen; users can then use the cursor keys to navigate the file.

linked file   The files that represent the same data as other files.

ll command   An alias for the ls -l command; it gives a long file listing.

log file   A file that contains past system events.

ls command   A Linux command used to list the files in a given directory.

more command   A Linux command used to display a text file page-by-page and line-by-line on the terminal screen.

named pipe file   A temporary connection that sends information from one command or process in memory to another; it can also be represented by a file on the filesystem.

nano editor   A user-friendly terminal text editor that uses Ctrl key combinations to perform basic functions.

od command   A Linux command used to display the contents of a file in octal format.

parent directory The directory that is one level closer to the root directory in the directory tree relative to your current directory.

pwd (print working directory) command A Linux command used to display the current directory in the directory tree.

regexp *See* regular expressions.

regular expressions The special metacharacters used to match patterns of text within text files; they are commonly used by text tool commands, including grep.

relative pathname The pathname of a target directory relative to your current directory in the tree.

socket file A named pipe connecting processes on two different computers; it can also be represented by a file on the filesystem.

special device file A file used to identify hardware devices such as hard disks and serial ports.

strings command A Linux command used to search for and display text characters in a binary file.

subdirectory A directory that resides within another directory in the directory tree.

Tab-completion feature A feature of the BASH shell that fills in the remaining characters of a unique filename or directory name when the user presses Tab.

tac command A Linux command that displays a file on the screen, beginning with the last line of the file and ending with the first line of the file.

tail command A Linux command used to display lines of text at the end of a file; by default, the tail command displays the last 10 lines of the file.

text file A file that stores information in a readable text format.

text tools The programs that allow for the creation, modification, and searching of text files.

vi editor A powerful command-line text editor available on most UNIX and Linux systems.

wildcard metacharacters The metacharacters used to match certain characters in a file or directory name; they are often used to specify multiple files.

Review Questions

1. A directory is a type of file. True or False?

2. Which command would a user type on the command line to find out which directory in the directory tree he is currently located in?

   a. pd

   b. cd

   c. where

   d. pwd

3. Which of the following is an absolute pathname? (Choose all that apply.)

    a.   Home/resume

    b.   C:\myfolder\resume

    c.   resume

    d.   /home/resume

    e.   C:home/resume

4. A special device file is used to _____.

    a.   enable proprietary custom-built devices to work with Linux

    b.   represent hardware devices such as hard disk drives and ports

    c.   keep a list of device settings specific to each individual user

    d.   do nothing in Linux

5. If a user's current directory is /home/mary/project1, which command could she use to move to the etc directory directly under the root?

    a.   `cd ..`

    b.   `cd /home/mary/etc`

    c.   `cd etc`

    d.   `cd /etc`

    e.   `cd \etc`

6. After typing the `ls -a` command, you notice that there is a file whose filename begins with a dot (.). What does this mean?

    a.   It is a binary file.

    b.   It is a system file.

    c.   It is a file in the current directory.

    d.   It is a hidden file.

7. After typing the `ls -F` command, you notice a filename that ends with an asterisk (*) character. What does this mean?

    a.   It is a hidden file.

    b.   It is a linked file.

    c.   It is a special device file.

    d.   It is an executable file.

8. The vi editor can function in which two of the following modes? (Choose both that apply.)

    a.   text

    b.   command

    c.   input

    d.   interactive

    e.   insert

9. The `less` command offers less functionality than the `more` command. True or False?

10. Which command searches for and displays any text contents of a binary file?

    a. `text`

    b. `strings`

    c. `od`

    d. `less`

11. How can a user switch from insert mode to command mode when using the vi editor?

    a. Press the Ctrl+Alt+Del keys simultaneously.

    b. Press the Del key.

    c. Type in a : character.

    d. Press the Esc key.

12. If "resume" is the name of a file in the home directory off the root of the filesystem and your present working directory is home, what is the relative name for the file named resume?

    a. /home/resume

    b. /resume

    c. resume

    d. \home\resume

13. What will the following wildcard regular expression return: file[a-c]?

    a. filea-c

    b. filea, filec

    c. filea, fileb, filec

    d. fileabc

14. What will typing `q!` at the : prompt in command mode do when using the vi editor?

    a. quit because no changes were made

    b. quit after saving any changes

    c. nothing because the ! is a metacharacter

    d. quit without saving any changes

15. A user types in the command `head /poems/mary`. What will be displayed on the terminal screen?

    a. the first line of the file mary

    b. the header for the file mary

    c. the first 20 lines of the file mary

    d. the last 10 lines of the file mary

    e. the first 10 lines of the file mary

16. The `tac` command _____.

    a. is not a valid Linux command

    b. displays the contents of hidden files

    c. displays the contents of a file in reverse order, last word on the line first and first word on the line last

    d. displays the contents of a file in reverse order, last line first and first line last

17. How can you specify a text pattern that must be at the beginning of a line of text using a regular expression?

    a. Precede the string with a /.

    b. Follow the string with a \.

    c. Precede the string with a $.

    d. Precede the string with a ^.

18. Linux has only one root directory per directory tree. True or False?

19. Using wildcard metacharacters, how can you indicate a character that is *not* a or b or c or d?

    a. [^abcd]

    b. not [a-d]

    c. [!a-d]

    d. !a-d

20. A user typed in the command `pwd` and saw the following output: /home/jim/sales/pending. How could that user navigate to the /home/jim directory?

    a. `cd ..`

    b. `cd /jim`

    c. `cd ../..`

    d. `cd ./.`

Hands-On Projects

These projects should be completed in the order given. The hands-on projects presented in this chapter should take a total of three hours to complete. The requirements for this lab include:

- A computer with Fedora Linux installed according to Hands-On Project 2-2.

Project 3-1

In this hands-on project, you log in to the computer and navigate the file structure.

1. Turn on your computer. After your Linux system has been loaded, switch to a command-line terminal (tty2) by pressing **Ctrl+Alt+F2** and log in to the terminal using the user name of **root** and the password of **secret**.

2. At the command prompt, type **pwd** and press **Enter** to view the current working directory. What is your current working directory?

3. At the command prompt, type **cd** and press **Enter**. At the command prompt, type **pwd** and press **Enter** to view the current working directory. Did your current working directory change? Why or why not?

4. At the command prompt, type **cd .** and press **Enter**. At the command prompt, type **pwd** and press **Enter** to view the current working directory. Did your current working directory change? Why or why not?

5. At the command prompt, type **cd ..** and press **Enter**. At the command prompt, type **pwd** and press **Enter** to view the current working directory. Did your current working directory change? Why or why not?

6. At the command prompt, type **cd root** and press **Enter**. At the command prompt, type **pwd** and press **Enter** to view the current working directory. Did your current working directory change? Where are you now? Did you specify a relative or absolute pathname to your home directory when you used the **cd root** command?

7. At the command prompt, type **cd etc** and press **Enter**. What error message did you receive and why?

8. At the command prompt, type **cd /etc** and press **Enter**. At the command prompt, type **pwd** and press **Enter** to view the current working directory. Did your current working directory change? Did you specify a relative or absolute pathname to the /etc directory when you used the **cd /etc** command?

9. At the command prompt, type **cd /** and press **Enter**. At the command prompt, type **pwd** and press **Enter** to view the current working directory. Did your current working directory change? Did you specify a relative or absolute pathname to the / directory when you used the **cd /** command?

10. At the command prompt, type **cd ~user1** and press **Enter**. At the command prompt, type **pwd** and press **Enter** to view the current working directory. Did your current working directory change? Which command discussed earlier performs the same function as the **cd ~** command?

11. At the command prompt, type **cd Desktop** and press **Enter** (be sure to use a capital D). At the command prompt, type **pwd** and press **Enter** to view the current working directory. Did your current working directory change? Where are you now? What kind of pathname did you use here (absolute or relative)?

12. Currently, you are in a subdirectory of user1's home folder, three levels below the root. To go up three parent directories to the / directory, type **cd ../../..** and press **Enter** at the command prompt. Next, type **pwd** and press **Enter** to ensure that you are in the / directory.

13. At the command prompt, type **cd /etc/samba** and press **Enter** to change the current working directory using an absolute pathname. Next, type **pwd** and press **Enter** at the command prompt to ensure that you have changed to the /etc/samba directory. Next, type in the command **cd ../sysconfig** at the command prompt and press **Enter**. Type **pwd** and press **Enter** to view your current location. Explain how the relative

pathname seen in the **cd ../sysconfig** command specified your current working directory.

14. At the command prompt, type **cd ../../home/user1/Desktop** and press **Enter** to change your current working directory to the Desktop directory underneath user1's home directory. Verify that you are in the target directory by typing the **pwd** command at a command prompt and pressing **Enter**. Would it have been more advantageous to use an absolute pathname to change to this directory instead of the relative pathname that you used?

15. Type **exit** and press **Enter** to log out of your shell.

Project 3-2

In this hands-on project, you navigate the Linux filesystem using the Tab-completion feature of the BASH shell.

1. Switch to a command-line terminal (tty2) by pressing **Ctrl+Alt+F2** and log in to the terminal using the user name of **root** and the password of **secret**.

2. At the command prompt, type **cd /** and press **Enter**.

3. Next, type **cd r** at the command prompt and press **Tab**. What is displayed on the screen and why? How many subdirectories under the root begin with "r"?

4. Press the **Ctrl** and **c** keys simultaneously to cancel the command and return to an empty command prompt.

5. At the command prompt, type **cd b** and press **Tab**. Did the display change? Why did you hear a beep?

6. Press **Tab** again. How many subdirectories under the root begin with "b"?

7. Type the letter **i**. Notice that the command now reads cd bi. Press **Tab** again. Which directory did it expand to? Why? Press the **Ctrl** and **c** keys simultaneously to cancel the command and return to an empty command prompt.

8. At the command prompt, type **cd m** and press **Tab**. Press **Tab** once again after hearing the beep. How many subdirectories under the root begin with "m"?

9. Type the letter **e**. Notice that the command now reads cd me. Press **Tab**.

10. Press **Enter** to execute the command at the command prompt. Next, type the **pwd** command and press **Enter** to verify that you are in the /media directory.

11. Type **exit** and press **Enter** to log out of your shell.

Project 3-3

In this hands-on project, you examine files and file types using the ls and file commands.

1. Switch to a command-line terminal (tty2) by pressing **Ctrl+Alt+F2** and log in to the terminal using the user name of **root** and the password of **secret**.

2. At the command prompt, type **cd /etc** and press **Enter**. Verify that you are in the /etc directory by typing **pwd** at the command prompt and pressing **Enter**.

3. At the command prompt, type **ls** and press **Enter**. What do you see listed in the four columns? Do any of the files have extensions? What is the most common extension you see and what does it indicate? Is the list you are viewing on the screen the entire contents of /etc?

4. At the command prompt, type **ls | more** and then press **Enter** (the | symbol is usually near the Enter key on the keyboard and is obtained by pressing the Shift and \ keys in combination). What does the display show? Notice the highlighted --More-- prompt at the bottom of the screen. Press **Enter**. Press **Enter** again. Press **Enter** once more. Notice that each time you press Enter, you advance one line further into the file. Next, press the **Spacebar**. Press the **Spacebar** again. Notice that with each press of the Spacebar, you advance one full page into the displayed directory contents. Press the **h** key to get a Help screen. Examine the command options.

5. Press the **q** key to quit the more command and return to an empty command prompt.

6. At the command prompt, type **ls | less** and then press **Enter**. What does the display show? Notice the : at the bottom of the screen. Press **Enter**. Press **Enter** again. Press **Enter** once more. Notice that each time you press Enter, you advance one line further into the file. Next, press the **Spacebar**. Press the **Spacebar** again. Notice that with each press of the Spacebar, you advance one full page into the displayed directory contents. Press the **h** key to get a Help screen. Examine the command options, and then press **q** to return to the command output.

7. Press the ↑ (up cursor key) key. Press ↑ again. Press ↑ once more. Notice that each time you press the ↑ key, you go up one line in the file display toward the beginning of the file. Next, press the ↓ (down arrow) key. Press ↓ again. Press ↓ once more. Notice that each time you press the ↓ key, you move forward into the file display.

8. Press the **q** key to quit the less command and return to a shell command prompt.

9. At the command prompt, type **cd** and press **Enter**. At the command prompt, type **pwd** and press **Enter**. What is your current working directory? At the command prompt, type **ls** and press **Enter**.

10. At the command prompt, type **ls /etc** and press **Enter**. How does this output compare with what you saw in Step 9? Has your current directory changed? Verify your answer by typing **pwd** at the command prompt and pressing **Enter**. Notice that you were able to list the contents of another directory by giving the absolute name of it as an argument to the ls command without leaving the directory in which you are currently located.

11. At the command prompt, type **ls /etc/skel** and press **Enter**. Did you see a listing of any files? At the command prompt, type **ls -a /etc/skel** and press **Enter**. What is special about these files? What do the first two entries in the list (. and ..) represent?

12. At the command prompt, type **ls -aF /etc/skel** and press **Enter**. Which file types are available in the /etc/skel directory?

13. At the command prompt, type **ls /bin** and press **Enter**. Did you see a listing of any files? At the command prompt, type **ls -F /bin** and press **Enter**. What file types are present in the /bin directory?

14. At the command prompt, type **ls /boot** and press **Enter**. Next type **ls -l /boot** and press **Enter**. What additional information is available on the screen? What types of files are available in the /boot directory? At the command prompt, type **ll /boot** and press **Enter**. Is the output any different from that of the **ls -l /boot** command you just entered? Why or why not?

15. At the command prompt, type **file /etc** and press **Enter**. What type of file is etc?

16. At the command prompt, type **file /etc/inittab** and press **Enter**. What type of file is /etc/inittab?

17. At the command prompt, type **file /boot/*** to see the types of files in the /boot directory. Is this information more specific than the information you gathered in Step 14?

18. Type **exit** and press **Enter** to log out of your shell.

Project 3-4

In this hands-on project, you display file contents using the cat, tac, head, tail, strings, and od commands.

1. Switch to a command-line terminal (tty2) by pressing **Ctrl+Alt+F2** and log in to the terminal using the user name of **root** and the password of **secret**.

2. At the command prompt, type **cat /etc/hosts** and press **Enter** to view the contents of the file hosts, which reside in the directory /etc. Next, type **cat -n /etc/hosts** and press **Enter**. How many lines does the file have? At the command prompt, type **tac /etc/hosts** and press **Enter** to view the same file in reverse order. The output of both commands should be visible on the same screen. Compare them.

3. To see the contents of the same file in octal format instead of ASCII text, type **od /etc/hosts** at the command prompt and press **Enter**.

4. At the command prompt, type **cat /etc/inittab** and press **Enter**.

5. At the command prompt, type **head /etc/inittab** and press **Enter**. What is displayed on the screen? How many lines are displayed, which ones are they, and why?

6. At the command prompt, type **head -5 /etc/inittab** and press **Enter**. How many lines are displayed and why? Next, type **head -3 /etc/inittab** and press **Enter**. How many lines are displayed and why?

7. At the command prompt, type **tail /etc/inittab** and press **Enter**. What is displayed on the screen? How many lines are displayed, which ones are they, and why?

8. At the command prompt, type **tail -5 /etc/inittab** and press **Enter**. How many lines are displayed and why? Type the **cat -n /etc/inittab** command at a command prompt and press **Enter** to justify your answer.

9. At the command prompt, type **file /bin/nice** and press **Enter**. What type of file is it? Should you use a text tool command on this file?

10. At the command prompt, type **strings /bin/nice** and press **Enter**. Notice that you are able to see some text within this binary file. Next, type **strings /bin/nice | more** to view the same content page-by-page. When finished, press **q** to quit the more command.

11. Type **exit** and press **Enter** to log out of your shell.

Project 3-5

In this hands-on project, you create and edit text files using the vi editor.

1. Switch to a command-line terminal (tty2) by pressing **Ctrl+Alt+F2** and log in to the terminal using the user name of **root** and the password of **secret**.

2. At the command prompt, type **pwd**, press **Enter**, and ensure that /root is displayed, showing that you are in the root user's home folder. At the command prompt, type **vi sample1** and press **Enter** to open the vi editor and create a new text file called sample1. Notice that this name appears at the bottom of the screen along with the indication that it is a new file.

3. At the command prompt, type **My letter** and press **Enter**. Why was nothing displayed on the screen? To switch from command mode to insert mode to allow the typing of text, press **i**. Notice that the word "Insert" appears at the bottom of the screen. Next, type **My letter** and notice that this text is displayed on the screen. What types of tasks can be accomplished in insert mode?

4. Press **Esc**. Did the cursor move? What mode are you in now? Press ← two times until the cursor is under the last "t" in "letter." Press the **x** key. What happened? Next, type **i** to enter insert mode and type the letter *h*. Did the letter "h" get inserted before or after the cursor?

5. Press **Esc** to switch back to command mode and then move your cursor to the end of the line. Next, type the letter "**o**" to open a line underneath the current line and enter insert mode.

6. Type the following:

   It might look like I am doing nothing, but at the cellular level I can assure you that I am quite busy.

   Notice that the line wraps to the next line partway through the sentence. Though displayed over two lines on the screen, this sentence is treated as one continuous line of text in vi. Press **Esc** to return to command mode, and then press ↑. Where does the cursor move? Use the cursor keys to navigate to the letter "l" at the beginning of the word "level" and press the **i** key to enter insert mode. Press **Enter** while in insert mode. Next, press **Esc** to return to command mode and then press ↑. Where does the cursor move?

7. Type **dd** three times to delete all lines in the file.

8. Type **i** to enter insert mode, and then type:

   Hi there, I hope this day finds you well.

   and press **Enter**. Press **Enter** again. Type:

   Unfortunately we were not able to make it to your dining

   and press **Enter**. Type:

   room this year while vacationing in Algonquin Park – I

   and press **Enter**. Type:

   especially wished to see the model of the Highland Inn

and press **Enter**. Type:

and the train station in the dining room.

and press **Enter**. Press **Enter** again. Type:

I have been reading on the history of Algonquin Park but

and press **Enter**. Type:

no where could I find a description of where the Highland

and press **Enter**. Type:

Inn was originally located on Cache lake.

and press **Enter**. Press **Enter** again. Type:

If it is no trouble, could you kindly let me know such that

and press **Enter**. Type:

I need not wait until next year when I visit your lodge?

and press **Enter**. Press **Enter** again. Type:

Regards,

and press **Enter**. Type:

Mackenzie Elizabeth

and press **Enter**. You should now have the sample letter used in this chapter on your screen. It should resemble the letter in Figure 3-4.

9. Press **Esc** to switch to command mode. Next, press the **Shift** and **;** keys simultaneously to open the **:** prompt at the bottom of the screen. At this prompt, type **w** and press **Enter** to save the changes you have made to the file. What is displayed at the bottom of the file when you are finished?

10. Press the **Shift** and **;** keys simultaneously to open the **:** prompt at the bottom of the screen again, type **q**, and then press **Enter** to exit the vi editor.

11. At the command prompt, type **ls** and press **Enter** to view the contents of your current directory. Notice that there is now a file called sample1 listed.

12. Next, type **file sample1** and press **Enter**. What type of file is sample1? At the command prompt, type **cat sample1** and press **Enter**.

13. At the command prompt, type **vi sample1** and press **Enter** to open the letter again in the vi editor. What is displayed at the bottom of the screen? How does this compare with Step 9?

14. Press the **F1** key to display a help file for vi and its commands. Use the Page Down and Page Up keys to navigate the help file. When finished, press the **Shift** and **;** keys simultaneously to open the **:** prompt at the bottom of the screen again, type **q**, and then press **Enter** to exit the Help screen.

15. Use the cursor keys to navigate to the bottom of the document. Press the **Shift** and **;** keys simultaneously to open the **:** prompt at the bottom of the screen again, type **!date**, and press **Enter**. The current system date and time appear at the bottom of the screen. As indicated, press **Enter** to return to the document. Press the **Shift** and **;** keys simultaneously again to open the **:** prompt at the bottom of the screen again, type **r !date**, and press **Enter**. What happened and why?

16. Use the cursor keys to position your cursor on the line in the document that displays the current date and time, and type **yy** to copy it to the buffer in memory. Next, use the cursor keys to position your cursor on the first line in the document, and type **P** (capitalized) to paste the contents of the memory buffer above your current line. Does the original line remain at the bottom of the document?

17. Use the cursor keys to position your cursor on the line at the end of the document that displays the current date and time, and type **dd** to delete it.

18. Use the cursor keys to position your cursor on the "t" in the word "there" on the second line of the file that reads **Hi there, I hope this day finds you well.**, type **dw** to delete the word. Next, type **i** to enter insert mode, type the word **Bob**, and then press **Esc** to switch back to command mode.

19. Press the **Shift** and **;** keys simultaneously to open the **:** prompt at the bottom of the screen again, type **w sample2**, and press **Enter**. What happened and why?

20. Press **i** to enter insert mode, and type the word **test**. Next, press **Esc** to switch to command mode. Press the **Shift** and **;** keys simultaneously to open the **:** prompt at the bottom of the screen again, type **q**, and press **Enter** to quit the vi editor. Were you able to quit? Why not?

21. Press the **Shift** and **;** keys simultaneously to open the **:** prompt at the bottom of the screen again, type **q!**, and press **Enter** to quit the vi editor and discard any changes since the last save.

22. At the command prompt, type **ls** and press **Enter** to view the contents of your current directory. Notice that there is now a file called sample2, which was created in Step 19.

23. At the command prompt, type **vi sample2** and press **Enter** to open the letter again in the vi editor.

24. Use the cursor keys to position your cursor on the line that reads **Hi Bob, I hope this day finds you well.**

25. Press the **Shift** and **;** keys simultaneously to open the **:** prompt at the bottom of the screen, type **s/Bob/Barb/g**, and press **Enter** to change all occurrences of "Bob" to "Barb" on the current line.

26. Press the **Shift** and **;** keys simultaneously to open the **:** prompt at the bottom of the screen again, type **1,$ s/to/TO/g**, and press **Enter** to change all occurrences of the word "to" to "TO" for the entire file.

27. Press the **u** key to undo the last function performed. What happened and why?

28. Press the **Shift** and **;** keys simultaneously to open the **:** prompt at the bottom of the screen again, type **wq**, then press **Enter** to save your document and quit the vi editor.

29. At the command prompt, type **vi sample3** and press **Enter** to open a new file called sample3 in the vi editor. Type **i** to enter insert mode. Next, type **P.S. How were the flies this year?** Press the **Esc** key when finished.

30. Press the **Shift** and **;** keys simultaneously to open the **:** prompt at the bottom of the screen again, type **wq,** then press **Enter** to save your document and quit the vi editor.

31. At the command prompt, type **vi sample1,** press **Enter** to open the file sample1 again, and use the cursor keys to position your cursor on the line that reads "Mackenzie Elizabeth."

32. Press the Shift and **;** keys simultaneously to open the **:** prompt at the bottom of the screen again, type **r sample3,** and press **Enter** to insert the contents of the file sample3 below your current line.

33. Press the Shift and **;** keys simultaneously to open the **:** prompt at the bottom of the screen, type **s/flies/flies and bears/g,** and press **Enter.** What happened and why?

34. Press the **Shift** and **;** keys simultaneously to open the **:** prompt at the bottom of the screen again, type **set number,** and press **Enter** to turn on line numbering.

35. Press the **Shift** and **;** keys simultaneously to open the **:** prompt at the bottom of the screen again, type **set nonumber,** and press **Enter** to turn off line numbering.

36. Press the **Shift** and **;** keys simultaneously to open the **:** prompt at the bottom of the screen again, type **set all,** and press **Enter** to view all vi parameters. Press **Enter** to advance through the list and press **q** when finished to return to the vi editor.

37. Press the **Shift** and **;** keys simultaneously to open the **:** prompt at the bottom of the screen again, type **wq,** and press **Enter** to save your document and quit the vi editor.

38. Type **exit** and press **Enter** to log out of your shell.

Project 3-6

In this hands-on project, you use the ls command alongside wildcard metacharacters in your shell to explore the contents of your home directory.

1. Switch to a command-line terminal (tty2) by pressing **Ctrl+Alt+F2** and log in to the terminal using the user name of **root** and the password of **secret.**

2. At the command prompt, type **pwd,** press **Enter,** and ensure that **/root** is displayed, showing that you are in the root user's home folder. At the command prompt, type **ls.** How many files with a name beginning with the word "sample" exist in **/root?**

3. At the command prompt, type **ls *** and press **Enter.** What is listed and why?

4. At the command prompt, type **ls sample** and press **Enter.** What is listed and why?

5. At the command prompt, type **ls sample?** and press **Enter.** What is listed and why?

6. At the command prompt, type **ls sample??** and press **Enter.** What is listed and why?

7. At the command prompt, type **ls sample[13]** and press **Enter.** What is listed and why?

8. At the command prompt, type **ls sample[!13]** and press **Enter.** What is listed and why? How does this compare with the results from Step 7?

9. At the command prompt, type **ls sample[1-3]** and press **Enter**. What is listed and why?

10. At the command prompt, type **ls sample[!1-3]** and press **Enter**. What is listed and why? How does this compare with the results from Step 9?

11. Type **exit** and press **Enter** to log out of your shell.

Project 3-7

In this hands-on project, you use the grep and egrep commands alongside regular expression metacharacters to explore the contents of text files.

1. Switch to a command-line terminal (tty2) by pressing **Ctrl+Alt+F2** and log in to the terminal using the user name of **root** and the password of **secret**.

2. At the command prompt, type **grep "Inn" sample1** and press **Enter**. What is displayed and why?

3. At the command prompt, type **grep -v "Inn" sample1** and press **Enter**. What is displayed and why? How does this compare with the results from Step 2?

4. At the command prompt, type **grep "inn" sample1** and press **Enter**. What is displayed and why?

5. At the command prompt, type **grep -i "inn" sample1** and press **Enter**. What is displayed and why? How does this compare with the results from Steps 2 and 4?

6. At the command prompt, type **grep "I" sample1** and press **Enter**. What is displayed and why?

7. At the command prompt, type **grep "I" sample1** and press **Enter**. What is displayed and why? How does it differ from the results from Step 6 and why?

8. At the command prompt, type **grep "t.e" sample1** and press **Enter**. What is displayed and why?

9. At the command prompt, type **grep "w...e" sample1** and press **Enter**. What is displayed and why?

10. At the command prompt, type **grep " ^I" sample1** and press **Enter**. What is displayed and why?

11. At the command prompt, type **grep "^I" sample1** and press **Enter**. What is displayed and why? How does this differ from the results in Step 10 and why?

12. At the command prompt, type **grep "(we|next)" sample1** and press **Enter**. Is anything displayed? Why?

13. At the command prompt, type **egrep "(we|next)" sample1** and press **Enter**. What is displayed and why?

14. At the command prompt, type **grep "Inn$" sample1** and press **Enter**. What is displayed and why?

15. At the command prompt, type **grep "?$" sample1** and press **Enter**. What is displayed and why? Does the ? metacharacter have special meaning here? Why?

16. At the command prompt, type **grep "^$" sample1** and press **Enter**. Is anything displayed? (*Hint:* Be certain to look closely!) Can you explain the output?

17. Type **exit** and press **Enter** to log out of your shell.

Discovery Exercises

1. You are the systems administrator for a scientific research company that employs over 100 scientists who write and run Linux programs to analyze their work. All of these programs are stored in each scientist's home directory on the Linux system. One scientist has left the company, and you are instructed to retrieve any work from that scientist's home directory. When you enter the home directory for that user, you notice that there are very few files and only two directories (one named Projects and one named Lab). List the commands that you would use to navigate through this user's home directory and view filenames and file types. If there are any text files, what commands could you use to view their contents?

2. When you type the pwd command, you notice that your current location on the Linux filesystem is the /usr/local directory. Answer the following questions, assuming that your current directory is /usr/local for each question:

   a. Which command could you use to change to the /usr directory using an absolute pathname?

   b. Which command could you use to change to the /usr directory using a relative pathname?

   c. Which command could you use to change to the /usr/local/share/info directory using an absolute pathname?

   d. Which command could you use to change to the /usr/local/share/info directory using a relative pathname?

   e. Which command could you use to change to the /etc directory using an absolute pathname?

   f. Which command could you use to change to the /etc directory using a relative pathname?

3. Using wildcard metacharacters and options to the ls command, view the following:

   a. All the files that end with .cfg under the /etc directory

   b. All hidden files in the /home/user1 directory

   c. The directory names that exist under the /var directory

   d. All the files that start with the letter "a" underneath the /bin directory

   e. All the files that have exactly three letters in their filenames in the /bin directory

   f. All files that have exactly three letters in their filenames and end with either the letter "t" or the letter "h" in the /bin directory

4. Explore the manual pages for the ls, grep, cat, od, tac, head, tail, pwd, cd, strings, and vi commands. Experiment with what you learned on the file sample1 that you created earlier.

5. The famous quote from Shakespeare's *Hamlet*, "To be or not to be," can be represented by the following regular expression:

    `(2b|[^b]{2})`

    If you used this expression when searching a text file using the `egrep` command (**`egrep "(2b|[^b]{2})" filename`**), what would be displayed? Try this command on a file that you have created. Why does it display what it does? That is the question.

6. The vi editor comes with a 30-minute tutorial on its usage. Start this tutorial by typing **vimtutor** at a command prompt and follow the directions. Provided you have a functional Web browser and an Internet connection, explore the resources available at *www.vim.org*.

7. Enter the following text into a new document called question7 using the vi editor. Next, use the vi editor to fix the mistakes in the file using the information in Table 3-5, Table 3-6, and Table 3-7 as well as the examples provided in this chapter.

    ```
    Hi there,
    Unfortunately we were not able to make it to your dining room
    Unfortunately we were not able to make it to your dining room
    this year while vacationing in Algonuin Park - I especially wished
    to see the model of the highland inn and the train station in the
        dining rooms.
    I have been readng on the history of Algonuin Park but
    no where could I find a description of where the Highland Inn was
    originally located on Cache lake.

    If it is not trouble, could you kindly let me that I need
    not wait until next year when we visit Lodge?

    I hope this day finds you well.
    Regard
    Elizabeth Mackenzie
    ```

8. The knowledge gained from using the vi editor can be transferred easily to the Emacs editor. Perform Question 7 using the Emacs editor instead of the vi editor.

9. When you use the vi editor and change environment settings at the : prompt, such as : `set number` to enable line numbering, those changes are lost when you exit the vi editor. To continuously apply the same environment settings, you can choose to put the `set` commands in a special hidden file in their home directory called .exrc; this .exrc file is then applied each time you open the vi editor. Enter the vi editor and find three environment settings that you want to change in addition to line numbering. Then create a new file called .exrc in your home directory, and enter the four lines changing these vi environment settings (do not start each line with a : character, just enter the `set` command—for example, `set number`). When finished, open the vi editor to edit a new file, and test to see whether the settings were applied automatically.

## chapter 4

Linux Filesystem Management

After completing this chapter, you will be able to:

- Find files and directories on the filesystem
- Understand and create linked files
- Explain the function of the Filesystem Hierarchy Standard
- Use standard Linux commands to manage files and directories
- Modify file and directory ownership
- Define and change Linux file and directory permissions
- Identify the default permissions created on files and directories
- Apply special file and directory permissions

In the previous chapter, you learned about navigating the Linux filesystem as well as viewing and editing files. This chapter focuses on the organization of files on the Linux filesystem as well as their linking and security. First, you explore standard Linux directories using the Filesystem Hierarchy Standard. Next, you explore common commands used to manage files and directories, followed by a discussion on finding files and directories. Finally, you learn about file and directory linking and common and special permissions available for files and directories.

The Filesystem Hierarchy Standard

The many thousands of files on a typical Linux system are organized into directories in the Linux directory tree. It's a complex system, made even more complex in the past by the fact that different Linux distributions were free to place files in different locations. This meant that you could waste a great deal of time searching for a configuration file on a Linux system with which you were unfamiliar. To simplify the task of finding specific files, the **Filesystem Hierarchy Standard (FHS)** was created.

FHS defines a standard set of directories for use by all Linux and UNIX systems, as well as the file and subdirectory contents of each directory. This ensures that, because the filename and location follow a standard convention, a Fedora Linux user will find the correct configuration file on a SuSE Linux or Hewlett-Packard UNIX computer with little difficulty. The FHS also gives Linux software developers the ability to locate files on a Linux system regardless of the distribution, allowing them to create software that is not distribution-specific.

A comprehensive understanding of the standard types of directories found on Linux systems is valuable when locating and managing files and directories; some standard UNIX and Linux directories defined by FHS and their descriptions are found in Table 4-1. These directories are discussed throughout this chapter and subsequent chapters.

To read the complete Filesystem Hierarchy Standard definition, visit the Internet at *www.pathname.com/fhs/*.

Managing Files and Directories

As mentioned earlier, using a Linux system involves navigating several directories and manipulating the files inside them. Thus, an efficient Linux user must understand how to create directories as needed, copy or move files from one directory to another, and delete files and directories. These tasks are commonly referred to as file management tasks.

Following is an example of a directory listing displayed by a user who is logged in as the root user:

```
[root@server1 ~]# pwd
/root
[root@server1 ~]# ls -F
current@  myprogram*  project   project12  project2  project4
Desktop/  myscript    project1  project13  project3  project5
[root@server1 ~]#_
```

Directory	Description
/bin	Contains binary commands for use by all users
/boot	Contains the Linux kernel and files used by the boot loader
/dev	Contains device files
/etc	Contains system-specific configuration files
/home	Is the default location for user home directories
/lib	Contains shared program libraries (used by the commands in /bin and /sbin) as well as kernel modules
/media	Contains subdirectories used for accessing (mounting) filesystems on removable media devices such as floppy disks, DVDs, and USB flash drives
/mnt	Is an empty directory used for temporarily accessing filesystems on removable media devices
/opt	Stores additional software programs
/proc	Contains process and kernel information
/root	Is the root user's home directory
/sbin	Contains system binary commands (used for administration)
/tmp	Holds temporary files created by programs
/usr	Contains most system commands and utilities—contains the following directories: /usr/bin—User binary commands /usr/games—Educational programs and games /usr/include—C program header files /usr/lib—Libraries /usr/local—Local programs /usr/sbin—System binary commands /usr/share—Files that are architecture independent /usr/src—Source code /usr/X11R6—The X Window System
/usr/local	Is the location for most additional programs
/var	Contains log files and spools

Table 4-1   Linux directories defined by the Filesystem Hierarchy Standard

As shown in the preceding output, only one directory (Desktop), two executable files (myprogram and myscript), and several project-related files (project) exist on this sample system. Although this directory structure is not cluttered and appears in an easy-to-read format on the terminal screen, typical home directories on a Linux system contain many more files; a typical Linux user might have over 100 files in his home directory. As a result, it is good practice to organize these files into subdirectories based on file purpose. Because several project files are in the root user's home directory in the preceding output, you could create a subdirectory called proj_files to contain the project-related files and decrease the size of the directory listing. To do this, you use the **mkdir (make directory) command**, which takes arguments specifying the absolute or relative pathnames of the directories to create. To create a proj_files directory underneath the current directory, you can use the mkdir command with a relative pathname:

```
[root@server1 ~]# mkdir proj_files
[root@server1 ~]# ls -F
```

```
current@ myprogram* project   project12  project2   project4 proj_files/
Desktop/ myscript*  project1  project13  project3   project5
[root@server1 ~]#_
```

Now, you can move the project files into the proj_files subdirectory by using the **mv (move)** **command.** The mv command requires two arguments at minimum: the **source file/directory** and the **target file/directory.** For example, to move the /etc/sample1 file to the /root directory, you could use the command mv /etc/sample1 /root.

If you want to move several files, you include one source argument for each file you want to move, then include the target directory as the last argument. For example, to move the /etc/ sample1 and /etc/sample2 files to the /root directory, you could use the command mv /etc/ sample1 /etc/sample2 /root.

Note that both the source (or sources) and the destination can be absolute or relative pathnames, and the source can contain wildcards if several files are to be moved. For example, to move all of the project files to the proj_files directory, you could type mv with the source argument project* (to match all files starting with the letters "project") and the target argument proj_files (relative pathname to the destination directory), as shown in the following output:

```
[root@server1 ~]# mv project*  proj_files
[root@server1 ~]# ls -F
current@ Desktop/ myprogram* myscript*  proj_files/
[root@server1 ~]# ls -F proj_files
project  project1  project12  project13  project2  project3  project4
project5
[root@server1 ~]#_
```

In the preceding output, the current directory listing does not show the project files anymore, yet the listing of the proj_files subdirectory indicates that they were moved successfully.

 If the target is the name of a directory, the mv command moves those files to that directory. If the target is a filename of an existing file in a certain directory and there is one source file, the mv command overwrites the target with the source. If the target is a filename of a nonexistent file in a certain directory, the mv command creates a new file with that filename in the target directory and moves the source file to that file.

Another important use of the mv command is to rename files, which is simply moving a file to the same directory but with a different filename. To rename the myscript file from earlier examples to myscript2, you can use the following mv command:

```
[root@server1 ~]# ls -F
current@ Desktop/ myprogram* myscript*  proj_files/
[root@server1 ~]# mv myscript  myscript2
[root@server1 ~]# ls -F
current@ Desktop/ myprogram* myscript2*  proj_files/
[root@server1 ~]#_
```

Similarly, the mv command can rename directories. If the source is the name of an existing directory, it is renamed to whatever directory name is specified as the target.

The mv command works similarly to a cut-and-paste operation in which the file is copied to a new directory and deleted from the source directory. In some cases, however, you might want to keep the file in the source directory and instead insert a copy of the file in the target directory. You can do this using the **cp (copy) command**. Much like the mv command, the cp command takes two arguments at minimum. The first argument specifies the source file/directory to be copied and the second argument specifies the target file/directory. If several files need to be copied to a destination directory, simply specify several source arguments, with the final argument on the command line serving as the target directory. Each argument can be an absolute or relative pathname and can contain wildcards or the special metacharacters "." (which specifies the current directory) and ".." (which specifies the parent directory). For example, to make a copy of the file /etc/hosts in the current directory (/root), you can specify the absolute pathname to the /etc/hosts file (/etc/hosts) and the relative pathname indicating the current directory (.):

```
[root@server1 ~]# cp /etc/hosts .
[root@server1 ~]# ls -F
current@ Desktop/ hosts myprogram* myscript2* proj_files/
[root@server1 ~]#_
```

You can also make copies of files in the same directory. To make a copy of the hosts file called hosts2 in the current directory, type the following command:

```
[root@server1 ~]# cp hosts hosts2
[root@server1 ~]# ls -F
current@ Desktop/ hosts hosts2 myprogram* myscript2* proj_files/
[root@server1 ~]#_
```

Despite their similarities, the mv and cp commands work on directories differently. The mv command renames a directory, whereas the cp command creates a whole new copy of the directory and its contents. To copy a directory full of files in Linux, you must tell the cp command that the copy will be **recursive** (involve files and subdirectories too) by using the -R option. The following example demonstrates copying the proj_files directory and all of its contents to the /home/user1 directory without and with the -R option:

```
[root@server1 ~]# ls -F
current@ Desktop/ hosts myprogram* myscript2* proj_files/
[root@server1 ~]# ls -F /home/user1
Desktop/
[root@server1 ~]# cp  proj_files /home/user1
cp: omitting directory 'proj_files'
[root@server1 ~]# ls -F /home/user1
Desktop/
[root@server1 ~]# cp -R proj_files /home/user1
[root@server1 ~]# ls -F /home/user1
Desktop/ proj_files/
[root@server1 ~]#_
```

If the target is a file that exists, both the mv and cp commands warn the user that the target file will be overwritten and then ask whether to continue. This is not a feature of the command as normally invoked but is a feature of the default configuration in Fedora Linux because the BASH shell in Fedora Linux contains aliases to the cp and mv commands.

Aliases are special variables in memory that point to commands; they are fully discussed in Chapter 7.

When you type mv, you are actually running the mv command with the –i option without realizing it. If the target file already exists, both the mv command and the mv command with the –i option interactively prompt the user to choose whether to overwrite the existing file. Similarly, when you type the cp command, you are actually running the cp –i command, which prevents the accidental overwriting of files. To see the aliases present in your current shell, simply type alias, as shown in the following output:

```
[root@server1 ~]# alias
alias cp='cp -i'
alias l.='ls -d .* --color=auto'
alias ll='ls -l --color=auto'
alias ls='ls --color=auto'
alias mv='mv -i'
alias rm='rm -i'
alias which='alias | /usr/bin/which --tty-only --read-alias --show-dot
--show-tilde'
[root@server1 ~]#_
```

If you want to override this interactive option, which is known as **interactive mode,** use the –f (force) option to override the choice, as shown in the following example. In this example, the root user tries to rename the hosts file using the name "hosts2," a name already assigned to an existing file. The example shows the user attempting this task both without and with the –f option to the mv command:

```
[root@server1 ~]# ls -F
current@  Desktop/  hosts  hosts2  myprogram*  myscript2*  proj_files/
[root@server1 ~]# mv hosts hosts2
mv: overwrite 'hosts2'? n
[root@server1 ~]# mv -f hosts hosts2
[root@server1 ~]# ls -F
current@  Desktop/  hosts2  myprogram*  myscript2*  proj_files/
[root@server1 ~]#_
```

Creating directories, copying, and moving files are file management tasks that preserve or create data on the hard disk. To remove files or directories, you must use either the rm command or the rmdir command.

The **rm (remove) command** takes a list of arguments specifying the absolute or relative pathnames of files to remove. As with most commands, wildcards can be used to simplify the process of removing multiple files. After a file has been removed from the filesystem, it cannot be recovered. As a result, the rm command is aliased in Fedora Linux to the rm command with the –i option, which interactively prompts the user to choose whether to continue with the deletion. Like the cp and mv commands, the rm command accepts the –f option to override this choice and immediately delete the file. The use of the rm and rm −f commands to remove the current and hosts2 files is demonstrated in the following example:

```
[root@server1 ~]# ls -F
current@ Desktop/ hosts2 myprogram* myscript2* proj_files/
[root@server1 ~]# rm current
rm: remove 'current'? y
[root@server1 ~]# rm -f hosts2
[root@server1 ~]# ls -F
Desktop/ myprogram* myscript2* proj_files/
[root@server1 ~]# _
```

To remove a directory, you can use the **rmdir (remove directory) command**; however, the rmdir command only removes a directory if it contains no files. To remove a directory and the files inside, you must use the rm command and specify that a directory full of files should be removed. As explained earlier in this chapter, you need to use the recursive option (−R) with the cp command to copy directories; to remove a directory full of files, you can also use a recursive option (−R) with the rm command. If, for example, the root user wants to remove the proj_files subdirectory and all of the files within it without being prompted to confirm each file deletion, the command she must use is rm −Rf proj_files, as shown in the following example:

```
[root@server1 ~]# ls -F
Desktop/ myprogram* myscript2* proj_files/
[root@server1 ~]# rmdir  proj_files
rmdir: 'proj_files': Directory not empty
[root@server1 ~]# rm -Rf  proj_files
[root@server1 ~]# ls -F
Desktop/ myprogram* myscript2*
[root@server1 ~]# _
```

In many commands, such as rm and cp, the −r and the −R options have the same meaning (recursive).

The −R option to the rm command is dangerous if you are not certain which files exist in the directory to be deleted recursively. As a result, the −R option to the rm command is commonly referred to as the −résumé option; if you use it incorrectly, you might need to prepare your résumé.

It is important to note that the aforementioned file management commands are commonly used by Linux users, developers, and administrators alike. Table 4-2 shows a summary of these common file management commands.

Finding Files

Before using the file management commands mentioned in the preceding section, you must know the locations of the files involved. The fastest method to search for files in the Linux

Command	Description
mkdir	Creates directories
rmdir	Removes empty directories
mv	Moves/renames files and directories
cp	Copies files and directories full of files (with the –r option)
alias	Displays BASH shell aliases
rm	Removes files and directories full of files (with the –r option)

Table 4-2   Common Linux file management commands

directory tree is to use the **locate command**. For example, to view all of the files underneath the root directory with the filename "inittab," or with "inittab" as part of the filename, you can simply type locate inittab at a command prompt, which produces the following output:

```
[root@server1 ~]# locate inittab
/etc/inittab
/usr/share/man/man5/inittab.5.gz
/usr/share/vim/vim72/syntax/inittab.vim
[root@server1 ~]# _
```

The locate command looks in a premade database that contains a list of all the files on the system. This database is indexed much like a textbook for fast searching, yet can become outdated as files are added and removed from the system, which happens on a regular basis. As a result, the database used for the locate command (/var/lib/mlocate/mlocate.db) is updated each day automatically and can be updated manually by running the updatedb command at a command prompt.

As the locate command searches all files on the filesystem, it returns too much information to display on the screen. To make the output easier to read, you can use the more (or less) command to pause the output, as in locate inittab | more. To prevent the problem entirely, you can do more specific searches.

A slower, yet more versatile method for locating files on the filesystem is to use the **find command**. The find command does not use a premade index of files but instead searches the directory tree recursively, starting from a certain directory, for files that meet a certain criterion. The format of the find command is as follows:

```
find  <start directory>  -criteria  <what to find>
```

For example, to find any files named "inittab" underneath the /etc directory, you can use the command find /etc –name inittab and receive the following output:

```
[root@server1 ~]# find /etc -name inittab
/etc/inittab
[root@server1 ~]# _
```

You can also use wildcard metacharacters with the find command; however, these wildcards must be protected from shell interpretation, as they must only be interpreted by the find command. To do this, ensure that any wildcard metacharacters are enclosed within quote characters. An example of using the find command with wildcard metacharacters to find all files that start with the letters "host" underneath the /etc directory is shown in the following output:

```
[root@server1 ~]# find /etc -name "host*"
etc/hosts.allow
/etc/avahi/hosts
/etc/hosts.atm
/etc/BackupPC/hosts
/etc/hosts
/etc/host.conf
/etc/hosts.deny
/etc/sysconfig/networking/profiles/default/hosts
[root@server1 ~]# _
```

Although name is the most common criterion used with the find command, many other criteria can be used with the find command as well. To find all files starting from the /var directory that have a size greater than 4096K (Kilobytes), you can use the following command:

```
[root@server1 ~]# find /var -size +4096k
/var/tmp/kdecache-bob/kpc/kde-icon-cache.index
/var/tmp/kdecache-bob/kpc/plasma_theme_default.data
/var/tmp/kdecache-bob/kpc/kde-icon-cache.data
/var/tmp/kdecache-bob/kpc/plasma_theme_default.index
/var/tmp/kdecache-bozo/kpc/kde-icon-cache.index
/var/tmp/kdecache-bozo/kpc/plasma_theme_default.data
/var/tmp/kdecache-bozo/kpc/kde-icon-cache.data
/var/tmp/kdecache-bozo/kpc/plasma_theme_default.index
/var/cache/abrt/ccpp-1280847743-3253/coredump
/var/lib/mlocate/mlocate.db
/var/lib/rpm/Basenames
/var/lib/rpm/Packages
/var/lib/rpm/Filedigests
[root@server1 ~]# _
```

As well, if you want to find all the directories only underneath the /boot directory, you can type the following command:

```
[root@server1 ~]# find /boot -type d
boot
/boot/grub
/boot/efi
/boot/efi/EFI
/boot/efi/EFI/redhat
[root@server1 ~]# _
```

Table 4-3 provides a list of some common criteria used with the find command.

Although the find command can be used to search for files based on many criteria, it might take several minutes to complete the search if the number of directories and files being searched is large. To reduce the time needed to search, narrow down the directories searched by specifying a subdirectory when possible. It takes less time to search the /usr/local/bin

Criteria	Description
-amin -x	Searches for files that were accessed less than x minutes ago
-amin +x	Searches for files that were accessed more than x minutes ago
-atime -x	Searches for files that were accessed less than x days ago
-atime +x	Searches for files that were accessed more than x days ago
-empty	Searches for empty files or directories
-fstype x	Searches for files if they are on a certain filesystem x (where x could be ext2, ext3, and so on)
-group x	Searches for files that are owned by a certain group or GID (x)
-inum x	Searches for files that have an inode number of x
-mmin -x	Searches for files that were modified less than x minutes ago
-mmin +x	Searches for files that were modified more than x minutes ago
-mtime -x	Searches for files that were modified less than x days ago
-mtime +x	Searches for files that were modified more than x days ago
-name x	Searches for a certain filename x (x can contain wildcards)
-regexp x	Searches for certain filenames using regular expressions instead of wildcard metacharacters
-size -x	Searches for files with a size less than x
-size x	Searches for files with a size of x
-size +x	Searches for files with a size greater than x
-type x	Searches for files of type x where x is: • b for block files • c for character files • d for directory files • p for named pipes • f for regular files • l for symbolic links (shortcuts) • s for sockets
-user x	Searches for files owned by a certain user or UID (x)

Table 4-3 Common criteria used with the `find` command

directory and its subdirectories, compared to searching the /usr directory and all of its subdirectories. As well, if the filename that you are searching for is an executable file, that file can likely be found in less time using the **which command**. The which command only searches directories that are listed in a special variable called the **PATH variable** in the current BASH shell. Before exploring the which command, you must understand the usage of PATH.

Executable files can be stored in directories scattered around the directory tree. Recall from FHS that most executable files are stored in directories named bin or sbin, yet there are over 20 bin and sbin directories scattered around the directory tree after a typical Fedora Linux installation. To ensure that users do not need to specify the full pathname to commands such as ls (which is the executable file /bin/ls), there exists a special variable called PATH that is placed into memory each time a user logs in to the Linux system. Recall that you can see the contents of a certain variable in memory by using the $ metacharacter with the echo command:

```
[root@server1 ~]# echo $PATH
/usr/lib/qt-3.3/bin:/usr/kerberos/sbin:/usr/kerberos/bin:
/usr/lib/ccache:/usr/local/sbin:/usr/local/bin:/sbin:/bin:
/usr/sbin:/usr/bin:/root/bin
[root@server1 ~]# _
```

The PATH variable lists directories that are searched for executable files if a relative or absolute pathname was not specified when executing a command on the command line. In the preceding output, when a user types the ls command on the command line and presses Enter, the system recognizes that the command was not an absolute pathname (for example, /bin/ls) or relative pathname (for example, ../../bin/ls) and then proceeds to look for the ls executable file in the /usr/lib/qt-3.3/bin directory, then the /usr/kerberos/sbin directory, then the /usr/kerberos/bin directory, and so on. If all the directories in the PATH variable are searched and no ls command is found, the shell gives an error message to the user stating that the command was not found. In the preceding output, the /bin directory is in the PATH variable and, thus, the ls command is found and executed, but not until the previous directories in the PATH variable are searched first.

To search the directories in the PATH variable for the file called "grep," you could use the word "grep" as an argument for the which command and receive the following output:

```
[root@server1 ~]# which grep
/bin/grep
[root@server1 ~]# _
```

If the file being searched does not exist in the PATH variable directories, the which command lets you know in which directories it was not found, as shown in the following output:

```
[root@server1 ~]# which grepper
/usr/bin/which: no grepper in (/usr/lib/qt-3.3/bin:/usr/kerberos/sbin:
/usr/kerberos/bin:/usr/lib/ccache:/usr/local/sbin:/usr/local/bin:
/sbin:/bin:/usr/sbin:/usr/bin:/root/bin)
[root@server1 ~]# _
```

Linking Files

Files can be linked to one another in two ways. In a **symbolic link,** or symlink, one file is a pointer, or shortcut, to another file. In a **hard link,** two files share the same data.

To better understand how files are linked, you must understand how files are stored on a filesystem. On a structural level, a filesystem has three main sections:

- The superblock
- The inode table
- Data blocks

The **superblock** is the section that contains information about the filesystem in general, such as the number of inodes and data blocks, as well as how much data a data block stores in

Kilobytes. The **inode table** consists of several **inodes** (information nodes); each inode describes one file or directory on the filesystem and contains a unique inode number for identification. What is more important, the inode stores information such as the file size, data block locations, last date modified, permissions, and ownership. When a file is deleted, only its inode (which serves as a pointer to the actual data) is deleted. The data that makes up the contents of the file as well as the filename are stored in **data blocks**, which are referenced by the inode. In filesystem-neutral terminology, blocks are known as allocation units because they are the unit by which disk space is allocated for storage.

 Each file and directory must have an inode. All files except for special device files also have data blocks associated with the inode. Special device files are discussed in Chapter 5.

 Recall that directories are simply files that are used to organize other files; they too have an inode and data blocks, but their data blocks contain a list of filenames that are located within the directory.

Hard-linked files are direct copies of one another, as they share the same inode and inode number. All hard-linked files have the same size, and when one file is modified, the other hard-linked files are updated as well. This relationship between hard-linked files can be seen in Figure 4-1. You can hard-link a file an unlimited number of times; however, the hard-linked files must reside on the same filesystem. This is because inode numbers are defined to be unique only on the same filesystem and hard links are recognized by ignoring this unique inode number rule.

To create a hard link, you must use the **ln (link) command** and specify two arguments: the existing file to hard-link and the target file that will be created as a hard link to the existing file. Each argument can be the absolute or relative pathname to a file.

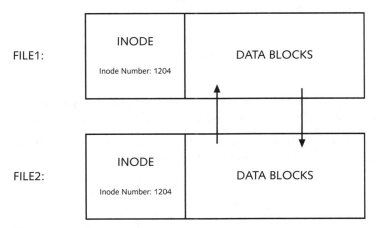

Figure 4-1 The structure of hard-linked files

Source: Course Technology/Cengage Learning

Take, for example, the following contents of the root user's home directory:

```
[root@server1 ~]# ls -l
total 520
drwx------    3 root     root       4096 Apr  8 07:12 Desktop
-rwxr-xr-x    1 root     root     519964 Apr  7 09:59 file1
-rwxr-xr-x    1 root     root       1244 Apr 27 18:17 file3
[root@server1 ~]# _
```

Suppose you want to make a hard link to file1 and call the new hard link file2, as shown in Figure 4-1. To accomplish this, you issue the command ln file1 file2 at the command prompt; a file called file2 is created and hard-linked to file1. To view the hard-linked filenames after creation, you can use the ls –l command:

```
[root@server1 ~]# ln file1 file2
[root@server1 ~]# ls -l
total 1032
drwx------    3 root     root       4096 Apr  8 07:12 Desktop
-rwxr-xr-x    2 root     root     519964 Apr  7 09:59 file1
-rwxr-xr-x    2 root     root     519964 Apr  7 09:59 file2
-rwxr-xr-x    1 root     root       1244 Apr 27 18:17 file3
[root@server1 ~]# _
```

Notice from the preceding long listing that file1 and file2 share the same inode, as they have the same size, permissions, ownership, modification date, and so on. Also note that the link count (the number after the permission set) for file1 has increased from the number one to the number two in the preceding output. A link count of one indicates that only one inode is shared by the file. A file that is hard-linked to another file shares two inodes and, thus, has a link count of two. Similarly, a file that is hard-linked to three other files shares four inodes and, thus, has a link count of four.

Although hard links share the same inode, deleting a hard-linked file does not delete all the other hard-linked files. Removing a hard link can be achieved by removing one of the files, which then lowers the link count.

To view the inode number of hard-linked files to verify that they are identical, you can use the –i option to the ls command in addition to any other options. The inode number is placed on the left of the directory listing on each line, as shown in the following output:

```
[root@server1 ~]# ls -li
total 1032
37595 drwx------    3 root     root       4096 Apr  8 07:12 Desktop
 1204 -rwxr-xr-x    2 root     root     519964 Apr  7 09:59 file1
 1204 -rwxr-xr-x    2 root     root     519964 Apr  7 09:59 file2
17440 -rwxr-xr-x    1 root     root       1244 Apr 27 18:17 file3
[root@server1 ~]# _
```

NOTE Directory files are not normally hard-linked, as the result would consist of two directories that contain the same contents. However, the root user has the ability to hard-link directories in some cases, using the –F or –d option to the ln command. Only directories that have files regularly added and need to maintain identical file contents are typically hard-linked.

Symbolic links (shown in Figure 4-2) are different from hard links because they do not share the same inode and inode number with their target file; one is merely a pointer to the other; thus, the files have different sizes. The data blocks in a symbolically linked file contain only the pathname to the target file. When a user edits a symbolically linked file, he is actually editing the target file. Thus, if the target file is deleted, the symbolic link serves no function, as it points to a nonexistent file.

Symbolic links are sometimes referred to as "soft links" or "symlinks."

To create a symbolic link, you use the -s option to the ln command. To create a symbolic link to file3 called file4, as in Figure 4-2, you can type ln -s file3 file4 at the command prompt. As with hard links, the arguments specified can be absolute or relative pathnames. To view the symbolically linked filenames after creation, you can use the ls -l command, as shown in the following example:

```
[root@server1 ~]# ln -s file3 file4
[root@server1 ~]# ls -l
total 1032
drwx- - - - -   3 root    root      4096  Apr  8 07:12 Desktop
-rwxr-xr-x   2 root    root    519964  Apr  7 09:59 file1
-rwxr-xr-x   2 root    root    519964  Apr  7 09:59 file2
-rwxr-xr-x   1 root    root      1244  Apr 27 18:17 file3
lrwxrwxrwx   1 root    root         5  Apr 27 19:05 file4 -> file3
[root@server1 ~]# _
```

Notice from the preceding output that file4 does not share the same inode, because the permissions, size, and modification date are different from file3. In addition, symbolic links are easier to identify than hard links; the file type character (before the permissions) is l, which indicates a symbolic link, and the filename points to the target using an arrow.

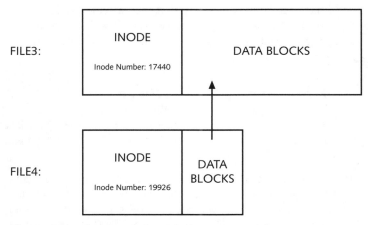

Figure 4-2 The structure of symbolically linked files

Source: Course Technology/Cengage Learning

The `ls -F` command also indicates symbolic links by appending an @ symbol, as shown in the following output:

```
[root@server1 ~]# ls -F
Desktop/ file1*  file2*  file3*  file4@
[root@server1 ~]# _
```

Another difference between hard links and symbolic links is that symbolic links need not reside on the same filesystem as their target. Instead, they point to the target filename and do not require the same inode, as shown in the following output:

```
[root@server1 ~]# ls -li
total 1032
37595 drwx- - - - -   3 root    root      4096 Apr  8 07:12 Desktop
 1204 -rwxr-xr-x      2 root    root    519964 Apr  7 09:59 file1
 1204 -rwxr-xr-x      2 root    root    519964 Apr  7 09:59 file2
17440 -rwxr-xr-x      1 root    root      1244 Apr 27 18:17 file3
19926 lrwxrwxrwx      1 root    root         5 Apr 27 19:05 file4 -> file3
[root@server1 ~]# _
```

NOTE Unlike hard links, symbolic links are commonly made to directories to simplify navigating the filesystem tree. Also, symbolic links made to directories are typically used to maintain compatibility with other UNIX and Linux systems. On Fedora Linux, the /etc/init.d directory is symbolically linked to the /etc/rc.d/init.d directory and the /usr/tmp directory is symbolically linked to the /var/tmp directory for this reason.

File and Directory Permissions

Recall that all users must log in with a user name and password to gain access to a Linux system. After logging in, a user is identified by her user name and group memberships; all access to resources depends on whether the user name and group memberships have the required **permission**. Thus, a firm understanding of ownership and permissions is necessary to operate a Linux system in a secure manner and to prevent unauthorized users access to sensitive files, directories, and commands.

File and Directory Ownership

When a user creates a file or directory, that user's name and **primary group** become the owner and group owner of the file, respectively. This affects the permission structure, as you see in the next section; however, it also determines who has the ability to modify file and directory permissions and ownership. Only two users on a Linux system can modify permissions on a file or directory or change its ownership: the owner of the file or directory and the root user.

To view your current user name, you can use the `whoami` command. To view your group memberships and primary group, you can use the `groups` command. An example of these two commands when logged in as the root user is shown in the following output:

```
[root@server1 ~]# whoami
root
[root@server1 ~]# groups
root bin daemon sys adm disk wheel
[root@server1 ~]# _
```

Notice from the preceding output that the root user is a member of seven groups, yet the root user's primary group is also called "root," as it is the first group mentioned in the output of the group's command. If this user creates a file, the owner is "root" and the group owner is also "root." To quickly create an empty file, you can use the **touch** command:

```
[root@server1 ~]# touch file1
[root@server1 ~]# ls -l
total 4
drwx------    3 root      root      4096 Apr  8 07:12 Desktop
-rw-r--r--    1 root      root         0 Apr 29 15:40 file1
[root@server1 ~]# _
```

Notice from the preceding output that the owner of file1 is "root" and the group owner is the "root" group. To change the ownership of a file or directory, you can use the **chown (change owner) command**, which takes two arguments at minimum: the new owner and the files or directories to change. Both arguments can be absolute or relative pathnames, and you can also change permissions recursively throughout the directory tree using the -R option to the chown command. To change the ownership of file1 to the user "user1" and the ownership of the directory Desktop and all of its contents to "user1" as well, you can enter the following commands:

```
[root@server1 ~]# chown user1 file1
[root@server1 ~]# chown -R user1 Desktop
[root@server1 ~]# ls -l
total 4
drwx------    3 user1     root      4096 Apr  8 07:12 Desktop
-rw-r--r--    1 user1     root         0 Apr 29 15:40 file1
[root@server1 ~]# ls -l Desktop
total 16
-rw------    1 user1     root       163 Mar 29 09:58 Floppy
-rw-r--r--    1 user1     root      3578 Mar 29 09:58 Home
-rw-r--r--    1 user1     root      1791 Mar 29 09:58 Start Here
drwx------    2 user1     root      4096 Mar 29 09:58 Trash
[root@server1 ~]# _
```

Recall that the owner of a file or directory and the root user have the ability to change ownership of a particular file or directory. If a regular user changes the ownership of a file or directory that he owns, that user cannot gain back the ownership. Instead, the new owner of that file or directory must change it to the original user. However, the previous examples involve the root user, who always has the ability to regain the ownership:

```
[root@server1 ~]# chown root file1
[root@server1 ~]# chown -R root Desktop
[root@server1 ~]# ls -l
total 4
drwx------    3 root      root      4096 Apr  8 07:12 Desktop
-rw-r--r--    1 root      root         0 Apr 29 15:40 file1
[root@server1 ~]# ls -l Desktop
```

```
total 16
-rw------    1 root    root     163 Mar 29 09:58 Floppy
-rw-r--r--   1 root    root    3578 Mar 29 09:58 Home
-rw-r--r--   1 root    root    1791 Mar 29 09:58 Start Here
drwx-----    2 root    root    4096 Mar 29 09:58 Trash
[root@server1 ~]# _
```

Just as the chown command can be used to change the owner of a file or directory, you can use the **chgrp (change group) command** to change the group owner of a file or directory. The chgrp command takes two arguments at minimum: the new group owner and the files or directories to change. As with the chown command, the chgrp command also accepts the -R option to change group ownership recursively throughout the directory tree. To change the group owner of file1 and the Desktop directory recursively throughout the directory tree, you can execute the following commands:

```
[root@server1 ~]# chgrp sys file1
[root@server1 ~]# chgrp -R sys Desktop
[root@server1 ~]# ls -l
total 4
drwx-----    3 root    sys     4096 Apr  8 07:12 Desktop
-rw-r--r--   1 root    sys        0 Apr 29 15:40 file1
[root@server1 ~]# ls -l Desktop
total 16
-rw------    1 root    sys      163 Mar 29 09:58 Floppy
-rw-r--r--   1 root    sys     3578 Mar 29 09:58 Home
-rw-r--r--   1 root    sys     1791 Mar 29 09:58 Start Here
drwx-----    2 root    sys     4096 Mar 29 09:58 Trash
[root@server1 ~]# _
```

Regular users can change the group of a file or directory only to a group to which they belong.

Normally, you change both the ownership and group ownership on a file when that file needs to be maintained by someone else. As a result, you can change both the owner and the group owner at the same time using the chown command. To change the owner to "user1" and the group owner to "root" for file1 and the directory Desktop recursively, you can enter the following commands:

```
[root@server1 ~]# chown user1.root file1
[root@server1 ~]# chown -R user1.root Desktop
[root@server1 ~]# ls -l
total 4
drwx-----    3 user1   root    4096 Apr  8 07:12 Desktop
-rw-r--r--   1 user1   root       0 Apr 29 15:40 file1
[root@server1 ~]# ls -l Desktop
total 16
-rw------    1 user1   root     163 Mar 29 09:58 Floppy
-rw-r--r--   1 user1   root    3578 Mar 29 09:58 Home
```

```
-rw-r--r--    1 user1    root     1791 Mar 29 09:58 Start Here
drwx-----    2 user1    root     4096 Mar 29 09:58 Trash
[root@server1 ~]# _
```

Note that there must be no spaces before and after the . character in the chown commands shown in the preceding output.

You can also use the : character instead of the . character in the chown command to change both the owner and group ownership (for example, chown –R user1:root Desktop).

To protect your system's security, you should ensure that most files residing in a user's home directory are owned by that user; some files in a user's home directory (especially the hidden files and directories) require this to function properly. To change the ownership back to the root user for file1 and the Desktop directory to avoid future problems, you can type the following:

```
[root@server1 ~]# chown root.root file1
[root@server1 ~]# chown -R root.root Desktop
[root@server1 ~]# ls -l
total 4
drwx-----    3 root     root     4096 Apr  8 07:12 Desktop
-rw-r--r--    1 root     root        0 Apr 29 15:40 file1
[root@server1 root]# ls -l Desktop
total 16
-rw------    1 root     root      163 Mar 29 09:58 Floppy
-rw-r--r--    1 root     root     3578 Mar 29 09:58 Home
-rw-r--r--    1 root     root     1791 Mar 29 09:58 Start Here
drwx-----    2 root     root     4096 Mar 29 09:58 Trash
[root@server1 ~]# _
```

You can override who is allowed to change ownership and permissions using a system setting. Many Linux distributions, including Fedora 13 Linux, use this system setting by default to restrict regular (non-root) users from changing the ownership and group ownership of files and directories. This prevents these users from bypassing disk quota restrictions, which rely on the ownership of files and directories to function properly. Disk quotas are discussed in Chapter 5.

Managing File and Directory Permissions

Every file and directory file on a Linux filesystem contains information regarding permissions in its inode. The section of the inode that stores permissions is called the **mode** of the file and is divided into three sections based on the users who receive the permissions to that file or directory:

- User (owner) permissions
- Group (group owner) permissions
- Other (everyone else on the Linux system) permissions

Furthermore, you can assign to each of these users the following regular permissions:

- Read
- Write
- Execute

Interpreting the Mode Recall that the three sections of the mode and the permissions that you can assign to each section are viewed when you perform an `ls -l` command; a detailed depiction of this is shown in Figure 4-3. It is important to note that the root user supersedes all file and directory permissions; in other words, the root user has all permissions to every file and directory regardless of what the mode of the file or directory indicates.

Consider the root user's home directory listing shown in the following example:

```
[root@server1 ~]# ls -l
total 28
drwx------    3 root     root         4096 Apr  8 07:12 Desktop
-r---w---x    1 bob      proj          282 Apr 29 22:06 file1
-------rwx    1 root     root          282 Apr 29 22:06 file2
-rwxrwxrwx    1 root     root          282 Apr 29 22:06 file3
----------    1 root     root          282 Apr 29 22:06 file4
-rw-r--r--    1 root     root          282 Apr 29 22:06 file5
-rw-r--r--    1 user1    sys           282 Apr 29 22:06 file6
[root@server1 ~]# _
```

Note from the preceding output that all permissions (as shown in Figure 4-3) need not be on a file or directory; if the permission is unavailable, a dash (the hyphen character on your keyboard, -) replaces its position in the mode. Be sure not to confuse the character to the left of the mode (which determines the file type) with the mode, as it is unrelated to the permissions on the file or directory. From the preceding output, the Desktop directory gives the **user** or **owner** of the directory (the root user) read, write, and execute permission, yet members of the **group** (the root group) do not receive any permissions to the directory. Note that **other** (everyone on the system) does not receive permissions to this directory either.

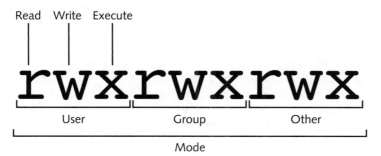

Figure 4-3 The structure of a mode

Source: Course Technology/Cengage Learning

Permissions are not additive; the system assigns the first set of permissions that are matched in the mode order: user, group, other. Let us assume that the bob user is a member of the proj group. In this case, the file called file1 in the preceding output gives the user or owner of the file (the bob user) read permission, gives members of the group (the proj group) write permission, and gives other (everyone else on the system) execute permission only. Because permissions are not additive, the user "bob" shall only receive read permission to file1 from the system.

Linux permissions should not be assigned to other only. Although file2 in our example does not give the user or group any permissions, all other users receive read, write, and execute permission via the other category. Thus, file2 should not contain sensitive data, because many users have full access to it. For the same reason, it is bad form to assign all permissions to a file that contains sensitive data, as shown with file3 in the preceding example.

On the contrary, it is possible to have a file that has no permissions assigned to it, as shown in the preceding file4. In this case, the only user who has permissions to the file is the root user.

The permission structure that you choose for a file or directory might result in too few or too many permissions. You can follow some general guidelines to avoid these situations. The owner of a file or directory is typically the person who maintains it; members of the group are typically users in the same company department and must have limited access to the file or directory. As a result, most files and directories that you find on a Linux filesystem have more permissions assigned to the user of the file/directory than to the group of the file/directory, and the other category has either the same permissions or less than the group of the file/directory, depending on how private that file or directory is. The file file5 in the previous output depicts this common permission structure. In addition, files in a user's home directory are typically owned by that user; however, you might occasionally find files that are not. For these files, their permission definitions change, as shown in the previous file1 and file6. The user or owner of file6 is user1, who has read and write permissions to the file. The group owner of file6 is the sys group; thus, any members of the sys group have read permission to the file. Finally, everyone on the system receives read permission to the file via the other category. Regardless of the mode, the root user receives all permissions to this file.

Interpreting Permissions   After you understand how to identify the permissions that are applied to user, group, and other on a certain file or directory, you can interpret the function of those permissions. Permissions for files are interpreted differently than those for directories. Also, if a user has a certain permission on a directory, that user does not have the same permission for all files or subdirectories within that directory; file and directory permissions are treated separately by the Linux system. Table 4-4 shows a summary of the different permissions and their definitions.

The implications of the permission definitions described in Table 4-4 are important to understand. If a user has the read permission to a text file, that user can use, among others, the `cat`, `more`, `head`, `tail`, `less`, `strings`, and `od` commands to view its contents. That same user can also open that file with a text editor such as vi; however, the user does not have the ability to save any changes to the document unless that user has the write permission to the file as well.

Recall that some text files contain instructions for the shell to execute and are called shell scripts. Shell scripts can be executed in much the same way that binary compiled programs

Permission	Definition for Files	Definition for Directories
Read	Allows a user to open and read the contents of a file	Allows a user to list the contents of the directory (if she has also been given execute permission)
Write	Allows a user to open, read, and edit the contents of a file	Allows a user to add or remove files to and from the directory (if she has also been given execute permission)
Execute	Allows a user to execute the file in memory (if it is a program file or script)	Allows a user to enter the directory and work with directory contents

Table 4-4 **Linux permissions**

are; the user who executes the shell script must then have execute permission to that file to execute it as a program.

It is important to avoid giving execute permission to files that are not programs or shell scripts. This ensures that these files will not be executed accidentally, causing the shell to interpret the contents.

Remember that directories are simply special files that have an inode and a data section, yet the contents of the data section are a list of that directory's contents. If you want to read that list, using the ls command for example, then you require the read permission to the directory. To modify that list, by adding or removing files, you require the write permission to the directory. Thus, if you want to create a new file in a directory with a text editor such as vi, you must have the write permission to that directory. Similarly, when a source file is copied to a target directory with the cp command, a new file is created in the target directory, and you must have the write permission to the target directory for the copy to be successful. Conversely, to delete a certain file, you must have the write permission to the directory that contains that file. It is also important to note that a user who has the write permission to a directory has the ability to delete all files and subdirectories within it.

The execute permission on a directory is sometimes referred to as the search permission, and it works similarly to a light switch. When a light switch is turned on, you can navigate a room and use the objects within it. However, when a light switch is turned off, you cannot see the objects in the room, nor can you walk around and view them. A user who does not have the execute permission to a directory is prevented from listing the directory's contents, adding and removing files, and working with files and subdirectories inside that directory, regardless of what permissions the user has to them. In short, a quick way to deny a user from accessing a directory and all of its contents in Linux is to take away the execute permission on that directory. Because the execute permission on a directory is crucial for user access, it is commonly given to all users via the other category, unless the directory must be private.

Changing Permissions To change the permissions for a certain file or directory, you can use the **chmod (change mode) command**. The chmod command takes two arguments at minimum; the first argument specifies the criteria used to change the permissions (Table 4-5), and the remaining arguments indicate the filenames to change.

Category	Operation	Permission
u (user)	+ (adds a permission)	r (read)
g (group)	- (removes a permission)	w (write)
o (other)	= (makes a permission equal to)	x (execute)
a (all categories)		

Table 4-5 Criteria used within the `chmod` command

Take, for example, the directory list used earlier:

```
[root@server1 ~]# ls -l
total 28
drwx------     3 root     root        4096 Apr  8 07:12 Desktop
-r---w---x     1 bob      proj         282 Apr 29 22:06 file1
-------rwx     1 root     root         282 Apr 29 22:06 file2
-rwxrwxrwx     1 root     root         282 Apr 29 22:06 file3
----------     1 root     root         282 Apr 29 22:06 file4
-rw-r--r--     1 root     root         282 Apr 29 22:06 file5
-rw-r--r--     1 user1    sys          282 Apr 29 22:06 file6
[root@server1 ~]# _
```

To change the mode of file1 to rw-r--r--, you must add the write permission to the user of the file, add the read permission and take away the write permission for the group of the file, and add the read permission and take away the execute permission for other.

From the information listed in Table 4-5, you can use the following command:

```
[root@server1 ~]# chmod u+w,g+r-w,o+r-x file1
[root@server1 ~]# ls -l
total 28
drwx------     3 root     root        4096 Apr  8 07:12 Desktop
-rw-r--r--     1 bob      proj         282 Apr 29 22:06 file1
----r--rwx     1 root     root         282 Apr 29 22:06 file2
-rwxrwxrwx     1 root     root         282 Apr 29 22:06 file3
----------     1 root     root         282 Apr 29 22:06 file4
-rw-r--r--     1 root     root         282 Apr 29 22:06 file5
-rw-r--r--     1 user1    sys          282 Apr 29 22:06 file6
[root@server1 ~]# _
```

You should ensure that there are no spaces between any criteria used in the `chmod` command, because all criteria make up the first argument only.

You can also use the = criteria from Table 4-5 to specify the exact permissions to change. To change the mode on file2 in the preceding output to the same as file1 (rw-r--r--), you can use the following `chmod` command:

```
[root@server1 ~]# chmod u=rw,g=r,o=r file2
[root@server1 ~]# ls -l
```

```
total 28
drwx------      3 root     root       4096 Apr  8 07:12 Desktop
-rw-r--r--      1 bob      proj        282 Apr 29 22:06 file1
-rw-r--r--      1 root     root        282 Apr 29 22:06 file2
-rwxrwxrwx      1 root     root        282 Apr 29 22:06 file3
----------      1 root     root        282 Apr 29 22:06 file4
-rw-r--r--      1 root     root        282 Apr 29 22:06 file5
-rw-r--r--      1 user1    sys         282 Apr 29 22:06 file6
[root@server1 ~]# _
```

If the permissions to be changed are identical for the user, group, and other categories, you can use the "a" character to refer to all categories as shown in Table 4-5 and in the following example when adding the execute permission to user, group, and other for file1:

```
[root@server1 ~]# chmod a+x file1
[root@server1 ~]# ls -l
total 28
drwx------      3 root     root       4096 Apr  8 07:12 Desktop
-rwxr-xr-x      1 bob      proj        282 Apr 29 22:06 file1
-rw-r--r--      1 root     root        282 Apr 29 22:06 file2
-rwxrwxrwx      1 root     root        282 Apr 29 22:06 file3
----------      1 root     root        282 Apr 29 22:06 file4
-rw-r--r--      1 root     root        282 Apr 29 22:06 file5
-rw-r--r--      1 user1    sys         282 Apr 29 22:06 file6
[root@server1 ~]# _
```

However, if there is no character specifying the category of user to affect, all users are assumed, as shown in the following example when adding the execute permission to user, group, and other for file2:

```
[root@server1 ~]# chmod +x file2
[root@server1 ~]# ls -l
total 28
drwx------      3 root     root       4096 Apr  8 07:12 Desktop
-rwxr-xr-x      1 bob      proj        282 Apr 29 22:06 file1
-rwxr-xr-x      1 root     root        282 Apr 29 22:06 file2
-rwxrwxrwx      1 root     root        282 Apr 29 22:06 file3
----------      1 root     root        282 Apr 29 22:06 file4
-rw-r--r--      1 root     root        282 Apr 29 22:06 file5
-rw-r--r--      1 user1    sys         282 Apr 29 22:06 file6
[root@server1 ~]# _
```

All of the aforementioned chmod examples use the symbols listed in Table 4-5 as the criteria for changing the permissions on a file or directory. You might instead choose to use numeric criteria with the chmod command to change permissions. All permissions are stored in the inode of a file or directory as binary powers of two:

- read = 2^2 = 4
- write = 2^1 = 2
- execute = 2^0 = 1

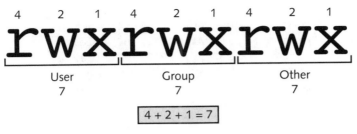

Figure 4-4 Numeric representation of the mode

Source: Course Technology/Cengage Learning

Thus, the mode of a file or directory can be represented using the numbers 421421421 instead of rwxrwxrwx. Because permissions are grouped into the categories user, group, and other, you can then simplify this further by using only three numbers, one for each category that represents the sum of the permissions, as depicted in Figure 4-4.

Similarly, to represent the mode rw-r--r--, you can use the numbers 644 because user has read and write (4 + 2 = 6) permission, group has read (4) permission, and other has read (4) permission. The mode rwxr-x--- can also be represented by 750 because user has read, write, and execute (4 + 2 + 1 = 7) permission, group has read and execute (4 + 1 = 5) permission, and other has nothing (0). Table 4-6 provides a list of the different permissions and their corresponding numbers.

To change the mode of the file1 file used earlier to r-xr-----, you can use the command chmod 540 file1, as shown in the following example:

```
[root@server1 ~]# chmod 540 file1
[root@server1 ~]# ls -l
total 28
drwx------    3 root    root    4096 Apr  8 07:12 Desktop
-r-xr-----    1 bob     proj     282 Apr 29 22:06 file1
-rwxr-xr-x    1 root    root     282 Apr 29 22:06 file2
```

Mode (One Section Only)	Corresponding Number
rwx	4 + 2 + 1 = **7**
rw-	4 + 2 = **6**
r-x	4 + 1 = **5**
r--	**4**
-wx	2 + 1 = **3**
-w-	**2**
--x	**1**
---	**0**

Table 4-6 Numeric representations of the permissions in a mode

```
-rwxrwxrwx   1 root    root     282 Apr 29 22:06 file3
----------   1 root    root     282 Apr 29 22:06 file4
-rw-r--r--   1 root    root     282 Apr 29 22:06 file5
-rw-r--r--   1 user1   sys      282 Apr 29 22:06 file6
[root@server1 ~]# _
```

Similarly, to change the mode of all files in the directory that start with the word "file" to 644 (which is common permissions for files), you can use the following command:

```
[root@server1 ~]# chmod 644 file*
[root@server1 ~]# ls -l
total 28
drwx------   3 root    root    4096 Apr  8 07:12 Desktop
-rw-r--r--   1 bob     proj     282 Apr 29 22:06 file1
-rw-r--r--   1 root    root     282 Apr 29 22:06 file2
-rw-r--r--   1 root    root     282 Apr 29 22:06 file3
-rw-r--r--   1 root    root     282 Apr 29 22:06 file4
-rw-r--r--   1 root    root     282 Apr 29 22:06 file5
-rw-r--r--   1 user1   sys      282 Apr 29 22:06 file6
[root@server1 ~]# _
```

Like the chown and chgrp commands, the chmod command can also be used to change the permission on a directory and all of its contents recursively by using the −R option, as shown in the following example when changing the mode of the Desktop directory:

```
[root@server1 ~]# chmod −R 755 Desktop
[root@server1 ~]# ls -l
total 28
drwxr-xr-x   3 root    root    4096 Apr  8 07:12 Desktop
-rw-r--r--   1 bob     proj     282 Apr 29 22:06 file1
-rw-r--r--   1 root    root     282 Apr 29 22:06 file2
-rw-r--r--   1 root    root     282 Apr 29 22:06 file3
-rw-r--r--   1 root    root     282 Apr 29 22:06 file4
-rw-r--r--   1 root    root     282 Apr 29 22:06 file5
-rw-r--r--   1 user1   sys      282 Apr 29 22:06 file6
[root@server1 ~]# ls -l Desktop
total 16
-rwxr-xr-x   1 root    root     163 Mar 29 09:58 Floppy
-rwx-r-xr-x  1 root    root    3578 Mar 29 09:58 Home
-rwx-r-xr-x  1 root    root    1791 Mar 29 09:58 Start Here
drwxr-xr-x   2 root    root    4096 Mar 29 09:58 Trash
[root@server1 ~]# _
```

Default Permissions

Recall that permissions provide security for files and directories by allowing only certain users access, and that there are common guidelines for setting permissions on files and directories, so that permissions are not too strict or too permissive. Also important to maintaining security are the permissions that are given to new files and directories after they are created. New files are given rw-rw-rw- by the system when they are created (because execute should not be given unless necessary), and new directories are given rwxrwxrwx by the system when they are created. These default permissions are too permissive for most files, as they allow other full access to directories and nearly full access to files. Hence, a special variable on the system called the **umask** (user mask) takes away permissions on new files and directories immediately after they are created. The most common umask that you will find is 022, which specifies that nothing (0) is taken away from the user, write permission (2) is taken away from members of the group, and write permission (2) is taken away from other on new files and directories when they are first created and given permissions by the system.

 Keep in mind that the umask applies only to newly created files and directories; it is never used to modify the permissions of existing files and directories. You must use the chmod command to modify existing permissions.

An example of how a umask of 022 can be used to alter the permissions of a new file or directory after creation is shown in Figure 4-5.

To verify the umask used, you can use the **umask command** and note the final three digits in the output. To ensure that the umask functions as shown in Figure 4-5, simply create a new file using the touch command and a new directory using the mkdir command, as shown in the following output:

```
[root@server1 ~]# ls -l
total 28
drwx------    3 root     root     4096 Apr 8 07:12 Desktop
[root@server1 ~]# umask
0022
[root@server1 ~]# mkdir dir1
[root@server1 ~]# touch file1
[root@server1 ~]# ls -l
total 8
drwx------    3 root     root     4096 Apr 8 07:12 Desktop
drwxr-xr-x    2 root     root     4096 May 3 21:39 dir1
-rw-r--r--    1 root     root        0 May 3 21:40 file1
[root@server1 ~]# _
```

	New Files	New Directories
Permissions assigned by system	rw-rw-rw-	rwxrwxrwx
- umask	0 2 2	0 2 2
= resulting permissions	rw-r--r--	rwxr-xr-x

Figure 4-5 Performing a umask 022 calculation

Source: Course Technology/Cengage Learning

	New Files	New Directories
Permissions assigned by system	rw-rw-rw-	rwxrwxrwx
- umask	0 0 7	0 0 7
= resulting permissions	rw-rw----	rwxrwx---

Figure 4-6 Performing a umask 007 calculation

Source: Course Technology/Cengage Learning

Because the umask is a variable stored in memory, it can be changed. To change the current umask, you can specify the new umask as an argument to the umask command. Suppose, for example, you want to change the umask to 007; the resulting permissions on new files and directories is calculated in Figure 4-6.

To change the umask to 007 and view its effect, you can type the following commands on the command line:

```
[root@server1 ~]# ls -l
total 8
drwx------   3 root     root     4096 Apr 8 07:12 Desktop
drwxr-xr-x   2 root     root     4096 May 3 21:39 dir1
-rw-r--r--   1 root     root        0 May 3 21:40 file1
[root@server1 ~]# umask 007
[root@server1 ~]# umask
0007
[root@server1 ~]# mkdir dir2
[root@server1 ~]# touch file2
[root@server1 ~]# ls -l
total 12
drwx------   3 root     root     4096 Apr 8 07:12 Desktop
drwxr-xr-x   2 root     root     4096 May 3 21:39 dir1
drwxrwx---   2 root     root     4096 May 3 21:41 dir2
-rw-r--r--   1 root     root        0 May 3 21:40 file1
-rw-rw----   1 root     root        0 May 3 21:41 file2
[root@server1 ~]# _
```

Special Permissions

Read, write, and execute are the regular file permissions that you would use to assign security to files; however, you can optionally use three more special permissions on files and directories:

- SUID (Set User ID)
- SGID (Set Group ID)
- Sticky bit

Defining Special Permissions The SUID has no special function when set on a directory; however, if the SUID is set on a file and that file is executed, the person who executed the file temporarily becomes the owner of the file while it is executing. Many commands on a typical Linux system have this special permission set; the ping command (/bin/ping) that is used to test network connectivity is one such file. Because this file is owned by the root user, when a regular user executes the ping command, that user temporarily becomes the root user while the ping command is executing in memory. This ensures that any user can test network connectivity, with all rights to do so on the system. Furthermore, the SUID can only be applied to binary compiled programs. The Linux kernel does not let you apply the SUID to a shell script, because shell scripts are easy to edit and, thus, pose a security hazard to the system.

Contrary to the SUID, the SGID has a function when applied to both files and directories. Just as the SUID allows regular users to execute a binary compiled program and become the owner of the file for the duration of execution, the SGID allows regular users to execute a binary compiled program and become a member of the group that is attached to the file. Thus, if a file is owned by the group "sys" and also has the SGID permission, any user who executes that file will be a member of the group "sys" during execution. If a command or file requires the user executing it to have the same permissions applied to the sys group, setting the SGID on the file simplifies assigning rights to the file for user execution.

The SGID also has a special function when placed on a directory. When a user creates a file, recall that that user's name and primary group become the owner and group owner of the file, respectively. However, if a user creates a file in a directory that has the SGID permission set, that user's name becomes the owner of the file and the directory's group becomes the group owner of the file.

Finally, the sticky bit was used on files in the past to lock them in memory; however, today the sticky bit performs a useful function only on directories. As explained earlier in this chapter, the write permission applied to a directory allows you to add and remove any file to or from that directory. Thus, if you have the write permission to a certain directory but no permission to files within it, you could delete all of those files. Consider a company that requires a common directory that gives all employees the ability to add files; this directory must give everyone the write permission.

Unfortunately, the write permission also gives all employees the ability to delete all files and directories within, including the ones that others have added to the directory. If the sticky bit is applied to this common directory in addition to the write permission, employees can add files to the directory but only delete those files that they have added and not others.

 Note that all special permissions also require the execute permission to work properly; the SUID and SGID work on executable files, and the SGID and sticky bit work on directories (which must have execute permission for access).

Setting Special Permissions The mode of a file that is displayed using the ls -l command does not have a section for special permissions. However, because special permissions require execute, they mask the execute permission when displayed using the ls -l command, as shown in Figure 4-7.

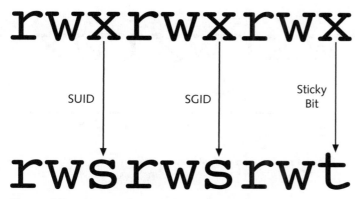

Figure 4-7 Representing special permissions in the mode

Source: Course Technology/Cengage Learning

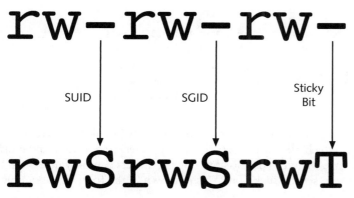

Figure 4-8 Representing special permission in the absence of the execute permission

Source: Course Technology/Cengage Learning

The system allows you to set special permissions even if the file or directory does not have execute permission. However, the special permissions will not perform their function. If the special permissions are set on a file or directory without execute permissions, then the ineffective special permissions are capitalized, as shown in Figure 4-8.

To set the special permissions, you can visualize them to the left of the mode, as shown in Figure 4-9.

Thus, to set all of the special permissions on a certain file or directory, you can use the command chmod 7777 name, as indicated in Figure 4-9. However, the SUID and SGID bits are typically set on files. To change the permissions on the file1 file used earlier so that other has the ability to view and execute the file as the owner and a member of the group, you can use the command chmod 6755 file1, as shown in the following example:

```
[root@server1 ~]# ls -l
total 12
drwx------    3 root     root     4096 Apr 8 07:12 Desktop
drwxr-xr-x    2 root     root     4096 May 3 21:39 dir1
drwx------    2 root     root     4096 May 3 21:41 dir2
```

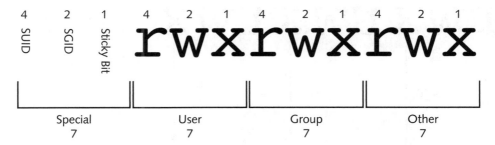

Figure 4-9 Numeric representation of regular and special permissions

Source: Course Technology/Cengage Learning

```
-rw-r--r--      1 root     root         0 May 3 21:40 file1
-rw-------      1 root     root         0 May 3 21:41 file2
[root@server1 ~]# chmod 6755 file1
[root@server1 ~]# ls -l
total 12
drwx------      3 root     root      4096 Apr 8 07:12 Desktop
drwxr-xr-x      2 root     root      4096 May 3 21:39 dir1
drwx------      2 root     root      4096 May 3 21:41 dir2
-rwsr-sr-x      1 root     root         0 May 3 21:40 file1
-rw-------      1 root     root         0 May 3 21:41 file2
[root@server1 ~]# _
```

Similarly, to set the sticky bit permission on the directory dir1 used earlier, you can use the command chmod 1777 dir1, which allows all users (including other) to add files to the dir1 directory. This is because you gave the write permission; however, users can only delete the files that they own in dir1, because you set the sticky bit. This is shown in the following example:

```
[root@server1 ~]# ls -l
total 12
drwx------      3 root     root      4096 Apr 8 07:12 Desktop
drwxr-xr-x      2 root     root      4096 May 3 21:39 dir1
drwx------      2 root     root      4096 May 3 21:41 dir2
-rwsr-sr-x      1 root     root         0 May 3 21:40 file1
-rw-------      1 root     root         0 May 3 21:41 file2
[root@server1 ~]# chmod 1777 dir1
[root@server1 ~]# ls -l
total 12
drwx------      3 root     root      4096 Apr 8 07:12 Desktop
drwxrwxrwt      2 root     root      4096 May 3 21:39 dir1
drwx------      2 root     root      4096 May 3 21:41 dir2
-rwsr-sr-x      1 root     root         0 May 3 21:40 file1
-rw-------      1 root     root         0 May 3 21:41 file2
[root@server1 ~]# _
```

Also, remember that assigning special permissions without execute permission renders those permissions useless. For example, you may forget to give execute permission to either user, group, or other, and the long listing covers the execute permission with a special permission. In that case, the special permission is capitalized, as shown in the following example when dir2 is not given execute permission underneath the position in the mode that indicates the sticky bit (t):

```
[root@server1 ~]# ls -l
total 12
drwx------    3 root    root    4096 Apr 8 07:12 Desktop
drwxrwxrwt    2 root    root    4096 May 3 21:39 dir1
drwx------    2 root    root    4096 May 3 21:41 dir2
-rwsr-sr-x    1 root    root       0 May 3 21:40 file1
-rw-------    1 root    root       0 May 3 21:41 file2
[root@server1 ~]# chmod 1770 dir2
[root@server1 ~]# ls -l
total 12
drwx------    3 root    root    4096 Apr 8 07:12 Desktop
drwxrwxrwt    2 root    root    4096 May 3 21:39 dir1
drwxrwx--T    2 root    root    4096 May 3 21:41 dir2
-rwsr-sr-x    1 root    root       0 May 3 21:40 file1
-rw-------    1 root    root       0 May 3 21:41 file2
[root@server1 ~]# _
```

Chapter Summary

- The Linux directory tree obeys the Filesystem Hierarchy Standard, which allows Linux users and developers to locate system files in standard directories.

- Many file management commands exist to create, change the location of, or remove files and directories. The most common of these are cp, mv, rm, rmdir, and mkdir.

- You can find files on the filesystem using a preindexed database (the locate command) or by searching the directories listed in the PATH variable (the which command). However, the most versatile command used to find files is the find command, which searches for files based on a wide range of criteria.

- Files can be linked two different ways. In a symbolic link, one file serves as a pointer to another file. In a hard link, one file is a linked duplicate of another file.

- Each file and directory has an owner and a group owner. In the absence of system restrictions, the owner of the file or directory has the ability to change permissions and give ownership to others.

- Permissions can be set on the user or owner of a file, members of the group of the file, as well as everyone on the system (other).

- There are three regular file and directory permissions (read, write, execute) and three special file and directory permissions (SUID, SGID, sticky bit). These permissions have separate definitions for files and directories.

- Permissions can be changed using the chmod command by specifying symbols or numbers to represent the changed permissions.

- To ensure security, new files and directories receive default permissions from the system, less the value of the umask variable.

- The root user has all permissions to all files and directories on the Linux filesystem. Similarly, the root user can change the ownership of any file or directory on the Linux filesystem.

Key Terms

/bin directory   The directory that contains binary commands for use by all users.

/boot directory   The directory that contains the Linux kernel and files used by the boot loader data block.

/dev directory   The directory that contains device files.

/etc directory   The directory that contains system-specific configuration files.

/home directory   The default location for user home directories.

/lib directory   The directory that contains shared program libraries (used by the commands in /bin and /sbin) as well as kernel modules.

/media directory   A directory typically used for mounting removable media devices.

/mnt directory   An empty directory used for temporarily mounting media.

/opt directory   The directory that stores additional software programs.

/proc directory   The directory that contains process and kernel information.

/root directory   The root user's home directory.

/sbin directory   The directory that contains system binary commands (used for administration).

/tmp directory   The directory that holds temporary files created by programs.

/usr directory   The directory that contains most system commands and utilities.

/usr/local directory   The location for most additional programs.

/var directory   The directory that contains log files and spools.

`chgrp (change group)` **command**   The command used to change the group owner of a file or directory.

`chmod (change mode)` **command**   The command used to change the mode (permissions) of a file or directory.

`chown (change owner)` **command**   The command used to change the owner and group owner of a file or directory.

`cp (copy)` **command**   The command used to create copies of files and directories.

data blocks   A filesystem allocation unit in which the data that makes up the contents of the file as well as the filename are stored.

Filesystem Hierarchy Standard (FHS)   A standard outlining the location of set files and directories on a Linux system.

`find` **command**   The command used to find files on the filesystem using various criteria.

group   When used in the mode of a certain file or directory, the collection of users who have ownership of that file or directory.

hard link   A file joined to other files on the same filesystem that shares the same inode.

inode   The portion of a file that stores information on the file's attributes, access permissions, location, ownership, and file type.

inode table   The collection of inodes for all files and directories on a filesystem.

interactive mode   The mode that file management commands use when a file can be overwritten; the system interacts with a user, asking the user to confirm the action.

`ln (link) command`   The command used to create hard and symbolic links.

`locate command`   The command used to locate files from a file database.

`mkdir (make directory) command`   The command used to create directories.

mode   The part of the inode that stores information on access permissions.

`mv (move) command`   The command used to move/rename files and directories.

other   When used in the mode of a certain file or directory, refers to all users on the Linux system.

owner   The user whose name appears in a long listing of a file or directory and who has the ability to change permissions on that file or directory.

PATH variable   A variable that stores a list of directories that will be searched in order when commands are executed without an absolute or relative pathname.

permissions   A list that identifies who can access a file or folder and their level of access.

primary group   The default group to which a user belongs.

recursive   A term referring to itself and its own contents; a recursive search includes all subdirectories in a directory and their contents.

`rm (remove) command`   The command used to remove files and directories.

`rmdir (remove directory) command`   The command used to remove empty directories.

source file/directory   The portion of a command that refers to the file or directory from which information is taken.

superblock   The portion of a filesystem that stores critical information, such as the inode table and block size.

symbolic link   A pointer to another file on the same or another filesystem; commonly referred to as a shortcut.

target file/directory   The portion of a command that refers to the file or directory to which information is directed.

`touch command`   The command used to create new files. It was originally used to update the time stamp on a file.

umask   A special variable used to alter the permissions on all new files and directories by taking away select default file and directory permissions.

`umask command`   The command used to view and change the umask variable.

user   When used in the mode of a certain file or directory, the owner of that file or directory.

`which command`   The command used to locate files that exist within directories listed in the PATH variable.

Review Questions

1. A symbolic link is also known as a soft link and is depicted by an @ symbol appearing at the beginning of the filename when viewed using the ls –l command. True or False?

2. What was created to define a standard directory structure and common file location for Linux?

   a. FSH

   b. X.500

   c. FHS

   d. root directory

3. There is no real difference between the "S" and "s" special permissions when displayed using the ls –l command. One just means it is on a file and the other that it is on a directory. True or False?

4. The default permissions given by the system prior to analyzing the umask are _____ for directories and _____ for files.

   a. rw-rw-rw- and rw-rw-rw-

   b. rw-rw-rw- and r--r--r--

   c. rw-rw-rw- and rwxrwxrwx

   d. rwxrwxrwx and rw-rw-rw-

   e. rwxrw-rw- and rwx-rw-rw-

5. What must a user do to run cp or mv interactively and be asked if she wants to overwrite an existing file?

   a. There is no choice, because the new file will overwrite the old one by default.

   b. Type interactive cp or interactive mv.

   c. Type cp -i or mv -i.

   d. Type cp –interactive or mv -interactive.

   e. Just type cp or mv, because they run in interactive mode by default.

6. The root user utilizes the chgrp command to give ownership of a file to another user. What must the root user do to regain ownership of the file?

   a. Run chgrp again listing the root user as the new owner.

   b. Nothing, because this is a one-way, one-time action.

   c. Have the new owner run chgrp and list the root user as the new owner.

   d. Run chown and list the root user as the new owner.

7. After typing the ls –F command, you see the following line in the output:

   -rw-r-xr--   1 user1   root   0 Apr 29 15:40 file1

What does this mean?

a. User1 has read and write permission, members of the root group have read and execute permissions, and all others have read permissions to the file.

b. Members of the root group have read and write permissions, user1 has read and execute permission, and all others have read permissions to the file.

c. All users have read and write permissions, members of the root group have read and execute permissions, and user1 has read permission to the file.

d. User1 has read and write permission, all others have read and execute permissions, and members of the root group have read permissions to the file.

8. After typing the command umask 731, the permissions on all subsequently created files and directories will be affected. In this case, what will be the permissions on all new files?

a. rw-rw-rw-

b. rwxrw-r--

c. ---r--rw-

d. ----wx--x

9. When you change the data in a file that is hard-linked to three others, _____.

a. only the data in the file you modified is affected

b. only the data in the file you modified and any hard-linked files in the same directory are affected

c. the data in the file you modified and the data in all hard-linked files are modified, because they have different inodes

d. the data in the file you modified as well as the data in all hard-linked files are modified, because they share the same data and all have the same inode and file size

10. The command chmod 317 file1 would produce which of the following lines in the ls command?

a. --w-r--rwx 1 user1 root 0 Apr 29 15:40 file1

b. --wx--xrwx 1 user1 root 0 Apr 29 15:40 file1

c. -rwxrw-r-x 1 user1 root 0 Apr 29 15:40 file1

d. --w-rw-r-e 1 user1 root 0 Apr 29 15:40 file1

11. Which of the following commands will change the user ownership and group ownership of file1 to user1 and root, respectively?

a. chown user1:root file1

b. chown user1 : root file1

c. This cannot be done, because user and group ownership properties of a file must be modified separately.

d. chown root:user1 file1

e. chown root : user1 file1

12. What does the /var directory contain?

    a. various additional programs

    b. spools and log files

    c. temporary files

    d. files that are architecture independent

    e. local variance devices

13. What does the mv command do? (Choose all that apply.)

    a. It makes a volume.

    b. It makes a directory.

    c. It moves a directory.

    d. It moves a file.

14. A file has the following permissions: *r----x-w-*. The command chmod 143 would have the same effect as the command _____. (Choose all that apply.)

    a. chmod u+x-r,g+r-x,o+w file1

    b. chmod u=w,g=rw,o=rx file1

    c. chmod u-r-w,g+r-w,o+r-x file1

    d. chmod u=x,g=r,o=wx file1

    e. chmod u+w,g+r-w,o+r-x file1

    f. chmod u=rw,g=r,o=r file1

15. The which command _____.

    a. can only be used to search for executables

    b. searches for a file in all directories, starting from the root

    c. is not a valid Linux command

    d. searches for a file only in directories that are in the PATH variable

16. Hard links need to reside on the same filesystem as the target, whereas symbolic links need not be on the same filesystem as the target. True or False?

17. When applied to a directory, the SGID special permission _____.

    a. causes all new files created in the directory to have the same group membership as the directory, and not the entity that created them

    b. cannot be used, because it is applied only to files

    c. allows users to use more than two groups for files that they create within the directory

    d. causes users to have their permissions checked before they are allowed to access files in the directory

18. Which command do you use to rename files and directories?

    a. cp

    b. mv

    c. rn

    d. rename

19. What are the three standard Linux permissions?

    a. full control, read-execute, write

    b. read, write, modify

    c. execute, read, write

    d. read, write, examine

20. Given the following output from the `ls` command, how many files are linked with file1?

```
drwxr-xr-x    3 root    root      4096 Apr  8 07:12 Desktop
-rw-r--r--    3 root    root       282 Apr 29 22:06 file1
-rw-r--r--    1 root    root       282 Apr 29 22:06 file2
-rw-r--r--    4 root    root       282 Apr 29 22:06 file3
-rw-r--r--    2 root    root       282 Apr 29 22:06 file4
-rw-r--r--    1 root    root       282 Apr 29 22:06 file5
-rw-r--r--    1 user1   sys        282 Apr 29 22:06 file6
```

    a. one

    b. two

    c. three

    d. four

Hands-On Projects

These projects should be completed in the order given. The hands-on projects presented in this chapter should take a total of three hours to complete. The requirements for this lab include:

- A computer with Fedora 13 installed according to Hands-On Project 2-2
- Completion of all hands-on projects in Chapter 3

Project 4-1

In this hands-on project, you log in to the computer and create new directories.

1. Turn on your computer. After your Linux system has loaded, switch to a command-line terminal (tty2) by pressing **Ctrl+Alt+F2**. Log in to the terminal using the user name of **root** and the password of **secret**.

2. At the command prompt, type **ls -F** and press **Enter**. Note the contents of your home folder.

3. At the command prompt, type **mkdir mysamples** and press **Enter**. Next, type **ls -F** at the command prompt and press **Enter**. How many files and subdirectories are there? Why?

4. At the command prompt, type **cd mysamples** and press **Enter**. Next, type **ls -F** at the command prompt and press **Enter**. What are the contents of the subdirectory mysamples?

5. At the command prompt, type **mkdir undermysamples** and press **Enter**. Next, type **ls -F** at the command prompt and press **Enter**. What are the contents of the subdirectory mysamples?

6. At the command prompt, type **mkdir todelete** and press **Enter**. Next, type **ls -F** at the command prompt and press **Enter**. Does the subdirectory todelete you just created appear listed in the display?

7. At the command prompt, type **cd ..** and press **Enter**. Next, type **ls -R** and press **Enter**. Notice that the subdirectory mysamples and its subdirectory undermysamples are both displayed. You have used the recursive option with the ls command.

8. At the command prompt, type **cd ..** and press **Enter**. At the command prompt, type **pwd** and press **Enter**. What is your current directory?

9. At the command prompt, type **mkdir foruser1** and press **Enter**. At the command prompt, type **ls -F** and press **Enter**. Does the subdirectory you just created appear listed in the display?

10. Type **exit** and press **Enter** to log out of your shell.

Project 4-2

In this hands-on project, you copy files using the cp command.

1. Switch to a command-line terminal (tty2) by pressing **Ctrl+Alt+F2** and log in to the terminal using the user name of **root** and the password of **secret**.

2. Next, type **ls -F** at the command prompt and press **Enter**. Note the contents of your home folder.

3. At the command prompt, type **cp sample1** and press **Enter**. What error message was displayed and why?

4. At the command prompt, type **cp sample1 sample1A** and press **Enter**. Next, type **ls -F** at the command prompt and press **Enter**. How many files are there, and what are their names? Why?

5. At the command prompt, type **cp sample1 mysamples/sample1B** and press **Enter**. Next, type **ls -F** at the command prompt and press **Enter**. How many files are there, and what are their names? Why?

6. At the command prompt, type **cd mysamples** and press **Enter**. Next, type **ls -F** at the command prompt and press **Enter**. Was sample1B copied successfully?

7. At the command prompt, type **cp /root/sample2 .** and press **Enter**. Next, type **ls -F** at the command prompt and press **Enter**. How many files are there, and what are their names? Why?

8. At the command prompt, type **cp sample1B ..** and press **Enter**. Next, type **cd ..** at the command prompt and press **Enter**. At the command prompt, type **ls -F** and press **Enter**. Was the sample1B file copied successfully?

9. At the command prompt, type **cp sample1 sample2 sample3 mysamples** and press **Enter**. What message do you get and why? Choose **y** and press **Enter**. Next, type **cd mysamples** at the command prompt and press **Enter**. At the command prompt, type **ls -F** and press **Enter**. How many files are there, and what are their names? Why?

10. At the command prompt, type **cd ..** and press **Enter**. Next, type **cp mysamples mysamples2** at the command prompt and press **Enter**. What error message did you receive? Why?

11. At the command prompt, type **cp –R mysamples mysamples2** and press **Enter**. Next, type **ls –F** at the command prompt and press **Enter**. Was the directory copied successfully? Type **ls –F mysamples2** at the command prompt and press **Enter**. Were the contents of mysamples successfully copied to mysamples2?

12. Type **exit** and press **Enter** to log out of your shell.

Project 4-3

In this hands-on project, you use the mv command to rename files and directories.

1. Switch to a command-line terminal (tty2) by pressing **Ctrl+Alt+F2** and log in to the terminal using the user name of **root** and the password of **secret**.

2. Next, type **ls -F** at the command prompt and press **Enter**. Note the contents of your home folder.

3. At the command prompt, type **mv sample1** and press **Enter**. What error message was displayed and why?

4. At the command prompt, type **mv sample1 sample4** and press **Enter**. Next, type **ls -F** at the command prompt and press **Enter**. How many files are listed, and what are their names? What happened to sample1?

5. At the command prompt, type **mv sample4 mysamples** and press **Enter**. Next, type **ls -F** at the command prompt and press **Enter**. How many files are there, and what are their names? Where did sample4 go?

6. At the command prompt, type **cd mysamples** and press **Enter**. Next, type **ls -F** at the command prompt and press **Enter**. Notice that the sample4 file you moved in Step 5 was moved here.

7. At the command prompt, type **mv sample4 ..** and press **Enter**. Next, type **ls -F** at the command prompt and press **Enter**. How many files are there, and what are their names? Where did the sample4 file go?

8. At the command prompt, type **cd ..** and press **Enter**. Next, type **ls -F** at the command prompt, and press **Enter** to view the new location of sample4.

9. At the command prompt, type **mv sample4 mysamples/sample2** and press **Enter**. What message appeared on the screen and why?

10. Type **y** and press **Enter** to confirm you want to overwrite the file in the destination folder.

11. At the command prompt, type **mv sample? mysamples** and press **Enter**. Type **y** and press **Enter** to confirm you want to overwrite the file sample3 in the destination folder.

12. At the command prompt, type **ls -F** and press **Enter**. How many files are there and why?

13. At the command prompt, type **mv sample1* mysamples** and press **Enter**. Type **y** and press **Enter** to confirm you want to overwrite the file sample1B in the destination directory.

14. At the command prompt, type **ls -F** and press **Enter**. Notice that there are no sample files in the /root directory.

15. At the command prompt, type **cd mysamples** and press **Enter**. Next, type **ls -F** at the command prompt and press **Enter**. Notice that all files originally in /root have been moved to this directory.

16. At the command prompt, type **cd ..** and press **Enter**. Next, type **ls -F** at the command prompt and press **Enter**. Type **mv mysamples samples** and press **Enter**. Next, type **ls -F** at the command prompt and press **Enter**. Why did you not need to specify the recursive option to the mv command to rename the mysamples directory to samples?

17. Type **exit** and press **Enter** to log out of your shell.

Project 4-4

In this hands-on project, you make and view links to files and directories.

1. Switch to a command-line terminal (tty2) by pressing **Ctrl+Alt+F2** and log in to the terminal using the user name of **root** and the password of **secret**.

2. At the command prompt, type **cd samples** and press **Enter**. Next, type **ls -F** at the command prompt and press **Enter**. What files do you see? Next, type **ls -l** at the command prompt and press **Enter**. What is the link count for the sample1 file?

3. At the command prompt, type **ln sample1 hardlinksample** and press **Enter**. Next, type **ls -F** at the command prompt and press **Enter**. Does anything in the terminal output indicate that sample1 and hardlinksample are hard-linked? Next, type **ls -l** at the command prompt and press **Enter**. Does anything in the terminal output indicate that sample1 and hardlinksample are hard-linked? What is the link count for sample1 and hardlinksample? Next, type **ls -li** at the command prompt and press **Enter** to view the inode numbers of each file. Do the two hard-linked files have the same inode number?

4. At the command prompt, type **ln sample1 hardlinksample2** and press **Enter**. Next, type **ls -l** at the command prompt and press **Enter**. What is the link count for the files sample1, hardlinksample, and hardlinksample2? Why?

5. At the command prompt, type **vi sample1** and press **Enter**. Enter a sentence of your choice into the vi editor, then save your document and quit the vi editor.

6. At the command prompt, type **cat sample1** and press **Enter**. Next, type **cat hardlinksample** at the command prompt and press **Enter**. Next, type **cat hardlinksample2** at the command prompt and press **Enter**. Are the contents of each file the same? Why?

7. At the command prompt, type **ln –s sample2 symlinksample** and press **Enter**. Next, type **ls -F** at the command prompt and press **Enter**. Does anything in the terminal output indicate that sample2 and symlinksample are symbolically linked? Which file is the target file? Next, type **ls -l** at the command prompt and press **Enter**. Does anything in the terminal output indicate that sample2 and symlinksample are symbolically linked? Next, type **ls -li** at the command prompt and press **Enter** to view the inode numbers of each file. Do the two symbolically linked files have the same inode number?

8. At the command prompt, type **vi symlinksample** and press **Enter**. Enter a sentence of your choice into the vi editor, then save your document and quit the vi editor.

9. At the command prompt, type **ls -l** and press **Enter**. What is the size of the symlinksample file compared to sample2? Why? Next, type **cat sample2** at the command prompt and press **Enter**. What are the contents and why?

10. At the command prompt, type **ln –s /etc/sysconfig/network-scripts netscripts** and press **Enter**. Next, type **ls -F** at the command prompt and press **Enter**. What file type is indicated for netscripts? Next, type **cd netscripts** at the command prompt and press **Enter**. Type **pwd** at the command prompt and press **Enter** to view your current directory. What is your current directory? Next, type **ls -F** at the command prompt and press **Enter**. What files are listed? Next, type **ls -F /etc/sysconfig/network-scripts** at the command prompt and press **Enter**.

   Note that your netscripts directory is merely a pointer to the /etc/sysconfig/network-scripts directory. How can this type of linking be useful?

11. Type **exit** and press **Enter** to log out of your shell.

Project 4-5

In this hands-on project, you find files on the filesystem using the find, locate, and which commands.

1. Switch to a command-line terminal (tty2) by pressing **Ctrl+Alt+F2** and log in to the terminal using the user name of **root** and the password of **secret**.

2. At the command prompt, type **touch newfile** and press **Enter**. Next, type **locate newfile** at the command prompt and press **Enter**. Did the locate command find the file? Why?

3. At the command prompt, type **updatedb** and press **Enter**. When the command is finished, type **locate newfile** at the command prompt and press **Enter**. Did the locate command find the file? If so, how quickly did it find it? Why?

4. At the command prompt, type **find / -name "newfile"** and press **Enter**. Did the find command find the file? If so, how quickly did it find it? Why?

5. At the command prompt, type **find /root -name "newfile"** and press **Enter**. Did the find command find the file? How quickly did it find it? Why?

6. At the command prompt, type **which newfile** and press **Enter**. Did the which command find the file? Why? Type **echo $PATH** at the command prompt and press **Enter**. Is the /root directory listed in the PATH variable? Is the /bin directory listed in the PATH variable?

7. At the command prompt, type **which grep** and press **Enter**. Did the which command find the file? Why?

8. At the command prompt, type **find /root -name "sample"** and press **Enter**. What files are listed? Why?

9. At the command prompt, type **find /root -type l** and press **Enter**. (Note that the last character in this command is the lowercase letter "l" and not the number one.) What files are listed? Why?

10. At the command prompt, type **find /root -size 0** and press **Enter**. What types of files are listed? Type **find /root -size 0 | more** to see all of the files listed.

11. Type **exit** and press **Enter** to log out of your shell.

Project 4-6

In this hands-on project, you delete files and directories using the rmdir and rm commands.

1. Switch to a command-line terminal (tty2) by pressing **Ctrl+Alt+F2** and log in to the terminal using the user name of **root** and the password of **secret**.

2. At the command prompt, type **cd samples** and press **Enter**. At the command prompt, type **ls -R** and press **Enter**. Note the two empty directories todelete and undermysamples.

3. At the command prompt, type **rmdir undermysamples todelete** and press **Enter**. Did the command work? Why? Next, type **ls -F** at the command prompt and press **Enter**. Were both directories deleted successfully?

4. At the command prompt, type **rm sample1*** and press **Enter**. What message is displayed? Answer **n** to all three questions.

5. At the command prompt, type **rm -f sample1*** and press **Enter**. Why were you not prompted to continue? Next, type **ls -F** at the command prompt and press **Enter**. Were all three files deleted successfully?

6. At the command prompt, type **cd ..** and press **Enter**. Next, type **rmdir samples** at the command prompt and press **Enter**. What error message do you receive and why?

7. At the command prompt, type **rm -Rf samples** and press **Enter**. Next, type **ls -F** at the command prompt and press **Enter**. Were the samples directory and all the files within it deleted successfully?

8. Type **exit** and press **Enter** to log out of your shell.

Project 4-7

In this hands-on project, you apply and modify access permissions on files and directories and test their effects.

1. Switch to a command-line terminal (tty2) by pressing **Ctrl+Alt+F2** and log in to the terminal using the user name of **root** and the password of **secret**.

2. At the command prompt, type **touch permsample** and press **Enter**. Next, type **chmod 777 permsample** at the command prompt and press **Enter**.

3. At the command prompt, type **ls -l** and press **Enter**. Who has permissions to this file?

4. At the command prompt, type **chmod 000 permsample** and press **Enter**. Next, type **ls -l** at the command prompt and press **Enter**. Who has permissions to this file?

5. At the command prompt, type **rm -f permsample** and press **Enter**. Were you able to delete this file? Why?

6. At the command prompt, type **cd /** and press **Enter**. Next, type **pwd** at the command prompt and press **Enter**. What directory are you in? Type **ls -F** at the command prompt and press **Enter**. What directories do you see?

7. At the command prompt, type **ls -l** and press **Enter** to view the owner, group owner, and permissions on the foruser1 directory created in Hands-On Project 4-1. Who is the owner and group owner? If you were logged in as the user user1, in which category would you be placed (*user, group, other*)? What permissions do you have as this category (read, write, execute)?

8. At the command prompt, type **cd /foruser1** and press **Enter** to enter the foruser1 directory. Next, type **ls -F** at the command prompt and press **Enter**. Are there any files in this directory? Type **cp /etc/hosts .** at the command prompt and press **Enter**. Next, type **ls -F** at the command prompt and press **Enter** to ensure that a copy of the hosts file was made in your current directory.

9. Switch to a different command-line terminal (tty3) by pressing **Ctrl+Alt+F3** and log in to the terminal using the user name of **user1** and the password of **secret**.

10. At the command prompt, type **cd /foruser1** and press **Enter**. Were you successful? Why? Next, type **ls -F** at the command prompt and press **Enter**. Were you able to see the contents of the directory? Why? Next, type **rm -f hosts** at the command prompt and press **Enter**. What error message did you see? Why?

11. Switch back to your previous command-line terminal (tty2) by pressing **Ctrl+Alt+F2**. Note that you are logged in as the root user on this terminal.

12. At the command prompt, type **chmod o+w /foruser1** and press **Enter**. Were you able to change the permissions on the /foruser1 directory successfully? Why?

13. Switch back to your previous command-line terminal (tty3) by pressing **Ctrl+Alt+F3**. Note that you are logged in as the user1 user on this terminal.

14. At the command prompt, type **cd /foruser1** and press **Enter**. Next, type **rm -f hosts** at the command prompt and press **Enter**. Were you successful now? Why?

15. Switch back to your previous command-line terminal (tty2) by pressing **Ctrl+Alt+F2**. Note that you are logged in as the root user on this terminal.

16. At the command prompt, type **cd /foruser1** and press **Enter** to enter the foruser1 directory. Type **cp /etc/hosts .** at the command prompt and press **Enter** to place another copy of the hosts file in your current directory.

17. At the command prompt, type **ls –l** and press **Enter**. Who is the owner and group owner of this file? If you were logged in as the user user1, in which category would you be placed (*user, group, other*)? What permissions do you have as this category (read, write, execute)?

18. Switch back to your previous command-line terminal (tty3) by pressing **Ctrl+Alt+F3**. Note that you are logged in as the user1 user on this terminal.

19. At the command prompt, type **cd /foruser1** and press **Enter** to enter the foruser1 directory. Type **cat hosts** at the command prompt and press **Enter**. Were you successful? Why? Next, type **vi hosts** at the command prompt to open the hosts file in the vi editor. Delete the first line of this file and save your changes. Were you successful? Why? Exit the vi editor and discard your changes.

20. Switch back to your previous command-line terminal (tty2) by pressing **Ctrl+Alt+F2**. Note that you are logged in as the root user on this terminal.

21. At the command prompt, type **chmod o+w /foruser1/hosts** and press **Enter**.

22. Switch back to your previous command-line terminal (tty3) by pressing **Ctrl+Alt+F3**. Note that you are logged in as the user1 user on this terminal.

23. At the command prompt, type **cd /foruser1** and press **Enter** to enter the foruser1 directory. Type **vi hosts** at the command prompt to open the hosts file in the vi editor. Delete the first line of this file and save your changes. Why were you successful this time? Exit the vi editor.

24. At the command prompt, type **ls -l** and press **Enter**. Do you have permission to execute the hosts file? Should you make this file executable? Why? Next, type **ls –l /bin** at the command prompt and press **Enter**. Note how many of these files to which you have execute permission. Type **file /bin/*** at the command prompt and press **Enter** to view the file types of the files in the /bin directory. Should these files have the execute permission?

25. Type **exit** and press **Enter** to log out of your shell.

26. Switch back to your previous command-line terminal (tty2) by pressing **Ctrl+Alt+F2**. Note that you are logged in as the root user on this terminal.

27. Type **exit** and press **Enter** to log out of your shell.

Project 4-8

In this hands-on project, you view and manipulate the default file and directory permissions using the umask variable.

1. Switch to a command-line terminal (tty3) by pressing **Ctrl+Alt+F3** and log in to the terminal using the user name of **user1** and the password of **secret**.

2. At the command prompt, type **ls -l** and press **Enter**. What files do you see?

3. At the command prompt, type **umask** and press **Enter**. What is the default umask variable?

4. At the command prompt, type **touch utest1** and press **Enter**. Next, type **ls -l** at the command prompt and press **Enter**. What are the permissions on the utest1 file? Do these agree with the calculation in Figure 4-5? Create a new directory by typing the command **mkdir udir1** at the command prompt and pressing **Enter**. Next, type **ls -l** at the command prompt and press **Enter**. What are the permissions on the udir1 directory? Do these agree with the calculation in Figure 4-5?

5. At the command prompt, type **umask 007** and press **Enter**. Next, type **umask** at the command prompt and press **Enter** to verify that your umask variable has been changed to 007.

6. At the command prompt, type **touch utest2** and press **Enter**. Next, type **ls -l** at the command prompt and press **Enter**. What are the permissions on the utest2 file? Do these agree with the calculation in Figure 4-6? Create a new directory by typing the command **mkdir udir2** at the command prompt and pressing **Enter**. Next, type **ls -l** at the command prompt and press **Enter**. What are the permissions on the udir2 directory? Do these agree with the calculation in Figure 4-6?

7. Type **exit** and press **Enter** to log out of your shell.

Project 4-9

In this hands-on project, you view and change file and directory ownership using the chown and chgrp commands.

1. Switch to a command-line terminal (tty3) by pressing **Ctrl+Alt+F3** and log in to the terminal using the user name of **root** and the password of **secret**.

2. At the command prompt, type **touch ownersample** and press **Enter**. Next, type **mkdir ownerdir** at the command prompt and press **Enter**. Next, type **ls -l** at the command prompt and press **Enter** to verify that the file ownersample and directory ownerdir were created and that root is the owner and who is the group owner of each.

3. At the command prompt, type **chgrp sys owner*** and press **Enter** to change the group ownership to the sys group for both ownersample and ownerdir. Why were you successful?

4. At the command prompt, type **chown user1 owner*** and press **Enter** to change the ownership to the root user for both ownersample and ownerdir. Why were you successful?

5. At the command prompt, type **chown root.root owner*** and press **Enter** to change the ownership and group ownership back to the root user for both ownersample and ownerdir. Although you are not the current owner of these files, why did you not receive an error message?

6. At the command prompt, type **mv ownersample ownerdir** and press **Enter**. Next, type **ls -lR** at the command prompt and press **Enter** to note that the ownersample file now exists within the ownerdir directory and that both are owned by root.

7. At the command prompt, type **chown –R user1 ownerdir** and press **Enter**. Next, type **ls –lR** at the command prompt and press **Enter**. Who owns the ownerdir directory and ownersample file? Why?

8. At the command prompt, type **rm -Rf ownerdir** and press **Enter**. Why were you able to delete this directory without being the owner of it?

9. Type **exit** and press **Enter** to log out of your shell.

Project 4-10

In this hands-on project, you view and set special permissions on files and directories.

1. Switch to a command-line terminal (tty3) by pressing **Ctrl+Alt+F3** and log in to the terminal using the user name of **user1** and the password of **secret**.

2. At the command prompt, type **touch specialfile** and press **Enter**. Next, type **ls –l** at the command prompt and press **Enter** to verify that specialfile was created successfully. Who is the owner and who is the group owner of specialfile?

3. At the command prompt, type **chmod 4777 specialfile** and press **Enter**. Next, type **ls -l** at the command prompt and press **Enter**. Which special permission is set on this file? If this file were executed by another user, who would that user be during execution?

4. At the command prompt, type **chmod 6777 specialfile** and press **Enter**. Next, type **ls -l** at the command prompt and press **Enter**. Which special permissions are set on this file? If this file were executed by another user, who would that user be during execution and which group would that user be a member of?

5. At the command prompt, type **chmod 6444 specialfile** and press **Enter**. Next, type **ls –l** at the command prompt and press **Enter**. Can you tell if execute is not given underneath the special permission listings? Would the special permissions retain their meaning in this case?

6. Switch to a command-line terminal (tty2) by pressing **Ctrl+Alt+F2** and log in to the terminal using the user name of **root** and the password of **secret**.

7. At the command prompt, type **mkdir /public** and press **Enter**. Next, type **chmod 1777 /public** at the command prompt and press **Enter**. Which special permission is set on this directory? Who can add or remove files to and from this directory?

8. At the command prompt, type **touch /public/rootfile** and press **Enter**.

9. Type **exit** and press **Enter** to log out of your shell.

10. Switch back to your previous command-line terminal (tty3) by pressing **Ctrl+Alt+F3**. Note that you are logged in as the user1 user on this terminal.

11. At the command prompt, type **touch /public/user1file** and press **Enter**. Next, type **ls -l /public** at the command prompt and press **Enter**. What files exist in this directory, and who are the owners?

12. At the command prompt, type **rm /public/user1file** and press **Enter**. Were you prompted to confirm the deletion of the file?

13. At the command prompt, type **rm /public/rootfile** and press **Enter**. What message did you receive? Why? Press **y**. Note the error message that you receive.

14. Type **exit** and press **Enter** to log out of your shell.

Discovery Exercises

1. Use the **ls** command with the **-F** option to explore directories described in the Filesystem Hierarchy Standard starting with /bin. Do you recognize any of the commands in /bin? Explore several other FHS directories and note their contents. Refer to Table 4-1 for a list of directories to explore. Further, visit *www.pathname.com/fhs/* and read about the Filesystem Hierarchy Standard. What benefits does it offer Linux?

2. Write the commands required for the following tasks. Try out each command on your system to ensure that it is correct:

   a. Make a hierarchical directory structure under /root that consists of one directory containing three subdirectories.

   b. Copy two files into each of the subdirectories.

   c. Create one more directory with three subdirectories beneath it and move files from the subdirectories containing them to the counterparts you just created.

   d. Hard-link three of the files. Examine their inodes.

   e. Symbolically link two of the files and examine their link count and inode information.

   f. Make symbolic links from your home directory to two directories in this structure and examine the results.

   g. Delete the symbolic links in your home directory and the directory structure you created under /root.

3. Write the commands that can be used to perform the following tasks. (*Hint:* Try each out on the system to check your results.)

   a. Find all files on the system that have the word "test" as part of their filenames.

   b. Search the PATH variable for the pathname to the awk command.

   c. Find all files in the /usr directory and subdirectories that are larger than 50 Kilobytes in size.

   d. Find all files in the /usr directory and subdirectories that are less than 70 Kilobytes in size.

   e. Find all files in the / directory and subdirectories that are symbolic links.

   f. Find all files in the /var directory and subdirectories that were accessed less than 60 minutes ago.

   g. Find all files in the /var directory and subdirectories that were accessed less than six days ago.

   h. Find all files in the /home directory and subdirectories that are empty.

   i. Find all files in the /etc directory and subdirectories that are owned by the group bin.

4. For each of the following modes, write the numeric equivalent (for example, 777):

   a. rw-r--r--

   b. r--r--r--

   c. ---rwxrw-

   d. -wxr-xrw-

   e. rw-rw-rwx

   f. -w-r-----

5. Fill in the permissions in Table 4-7 with checkmarks, assuming that all four files are in the directory /public, which has a mode of rwxr-xr-x.

6. Fill in the permissions in Table 4-8 with checkmarks, assuming that all four files are in the directory /public, which has a mode of rwx--x---.

Filename	Mode		Read	Edit	Execute	List	Delete
sample1	rw-rw-rw-	User Group Other					
sample2	r--r-----	User Group Other					
sample3	rwxr-x---	User Group Other					
sample4	r-x------	User Group Other					

Table 4-7   **Permissions table for Discovery Exercise 5**

Filename	Mode		Read	Edit	Execute	List	Delete
sample1	rwxr--r--	User Group Other					
sample2	r-xr--rw-	User Group Other					
sample3	--xr-x---	User Group Other					
sample4	r-xr--r--	User Group Other					

Table 4-8   **Permissions table for Discovery Exercise 6**

7. For each of the following umasks, calculate the default permissions given to new files and new directories:

    a. 017

    b. 272

    c. 777

    d. 000

    e. 077

    f. 027

8. For each of the umasks in Discovery Exercise 7, list the umasks that are reasonable to use to increase security on your Linux system, and explain why.

9. Starting from the Linux default permissions for files and directories, what umask would you use to ensure that for all new _____?

    a. directories, the owner would have read, write, and execute; members of the group would have read and execute; and others would have read

    b. files, the owner would have read and execute; the group would have read, write, and execute; and others would have execute

    c. files, the owner would have write; the group would have read, write, and execute; and others would have read and write

    d. directories, the owner would have read, write, and execute; the group would have read, write, and execute; and others would have read, write, and execute

    e. directories, the owner would have execute; the group would have read, write, and execute; and others would have no permissions

    f. files, the owner would have read and write; the group would have no permissions; and others would have write

    g. directories, the owner would have read, write, and execute; the group would have read; and others would have read and execute

    h. directories, the owner would have write; the group would have read, write, and execute; and others would have read, write, and execute

    i. files, the owner would have no permissions; the group would have no permissions; and others would have no permissions

10. What chmod command would you use to impose the following permissions?

    a. On a directory such that the owner would have read, write, and execute; the group would have read and execute; and others would have read

    b. On a file such that the owner would have read and write; the group would have no permissions; and others would have write

    c. On a file such that the owner would have write; the group would have read, write, and execute; and others would have read and write

    d. On a file such that the owner would have read and execute; the group would have read, write, and execute; and others would have execute

e. On a directory such that the owner would have execute; the group would have read, write, and execute; and others would have no permissions

f. On a directory such that the owner would have write; the group would have read, write, and execute; and others would have read, write, and execute

g. On a directory such that the owner would have read, write, and execute; the group would have read; and others would have read and execute

h. On a directory such that the owner would have read, write, and execute; the group would have read, write, and execute; and others would have read, write, and execute

i. On a file such that the owner would have no permissions; the group would have no permissions; and others would have no permissions

## chapter 5

Linux Filesystem Administration

After completing this chapter, you will be able to:

- Identify the structure and types of device files in the /dev directory
- Understand common filesystem types and their features
- Mount and unmount filesystems to and from the Linux directory tree
- Create and manage filesystems on floppy disks, CDs, DVDs, USB storage devices, FireWire storage devices, and hard disk partitions
- Create and use ISO images
- Use the LVM to create and manage logical volumes
- Monitor free space on mounted filesystems
- Check filesystems for errors
- Use hard disk quotas to limit user space usage

Navigating the Linux directory tree and manipulating files are common tasks that are performed on a daily basis by all users. However, administrators must provide this directory tree for users, as well as manage and fix the disk devices that support it. In this chapter, you learn about the various device files that represent disk devices and the different filesystems that can be placed on those devices. Next, you learn how to create and manage filesystems on floppy disks, CDs, DVDs, ISO images, and USB and FireWire-based storage devices as well as learn standard hard disk partitioning, LVM configuration, and filesystem management. Finally, this chapter concludes with a discussion of disk usage, filesystem errors, and restricting users' ability to store files.

The /dev Directory

Fundamental to administering the disks used to store information is an understanding of how these disks are specified by the Linux operating system. Most devices on a Linux system (such as disks, terminals, and serial ports) are represented by a file on the hard disk called a **device file**. There is one file per device, and these files are typically found in the **/dev directory**. This allows you to specify devices on the system by using the pathname to the file that represents it in the /dev directory. To specify the first floppy disk in the Linux system, you can type the pathname /dev/fd0 (floppy disk 0) in the appropriate section of a command. In addition, to represent the second floppy disk in the Linux system, you can specify the pathname to the file /dev/fd1 (floppy disk 1).

Furthermore, each device file specifies how data should be transferred to and from the device. You have two methods for transferring data to and from a device. The first method involves transferring information character-by-character to and from the device. Devices that transfer data in this fashion are referred to as **character devices**. The second method transfers chunks or blocks of information at a time by using physical memory to buffer the transfer. Devices that use this method of transfer are called **block devices**, and they can transfer information much faster than character devices. Device files that represent disks, such as floppy disks, CD-ROMs, DVDs, USB flash drives, and hard disks, are typically block device files because a fast data transfer rate is preferred. Tape drives and most other devices, however, are typically represented by character device files.

To see whether a particular device transfers data character-by-character or block-by-block, recall that the ls –l command displays a c or b character in the type column indicating the type of device file. To view the type of the file /dev/fd0, you can use the following command:

```
[root@server1 ~]# ls -l /dev/fd0
brw-rw----  1 root     floppy    2,    0 Feb 23 16:02  /dev/fd0
[root@server1 ~]#_
```

 Floppy disk drives are not standard on newer computers today. As a result, Fedora 13 does not load the floppy driver and create the /dev/fd0 device file by default. To load the floppy driver manually (which also creates the /dev/fd0 device file), you can type modprobe floppy at a command prompt as the root user.

From the leftmost character in the preceding output, you can see that the /dev/fd0 file is a block device file. Table 5-1 provides a list of some common device files and their types.

Device File	Description	Block or Character
/dev/fd0	First floppy disk on the system	Block
/dev/fd1	Second floppy disk on the system	Block
/dev/hda1	First primary partition on the first IDE hard disk drive (primary master)	Block
/dev/hdb1	First primary partition on the second IDE hard disk drive (primary slave)	Block
/dev/hdc1	First primary partition on the third IDE hard disk drive (secondary master)	Block
/dev/hdd1	First primary partition on the fourth IDE hard disk drive (secondary slave)	Block
/dev/sda1	First primary partition on the first SATA/SCSI hard disk drive	Block
/dev/sdb1	First primary partition on the second SATA/SCSI hard disk drive	Block
/dev/loop0	The first loopback interface	Block
/dev/tty1	First local terminal on the system (Ctrl+Alt+F1)	Character
/dev/tty2	Second local terminal on the system (Ctrl+Alt+F2)	Character
/dev/ttyS0	First serial port on the system (COM1)	Character
/dev/ttyS1	Second serial port on the system (COM2)	Character
/dev/psaux	PS/2 mouse port	Character
/dev/lp0	First parallel port on the system (LPT1)	Character
/dev/null	Device file that represents nothing; any data sent to this device is discarded	Character
/dev/st0	First SCSI tape device in the system	Character
/dev/bus/usb/*	USB device files	Character

Table 5-1   Common device files

After a typical Fedora Linux installation, over 700 different device files are in the /dev directory; some of these device files represent devices that might not exist on the particular Linux system and, hence, are never used. Providing this large number of redundant device files on a Linux system does not require much disk space because all device files consist of inodes and no data blocks; as a result, the entire contents of the /dev directory are usually less than 700 Kilobytes in size, which could easily fit on a floppy disk. When the ls -l command is used to view device files, the portion of the listing describing the file size in Kilobytes is replaced by two numbers: the major number and the minor number. The **major number** of a device file points to the device driver for the device in the Linux kernel; several different devices can share the same major number if they are of the same general type (that is, two different floppy disk drives might share the same major number). The **minor number** indicates the particular device itself; the first floppy disk drive in the computer will have a different minor number than the second floppy disk drive in the computer. In the following output, you see that /dev/fd0 and /dev/fd1 share the major number of 2, yet the minor number for /dev/fd0 is 0 and the minor number for /dev/fd1 is 1, which differentiates them from one another.

```
[root@server1 ~]# ls -l  /dev/fd0   /dev/fd1
brw-rw----  1   root    floppy   2,   0 Feb  23  16:02  /dev/fd0
brw-rw----  1   root    floppy   2,   1 Feb  23  16:02  /dev/fd1
[root@server1 ~]#_
```

Together, the device file type (block or character), the major number (device driver), and the minor number (specific device) make up the unique characteristics of each device file. To create a device file, you simply need to know these three pieces of information.

If a device file becomes corrupted, it is usually listed as a regular file instead of a block or character special file. Recall from Chapter 4 that the find /dev -type f command can be used to search for regular files underneath the /dev directory to identify whether corruption has taken place. If you find a corrupted device file, or accidentally delete a device file, the **mknod command** can be used to re-create the device file if you know the type, major number, and minor number. An example of re-creating the /dev/fd0 block device file used earlier with a major number of 2 and a minor number of 0 is shown in the following example:

```
[root@server1 ~]# ls -l /dev/fd0
brw-rw----    1 root    floppy     2,    0 Feb  23  16:02  /dev/fd0
[root@server1 ~]# rm -f /dev/fd0
[root@server1 ~]# ls -l /dev/fd0
[root@server1 ~]# mknod /dev/fd0 b 2     0
[root@server1 ~]# ls -l /dev/fd0
brw-rw--rw--  1 root    root       2,    0 May   8  13:26  /dev/fd0
[root@server1 ~]#_
```

However, if you do not know the type, major number, or minor number of the device, you can use the **/dev/MAKEDEV command** to re-create the device based on the common name, as shown here:

```
[root@server1 ~]# ls -l /dev/fd0
brw-rw--rw--  1 root    root       2,    0 May   8  13:26  /dev/fd0
[root@server1 ~]# rm -f /dev/fd0
[root@server1 ~]# ls -l /dev/fd0
[root@server1 ~]# /dev/MAKEDEV fd0
[root@server1 ~]# ls -l /dev/fd0
brw-rw----    1 root    floppy     2,    0 May   8  13:30  /dev/fd0
[root@server1 ~]#_
```

Recall from earlier in this chapter that many device files present in the /dev directory are never used. To see a list of devices that are currently used on the system and their major numbers, you can view the contents of the **/proc/devices** file, as shown here:

```
[root@server1 ~]# cat /proc/devices
Character devices:
  1   mem
  4   /dev/vc/0
  4   tty
  4   ttyS
  5   /dev/tty
  5   /dev/console
  5   /dev/ptmx
```

```
  7  vcs
 10  misc
 13  input
 14  sound
 21  sg
 29  fb
116  alsa
128  ptm
136  pts
162  raw
180  usb
189  usb_device
202  cpu/msr
203  cpu/cpuid
226  drm
250  hidraw
251  usbmon
252  bsg
253  pcmcia
254  rtc

Block devices:
  1  ramdisk
  2  fd
  7  loop
  8  sd
  9  md
 11  sr
 65  sd
 69  sd
 70  sd
 71  sd
128  sd
134  sd
135  sd
253  device-mapper
254  mdp
[root@server1 ~]#_
```

Filesystems

Recall from Chapter 2 that files must be stored on the hard disk in a defined format called a **filesystem,** so that the operating system can work with them. The type of filesystem used determines how files are managed on the physical hard disk. Each filesystem can have different methods for storing files and features that make the filesystem robust against errors. Although many different types of filesystems are available, all filesystems have three common components, as discussed in Chapter 4: the superblock, the inode table, and the data blocks. On a structural level, these three components work together to organize files and allow rapid access to and retrieval of data. All storage media, such as floppy disks, hard disks, and DVDs, need to contain a filesystem before they can be used.

 Creating a filesystem on a device is commonly referred to as **formatting**.

Filesystem Types

As mentioned, many filesystems are available for use in the Linux operating system. Each has its own strengths and weaknesses, thus some are better suited to some tasks and not as well suited to others. One benefit of Linux is that you need not use only one type of filesystem on the system; you can use several different devices formatted with different filesystems under the same directory tree. In addition, files and directories appear the same throughout the directory tree regardless of whether there is one filesystem or 20 different filesystems in use by the Linux system. Table 5-2 lists some common filesystems available for use in Linux.

Filesystem	Description
bfs	Boot File System—A small, bootable filesystem used to hold the files necessary for system startup; it is commonly used on UNIX systems.
cramfs	Compressed ROM filesystem—A read-only filesystem typically used on embedded Linux systems to host system files in a small amount of storage space.
ext2	Second extended filesystem—The traditional filesystem used on Linux, it supports access control lists (individual user permissions). In addition, it retains its name from being the new version of the original extended filesystem, based on the Minix filesystem.
ext3	Third extended filesystem—A variation on ext2 that allows for journaling and, thus, has a faster startup and recovery time.
ext4	Fourth extended filesystem—A variation on ext3 that has larger filesystem support and speed enhancements.
hfs, hfsplus	Hierarchical File System—A filesystem native to Apple Macintosh computers.
hpfs	High Performance File System—An IBM proprietary OS/2 filesystem that provides long filename support and is optimized to manipulate data on large disk volumes.
iso9660	ISO 9660 filesystem—A filesystem that originated from the International Organization for Standardization (ISO) recommendation 9660 and is used to access data stored on CDs and DVDs.
minix	MINIX filesystem—The filesystem used by Linus Torvalds in the early days of Linux development.
msdos	FAT filesystem.—The filesystem used on DOS and Windows computers.
ntfs	New Technology File System—A Microsoft proprietary filesystem developed for its Windows operating systems.
reiserfs	REISERFS filesystem—A journalizing filesystem similar to ext3 and more suited for use with databases.
udf	Universal Disk Format filesystem—A filesystem used by software programs that write to a CD-RW or DVD-RW drive.
vfat	Virtual FAT filesystem—A filesystem used by DOS and Windows computers that supports long file names.

Filesystem	Description
vxfs	Veritas filesystem—A journalizing filesystem that offers large file support and supports access control lists (individual user permissions) and is commonly used by major versions of UNIX.
xfs	X filesystem—A high-performance filesystem created by Silicon Graphics for use on their IRIX UNIX systems. Many Linux administrators prefer to use xfs on systems that need to quickly write large numbers of files to the hard disk.

Table 5-2 Common Linux filesystems

For a full listing of filesystem types and their features, you can refer to the Filesystem HOWTO on the Internet at *www.tldp.org/HOWTO/Filesystems-HOWTO.html*.

Filesystem support is typically built in to the Linux kernel or added as a package on most distributions. Fedora 13 has native support for cramfs, ext2, ext3, ext4, hfs, hfsplus, iso9660, ntfs, udf, vfat, and xfs by default.

Mounting

The term **mounting** originated in the 1960s when information was stored on large tape reels that had to be mounted on computers to make the data available. Today, the term still refers to making data available. More specifically, it refers to the process whereby a device is made accessible to users via the logical directory tree. This device is attached to a certain directory on the directory tree called a **mount point**. Users can then create files and subdirectories in this mount point directory, and then store the files on the filesystem that was mounted to that particular directory.

Remember that directories are merely files that do not contain data; instead, they contain a list of files and subdirectories organized within them. Thus, it is easy for the Linux system to cover up directories to prevent user access to that data. This is essentially what happens when a device is mounted to a certain directory; the mount point directory is temporarily covered up by that device while the device remains mounted. Any file contents that were present in the mount point directory prior to mounting are not lost; when the device is unmounted, the mount point directory is uncovered, and the previous file contents are revealed. Suppose, for example, that you mount a floppy device that contains a filesystem to the /mnt directory. The /mnt directory is an empty directory that is commonly used as a temporary mount point for mounting removable media devices. Before mounting, the directory structure would resemble that depicted in Figure 5-1. After the floppy is mounted to the /mnt directory, the contents of the /mnt directory would be covered up by the floppy filesystem, as illustrated in Figure 5-2.

If a user then stores a file in the /mnt directory, as shown in Figure 5-2, that file will be stored on the floppy disk device. Similarly, if a user creates a subdirectory under the /mnt directory depicted in Figure 5-2, that subdirectory will be made on the floppy disk.

It is important to note that any existing directory can be used as a mount point. If a user mounts a floppy device to the /bin directory, all files in the /bin directory are covered up during the time that floppy disk is mounted, including the command used to unmount the

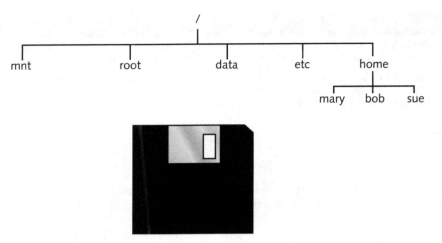

Figure 5-1 The directory structure prior to mounting

Source: Course Technology/Cengage Learning

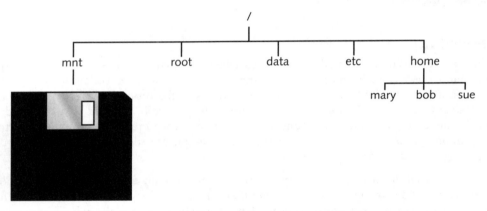

Figure 5-2 The directory structure after mounting a floppy device

Source: Course Technology/Cengage Learning

floppy. Thus, it is a safe practice to create empty directories used specifically for mounting devices to avoid making existing files inaccessible to users.

Most systems today have several removable media devices, such as CDs DVDs, USB flash drives, and USB hard drives that may be connected to your PC for long periods of time. As a result, it is considered good form to create subdirectories under the /media directory on your Linux system to mount these removable media devices and only use the /mnt directory to temporarily mount devices. For example, you could mount your floppy to the /media/floppy directory and your DVD to the /media/DVD directory. You could then access the files on your floppy disk by navigating to the /media/floppy directory, as well as access the files on your DVD by navigating to the / media/DVD directory.

When the Linux system is first turned on, a filesystem present on the hard drive is mounted to the / directory. This is referred to as the **root filesystem** and contains most of the operating system files. Other filesystems present on hard disks inside the computer can also be mounted to various mount point directories underneath the / directory at boot time, as well as via entries in the filesystem table (**/etc/fstab**) discussed in the following sections.

The **mount command** is used to mount devices to mount point directories, and the **umount command** is used to unmount devices from mount point directories; both of these commands are discussed throughout the remainder of this chapter.

Working with Floppy Disks

When transferring small amounts of information from computer to computer in the past, it was commonplace to use floppy disk removable media to store the files. Today, floppy disks are not available on all systems, but we will examine them here as they are an easy way to practice and learn the commands that are commonly used to work with filesystems. Recall that each disk device must be formatted with a filesystem prior to being used to store files. To do this, you can use the **mkfs** (**make filesystem**) **command** and specify the filesystem type using the −t switch and the device file representing the floppy disk device. To format the floppy disk inside the first floppy disk drive in the computer with the ext2 filesystem, place a floppy disk in the floppy disk drive and type the following command:

```
[root@server1 ~]# mkfs -t ext2 /dev/fd0
mke2fs 1.41.4 (27-Jan-2009)
Filesystem label=
OS type: Linux
Block size=1024 (log=0)
Fragment size=1024 (log=0)
184 inodes, 1440 blocks
72 blocks (5.00%) reserved for the super user
First data block=1
1 block group
8192 blocks per group, 8192 fragments per group
184 inodes per group

Writing inode tables: done
Writing superblocks and filesystem accounting information: done

This filesystem will be automatically checked every 24 mounts or
180 days, whichever comes first. Use tune2fs -c or -i to override.
[root@server1 ~]#_
```

Alternatively, you can specify a different filesystem after the −t option, such as the DOS FAT filesystem. This results in a different output from the mkfs command, as shown in the following example:

```
[root@server1 ~]# mkfs -t msdos /dev/fd0
mkfs.msdos 3.0.9 (31 Jan 2010)
[root@server1 ~]#_
```

If you do not specify the filesystem using the mkfs command, the default filesystem assumed is the ext2 filesystem, as shown in the following example:

```
[root@server1 ~]# mkfs /dev/fd0
mke2fs  1.41.4  (27-Jan-2009)
Filesystem label=
OS type: Linux
Block size=1024 (log=0)
Fragment size=1024 (log=0)
184 inodes, 1440 blocks
72 blocks (5.00%) reserved for the super user
First data block=1
1 block group
8192 blocks per group, 8192 fragments per group
184 inodes per group

Writing inode tables: done
Writing superblocks and filesystem accounting information: done

This filesystem will be automatically checked every 24 mounts or
180 days, whichever comes first. Use tune2fs -c or -i to override.
[root@server1 ~]#_
```

Although the most common command to create filesystems is the mkfs command, other variants and shortcuts to the mkfs command exist. For example, to create an ext2 filesystem, you could type mke2fs /dev/fd0 on the command line. Other alternatives to the mkfs command are listed in Table 5-3.

After a floppy disk has been formatted with a filesystem, it must be mounted on the directory tree before it can be used. A list of currently mounted filesystems can be obtained by using the mount command with no options or arguments, which reads the information listed in the /etc/mtab (mount table) file, as shown in the following output:

```
[root@server1 ~]# mount
/dev/sda1  on  /  type ext4 (rw)
proc  on  /proc type proc (rw)
sysfs  on  /sys type sysfs (rw)
devpts  on  /dev/pts type devpts (rw,gid=5,mode=620)
tmpfs  on  /dev/shm type tmpfs (rw)
none  on  /proc/sys/fs/binfmt_misc type binfmt_misc (rw)
sunrpc  on  /var/lib/nfs/rpc_pipefs type rpc_pipefs (rw)
[root@server1 ~]# cat /etc/mtab
/dev/sda1  / ext4 rw  0  0
proc  /proc proc rw  0  0
sysfs  /sys sysfs rw  0  0
devpts  /dev/pts devpts rw,gid=5,mode=620  0  0
tmpfs  /dev/shm tmpfs rw  0  0
none  /proc/sys/fs/binfmt_misc binfmt_misc rw  0  0
sunrpc  /var/lib/nfs/rpc_pipefs rpc_pipefs  rw  0  0
[root@server1 ~]#_
```

Command	Filesystem It Creates
`mkfs`	Filesystems of most types

`mkdosfs`
`mkfs.msdos`
`mkfs.vfat`
	FAT

`mkfs.ext2`
`mke2fs`
`mke2fs -t ext2`
	ext2

`mkfs.ext3` `mke2fs -t ext3`	ext3
`mkfs.ext4` `mke2fs -t ext4`	ext4
`mkisofs`	ISO
`mkreiserfs` `mkfs.reiserfs`	REISERFS
`mkfs.xfs`	XFS
`mkntfs` `mkfs.ntfs`	NTFS

Table 5-3 **Commands used to create filesystems**

From the preceding output, you can see that the device /dev/sda1 is mounted on the **/** directory and contains an ext4 filesystem. The other filesystems listed are special filesystems that are used by the system and are discussed later in this book.

To mount a device on the directory tree, you can use the `mount` command with options and arguments to specify the filesystem type, the device to mount, and the directory on which to mount the device (mount point). It is important to ensure that no user is currently using the mount point directory; otherwise, the system gives you an error message and the disk is not mounted. To check whether the /media/floppy directory is being used by any users, you can use the **fuser command** with the –u option, as shown in the following output:

```
[root@server1 ~]# fuser -u /media/floppy
[root@server1 ~]#_
```
The preceding output indicates the /media/floppy directory is not being used by any user processes. To mount the first floppy device formatted with the ext2 filesystem to the /media/floppy directory, simply type the following command:

```
[root@server1 ~]# mount -t ext2 /dev/fd0 /media/floppy
[root@server1 ~]# mount
/dev/sda1 on / type ext4 (rw)
proc on /proc type proc (rw)
sysfs on /sys type sysfs (rw)
```

```
devpts on /dev/pts type devpts (rw,gid=5,mode=620)
tmpfs on /dev/shm type tmpfs (rw)
none on /proc/sys/fs/binfmt_misc type binfmt_misc (rw)
sunrpc on /var/lib/nfs/rpc_pipefs type rpc_pipefs (rw)
/dev/fd0 on /media/floppy type ext2 (rw)
[root@server1 ~]#_
```

 If you omit the −t option to the mount command, it attempts to automatically detect the filesystem on the device. Thus, the command mount /dev/fd0 /media/floppy will perform the same action as the mount command shown in the preceding output.

Notice that /dev/fd0 appears mounted to the /media/floppy directory in the preceding output of the mount command. To access and store files on the floppy device, you can now treat the /media/floppy directory as the root of the floppy disk. When an ext2 filesystem is created on a disk device, one directory called lost+found is created by default and used by the fsck command discussed later in this chapter. To explore the recently mounted floppy filesystem, you can use the following commands:

```
[root@server1 ~]# cd /media/floppy
[root@server1 floppy]# pwd
/media/floppy
[root@server1 floppy]# ls -F
lost+found/
[root@server1 floppy]#_
```

To copy files to the floppy device, simply specify the /media/floppy directory as the target for the cp command, as shown next:

```
[root@server1 floppy]# cd /etc
[root@server1 etc]# cat issue
Fedora release 13 (Goddard)
Kernel \r on an \m (\l)
[root@server1 etc]# cp issue /media/floppy
[root@server1 etc]# cd /media/floppy
[root@server1 floppy]# ls -F
issue  lost+found/
[root@server1 floppy]# cat issue
Fedora release 13 (Goddard)
Kernel \r on an \m (\l)
[root@server1 floppy]#_
```

Similarly, you can create subdirectories underneath the floppy device to store files; these subdirectories are referenced underneath the mount point directory. To make a directory called workfiles on the floppy mounted in the previous example and copy the /etc/inittab file to it, you can use the following commands:

```
[root@server1 floppy]# pwd
/media/floppy
[root@server1 floppy]# ls -F
```

```
issue   lost+found/
[root@server1  floppy]# mkdir workfiles
[root@server1  floppy]# ls -F
issue   lost+found/  workfiles/
[root@server1  floppy]# cd workfiles
[root@server1  workfiles]# pwd
/media/floppy/workfiles
[root@server1  workfiles]# cp /etc/inittab .
[root@server1  workfiles]# ls -F
inittab
[root@server1  workfiles]#_
```

Even though you can eject the floppy disk from the floppy disk drive without permission from the system, doing so is likely to cause error messages to appear on the terminal screen. Before a floppy is ejected, it must be properly unmounted using the umount command. The umount command can take either the name of the device to unmount or the mount point directory as an argument. Similar to mounting a floppy disk, unmounting a floppy disk requires that the mount point directory have no users using it. If you try to unmount the floppy disk mounted to the /media/floppy directory while it is being used, you receive an error message similar to the one in the following example:

```
[root@server1 floppy]# pwd
/media/floppy
[root@server1 floppy]# umount /media/floppy
umount: /media/floppy: device is busy.
        (In some cases useful info about processes that
        use the device is found by lsof(8) or fuser(1))
[root@server1 floppy]# fuser -u /media/floppy
/media/floppy:           17368c(root)
[root@server1 floppy]# cd /root
[root@server1 ~]# umount /media/floppy
[root@server1 ~]# mount
/dev/sda1 on / type ext4 (rw)
proc on /proc type proc (rw)
sysfs on /sys type sysfs (rw)
devpts on /dev/pts type devpts (rw,gid=5,mode=620)
tmpfs on /dev/shm type tmpfs (rw)
none on /proc/sys/fs/binfmt_misc type binfmt_misc (rw)
sunrpc on /var/lib/nfs/rpc_pipefs type rpc_pipefs (rw)
[root@server1 ~]#_
```

Notice from the preceding output that you were still using the /media/floppy directory because it was the current working directory. The fuser command also indicated that the root user had a process using the directory. After the current working directory was changed, the umount command was able to unmount the floppy from the /media/floppy directory, and the output of the mount command indicated that the floppy disk was no longer mounted.

Recall that mounting simply attaches a disk device to the Linux directory tree so that you can treat the device like a directory full of files and subdirectories. A device can be mounted to any existing directory. However, if the directory contains files, those files are inaccessible until the device is unmounted. Suppose, for example, that you create a directory called /flopper for mounting floppy disks and a file inside called samplefile, as shown in the following output:

```
[root@server1 ~]# mkdir  /flopper
[root@server1 ~]# touch  /flopper/samplefile
[root@server1 ~]# ls -F  /flopper
samplefile
[root@server1 ~]#_
```

If the floppy disk used earlier is mounted to the /flopper directory, a user who uses the /flopper directory will be using the floppy disk; however, when nothing is mounted to the /flopper directory, the previous contents are available for use:

```
[root@server1 ~]# mount -t ext2 /dev/fd0 /flopper
[root@server1 ~]# mount
/dev/sda1 on / type ext4 (rw)
proc on /proc type proc (rw)
sysfs on /sys type sysfs (rw)
devpts on /dev/pts type devpts (rw,gid=5,mode=620)
tmpfs on /dev/shm type tmpfs (rw)
none on /proc/sys/fs/binfmt_misc type binfmt_misc (rw)
sunrpc on /var/lib/nfs/rpc_pipefs type rpc_pipefs (rw)
[root@server1 ~]# ls -F  /flopper
issue lost+found/ workfiles/
[root@server1 ~]# umount /flopper
[root@server1 ~]# ls -F  /flopper
samplefile
[root@server1 ~]#_
```

The mount command used in the preceding output specifies the filesystem type, the device to mount, and the mount point directory. To save time typing on the command line, you can alternatively specify one argument and allow the system to look up the remaining information in the /etc/fstab (filesystem table) file. The /etc/fstab file has a dual purpose; it is used to mount devices at boot time and is consulted when a user does not specify enough arguments on the command line when using the mount command.

The /etc/fstab file has six fields:

\<device to mount>   \<mount point>   \<type>   \<mount options>   \<dump#>   \<fsck#>

The device to mount can be the path to a device file (for example, /dev/sda1) or the boot loader label that describes the volume to mount (for example, UUID=db545f1d-c1ee-4b70-acbe-3dc61b 41db20). The mount point specifies where to mount the device. The type can be a specific value (such as ext4) or can be automatically detected. The mount options are additional options that the mount command accepts when mounting the volume (such as read only, or "ro"). Any filesystems with the mount option "noauto" are not automatically mounted at boot time; a complete list of options that the mount command accepts can be found by viewing the manual page for the mount command.

The dump# is used by the dump command (discussed in Chapter 11) when backing up filesystems; a 1 in this field indicates that the filesystem should be backed up, whereas a 0 indicates that no backup is necessary. The fsck# is used by the `fsck` command (discussed later in this chapter) when checking filesystems at boot time for errors; any filesystems with a 1 in this field are checked first before any filesystems with a number 2, and filesystems with a number 0 are not checked.

To mount all filesystems in the /etc/fstab file that are intended to mount at boot time, you can simply type the `mount -a` command.

The following output displays the contents of a sample /etc/fstab file:

```
[root@server1 ~]# cat /etc/fstab
#
# /etc/fstab
# Created by anaconda on Mon Aug 2 09:34:19 2010
#
# Accessible filesystems, by reference, are maintained under'/dev/disk'
# See man pages fstab(5), findfs(8), mount(8) and/or blkid(8) for info
#
/dev /sda1      /               ext4            defaults            1 1
/dev /sda2      swap            swap            defaults            0 0
tmpfs           /dev/shm        tmpfs           defaults            0 0
devpts          /dev/pts        devpts          gid=5,mode=620      0 0
sysfs           /sys            sysfs           defaults            0 0
proc            /proc           proc            defaults            0 0
/dev/fd0        /media/floppy   auto            noauto              0 0
[root@server1 ~]# _
```

Thus, to mount the first floppy device (/dev/fd0) to the /media/floppy directory and automatically detect the type of filesystem on the device, simply specify enough information for the mount command to find the appropriate line in the /etc/fstab file:

```
[root@server1 ~]# mount /dev/fd0
[root@server1 ~]# mount
/dev/sda1 on / type ext4 (rw)
proc on /proc type proc (rw)
sysfs on /sys type sysfs (rw)
devpts on /dev/pts type devpts (rw,gid=5,mode=620)
tmpfs on /dev/shm type tmpfs (rw)
none on /proc/sys/fs/binfmt_misc type binfmt_misc (rw)
sunrpc on /var/lib/nfs/rpc_pipefs type rpc_pipefs (rw)
/dev/fd0 on /media/floppy type ext2 (rw)
[root@server1 ~]# umount /dev/fd0
[root@server1 ~]#_
```

The mount command in the preceding output succeeded because a line in /etc/fstab described the mounting of the /dev/fd0 device.

Command	Description
`mount`	Displays mounted filesystems
`mount -t <type> <device> <mount point>`	Mounts a `<device>` of a certain `<type>` to a `<mount point>` directory
`fuser -u <directory>`	Displays the users using a particular directory
`umount <mount point>` or `umount <device>`	Unmounts a `<device>` from its `<mount point>` directory

Table 5-4   Useful commands when mounting and unmounting floppy disks

Alternatively, you could specify the mount point as an argument to the `mount` command to mount the same device via the correct entry in /etc/fstab:

```
[root@server1 ~]# mount /media/floppy
[root@server1 ~]# mount
/dev/sda1 on / type ext4 (rw)
proc on /proc type proc (rw)
sysfs on /sys type sysfs (rw)
devpts on /dev/pts type devpts (rw,gid=5,mode=620)
tmpfs on /dev/shm type tmpfs (rw)
none on /proc/sys/fs/binfmt_misc type binfmt_misc (rw)
sunrpc on /var/lib/nfs/rpc_pipefs type rpc_pipefs (rw)
/dev/fd0 on /media/floppy type ext2 (rw)
[root@server1 ~]# umount /media/floppy
[root@server1 ~]#_
```

Table 5-4 lists commands that are useful when mounting and unmounting floppy disks.

Working with CDs, DVDs, and ISO Images

Most software that is not downloaded from the Internet is packaged on CDs and DVDs because they have a much larger storage capacity than floppy disks; one DVD can store more than 3,000 times the data a floppy disk can store. Like floppies, CDs and DVDs can be mounted with the `mount` command and unmounted with the `umount` command, as shown in Table 5-4; however, the device file used with these commands is different. The device files used by CD-ROM and DVD-ROM drives, as well as CD-RW and DVD-RW drives (which can record to blank CDs or DVDs), depend on the technology used by the drive itself. If your computer has a PATA CD-ROM, CD-RW, DVD-ROM, or DVD-RW drive, you can refer to it using one of the following four standard PATA hard drive configurations (discussed in Chapter 2):

- Primary master (/dev/hda)
- Primary slave (/dev/hdb)
- Secondary master (/dev/hdc)
- Secondary slave (/dev/hdd)

However, if you have a SATA or SCSI CD-ROM, CD-RW, DVD-ROM, or DVD-RW drive, Linux may use many different names, depending on your actual CD or DVD drive:

- First SATA/SCSI drive (/dev/sda, /dev/scd0, /dev/sr0, and /dev/sg0)
- Second SATA/SCSI drive (/dev/sdb, /dev/scd1, /dev/sr1, and /dev/sg1)
- Third SATA/SCSI drive (/dev/sdc, /dev/scd2, /dev/sr2, and /dev/sg2)
- And so on

For example, if your system has a single SATA or SCSI CD-ROM or CD-RW drive, you would typically use /dev/sda or /dev/scd0 to read CDs. However, if your system has a SATA or SCSI DVD-ROM or DVD-RW, you would typically use /dev/sr0 to read CDs and DVDs. If you use **disk-burning software** to record to a CD-RW or DVD-RW drive, the disk-burning software typically uses /dev/sg0.

Nearly all DVD-ROM and DVD-RW drives can also work with CDs.

There are many OSS disk-burning softwares available for Linux. Fedora 13 comes with the Brasero Disc Burner program. You can access the Brasero Disc Burner program by navigating to Applications, Sound & Video, Brasero Disc Burner within the GNOME desktop environment.

To make the identification of your CD-ROM, CD-RW, DVD-ROM, or DVD-RW drive easier, Fedora Linux creates several symbolic links within the /dev directory:

- /dev/cdrom—A symbolic link to the correct device file for your first CD-ROM drive
- /dev/cdrw—A symbolic link to the correct device file for your first CD-RW drive
- /dev/dvd—A symbolic link to the correct device file for your first DVD-ROM drive
- /dev/dvdrw—A symbolic link to the correct device file for your first DVD-RW drive

For example, if your system contains a PATA CD-ROM drive that is configured as a secondary slave, a long listing of /dev/cdrom shows the following:

```
[root@server1 ~]# ls -l /dev/cdrom
lrwxrwxrwx 1 root root 8 Aug 10 11:19 /dev/cdrom -> /dev/hdd
[root@server1 ~]#_
```

However, if your system has a SATA DVD-RW drive, each symbolic link will point to /dev/sr0, as shown here:

```
[root@server1 ~]# ll /dev/cdrom
lrwxrwxrwx    1 root    root    3  Aug   10   12:39   /dev/cdrom -> sr0
[root@server1 ~]# ll /dev/cdrw
lrwxrwxrwx    1 root    root    3  Aug   10   12:39   /dev/cdrw -> sr0
[root@server1 ~]# ll /dev/dvd
lrwxrwxrwx    1 root    root    3  Aug   10   12:39   /dev/dvd -> sr0
[root@server1 ~]# ll /dev/dvdrw
lrwxrwxrwx    1 root    root    3  Aug   10   12:39   /dev/dvdrw -> sr0
[root@server1 ~]#_
```

In addition, CDs and DVDs typically use the iso9660 filesystem type and are read-only when accessed using Linux (recall that you must use disk-burning software to record to a CD or DVD via a CD-RW or DVD-RW drive). Thus, to mount a CD or DVD to a directory, you should use the filesystem type of iso9660 and add the –r (read-only) option to the mount command. To mount a sample CD to the /media/cd directory and view its contents, you could use the following commands:

```
[root@server1 ~]# mount -r -t iso9660 /dev/cdrom /media/cd
[root@server1 ~]# mount
/dev/sda1 on / type ext4 (rw)
proc on /proc type proc (rw)
sysfs on /sys type sysfs (rw)
devpts on /dev/pts type devpts (rw,gid=5,mode=620)
tmpfs on /dev/shm type tmpfs (rw)
none on /proc/sys/fs/binfmt_misc type binfmt_misc (rw)
sunrpc on /var/lib/nfs/rpc_pipefs type rpc_pipefs (rw)
/dev/cdrom on /media/cd type iso9660 (ro)
[root@server1 ~]# ls -l /media/cd
autorun.inf* install* graphics/ jungle/ jungle.txt* joystick/
[root@server1 ~]# umount /media/cd
[root@server1 ~]#_
```

 The /media/cd directory must exist for the mount command to succeed in the previous example.

As with floppies, you can modify the /etc/fstab file such that you can specify only a single argument to the mount command to mount a CD or DVD. Also remember that the mount point directory must not be in use to successfully mount or unmount CDs and DVDs; the fuser command can be used to verify this.

Unlike floppy disks, CDs and DVDs cannot be ejected from the drive until they are properly unmounted, because the mount command locks the CD-ROM, CD-RW, DVD-ROM, or DVD-RW drive as a precaution.

When you insert a CD or DVD while in a GUI environment, it is automatically mounted by the system to a directory underneath the /media directory that is named for the label on the CD or DVD (specified in the disk-burning software). For example, if you insert a DVD with a label of "Pictures" into your system while logged in to a GUI environment, the system will automatically create a /media/Pictures directory and mount the device to this directory, as shown here:

```
[root@server1 ~]# mount
/dev/sda1 on / type ext4 (rw)
proc on /proc type proc (rw)
sysfs on /sys type sysfs (rw)
devpts on /dev/pts type devpts (rw,gid=5,mode=620)
tmpfs on /dev/shm type tmpfs (rw)
none on /proc/sys/fs/binfmt_misc type binfmt_misc (rw)
```

```
sunrpc on /var/lib/nfs/rpc_pipefs type rpc_pipefs (rw)
gvfs-fuse-daemon on /home/bob/.gvfs type fuse.gvfs-fuse-daemon (rw,
nosuid,nodev,user=bob)
/dev/sr0 on /media/Pictures type iso9660 (ro,nosuid,nodev,uhelper=
udisks,uid=501,gid=501,iocharset=utf8,mode=0400,dmode=0500)
[root@server1 ~]#_
```

In addition, the system will place a shortcut to the /media/Pictures directory on your desktop with a DVD icon so that you can easily access the contents of your DVD, as shown in Figure 5-3.

You can right-click the icon that represents the DVD shown in Figure 5-3 and select Eject to unmount the DVD from the /media/Pictures directory and force the DVD drive to eject the DVD.

The iso9660 filesystem type is not limited to CDs and DVDs. You can also create image files, called **ISO images,** that contain other files. Most operating system software available from the Internet, such as Linux distributions and BSD UNIX, is available as an ISO image file. Once downloaded, ISO images can be easily written to a CD or DVD using disk-burning software or mounted and accessed by your Linux system. If you download an ISO image called sample.iso, you can mount it to the /mnt directory as a loopback device, which allows your system to access the contents of the sample.iso file, using the following command:

```
[root@server1 ~]# mount
[root@server1 ~]# mount -o loop -t iso9660 sample.iso /mnt
/dev/sda1 on / type ext4 (rw)
proc on /proc type proc (rw)
```

Figure 5-3 Accessing a DVD within the GNOME desktop environment

Source: Course Technology/Cengage Learning

```
sysfs on /sys type sysfs (rw)
devpts on /dev/pts type devpts (rw,gid=5,mode=620)
tmpfs on /dev/shm type tmpfs (rw)
none on /proc/sys/fs/binfmt_misc type binfmt_misc (rw)
sunrpc on /var/lib/nfs/rpc_pipefs type rpc_pipefs (rw)
/dev/loop0 on /mnt type iso9660 (rw)
[root@localhost ~]# ls /mnt
setup.exe tools binaries
[root@server1 ~]#_
```

You can then manipulate, execute, and edit files within the /mnt directory or copy files from the /mnt directory to another directory to extract the contents of the ISO image file.

To create an ISO image from a directory of files, simply use the **mkisofs command**. The following command creates an ISO image called newimage.iso from all the information in the /data directory with Joliet (-J) and Rock Ridge (-R) support for other computers that may access the ISO image:

```
[root@localhost ~]# mkisofs –RJ –o newimage.iso /data
[root@localhost ~]# mount –o loop –t iso9660 newimage.iso /mnt
/dev/sda1 on / type ext4 (rw)
proc on /proc type proc (rw)
sysfs on /sys type sysfs (rw)
devpts on /dev/pts type devpts (rw,gid=5,mode=620)
tmpfs on /dev/shm type tmpfs (rw)
none on /proc/sys/fs/binfmt_misc type binfmt_misc (rw)
sunrpc on /var/lib/nfs/rpc_pipefs type rpc_pipefs (rw)
/dev/loop0 on /mnt type iso9660 (rw)
[root@server1 ~]#_
```

Working with Hard Disks

Hard disks come in three flavors: PATA, SATA, and SCSI. PATA hard disks must be set to one of four configurations, each of which has a different device file:

- Primary master (/dev/hda)
- Primary slave (/dev/hdb)
- Secondary master (/dev/hdc)
- Secondary slave (/dev/hdd)

SATA and SCSI hard disks typically have faster data transfer speeds than PATA hard disks, and most systems allow for the connection of more than four SATA or SCSI hard disks. As a result of these benefits, both SATA and SCSI hard disks are well suited to Linux servers that require a great deal of storage space for programs and user files. However, SATA and SCSI hard disks have different device files associated with them:

- First SCSI hard disk drive (/dev/sda)
- Second SCSI hard disk drive (/dev/sdb)
- Third SCSI hard disk drive (/dev/sdc)

- Fourth SCSI hard disk drive (/dev/sdd)
- Fifth SCSI hard disk drive (/dev/sde)
- Sixth SCSI hard disk drive (/dev/sdf)
- And so on

Standard Hard Disk Partitioning

Recall that hard disks have the largest storage capacity of any device that you use to store information on a regular basis. As helpful as this storage capacity can be, it also poses some problems; as the size of a disk increases, organization becomes more difficult, and the chance of error increases. To solve these problems, Linux administrators typically divide a hard disk into smaller, more usable sections called **partitions**. Each partition can contain a separate file-system and can be mounted to different mount point directories. Recall from Chapter 2 that Linux requires two partitions at minimum: a partition that is mounted to the root directory (the root partition) and a partition used to hold virtual memory (the swap partition). The swap partition does not require a filesystem because it is written to and maintained by the operating system alone. It is good practice, however, to use more than just two partitions on a Linux system. This division can be useful to:

- Segregate different types of data—for example, home directory data is stored on a separate partition mounted to /home.
- Allow for the use of more than one type of filesystem on one hard disk drive—for example, some filesystems are tuned for database use.
- Reduce the chance that filesystem corruption will render a system unusable; if the partition that is mounted to the /home directory becomes corrupted, it does not affect the system because operating system files are stored on a separate partition mounted to the / directory.
- Speed up access to stored data by keeping filesystems as small as possible.

Segregation of data into physically separate areas of the hard disk drive can be exceptionally useful from an organizational standpoint. Keeping different types of data on different partitions allows you to manipulate one type of data without affecting the rest of the system. This also reduces the likelihood that filesystem corruption will affect all files in the directory tree. Access speed is improved because a smaller area needs to be searched by the magnetic heads in a hard disk drive to locate data. This process is similar to searching for a penny in a 20,000-square-foot warehouse. It takes much less time to find the penny if that warehouse is divided into four separate departments of 5,000 square feet each and you know in which department the penny is located. Searching and maneuvering is much quicker and easier in a smaller, defined space than in a larger one.

On a physical level, hard disks are circular metal platters that spin at a fast speed. Data is read off these disks in concentric circles called **tracks**; each track is divided into **sectors** of information, and sectors are combined into more usable **blocks** of data, as shown in Figure 5-4. Most hard disk drives have several platters inside them, organized on top of each other such that they can be written to simultaneously speed up data transfer. A series consisting of the same concentric track on all of the metal platters inside a hard disk drive is known as a **cylinder**.

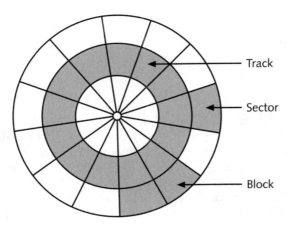

Figure 5-4 The physical areas of a hard disk

Source: Course Technology/Cengage Learning

Today, some PCs contain **Solid-State Drives (SSDs)** instead of hard disks as their main file storage. SSDs use flash memory to store data on non-volatile memory chips instead of metal platters. However, SSDs use circuitry within the drive itself to divide data into logical tracks, sectors, blocks, and cylinders to ensure that the OS can work with SSDs like any hard disk. This allows you to create partitions and filesystems on an SSD in the same way that you would a hard disk. Today, SSDs are much slower at reading and writing data compared with hard disks. As a result, they are typically used on laptops and netbooks and not in Linux servers.

Partition definitions are stored in the first readable sector of the hard disk, known as the Master Boot Record (MBR) or master boot block (MBB). Large hard disks (> 2TB) use a GUID Partition Table (GPT) in place of an MBR to allow for the additional addressing of sectors. If the MBR or GPT area of the hard disk becomes corrupted, the entire contents of the hard disk might be lost.

It is common for Linux servers to have several hard disks. In these situations, it is also common to configure one partition on each hard disk and mount each partition to different directories on the directory tree. Thus, if one partition fails, an entire hard disk can be replaced with a new one and the data retrieved from a backup source.

Recall from Chapter 2 that hard disks can contain up to four primary partitions; to overcome this limitation, you can use an extended partition in place of one of these primary partitions. An extended partition can then contain many more subpartitions called logical drives. Because it is on these partitions that you place a filesystem, there exist device files that refer to the various types of partitions that you can have on a hard disk. These device files start with the name of the hard disk (/dev/hda, /dev/hdb, /dev/sda, /dev/sdb, and so on) and append a number indicating the partition on that hard disk. The first primary partition is given the number 1, the second primary partition is given the number 2, the third primary partition is given the number 3, and the fourth primary partition is given the number 4. If

Partition	PATA Device Name (Assuming /dev/hda)	SATA/SCSI Device Name (Assuming /dev/sda)
1st primary partition	/dev/hda1	/dev/sda1
2nd primary partition	/dev/hda2	/dev/sda2
3rd primary partition	/dev/hda3	/dev/sda3
4th primary partition	/dev/hda4	/dev/sda4
1st logical drive in the extended partition	/dev/hda5	/dev/sda5
2nd logical drive in the extended partition	/dev/hda6	/dev/sda6
3rd logical drive in the extended partition	/dev/hda7	/dev/sda7
4th logical drive in the extended partition	/dev/hda8	/dev/sda8
5th logical drive in the extended partition	/dev/hda9	/dev/sda9
nth logical drive in the extended partition	/dev/hda$n$	/dev/sda$n$

Table 5-5 Common hard disk partition device files for **/dev/hda** and **/dev/sda**

any one of these primary partitions is labeled as an extended partition, the logical drives within are named starting with number 5. Table 5-5 lists some common hard disk partition names.

Note from Table 5-5 that any one of the primary partitions can be labeled as an extended partition. Also, for different disk drives than those listed in Table 5-5 (for example, /dev/hdc), the partition numbers remain the same (for example, /dev/hdc1, /dev/hdc2, and so on).

Hard disk partitions can be created specific to a certain filesystem. To create a partition that will later be formatted with an ext2, ex3, or ext4 filesystem, you should create a Linux partition (also known as type 83). Similarly, you should create a Linux swap partition (also known as type 82) if that partition is intended for use as virtual memory. This explicit choice of partition type allows for partitions that better suit the needs of a filesystem.

A typical Linux hard disk structure for the primary master PATA hard disk (/dev/hda) can contain a partition for the / filesystem (/dev/hda1) and an extended partition (/dev/hda2) that further contains a swap partition (/dev/hda5) and some free space, as shown in Figure 5-5.

A more complicated Linux hard disk structure for the first SCSI hard disk might involve preserving the Windows operating system partition, allowing a user to boot into and use the Linux operating system or boot into and use the Windows operating system. This is known as dual booting and is discussed in Chapter 6.

In Figure 5-6, the Windows partition was created as a primary partition (/dev/sda1) and the Linux partitions are contained within the extended partition (/dev/sda2). Figure 5-6 also creates a separate filesystem for users' home directories mounted to /home (/dev/sda6).

Working with Standard Hard Disk Partitions

Recall that the creation of partitions can be accomplished at installation using the graphical installation program. To create partitions after installation, you can use the **fdisk command**.

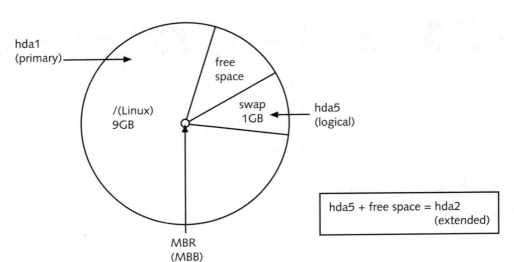

Figure 5-5 A sample Linux partitioning strategy

Source: Course Technology/Cengage Learning

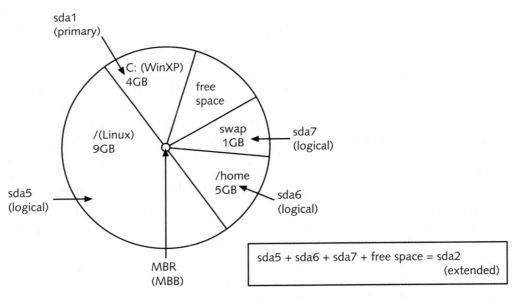

Figure 5-6 A sample dual-boot Linux partitioning strategy

Source: Course Technology/Cengage Learning

To use the `fdisk` command, simply specify the hard disk to partition as an argument. An example of using fdisk with the first SATA hard disk (/dev/sda) is shown in the following output:

```
[root@server1 ~]# fdisk /dev/sda
WARNING: DOS-compatible mode is deprecated. It's strongly recommended to
         switch off the mode (command 'c') and change display units to sec-
         tors (command 'u').

Command (m for help):_
```

Note from the preceding output that the `fdisk` command displays a prompt for the user to accept `fdisk` commands; a list of possible `fdisk` commands can be seen if the user presses the m key at this prompt, as shown in the following example:

```
Command (m for help): m
Command action
   a   toggle a bootable flag
   b   edit bsd disklabel
   c   toggle the dos compatibility flag
   d   delete a partition
   l   list known partition types
   m   print this menu
   n   add a new partition
   o   create a new empty DOS partition table
   p   print the partition table
   q   quit without saving changes
   s   create a new empty Sun disklabel
   t   change a partition's system id
   u   change display/entry units
   v   verify the partition table
   w   write table to disk and exit
   x   extra functionality (experts only)

Command (m for help):_
```

To print a list of the partitions currently set on /dev/sda, you could press the p key at the fdisk prompt:

```
Command (m for help): p

Disk /dev/sda: 80.0 GB, 80026361856 bytes
255 heads, 63 sectors/track, 9729 cylinders
Units = cylinders of 16065 * 512 = 8225280 bytes
Sector size (logical/physical): 512 bytes / 512 bytes
I/O size (minimum/optimal): 512 bytes / 512 bytes
Disk identifier: 0xa84aa84a
```

Device	Boot	Start	End	Blocks	Id	System
/dev/sda1	*	1	3825	30720000	83	Linux
/dev/sda2		3825	4335	4096000	82	Linux swap / Solaris
/dev/sda3		4335	4457	983828+	83	Linux

```
Command (m for help):_
```

Notice that the device names appear on the left side of the preceding output, including the partition that is booted to (/dev/sda1), the start and end locations of partitions on the physical hard disk (start and end cylinders), the number of total blocks for storing information in the partition, as well as the partition type and description (83 is a Linux partition; 82 is a Linux swap partition). A Linux partition can contain a Linux filesystem—for example, ext4.

To remove the /dev/sda3 partition and all the data contained on the filesystem within, you could use the d key, as noted earlier:

```
Command (m for help): d
Partition number (1-4): 3

Command (m for help): p

Disk /dev/sda: 80.0 GB, 80026361856 bytes
255 heads, 63 sectors/track, 9729 cylinders
Units = cylinders of 16065 * 512 = 8225280 bytes
Sector size (logical/physical): 512 bytes / 512 bytes
I/O size (minimum/optimal): 512 bytes / 512 bytes
Disk identifier: 0xa84aa84a

   Device Boot    Start      End      Blocks   Id  System
/dev/sda1     *        1     3825    30720000   83  Linux
/dev/sda2            3825     4335     4096000   82  Linux swap / Solaris
Command (m for help):_
```

To create an extended partition using the fourth primary partition (/dev/sda4) with two logical drives (/dev/sda5 and /dev/sda6), you could use the n key, as noted earlier, and specify the partition to create, the starting cylinder on the hard disk, and the size in blocks (+10G makes a 10GB partition):

```
Command (m for help): n
Command action
e    extended
p    primary partition (1-4)
e
Partition number (1-4): 4
First cylinder (4335-9729, default 4335): 4335
Last cylinder, +cylinders or +size{K,M,G} (4335-9729, default 9729): +10G

Command (m for help): p

Disk /dev/sda: 80.0 GB, 80026361856 bytes
255 heads, 63 sectors/track, 9729 cylinders
Units = cylinders of 16065 * 512 = 8225280 bytes
Sector size (logical/physical): 512 bytes / 512 bytes
I/O size (minimum/optimal): 512 bytes / 512 bytes
Disk identifier: 0xa84aa84a

   Device Boot    Start      End      Blocks   Id  System
/dev/sda1     *        1     3825    30720000   83  Linux
/dev/sda2            3825     4335     4096000   82  Linux swap / Solaris
/dev/sda4            4335     5551     9771383+   5  Extended

Command (m for help): n
```

```
Command action
l    logical (5 or over)
p    primary partition (1-4)
l
First cylinder (4335-5551, default 4335): 4335
Last cylinder, +cylinders or +size{K,M,G} (4335-5551, default 5551):+7GB

Command (m for help): p

Disk /dev/sda: 80.0 GB, 80026361856 bytes
255 heads, 63 sectors/track, 9729 cylinders
Units = cylinders of 16065 * 512 = 8225280 bytes
Sector size (logical/physical): 512 bytes / 512 bytes
I/O size (minimum/optimal): 512 bytes / 512 bytes
Disk identifier: 0xa84aa84a

   Device Boot      Start         End      Blocks   Id  System
/dev/sda1   *           1        3825    30720000   83  Linux
/dev/sda2            3825        4335     4096000   82  Linux swap / Solaris
/dev/sda4            4335        5551     9771383+   5  Extended
/dev/sda5            4335        5249     7345537   83  Linux

Command (m for help): n
Command action
l    logical (5 or over)
p    primary partition (1-4)
l
First cylinder (5250-5551, default 5250): 5250
Last cylinder, +cylinders or +size{K,M,G} (5250-5551, default 5551): _
Using default value 5551

Command (m for help): p

Disk /dev/sda: 80.0 GB, 80026361856 bytes
255 heads, 63 sectors/track, 9729 cylinders
Units = cylinders of 16065 * 512 = 8225280 bytes
Sector size (logical/physical): 512 bytes / 512 bytes
I/O size (minimum/optimal): 512 bytes / 512 bytes
Disk identifier: 0xa84aa84a

   Device Boot      Start         End      Blocks   Id  System
/dev/sda1   *           1        3825    30720000   83  Linux
/dev/sda2            3825        4335     4096000   82  Linux swap / Solaris
/dev/sda4            4335        5551     9771383+   5  Extended
/dev/sda5            4335        5249     7345537   83  Linux
/dev/sda6            5250        5551     2425783+  83  Linux

Command (m for help):_
```

Notice from the preceding output that the default type for new partitions created with fdisk is 83 (Linux); to change this, you can type the t key at the fdisk prompt. To change the /dev/sda6 partition to type 82 (Linux swap), you can do the following at the fdisk prompt:

```
Command (m for help): t
Partition number (1-6): 6
Hex code (type L to list codes): L
```

0	Empty	24	NEC DOS	81	Minix / old Lin	bf	Solaris	
1	FAT12	39	Plan 9	82	Linux swap / So	c1	DRDOS/sec (FAT-	
2	XENIX root	3c	PartitionMagic	83	Linux	c4	DRDOS/sec (FAT-	
3	XENIX usr	40	Venix 80286	84	OS/2 hidden C:	c6	DRDOS/sec (FAT-	
4	FAT16 <32M	41	PPC PReP Boot	85	Linux extended	c7	Syrinx	
5	Extended	42	SFS	86	NTFS volume set	da	Non-FS data	
6	FAT16	4d	QNX4.x	87	NTFS volume set	db	CP/M / CTOS / .	
7	HPFS/NTFS	4e	QNX4.x 2nd part	88	Linux plaintext	de	Dell Utility	
8	AIX	4f	QNX4.x 3rd part	8e	Linux LVM	df	BootIt	
9	AIX bootable	50	OnTrack DM	93	Amoeba	e1	DOS access	
a	OS/2 Boot Manag	51	OnTrack DM6 Aux	94	Amoeba BBT	e3	DOS R/O	
b	W95 FAT32	52	CP/M	9f	BSD/OS	e4	SpeedStor	
c	W95 FAT32 (LBA)	53	OnTrack DM6 Aux	a0	IBM Thinkpad hi	eb	BeOS fs	
e	W95 FAT16 (LBA)	54	OnTrackDM6	a5	FreeBSD	ee	GPT	
f	W95 Ext'd (LBA)	55	EZ-Drive	a6	OpenBSD	ef	EFI (FAT-12/16/	
10	OPUS	56	Golden Bow	a7	NeXTSTEP	f0	Linux/PA-RISC b	
11	Hidden FAT12	5c	Priam Edisk	a8	Darwin UFS	f1	SpeedStor	
12	Compaq diagnost	61	SpeedStor	a9	NetBSD	f4	SpeedStor	
14	Hidden FAT16 <3	63	GNU HURD or Sys	ab	Darwin boot	f2	DOS secondary	
16	Hidden FAT16	64	Novell Netware	af	HFS / HFS+	fb	VMware VMFS	
17	Hidden HPFS/NTF	65	Novell Netware	b7	BSDI fs	fc	VMware VMKCORE	
18	AST SmartSleep	70	DiskSecure Mult	b8	BSDI swap	fd	Linux raid auto	
1b	Hidden W95 FAT3	75	PC/IX	bb	Boot Wizard hid	fe	LANstep	
1c	Hidden W95 FAT3	80	Old Minix	be	Solaris boot	ff	BBT	
1e	Hidden W95 FAT1							

```
Hex code (type L to list codes): 82
Changed system type of partition 6 to 82 (Linux swap / Solaris)
Command (m for help): p

Disk /dev/sda: 80.0 GB, 80026361856 bytes
255 heads, 63 sectors/track, 9729 cylinders
Units = cylinders of 16065 * 512 = 8225280 bytes
Sector size (logical/physical): 512 bytes / 512 bytes
I/O size (minimum/optimal): 512 bytes / 512 bytes
Disk identifier: 0xa84aa84a

   Device  Boot    Start    End    Blocks     Id  System
/dev/sda1    *        1     3825   30720000   83  Linux
/dev/sda2           3825    4335    4096000   82  Linux swap / Solaris
/dev/sda4           4335    5551    9771383+    5  Extended
```

```
/dev/sda5                4335      5249      7345537   83    Linux
/dev/sda6                5250      5551      2425783+  82    Linux swap / Solaris

Command (m for help):_
```

Finally, to save partition changes to the hard disk and attempt to reload the new partition information back into memory, simply use the w key at the fdisk prompt:

```
Command (m for help): w
The partition table has been altered!

Calling ioctl() to re-read partition table.

WARNING: Re-reading the partition table failed with error 16:
   Device or resource busy.
The kernel still uses the old table. The new table will be used at
the next reboot or after you run partprobe(8) or kpartx(8)
Syncing disks.
[root@server1 ~]#_
```

If the fdisk command indicates that the new partition information must be reloaded manually (as in the preceding example), simply reboot your machine. This is the most reliable way to ensure that the MBR or GPT is reloaded into memory successfully. For this reason, it is good form to always reboot your machine after running fdisk.

An easier alternative to fdisk is the **cfdisk command,** which displays the interactive graphical utility shown in Figure 5-7. You can use this utility to quickly create, manipulate, and delete partitions using choices at the bottom of the screen that you can navigate using your cursor keys. As with fdisk, after making changes using the cfdisk command, you should reboot your system to ensure that the MBR or GPT is reloaded into memory successfully.

After the machine has rebooted, you can then use the mkfs, mount, and umount commands discussed earlier, specifying the partition device file as an argument. To create an ext4 filesystem on the /dev/sda5 partition created earlier, you can use the following command:

```
[root@server1 ~]# mkfs -t ext4 /dev/sda5
mke2fs 1.41.10 (10-Feb-2009)
Filesystem label=
OS type: Linux
Block size=4096 (log=2)
Fragment size=4096 (log=2)
Stride=0 blocks, Stripe width=0 blocks
459648 inodes, 1836384 blocks
91819 blocks (5.00%) reserved for the super user
First data block=0
Maximum filesystem blocks=1883242496
57 block groups
32768 blocks per group, 32768 fragments per group
8064 inodes per group
Superblock backups stored on blocks:
        32768, 98304, 163840, 229376, 294912, 819200, 884736, 1605632
```

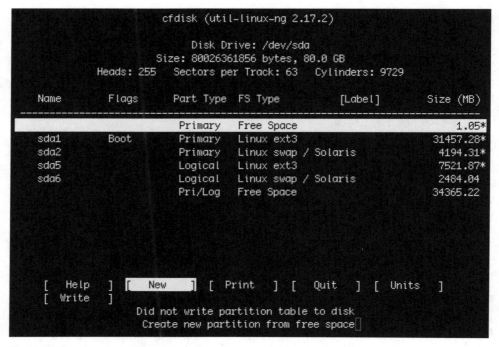

Figure 5-7 The cfdisk utility

Source: Course Technology/Cengage Learning

```
Writing inode tables: done
Creating journal (32768 blocks): done
Writing superblocks and filesystem accounting information: done
```

This filesystem will be automatically checked every 35 mounts or 180 days, whichever comes first. Use tune2fs -c or -i to override.
[root@server1 ~]#_

To mount this ext4 filesystem to a new mount point directory called /data and view the contents, you can use the following commands:

```
[root@server1 ~]# mkdir /data
[root@server1 ~]# mount -t ext4 /dev/sda5 /data
[root@server1 ~]# mount
/dev/sda1 on / type ext4 (rw)
proc on /proc type proc (rw)
sysfs on /sys type sysfs (rw)
devpts on /dev/pts type devpts (rw,gid=5,mode=620)
tmpfs on /dev/shm type tmpfs (rw)
none on /proc/sys/fs/binfmt_misc type binfmt_misc (rw)
sunrpc on /var/lib/nfs/rpc_pipefs type rpc_pipefs (rw)
/dev/sda5 on /data type ext4 (rw)
[root@server1 ~]# ls -F /data
```

```
lost+found/
[root@server1 ~]#_
```

To allow the system to mount this filesystem automatically at every boot, simply edit the
/etc/fstab file such that it has the following entry for /dev/sda5:

```
[root@server1 ~]# cat /etc/fstab
#
# /etc/fstab
# Created by anaconda on Mon Aug 2 09:34:19 2010
#
# Accessible filesystems, by reference, are maintained under'/dev/disk'
# See man pages fstab(5), findfs(8), mount(8) and/or blkid(8) for info
#
/dev/sda1     /              ext4     defaults        1 1
/dev/sda2     swap           swap     defaults        0 0
tmpfs         /dev/shm       tmpfs    defaults        0 0
devpts        /dev/pts       devpts   gid=5,mode=620  0 0
sysfs         /sys           sysfs    defaults        0 0
proc          /proc          proc     defaults        0 0
/dev/fd0      /media/floppy  auto     noauto          0 0
/dev/sda5     /data          ext4     defaults        0 0
[root@server1 ~]#_
```

Although swap partitions do not contain a filesystem, you must still be prepared to swap
partitions and activate them for use on the Linux system. To do this, you can use the
mkswap command to prepare the swap partition, and the **swapon command** to activate it.
To prepare and activate the /dev/sda6 partition that we created earlier as virtual memory,
you can use the following commands:

```
[root@server1 ~]# mkswap /dev/sda6
Setting up swapspace version 1, size = 2425776 KiB
no label, UUID=2fdc6d60-f7fa-4ee4-93ad-4191e60888db
[root@server1 ~]# swapon /dev/sda6
[root@server1 ~]# mount
```

 You can also use the **swapoff command** to deactivate a swap
partition.

Next, you can edit the /etc/fstab file to ensure that the new /dev/sda6 partition is activated as
virtual memory, as shown here:

```
[root@server1 ~]# cat /etc/fstab
#
# /etc/fstab
# Created by anaconda on Mon Aug 2 09:34:19 2010
#
```

```
# Accessible filesystems, by reference, are maintained under'/dev/disk'
# See man pages fstab(5), findfs(8), mount(8) and/or blkid(8) for info
#
/dev/sda1         /              ext4      defaults         1 1
/dev/sda2         swap           swap      defaults         0 0
tmpfs             /dev/shm       tmpfs     defaults         0 0
devpts            /dev/pts       devpts    gid=5,mode=620   0 0
sysfs             /sys           sysfs     defaults         0 0
proc              /proc          proc      defaults         0 0
/dev/fd0          /media/floppy  auto      noauto           0 0
/dev/sda5         /data          ext4      defaults         0 0
/dev/sda6         swap           swap      defaults         0 0
[root@server1 ~]#_
```

Working with the LVM

In the previous section, you learned how to create standard hard disk partitions. You also learned how to create filesystems on those partitions and mount the filesystems to a directory within the Linux filesystem hierarchy.

Instead of creating and mounting filesystems that reside on standard partitions, you can use the **Logical Volume Manager** (**LVM**) to create volumes. These volumes can contain a filesystem and be mounted to directories within the Linux filesystem hierarchy. Using volumes to host filesystems is far more flexible than using standard partitions because it allows you to select free space from unused partitions across multiple hard disks in your computer. This free space is then pooled together into a single group from which volumes can be created. These volumes can then be formatted with a filesystem and mounted to a directory on the Linux filesystem hierarchy. Furthermore, additional hard disks can easily be added to the LVM, where existing volumes can take advantage of the additional storage space.

The LVM consists of several different components:

- **Physical volumes** (**PVs**) are unused partitions on hard disks that the LVM can use to store information.

- A **volume group** (**VG**) contains one or more PVs. It represents the pool of hard disk storage space that is available to the LVM for creating logical volumes. Additional PVs can easily be added to a VG after creation.

- **Logical volumes** (**LVs**) are the usable volumes that are created by the LVM from the available storage space within a VG. LVs contain a filesystem and are mounted to a directory in the Linux filesystem hierarchy. In addition, LVs can be resized easily by the LVM to use more or less storage space.

The LVM subsystem in Linux manages the storage of all data that is saved to LVs. The physical location of the data is transparent to the user. Furthermore, the LVM has error correction abilities that minimize the chance that data will become corrupted or lost. Figure 5-8 illustrates the relationships between LVM components in a sample LVM configuration that creates four different PVs from the standard partitions on three different hard disks. These PVs are added to a VG that is divided into three LVs that are each mounted to a directory on the Linux filesystem hierarchy (/directory1, /directory2, and /directory3).

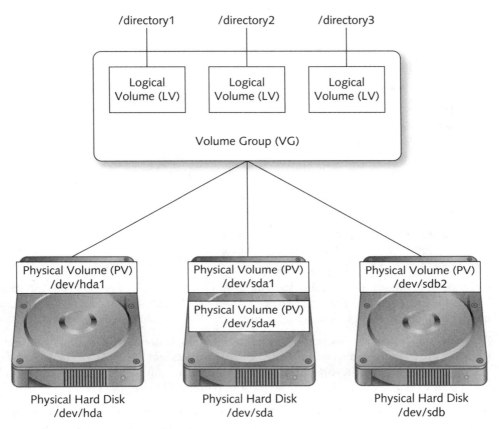

Figure 5-8 A sample LVM configuration

Source: Course Technology/Cengage Learning

To configure the LVM, you must first create one or more PVs that reference an unused partition on a hard disk in your computer. For example, suppose you used the fdisk command to create a new partition called /dev/sda4. Rather than placing a filesystem on /dev/sda4, you could instead allow the LVM to use the /dev/sda4 partition using the **pvcreate command**, as shown here:

```
root@server1 ~]# pvcreate /dev/sda4
Physical volume "/dev/sda4" successfully created
[root@server1 ~]#_
```

You should use the pvcreate command to create PVs for each unused partition that you want to be used by the LVM. For simplicity in code output, we will only create a single PV in this section to demonstrate the configuration of LVM.

The **pvdisplay command** can be used to display detailed information about each PV. The following pvdisplay command indicates that /dev/sda4 has 32GB of available space:

```
[root@server1 ~]# pvdisplay
"/dev/sda4" is a new physical volume of "32.00 GiB"
--- NEW Physical volume ---
```

```
PV Name          /dev/sda4
VG Name
PV Size          32.00 GiB
Allocatable      NO
PE Size          0
Total PE         0
Free PE          0
Allocated PE     0
PV UUID          YZDmIG-0qFU-54AT-ioB6-bjKa-sHcC-i8IJo0
[root@server1 ~]#_
```

Once you have created PVs, you can create a VG that uses the space in the PVs using the **vgcreate command**. For example, to create a VG called vg00 that uses the /dev/sda4 PV, you could use the following vgcreate command:

```
[root@server1 ~]# vgcreate vg00 /dev/sda4
Volume group "vg00" successfully created
[root@server1 ~]#_
```

To create a VG that uses multiple PVs, simply add multiple device arguments to the vgcreate command. For example, the vgcreate vg00 /dev/sda5 /dev/sdb1 /dev/sdc3 command would create a VG called vg00 that uses three PVs (/dev/sda5, /dev/sdb1, and /dev/sdc3).

When creating a VG, it is important to choose the block size for saving data because it cannot be safely changed later. This is called the **physical extent (PE) size** of the VG. A large PE size results in larger write operations and a larger maximum filesystem size for LVs. For example, a PE size of 32MB will allow for a maximum LV size of 2TB.

By default, the vgcreate command chooses an appropriate PE size according to the current sizes of the PVs that are associated with the VG, but you can use the -s or -physicalextentsize options to the vgcreate command to select a different PE size during VG creation.

The **vgdisplay command** can be used to display detailed information about each VG. The following vgdisplay command indicates that /dev/sda4 has over 31GB of available space:

```
[root@server1 ~]# vgdisplay
--- Volume group ---
  VG Name               vg00
  System ID
  Format                lvm2
  Metadata Areas        1
  Metadata Sequence No  1
  VG Access             read/write
  VG Status             resizable
  MAX LV                0
  Cur LV                0
  Open LV               0
  Max PV                0
  Cur PV                1
  Act PV                1
```

```
VG Size                32.00 GiB
PE Size                4.00 MiB
Total PE               8192
Alloc PE / Size        0 / 0
Free PE / Size         8192 / 32.00 GiB
VG UUID                C2jrUC-LZmR-0tSX-bLqj-43S0-8U7i-0ajUgP
[root@server1 ~]#_
```

Next, you can create LVs from the available space in your VG using the **lvcreate com-mand** and view your results using the **lvdisplay command**. The following commands cre-ate an LV called "data" that uses 15GB of space from vg00, as well as an LV called "extras" that uses 16GB of space from vg00, and displays the results.

```
[root@server1 ~]# lvcreate -L 15GB -n data vg00
  Logical volume "data" created
[root@server1 ~]# lvcreate -L 16GB -n extras vg00
  Logical volume "extras" created
[root@server1 ~]# lvdisplay
--- Logical volume ---
  LV Name              /dev/vg00/data
  VG Name              vg00
  LV UUID              hMCr4Z-JNrO-lVcf-5SZk-8UJg-B0ri-Am3siP
  LV Write Access      read/write
  LV Status            available
  # open               0
  LV Size              15.00 GiB
  Current LE           3840
  Segments             1
  Allocation           inherit
  Read ahead sectors   auto
  - currently set to   256
  Block device         253:0

  --- Logical volume ---
  LV Name              /dev/vg00/extras
  VG Name              vg00
  LV UUID              yUH5xW-U81b-CD3t-N22K-70gD-xHpm-TTHQca
  LV Write Access      read/write
  LV Status            available
  # open               0
  LV Size              16.00 GiB
  Current LE           4096
  Segments             1
  Allocation           inherit
  Read ahead sectors   auto
  - currently set to   256
  Block device         253:1

[root@server1 ~]#_
```

Notice from the preceding output that the new VGs can be accessed using the device files /dev/vg00/data and /dev/vg00/extras. You can also refer to your new VGs using the device files /dev/mapper/vg00-data and /dev/mapper/vg00-extras, which are typically used by the system when accessing the filesystems on your VGs.

You can work with these files as you would normally work with any other hard disk partition device file. For example, to create an ext4 filesystem on these devices and mount them to the appropriate directories on the filesystem, you could use the following commands:

```
[root@server1 ~]# mke2fs -t ext4 /dev/vg00/data
mke2fs 1.41.10 (10-Feb-2009)
Filesystem label=
OS type: Linux
Block size=4096 (log=2)
Fragment size=4096 (log=2)
Stride=0 blocks, Stripe width=0 blocks
983040 inodes, 3932160 blocks
196608 blocks (5.00%) reserved for the super user
First data block=0
Maximum filesystem blocks=4026531840
120 block groups
32768 blocks per group, 32768 fragments per group
8192 inodes per group
Superblock backups stored on blocks:
        32768, 98304, 163840, 229376, 294912, 819200, 884736, 1605632,
        2654208
Writing inode tables: done
Creating journal (32768 blocks): done
Writing superblocks and filesystem accounting information: done
This filesystem will be automatically checked every 33 mounts or
180 days, whichever comes first. Use tune2fs -c or -i to override.
[root@server1 ~]# mke2fs -t ext4 /dev/vg00/extras
mke2fs 1.41.10 (10-Feb-2009)
Filesystem label=
OS type: Linux
Block size=4096 (log=2)
Fragment size=4096 (log=2)
Stride=0 blocks, Stripe width=0 blocks
1048576 inodes, 4194304 blocks
209715 blocks (5.00%) reserved for the super user
First data block=0
Maximum filesystem blocks=0
128 block groups
32768 blocks per group, 32768 fragments per group
8192 inodes per group
Superblock backups stored on blocks:
        32768, 98304, 163840, 229376, 294912, 819200, 884736, 1605632,
        2654208, 4096000
Writing inode tables: done
```

```
Creating journal (32768 blocks): done
Writing superblocks and filesystem accounting information: done
This filesystem will be automatically checked every 35 mounts or
180 days, whichever comes first. Use tune2fs -c or -i to override.
[root@server1 ~]# mkdir /data
[root@server1 ~]# mkdir /extras
[root@server1 ~]# mount /dev/vg00/data /data
[root@server1 ~]# mount /dev/vg00/extras /extras
[root@server1 ~]# mount
/dev/sda1 on / type ext4 (rw)
proc on /proc type proc (rw)
sysfs on /sys type sysfs (rw)
devpts on /dev/pts type devpts (rw,gid=5,mode=620)
tmpfs on /dev/shm type tmpfs (rw)
none on /proc/sys/fs/binfmt_misc type binfmt_misc (rw)
sunrpc on /var/lib/nfs/rpc_pipefs type rpc_pipefs (rw)
/dev/mapper/vg00-data on /data type ext4 (rw)
/dev/mapper/vg00-extras on /extras type ext4 (rw)
[root@server1 ~]#_
```

Next, you can edit the /etc/fstab file to ensure that your new logical volumes are automatically mounted at system startup, as shown here:

```
[root@server1 ~]# cat /etc/fstab
#
# /etc/fstab
# Created by anaconda on Mon Aug 2 09:34:19 2010
#
# Accessible filesystems, by reference, are maintained under'/dev/disk'
# See man pages fstab(5), findfs(8), mount(8) and/or blkid(8) for info
#
/dev/sda1            /               ext4      defaults            1 1
/dev/sda2            swap            swap      defaults            0 0
tmpfs               /dev/shm        tmpfs     defaults            0 0
devpts              /dev/pts        devpts    gid=5,mode=620      0 0
sysfs               /sys            sysfs     defaults            0 0
proc                /proc           proc      defaults            0 0
/dev/fd0            /media/floppy   auto      noauto              0 0
/dev/sda5           /data           ext4      defaults            0 0
/dev/sda6           swap            swap      defaults            0 0
/dev/vg00/data      /data           ext4      defaults            0 0
/dev/vg00/extras    /extras         ext4      defaults            0 0
[root@server1 ~]#_
```

Three other useful commands that can display information about the PVs, VGs, and LVs that are configured on your system are the **pvscan command**, the **vgscan command**, and the **lvscan command**, respectively. Also, you can add additional storage space to your LVs after configuration. More specifically, you can add another PV using the pvcreate command, add this PV to your existing VG using the **vgextend command**, and then increase the size of your LVs to use the additional space using the **lvextend command**. Before using these commands, always consult the manual pages to ensure that you are using the command options and arguments that will perform the desired actions.

Working with USB and FireWire-Based Storage Devices

Because of their large capacity and portability, removable storage devices are commonly used today to store backups of data, pictures, music, movies, programs, and documents. These devices, which typically connect to your PC via high-speed USB or FireWire cables, include the following:

- Flash memory drives
- External hard drives
- Digital cameras (that contain flash memory cards)
- Media players

Nearly all removable storage device manufacturers emulate the SCSI protocol in the firmware of the device itself. As a result, Linux recognizes removable media devices that connect to your PC via USB or FireWire cables as SCSI devices and automatically mounts them to a new directory under the /media directory named for the label on the device.

Consider the example shown in Figure 5-9 that shows the filesystems available when you double-click the Computer icon in the GNOME desktop environment.

In addition to the / filesystem and the two logical volumes stored in the vg00 volume group, Figure 5-9 shows a USB flash memory drive with the label BLUE2GB, two different flash memory cards from the KODAK EasyShare CX7330 digital camera, and an Apple iPod. Because these were inserted into the computer in this same order, Linux mounted them as follows:

- The filesystem on the USB flash memory drive was recognized as /dev/sdb1 and mounted to the /media/BLUE2GB directory.
- The filesystems on the two memory cards within the Kodak EasyShare CX7330 digital camera were recognized as /dev/sdc1 and /dev/sdc2 and were mounted to the /media/Kingston and /media/827462-28 directories, respectively (Kingston and 827462-28 were the labels on the flash memory cards within the Kodak EasyShare CX7330 digital camera).
- The filesystem on the Apple iPod was recognized as /dev/sdd1 and mounted to the /media/Jason_iPod directory (Jason_iPod was the label on the iPod filesystem).

As you can see from this example, it is difficult to tell how Linux will recognize USB and FireWire removable media devices until they are plugged into the computer because there could be multiple removable devices plugged into the computer at the same time. Because it is common to work with removable media devices within a GUI environment, understanding the device names and mount point directories used by the devices themselves is often irrelevant. You can work with the files on removable media devices by accessing the appropriate icons that represent the devices in the GUI environment. Before unplugging the removable media device, you can right-click the icon that represents it within the GUI environment and choose Safely Remove Drive to unmount the volume.

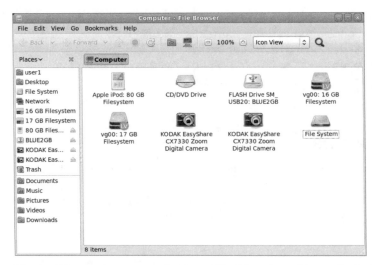

Figure 5-9 Viewing mounted USB and FireWire removable media devices

Source: Course Technology/Cengage Learning

However, if you want to use commands to work with the files on removable media devices, or if you want to manipulate the partitions and filesystems on them, then you must know the device file used to identify each device as well as the mount point directory for each mounted device. In that case, it is best to plug your removable media device into your computer and run the mount command to identify the device file that is used to identify the removable media device as well as the mount point directory that it was automatically mounted to. You can then use the filesystem management commands within this chapter to manipulate the device. For example, you could unmount the USB flash memory drive, reformat it with the ext4 filesystem, and remount it to the /media/FlashDrive directory using the following commands:

```
[root@server1 ~]# umount /dev/sdb1
[root@server1 ~]# mke2fs -t ext4 /dev/sdb1
mke2fs 1.41.10 (10-Feb-2009)
Filesystem label=
OS type: Linux
Block size=4096 (log=2)
Fragment size=4096 (log=2)
Stride=0 blocks, Stripe width=0 blocks
122400 inodes, 489464 blocks
24473 blocks (5.00%) reserved for the super user
First data block=0
Maximum filesystem blocks=503316480
15 block groups
32768 blocks per group, 32768 fragments per group
8160 inodes per group
Superblock backups stored on blocks:
        32768, 98304, 163840, 229376, 294912
Writing inode tables: done
Creating journal (8192 blocks): done
Writing superblocks and filesystem accounting information: done
```

```
This filesystem will be automatically checked every 33 mounts or
180 days, whichever comes first. Use tune2fs -c or -i to override.
[root@server1 ~]# mkdir /media/FlashDrive
[root@server1 ~]# mount -t ext4 /dev/sdb1 /media/FlashDrive
[root@server1 ~]#_
```

Monitoring Filesystems

After filesystems are created on devices and those devices are mounted to the directory tree, they should be checked periodically for errors, disk space usage, and inode usage. This minimizes the problems that can occur as a result of a damaged filesystem and reduces the likelihood that a file cannot be saved due to insufficient disk space.

Disk Usage

Several filesystems can be mounted to the directory tree. As mentioned earlier, the more filesystems that are used, the less likely a corrupted filesystem will interfere with normal system operations. Conversely, using more filesystems typically results in less hard disk space per filesystem and might result in system errors if certain filesystems fill up with data. Many users create filesystems for the /, /usr, and /var directories during installation. The /usr directory contains most utilities and installed programs on a Linux system, and should have enough space for future software installations. The /var directory grows in size continuously as it stores log files. Old log files should be removed periodically to leave room for new ones. The / filesystem is the most vital of these and should always contain a great deal of free space used as working space for the operating system. As a result, the / filesystem should be monitored frequently. If free space on the / filesystem falls below 10 percent, the system might suffer from poorer performance or cease to operate.

The easiest method for monitoring free space by mounted filesystems is to use the **df** (**disk free space**) **command**, as shown in the following output:

```
[root@server1 ~]# df
Filesystem              1K-blocks     Used   Available   Use%   Mounted on
/dev/sda1               30237648   7227280    21474368    26%   /
tmpfs                     480640       272      480368     1%   /dev/shm
/dev/mapper/vg00-data   15481840    169456   14525952     2%   /data
/dev/mapper/vg00-extras 16513960    176108   15498992     2%   /extras
[root@server1 ~]#_
```

From the preceding output, the only filesystems used are the / filesystem, the /data filesystem, and the /extras filesystem; the /usr and /var directories are simply directories on the / filesystem, which increases the importance of monitoring the / filesystem. Because the / filesystem is 26 percent used in the preceding output, there is no immediate concern. However, log files and software installed in the future will increase this number and might warrant the purchase of an additional hard disk for data to reside on.

Alternatively, you can view the output of the df command in a more user-friendly (or human-readable) format by using the –h option, which prints sizes in the most convenient format (G = gigabyte, M = megabyte), as shown here:

```
[root@server1 ~]# df -h
Filesystem                  Size   Used   Avail   Use%   Mounted on
/dev/sda1                   29G    6.9G   21G     26%    /
tmpfs                       470M   272K   470M    1%     /dev/shm
/dev/mapper/vg00-data       15G    166M   14G     2%     /data
/dev/mapper/vg00-extras     16G    172M   15G     2%     /extras
[root@server1 ~]#_
```

It is important to remember that the df command only views mounted filesystems; thus, to get statistics on free disk space on a floppy filesystem, you should mount it prior to viewing the output of the df command:

```
[root@server1 ~]# mount /dev/fd0
[root@server1 ~]# df
Filesystem                  1K-blocks     Used   Available Use%  Mounted on
/dev/sda1                   30237648   7227280    21474368  26%  /
tmpfs                         480640       272      480368   1%  /dev/shm
/dev/mapper/vg00-data       15481840    169456    14525952   2%  /data
/dev/mapper/vg00-extras     16513960    176108    15498992   2%  /extras
/dev/fd0                        1412        17        1323   2%  /mnt/floppy
[root@server1 ~]# umount /dev/fd0
[root@server1 ~]# df
Filesystem                  1K-blocks     Used   Available  Use%  Mounted on
/dev/sda1                   30237648   7227280    21474368   26%  /
tmpfs                         480640       272      480368    1%  /dev/shm
/dev/mapper/vg00-data       15481840    169456    14525952    2%  /data
/dev/mapper/vg00-extras     16513960    176108    15498992    2%  /extras
[root@server1 ~]#_
```

If a filesystem is approaching full capacity, it might be useful to examine which directories on that filesystem are taking up the most disk space so that you can remove files or move them from that directory to another filesystem that has sufficient space. To view the size of a directory and its contents in Kilobytes, you can use the **du (directory usage) command**. If the directory is large, you should use either the more or less command to view the output page-by-page, as shown with the following /usr directory:

```
[root@server1 ~]# du /usr |more
4          /usr/include/ncursesw
120        /usr/include/rpc
64         /usr/include/arpa
260        /usr/include/QtTest
20         /usr/include/QtAssistant
156        /usr/include/QtWebKit
76         /usr/include/gconf/2/gconf
80         /usr/include/gconf/2
```

```
84              /usr/include/gconf
24              /usr/include/xulrunner-sdk-1.9.2/mozilla/storage
108             /usr/include/xulrunner-sdk-1.9.2/mozilla
132             /usr/include/xulrunner-sdk-1.9.2/oggz
24              /usr/include/xulrunner-sdk-1.9.2/ogg
60              /usr/include/xulrunner-sdk-1.9.2/oggplay
20              /usr/include/xulrunner-sdk-1.9.2/sydneyaudio
16              /usr/include/xulrunner-sdk-1.9.2/vorbis
60              /usr/include/xulrunner-sdk-1.9.2/fishsound
112             /usr/include/xulrunner-sdk-1.9.2/theora
20996           /usr/include/xulrunner-sdk-1.9.2
92              /usr/include/gupnp-1.0/libgupnp
96              /usr/include/gupnp-1.0
48              /usr/include/pixman-1
116             /usr/include/sasl
--More--
```

To view only a summary of the total size of a directory, simply use the –s switch to the du command, as shown in the following example with the /usr directory:

```
[root@server1 ~]# du -s /usr
5719324  /usr
[root@server1 ~]# _
```

As with the df command, the du command also accepts the –h option to make the view more human-readable; the following indicates that the total size of the /usr directory is 5.5 GB:

```
[root@server1 ~]# du -hs /usr
5.5G /usr
[root@server1 ~]# _
```

Recall that every filesystem has an inode table that contains the inodes for the files and directories on the filesystem; this inode table is made during filesystem creation and is usually proportionate to the size of the filesystem. Each file and directory uses one inode; thus, a filesystem with several small files might use up all of the inodes in the inode table and prevent new files from being created on the filesystem. To view the total number of inodes and free inodes for an ext2, ext3, or ext4 filesystem, you can use the dumpe2fs command with the –h switch, as shown in the following output:

```
[root@server1 ~]# df
Filesystem              1K-blocks        Used    Available  Use% Mounted on
/dev/sda1                30237648     7227280     21474368   26% /
tmpfs                      480640         272       480368    1% /dev/shm
/dev/mapper/vg00-data    15481840      169456     14525952    2% /data
/dev/mapper/vg00-extras  16513960      176108     15498992    2% /extras
[root@server1 ~]# dumpe2fs -h /dev/sda1
dumpe2fs 1.41.10 (10-Feb-2009)
```

```
Filesystem volume name:     <none>
Last mounted on:            /
Filesystem UUID:            db545f1d-c1ee-4b70-acbe-3dc61b41db20
Filesystem magic number:    0xEF53
Filesystem revision #:      1 (dynamic)
Filesystem  features:       has_journal  ext_attr  resize_inode  dir_index
file type needs_recovery extent flex_bg sparse_super large_file huge_file
uninit_bg dir_nlink extra_isize
Filesystem flags:           signed_directory_hash
Default mount options:      user_xattr acl
Filesystem state:           clean
Errors behavior:            Continue
Filesystem OS type:         Linux
Inode count:                1921360
Block count:                7680000
Reserved block count:       384000
Free blocks:                5752659
Free inodes:                1663809
First block:                0
Block size:                 4096
Fragment size:              4096
Reserved GDT blocks:        1022
Blocks per group:           32768
Fragments per group:        32768
Inodes per group:           8176
Inode blocks per group:     511
Flex block group size:      16
Filesystem created:         Mon Aug 2 09:27:13 2010
Last mount time:            Thu Aug 12 10:55:03 2010
Last write time:            Mon Aug 2 10:24:23 2010
Mount count:                20
Maximum mount count:        -1
Last checked:               Mon Aug 2 09:27:13 2010
Check interval:             0 (<none>)
Lifetime writes:            13 GB
Reserved blocks uid:        0 (user root)
Reserved blocks gid:        0 (group root)
First inode:                11
Inode size:                 256
Required extra isize:       28
Desired extra isize:        28
Journal inode:              8
First orphan inode:         1705241
Default directory hash:     half_md4
Directory Hash Seed:      cab24941-82b1-43a5-8b3f-18a93adbfd94
```

5

```
Journal backup:         inode blocks
Journal features:       journal_incompat_revoke
Journal size:           128M
Journal length:         32768
Journal sequence:       0x000031fe
Journal start:          1
[root@server1 ~]# _
```

In the preceding output, you can see that there are 1,921,360 inodes in the inode table and that 1,663,809 of them are free to use when creating new files and directories.

Checking Filesystems for Errors

Filesystems themselves can accumulate errors over time. These errors are often referred to as **filesystem corruption** and are common on most filesystems. Those filesystems that are accessed frequently are more prone to corruption than those that are not. As a result, such filesystems should be checked regularly for errors. The most common filesystem corruption occurs because a system was not shut down properly using the shutdown, poweroff, halt, or reboot commands. Data is stored in memory for a short period of time before it is written to a file on the hard disk. This process of saving data to the hard disk is called **syncing**. If the computer's power is turned off, data in memory might not be synced properly to the hard disk and corruption might occur. Filesystem corruption can also occur if the hard disks are used frequently for time-intensive tasks such as database access. As the usage of any system increases, so does the possibility for operating system errors when writing to the hard disks. Along the same lines, the physical hard disks themselves are mechanical in nature and can wear over time. Some areas of the hard disk platter might become unusable if they cannot hold a magnetic charge; these areas are known as **bad blocks**. When the operating system finds a bad block, it puts a reference to that bad block in the bad blocks table on the filesystem. Any entries in the bad blocks table are not used for any future disk storage.

To check a filesystem for errors, you can use the **fsck (filesystem check) command**, which can check filesystems of many different types. The fsck command takes an option specifying the filesystem type and an argument specifying the device to check; if the filesystem type is not specified, the filesystem is detected automatically. It is also important to note that the filesystem being checked must be unmounted beforehand for the fsck command to work properly, as shown here:

```
[root@server1 ~]# fsck /dev/vg00/data
fsck from util-linux-ng 2.17.2
e2fsck 1.41.10 (10-Feb-2009)
/dev/mapper/vg00-data is mounted.

WARNING!!! Running e2fsck on a mounted filesystem may cause
SEVERE filesystem damage.

Do you really want to continue (y/n)? n

check aborted.
[root@server1 ~]# umount /dev/vg00/data
[root@server1 ~]# fsck /dev/vg00/data
```

```
fsck from util-linux-ng 2.17.2
e2fsck 1.41.10 (10-Feb-2009)
/dev/mapper/vg00-data:  clean,  11/983040  files,  104064/3932160  blocks
[root@server1 ~]# _
```

NOTE   Because the / filesystem cannot be unmounted, you should only run the `fsck` command on the / filesystem from single-user mode (discussed in Chapter 8), or from System Recovery mode (discussed in Chapter 6).

Notice from the preceding output that the `fsck` command does not give lengthy output on the terminal screen when checking the filesystem; this is because the `fsck` command only performs a quick check for errors unless the −f option is used to perform a full check, as shown in the following example:

```
[root@server1 ~]# fsck -f /dev/vg00/data
fsck from util-linux-ng 2.17.2
e2fsck 1.41.10 (10-Feb-2009)
Pass 1: Checking inodes, blocks, and sizes
Pass 2: Checking directory structure
Pass 3: Checking directory connectivity
Pass 4: Checking reference counts
Pass 5: Checking group summary information
/dev/mapper/vg00-data:   11/983040    files   (0.0%    non-contiguous),
104064/3932160 blocks
[root@server1 ~]# _
```

Table 5-6 displays a list of common options used with the `fsck` command.

If the `fsck` command finds a corrupted file, it displays a message to the user asking whether to fix the error; to avoid these messages, you may use the −a or −y options listed in Table 5-6 to specify that the `fsck` command should automatically repair any corruption. If there are files that the `fsck` command cannot repair, it places them in the lost+found directory on that filesystem and renames the file to the inode number.

To view the contents of the lost+found directory, simply mount the device and view the contents of the lost+found directory immediately underneath the mount point. Because it is difficult to identify lost files by their inode number, most users delete the contents of this directory periodically. Recall that the lost+found directory is automatically created when an ext2, ext3, or ext4 filesystem is created.

Just as you can use the `mke2fs` command to make an ext2, ext3, or ext4 filesystem, you can use the `e2fsck` command to check an ext2, ext3, or ext4 filesystem. The `e2fsck` command accepts more options and can check a filesytem more thoroughly than `fsck`. For example, by using the −c option to the `e2fsck` command, you can check for bad blocks on the hard disk and add them to a bad block table on the filesystem so that they are not used in the future, as shown in the following example:

```
[root@server1 ~]# e2fsck -c /dev/vg00/data
e2fsck 1.41.10 (10-Feb-2009)
Checking for bad blocks (read-only test): done
```

Option	Description
-f	Performs a full filesystem check
-a or -y	Allows fsck to automatically repair any errors
-A	Checks all filesystems in /etc/fstab that have a 1 or 2 in the sixth field
-Cf	Performs a full filesystem check and displays a progress line
-AR	Checks all filesystems in /etc/fstab that have a 1 or 2 in the sixth field but skips the / filesystem
-V	Displays verbose output

Table 5-6 Common options to the `fsck` command

```
/dev/vg00/data: Updating bad block inode.
Pass 1: Checking inodes, blocks, and sizes
Pass 2: Checking directory structure
Pass 3: Checking directory connectivity
Pass 4: Checking reference counts
Pass 5: Checking group summary information

/dev/vg00/data: ***** FILE SYSTEM WAS MODIFIED *****
/dev/vg00/data: 11/983040 files (0.0% non-contiguous), 104064/3932160 blocks
[root@server1 ~]#_
```

 The `badblocks` command can be used to perform the same function as the `e2fsck` command with the −c option.

Recall from earlier in this chapter that the `fsck` command is run at boot time when filesystems are mounted from entries in the /etc/fstab file. Any entries in /etc/fstab that have a 1 in the sixth field are checked first, followed by entries that have a 2 in the sixth field. However, typically every 20 to 40 times an ext2, ext3, or ext4 filesystem is mounted (alternatively, every 180 days), a full filesystem check is forced. This might delay booting for several minutes or even hours depending on the size of the filesystems being checked. To change this interval, you can use the −i option to the **tune2fs command**, as shown here:

```
[root@server1 ~]# tune2fs -i 0 /dev/vg00/data
tune2fs 1.41.10 (10-Feb-2009)
Setting interval between check 0 seconds
[root@server1 ~]# _
```

The `tune2fs` command can be used to change or "tune" filesystem parameters after a filesystem has been created. Changing the interval between checks to 0 seconds, as shown in the preceding example, disables filesystem checks.

Hard Disk Quotas

If there are several users on a Linux system, there must be enough hard disk space to support the files that each user is expected to store on the hard disk. However, if hard disk space is limited or company policy limits disk usage, you should impose limits on filesystem usage. These restrictions, called **hard disk quotas**, can be applied to users or groups of users. Furthermore, **quotas** can restrict how many files and directories a user can create (that is, restrict the number of inodes created) on a particular filesystem, or the total size of all files that a user can own on a filesystem. Two types of quota limits are available: soft limits and hard limits. **Soft limits** are hard disk quotas that the user can exceed for a certain period of time (seven days by default), whereas **hard limits** are rigid quotas that the user cannot exceed. Quotas are typically enabled at boot time if there are quota entries in /etc/fstab, but can also be turned on and off afterward by using the **quotaon** and **quotaoff commands**, respectively.

To set up quotas for the /data filesystem and restrict the user user1, you can carry out the following steps:

1. Edit the /etc/fstab file to add the usrquota and grpquota mount options for the /data filesystem. The resulting /etc/fstab file should look like the following:

```
[root@server1 ~]# cat /etc/fstab
#
# /etc/fstab
# Created by anaconda on Mon Aug 2 09:34:19 2010
#
# Accessible filesystems, by reference, are maintained under'/dev/disk'
# See man pages fstab(5), findfs(8), mount(8) and/or blkid(8) for info
#
/dev/sda1            /               ext4        defaults        1 1
/dev/sda2            swap            swap        defaults        0 0
tmpfs               /dev/shm        tmpfs       defaults        0 0
devpts              /dev/pts        devpts      gid=5,mode=620  0 0
sysfs               /sys            sysfs       defaults        0 0
proc                /proc           proc        defaults        0 0
/dev/fd0            /media/floppy   auto        noauto          0 0
/dev/sda5            /data           ext4        defaults        0 0
/dev/sda6            swap            swap        defaults        0 0
/dev/vg00/data       /data           ext4        defaults        0 0
/dev/vg00/extras     /extras         ext4
defaults,usrquota,grpquota 0 0
[root@server1 ~]# _
```

2. Remount the /data filesystem as read-write to update the system with the new options from /etc/fstab. The command to do this is:

```
[root@server1 ~]# mount /data -o remount,rw
[root@server1 ~]# _
```

3. Create two files in the root of the filesystem called aquota.user and aquota.group. For the /data filesystem, you should create the files /data/aquota.user and /data/aquota.group. Following this, run the quotacheck –mavug command, which looks on the system for file

ownership and updates the quota database for all filesystems with quota options listed in /etc/fstab (-a), giving verbose output (-v) for all users and groups (-u and -g) even if the filesystem is used by other processes (-m). This places information in the aquota.user and aquota.group files.

```
[root@server1 ~]# touch /aquota.user
[root@server1 ~]# touch /aquota.group
[root@server1 ~]# quotacheck -mavug
quotacheck: Your kernel probably supports journaled quota but you are not
using it. Consider switching to journaled quota to avoid running quota-
check after an unclean shutdown.
quotacheck: WARNING - Quotafile /data/aquota.user was probably trun-
cated. Cannot save quota settings...
quotacheck: WARNING - Quotafile /data/aquota.group was probably trun-
cated. Cannot save quota settings...
quotacheck: Scanning /dev/mapper/vg00-data [/data] done
quotacheck: Checked 22249 directories and 337809 files
[root@server1 ~]# _
```

 You can safely ignore any warnings at the beginning of the quotacheck output at this stage because they are the result of newly created aquota.user and aquota.group files that have not been used yet.

4. Use the quotaon -avug command to turn user and group quotas on for all filesystems that have quotas configured:

```
[root@server1 ~]# quotaon -avug
/dev/mapper/vg00-data [/data] : group quotas turned on
/dev/mapper/vg00-data [/data] : user quotas turned on
[root@server1 ~]# _
```

 You can also enable and disable quotas for individual filesystems. For example, you can use the quotaon /data command to enable quotas for the /data filesystem and the quotaoff /data command to disable them.

5. Edit the quotas for certain users by using the **edquota command** as follows: edquota -u <username>. This brings up the vi editor and allows you to set soft and hard quotas for the number of blocks a user can own on the filesystem (typically, 1 block = 1 Kilobyte) and the total number of inodes (files and directories) that a user can own on the filesystem. A soft limit and hard limit of zero (0) indicates that there is no limit. To set a hard limit of 20MB (=20480KB) and 1,000 inodes, as well as a soft limit of 18MB (=18432KB) and 900 inodes, you can do the following:

```
[root@server1 ~]# edquota –u user1
Disk quotas for user user1 (uid 500):
```

Filesystem	blocks	soft	hard	inodes	soft	hard
/dev/mapper/vg00-data	1188	0	0	326	0	0

```
~
~
~
```

```
~
"/tmp//EdP.aclpslv" 3L, 216C
```

Next, place the appropriate values in the columns provided, and then save and quit the vi editor:

```
Disk quotas for user user1 (uid 500):
Filesystem              blocks    soft    hard   inodes   soft   hard
/dev/mapper/vg00-data     1188   18432   20480      326    900   1000
~
~
~
~
:wq
"/tmp/EdP.aclpslv" 3L, 216C written
[root@server1 ~]# _
```

6. Edit the time limit for which users can go beyond soft quotas by using the edquota -u -t command. The default time limit for soft quotas is seven days, but it can be changed as follows:

```
[root@server1 ~]# edquota -u -t
Grace period before enforcing soft limits for users:
Time units may be: days, hours, minutes, or seconds
Filesystem              Block grace period      Inode grace period
/dev/mapper/vg00-data        7days                   7days
~
~
~
"/tmp//EdP.a1vzfSy" 4L, 233C
```

7. Ensure that quotas were updated properly by gathering a report for quotas by user on the /data filesystem using the **repquota command**, as shown in the following output:

```
[root@server1 ~]# repquota /data
*** Report for user quotas on device /dev/mapper/vg00-data
Block grace time: 7days; Inode grace time: 7days
                    Block limits              File limits
User       used    soft    hard   grace   used   soft   hard  grace
-- -- - - - - - - - - - - - - - - - - - - - - - - - - - - - - - - - -
root -- 6420573       0       0           376520      0      0
user1 --    1188   18432   20480              326    900   1000
[root@server1 ~]# _
```

Note that most users in the preceding output are system users and do not have quotas applied to them. These users are discussed in Chapter 10.

The aforementioned commands are only available to the root user; however, regular users can view their own quotas using the **quota command**. The root user can also use the quota command to view quotas of other users:

```
[root@server1 ~]# quota
Disk quotas for user root (uid 0): none
```

```
[root@server1 ~]# quota -u user1
Disk quotas for user user1 (uid 500):
Filesystem       blocks quota limit  grace  files quota limit grace
/dev/mapper/vg00-data
                 1188 18432 20480            326   900  1000
[root@server1 ~]# _
```

Chapter Summary

- Disk devices are represented by device files that reside in the /dev directory. These device files specify the type of data transfer, the major number of the device driver in the Linux kernel, and the minor number of the specific device.

- Each disk device must contain a filesystem, which is then mounted to the Linux directory tree for usage using the mount command. The filesystem can later be unmounted using the umount command. The directory used to mount the device must not be in use by any logged-in users for mounting and unmounting to take place.

- Hard disks must be partitioned into distinct sections before filesystems are created on those partitions. The fdisk command can be used to partition a hard disk.

- Many different filesystems are available to Linux; each filesystem is specialized for a certain purpose, and several different filesystems can be mounted to different mount points on the directory tree. You can create a filesystem on a device using the mkfs command and its variants.

- The LVM can be used to create logical volumes from the free space within multiple partitions on the various hard disks within your system. Like standard hard disk partitions, logical volumes can contain a filesystem and be mounted to the Linux directory tree. They allow for the easy expansion and reconfiguration of storage.

- USB and FireWire storage devices are recognized as SCSI disks by the Linux system.

- It is important to monitor disk usage using the df, du, and dumpe2fs commands to avoid running out of storage space. Similarly, it is important to check disks for errors using the fsck command and its variants.

- If hard disk space is limited, you can use hard disk quotas to limit the space that each user has on filesystems.

Key Terms

/dev directory   The directory off the root where device files are typically stored.

/dev/MAKEDEV command   The command used to re-create a device file if one or more of the following pieces of device information is unknown: major number, minor number, or type (character or block).

/etc/fstab   A file used to specify which filesystems to mount automatically at boot time and queried by the mount command if an insufficient number of arguments is specified.

/etc/mtab   A file that stores a list of currently mounted filesystems.

/proc/devices   A file that contains currently used device information.

bad blocks   The areas of a storage medium unable to store data properly.

block   The unit of data commonly used by filesystem commands; a block can contain several sectors.

block devices   The storage devices that transfer data to and from the system in chunks of many data bits by caching the information in RAM; they are represented by block device files.

`cfdisk` **command**   A command used to partition hard disks; it displays a graphical interface in which the user can select partitioning options.

character devices   The storage devices that transfer data to and from the system one data bit at a time; they are represented by character device files.

cylinder   A series of tracks on a hard disk that are written to simultaneously by the magnetic heads in a hard disk drive.

device file   A file used by Linux commands that represents a specific device on the system; these files do not have a data section and use major and minor numbers to reference the proper driver and specific device on the system, respectively.

`df (disk free space)` **command**   A command that displays disk free space by filesystem.

disk-burning software   Software that can be used to record data to CD-RW or DVD-RW media.

`du (directory usage)` **command**   A command that displays directory usage.

`edquota` **command**   A command used to specify quota limits for users and groups.

`fdisk` **command**   A command used to create, delete, and manipulate partitions on hard disks.

filesystem   The organization imposed on a physical storage medium that is used to manage the storage and retrieval of data.

filesystem corruption   The errors in a filesystem structure that prevent the retrieval of stored data.

formatting   The process in which a filesystem is placed on a disk device.

`fsck (filesystem check)` **command**   A command used to check the integrity of a filesystem and repair damaged files.

`fuser` **command**   A command used to identify any users or processes using a particular file or directory.

hard disk quotas   The limits on the number of files, or total storage space on a hard disk drive, available to a user.

hard limit   A hard disk quota that the user cannot exceed.

ISO images   Files that contain an ISO 9660 filesystem within.

logical volume (LV)   A volume that is managed by the LVM and composed of free space within a VG.

Logical Volume Manager (LVM)   A set of software components within Linux that can be used to manage the storage of information across several different hard disks on a Linux system.

`lvcreate` **command**   A command used to create LVM logical volumes.

`lvdisplay` **command**   A command used to view LVM logical volumes.

`lvextend` **command**   A command used to add additional space from volume groups to existing LVM logical volumes.

`lvscan` **command**   A command used to view LVM logical volumes.

major number The number used by the kernel to identify which device driver to call to interact properly with a given category of hardware; hard disk drives, CD-ROMs, and video cards are all categories of hardware; similar devices share a common major number.

minor number The number used by the kernel to identify which specific hardware device, within a given category, to use a driver to communicate with; *see also* major number.

mkfs (make filesystem) command A command used to format or create filesystems.

mkisofs command A command used to create an ISO image from one or more files on the filesystem.

mknod command A command used to re-create a device file, provided the major number, minor number, and type (character or block) are known.

mkswap command A command used to prepare newly created swap partitions for use by the Linux system.

mount command A command used to mount filesystems on devices to mount point directories.

mounting A process used to associate a device with a directory in the logical directory tree such that users can store data on that device.

mount point The directory in a file structure to which something is mounted.

partition A physical division of a hard disk drive.

physical extent (PE) size The block size used by the LVM when storing data on a volume group.

physical volume (PV) A hard disk partition that is used by the LVM.

pvcreate command A command used to create LVM physical volumes.

pvdisplay command A command used to view LVM physical volumes.

pvscan command A command used to view LVM physical volumes.

quota command A command used to view disk quotas imposed on a user.

quotaoff command A command used to deactivate disk quotas.

quotaon command A command used to activate disk quotas.

quotas The limits that can be imposed on users and groups for filesystem usage.

repquota command A command used to produce a report on quotas for a particular filesystem.

root filesystem The filesystem that contains most files that make up the operating system; it should have enough free space to prevent errors and slow performance.

sector The smallest unit of data storage on a hard disk; sectors are arranged into concentric circles called tracks and can be grouped into blocks for use by the system.

soft limit A hard disk quota that the user can exceed for a certain period of time.

Solid-State Drives (SSDs) Hard disk devices that use flash memory chips for storage instead of electromagnetic platters.

swapoff command A command used to disable a partition for use as virtual memory on the Linux system.

swapon command A command used to enable a partition for use as virtual memory on the Linux system.

syncing The process of writing data to the hard disk drive that was stored in RAM.

track The area on a hard disk that forms a concentric circle of sectors.

tune2fs command   A command used to modify ext2 and ext3 filesystem parameters.

umount command   A command used to break the association between a device and a directory in the logical directory tree.

vgcreate command   A command used to create LVM volume groups.

vgdisplay command   A command used to view LVM volume groups.

vgextend command   A command used to add additional physical volumes to an LVM volume group.

vgscan command   A command used to view LVM volume groups.

volume group (VG)   A group of physical volumes that are used by the LVM.

Review Questions

1. You find that a device file in the /dev directory has become corrupted. You know that this device is /dev/tty3 and that it is a character device file. What should you do?

   a.   Use the `fsck` command to repair the file.

   b.   Use the `mknod` command to re-create the file.

   c.   Use the `/dev/MAKEDEV` command to re-create the file.

   d.   Nothing; without the minor number, you cannot re-create the file.

2. After a partition on a hard disk drive is formatted with a filesystem, all partitions on that hard disk drive must use the same filesystem. True or False?

3. You want to see the filesystems that are presently in use on the system. What command could you use?

   a.   `cat /etc/fstab`

   b.   `ls -l /etc/fstab`

   c.   `cat /etc/mtab`

   d.   `/etc/mtab`

4. Jim has just purchased two new SCSI hard disk drives and a controller card for them. He properly installs the hardware in his machine. Before he can use them for data storage and retrieval, what must he do? (Choose all that apply.)

   a.   Mount the two hard drives so they are accessible by the operating system.

   b.   Mount a filesystem to each of the hard disk drives.

   c.   Use the `fdisk` command to create one or more partitions on each of the hard disk drives.

   d.   Use the vi editor to edit /etc/mtab and create an entry for the controller card and the hard disk drives.

   e.   Mount any partitions created on the two hard drives so that they are accessible by the operating system.

   f.   Format any partitions created with a valid filesystem recognized by Linux.

5. Given the following output from /etc/fstab, which filesystems will be automatically checked on boot by the fsck command?

/dev/sda1	/	ext4	defaults	1 1
none	/dev/pts	devpts	gid=5,mode=620	1 0
none	/proc	proc	defaults	0 1
none	/dev/shm	tmpfs	defaults	1 0
/dev/sdc2	swap	swap	defaults	0 1
/dev/dvd	/media/dvd	iso9660	noauto,ro	0 0
/dev/fd0	/media/floppy	auto	noauto	0 0

a. none, as fsck must be run manually for each filesystem

b. /, /dev/pts, and /dev/shm

c. /, /proc, and swap

d. all of them, as fsck is run automatically at boot for all filesystems

6. A user mounts a device to a mount point directory and realizes afterward that there are files previously found within the mount point directory that are needed. What should this user do?

a. Nothing; the files are lost and cannot ever be accessed.

b. Nothing; the files could not have been there because you can only mount to empty directories.

c. Unmount the device from the directory.

d. Run the fsck command to recover the file.

e. Look in the lost+found directory for the file.

7. Which command is used to display the amount of free space that exists on a filesystem?

a. fsck

b. quota

c. du

d. df

8. What must you do to successfully run the fsck command on a filesystem?

a. Run the fsck command with the -u option to automatically unmount the filesystem first.

b. Choose yes when warned that running fsck on a mounted filesystem can cause damage.

c. Unmount the filesystem.

d. Ensure that the filesystem is mounted.

9. Character devices typically transfer data more quickly than block devices. True or False?

10. What does the `du /var` command do?

    a. shows the users connected to the /var directory

    b. shows the size of all directories within the /var directory

    c. dumps the /var directory

    d. displays the amount of free space in the /var directory

11. What does the command `dumpe2fs -h` do?

    a. backs up an ext2 filesystem

    b. displays the number of inodes used and available in an ext2 filesystem

    c. dumps an ext2 filesystem

    d. not a valid command

12. The first floppy drive on the system is not responding. You enter the `file /dev/fd0` command and receive the following output. What is the problem?

    ```
    [root@server1 root]# file /dev/fd0
    /dev/fd0:   ASCII text
    [root@server1 root]#
    ```

    a. The floppy drive cable has come loose.

    b. There is no floppy disk in the drive.

    c. The device file has become corrupt.

    d. The floppy drive is seen as a character device.

13. Which of the following statements are true? (Choose all that apply.)

    a. Quotas can only limit user space.

    b. Quotas can only limit the number of files a user can own.

    c. Quotas can limit both user space and the number of files a user can own.

    d. Hard limits can never be exceeded.

    e. Hard limits allow a user to exceed them for a certain period of time.

    f. Soft limits can never be exceeded.

    g. Soft limits allow a user to exceed them for a certain period of time.

    h. Either a hard limit or a soft limit can be set, but not both concurrently.

14. A device file _____. (Choose all that apply.)

    a. has no inode section

    b. has no data section

    c. has no size

    d. displays a major and minor number in place of a file size

    e. has a fixed size of 300 Kilobytes

15. Which of the following statements regarding LVM structure is correct?

    a. PVs are collections of VGs.

    b. LVs are created from the free space available within PVs.

    c. VGs are composed of one or more PVs.

    d. PVs use the space within LVs to create VGs.

16. The lvextend command can be used to add additional unused space within a volume group to an existing logical volume. True or False?

17. You plug a USB flash memory drive into a system that has two SATA hard disks. How will the partition on this USB flash memory drive be identified by Linux?

    a. /dev/sda1

    b. /dev/sda2

    c. /dev/sdb1

    d. /dev/sdc1

18. Which command mounts all existing filesystems in /etc/fstab?

    a. mount -f

    b. mount -a

    c. mount /etc/fstab

    d. mount /etc/mtab

19. A user runs the fsck command with the -a option on a filesystem that is showing signs of corruption. How would that user locate any files the system was unable to repair?

    a. Look in the root of the filesystem.

    b. The system prompts the user for a target location when it comes across a file it cannot repair.

    c. Mount the filesystem and check the lost+found directory underneath the mount point.

    d. View the contents of the directory /lost+found.

20. Which command is used to format a partition on a hard disk drive with the ext4 filesystem?

    a. format_ext4 *device*

    b. ext4mkfs *device*

    c. mke2fs –t ext4 *device*

    d. makeext4FS *device*

Hands-On Projects

These projects should be completed in the order given. The hands-on projects presented in this chapter should take a total of three hours to complete. The requirements for this lab include:

- A computer with Fedora 13 installed according to Hands-On Project 2-2
- A 3.5-inch, high-density floppy disk or a USB flash memory drive

Project 5-1

In this hands-on project, you view and create device files.

1. Turn on your computer. After your Linux system is loaded, switch to a command-line terminal (tty2) by pressing Ctrl+Alt+F2 and log in to the terminal using the user name of **root** and the password of **secret**.

2. At the command prompt, type **ls –l /dev/tty6** and press **Enter**. What device does /dev/tty6 represent? Is this file a block or character device file? Why? What are the major and minor numbers for this file?

3. At the command prompt, type **rm –f /dev/tty6** and press **Enter**. Next, type **ls –l /dev/tty6** at the command prompt and press **Enter**. Was the file removed successfully?

4. Switch to the command-line terminal (tty6) by pressing **Ctrl+Alt+F6** and attempt to log in to the terminal using the user name of **root** and the password of **secret**. Were you successful?

5. Switch back to the command-line terminal (tty2) by pressing **Ctrl+Alt+F2**, type the command **mknod /dev/tty6 c 4 6** at the command prompt and press **Enter**. What did this command do? What other command can be used to do the same function? Next, type **ls –l /dev/tty6** at the command prompt and press **Enter**. Was the file re-created successfully?

6. At the command prompt, type **reboot** and press **Enter**. After your Linux system has loaded, switch to a command-line terminal (tty6) by pressing **Ctrl+Alt+F6** and log in to the terminal using the user name of **root** and the password of **secret**. Why were you successful?

7. At the command prompt, type **ls –l /dev/tty?** and press **Enter**. What is similar among all these files? Is the major number different for each file? Is the minor number different for each file? Why?

8. At the command prompt, type **find /dev** and press **Enter** to list all of the filenames underneath the /dev directory. Are there many files? Next, type **du –s /dev** at the command prompt and press **Enter**. How large in Kilobytes are all files within the /dev directory? Why?

9. At the command prompt, type **cat /proc/devices | more** and press **Enter**. Which devices and major numbers are present on your system? What character device has a major number of 4? How does this compare with what you observed in Step 2?

10. Type **exit** and press **Enter** to log out of your shell.

Project 5-2

In this hands-on project, you create filesystems on floppy disks or USB flash drives, mount them to the directory tree, and view their contents.

1. If you are performing this project using a floppy disk, proceed to Step 4. Alternatively, if you are performing this project using a USB flash drive, log in to your GNOME desktop environment as **sample user one** with the password of **secret**. Once GNOME has loaded, insert your USB flash drive into your computer and wait for its icon to be displayed on your desktop.

2. Open a terminal within your GNOME desktop environment, type **mount** at the command prompt and press **Enter**. Note the device file used by your USB flash drive (i.e., /dev/sdb1).

3. Next, type **umount *device_file*** where ***device_file*** is the device file for your USB flash drive. Leave your USB flash drive plugged into your computer and log out of the GNOME desktop environment.

4. Switch to a command-line terminal (tty2) by pressing **Ctrl+Alt+F2** and log in to the terminal using the user name of **root** and the password of **secret**.

5. If you are performing this project using a USB flash drive, proceed to Step 6. If you are performing this project using a floppy disk, insert a floppy disk into your computer. Next, type **modprobe floppy** and press **Enter** to load the floppy driver into the Linux kernel.

6. At the command prompt, type **mkdir /mymount** and press **Enter** to create a new mount point directory. Next, type **ls –F /mymount** at the command prompt and press **Enter**. Are there any files in the /mymount directory? Next, type **cp /etc/ hosts /mymount** at the command prompt and press **Enter**. Next, type **ls –F /mymount** at the command prompt and press **Enter** to verify that the hosts file was copied successfully.

7. At the command prompt, type **mkfs –t ext2 *device_file*** and press **Enter**, where ***device_file*** is /dev/fd0 if you are performing this project using a floppy disk, or the device file that you noted in Step 2 if you are performing this project using a USB flash drive.

8. At the command prompt, type **mount –t ext2 *device_file* /mymount** and press **Enter**, where ***device_file*** is /dev/fd0 if you are performing this project using a floppy disk, or the device file that you noted in Step 2 if you are performing this project using a USB flash drive. Next, type **mount** at the command prompt and press **Enter**. Was your device successfully mounted to the /mymount directory?

9. At the command prompt, type **ls -F /mymount** and press **Enter**. What files do you see? Why? What happened to the hosts file? Next, type **cp /etc/inittab /mymount** at the command prompt and press **Enter**. At the command prompt, type **ls -F /mymount** and press **Enter** to verify that the file was copied to your device.

10. At the command prompt, type **umount /mymount** and press **Enter**. Next, type **mount** at the command prompt and press **Enter**. Was the device successfully unmounted from the /mymount directory?

11. At the command prompt, type `ls -F /mymount` and press **Enter**. What files do you see? Why? What happened to the inittab file and lost+found directory? Is the hosts file present?

12. At the command prompt, type `mount -t ext2 device_file /mymount` and press **Enter**, where `device_file` is /dev/fd0 if you are performing this project using a floppy disk, or the device file that you noted in Step 2 if you are performing this project using a USB flash drive.

13. At the command prompt, type `cd /mymount` and press **Enter**. Next, type `ls -F` and press **Enter**. Are the inittab file and lost+found directory available again?

14. At the command prompt, type `fuser -u /mymount` and press **Enter**. Who is using the /mymount directory? Next, type `cd` at the command prompt and press **Enter** to return to your home directory. Next, type `umount /mymount` at the command prompt and press **Enter**. Did you receive an error message? Type `mount` at the command prompt and press **Enter** to verify that the device was successfully unmounted from the /mymount directory.

15. Remove the floppy disk or USB flash drive from your computer.

16. Type `exit` and press **Enter** to log out of your shell.

Project 5-3

In this hands-on project, you mount DVDs to the directory tree and view their contents.

1. Switch to a command-line terminal (tty2) by pressing **Ctrl+Alt+F2** and log in to the terminal using the user name of **root** and the password of **secret**.

2. At the command prompt, type `ls -l /dev/dvd` and press **Enter**. What device file does the /dev/dvd symbolic link point to?

3. Next, insert your Fedora 13 installation DVD in your computer's DVD drive. At the command prompt, type `mount -r -t iso9660 /dev/dvd /mymount` and press **Enter**. Next, type `mount` at the command prompt and press **Enter**. Was the DVD successfully mounted to the /mymount directory?

4. At the command prompt, type `ls -F /mymount` and press **Enter**. What files do you see? Why? Next, type `cd /mymount/Packages` at the command prompt and press **Enter**. At the command prompt, type `ls -F` and press **Enter** to view the software packages used to install your Linux operating system.

5. At the command prompt, type `cd` and press **Enter** to return to your home directory. Next, type `umount /mymount` at the command prompt and press **Enter**. Was the DVD successfully unmounted from the /mymount directory? Type the `mount` command at a command prompt and press **Enter** to verify this.

6. Eject the DVD from the DVD drive.

7. Type `exit` and press **Enter** to log out of your shell.

8. Switch to the graphical terminal (tty1 or tty7) by pressing **Ctrl+Alt+F1** or **Ctrl+Alt+F7** and log in to the GNOME desktop environment as **sample user one**, using the password of **secret**.

9. Next, insert the first Fedora 13 installation DVD into your computer's DVD drive and wait for a few seconds. Is there an icon placed on the desktop for your DVD device?

10. Open a terminal in the GNOME desktop environment. At the command prompt, type **mount** and press **Enter**. What mount point directory did your desktop environment mount the DVD to? Close your terminal when finished.

11. Right-click the icon that represents your DVD and select **Eject** from the menu to unmount and eject your device. Remove the DVD from your computer and log out of the GNOME desktop environment.

Project 5-4

In this hands-on project, you work with standard hard disk partitions. You will first create a hard disk partition using the fdisk utility. Next, you create an ext4 filesystem on the partition and mount it to the directory tree. Finally, you use the /etc/fstab file to automatically mount the partition at boot time.

1. Switch to a command-line terminal (tty2) by pressing **Ctrl+Alt+F2** and log in to the terminal using the user name of **root** and the password of **secret**.

2. At the command prompt, type **fdisk *device_file*** and press **Enter**, where ***device_file*** is the device file for your first hard disk (/dev/sda if you have a SCSI or SATA hard disk, or /dev/hda if you have a PATA hard disk). At the fdisk prompt, type **m** and press **Enter** to view the various fdisk commands.

3. At the fdisk prompt, type **p** and press **Enter** to view the partition table on your hard disk. Which two partitions are present? When were they created? What are their types?

4. At the fdisk prompt, type **n** and press **Enter** to create a new partition. Next, type **p** to select a primary partition and press **Enter**. When prompted for the partition number, type **3** and press **Enter**. When prompted for the start cylinder, observe the valid range within the brackets and press **Enter** to select the default (the first available cylinder). When prompted for the end cylinder, type **+10GB** and press **Enter** to create a 10GB partition.

5. At the fdisk prompt, type **p** and press **Enter** to view the partition table on your hard disk. How many partitions are present? What type of partition is /dev/hda3 or /dev/sda3?

6. At the fdisk prompt, type **l** and press **Enter** to view the different partition types. Which character would you type at the fdisk prompt to change the type of partition?

7. At the fdisk prompt, type **w** and press **Enter** to save the changes to the hard disk and exit the fdisk utility.

8. At the command prompt, type **reboot** and press **Enter** to reboot your machine and ensure that the partition table was read into memory correctly. After your Linux system has been loaded, switch to a command-line terminal (tty2) by pressing **Ctrl+Alt+F2** and log in to the terminal using the user name of **root** and the password of **secret**.

9. At the command prompt, type **mke2fs –t ext4 *device_file*** and press **Enter**, where ***device_file*** is the device file for the third partition on your first hard

disk (/dev/sda3 if you have a SCSI or SATA hard disk, or /dev/hda3 if you have a PATA hard disk).

10. At the command prompt, type **mkdir /newmount** and press **Enter** to create a mount point directory underneath the / directory for mounting the third partition on your first hard disk.

11. At the command prompt, type **mount –t ext4** *device_file* **/newmount** and press **Enter**, where *device_file* is the device file for the third partition on your first hard disk (/dev/sda3 if you have a SCSI or SATA hard disk, or /dev/hda3 if you have a PATA hard disk). This will mount your third partition to the /newmount directory. Next, type the **mount** command and press **Enter** to verify that the filesystem was mounted correctly.

12. At the command prompt, type **ls –F /newmount** and press **Enter**. Is the lost+found directory present? Next, type **cp /etc/hosts /newmount** at the command prompt and press **Enter** to copy the hosts file to the new partition. Verify that the copy was successful by typing the **ls –F /newmount** command at the command prompt again, and press **Enter**.

13. At the command prompt, type **umount /newmount** and press **Enter**. Next, type the **mount** command and press **Enter** to verify that the filesystem was unmounted correctly.

14. At the command prompt, type **vi /etc/fstab** and press **Enter**. Observe the contents of the file. Add a line to the bottom of the file, as shown here, where *device_file* is the device file for the third partition on your first hard disk (/dev/sda3 if you have a SCSI or SATA hard disk, or /dev/hda3 if you have a PATA hard disk):

    ```
    device_file    /newmount    ext4    defaults    0    0
    ```

15. Save your changes and quit the vi editor.

16. At the command prompt, type **reboot** and press **Enter**. After your Linux system has been loaded, switch to a command-line terminal (tty2) by pressing **Ctrl+Alt+F2** and log in to the terminal using the user name of **root** and the password of **secret**.

17. At the command prompt, type **mount** and press **Enter**. Is the third partition on your hard disk mounted? Why?

18. At the command prompt, type **umount /newmount** and press **Enter**. Next, type the **mount** command to verify that the filesystem was unmounted correctly.

19. At the command prompt, type **mount -a** and press **Enter**. Next, type the **mount** command and press **Enter**. Is the third partition on your hard disk mounted? Why?

20. Type **exit** and press **Enter** to log out of your shell.

Project 5-5

In this hands-on project, you configure the LVM to host two logical volumes. Next, you format these logical volumes and mount them to the directory tree, as well as edit the /etc/fstab file to ensure that they are mounted at boot time.

1. Switch to a command-line terminal (tty2) by pressing **Ctrl+Alt+F2** and log in to the terminal using the user name of **root** and the password of **secret**.

2. At the command prompt, type **fdisk *device_file*** and press **Enter**, where ***device_file*** is the device file for your first hard disk (/dev/sda if you have a SCSI or SATA hard disk, or /dev/hda if you have a PATA hard disk). At the fdisk prompt, type **m** and press **Enter** to view the various fdisk commands.

3. At the fdisk prompt, type **n** and press **Enter** to create a new partition. Next, type **p** to select a primary partition and press **Enter**. When prompted for the partition number, type **4** and press **Enter**. When prompted for the start cylinder, observe the valid range within the brackets and press **Enter** to select the default (the first available cylinder). When prompted for the end cylinder, press **Enter** to select the default of the last available cylinder on your hard disk.

4. At the fdisk prompt, type **p** and press **Enter** to view the partition table on your hard disk. How many partitions are present? What type of partition is /dev/hda4 or /dev/sda4?

5. At the fdisk prompt, type **w** and press **Enter** to save the changes to the hard disk and exit the fdisk utility.

6. At the command prompt, type **reboot** and press **Enter** to reboot your machine and ensure that the partition table was read into memory correctly. After your Linux system has been loaded, switch to a command-line terminal (tty2) by pressing **Ctrl+Alt +F2** and log in to the terminal using the user name of **root** and the password of **secret**.

7. At the command prompt, type **pvcreate *device_file*** and press **Enter**, where ***device_file*** is the device file for the fourth partition on your first hard disk (/dev/sda4 if you have a SCSI or SATA hard disk, or /dev/hda4 if you have a PATA hard disk). What does this command do?

8. At the command prompt, type **vgcreate vg00 *device_file*** and press **Enter**, where ***device_file*** is the device file for the fourth partition on your first hard disk (/dev/ sda4 if you have a SCSI or SATA hard disk, or /dev/hda4 if you have a PATA hard disk). What does this command do?

9. At the command prompt, type **lvcreate –L 4GB –n volume1 vg00** and press **Enter** to create a 4GB logical volume called volume1 from the vg00 volume group.

10. At the command prompt, type **lvcreate –L 6GB –n volume2 vg00** and press **Enter** to create a 6GB logical volume called volume2 from the vg00 volume group.

11. At the command prompt, type **mke2fs –t ext4 /dev/vg00/volume1** and press **Enter** to format the volume1 logical volume using the ext4 filesystem. Next, type **mke2fs –t ext4 /dev/vg00/volume2** and press **Enter** to format the volume2 logical volume using the ext4 filesystem.

12. At the command prompt, type **mkdir /volume1** and press **Enter** to create a mount point for the volume1 logical volume. Next, type **mkdir /volume2** and press **Enter** to create a mount point for the volume2 logical volume.

13. At the command prompt, type **mount –t ext4 /dev/vg00/volume1 /volume1** and press **Enter** to mount the volume1 logical volume to the /volume1 directory. Next, type **mount –t ext4 /dev/vg00/volume2 /volume2** and press **Enter** to mount the volume2 logical volume to the /volume2 directory. When finished, type **mount** and press **Enter** to verify that both filesystems are mounted.

14. At the command prompt, type **ls –F /volume1 /volume2** and press **Enter**. Is there a lost+found directory underneath each directory? Why?

15. At the command prompt, type **vi /etc/fstab** and press **Enter**. Add the following lines to the bottom of the file, as shown here, to ensure that the volume1 and volume2 logical volumes are mounted at boot time:

```
/dev/vg00/volume1      /volume1    ext4    defaults    0 0
/dev/vg00/volume2      /volume2    ext4    defaults    0 0
```

16. Save your changes and quit the vi editor.

17. At the command prompt, type **reboot** and press **Enter**. After your Linux system has been loaded, switch to a command-line terminal (tty2) by pressing **Ctrl+Alt+F2** and log in to the terminal using the user name of **root** and the password of **secret**.

18. At the command prompt, type **mount** and press **Enter**. Are volume1 and volume2 mounted? Why?

19. At the command prompt, type the following commands in turn (pressing **Enter** after each one) and review the information regarding your computer's physical and logical volumes:
    pvdisplay
    pvscan
    vgdisplay
    vgscan
    lvdisplay
    lvscan

20. Type **exit** and press **Enter** to log out of your shell.

Project 5-6

In this hands-on project, you view disk usage and check filesystems for errors.

1. Switch to a command-line terminal (tty2) by pressing **Ctrl+Alt+F2** and log in to the terminal using the user name of **root** and the password of **secret**.

2. At the command prompt, type **df** and press **Enter**. What filesystems are displayed? Can you see the swap partition? Why?

3. At the command prompt, type **dumpe2fs –h /dev/vg00/volume1 | more** and press **Enter**. How many inodes are available to this filesystem? How many inodes are free to be used? Why?

4. At the command prompt, type **fsck /dev/vg00/volume1** and press **Enter**. What error message do you receive and why? Type **n** at the prompt to quit the fsck command.

5. At the command prompt, type **umount /volume1** and press **Enter**. Next, type the **mount** command and press **Enter** to verify that the filesystem was unmounted correctly.

6. At the command prompt, type **fsck /dev/vg00/volume1** and press **Enter**. How long did the filesystem check take and why?

7. At the command prompt, type **fsck –f /dev/vg00/volume1** and press **Enter**. How long did the filesystem check take and why?

8. At the command prompt, type **fsck -Cf /dev/vg00/volume1** and press **Enter**. What does the -C option do when displaying the results to the terminal screen?

9. At the command prompt, type **e2fsck -c /dev/vg00/volume1** and press **Enter**. What does this command do?

10. At the command prompt, type **tune2fs -i 0 /dev/vg00/volume1** and press **Enter** to change the interval for forced checks so that they are avoided. Is this a good idea for the ext4 filesystem? Why?

11. At the command prompt, type **mount /dev/vg00/volume1** and press **Enter**. Next type the **mount** command and press **Enter** to verify that the filesystem was mounted correctly.

12. Type **exit** and press **Enter** to log out of your shell.

Project 5-7

In this hands-on project, you enable, set, and view disk quotas for the /newmount filesystem created earlier.

1. Switch to a command-line terminal (tty2) by pressing **Ctrl+Alt+F2** and log in to the terminal using the user name of **root** and the password of **secret**.

2. At the command prompt, type **chmod 777 /newmount** to give all users the ability to create files within the /newmount directory.

3. Switch to a command-line terminal (tty3) by pressing **Ctrl+Alt+F3** and log in to the terminal using the user name of **user1** and the password of **secret**.

4. At the command prompt, type **touch /newmount/samplefile** to create a file in /newmount that is owned by the user user1.

5. Type **exit** and press **Enter** to log out of your shell.

6. Switch to a command-line terminal (tty2) by pressing **Ctrl+Alt+F2**.

7. At the command prompt, type **vi /etc/fstab** and press **Enter**. Observe the options for the /newmount filesystem. If your system uses a SATA or SCSI hard disk, change the line that mounts /dev/sda3 to the following:

   ```
   /dev/sda3    /newmount    ext4    defaults,usrquota,grpquota    0 0
   ```

   If your system uses a PATA hard disk, change the line that mounts /dev/hda3 to the following:

   ```
   /dev/hda3    /newmount    ext4    defaults,usrquota,grpquota    0 0
   ```

8. Save your changes and quit the vi editor.

9. Remount the filesystem as read-write by typing the command **mount /newmount -o remount,rw** and press **Enter**.

10. At the command prompt, type **touch /newmount/aquota.user** and press **Enter**.

11. At the command prompt, type **touch /newmount/aquota.group** and press **Enter**.

12. At the command prompt, type **quotacheck -mavug** and press **Enter**. What does this command do? Next, type **ls -l /newmount** and press **Enter**. What are the sizes of the aquota.user and aquota.group files? What are these files used for?

13. At the command prompt, type **quotaon -avug** and press **Enter** to activate quotas for all partitions that have quota options defined within /etc/fstab.

14. At the command prompt, type **edquota –u user1** and press **Enter**. Are there any quota limits applied to the user user1 by default? Change the value of the soft quota for blocks to **50,000** and the value of the hard quota for blocks to **60,000**. Similarly, change the value of the soft quota for inodes to **300** and the value of the hard quota for inodes to **400**. How many files and directories can user1 create on this partition? How much space can user1 use in total on this partition?

15. Save your changes and quit the vi editor.

16. At the command prompt, type **edquota –u -t** and press **Enter**. Change the time limit for users who extend the soft limit to **5 days** for both inodes and blocks.

17. Save your changes and quit the vi editor.

18. At the command prompt, type **repquota /newmount** and press **Enter**. Are the quota changes you made for the user user1 visible? How many files has user1 stored on this volume so far?

19. At the command prompt, type **quota –u user1** and press **Enter**. How do the values compare with those from the previous step?

20. Type **exit** and press **Enter** to log out of your shell.

5

Discovery Exercises

1. Answer the following questions regarding your system by using the commands listed in this chapter. For each question, write the command you used to obtain the answer.

   a. What is the total number of inodes in the root filesystem? How many are currently utilized? How many are available for use?

   b. What filesystems are currently mounted on your system?

   c. What filesystems are available to be mounted on your system?

   d. What filesystems will be automatically mounted at boot time?

2. List the major numbers for the following devices:

   a. fd0

   b. fd1

   c. fd3

   d. hda1

   e. hda2

   f. hda3

   g. sda1

   h. sda2

   i. sda3

   How do they compare? Is there a pattern? Why or why not?

3. Use the Internet to gather information on four filesystems compatible with Linux. For each filesystem, list the situations for which the filesystem was designed and the key features that the filesystem provides.

4. You have a Linux system that has a 1,000GB hard disk drive, which has a 90GB partition containing an ext4 filesystem mounted to the / directory and a 4GB swap partition. Currently, this Linux system is only used by a few users for storing small files; however, the department manager wants to upgrade this system and use it to run a database application that will be used by 100 users. The database application and the associated data will take up over 200GB of hard disk space. In addition, these 100 users will store their personal files on the hard disk of the system. Each user must have a maximum of 5GB of storage space. The department manager has made it very clear that this system must not exhibit any downtime as a result of hard disk errors. How much hard disk space will you require, and what partitions would you need to ensure that the system will perform as needed? Where would these partitions be mounted? What quotas would you implement? What commands would you need to run, and what entries to /etc/fstab would you need to create? Justify your answers.

5. You have several filesystems on your hard disk that are mounted to separate directories on the Linux directory tree. The /dev/sdc6 filesystem was unable to be mounted at boot time. What could have caused this? What commands could you use to find more information about the nature of the problem?

## chapter 6

Advanced Installation

After completing this chapter, you will be able to:

- Describe the types and configurations of SCSI devices
- Explain the different levels of RAID and types of RAID configurations
- Describe how to install Linux from source files on CDs, USB flash memory drives, hard disks, or network servers
- Install Fedora Linux using a kickstart file
- Troubleshoot the installation process
- Access an installed system using System Rescue

In Chapter 2, you examined a standard DVD-based installation process using common hardware components and practices. This chapter examines specialized hardware configurations that will affect your choices during the Linux installation process. In addition, you explore various methods for installing Linux and common installation problems. Finally, this chapter discusses how to access and use System Rescue.

Advanced Storage Configuration

Throughout the Linux installation process, described in Chapter 2, you are prompted for configuration information such as language, keyboard layout, date and time zone, root password, package selection, and storage configuration. The storage that you configure during installation depends on your specific storage technologies and the space needs of your Linux system. In this section, we examine the configuration of advanced storage technologies that are commonly used on Linux servers, including SCSI and RAID.

 You can choose from many different advanced storage technologies. However, because many of these technologies involve proprietary hardware and are used primarily on specialized systems, this discussion is limited to two general-use technologies, SCSI and RAID. To learn more about configuring other advanced storage technologies during a Fedora 13 installation, visit *http://docs.fedoraproject.org/en-US/Fedora/13/html/Installation_Guide/*.

SCSI Hard Disk Configuration

The Small Computer System Interface (SCSI) was designed as a way to connect multiple peripherals to the system in a scalable, high-speed manner. In most systems, a SCSI device is connected to a controller card, which, in turn, connects all devices attached to it to the system. However, many other types of SCSI disk configurations and technologies are available, including Parallel SCSI, Serial Attached SCSI, and iSCSI.

Parallel SCSI Configuration Parallel SCSI, which is the traditional SCSI technology, relies on ribbon cables to transmit information between the hard disk and SCSI controller. Disk devices can attach to the SCSI controller card via one cable with several connectors for the devices to plug in to. Information is then sent from device to device along this cable in a daisy-chain fashion. To prevent signals from bouncing back and forth on the cable, each end of the cable must be terminated with a device that stops signals from being perpetuated. This device is called a **terminator**. Typically, one terminator is on the controller card itself, as shown in the top half of Figure 6-1. Some systems that have several hard drives attached to one controller, however, typically place the controller in the middle of the daisy chain, as shown in the bottom half of Figure 6-1.

SCSI disk drives must be configured such that each hard disk drive can be uniquely identified by the system; this is accomplished by assigning a unique ID number known as a **SCSI ID** or **target ID** to each device. Most Parallel SCSI controllers support up to 15 devices and identify these devices with the numbers 0–15 (one number must be reserved for the controller card itself). This SCSI ID also gives priority to the device. The highest priority device is given the number 7, followed by 6, 5, 4, 3, 2, 1, 0, 15, 14, 13, 12, 11, 10, 9, and 8.

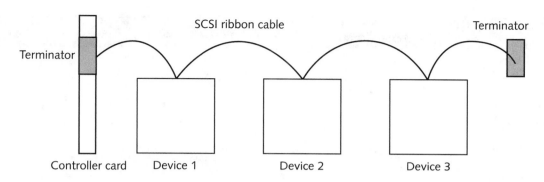

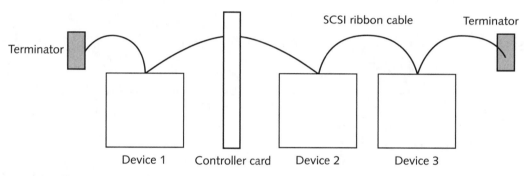

Figure 6-1 Connecting Parallel SCSI devices

Source: Course Technology/Cengage Learning

 The SCSI ID of a SCSI hard disk can be configured using software on the SCSI controller or using jumper switches on the physical hard drive itself.

 Some SCSI devices act as a gateway to other devices; if this is the case, each device is associated with a unique **Logical Unit Number (LUN)**.

Parallel SCSI technology has evolved over time; it was initially adopted as an industry-defined standard in 1986. At that time, SCSI used an 8-bit-wide data path on a controller card that held up to seven devices and had a data transfer speed of 5MB per second. This was commonly referred to as SCSI-1 (SCSI Standard 1). By 1994, it had evolved to a standard that used a 16-bit-wide data path on a controller card that could hold up to 15 devices and had a transfer speed of 20MB per second. This advent was referred to as SCSI-2 (SCSI Standard 2). SCSI-3 was introduced a short time later and provided speeds of over 160MB per second. Table 6-1 describes various SCSI technologies.

SCSI Type	Speed (MB/s)	Bus Width (Bits)	Connector	Number of Devices Supported
SCSI-1 (Narrow/ Slow)	5	8	50-pin Centronics or 50-pin LPT (Line Port Terminal) type	7
SCSI-2 (Fast)	10	8	50-pin LPT type	7
SCSI-2 (Wide)	20	16	68-pin LPT type	15
SCSI-3 (Ultra)	40	16	68-pin LPT type or 80-pin SCA (Single Connector Adapter) type	15
SCSI-3 (Ultra2 Wide)	80	16	68-pin LPT type or 80-pin SCA (Single Connector Adapter) type	15
SCSI-3 (Ultra3 Wide)	160	16	68-pin LPT type or 80-pin SCA (Single Connector Adapter) type	15
SCSI-3 (Ultra320)	320	16	68-pin LPT type or 80-pin SCA (Single Connector Adapter) type	15
SCSI-3 (Ultra640)	640	16	68-pin LPT type or 80-pin SCA (Single Connector Adapter) type	15

Table 6-1 Common SCSI standards

Before you install a Linux system, you must ensure that you configure your Parallel SCSI devices properly. First, verify that all of your SCSI components (SCSI controller, cables, connectors, hard disks, terminators) support the same technology, as listed in Table 6-1. Next, ensure that your SCSI components are connected properly, as shown earlier in Figure 6-1. Finally, make sure your system recognizes the hard drives at system startup. To do this, examine the system BIOS or enter the SCSI BIOS on your SCSI controller card. When you start the Linux installation, your SCSI hard disks will be detected automatically as /dev/sda, /dev/sdb, and so on.

Most SCSI controllers add a second BIOS to your system that is started after the system BIOS. You can interact with this SCSI BIOS at system startup by pressing a key combination that is unique to your SCSI controller manufacturer. For example, Adaptec SCSI controllers allow you to enter the SCSI BIOS by pressing the Ctrl+A key combination at system startup.

Serial Attached SCSI (SAS) Configuration Serial Attached SCSI (SAS) is a recent SCSI technology that can transfer data at up to 768MB/s. Up to 65,535 Serial Attached SCSI hard disks can be connected to a single SCSI controller via serial cables with small serial connectors (between 7 and 36 pins).

Before you install Linux on a system that includes Serial Attached SCSI hard disks, you must connect the hard disks to the SCSI controller via the correct serial cable. Then, you must ensure that the hard disks are detected properly by the system or SCSI BIOS. All other Serial

Attached SCSI configuration (SCSI ID, LUN, etc.) is performed automatically by the SCSI controller, but can be changed manually if you access the SCSI BIOS.

As with Parallel SCSI disks, your Linux installation will detect your Serial Attached SCSI hard disks using /dev/sda, /dev/sdb, and so on.

FireWire (IEEE 1394) is also a serial-based SCSI transfer protocol. It can be used to transfer data to an external hard disk at speeds of over 800MB per second. Unfortunately, FireWire hard disks are not supported for hosting the Linux operating system during installation. Like USB hard disks, they are only intended to be used as removable media, and are treated like USB hard disks by the Linux OS.

iSCSI Configuration Internet SCSI (iSCSI) is a recent SCSI technology that uses network cables to transfer data to and from remote hard disks that reside on your organization's intranet (internal TCP/IP network) or on the Internet. The computer connected to a remote hard disk via iSCSI is referred to as an **iSCSI initiator,** and the remote hard disk is called the **iSCSI target.** An iSCSI initiator can consist of a software component that is part of the Linux OS, or it can consist of a hardware component that is part of the iSCSI-compliant network card. iSCSI targets are typically contained within external network-attached devices that contain multiple hard disks (some iSCSI devices contain over 30 hard disks).

A single iSCSI target can be used by multiple computers, or iSCSI initiators. The computers that use the same iSCSI target are said to be part of the same **Storage Area Network (SAN)**. iSCSI is often referred to as a SAN technology as a result.

The configuration settings for remote iSCSI devices vary by manufacturer. To connect the Linux computer to the remote iSCSI device, you must specify the configuration settings while installing Linux. This means you must understand the configuration settings used by your iSCSI device (name, authentication information, etc.) and ensure that your computer has an iSCSI-compliant network card before starting the installation process. During installation, you need to select Specialized Storage Devices (instead of Basic Storage Devices) when prompted for the storage type, as shown earlier in Figure 2-6. You can then click Add Advanced Target and supply the TCP/IP configuration of your computer's network card as well as the configuration settings needed to connect to the remote iSCSI device. Following this, the installation will proceed and allow you to create Linux filesystems on your iSCSI device (i.e., /dev/sda).

RAID Configuration

Recall that you typically create several partitions during installation to decrease the likelihood that the failure of a filesystem on one partition will affect the rest of the system. These partitions should be spread across several different hard disks to minimize the impact of a hard disk failure; if one hard disk fails, the data on the other hard disks is unaffected.

If a hard disk failure occurs, you must power down the computer, replace the failed hard disk drive, power on the computer, and restore the data that was originally on the hard disk drive from a backup source such as a tape device. The whole process can take several hours. However, with some systems, such as database servers, no amount of downtime is acceptable. In such situations, hard disk configurations that minimize the time required to recover from a hard disk failure are required. Such **fault-tolerant** configurations are typically implemented by a **redundant array of independent disks (RAID)**. Note that RAID has other uses besides creating a fault-tolerant system. It can be used to speed up access to hard disks or combine multiple hard disks into a single volume.

Course Technology/Cengage LearningCurrently, seven basic RAID configurations, ranging from level 0 to level 6, are available. RAID level 0 configurations are not fault tolerant. One type of RAID level 0, known as **spanning**, consists of two hard disks that the system sees as one large volume. Using this technology, you could, for example, combine two 1TB hard disks into one 2TB partition. Spanning is useful when you need a large amount of storage space in a single volume without fault tolerance.

In another type of RAID level 0, called **disk striping,** an individual file is divided into sections and saved concurrently on multiple disks, one section per disk. For example, suppose you have a disk striping configuration made up of three disks. In that case, when you save a file, it is divided into three sections, with each section written to separate hard disk devices concurrently, in a third of the amount of time it would take to save the entire file on one hard disk device. Note that the system can also read the same file in one-third the amount of time it would take if the file were stored on a single hard drive. Disk striping is useful when you need to speed up disk access, but it is not fault tolerant. If one hard disk fails in a RAID level 0 configuration, all data is lost.

RAID level 1, which is often referred to as **disk mirroring,** provides fault tolerance in the case of a hard disk failure. In this RAID configuration, the same data is written to two separate hard disks at the same time. This results in two hard disks with identical information. If one fails, the copy can replace the failed hard disk in a short period of time. The only drawback to RAID level 1 is the cost, because you need to purchase twice the hard disk space needed for a given computer.

RAID level 2 is no longer used and was a variant of RAID level 0 that allowed for error and integrity checking on hard disk drives. Modern hard disk drives do this intrinsically.

RAID level 3 is disk striping with a parity bit, or marker, that indicates what data is where. It requires a minimum of three hard disk drives to function, with one of the hard disks used to store the parity information. Should one of the hard disks containing data fail, you can replace the hard disk drive and regenerate the data using the parity information stored on the parity disk. If the parity disk fails, the system must be restored from a backup device.

RAID level 4 is only a slight variant of RAID level 3. RAID level 4 offers greater access speed than RAID level 3, because it can store data in blocks and, thus, does not need to access all disks in the array at once to read data.

RAID level 5 replaces RAID levels 3 and 4, and is the most common RAID configuration as of this writing. It is commonly referred to as **disk striping with parity**. As with RAID levels 3 and 4, it requires a minimum of three hard disk drives for implementation; however, the parity information is not stored on a separate drive, but is intermixed with data on the drives that make up the set. This offers better performance and fault tolerance; if any drive in the RAID configuration fails, the information on the other drives can be used to regenerate the lost information after the failed hard disk has been replaced. If two hard disks fail, the system must be restored from a backup device. Figure 6-2 shows how a RAID level 5 configuration can be restored using parity information. The parity bits shown in Figure 6-2 are a sum of the information on the other two disks ($22 + 12 = 34$).

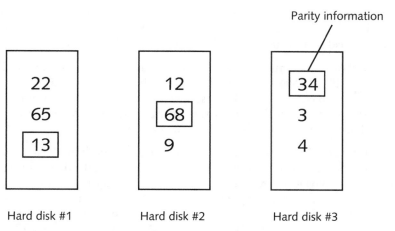

Figure 6-2 Organization of data on RAID level 5

Source: Course Technology/Cengage Learning

If the third hard disk fails, the information can be regenerated, because only one element is missing from each equation:

$$22 + 12 = 34$$
$$68 - 65 = 3$$
$$13 - 9 = 4$$

RAID level 6 is basically the same as RAID level 5 but adds a second set of parity bits for added fault tolerance and allows up to two simultaneous hard disk drive failures while remaining fault tolerant.

 RAID levels are often combined; RAID level 15 refers to a Stripe Set with Parity (RAID level 5) that is mirrored (RAID level 1) to another Stripe Set with Parity.

RAID configurations can be handled by software running on an operating system (called **software RAID**) but are more commonly handled by the hardware contained within a SCSI or SATA hard disk controller (called **hardware RAID**), or by the system BIOS (called **firmware RAID**).

 Most firmware RAID devices only support RAID levels 0 and 1.

To configure hardware RAID, you must use the RAID setup utility for your specific SCSI or SATA hard disk controller. You can access this setup utility by entering the system or SCSI BIOS at system startup or by using a manufacturer-supplied boot CD or DVD. After you have configured your hardware RAID volumes within the setup utility, they will automatically appear as standard hard disk volumes to the Linux installation program. For example, if you configure three hard disks in a RAID level 5 volume using the RAID setup utility, they will appear as a single volume (/dev/sda1) to the Fedora installation program. You can then place a filesystem on /dev/sda1 as you would any other physical hard disk.

To configure firmware RAID, you must first configure a RAID volume using the RAID setup utility within the system BIOS. Next, during the Fedora 13 installation, select Specialized Storage Devices (instead of Basic Storage Devices) when prompted for the storage type, as shown earlier in Figure 2-6. You can then select the Firmware RAID tab and select the firmware RAID volumes that you would like to use for Linux installation.

Unlike hardware or firmware RAID, software RAID is configured entirely during the Fedora installation process (provided that your system has more than one hard disk). To configure software RAID, select Basic Storage Devices when prompted for the storage type, as shown earlier in Figure 2-6. Later in the process, when prompted for your partitioning strategy (shown earlier in Figure 2-10), select Create Custom Layout. Next, click the Create button shown in Figure 2-11 and select RAID Partition from the Create Storage dialog box shown in Figure 2-12. You will then be prompted to choose the level and size of RAID volume to create from the free space on the available hard disks within your system, as well as the volume's desired filesystem. Your first RAID volume will use the device file /dev/md0 (multiple disk, first volume), your second RAID volume will use the device file /dev/md1 (multiple disk, second volume), and so on.

Installation Methods

Modern workstations and servers contain a DVD device that can be used to start a DVD-based Fedora installation such as the one discussed in Chapter 2. You can obtain the Fedora DVD easily by downloading the **ISO image** from *http://fedoraproject.org*. Next, you need to burn the ISO image to a DVD using disk burning software (provided that you have a DVD-RW drive in your computer) and boot your computer using the DVD to start the Linux installation.

In addition to the full Fedora 13 DVD ISO image, a LiveCD ISO image is available at *http://fedoraproject.org*. This LiveCD image is smaller than the ISO image intended for DVD, and can be written to a CD. When you boot from this CD, a full Fedora 13 Linux system loads into your computer's memory so that you can use Linux before installing it to your hard drive. Because the LiveCD image does not contain all of the software that we use in this textbook, you should not download and use the LiveCD ISO image to perform the textbook exercises.

Although a DVD-based installation is the most common installation method for Linux computers at the time of this writing, other methods can be used to install Linux. For example, you can install Linux from multiple CDs, a USB flash memory drive, ISO image files on hard disk, or from shared ISO images that are hosted on network servers using the NFS, FTP, or HTTP protocol.

CD Installation

In many companies, when server hardware reaches a certain age, it is replaced with new hardware, and the old hardware is repurposed. Because Linux typically uses less hardware resources than Windows and does not require licensing costs, it is often installed on these servers to prolong their useful life on the company network.

However, most legacy computers have CD drives instead of DVD drives. Rather than adding a DVD drive to these computers, you can instead download six Fedora 13 CD ISO images from *http://fedoraproject.org* and burn them to six CDs using disk burning software. In this case, only the first CD contains the installation program, so you only need to boot the computer using the first CD and make the appropriate choices during the Fedora installation program. During the file copy stage, you will be prompted to insert the remaining CDs when the installation program requires the files they contain. At the end of the Fedora installation, the last CD is ejected, your system reboots, and then the firstboot wizard appears to help you finalize the installation.

USB Flash Drive Installation

Most modern computers have a BIOS that allows the computer to boot from a flash memory drive that is inserted into a USB slot. If your computer does not have a CD or DVD drive, you can use a USB flash memory drive to install Fedora Linux.

To do this, first download the DVD Fedora 13 ISO image from *http://fedoraproject.org* and use **disk imaging software** to write the ISO image to the USB flash memory drive. This overwrites the existing filesystem and all files on the USB flash memory drive, replacing them with a bootable image of the Fedora 13 installation media.

If you want to use a Windows computer to write the ISO image to the USB flash memory drive, you can use one of several free utilities, such as LiveUSB Creator, available from *https://fedorahosted.org/liveusb-creator/*. If you already have an installed Linux system, you can instead use the `dd command` to write the ISO image to your USB flash memory drive. The dd command takes two arguments: an input file (`if`) that represents the ISO image and an output file (`of`) that represents the device that the ISO image should be written to in a sector-by-sector fashion. For example, if you want to write the /root/Fedora13.iso image to your USB stick recognized as /dev/sdb1, you can use the command `dd if=/root/Fedora13.iso of=/dev/sdb1`.

Next, insert your USB flash memory drive into a free USB slot, boot your computer from the flash memory drive, and complete the Fedora installation as described in Chapter 2.

Hard Disk Installation

Not everyone installs Linux from CD, DVD, or USB flash memory drive. If you have downloaded the Fedora 13 DVD ISO image from the Internet to a FAT, FAT32, ext2, ext3, or ext4 filesystem, you can install Linux directly from the downloaded ISO image on the hard disk, provided that you have free space outside the partition that contains the Fedora 13 DVD ISO image.

To start the installation, first boot from either the Fedora 13 DVD, the first Fedora 13 CD, or a USB flash memory drive imaged with the Fedora 13 installation program. When you reach the welcome screen shown in Figure 2-1, press Tab on your keyboard and add `ask-method` to the end of the boot options line, as shown in Figure 6-3. This forces the Fedora installation program to perform a nonstandard installation and prompt you for the location of the Fedora 13 installation files.

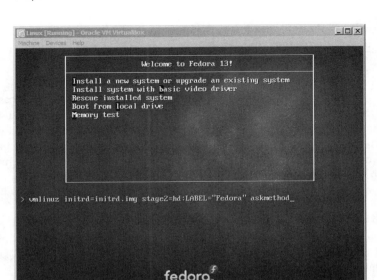

Figure 6-3 Selecting a nonstandard installation method
Source: Course Technology/Cengage Learning

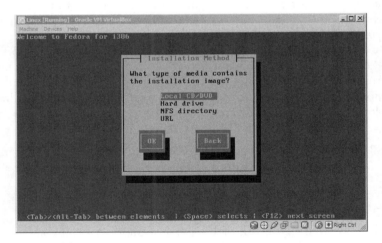

Figure 6-4 Selecting the installation media location
Source: Course Technology/Cengage Learning

Next, you are prompted to choose an installation language (such as English) and keyboard layout (such as US) using a text interface. Then, you are prompted for the location of the Fedora 13 installation media, as shown in Figure 6-4.

After you choose Hard drive and select OK, you are prompted for the hard disk and directory that contain the Fedora 13 ISO image. If you copied the Fedora 13 ISO image to the fedoraISO directory under the root of the filesystem on the first partition of your SATA hard disk, you would specify the device file and path shown in Figure 6-5.

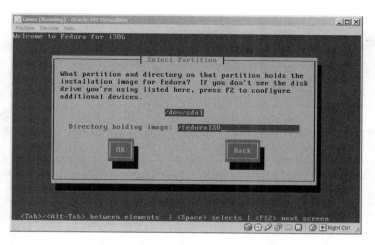

Figure 6-5 Specifying the location of the Fedora ISO image on the hard disk
Source: Course Technology/Cengage Learning

The installation program then locates the ISO image and proceeds with the Fedora installation process as described in Chapter 2.

Network-Based Installations

Though less common than DVD, CD, USB flash memory drive, or hard disk installations, a network-based installation is also an option. In this type of installation, the installation media is stored on another computer that is accessible across a network. To begin this type of installation, you download the Fedora 13 DVD ISO image to a server and, using one of the following protocols, share it with the computer on which you plan to install Fedora:

- Network File System (NFS)
- File Transfer Protocol (FTP)
- Hypertext Transfer Protocol (HTTP)

Configuring NFS, FTP, and HTTP is discussed in Chapter 14.

Next, you boot the computer on which you plan to install Fedora 13. You can boot the computer from either the Fedora 13 DVD, the first Fedora 13 CD, or a USB flash memory drive imaged with the Fedora 13 installation program using a disk imaging software. When you reach the welcome screen shown in Figure 2-1, press Tab on your keyboard and add `ask-method` to the end of the boot options line, as shown earlier in Figure 6-3.

Next, choose an installation language (such as English), a keyboard layout (such as US), and select a network installation method. If you want to connect to a server that hosts the ISO image using NFS, select NFS directory in the Installation Method screen shown in Figure 6-4. You are then prompted to configure the IP settings on your computer's network adapter. After that, you are prompted for the location of the NFS server and ISO image. Assuming you copied

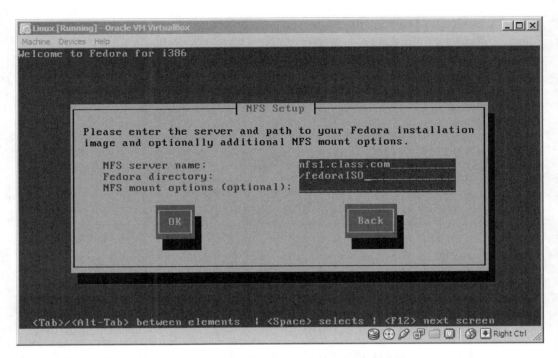

Figure 6-6 Specifying the location of the Fedora ISO image on an NFS server

Source: Course Technology/Cengage Learning

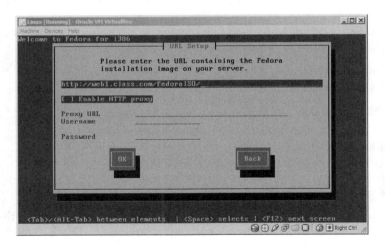

Figure 6-7 Specifying the location of the Fedora ISO image on an HTTP server

Source: Course Technology/Cengage Learning

the ISO image to the shared /fedoraISO directory on the NFS server nfs1.class.com, you would specify the settings shown in Figure 6-6.

Alternatively, if you want to connect to a server that hosts the ISO image using FTP or HTTP, you must select URL from the screen shown in Figure 6-4 and then configure the IP settings on your computer's network adapter. Next, you are prompted for the HTTP or FTP URL that specifies the location of the ISO image. For example, if you copied the Fedora 13 ISO image to the fedoraISO directory under the root of your FTP server ftp1.class.com, you would specify ftp://ftp1.class.com/fedoraISO/. If you instead copied the Fedora 13 ISO image to the fedoraISO directory under the root of your HTTP server web1.class.com, you could specify the URL shown in Figure 6-7. If your computer has to pass through a proxy server to gain access to the FTP or HTTP server, you must also supply the name of the proxy server and the appropriate login information at this point.

After you choose the location of the ISO image on an NFS, FTP, or HTTP server, you can proceed with the remainder of the Fedora installation process as described in Chapter 2.

Automating Linux Installations

Some organizations deploy several Linux servers and workstations that require the same or similar configuration. Rather than working through the installation screens one-by-one on each computer, it's more efficient for these organizations to automate the installation process via installation scripts.

Many Linux distributions, including Fedora, provide an installation program that accepts a script file that specifies typical choices when you install the operating system. In Fedora, this script is called the **kickstart file**. After a normal Fedora Linux installation, the installation program creates a sample kickstart file called /root/anaconda-ks.cfg that contains the choices you made during the installation program. A sample /root/anaconda-ks.cfg file is shown in the following output:

```
[root@server1 ~]# cat ks.cfg
# Kickstart file automatically generated by anaconda.
#version=DEVEL
install
cdrom
lang en_US.UTF-8
keyboard us
timezone --utc America/New_York
rootpw --iscrypted
$6$rzadEpg.23n9I4s6$JQa0iwv.H8Ea4XAVrFR4eNLTs/LVF5LDAahRXA14ZZfbS/
LMF1GP0QOxdw8cWGe.umOQp2NhHx6Ipgb7Gub9N.
selinux --enforcing
authconfig --enableshadow --passalgo=sha512 --enablefingerprint
firewall --service=ssh
# The following is the partition information you requested
# Note that any partitions you deleted are not expressed
# here so unless you clear all partitions first, this is
# not guaranteed to work
#clearpart --none --drives=sda
#ignoredisk --only-use=sda

#part / --fstype=ext4 --size=30000
```

```
#part swap --size=4000

bootloader --location=mbr --driveorder=sda --append="rhgb quiet"

%packages
@admin-tools
@authoring-and-publishing
@base
@core
@dns-server
@development-libs
@development-tools
@dial-up
@directory-server
@editors
@electronic-lab
@ftp-server
@eclipse
@fedora-packager
@fonts
@gnome-desktop
@gnome-software-development
@games
@graphical-internet
@graphics
@hardware-support
@input-methods
@java
@java-development
@kde-desktop
@kde-software-development
@legacy-fonts
@mail-server
@mysql
@network-server
@news-server
@office
@online-docs
@sql-server
@printing
@server-cfg
@sound-and-video
@system-tools
@text-internet
@web-server
@smb-server
@x-software-development
@base-x
```

```
@xfce-desktop
kpackagekit
system-config-network
scribus
xfsprogs
mtools
gpgme
gpm
bind
rpmdevtools
koji
mercurial
lua
pylint
rpmlint
plague-client
cmake
mock
bzr
pptp
samba
minicom
openoffice.org-opensymbol-fonts
qtcurve-gtk2
gvfs-obexftp
glibmm24-devel
gnome-vfs2-devel
libsigc++20-devel
libart_lgpl-devel
gnugo
kdegames
kdepim
konversation
ImageMagick
digikam
kipi-plugins
kdegraphics
gypsy
gpsd
xorg-x11-fonts-ISO8859-1-100dpi
urw-fonts
ghostscript-fonts
spambayes
qt-mysql
php-mysql
dnsmasq
openswan
ntpdate
```

6

```
rdesktop
fuse
ncftp
mesa-libGLU-devel
xorg-x11-apps
gdm
xscreensaver-extras
xscreensaver-base
xterm
xorg-x11-resutils-dnssec-conf
%end
[root@server1 ~]# _
```

Any line in a kickstart file that starts with a # symbol is a comment line and is ignored by the installation program.

It is good form to first create a copy of anaconda-ks.cfg called ks.cfg and edit the ks.cfg file to make any changes you feel necessary before you reuse it for future Fedora installations.

The kickstart file contains sections on system configuration, disk partitioning, and package selection. The section on disk partitioning is always commented out (with # symbols) for safety. Thus, you must at least change this section. To re-create the installation outlined in Project 2-2, simply create a copy of /root/anaconda-ks.cfg called /root/ks.cfg. Then delete the following section of the file:

```
#clearpart --none --drives=sda
#ignoredisk --only-use=sda

#part / --fstype=ext4 --size=30000
#part swap --size=4000
```

Next, replace the deleted portion with the following, which ensures that the MBR is rewritten, all existing partitions are removed, a 30,000MB ext4 partition is created and mounted to the / directory, and a 4,000MB swap partition is created and activated for use:

```
zerombr yes
clearpart --all
part / --fstype=ext4 --size=30000
part swap --size=4000
```

If you need to make major changes to the kickstart file, you should install the **Kickstart Configurator** tool by running the yum install system-config-kickstart command as the root user. Next, you can open a terminal within a GUI environment and execute the system-config-kickstart command to start the Kickstart Configurator shown in Figure 6-8.

Use the screens within the Kickstart Configurator to select the options you would like to configure during a future installation and then click File, Save to save these options to a new kickstart file.

Figure 6-8 The Kickstart Configurator

Source: Course Technology/Cengage Learning

The default filename used by the Kickstart Configurator is ks.cfg.

Once you have a kickstart file, place it on a CD, DVD, USB flash memory drive, or hard disk partition and boot from the Fedora DVD. At the Fedora installation welcome screen shown in Figure 2-1, ensure that Install a new system or upgrade an existing system is highlighted and press Tab to modify the boot options. At the end of the boot option line, append `ks=device:path` (where `device` is the device that contains the kickstart file, and `path` is the absolute pathname to the kickstart file on the filesystem), and then press Enter. If you placed the ks.cfg kickstart file in the root directory of a floppy, you would append the text `ks=floppy:/ks.cfg` to the boot options line. Alternatively, if the ks.cfg file is located on the root of a CD or DVD, you would append the text `ks=cdrom:/ks.cfg` to the boot options line. If you placed the ks.cfg file on a hard disk partition, you must specify the hard disk partition. For example, if the ks.cfg file is located in the /sample directory on the second partition of your first SCSI hard disk, you would append `ks=hd:sda2:/sample/ks.cfg` to the boot options line.

After you modify the boot options line to include the kickstart file, the installation process proceeds without prompting you for information. At the end of the installation process, your system reboots, after which you need to complete the firstboot wizard.

Troubleshooting Installation

Computers typically have different hardware BIOS configurations, so the installation process can vary from one computer to the next. You might encounter problems while installing Linux on one computer but not when installing it on another. These problems are usually related to hardware support or configuration, and are typically fixed with a change to the hardware configuration of the system. Furthermore, you can divide these problems into three categories based on when they occur:

- Problems starting the installation
- Problems during installation
- Problems after installation

Problems Starting the Installation

You will typically start a Linux installation by booting from a CD, DVD, or USB flash memory drive. For this to occur, you must ensure that the boot order located in the BIOS is set to look for an operating system on the CD-ROM, DVD, or USB flash memory drive before it looks to the hard disk. The BIOS on different computers can be radically different; in some cases, the BIOS will have sections labeled First Boot Device, Second Boot Device, and Third Boot Device, whereas others have a section labeled Boot Order. To ensure that you are changing the correct setting, consult the user's manual for your computer.

BIOS settings are stored in a memory chip on the computer, which is given a continuous supply of power via a small lithium battery attached to the computer's mainboard. If this battery dies, any changes to the BIOS settings are lost and default values are loaded. When this occurs, the system warns the user upon system startup with a message similar to "BIOS Error—Defaults Loaded—Press F1 to continue." In this case, the battery needs to be replaced before the boot order is changed; otherwise, the setting is lost when the computer is powered off.

Alternatively, on many computers, the BIOS allows you to choose the device to boot from at system startup by pressing a special key, such as F12. Consult your computer's user manual to learn if your system has this ability.

Problems During Installation

After the installation program has loaded, you are prompted for the method of installation. If you are installing Linux graphically, the installation program must first detect the video card and mouse in the computer and load the appropriate drivers into memory. If, after the initial welcome screen (Figure 2-1), the graphical installation screens do not appear, or appear as scrambled lines across the computer screen, the video card is probably not supported by the mode and resolution of the graphical installation. To solve this, you should restart the installation and select Install system with basic video driver at the initial welcome screen, shown in Figure 2-1.

If the graphical installation starts successfully but the mouse does not work, an alternative is to start a text-based installation. Simply restart the installation and press the Esc key before you see the initial welcome screen. When you see a boot: prompt, type `linux text`, as shown in Figure 6-9, and then press Enter. From here, you can proceed through the installation program in text mode. Figure 6-10 shows the text mode installation welcome screen.

On some older systems, the installation might freeze randomly during the installation; this is a result of improper device communication. To fix this, restart the computer and disable Plug-and-Play support in the computer's BIOS and then start the installation again. After the installation has completed, you can reenable Plug-and-Play support in the BIOS.

Sometimes, an installation ends abnormally and the screen displays a "fatal signal 11" error message. This indicates an error, known as a **segmentation fault**, in which a program has

Figure 6-9 Starting a text mode Fedora installation
Source: Course Technology/Cengage Learning

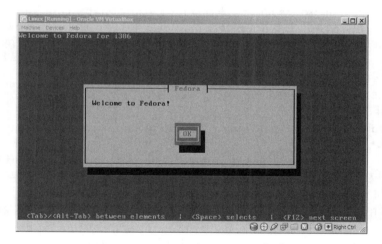

Figure 6-10 The Fedora welcome screen during a text mode installation
Source: Course Technology/Cengage Learning

accessed a certain area of RAM that was not assigned. Although this might be a software problem, when it occurs during installation it is likely a hardware problem. If a segmentation fault occurs when you are installing Linux, stop the installation and check the RAM for errors. As explained in Chapter 2, to check for RAM errors you boot from the Fedora 13 DVD and select Memory test at the installation welcome screen shown in Figure 2-1; this tests RAM using the memtest86 utility.

If you experience a segmentation fault during installation, and the memtest86 utility finds no RAM errors, you should assume that some other piece of hardware is faulty. Zeroing in on the right piece of hardware can be tricky. Often, you can fix segmentation faults by turning off the CPU cache memory or by increasing the number of memory wait states in the BIOS. Sometimes, RAM that contains no errors can still be the source of the problem if the memory is too slow for the mainboard (for example, if the memory is 70ns RAM and the mainboard requires 60ns RAM). In that case, you should replace the RAM. On some computers, the BIOS allows the user to change the voltage for the RAM and CPU; incorrect values could be the source of a segmentation fault. Other causes include an AMD K6 processor, laptop power management conflicts, and overclocked CPUs.

An **overclocked** CPU is a CPU that is faster than the speed for which the processor was designed. Although this might lead to increased performance, it also makes the processor hotter and can result in intermittent computer crashes.

If the installation fails with an error other than "fatal signal 11," consult the support documentation for your distribution of Linux, or check Internet newsgroups. Also, keep in mind that certain hardware devices, such as Winmodems, are not compatable with Linux; ensure that all hardware is listed on the Hardware Compatibility List for your Linux distribution prior to installation.

In some cases, the installation process fails to place a boot loader on the hard disk properly; this often occurs with older hard disk drives that have over 1,024 cylinders. To avoid this problem, ensure that the / partition starts before the 1,024th cylinder (the 8GB mark on most hard disks) or create a partition for the /boot directory that starts before the 1,024th cylinder.

Problems After Installation

Even after a successful Fedora Linux installation, problems might arise if the installation program failed to detect the computer's hardware properly or if certain programs were not installed as expected. To ensure no such problems occurred, check the **installation log files** after installation, and then verify system settings to ensure that all hardware was detected with the correct values.

The installation log files are files created by the installation program that record the events that occur during the installation process, including errors. Two installation log files are created by the Fedora installation program: /root/install.log, which contains a list of packages that were installed as well as a list of those that were not installed; and /root/install.log. syslog, which lists all of the system events that occurred during the installation, such as the creation of user and group accounts.

To verify hardware settings, you can examine the content of the /proc directory or boot-up log files. The /proc directory is mounted to a special filesystem contained within RAM that lists system information made available by the Linux kernel; because this is an administrative filesystem, all files within are readable only by the root user. A listing of the /proc directory shows the following file and subdirectory contents:

```
[root@server1 ~]# ls -F /proc
1/      1259/   1708/   39/     7086/   7466/   bus/        meminfo
10/     1265/   1749/   4/      7087/   7471/   cgroups     misc
1014/   1270/   1757/   45/     7091/   7498/   cmdline     modules
1016/   1272/   18/     454/    7097/   7499/   cpuinfo     mounts@
```

```
1020/   1292/   19/   46/    7098/   7500/   crypto   mtrr
1041/   13/     2/    47/    7102/   7523/   devices   net@
1055/   1307/   20/   48/    7103/   7535/   diskstats   pagetype
1066/   1342/   21/   5/     7104/   7537/   dma   partitions
1067/   1351/   22/   6/     7105/   7539/   dri/   sched
1078/   1359/   23/   6829/  7107/   7541/   driver/   schedstat
1087/   1371/   24/   6833/  7108/   7547/   execdomains   scsi/
1099/   1379/   25/   688/   7109/   7724/   fb   self@
11/     14/     26/   6916/  7117/   7740/   filesystems   slabinfo
1108/   1407/   27/   6937/  7119/   7741/   fs/   softirqs
1118/   1410/   28/   6949/  7123/   7780/   interrupts   stat
1125/   1413/   29/   6960/  7125/   7783/   iomem   swaps
1129/   1417/   3/    6967/  7129/   7819/   ioports   sys/
1130/   1419/   30/   6977/  7131/   8/      irq/   sysrg
1145/   1439/   33/   6978/  7133/   824/    kallsyms   sysvipc/
1147/   147/    336/  7/     7174/   832/    kcore   timer_list
1174/   148/    338/  705/   7180/   865/    keys   timer
1175/   149/    34/   7060/  7182/   866/    key-users   tty/
1182/   15/     35/   7068/  7183/   867/    kmsg   uptime
1192/   1514/   36/   7070/  7264/   9/      kpagecount   version
12/     1553/   366/  7074/  727/    912/    kpageflags   vlocinfo
1217/   1562/   367/  7076/  7321/   914/    latency_stats   vmstat
1225/   16/     368/  7080/  7376/   acpi/   loadavg   zoneinfo
1226/   1698/   37/   7082/  7403/   asound/   locks
1255/   17/     38/   7083/  7405/   buddyinfo mdstat
[root@server1 ~]# _
```

The subdirectories that start with a number in the preceding output are used to display process information; other directories can contain kernel parameters. The files listed in the preceding output are text representations of various parts of the Linux system; they are updated regularly by the Linux kernel and can be viewed using standard text commands, such as cat or more.

To view the information that Linux has detected regarding a computer's CPUs, view the contents of the cpuinfo file in the /proc directory:

```
[root@server1 ~]# cat /proc/cpuinfo
processor       : 0
vendor_id       : AuthenticAMD
cpu family      : 15
model           : 72
model name      : AMD Turion(tm) 64 X2 Mobile Technology TL-50
stepping        : 2
cpu MHz         : 800.000
cache size      : 256 KB
physical id     : 0
siblings        : 2
core id         : 0
cpu cores       : 2
apicid          : 0
```

```
initial apicid      : 0
fdiv_bug            : no
hlt_bug             : no
f00f_bug            : no
coma_bug            : no
fpu                 : yes
fpu_exception       : yes
cpuid level         : 1
wp                  : yes
flags               : fpu vme de pse tsc msr pae mce cx8 apic sep mtrr pge mca
                      cmov pat pse36 clflush mmx fxsr sse sse2 ht syscall nx
                      mmxext fxsr_opt rdtscp lm 3dnowext 3dnow extd_apicid
                      pni cx16 lahf_lm cmp_legacy svm extapic cr8_legacy
bogomips            : 1603.35
clflush size        : 64
cache_alignment     : 64
address sizes       : 40 bits physical, 48 bits virtual
power management    : ts fid vid ttp tm stc
processor           : 1
vendor_id           : AuthenticAMD
cpu family          : 15
model               : 72
model name          : AMD Turion(tm) 64 X2 Mobile Technology TL-50
stepping            : 2
cpu MHz             : 800.000
cache size          : 256 KB
physical id         : 0
siblings            : 2
core id             : 1
cpu cores           : 2
apicid              : 1
initial apicid      : 1
fdiv_bug            : no
hlt_bug             : no
f00f_bug            : no
coma_bug            : no
fpu                 : yes
fpu_exception       : yes
cpuid level         : 1
wp                  : yes
flags               : fpu vme de pse tsc msr pae mce cx8 apic sep mtrr pge mca
                      cmov pat pse36 clflush mmx fxsr sse sse2 ht syscall nx
                      mmxext fxsr_opt rdtscp lm 3dnowext 3dnow extd_apicid
                      pni cx16 lahf_lm cmp_legacy svm extapic cr8_legacy
bogomips            : 1603.35
clflush size        : 64
cache_alignment     : 64
address sizes       : 40 bits physical, 48 bits virtual
```

```
power management    : ts fid vid ttp tm stc
[root@server1 ~]# _
```

The preceding output is from a computer with two processors (or processor cores) that run at 800MHz (processor 0 and processor 1), with 256KB of processor cache. If, for example, the computer in actuality has two processors and Linux failed to detect the second processor, you might need to change a setting in BIOS or research a solution to the problem on the mainboard or processor manufacturer's Web site.

After installation, you also need to ensure that Linux has detected the correct amount of RAM. To do this, you can view the contents of the /proc/meminfo file, as shown in the following output:

```
[root@server1 ~]# cat /proc/meminfo
MemTotal:              961284 kB
MemFree:                16444 kB
Buffers:                71592 kB
Cached:                618088 kB
SwapCached:                64 kB
Active:                453108 kB
Inactive:              391516 kB
Active(anon):           80972 kB
Inactive(anon):         78768 kB
Active(file):          372136 kB
Inactive(file):        312748 kB
Unevictable:               16 kB
Mlocked:                   16 kB
HighTotal:              74824 kB
HighFree:                 624 kB
LowTotal:              886460 kB
LowFree:                15820 kB
SwapTotal:            4095992 kB
SwapFree:             4094616 kB
Dirty:                    456 kB
Writeback:                  0 kB
AnonPages:             154900 kB
Mapped:                 73132 kB
Shmem:                   4796 kB
Slab:                   50960 kB
SReclaimable:           38160 kB
SUnreclaim:             12800 kB
KernelStack:             2088 kB
PageTables:              8772 kB
NFS_Unstable:               0 kB
Bounce:                     0 kB
WritebackTmp:               0 kB
CommitLimit:          4576632 kB
Committed_AS:          620996 kB
VmallocTotal:          122880 kB
```

6

```
VmallocUsed:             44444 kB
VmallocChunk:            63652 kB
HardwareCorrupted:           0 kB
HugePages_Total:             0
HugePages_Free:              0
HugePages_Rsvd:              0
HugePages_Surp:              0
Hugepagesize:             2048 kB
DirectMap4k:              8184 kB
DirectMap2M:            899072 kB
[root@server1 ~]# _
```

In the preceding output, the total amount of memory (MemTotal) is 961,284KB, or approximately 1GB. If this value is incorrect because the computer has 2GB of RAM, you may need to change a setting in BIOS or research a solution to the problem on the mainboard or RAM manufacturer's Web site.

In some cases, it's necessary to insert a device's driver into the Linux kernel as a module. This is typically true of sound cards, video cards, network cards, and USB devices. To see a list of modules currently inserted into the Linux kernel, view the /proc/modules file, as shown in the following output:

```
[root@server1 ~]# cat /proc/modules
vfat 6435 0 - Live 0xf7ed9000
fat 36677 1 vfat, Live 0xfb3cd000
usb_storage 34392 0 - Live 0xf9af1000
aes_i586 7078 1 - Live 0xf7ea0000
aes_generic 26388 1 aes_i586, Live 0xfaa8a000
fuse 46663 2 - Live 0xfa868000
sunrpc 159624 1 - Live 0xfab58000
ipv6 216224 26 - Live 0xfaae1000
cpufreq_ondemand 6732 1 - Live 0xfaa93000
powernow_k8 12761 1 - Live 0xfaa84000
uinput 5210 0 - Live 0xfa78b000
snd_hda_codec_idt 44127 1 - Live 0xf9f7a000
snd_hda_intel 20311 2 - Live 0xf9b5d000
snd_hda_codec 61515 2 snd_hda_codec_idt,snd_hda_intel, Live 0xf9b38000
arc4 1041 2 - Live 0xf9b1c000
ecb 1491 2 - Live 0xf9b13000
snd_hwdep 4704 1 snd_hda_codec, Live 0xf9b09000
rtl8180 23739 0 - Live 0xf9afc000
snd_seq 41363 0 - Live 0xf9ae4000
snd_seq_device 4867 1 snd_seq, Live 0xf8a16000
snd_pcm 59444 2 snd_hda_intel,snd_hda_codec, Live 0xf9ac2000
mac80211 163458 1 rtl8180, Live 0xf9a82000
eeprom_93cx6 1207 1 rtl8180, Live 0xf7fd0000
forcedeth 41902 0 - Live 0xf7f64000
i2c_nforce2 5522 0 - Live 0xf7f5d000
cfg80211 97351 2 rtl8180,mac80211, Live 0xf7f35000
```

```
snd_timer 15063 2 snd_seq,snd_pcm, Live 0xf7f0e000
snd 45127 12
snd_hda_codec_idt,snd_hda_intel,snd_hda_codec,snd_hwdep,snd_seq,
snd_seq_device,snd_pcm,snd_timer, Live 0xf7ee4000
soundcore 4842 1 snd, Live 0xf7e9c000
snd_page_alloc 5941 2 snd_hda_intel,snd_pcm, Live 0xf7e90000
k8temp 2771 0 - Live 0xf7e71000
3x59x 30376 0 -Live 0x14c3d000
rfkill 12905 2 cfg80211, Live 0xf7e7e000
microcode 10013 0 - Live 0xf7e5d000
joydev 7291 0 - Live 0xf7e3f000
ata_generic 2287 0 - Live 0xf8a1e000
pata_acpi 2211 0 - Live 0xf8a0e000
pata_amd 7358 3 - Live 0xf8a02000
nouveau 334926 2 - Live 0xf7f70000
ttm 43888 1 nouveau, Live 0xf7ef9000
drm_kms_helper 21663 1 nouveau, Live 0xf7edc000
drm 133962 4 nouveau,ttm,drm_kms_helper, Live 0xf7ea4000
i2c_algo_bit 3929 1 nouveau, Live 0xf7e73000
video 17109 1 nouveau, Live 0xf7e63000
output 1541 1 video, Live 0xf7e53000
i2c_core  19651  5  i2c_nforce2,nouveau,drm_kms_helper,drm,i2c_algo_bit,
Live 0xf7e49000
[root@server1 ~]# _
```

In the preceding output, you can see that the module for the 3COM 590c NIC card (3x59x) as well as the sound support module (soundcore) are inserted into the kernel. If a module that represents the driver for a particular hardware device is not in the kernel, you might need to add the module manually, as discussed in Chapter 13.

The /proc directory contains many more files than presented so far in this chapter. Table 6-2 describes some files that you will find useful when examining a system after installation.

Hardware is detected by the Linux kernel at system startup. However, this information is displayed too quickly to read; in fact, in the graphical Fedora startup screen it is hidden. Fortunately, the system logs all information regarding hardware detection and the startup of system processes in log files that can be viewed at a later time.

To view the hardware detected during boot time, you can use the dmesg command after system startup, as shown in the following output. This information is also stored in the /var/log/dmesg log file:

```
[root@server1 ~]# dmesg | tail
sd 2:0:0:0 [sdb] Mode Sense: 00 00 00 00
sd 2:0:0:0: [sdb] Assuming drive cache: write through
sd 2:0:0:0: [sdb] Assuming drive cache: write through
   sdb: sdb1
sd 2:0:0:0: [sdb] Assuming drive cache: write through
sd 2:0:0:0: [sdb] Attached SCSI removable disk
usb 1-2: USB disconnect, address 2
 [drm] nouveau 0000:00:05.0: Setting dpms mode 3 on lvds encoder
```

Filename	Contents
apm	Information about Advanced Power Management
cmdline	Current location of the Linux kernel
cpuinfo	Information regarding the processors in the computer
devices	List of the character and block devices that are currently in use by the Linux kernel
execdomains	List of execution domains for processes on the system; execution domains allow a process to execute in a specific manner
fb	List of framebuffer devices in use on the Linux system; typically, these include video adapter card devices
filesystems	List of filesystems supported by the Linux kernel
interrupts	List of IRQs in use on the system
iomem	List of memory addresses currently used
ioports	List of memory address ranges reserved for device use
kcore	A representation of the physical memory inside the computer; this file should not be viewed
kmsg	Temporary storage location for messages from the kernel
loadavg	Statistics on the performance of the processor
locks	List of files currently locked by the kernel
mdstat	Configuration of multiple-disk RAID hardware
meminfo	Information regarding physical and virtual memory on the Linux system
misc	List of miscellaneous devices (major number = 10)
modules	List of currently loaded modules in the Linux kernel
mounts	List of currently mounted filesystems
partitions	Information regarding partition tables loaded in memory on the system
pci	List of the PCI devices on the system and their configurations
scsi	Information on SCSI devices on the Linux system
swaps	Information on virtual memory utilization
version	Version information for the Linux kernel and libraries

Table 6-2   Files commonly found in the /proc directory

```
[drm] nouveau 0000:00:05.0: Calling LVDS script 6:
[drm] nouveau 0000:00:05.0: 0xD3CD: Parsing digital output script table
[root@server1 ~]# _
```

You can also view the system processes that started successfully or unsuccessfully during boot time by viewing the contents of the /var/log/messages log file. This file also contains messages from the system after boot time. A sample messages log file is shown in the following output:

```
[root@server1 ~]# tail /var/log/messages
Aug 18 16:49:54 localhost kernel: sd 2:0:0:0: [sdb] Assuming drive
cache: write through
```

```
Aug 18 16:49:54 localhost kernel: sdb: sdb1
Aug 18 16:49:54 localhost kernel: sd 2:0:0:0: [sdb] Assuming drive
cache: write through
Aug 18 16:49:54 localhost kernel: sd 2:0:0:0: [sdb] Attached SCSI
removable disk
Aug 18 16:50:14 localhost kernel: usb 1-2: USB disconnect, address 2
Aug 18 17:20:23 localhost kernel: [drm] nouveau 0000:00:05.0: Setting
dpms mode 3 on lvds encoder (output 0)
Aug 18 17:20:23 localhost kernel: [drm] nouveau 0000:00:05.0: Calling
LVDS script 6:
Aug 18 17:20:23 localhost kernel: [drm] nouveau 0000:00:05.0: 0xD3CD:
Parsing digital output script table
Aug 18 17:43:08 localhost NetworkManager[1118]: <info> (wlan0):
supplicant connection state: completed -> group handshake
Aug 18 17:43:08 localhost NetworkManager[1118]: <info> (wlan0):
supplicant connection state: group handshake -> completed
[root@server1 ~]# _
```

NOTE Log files can become very large over time. To save space on the filesystem, the system archives old copies of these log files in the /var/log directory and appends the date to them in the format YYYYMMDD. For example, to view the archive of /var/log/messages from August 22, 2010, you could view the /var/log/messages-20100822 file.

System Rescue

The installation files of most Linux distributions contain a small bootable Linux kernel and virtual filesystem that you can load into RAM and then use to fix problems that prevent Linux from functioning properly or loading at system startup. In particular, you can use this small bootable Linux kernel to fix problems related to the following: the boot loader; filesystems and partitions; the configuration file; and drivers.

In Fedora 13, this small bootable kernel is known as System Rescue. As explained in Chapter 2, you can boot from your Fedora 13 DVD and select Rescue installed system at the initial welcome screen, shown earlier in Figure 2-1, to start System Rescue. Next, you are prompted to choose your language and keyboard layout, and to indicate whether System Rescue should configure the network cards on your system. (You should choose to configure network cards if you need to obtain files or updates from across the network or Internet.) Following this, you see the screen shown in Figure 6-11.

This screen offers several options. Click Continue to allow System Rescue to mount your / (root) filesystem to the /mnt/sysimage directory in RAM, and to mount all other filesystems to the appropriate mount point directories underneath the /mnt/sysimage directory. If your filesystems are damaged, choose Skip instead. This bypasses mounting, so that you can repair the filesystem. If your system was subject to a security breach and you want to view any files that were modified maliciously, while at the same time ensuring that you can't make any changes to those files, choose Read-Only. This forces System Rescue to mount the filesystems on your hard disk underneath /mnt/sysimage as read-only.

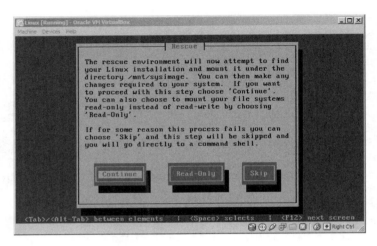

Figure 6-11 Selecting System Rescue mount options

Source: Course Technology/Cengage Learning

Next, no matter which choice you make, you see the menu shown in Figure 6-12, which allows you to access a BASH shell, run a system diagnostic test, or reboot the system.

If you choose the shell option, a BASH shell starts with access to a / (root) filesystem in RAM. This file system contains /bin, /usr/bin, /sbin, and /usr/sbin directories, which in turn contain commands (such as fdisk, fsck, and mkfs) that you can use to repair problems with your filesystem, as well as commands (such as vi and nano) that you can use to edit configuration files, and commands (cp, mv) that you can use to copy files from backup locations. If you chose to mount your / (root) filesystem to the /mnt/sysimage directory (in other words, if you clicked Continue in the screen shown in Figure 6-11), you can now list the contents of the /mnt/sysimage directory to view the files and subdirectories on the / (root) filesystem on your hard disk. Additionally, you can run the chroot /mnt/sysimage command to force your

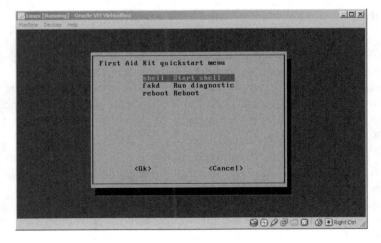

Figure 6-12 Selecting System Rescue options

Source: Course Technology/Cengage Learning

Figure 6-13 Using the System Rescue BASH shell

Source: Course Technology/Cengage Learning

System Rescue Linux kernel to set the / (root) directory of System Rescue to /mnt/sysimage in order to make it easier to navigate your / (root) filesystem on the hard disk. This is illustrated by the System Rescue commands shown in Figure 6-13.

> **NOTE** After running the `chroot /mnt/sysimage` command, System Rescue allows you root access to all of the files and commands on your / (root) filesystem, including the ability to change the root user's password!

Chapter Summary

- Many different SCSI standards have been developed since 1986. Parallel SCSI hard disks are uniquely identified by a SCSI ID and attach to a controller via a terminated cable. SAS is a newer SCSI technology that transfers information to hard disks using a serial cable. iSCSI is a SAN technology used to transfer information from iSCSI initiators to iSCSI targets across a TCP/IP network.

- RAID is often used within Linux servers to combine several hard disks into a single volume for speed or fault tolerance. It can be implemented by software that runs within the OS, hardware on a hard disk controller card, or by the system BIOS.

- The different levels of RAID determine how disks are combined and written to. RAID level 0 is not fault tolerant, whereas RAID levels 1 through 6 provide fault tolerance for data in the event of hard disk failure.

- Although Linux is typically installed from a DVD, you can also install it using files located on a CD, USB flash memory drive, or hard disk, as well as files stored on NFS, FTP, or HTTP servers.

- You can use a kickstart file to simplify the installation of Linux on several computers.

- Unsupported video cards, overclocked CPUs, PnP support, and improper RAM settings can cause an installation to fail.

- The /proc directory contains information regarding detected hardware on the system and is useful when verifying whether an installation was successful.

- You can use the System Rescue feature of the Fedora installation media to access and repair a damaged Linux installation.

Key Terms

dd command   A Linux command that can be used to write image files to a device such as a USB flash memory drive or hard disk.

disk imaging software   Software used to copy sectors between devices. For example, you can use disk imaging software to copy an ISO image to a disk device sector-by-sector, preserving the image's boot sector. An ISO image copied in this way can be used to start the system BIOS.

disk mirroring   A RAID configuration consisting of two identical hard disks to which identical data is written in parallel, thus ensuring fault tolerance. Also known as RAID 1.

disk striping   A RAID configuration in which a single file is divided into sections, which are then written to different hard disks concurrently to speed up access time; this type of RAID is not fault tolerant. Also known as RAID 0.

disk striping with parity   A RAID configuration that incorporates disk striping for faster file access, as well as parity information to ensure fault tolerance. Also known as RAID 5.

fault tolerant   Term used to describe a device that exhibits a minimum of downtime in the event of a failure.

File Transfer Protocol (FTP)   The most common protocol used to transfer files across the Internet.

firmware RAID   A RAID system controlled by the computer's BIOS.

hardware RAID   A RAID system controlled by hardware located on a disk controller card within the computer.

Hypertext Transfer Protocol (HTTP)   The protocol used to transfer information over the Internet.

installation log files   The files created at installation to record actions that occurred or failed during the installation process.

Internet SCSI (iSCSI)   A SCSI technology that transfers data via TCP/IP networks.

iSCSI initiator   The software and hardware components that can be used to transfer files to and from an iSCSI target.

iSCSI target   An external iSCSI storage device that hosts one or more hard disks.

ISO image   A file that contains an ISO filesystem.

Kickstart Configurator   A graphical utility that can be used to create a kickstart file.

kickstart file   A file that can be specified at the beginning of a Fedora Linux installation to automate the installation process.

Logical Unit Number (LUN)   A unique identifier for each device attached to any given node in a SCSI chain.

Network File System (NFS)   A distributed filesystem developed by Sun Microsystems that allows computers of differing types to access files shared on the network.

overclocked   Term used to describe a CPU that runs faster than the clock speed for which it has been rated.

Parallel SCSI   The traditional SCSI technology that transfers data across parallel cables.

redundant array of independent disks (RAID)   The process of combining the storage space of several hard disk drives into one larger, logical storage unit.

SCSI ID   A number that uniquely identifies and prioritizes devices attached to a SCSI controller.

segmentation fault   An error that software encounters when it cannot locate the information needed to complete its task.

Serial Attached SCSI (SAS)   A SCSI technology that transfers information in serial mode rather than the traditional parallel mode.

software RAID   A RAID system that is controlled by software running within the operating system.

spanning   A type of RAID level 0 that allows two or more devices to be represented as a single large volume.

Storage Area Network (SAN)   A group of computers that access the same storage device across a fast network.

target ID   *See also* SCSI ID.

terminator   A device used to terminate an electrical conduction medium to absorb the transmitted signal and prevent signal bounce.

Review Questions

1. SAS transfers data to SCSI disks via parallel cables. True or False?

2. Which of the following is used to describe a computer that is used to access an iSCSI hard disk across the network?

   a.   iSCSI target

   b.   iSCSI requestor

   c.   iSCSI initiator

   d.   iSCSI terminator

3. You want to view log files to get information about a problem you are having. In which directory will you likely find the log files?

   a.   /root/log

   b.   /sys/log

   c.   /var/log

   d.   /etc/log

4. Which of the following RAID levels is not fault tolerant?

   a.   RAID 0

   b.   RAID 1

   c.   RAID 4

   d.   RAID 5

5. Which directory does System Rescue use to mount the / (root) filesystem that is located on your hard disk?

   a. /media

   b. /mnt/sysimage

   c. /chroot

   d. /

6. Which of the following is not a type of RAID?

   a. hardware RAID

   b. software RAID

   c. firmware RAID

   d. serial RAID

7. Where is the /proc filesystem stored?

   a. in RAM

   b. on the hard disk drive in the / directory

   c. on the hard disk drive in the /etc directory

   d. on the hard disk drive in the /var directory

8. Which RAID level uses striping with parity?

   a. RAID 2

   b. RAID 4

   c. RAID 1

   d. RAID 5

9. The Fedora installation process automatically generates a sample kickstart configuration file called /root/anaconda-ks.cfg. True or False?

10. SCSI devices that use an 8-bit-wide data path use _____.

    a. an 8-pin connector

    b. a 15-pin connector

    c. a 50-pin connector

    d. a 68-pin connector

11. Which type of RAID requires that you choose Specialized Storage Devices during the Fedora installation?

    a. hardware RAID

    b. software RAID

    c. firmware RAID

    d. serial RAID

12. What stores the default boot order for a PC?

    a.   system BIOS

    b.   boot loader

    c.   the /proc/loader file

    d.   the MBR of the first hard disk

13. List the following SCSI IDs in proper priority order.

    a.   5

    b.   7

    c.   15

    d.   8

    e.   2

    f.   11

    g.   13

    h.   1

    i.   0

14. Which of the following can be used to simplify the deployment of several Linux servers in your organization?

    a.   disk burning software

    b.   an automatic software installation server

    c.   a kickstart file

    d.   an automated boot disk

15. Which RAID level is also referred to as mirroring?

    a.   RAID 0

    b.   RAID 1

    c.   RAID 4

    d.   RAID 5

16. A SCSI-3 controller card can always accommodate more devices than a SCSI-2 controller card. True or False?

17. Which of the following could result in a segmentation fault (fatal signal 11) during a Fedora installation? (Choose all that apply.)

    a.   RAM problems

    b.   overclocked CPU

    c.   damaged installation media

    d.   Plug-and-Play support

18. SCSI-1 is also referred to as _____.

   a. fast and wide

   b. slow and wide

   c. slow and narrow

   d. fast and narrow

19. You need to perform a Fedora installation from source files hosted on an FTP server across the network. What is the first step you should perform?

   a. Boot from local Fedora installation media and select the FTP server option from the welcome screen.

   b. Obtain a network boot floppy disk from *http://fedoraproject.org*.

   c. Download a network installation CD from *http://fedoraproject.com*.

   d. Boot from local Fedora installation media and modify the boot options to include `askmethod`.

20. Immediately after installation, you want to view the installation log files. Which files should you view? (Choose two answers.)

   a. /root/install.log

   b. /proc/install.log

   c. /root/install.log.syslog

   d. /proc/install.log.syslog

Hands-On Projects

These projects should be completed in the order given. The hands-on projects presented in this chapter should take a total of three hours to complete. The requirements for this lab include:

- A computer with Fedora 13 installed according to Hands-On Project 2-2

Project 6-1

In this hands-on project, you create and view a kickstart file using the Kickstart Configurator. Then you compare it to the kickstart file automatically generated by the Fedora installation program.

1. Turn on your computer. After your Linux system has been loaded, switch to a command-line terminal (tty2) by pressing **Ctrl+Alt+F2** and log in to the terminal using the user name of **root** and the password of **secret**.

2. At the command prompt, type **yum install system-config-kickstart** and press **Enter**. Your system locates the necessary packages stored in software repositories on the Internet.

3. When prompted to download and install these packages, type **y** and press **Enter**.

4. Switch to your graphical terminal (tty1 or tty7) by pressing **Ctrl+Alt+F1** or **Ctrl+Alt+F7** and log in to the GNOME desktop as **user1** with the password of **secret**.

5. Click **Applications**, choose **System Tools**, and click **Terminal** to open a BASH shell terminal.

6. At the command prompt, type `system-config-kickstart` and press **Enter** to start the Kickstart Configurator. Explore the various settings within the Kickstart Configurator and make selections of your choice.

7. Click the **File** menu and choose **Save**. At the Save File screen, ensure that **ks.cfg** is listed as the filename, and click **Save**. This saves your selections to the ks.cfg file in the /home/user1 directory.

8. Close the Kickstart Configurator and log out of the GNOME desktop.

9. Switch back to your command-line terminal (tty2) by pressing **Ctrl+Alt+F2**.

10. At the command prompt, type `less /home/user1/ks.cfg` and press **Enter**. View the entries created in the file by the Kickstart Configurator, and type **q** to quit when finished.

11. At the command prompt, type `less anaconda-ks.cfg` and press **Enter**. View the entries created in the file by the Fedora installation program in Hands-On Project 2-2. What differences exist? Type **q** to quit when finished.

12. Type `exit` and press **Enter** to log out of your shell.

Project 6-2

In this hands-on project, you perform a kickstart installation. Following the kickstart installation, you manually run the firstboot wizard to configure system settings.

1. Switch to a command-line terminal (tty2) by pressing **Ctrl+Alt+F2** and log in to the terminal using the user name of **root** and the password of **secret**.

2. At the command prompt, type `cp anaconda-ks.cfg ks.cfg` and press **Enter** to create a copy of the system-generated kickstart file. Next, type `vi ks.cfg` at the command prompt and press **Enter**. Delete the following section of the file:

   ```
   #clearpart --none --drives=sda
   #ignoredisk --only-use=sda
   #part / --fstype=ext4 --size=30000
   #part swap --size=4000
   ```

   Then replace the deleted text with the following:

   ```
   zerombr yes
   clearpart --all
   part / --fstype=ext4 --size=30000
   part swap --size=4000
   ```

   When finished, save your changes and quit the vi editor.

3. Place your Fedora 13 DVD in your DVD drive, type `reboot` at the command prompt and press **Enter** to reboot your computer. If DVD does not come before hard disk in your BIOS boot order, open the boot menu and select your DVD device to ensure that your system boots from your Fedora 13 DVD.

6

4. When you see the Fedora installation welcome screen, press **Tab**. If your hard disk is SATA or SCSI, append **ks=hd:sda1:/root/ks.cfg** to the boot options line and press **Enter**. Alternatively, if your hard disk is PATA, append **ks=hd:hda1:/root/ks.cfg** to the boot options line and press **Enter**. After you press Enter, your computer will typically need 20 to 100 minutes to install Fedora 13, depending on your hardware.

5. When installation is complete, click **Reboot** and remove your DVD.

6. Click **Forward** at the Welcome screen of the firstboot wizard.

7. At the License Information screen, click **Forward**.

8. At the Create User screen, enter the following information:

Username:	user1
Full Name:	sample user one
Password:	secret

9. When finished, click **Forward**. When prompted to use the password even though it is based on a dictionary word, click **Yes**.

10. At the Date and Time screen, confirm the local date and time and click **Forward**.

11. At the Hardware Profile screen, ensure that **Do not send profile** is selected and click **Finish**. Click **No, do not send** when prompted to reconsider sending your hardware profile.

12. Log in to the GNOME desktop environment as **sample user one**.

13. Open the **System** menu and navigate to **Administration, Network** and supply the root user password of **secret** when prompted.

14. Use the Network utility to configure the network interface on your system to obtain Internet access, using the configuration parameters provided by your instructor. Close the Network Configuration utility when finished.

15. Open the **System** menu again and navigate to **Administration, Firewall**. Supply the root user password of **secret** if prompted. Click **Disable** and then **Apply** followed by **Yes** to disable your firewall. Close the Firewall Configuration utility when finished.

16. Open the **System** menu again and navigate to **Administration, SELinux Management**. Supply the root user password of **secret** if prompted. Change the **System Default Enforcing Mode** to **Disabled** and close the SELinux Administration utility.

17. Log out of the GNOME desktop environment.

Project 6-3

In this hands-on project, you use System Rescue to check your root filesystem for errors and to change the root user's password.

1. Switch to a command-line terminal (tty2) by pressing **Ctrl+Alt+F2** and log in to the terminal using the user name of **root** and the password of **secret**.

2. Place your Fedora 13 DVD in your DVD drive, type **reboot** at the command prompt, and press **Enter** to reboot your computer. If DVD does not come before hard disk in your BIOS boot order, open the boot menu and select your DVD device to ensure that your system boots from your Fedora 13 DVD.

3. At the Fedora installation welcome screen, select **Rescue installed system** and press **Enter**.

4. Select **OK** to choose the English language.

5. Select **OK** to choose the US keyboard type.

6. Select **No** to prevent System Rescue from configuring the network interfaces on your system.

7. Select **Continue** to mount the / (root) filesystem on your hard disk to the /mnt/sysimage directory in RAM. When you see a message indicating that the mount operation was successful, select **OK**.

8. At the First Aid Kit quickstart menu, select **fakd** and press **Enter**. Were any errors detected on your system?

9. At the First Aid Kit quickstart menu, select **shell** to obtain a System Rescue BASH shell.

10. At the command prompt, type **pwd** and press **Enter**. What directory are you in?

11. At the command prompt, type **ls -F** and press **Enter**. Note the contents of the / (root) filesystem in RAM.

12. At the command prompt, type **ls –F /mnt/sysimage** and press **Enter**. What files and subdirectories are you viewing?

13. At the command prompt, type **umount /mnt/sysimage** and press **Enter**. Next, type **fsck –f /dev/sda1** and press **Enter** to check the / (root) filesystem on your hard disk for errors. Why should you check this filesystem using System Rescue instead of on a system that has booted normally?

14. At the command prompt, type **mount /mnt/sysimage** and press **Enter** to remount the / (root) filesystem on your hard disk to the /mnt/sysimage directory.

15. At the command prompt, type **chroot /mnt/sysimage** and press **Enter**. Next, type **pwd** and press **Enter**. What directory are you in? Type **ls –F** and press **Enter**. What files and subdirectories are you viewing and why?

16. At the command prompt, type **whoami** and press **Enter** to verify that you are the root user. Next, type **passwd** and press **Enter** to change the root user's password. Type **secret** when prompted and type **secret** again to confirm. Were you able to change the root user's password on the Linux system installed on the hard disk?

17. Type **exit** and press **Enter** to log out of your chroot session. Type **exit** again and press **Enter** to return to the First Aid Kit quickstart menu.

18. Choose **reboot** and press **Enter** to reboot your system, and then remove your DVD from the DVD drive.

Project 6-4

In this hands-on project, you view system information.

1. Switch to a command-line terminal (tty2) by pressing **Ctrl+Alt+F2** and log in to the terminal using the user name of **root** and the password of **secret**.

2. Type **less install.log** at the command prompt, press **Enter**, and view the entries in this file. Were there any errors during package installation? Type **q** to quit the less utility.

3. Type the **less install.log.syslog** command at the command prompt, press **Enter,** and view the entries in this file. What information is displayed in this file? Type **q** to quit the less utility.

4. At the command prompt, type **ls -F /proc** and press **Enter** to view the file and directory contents of the proc filesystem.

5. At the command prompt, type **less /proc/cpuinfo** and press **Enter.** Did the installation detect your CPU correctly? Type q to quit the less utility.

6. At the command prompt, type **less /proc/modules** and press **Enter.** What is displayed? What does each entry represent? Type **q** to quit the less utility.

7. At the command prompt, type **less /proc/meminfo** and press **Enter.** Does your Linux system recognize all the memory in your computer? If not, what could you do? Type **q** to quit the less utility.

8. At the command prompt, type **dmesg | less** and press **Enter.** Observe the entries. How do they correspond with the hardware information that you saw in Step 6? Type **q** to quit the less utility.

9. At the command prompt, type **less /var/log/messages** and press **Enter.** What does each entry represent? How do these entries correspond with the information seen in Step 8? Type **q** to quit the less utility.

10. Type **exit** and press **Enter** to log out of your shell.

Discovery Exercises

1. Determine the following about your system by viewing the appropriate files within the /proc directory:

   a. Where is the Linux kernel located?

   b. What version is your Linux kernel?

   c. What filesystems are supported by your Linux kernel?

   d. Are there any PCI devices in use on the system?

   e. What modules are loaded into the kernel?

   f. Gather information about the physical memory on your system.

2. Use the Internet to gather information on three different commercial iSCSI SAN enclosures that can be used to host Linux, and write a short report that compares and contrasts their features and cost. In what situations would you use each one?

3. Use the Internet to gather information on three different commercial hardware RAID controllers that perform RAID level 5, and write a short report that compares and contrasts their features and costs. In what situations would you use each one?

4. Search the Internet for information about five Linux installation problems that are different from those described in this chapter. How have other people solved these problems? If you had similar difficulties during installation, how could you get help?

5. Linux servers are typically stored in a locked server closet to prevent physical access by unauthorized persons. Given the steps that you performed in Project 6-3, describe why these physical restrictions are warranted.

## chapter 7

Working with the BASH Shell

After completing this chapter, you will be able to:

- Redirect the input and output of a command
- Identify and manipulate common shell environment variables
- Create and export new shell variables
- Edit environment files to create variables upon shell startup
- Describe the purpose and nature of shell scripts
- Create and execute basic shell scripts
- Effectively use common decision constructs in shell scripts

A solid understanding of shell features is vital to both administrators and users, who must interact with the shell on a daily basis. The first part of this chapter describes how the shell can manipulate command input and output using redirection and pipe shell metacharacters. Next, you explore the different types of variables present in a BASH shell after login, as well as their purpose and usage. Finally, this chapter ends with an introduction to creating and executing BASH shell scripts.

Command Input and Output

The BASH shell is responsible for providing a user interface and interpreting commands entered on the command line. In addition, the BASH shell can manipulate command input and output, provided the user specifies certain shell metacharacters on the command line alongside the command. Command input and output are represented by labels known as **file descriptors**. For each command that can be manipulated by the BASH shell, there are three file descriptors:

- Standard input (stdin)
- Standard output (stdout)
- Standard error (stderr)

Standard input (stdin) refers to the information processed by the command during execution; this often takes the form of user input typed on the keyboard. **Standard output (stdout)** refers to the normal output of a command, whereas **standard error (stderr)** refers to any error messages generated by the command. Both stdout and stderr are displayed on the terminal screen by default. All three components are depicted in Figure 7-1.

As shown in Figure 7-1, each file descriptor is represented by a number, with stdin represented by the number 0, stdout represented by the number 1, and stderr represented by the number 2.

Although all three descriptors are available to any command, not all commands use every descriptor. The `file /etc/hosts /etc/h` command in Figure 7-1 gives stdout (the listing

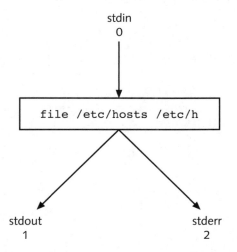

Figure 7-1 The three common file descriptors

Source: Course Technology/Cengage Learning

of the /etc/hosts file) and stderr (an error message indicating that the /etc/h file does not exist) to the terminal screen, as shown in the following output:

```
[root@server1 ~]# ls /etc/hosts /etc/h
ls: cannot access /etc/h: No such file or directory
/etc/hosts
[root@server1 ~]# _
```

Redirection

You can use the BASH shell to redirect stdout and stderr from the terminal screen to a file on the filesystem. To do this, include the > shell metacharacter followed by the absolute or relative pathname of the file. For example, to redirect only the stdout to a file called goodoutput for the command used in Figure 7-1, you append the number of the file descriptor (1) followed by the **redirection** symbol (>) and the file to redirect the stdout to (goodoutput), as shown in the following output:

```
[root@server1 ~]# ls /etc/hosts /etc/h 1>goodoutput
ls: cannot access /etc/h: No such file or directory
[root@server1 ~]# _
```

 You can include a space character after the > shell metacharacter, but it is not necessary.

In the preceding output, the stderr is still displayed to the terminal screen, because it was not redirected to a file. The listing of /etc/hosts was not displayed, however; instead, it was redirected to a file called goodoutput in the current directory. If the goodoutput file did not exist prior to running the command in the preceding output, it is created automatically. However, if the goodoutput file did exist prior to the redirection, the BASH shell clears its contents before executing the command. To see that the stdout was redirected to the goodoutput file, you can run the following commands:

```
[root@server1 ~]# ls -F
Desktop/  goodoutput
[root@server1 ~]# cat goodoutput
/etc/hosts
[root@server1 ~]# _
```

Similarly, you can redirect the stderr of a command to a file; simply specify file descriptor number 2, as shown in the following output:

```
[root@server1 ~]# ls /etc/hosts /etc/h 2>badoutput
/etc/hosts
[root@server1 ~]# cat badoutput
ls: cannot access /etc/h: No such file or directory
[root@server1 ~]# _
```

In the preceding output, only the stderr was redirected to a file called badoutput; thus, the stdout (a listing of /etc/hosts) was displayed on the terminal screen.

Because redirecting the stdout to a file for later use is more common than redirecting the stderr to a file, the BASH shell assumes stdout in the absence of a numeric file descriptor:

```
[root@server1 ~]# ls /etc/hosts /etc/h >goodoutput
ls: cannot access /etc/h: No such file or directory
[root@server1 ~]# cat goodoutput
/etc/hosts
[root@server1 ~]# _
```

In addition, you can redirect both stdout and stderr to separate files at the same time, as shown in the following output:

```
[root@server1 ~]# ls /etc/hosts /etc/h >goodoutput 2>badoutput
[root@server1 ~]# cat goodoutput
/etc/hosts
[root@server1 ~]# cat badoutput
ls: cannot access /etc/h: No such file or directory
[root@server1 ~]# _
```

 The order of redirection on the command line does not matter; the command `ls /etc/hosts /etc/h >goodoutput 2>badoutput` is the same as `ls /etc/hosts /etc/h 2>badoutput >goodoutput`.

It is important to use separate filenames to hold the contents of stdout and stderr; using the same filename for both causes a loss of data, because the system attempts to write both contents to the file at the same time:

```
[root@server1 ~]#ls /etc/hosts /etc/h >goodoutput 2>goodoutput
[root@server1 ~]# cat goodoutput
/etc/hosts
access /etc/h: No such file or directory
[root@server1 ~]# _
```

To redirect both stdout and stderr to the same file without any loss of data, you must use special notation. To specify that stdout be sent to the file goodoutput and stderr be sent to the same place as stdout, you can do the following:

```
[root@server1 ~]# ls /etc/hosts /etc/h >goodoutput 2>&1
[root@server1 ~]# cat goodoutput
ls: cannot access /etc/h: No such file or directory
/etc/hosts
[root@server1 ~]# _
```

Alternatively, you can specify that the stderr be sent to the file badoutput and stdout be sent to the same place as stderr:

```
[root@server1 ~]# ls /etc/hosts /etc/h 2>badoutput >&2
[root@server1 ~]# cat badoutput
ls: cannot access /etc/h: No such file or directory
/etc/hosts
[root@server1 ~]# _
```

In all of the examples used earlier, the contents of the files used to store the output from commands were cleared prior to use by the BASH shell. Another example of this is shown in the following output when redirecting the stdout of the `date` command to the file dateoutput:

```
[root@server1 ~]# date >dateoutput
[root@server1 ~]# cat dateoutput
Fri Aug 20 07:54:00 EDT 2010
[root@server1 ~]# date >dateoutput
[root@server1 ~]# cat dateoutput
Fri Aug 20 07:54:00 EDT 2010
[root@server1 ~]# _
```

To prevent the file from being cleared by the BASH shell and append output to the existing output, you can specify two > shell metacharacters alongside the file descriptor, as shown in the following output:

```
[root@server1 ~]# date >dateoutput
[root@server1 ~]# cat dateoutput
Fri Aug 20 07:54:32 EDT 2010
[root@server1 ~]# date >>dateoutput
[root@server1 ~]# cat dateoutput
Fri Aug 20 07:54:32 EDT 2010
Fri Aug 20 07:54:48 EDT 2010
[root@server1 ~]# _
```

You can also redirect a file to the stdin of a command using the < shell metacharacter. Because there is only one file descriptor for input, there is no need to specify the number 0 before the < shell metacharacter to indicate stdin, as shown here:

```
[root@server1 ~]# cat </etc/issue
Fedora release 13 (Goddard)
Kernel \r on an \m (\l)

[root@server1 ~]# _
```

In the preceding output, the BASH shell located and sent the /etc/issue file to the `cat` command as stdin. Because the `cat` command normally takes the filename to be displayed as an argument on the command line (for example, cat /etc/issue), there is no need to use stdin redirection with the `cat` command, as used in the previous example; however, some commands on the Linux system only accept files when they are passed by the shell through stdin. The **tr command** is one such command that can be used to replace characters in a file sent via stdin. To translate all of the lowercase r characters in the /etc/issue file to uppercase R characters, you can run the following command:

```
[root@server1 ~]# tr r R </etc/issue
FedoRa Release 13 (GoddaRd)
KeRnel \R on an \m (\l)

[root@server1 ~]# _
```

The preceding command does not modify the /etc/issue file; it simply takes a copy of the /etc/issue file, manipulates it, and then sends the stdout to the terminal screen. To save a copy of the stdout for later use, you can use stdin and stdout redirection together:

```
[root@server1 ~]# tr r R </etc/issue >newissue
[root@server1 ~]# cat newissue
FedoRa Release 13 (GoddaRd)
KeRnel \R on an \m (\l)

[root@server1 ~]# _
```

As with redirecting stdout and stderr in the same command, you should use different file-names when redirecting stdin and stdout. However, this is because the BASH shell clears a file that already exists before performing the redirection. An example of this is shown in the following output:

```
[root@server1 ~]# sort <newissue >newissue
[root@server1 ~]# cat newissue
[root@server1 ~]# _
```

The newissue file has no contents when displayed in the preceding output. This is because the BASH shell saw that output redirection was indicated on the command line, cleared the contents of the file newissue, then sorted the blank file and saved the output (nothing in our example) into the file newissue. Because of this feature of shell redirection, Linux administrators commonly use the command >filename at the command prompt to clear the contents of a file.

The contents of log files are typically cleared periodically using the command >/path/to/logfile.

Table 7-1 summarizes the different types of redirection discussed in this section.

Pipes

Note from Table 7-1 that redirection only occurs between a command and a file and vice versa. However, you can send the stdout of one command to another command as stdin. To do this, you use the | (**pipe**) shell metacharacter and specify commands on either side. The shell then sends the stdout of the command on the left to the command on the right, which then interprets the information as stdin. This process is depicted in Figure 7-2.

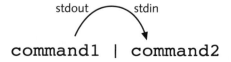

stdout   stdin

```
command1 | command2
```

Figure 7-2 Piping information from one command to another

Source: Course Technology/Cengage Learning

Command	Description
`1>file` `>file`	The stdout of the command is sent to a file instead of to the terminal screen.
`2>file`	The stderr of the command is sent to a file instead of to the terminal screen.
`1>fileA 2>fileB` `>fileA 2>fileB`	The stdout of the command is sent to fileA instead of to the terminal screen, and the stderr of the command is sent to fileB instead of to the terminal screen.

`1>file 2>&1`
`>file 2>&1`
`1>&2 2>file`
`command >&2 2>file`
	Both the stdout and the stderr are sent to the same file instead of to the terminal screen.

`1>>file` `>>file`	The stdout of the command is appended to a file instead of being sent to the terminal screen.
`2>>file`	The stderr of the command is appended to a file instead of being sent to the terminal screen.
`0<file` `<file`	The stdin of a command is taken from a file.

Table 7-1   **Common redirection examples**

 The whole command that includes the | (pipe) shell metacharacter is commonly referred to as a **pipe**.

 The pipe symbol can be created on most keyboards by pressing Shift+\.

For example, the stdout of the `ls -l /etc` command is too large to fit on one terminal screen. To send the stdout of this command to the `less` command, which views stdin page-by-page, you could use the following command:

```
[root@server1 ~]# ls -l /etc | less
total 3052
drwxr-xr-x.  3 root     root      4096 Aug  2 09:45 abrt
drwxr-xr-x.  4 root     root      4096 Aug  2 09:59 acpi
-rw-r--r--.  1 root     root        44 Aug 19 20:01 adjtime
drwxr-xr-x.  2 root     root      4096 Aug  2 09:58 akonadi
drwxr-xr-x.  4 root     root      4096 Aug  2 09:45 alchemist
-rw-r--r--.  1 root     root      1512 Mar 31 06:56 aliases
-rw-r-----.  1 root     smmsp    12288 Aug  2 09:56 aliases.db
drwxr-xr-x.  2 root     root      4096 Aug  2 10:07 alsa
drwxr-xr-x.  2 root     root      4096 Aug  6 19:35 alternatives
-rw-r--r--.  1 root     root       541 Feb 19 03:43 anacrontab
```

```
-rw-r--r--.  1 root      root      391 Sep 26  2008 ant.conf
drwxr-xr-x.  2 root      root     4096 Aug  2 10:17 ant.d
-rw-r--r--.  1 root      root      245 Dec 21  2009 anthy-conf
-rw-r--r--.  1 root      root      148 Sep 10  2008 asound.conf
-rw-------.  1 root      root        1 Mar 19 02:56 at.deny
-rw-r--r--.  1 root      root      186 Jul 26  2009 atmsigd.conf
drwxr-x---.  3 root      root     4096 Aug  2 09:45 audisp
drwxr-x---.  2 root      root     4096 Aug  2 09:45 audit
drwxr-xr-x.  4 root      root     4096 Aug  2 09:54 avahi
drwxr-x---.  3 backuppc  backuppc 4096 Aug  2 10:02 BackupPC
drwxr-xr-x.  2 root      root     4096 Aug  2 10:00 bash_completion.d
-rw-r--r--.  1 root      root     2631 Mar 31 06:56 bashrc
:
```

You need not have spaces around the | shell metacharacter. The following commands are equivalent: ls –l /etc|less and ls –l /etc | less.

A common use of piping is to reduce the amount of information displayed on the terminal screen from commands that display too much information. Take the following output from the mount command:

```
[root@server1 ~]# mount
/dev/sda1 on / type ext4 (rw)
proc on /proc type proc (rw)
sysfs on /sys type sysfs (rw)
devpts on /dev/pts type devpts (rw,gid=5,mode=620)
tmpfs on /dev/shm type tmpfs (rw)
/dev/sda3 on /oracle type ext4 (rw)
/dev/mapper/vg00-data on /data type ext4 (rw,usrquota,grpquota)
none on /proc/sys/fs/binfmt_misc type binfmt_misc (rw)
sunrpc on /var/lib/nfs/rpc_pipefs type rpc_pipefs (rw)
[root@server1 ~]# _
```

To view only those lines that contain the information regarding filesystems mounted from the first SATA hard disk (/dev/sda), you could send the stdout of the mount command to the grep command as stdin, as shown in the following output:

```
[root@server1 ~]# mount | grep /dev/sda
/dev/sda1 on / type ext4 (rw)
/dev/sda3 on /oracle type ext4 (rw)
[root@server1 ~]# _
```

The grep command in the preceding output receives the full output from the mount command and then displays only those lines that have /dev/sda in them. The grep command normally takes two arguments; the first specifies the text to search for and the second specifies the filename(s) to search within. The grep command used in the preceding output requires no second argument, because the material to search comes from stdin (the mount command) instead of from a file.

Furthermore, you can use more than one | shell metacharacter on the command line to pipe information from one command to another command in much the same fashion as an

Figure 7-3 Piping several commands

Source: Course Technology/Cengage Learning

assembly line in a factory. Typically, an assembly line goes through several departments, each of which performs a specialized task very well. For example, one department might assemble the product, another might paint the product, and yet another might package the product. Every product must pass through each department to be complete.

You can use Linux commands that manipulate data in the same way, connecting them into an assembly line via piping. Information is manipulated by one command, and then that manipulated information is sent to another command, which manipulates it further. The process continues until the information attains the form required by the user. The piping process is depicted in Figure 7-3.

Any command that can take stdin and transform it into stdout is called a **filter command**. It is important to note that commands such as `ls` and `mount` are not filter commands, because they do not accept stdin from other commands but instead find information from the system and display it to the user. As a result, these commands must be at the beginning of a pipe. Other commands, such as `vi`, are interactive and, as such, cannot exist between two pipe symbols, because they cannot take from stdin and give to stdout.

Several hundred filter commands are available to Linux users. Table 7-2 lists some common ones used throughout this book.

Command	Description
`sort`	Sorts lines in a file alphanumerically
`sort -r`	Reverse-sorts lines in a file alphanumerically
`wc`	Counts the number of lines, words, and characters in a file
`wc -l`	Counts the number of lines in a file
`wc -w`	Counts the number of words in a file
`wc -c`	Counts the number of characters in a file
`pr`	Formats a file for printing, with several options available; it places a date and page number at the top of each page
`pr -d`	Formats a file double-spaced
`tr`	Replaces characters in the text of a file
`grep`	Displays lines in a file that match a regular expression
`nl`	Numbers lines in a file
`awk`	Extracts, manipulates, and formats text using pattern-action statements
`sed`	Manipulates text using search-and-replace expressions

Table 7-2 Common filter commands

Take, for example, the prologue from Shakespeare's *Romeo and Juliet*:

```
[root@server1 ~]# cat prologue
Two households, both alike in dignity,
In fair Verona, where we lay our scene,
From ancient grudge break to new mutiny,
Where civil blood makes civil hands unclean.
From forth the fatal loins of these two foes
A pair of star-cross'd lovers take their life;
Whose misadventured piteous overthrows
Do with their death bury their parents' strife.
The fearful passage of their death-mark'd love,
And the continuance of their parents' rage,
Which, but their children's end, nought could remove,
Is now the two hours' traffic of our stage;
The which if you with patient ears attend,
What here shall miss, our toil shall strive to mend.
[root@server1 ~]# _
```

Now, suppose you want to replace all lowercase "a" characters with uppercase "A" characters in the preceding file, sort the contents by the first character on each line, double-space the output, and view the results page-by-page. To accomplish these tasks, you can use the following pipe:

```
[root@server1 ~]# cat prologue | tr a A | sort | pr -d | less
```

```
2010-08-20 08:06                                    Page 1
And the continuAnce of their pArents' rAge,
A pAir of stAr-cross'd lovers tAke their life;
Do with their deAth bury their pArents'  strife.
From Ancient grudge breAk to new mutiny,
From forth the fAtAl loins of these two foes
In fAir VeronA, where we lAy our scene,
Is now the two hours' trAffic of our stAge;
The feArful pAssAge of their deAth-mArk'd love,
The which if you with pAtient eArs Attend,
Two households, both Alike in dignity,
:
```

The command used in the preceding example displays the final stdout to the terminal screen via the less command. In many cases, you might want to display the results of the pipe while at the same time save a copy in a file on the hard disk. The filter command for this job is the **tee command**, which takes information from stdin and sends that information to a file, as well as to stdout.

To save a copy of the manipulated prologue before displaying it to the terminal screen with the less command, you can use the following command:

```
[root@server1 ~]# cat prologue|tr a A|sort|pr -d|tee newfile|less
2010-08-20 08:06                                    Page 1
And the continuAnce of their pArents' rAge,
```

```
A pAir of stAr-cross'd lovers tAke their life;
Do with their deAth bury their pArents' strife.
From Ancient grudge breAk to new mutiny,
From forth the fAtAl loins of these two foes
In fAir VeronA, where we lAy our scene,
Is now the two hours' trAffic of our stAge;
The feArful pAssAge of their deAth-mArk'd love,
The which if you with pAtient eArs Attend,
Two households, both Alike in dignity,
:q
[root@server1 ~]# _
[root@server1 ~]# cat newfile
2010-08-20 08:06                              Page 1
And  the  continuAnce  of  their  pArents'  rAge,
A  pAir  of  stAr-cross'd  lovers  tAke  their  life;
Do  with  their  deAth  bury  their  pArents'  strife.
From  Ancient  grudge  breAk  to  new  mutiny,
From  forth  the  fAtAl  loins  of  these  two  foes
In  fAir  VeronA,  where  we  lAy  our  scene,
Is  now  the  two  hours'  trAffic  of  our  stAge;
The  feArful  pAssAge  of  their  deAth-mArk'd  love,
The  which  if  you  with  pAtient  eArs  Attend,
Two  households,  both  Alike  in  dignity,
WhAt  here  shAll  miss,  our  toil  shAll  strive  to  mend.
Where  civil  blood  mAkes  civil  hAnds  uncleAn.
Which,  but  their  children's  end,  nought  could  remove,
Whose  misAdventured  piteous  overthrows
[root@server1 ~]# _
```

You can also combine redirection and piping, as long as input redirection occurs at the beginning of the pipe and output redirection occurs at the end of the pipe. An example of this is shown in the following output, which replaces all lowercase "a" characters with uppercase "A" characters in the prologue file used in the previous example, then sorts the file, numbers each line, and saves the output to a file called newprologue instead of sending the output to the terminal screen:

```
[root@server1 ~]# tr a A <prologue | sort | nl >newprologue
[root@server1 ~]# cat newprologue
     1  And the continuAnce of their pArents' rAge,
     2  A pAir of stAr-cross'd lovers tAke their life;
     3  Do with their deAth bury their pArents' strife.
     4  From Ancient grudge breAk to new mutiny,
     5  From forth the fAtAl loins of these two foes
     6  In fAir VeronA, where we lAy our scene,
     7  Is now the two hours' trAffic of our stAge;
     8  The feArful pAssAge of their deAth-mArk'd love,
     9  The which if you with pAtient eArs Attend,
    10  Two households, both Alike in dignity,
    11  WhAt here shAll miss, our toil shAll strive to mend.
```

```
 12  Where civil blood mAkes civil hAnds uncleAn.
 13  Which, but their children's end, nought could remove,
 14  Whose misAdventured piteous overthrows
[root@server1 ~]# _
```

Many Linux commands can be used to provide large amounts of useful text information. As a result, Linux administrators often use the sed and awk filter commands in conjunction with pipes to manipulate text information obtained from these commands.

The sed command is typically used to search for a certain string of text, and replaces that text string with another text string using the syntax s/search/replace/. For example, the following output demonstrates how sed can be used to search for the string "the" and replace it with the string "THE" in the prologue file used earlier:

```
[root@server1 ~]# cat prologue | sed s/the/THE/
Two households, both alike in dignity,
In fair Verona, where we lay our scene,
From ancient grudge break to new mutiny,
Where civil blood makes civil hands unclean.
From forth THE fatal loins of these two foes
A pair of star-cross'd lovers take THEir life;
Whose misadventured piteous overthrows
Do with THEir death bury their parents' strife.
The fearful passage of THEir death-mark'd love,
And THE continuance of their parents' rage,
Which, but THEir children's end, nought could remove,
Is now THE two hours' traffic of our stage;
The which if you with patient ears attend,
What here shall miss, our toil shall strive to mend.
[root@server1 ~]# _
```

Notice from the preceding output that sed only searched for and replaced the first occurrence of the string "the" in each line. To have sed replace all occurrences of the string "the" in each line, simply append a g to the search-and-replace expression:

```
[root@server1 ~]# cat prologue | sed s/the/THE/g
Two households, both alike in dignity,
In fair Verona, where we lay our scene,
From ancient grudge break to new mutiny,
Where civil blood makes civil hands unclean.
From forth THE fatal loins of THEse two foes
A pair of star-cross'd lovers take THEir life;
Whose misadventured piteous overthrows
Do with THEir death bury THEir parents' strife.
The fearful passage of THEir death-mark'd love,
And THE continuance of THEir parents' rage,
Which, but THEir children's end, nought could remove,
Is now THE two hours' traffic of our stage;
The which if you with patient ears attend,
What here shall miss, our toil shall strive to mend.
[root@server1 ~]# _
```

You can also tell sed the specific lines to search by prefixing the search-and-replace expression. For example, to force sed to replace the string "the" with "THE" globally on lines that contain the string "love," you can use the following command:

```
[root@server1 ~]# cat prologue | sed /love/s/the/THE/g
Two households, both alike in dignity,
In fair Verona, where we lay our scene,
From ancient grudge break to new mutiny,
Where civil blood makes civil hands unclean.
From forth the fatal loins of these two foes
A pair of star-cross'd lovers take THEir life;
Whose misadventured piteous overthrows
Do with their death bury their parents' strife.
The fearful passage of THEir death-mark'd love,
And the continuance of their parents' rage,
Which, but their children's end, nought could remove,
Is now the two hours' traffic of our stage;
The which if you with patient ears attend,
What here shall miss, our toil shall strive to mend.
[root@server1 ~]# _
```

You can also force sed to perform a search-and-replace on certain lines only. To replace the string "the" with "THE" globally on lines 5 to 8 only, you can use the following command:

```
[root@server1 ~]# cat prologue | sed 5,8s/the/THE/g
Two households, both alike in dignity,
In fair Verona, where we lay our scene,
From ancient grudge break to new mutiny,
Where civil blood makes civil hands unclean.
From forth THE fatal loins of THEse two foes
A pair of star-cross'd lovers take THEir life;
Whose misadventured piteous overthrows
Do with THEir death bury THEir parents' strife.
The fearful passage of their death-mark'd love,
And the continuance of their parents' rage,
Which, but their children's end, nought could remove,
Is now the two hours' traffic of our stage;
The which if you with patient ears attend,
What here shall miss, our toil shall strive to mend.
[root@server1 ~]# _
```

You can also use sed to remove unwanted lines of text. To delete all the lines that contain the word "the," you can use the following command:

```
[root@server1 ~]# cat prologue | sed /the/d
Two households, both alike in dignity,
In fair Verona, where we lay our scene,
From ancient grudge break to new mutiny,
Where civil blood makes civil hands unclean.
```

Whose misadventured piteous overthrows
The which if you with patient ears attend,
What here shall miss, our toil shall strive to mend.
[root@server1 ~]# _

Like sed, the awk command searches for patterns of text and performs some action on the text found. However, the awk command treats each line of text as a record in a database, and each word in a line as a database field. For example, the line "Hello, how are you?" has four fields: "Hello," "how," "are," and "you?". These fields can be referenced in the awk command using $1, $2, $3, and $4. For example, to display only the first and fourth words in the lines of the prologue file that contain the word "the," you can use the following command:

```
[root@server1 ~]# cat prologue | awk '/the/ {print $1, $4}'
From fatal
A star-cross'd
Do death
The of
And of
Which, children's
Is two
[root@server1 ~]# _
```

By default, the awk command uses space or tab characters as delimiters for each field in a line. Most configuration files on Linux systems, however, are delimited using the : (colon) character. To change the delimiter that awk uses, you can specify the −F option to the command. For example, the following example lists the last 10 lines of the colon-delimited file /etc/passwd, and views only the sixth and seventh fields for lines that contain the word "bob" in the last 10 lines of the file:

```
[root@server1 ~]# tail /etc/passwd
news:x:9:13:News server user:/etc/news:/sbin/nologin
smolt:x:490:474:Smolt:/usr/share/smolt:/sbin/nologin
backuppc:x:489:473::/var/lib/BackupPC:/sbin/nologin
pulse:x:488:472:PulseAudio System Daemon:/var/run/pulse:/sbin/nologin
gdm:x:42:468::/var/lib/gdm:/sbin/nologin
hsqldb:x:96:96::/var/lib/hsqldb:/sbin/nologin
jetty:x:487:467::/usr/share/jetty:/bin/sh
bozo:x:500:500:bozo the clown:/home/bozo:/bin/bash
bob:x:501:501:Bob Smith:/home/bob:/bin/bash
user1:x:502:502:sample user one:/home/user1:/bin/bash
[root@server1 ~]# tail /etc/passwd | awk −F : '/bob/ {print $6, $7}'
/home/bob /bin/bash
[root@server1 ~]# _
```

Both awk and sed allow you to specify regular expressions in the search pattern.

Shell Variables

A BASH shell has several **variables** in memory at any one time. Recall that a variable is simply a reserved portion of memory containing information that might be accessed. Most variables in the shell are referred to as **environment variables** because they are typically set by the system and contain information that the system and programs access regularly. Users can also create their own custom variables. These variables are called **user-defined variables**. In addition to these two types of variables, special variables are available that are useful when executing commands and creating new files and directories.

Environment Variables

Many environment variables are set by default in the BASH shell. To see a list of these variables and their current values, you can use the **set command**, as shown in the following output:

```
[root@server1 ~]# set
BASH=/bin/bash
BASHOPTS=checkwinsize:cmdhist:expand_aliases:extquote:force_fignore:
hostcomplete:interactive_comments:login_shell:progcomp:promptvars:
sourcepath
BASH_ALIASES=()
BASH_ARGC=()
BASH_ARGV=()
BASH_CMDS=()
BASH_LINENO=()
BASH_SOURCE=()
BASH_VERSINFO=([0]="4" [1]="1" [2]="2" [3]="1" [4]="release"
[5]="i386-redhat-linux-gnu")
BASH_VERSION='4.1.2(1)-release'
CCACHE_DIR=/var/cache/ccache
CCACHE_UMASK=002
COLORS=/etc/DIR_COLORS
COLUMNS=80
CVS_RSH=ssh
DIRSTACK=()
EUID=0
GROUPS=()
G_BROKEN_FILENAMES=1
HISTCONTROL=ignoredups
HISTFILE=/root/.bash_history
HISTFILESIZE=1000
HISTSIZE=1000
HOME=/root
HOSTNAME=localhost.localdomain
```

7

```
HOSTTYPE=i386
IFS=$'\t\n'
KDEDIRS=/usr
KDE_IS_PRELINKED=1
LANG=en_US.UTF-8
LESSOPEN='|/usr/bin/lesspipe.sh %s'
LINES=24
LOGNAME=root
LS_COLORS='rs=0:di=01;34:ln=01;36:mh=00:pi=40;33:so=01;35:
do=01;35:bd=40;33;01:cd=40;33;01:or=40;31;01:mi=01;05;37;41:
su=37;41:sg=30;43:ca=30;41:tw=30;42:ow=34;42:st=37;44:ex=01;32:*.
tar=01;31:*.tgz=01;31:*.arj=01;31:*.taz=01;31:*.lzh=01;31:*.
lzma=01;31:*.tlz=01;31:*.txz=01;31:*.zip=01;31:*.z=01;31:*.
Z=01;31:*.dz=01;31:*.gz=01;31:*.lz=01;31:*.xz=01;31:*.bz2=01;31:*.
tbz=01;31:*.tbz2=01;31:*.bz=01;31:*.tz=01;31:*.deb=01;31:*.
rpm=01;31:*.jar=01;31:*.rar=01;31:*.ace=01;31:*.zoo=01;31:*.
cpio=01;31:*.7z=01;31:*.rz=01;31:*.jpg=01;35:*.jpeg=01;35:*.
gif=01;35:*.bmp=01;35:*.pbm=01;35:*.pgm=01;35:*.ppm=01;35:*.
tga=01;35:*.xbm=01;35:*.xpm=01;35:*.tif=01;35:*.tiff=01;35:*.
png=01;35:*.svg=01;35:*.svgz=01;35:*.mng=01;35:*.pcx=01;35:*.
mov=01;35:*.mpg=01;35:*.mpeg=01;35:*.m2v=01;35:*.mkv=01;35:*.
ogm=01;35:*.mp4=01;35:*.m4v=01;35:*.mp4v=01;35:*.vob=01;35:*.
qt=01;35:*.nuv=01;35:*.wmv=01;35:*.asf=01;35:*.rm=01;35:*.
rmvb=01;35:*.flc=01;35:*.avi=01;35:*.fli=01;35:*.flv=01;35:*.
gl=01;35:*.dl=01;35:*.xcf=01;35:*.xwd=01;35:*.yuv=01;35:*.
cgm=01;35:*.emf=01;35:*.axv=01;35:*.anx=01;35:*.ogv=01;35:*.
ogx=01;35:*.aac=01;36:*.au=01;36:*.flac=01;36:*.mid=01;36:*.
midi=01;36:*.mka=01;36:*.mp3=01;36:*.mpc=01;36:*.ogg=01;36:*.
ra=01;36:*.wav=01;36:*.axa=01;36:*.oga=01;36:*.spx=01;36:*.
xspf=01;36:'
MACHTYPE=i386-redhat-linux-gnu
MAIL=/var/spool/mail/root
MAILCHECK=60
OPTERR=1
OPTIND=1
OSTYPE=linux-gnu
PATH=/usr/lib/qt-3.3/bin:/usr/kerberos/sbin:/usr/kerberos/bin:
/usr/lib/ccache:/usr/local/sbin:/usr/local/bin:/sbin:/bin:/usr/sbin:
/usr/bin:/root/bin
PIPESTATUS=([0]="0" [1]="0")
PPID=2142
PROMPT_COMMAND='echo -ne "\033]0;${USER}@${HOSTNAME%%.*}:${PWD/
#$HOME/~}"; echo -ne "\007"'
PS1='[\u@\h \W]\$ '
PS2='> '
PS4='+ '
```

```
PWD=/root
QTDIR=/usr/lib/qt-3.3
QTINC=/usr/lib/qt-3.3/include
QTLIB=/usr/lib/qt-3.3/lib
SHELL=/bin/bash
SHELLOPTS=braceexpand:emacs:hashall:histexpand:history:interactive-
comments:monitor
SHLVL=1
SSH_ASKPASS=/usr/libexec/openssh/gnome-ssh-askpass
SSH_CLIENT='10.0.1.2 51271 22'
SSH_CONNECTION='10.0.1.2 51271 10.0.1.8 22'
SSH_TTY=/dev/pts/0
TERM=xterm-color
UID=0
USER=root
[root@server1 ~]# _
```

Some environment variables shown in the preceding output are used by programs that require information about the system; the OSTYPE (Operating System TYPE) and SHELL (Pathname to shell) variables are examples from the preceding output. Other variables are used to set the user's working environment; the most common of these include the following:

- PS1—The default shell prompt
- HOME—The absolute pathname to the user's home directory
- PWD—The present working directory in the directory tree
- PATH—A list of directories to search for executable programs

The PS1 variable represents the BASH shell prompt. To view the contents of this variable only, you can use the **echo command** and specify the variable name prefixed by the $ shell metacharacter, as shown in the following output:

```
[root@server1 ~]# echo $PS1
[\u@\h \W]\$
[root@server1 ~]# _
```

Note that a special notation is used to define the prompt in the preceding output: \u indicates the user name, \h indicates the host name, and \W indicates the name of the current directory. A list of BASH notation can be found by navigating the manual page for the BASH shell.

To change the value of a variable, you specify the variable name followed immediately by an equal sign (=) and the new value. The following output demonstrates how you can change the value of the PS1 variable. The new prompt takes effect immediately and allows the user to type commands.

```
[root@server1 ~]# PS1="This is the new prompt: #"
This is the new prompt: # _
```

```
This is the new prompt: # date
Fri Aug 20 08:16:59 EDT 2010
This is the new prompt: # _
This is the new prompt: # who
user1     tty1       2010-08-20 07:47 (:0)
root      pts/0      2010-08-20 07:50 (10.0.1.2)
This is the new prompt: # _
This is the new prompt: # PS1="[\u@\h \W]#"
[root@server1 ~]# _
```

The HOME variable is used by programs that require the pathname to the current user's home directory to store or search for files; therefore, it should not be changed. If the root user logs in to the system, the HOME variable is set to /root; alternatively, the HOME variable is set to /home/user1 if the user named user1 logs in to the system. Recall that the ~ (tilde) shell metacharacter represents the current user's home directory; this shell metacharacter is a pointer to the HOME variable, as shown here:

```
[root@server1 ~]# echo $HOME
/root
[root@server1 ~]# echo ~
/root
[root@server1 ~]# HOME=/etc
[root@server1 ~]# echo $HOME
/etc
[root@server1 ~]# echo ~
/etc
[root@server1 ~]# _
```

Like the HOME variable, the PWD (Print Working Directory) variable is vital to the user's environment and should not be changed. PWD stores the current user's location in the directory tree. It is affected by the cd command and used by other commands, such as pwd, when the current directory needs to be identified. The following output demonstrates how this variable works:

```
[root@server1 ~]# pwd
/root
[root@server1 ~]# echo $PWD
/root
[root@server1 ~]# cd /etc
[root@server1 etc]# pwd
/etc
[root@server1 ~]# echo $PWD
/etc
[root@server1 ~]# _
```

The PATH variable is one of the most important variables in the BASH shell, as it allows users to execute commands by typing the command name alone. Recall that most commands are represented by an executable file on the hard drive. These executables are typically stored in directories named bin or sbin in various locations throughout the Linux directory tree. To execute the ls command, you could either type the absolute or relative pathname to the file (that is, /bin/ls or ../../bin/ls) or simply type the letters "ls" and allow the system to search the directories listed in the PATH variable for a command named ls. Sample contents of the PATH variable are shown in the following output:

```
[root@server1 ~]# echo $PATH
/usr/lib/qt-3.3/bin:/usr/kerberos/sbin:/usr/kerberos/bin:
/usr/lib/ccache:/usr/local/sbin:/usr/local/bin:/sbin:/bin:/usr/sbin:
/usr/bin:/root/bin
[root@server1 ~]# _
```

In this example, if the user had typed the command ls at the command prompt and pressed Enter, the shell would have noticed the lack of a / character in the pathname and proceeded to search for the file ls in the /usr/lib/qt-3.3/bin directory, then the /usr/kerberos/sbin directory, the /usr/kerberos/bin directory, the /usr/lib/ccache directory, the /usr/local/sbin directory, the /usr/local/bin directory, the /sbin directory, and then the /bin directory before finding the ls executable file. If no ls file is found in any directory in the PATH variable, the shell returns an error message, as shown here with a misspelled command:

```
[root@server1 ~]# lss
Command not found.
[root@server1 ~]# _
```

Thus, if a command is located within a directory that is listed in the PATH variable, you can simply type the name of the command on the command line to execute it. The shell will then find the appropriate executable file on the filesystem. All of the commands used in this book so far have been located in directories listed in the PATH variable. However, if the executable file is not in a directory listed in the PATH variable, the user must specify either the absolute or relative pathname to the executable file. The following example uses the myprogram file in the /root directory (a directory that is not listed in the PATH variable):

```
[root@server1 ~]# pwd
/root
[root@server1 ~]# ls -F
Desktop/ myprogram*
[root@server1 ~]# myprogram
Command not found.
[root@server1 ~]# /root/myprogram
This is a sample program.
[root@server1 ~]# ./myprogram
This is a sample program.
[root@server1 ~]# cp myprogram /bin
[root@server1 ~]# myprogram
This is a sample program.
[root@server1 ~]# _
```

After the myprogram executable file was copied to the /bin directory in the preceding output, the user was able to execute it by simply typing its name, because the /bin directory is listed in the PATH variable.

Table 7-3 provides a list of environment variables used in most BASH shells.

User-Defined Variables

You can set your own variables using the same method discussed earlier to change the contents of existing environment variables. To do so, you simply specify the name of the variable (known as the **variable identifier**) immediately followed by the equal sign (=) and the new

Variable	Description
BASH	The full path to the BASH shell
BASH_VERSION	The version of the current BASH shell
DISPLAY	The variable used to redirect the output of X Windows to another computer or device
ENV	The location of the BASH run-time configuration file (usually ~/.bashrc)
EUID	The effective UID (User ID) of the current user
HISTFILE	The filename used to store previously entered commands in the BASH shell (usually ~/.bash_history)
HISTFILESIZE	The number of previously entered commands that can be stored in the HISTFILE upon logout for use during the next login; it is typically 1,000 commands
HISTSIZE	The number of previously entered commands that will be stored in memory during the current login session; it is typically 1,000 commands
HOME	The absolute pathname of the current user's home directory
HOSTNAME	The host name of the Linux system
LOGNAME	The user name of the current user used when logging in to the shell
MAIL	The location of the mailbox file (where e-mail is stored)
OSTYPE	The current operating system
PATH	The directories to search for executable program files in the absence of an absolute or relative pathname containing a / character
PS1	The current shell prompt
PWD	The current working directory
RANDOM	The variable that creates a random number when accessed
SHELL	The absolute pathname of the current shell
TERM	The variable used to determine the terminal settings; it is typically set to "linux" or "xterm" on newer Linux systems and "console" on older Linux systems
TERMCAP	The variable used to determine the terminal settings on older systems that use a TERMCAP database (/etc/termcap)

Table 7-3 Common BASH environment variables

contents. When creating new variables, it is important to note the following features of variable identifiers:

- They can contain alphanumeric characters (0–9, A–Z, a–z), the – (dash) character, or the _ (underscore) character.
- They must not start with a number.
- They are typically capitalized to follow convention (for example, HOME, PATH, and so on).

To create a variable called MYVAR with the contents "This is a sample variable" and display its contents, you can use the following commands:

```
[root@server1 ~]# MYVAR="This is a sample variable"
[root@server1 ~]# echo $MYVAR
This is a sample variable
[root@server1 ~]# _
```

The preceding command created a variable that is available to the current shell. Most commands that are run by the shell are run in a separate **subshell**, which is created by the current shell. Any variables created in the current shell are not available to those subshells and the commands running within them. Thus, if a user creates a variable to be used within a certain program such as a database editor, that variable should be exported to all subshells using the **export command** to ensure that all programs started by the current shell have the ability to access the variable.

As explained earlier in this chapter, all environment variables in the BASH shell can be listed using the set command; user-defined variables are also indicated in this list. Similarly, to see a list of all exported environment and user-defined variables in the shell, you can use the **env command**. Because the outputs of set and env are typically large, you would commonly redirect the stdout of these commands to the grep command to display certain lines only.

To see the difference between the set and env commands as well as export the MYVAR variable created earlier, you can perform the following commands:

```
[root@server1 ~]# set | grep MYVAR
MYVAR='This is a sample variable.'
[root@server1 ~]# env | grep MYVAR
[root@server1 ~]# _
[root@server1 ~]# export MYVAR
[root@server1 ~]# env | grep MYVAR
MYVAR=This is a sample variable.
[root@server1 ~]# _
```

Not all environment variables are exported; the PS1 variable is an example of a variable that does not need to be available to subshells and is not exported as a result. However, it is good form to export user-defined variables, because they will likely be used by processes that run in subshells. This means that, to create and export a user-defined variable called MYVAR2, you can use the export command alone, as shown in the following output:

```
[root@server1 ~]# export MYVAR2="This is another sample variable"
[root@server1 ~]# set | grep MYVAR2
```

```
MYVAR2='This is another sample variable.'
_=MYVAR2
[root@server1 ~]# env | grep MYVAR2
MYVAR2=This is another sample variable.
[root@server1 ~]# _
```

Other Variables

Other variables are not displayed by the set or env commands; these variables perform specialized functions in the shell.

The UMASK variable used earlier in this textbook is an example of a special variable that performs a special function in the BASH shell and must be set by the umask command. Also recall that when you type the cp command, you are actually running an alias to the cp -i command. Aliases are shortcuts to commands stored in special variables that can be created and viewed using the **alias command**. To create an alias to the command mount -t ext2 /dev/fd0 /mnt/floppy called mf and view it, you can use the following commands:

```
[root@server1 ~]# alias mf="mount -t ext2 /dev/fd0 /mnt/floppy"
[root@server1 ~]# alias
alias cp='cp -i'
alias l.='ls -d .* --color=auto'
alias ll='ls -l --color=auto'
alias ls='ls --color=auto'
alias mf='mount -t ext2 /dev/fd0 /mnt/floppy'
alias mv='mv -i'
alias rm='rm -i'
alias which='alias | /usr/bin/which --tty-only --read-alias --
show-dot --show-tilde'
[root@server1 ~]# _
```

Now, you simply need to run the mf command to mount a floppy device that contains an ext2 filesystem to the /mnt/floppy directory, as shown in the following output:

```
[root@server1 ~]# mf
[root@server1 ~]# mount
/dev/sda1 on / type ext4 (rw)
proc on /proc type proc (rw)
sysfs on /sys type sysfs (rw)
devpts on /dev/pts type devpts (rw,gid=5,mode=620)
tmpfs on /dev/shm type tmpfs (rw)
/dev/sda3 on /oracle type ext4 (rw)
/dev/mapper/vg00-data on /data type ext4 (rw,usrquota,grpquota)
none on /proc/sys/fs/binfmt_misc type binfmt_misc (rw)
sunrpc on /var/lib/nfs/rpc_pipefs type rpc_pipefs (rw)
/dev/fd0 on /mnt/floppy type ext2 (rw)
[root@server1 ~]# _
```

You can also create aliases to multiple commands, provided they are separated by the ; shell metacharacter introduced in Chapter 2. To create and test an alias called dw that runs the date command followed by the who command, you can do the following:

```
[root@server1 ~]# alias dw="date;who"
[root@server1 ~]# alias
alias cp='cp -i'
alias dw='date;who'
alias l.='ls -d .* --color=auto'
alias ll='ls -l --color=auto'
alias ls='ls --color=auto'
alias mf='mount -t ext2 /dev/fd0 /mnt/floppy'
alias mv='mv -i'
alias rm='rm -i'
alias which='alias | /usr/bin/which --tty-only --read-alias --
show-dot --show-tilde'
[root@server1 ~]# dw
Fri Aug 20 08:32:14 EDT 2010
user1    tty1       2010-08-20  07:47  (:0)
root     pts/0      2010-08-20  07:50  (10.0.1.2)
[root@server1 ~]# _
```

It is important to use unique alias names, because the shell searches for them before it searches for executable files. If you create an alias called who, that alias would be used instead of the who command on the filesystem.

Environment Files

Recall that variables are stored in memory. When a user exits the BASH shell, all variables stored in memory are destroyed along with the shell itself. To ensure that variables are accessible to a shell at all times, you must place variables in a file that is executed each time a user logs in and starts a BASH shell. These files are called **environment files**. Some common BASH shell environment files and the order in which they are executed are listed next:

~/.bashrc

/etc/profile

~/.bash_profile

~/.bash_login

~/.profile

The ~/.bashrc (BASH run-time configuration) file is typically used to set aliases and variables that must be present in each BASH shell. It is executed immediately after login for all users on the system as well as when a new BASH shell is created after login.

The other environment files are only executed after login after the ~/.bashrc file has been executed. The /etc/profile file is always executed after login for all users on the system and sets most environment variables, such as HOME and PATH. After /etc/profile finishes executing, the home directory of the user is searched for the hidden environment files .bash_profile, .bash_login, and .profile. If these files exist, the first one found is executed; as a result, only one of these files is typically used. These hidden environment files allow a user to set customized variables independent of BASH shells used by other users on the system; any values assigned to variables in these files override those set in /etc/profile and ~/.bashrc, due to the order of execution.

To add a variable to any of these files, you simply add a line that has the same format as the command used on the command line. To add the MYVAR2 variable used previously to the .bash_profile file, simply edit the file using a text editor such as vi and add the line `export MYVAR2="This is another sample variable"` to the file.

Variables are not the only type of information that can be entered into an environment file; any command that can be executed on the command line can also be placed inside any environment file. If you want to set the UMASK to 077, display the date after each login, and create an alias, you can add the following lines to one of the hidden environment files in your home directory:

```
umask 077
date
alias dw="date;who"
```

Also, you might want to execute cleanup tasks upon exiting the shell; to do this, simply add those cleanup commands to the .bash_logout file in your home directory.

Shell Scripts

In the previous section, you learned that the BASH shell can execute commands that exist within environment files. The BASH shell also has the ability to execute other text files containing commands and special constructs. These files are referred to as **shell scripts** and are typically used to create custom programs that perform administrative tasks on Linux systems. Any command that can be entered on the command line in Linux can be entered into a shell script, because it is a BASH shell that interprets the contents of the shell script itself. The most basic shell script is one that contains a list of commands, one per line, for the shell to execute in order, as shown next in the text file called myscript:

```
[root@server1 ~]# cat myscript
#!/bin/bash
#this is a comment
date
who
ls -F /
[root@server1 ~]# _
```

The first line in the preceding shell script (`#!/bin/bash`) is called a **hashpling**; it specifies the pathname to the shell that interprets the contents of the shell script. Different shells can use different constructs in their shell scripts. Thus, it is important to identify which shell was used to create a particular shell script. The hashpling allows a user who uses the C shell the ability to use a BASH shell when executing the myscript shell script shown previously. The second line of the shell script is referred to as a comment because it begins with a # character and is ignored by the shell; the only exception to this is the hashpling on the first line of a shell script. The remainder of the shell script shown in the preceding output consists of three commands that will be executed by the shell in order: date, who, and ls.

If you have read permission to a shell script, you can execute the shell script by starting another BASH shell and specifying the shell script as an argument. To execute the myscript shell script shown earlier, you can use the following command:

```
[root@server1 ~]# bash myscript
Fri Aug  20 11:36:18 EDT 2010
user1  tty1      2010-08-20 07:47 (:0)
root   pts/0     2010-08-20 11:36 (10.0.1.2)
bin/   dev/      home/        media/  proc/    sbin/     sys/   var/
boot/  etc/      lib/         mnt/    public/  selinux/  tmp/
data/  extras/   lost+found/  opt/    root/    srv/      usr/
[root@server1 ~]# _
```

Alternatively, if you have read and execute permission to a shell script, you can execute the shell script like any other executable program on the system, as shown next using the myscript shell script:

```
[root@server1 ~]# chmod a+x myscript
[root@server1 ~]# ./myscript
Fri Aug 20 11:36:44 EDT 2010
user1  tty1      2010-08-20 07:47 (:0)
root   pts/0     2010-08-20 11:36 (10.0.1.2)
bin/   dev/      home/        media/  proc/    sbin/     sys/   var/
boot/  etc/      lib/         mnt/    public/  selinux/  tmp/
data/  extras/   lost+found/  opt/    root/    srv/      usr/
[root@server1 ~]# _
```

The preceding output is difficult to read, because the output from each command is not separated by blank lines or identified by a label. Utilizing the echo command results in a more user-friendly myscript, as shown next:

```
[root@server1 ~]# cat myscript
#!/bin/bash
echo "Today's date is:"
date
echo ""
echo "The people logged into the system include:"
who
echo ""
echo "The contents of the / directory are:"
ls -F /
[root@server1 ~]# ./myscript
Today's date is:
Fri Aug 20 11:35:34 EDT 2010

The people logged into the system include:
user1  tty1      2010-08-20 07:47 (:0)
root   pts/0     2010-08-20 11:36 (10.0.1.2)
```

```
The contents of the / directory are:
bin/    dev/    home/        media/  proc/     sbin/     sys/    var/
boot/   etc/    lib/         mnt/    public/   selinux/  tmp/
data/   extras/ lost+found/  opt/    root/     srv/      usr/
[root@server1 ~]# _
```

Escape Sequences

In the previous example, you used the echo command to manipulate data that appeared on the screen. The echo command also supports several special notations called **escape sequences**. You can use escape sequences to further manipulate the way text is displayed to the terminal screen, provided the −e option is specified to the echo command. Table 7-4 provides a list of these echo escape sequences.

The escape sequences listed in Table 7-4 can be used to further manipulate the output of the myscript shell script used earlier, as shown in the following example:

```
[root@server1 ~]# cat myscript
#!/bin/bash
echo -e "Today's date is: \c"
date
echo -e "\nThe people logged into the system include:"
who
echo -e "\nThe contents of the / directory are:"
ls -F /
[root@server1 ~]# ./myscript
Today's date is: Fri Aug 20 11:37:11 EDT 2010
```

Escape Sequence	Description
\???	An ASCII character represented by a three-digit octal number (???)
\\	Backslash
\a	ASCII beep
\b	Backspace
\c	Prevents a new line following the command
\f	Form feed
\n	New line
\r	Carriage return
\t	Horizontal tab
\v	Vertical tab

Table 7-4   Common echo escape sequences

```
The people logged into the system include:
user1    tty1      2010-08-20 07:47 (:0)
root     pts/0     2010-08-20 11:36 (10.0.1.2)

The contents of the / directory are:
bin/   dev/      home/        media/   proc/    sbin/     sys/   var/
boot/  etc/      lib/         mnt/     public/  selinux/  tmp/
data/  extras/   lost+found/  opt/     root/    srv/      usr/
[root@server1 ~]# _
```

Notice from the preceding output that the \c escape sequence prevented the newline character at the end of the output "Today's date is:" when myscript was executed. Similarly, newline characters (\n) were inserted prior to displaying "The people logged into the system include:" and "The contents of the / directory are:" to create blank lines between command outputs. This eliminated the need for using the echo " " command shown earlier.

Reading Standard Input

At times, a shell script might need input from the user executing the program; this input can then be stored in a variable for later use. The **read command** takes user input from stdin and places it in a variable specified by an argument to the read command. After the input has been read into a variable, the contents of that variable can then be used, as shown in the following shell script:

```
[root@server1 ~]# cat newscript
#!/bin/bash
echo -e "What is your name? -->\c"
read USERNAME
echo "Hello $USERNAME"
[root@server1 ~]# chmod a+x newscript
[root@server1 ~]# ./newscript
What is your name? --> Fred
Hello Fred
[root@server1 ~]# _
```

Note from the preceding output that the echo command used to pose a question to the user ends with --> to simulate an arrow prompt on the screen and the \c escape sequence to place the cursor after the arrow prompt; this is common among Linux administrators when writing shell scripts.

Decision Constructs

Decision constructs are the most common type of construct used in shell scripts. They alter the flow of a program based on whether a command in the program completed successfully or based on a decision that the user makes in response to a question posed by the program. Figures 7-4 and 7-5 illustrate some decision constructs.

The if Construct The most common type of decision construct, the if construct, has the following syntax:

```
if this is true
then
```

```
do these commands
elif this is true
then
do these commands
else
do these commands
fi
```

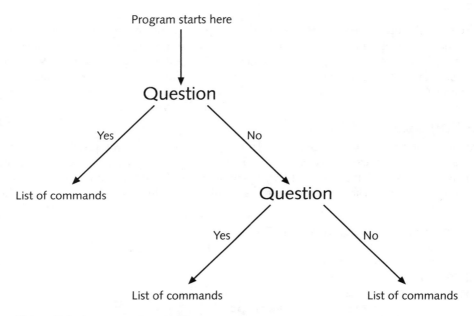

Figure 7-4 A two-question decision construct

Source: Course Technology/Cengage Learning

Figure 7-5 A command-based decision construct

Source: Course Technology/Cengage Learning

Some common rules govern if constructs:

1. elif (short for "else if") and else statements are optional.
2. You can have an unlimited number of elif statements.
3. The "do these commands" section can consist of multiple commands, one per line.
4. The "do these commands" section is typically indented from the left-hand side of the text file for readability, but does not need to be.
5. The end of the statement must be a backward "if" (fi).
6. The this is true part of the if syntax, shown earlier, can be a command or a **test statement:**
   - Commands return true if they perform their function properly.
   - Test statements are enclosed within square brackets [ ] or prefixed by the word "test" and used to test certain conditions on the system.

In the following example, a basic if construct is used to ensure that the /etc/hosts file is only copied to the /etc/sample directory if that directory could be created successfully:

```
[root@server1 ~]# cat testmkdir
#!/bin/bash
if mkdir /etc/sample
then
cp /etc/hosts /etc/sample
echo "The hosts file was successfully copied to /etc/sample"
else
echo "The /etc/sample directory could not be created."
fi
[root@server1 ~]# chmod a+x testmkdir
[root@server1 ~]# ./testmkdir
The hosts file was successfully copied to /etc/sample
[root@server1 ~]# _
```

In the preceding output, the mkdir /etc/sample command is always run. If it runs successfully, the shell script proceeds to the cp /etc/hosts /etc/sample and echo "The hosts file was successfully copied to /etc/sample" commands. If the mkdir /etc/sample command is unsuccessful, the shell script skips ahead and executes the echo "The /etc/sample directory could not be created." command. If there were more lines of text following the fi in the preceding shell script, they would be executed after the if construct regardless of its outcome.

Often, it is useful to use the if construct to alter the flow of the program given input from the user. Recall the myscript shell script used earlier:

```
[root@server1 ~]# cat myscript
#!/bin/bash
echo -e "Today's date is: \c"
date
echo -e "\nThe people logged into the system include:"
who
```

```
echo -e "\nThe contents of the / directory are:"
ls -F /
[root@server1 ~]# _
```

To ask the user whether to display the contents of the / directory, you could use the following if construct in the myscript file:

```
[root@server1 ~]# cat myscript
#!/bin/bash
echo -e "Today's date is: \c"
date
echo -e "\nThe people logged into the system include:"
who
echo -e "\nWould you like to see the contents of /? (y/n) -->\c"
read ANSWER
if [ $ANSWER = "y" ]
then
echo -e "\nThe contents of the / directory are:"
ls -F /
fi
[root@server1 ~]# ./myscript
Today's date is: Fri Aug 20 11:44:01 EDT 2010

The people logged into the system include:
user1    tty1      2010-08-20 07:47 (:0)
root     pts/0     2010-08-20 11:36 (10.0.1.2)

Would you like to see the contents of /? (y/n) --> y

The contents of the / directory are:
bin/    dev/      home/         media/   proc/     sbin/     sys/   var/
boot/   etc/      lib/          mnt/     public/   selinux/  tmp/
data/   extras/   lost+found/   opt/     root/     srv/      usr/
[root@server1 ~]# _
```

In the preceding output, the test statement [$ANSWER = "y"] is used to test whether the contents of the ANSWER variable are equal to the letter "y." Any other character in this variable causes this test statement to return false, and the directory listing is then skipped altogether. The type of comparison used previously is called a string comparison, because two values are compared for strings of characters; it is indicated by the operator of the test statement, which is the equal sign (=) in this example. Table 7-5 shows a list of common operators used in test statements and their definitions.

The test statement [$ANSWER = "y"] is equivalent to the test statement test $ANSWER = "y".

It is important to include a space character after the beginning square bracket and before the ending square bracket; otherwise, the test statement produces an error.

Test Statement	Returns True If:
[A = B]	String A is equal to String B.
[A != B]	String A is not equal to String B.
[A -eq B]	A is numerically equal to B.
[A -ne B]	A is numerically not equal to B.
[A -lt B]	A is numerically less than B.
[A -gt B]	A is numerically greater than B.
[A -le B]	A is numerically less than or equal to B.
[A -ge B]	A is numerically greater than or equal to B.
[-r A]	A is a file/directory that exists and is readable (r permission).
[-w A]	A is a file/directory that exists and is writable (w permission).
[-x A]	A is a file/directory that exists and is executable (x permission).
[-f A]	A is a file that exists.
[-d A]	A is a directory that exists.

Table 7-5 Common test statements

Test Statement	Returns True If:
[A = B -o C = D]	String A is equal to String B OR String C is equal to String D.
[A = B -a C = D]	String A is equal to String B AND String C is equal to String D.
[! A = B]	String A is NOT equal to String B.

Table 7-6 Special operators in test statements

You can combine any test statement with another test statement using the comparison operators -o (OR) and -a (AND). To reverse the meaning of a test statement, you can use the ! (NOT) operator. Table 7-6 provides some examples of using these operators in test statements.

One test statement can contain several -o, -a, and ! operators.

By modifying the myscript shell script in the previous output, you can proceed with the directory listing if the user enters "y" or "Y," as shown in the following example:

```
[root@server1 ~]# cat myscript
#!/bin/bash
echo -e "Today's date is: \c"
date
```

```
echo -e "\nThe people logged into the system include:"
who
echo -e "\nWould you like to see the contents of /?(y/n)-->\c"
read ANSWER
if [ $ANSWER = "y" -o $ANSWER = "Y" ]
then
echo -e "\nThe contents of the / directory are:"
ls -F /
fi
[root@server1 ~]# ./myscript
Today's date is: Fri Aug 20 11:51:22 EDT 2010

The people logged into the system include:
user1    tty1      2010-08-20 07:47 (:0)
root     pts/0     2010-08-20 11:36 (10.0.1.2)

Would you like to see the contents of /?(y/n)--> y

The contents of the / directory are:
bin/    dev/      home/        media/  proc/     sbin/     sys/  var/
boot/   etc/      lib/         mnt/    public/   selinux/  tmp/
data/   extras/   lost+found/  opt/    root/     srv/      usr/
[root@server1 ~]# _
```

The case Construct The if construct used earlier is well suited for a limited number of choices. In the following example, which uses the myscript example presented earlier, several elif statements perform tasks based on user input:

```
[root@server1 ~]# cat myscript
#!/bin/bash
echo -e "What would you like to see?
Todays date (d)
Currently logged in users (u)
The contents of the / directory (r)

Enter your choice(d/u/r)-->\c"
read ANSWER
if [ $ANSWER = "d" -o $ANSWER = "D" ]
then
echo -e "Today's date is: \c"
date
elif [ $ANSWER = "u" -o $ANSWER = "U" ]
then
echo -e "\nThe people logged into the system include:"
who
elif [ $ANSWER = "r" -o $ANSWER = "R" ]
then
echo -e "\nThe contents of the / directory are:"
ls -F /
```

```
fi
[root@server1 ~]# _
[root@server1 ~]# ./myscript
What would you like to see?
Todays date (d)
Currently logged in users (u)
The contents of the / directory (r)

Enter your choice(d/u/r)--> d
Today's date is: Fri Aug 20 11:53:02 EDT 2010
[root@server1 ~]# _
```

The preceding shell script becomes increasingly difficult to read as the number of choices available increases. Thus, when presenting several choices, it is commonplace to use a case construct. The syntax of the case construct is as follows:

```
case variable in
pattern1 )   do this
                 ;;
pattern2 )   do this
                 ;;
pattern3 )   do this
                 ;;
esac
```

The case statement compares the value of a variable with several different patterns of text or numbers. When a match occurs, the commands to the right of the pattern are executed (do this in the preceding syntax). As with the if construct, the case construct must be ended by a backward "case" (esac).

An example that simplifies the previous myscript example by using the case construct is shown in the following output:

```
[root@server1 ~]# cat myscript
#!/bin/bash
echo -e "What would you like to see?
Todays date (d)
Currently logged in users (u)
The contents of the / directory (r)

Enter your choice(d/u/r)-->\c"
read ANSWER

case $ANSWER in
   d | D ) echo -e "\nToday's date is: \c"
           date
           ;;
   u | U ) echo -e "\nThe people logged into the system include:"
           who
           ;;
```

```
   r | R ) echo -e "\nThe contents of the / directory are:"
        ls -F /
        ;;
     *) echo -e "Invalid choice! \a"
        ;;
esac
[root@server1 ~]# ./myscript
What would you like to see?
Todays date (d)
Currently logged in users (u)
The contents of the / directory (r)

Enter your choice(d/u/r)--> d
Today's date is: Fri Aug 20 11:57:08 EDT 2010
[root@server1 ~]# _
```

The preceding example prompts the user with a menu and allows the user to select an item that is then placed into the ANSWER variable. If the ANSWER variable is equal to the letter "d" or "D," the date command is executed; however, if the ANSWER variable is equal to the letter "u" or "U," the who command is executed, and if the ANSWER variable is equal to the letter "r" or "R," the ls command is executed. If the ANSWER variable contains something other than the aforementioned letters, the * (wildcard) shell metacharacter matches it and prints an error message to the screen. As with if constructs, any statements present in the shell script following the case construct are executed after the case construct.

The && and || Constructs   Although the if and case constructs are versatile, when only one decision needs to be made during the execution of a program, it's faster to use the && and || constructs. The syntax of these constructs is as follows:

```
command  &&  command
command  ||  command
```

For the preceding && syntax, the command on the right of the && construct is executed only if the command on the left of the && construct completed successfully. The opposite is true for the || syntax; the command on the right of the || construct is executed only if the command on the left of the || construct did not complete successfully.

Consider the testmkdir example presented earlier in this chapter:

```
[root@server1 ~]# cat testmkdir
#!/bin/bash
if mkdir /etc/sample
then
cp /etc/hosts /etc/sample
echo "The hosts file was successfully copied to /etc/sample"
else
echo "The /etc/sample directory could not be created."
fi
[root@server1 ~]# _
```

You can rewrite the preceding shell script utilizing the `&&` construct, as follows:

```
[root@server1 ~]# cat testmkdir
#!/bin/bash
mkdir /etc/sample && cp /etc/hosts /etc/sample
[root@server1 ~]# _
```

The preceding shell script creates the directory /etc/sample and only copies the /etc/hosts file to it if the `mkdir /etc/sample` command was successful. You can instead use the `||` construct to generate error messages if one of the commands fails to execute properly:

```
[root@server1 ~]# cat testmkdir
#!/bin/bash
mkdir /etc/sample || echo "Could not create /etc/sample"
cp /etc/hosts /etc/sample || echo "Could not copy /etc/hosts"
[root@server1 ~]# _
```

Loop Constructs

To execute commands repetitively, you can write shell scripts that contain loop constructs. Like decision constructs, **loop constructs** alter the flow of a program based on the result of a particular statement. But unlike decision constructs, which run different parts of a program depending on the results of the test statement, a loop construct simply repeats the entire program. Although several loop constructs are available within the BASH shell, the two most common are `for` and `while`.

The `for` Construct The `for` construct is the most useful looping construct for Linux administrators because it can be used to process a list of objects, such as files, directories, users, printers, and so on. The syntax of the `for` construct is as follows:

```
for var_name in string1  string2  string3  … …
do
these commands
done
```

When a `for` construct is executed, it creates a variable (var_name), sets its value equal to `string1`, and executes the commands between `do` and `done`, which can access the var_name variable. Next, the `for` construct sets the value of var_name to `string2`, and executes the commands between `do` and `done` again. Following this, the `for` construct sets the value of var_name to `string3` and executes the commands between `do` and `done` again. This process repeats as long as there are strings to process. Thus, if there are three strings, the `for` construct will execute three times. If there are 20 strings, the `for` construct will execute 20 times.

The following example uses the `for` construct to e-mail a list of users with a new schedule:

```
[root@server1 ~]# cat emailusers
#!/bin/bash
for  NAME  in bob sue mary jane frank lisa jason
do
mail -s "Your new project schedule" < newschedule $NAME
```

```
echo "$NAME was emailed successfully"
done
[root@server1 ~]# _
[root@server1 ~]# chmod a+x emailusers
[root@server1 ~]# ./emailusers
bob was emailed successfully
sue was emailed successfully
mary was emailed successfully
jane was emailed successfully
frank was emailed successfully
lisa was emailed successfully
jason was emailed successfully
[root@server1 ~]# _
```

When the for construct in the preceding example is executed, it creates a NAME variable and sets its value to bob. Then it executes the mail command to e-mail bob the contents of the newschedule file with a subject line of Your new project schedule. Next, it sets the NAME variable to sue and executes the mail command to send sue the same e-mail. This process is repeated until the last person receives the e-mail.

A more common use of the for construct within shell scripts is to process several files. The following example renames each file within a specified directory to include a .txt extension.

```
[root@server1 ~]# ls stuff
file1 file2 file3 file4 file5 file6 file7 file8
[root@server1 ~]# _
[root@server1 ~]# cat multiplerename
#!/bin/bash
echo -e "What directory has the files that you would like to rename?
   -->\c"
read DIR
for NAME in $DIR/*
do
mv $NAME $NAME.txt
done
[root@server1 ~]# _
[root@server1 ~]# chmod a+x multiplerename
[root@server1 ~]# ./multiplerename
What directory has the files that you would like to rename? --> stuff
[root@server1 ~]# ls stuff
file1.txt file2.txt file3.txt file4.txt file5.txt file6.txt
file7.txt file8.txt
[root@server1 ~]# _
```

When the for construct in the previous example is executed, it sets the list of strings to stuff/* (which expands to file1 file2 file3 file4 file5 file6 file7 file8). It then creates a NAME variable, sets its value to file1, and executes the mv command to rename file1 to file1.txt. Next, the for construct sets the value of the NAME variable to file2, and executes the mv command to rename file2 to file2.txt. This is repeated until all of the files have been processed.

The `while` Construct The `while` construct is another common loop construct used within shell scripts. Unlike the `for` construct, the `while` construct begins with a test statement. As long as (i.e. while) the test statement returns true, the commands within the loop construct are executed. When the test statement returns false, the commands within the `while` construct stop executing. A `while` construct typically contains a variable, called a **counter variable**, whose value changes each time through the loop. For the `while` construct to work properly, it must be set up so that, when the counter variable reaches a certain value, the test statement returns false. This prevents the loop from executing indefinitely.

The syntax of the `while` construct is as follows:

while *this returns true*
do
these commands
done

The following example illustrates the general use of the `while` construct:

```
[root@server1 ~]# cat echorepeat
#!/bin/bash
COUNTER=0
while [ $COUNTER -lt 7 ]
do
echo "All work and no play makes Jack a dull boy" >> /tmp/redrum
COUNTER=`expr $COUNTER + 1`
done
[root@server1 ~]# _
[root@server1 ~]# chmod a+x echorepeat
[root@server1 ~]# ./echorepeat
[root@server1 ~]# cat /tmp/redrum
All work and no play makes Jack a dull boy
All work and no play makes Jack a dull boy
All work and no play makes Jack a dull boy
All work and no play makes Jack a dull boy
All work and no play makes Jack a dull boy
All work and no play makes Jack a dull boy
All work and no play makes Jack a dull boy
[root@server1 ~]# _
```

The echorepeat shell script shown here creates a counter variable called COUNTER and sets its value to 0. Next, the `while` construct uses a test statement to determine whether the value of the COUNTER variable is less than 7 before executing the commands within the loop. Because the initial value of the COUNTER variable is 0, it appends the text All work and no play makes Jack a dull boy to the /tmp/redrum file and increments the value of the COUNTER variable to 1. Note the backquotes surrounding the `expr` command, which are required to numerically add 1 to the COUNTER variable (0 + 1 = 1). Because the value of the COUNTER variable at this stage (1) is still less than 7, the `while` construct executes the commands again. This process repeats until the value of the COUNTER variable is equal to 8.

 You can use `true` or `:` in place of a test statement to create a `while` construct that executes indefinitely.

Chapter Summary

- Three components are available to commands: standard input (stdin), standard output (stdout), and standard error (stderr). Not all commands use every component.

- Stdin is typically user input taken from the keyboard, whereas stdout and stderr are sent to the terminal screen by default.

- You can redirect the stdout and stderr of a command to a file using redirection symbols. Similarly, you can use redirection symbols to redirect a file to the stdin of a command.

- To redirect the stdout from one command to the stdin of another, you must use the pipe symbol (|).

- Most variables available to the BASH shell are environment variables that are loaded into memory after login from environment files.

- You can create your own variables in the BASH shell and export them to programs started by the shell. These variables can also be placed in environment files, so that they are loaded into memory on every shell login.

- The UMASK variable and command aliases are special variables that must be set using a certain command.

- Shell scripts can be used to execute several Linux commands.

- Decision constructs can be used within shell scripts to execute certain Linux commands based on user input or the results of a certain command.

- Loop constructs can be used within shell scripts to execute a series of commands repetitively.

Key Terms

;   A shell metacharacter used to chain multiple commands together for execution.

| A shell metacharacter used to pipe the stdout from one command to the stdin of another command.

<   A shell metacharacter used to obtain stdin from a file.

>   A shell metacharacter used to redirect stdout and stderr to a file.

alias command   A command used to create special variables that are shortcuts to longer command strings.

awk command   A filter command used to search for and display text.

counter variable   A variable that is altered by loop constructs to ensure that commands are not executed indefinitely.

decision construct   A special construct used in a shell script to alter the flow of the program based on the outcome of a command or contents of a variable. Common decision constructs include if, case, &&, and ||.

echo command   A command used to display or echo output to the terminal screen. It might utilize escape sequences.

env command   A command used to display a list of exported variables present in the current shell, except special variables.

environment files   The files used immediately after login to execute commands; they are typically used to load variables into memory.

environment variables   The variables that store information commonly accessed by the system or programs executing on the system—together, these variables form the user environment.

escape sequences   The character sequences that have special meaning inside the echo command. They are prefixed by the \ character.

export command   A command used to send variables to subshells.

file descriptors   The numeric labels used to define command input and command output.

filter command   A command that can take from stdin and send to stdout. In other words, a filter is a command that can exist in the middle of a pipe.

grep (Global Regular Expression Print) command   A program used to search one or more text files for a desired string of characters.

hashpling   The first line in a shell script, which defines the shell that will be used to interpret the commands in the script file.

loop construct   A special construct used in a shell script to execute commands repetitively. Common loop constructs include for and while.

pipe   A string of commands connected by | shell metacharacters.

read command   A command used to read stdin from a user into a variable.

redirection   The process of changing the default locations of stdin, stdout, and stderr.

sed command   A filter command used to search for and manipulate text.

set command   A command used to view all variables in the shell, except special variables.

shell scripts   The text files that contain a list of commands or constructs for the shell to execute in order.

sort command   A command used to sort lines in a file.

standard error (stderr)   A file descriptor that represents any error messages generated by a command.

standard input (stdin)   A file descriptor that represents information input to a command during execution.

standard output (stdout)   A file descriptor that represents the desired output from a command.

subshell   A shell started by the current shell.

tee command   A command used to take from stdin and send to both stdout and a specified file.

test statement   A statement used to test a certain condition and generate a True/False value.

tr command   A command used to transform or change characters received from stdin.

user-defined variables   The variables that are created by the user and are not used by the system. These variables are typically exported to subshells.

variable   An area of memory used to store information. Variables are created from entries in environment files when the shell is first created after login, and are destroyed when the shell is destroyed upon logout.

variable identifier   The name of a variable.

Review Questions

1. Because stderr and stdout represent the results of a command and stdin represents the input required for a command, only stderr and stdout can be redirected to/from a file. True or False?

2. Before a user-defined variable can be used by processes that run in subshells, that variable must be _____.

   a. imported

   b. validated by running the env command

   c. exported

   d. redirected to the BASH shell

3. The alias command can be used to make a shortcut to a single command. True or False?

4. Which of the following files is always executed immediately after a user logs in to a Linux system and receives a BASH shell?

   a. /etc/profile

   b. ~/.bash_profile

   c. ~/.bash_login

   d. ~/.profile

5. Which command could you use to see a list of all environment and user-defined shell variables as well as their current values?

   a. ls /var

   b. env

   c. set

   d. echo

6. Every if construct begins with if and must be terminated with _____.

   a. end

   b. endif

   c. stop

   d. fi

7. Which of the following will display the message welcome home if the `cd /home/user1` command is successfully executed?

    a. `cd /home/user1 && echo "welcome home"`

    b. `cat "welcome home" || cd /home/user1`

    c. `cd /home/user1 || cat "welcome home"`

    d. `echo "welcome home" && cd /home/user1`

8. The current value for the HOME variable is displayed by which of the following commands? (Choose all that apply.)

    a. `echo HOME=`

    b. `echo ~`

    c. `echo $HOME`

    d. `echo ls HOME`

9. Which of the following file descriptor numbers represents stdout?

    a. 2

    b. 0

    c. 1

    d. 3

10. Which of the following operators reverses the meaning of a test statement?

    a. `#!`

    b. `-o`

    c. `-a`

    d. `!`

11. What would be the effect of using the `alias` command to make an alias for the `date` command named `cat` in honor of your favorite pet?

    a. It cannot be done because there already is an environment variable cat associated with the `cat` command.

    b. It cannot be done because there already is a `cat` command on the system.

    c. When you use the `cat` command at the command prompt with the intention of viewing a text file, the date appears instead.

    d. There is no effect until the alias is imported, because it is a user-declared variable.

12. How do you indicate a comment line in a shell script?

    a. There are no comment lines in a shell script.

    b. Begin the line with `#!`.

    c. Begin the line with `!`.

    d. Begin the line with `#`.

13. You have redirected stderr to a file called Errors. You view the contents of this file afterward and notice that there are six error messages. After repeating the procedure, you notice that there are only two error messages in this file. Why?

    a. After you open the file and view the contents, the contents are lost.

    b. The system generated different stdout.

    c. You did not append the stderr to the Error file, and, as a result, it was overwritten when the command was run a second time.

    d. You must specify a new file each and every time you redirect, because the system creates the specified file by default.

14. The sed and awk commands are filter commands commonly used to format data within a pipe. True or False?

15. What is wrong with the following command string: ls /etc/hosts >listofhostfile?

    a. Nothing is wrong with the command.

    b. The file descriptor was not declared; unless 1 for stdout or 2 for stderr is indicated, the command will fail.

    c. The ls command is one of the commands that cannot be used with redirection. You must use | to pipe instead.

    d. The file listofhostfile will always only contain stderr because a file descriptor was not declared.

16. Which of the following is not necessarily generated by every command on the system? (Choose all that apply.)

    a. standard input

    b. standard deviation

    c. standard output

    d. standard error

17. Which construct can be used in a shell script to read stdin and place it in a variable?

    a. read

    b. sum

    c. verify

    d. test

18. A for construct is a loop construct that processes a specified list of objects. As a result, it is executed as long as there are remaining objects to process. True or False?

19. What does >> accomplish when entered on the command line after a command?

    a. It redirects both stderr and stdout to the same location.

    b. It does not accomplish anything.

    c. It redirects stderr and stdin to the same location.

    d. It appends stdout to a file.

20. Consider the following shell script:

```
echo -e "What is your favorite color?--> \c"
read REPLY
if [ "$REPLY" = "red" -o "$REPLY" = "blue" ]
then
echo "The answer is red or blue."
else
echo "The answer is not red nor blue."
fi
```

What would be displayed if a user executes the program and answers Blue when prompted?

a. The answer is red or blue.

b. The answer is neither red nor blue.

c. The code would cause an error.

d. The answer is red or blue. The answer is not red nor blue.

Hands-On Projects

These projects should be completed in the order given. The hands-on projects presented in this chapter should take a total of three hours to complete. The requirements for this lab include:

- A computer with Fedora 13 installed according to Hands-On Project 2-2.

Project 7-1

In this hands-on project, you use the shell to redirect the stdout and stderr to a file and take stdin from a file.

1. Switch to a command-line terminal (tty2) by pressing **Ctrl+Alt+F2** and log in to the terminal using the user name of **root** and the password of **secret**.

2. At the command prompt, type **touch sample1 sample2** and press **Enter** to create two new files named sample1 and sample2 in your home directory. Verify their creation by typing **ls –F** at the command prompt and press **Enter**.

3. At the command prompt, type **ls -l sample1 sample2 sample3** and press **Enter**. Is there any stdout displayed on the terminal screen? Is there any stderr displayed on the terminal screen? Why?

4. At the command prompt, type **ls -l sample1 sample2 sample3 > file** and press **Enter**. Is there any stdout displayed on the terminal screen? Is there any stderr displayed on the terminal screen? Why?

5. At the command prompt, type **cat file** and press **Enter**. What are the contents of file and why?

6. At the command prompt, type **ls -l sample1 sample2 sample3 2> file** and press **Enter**. Is there any stdout displayed on the terminal screen? Is there any stderr displayed on the terminal screen? Why?

7. At the command prompt, type **cat file** and press **Enter**. What are the contents of file and why? Were the previous contents retained? Why?

8. At the command prompt, type ls -l sample1 sample2 sample3 > file 2>file2 and press **Enter**. Is there any stdout displayed on the terminal screen? Is there any stderr displayed on the terminal screen? Why?

9. At the command prompt, type **cat file** and press **Enter**. What are the contents of file and why?

10. At the command prompt, type **cat file2** and press **Enter**. What are the contents of file2 and why?

11. At the command prompt, type ls -l sample1 sample2 sample3 > file 2>&1 and press **Enter**. Is there any stdout displayed on the terminal screen? Is there any stderr displayed on the terminal screen? Why?

12. At the command prompt, type **cat file** and press **Enter**. What are the contents of file and why?

13. At the command prompt, type ls -l sample1 sample2 sample3 >&2 2>file2 and press **Enter**. Is there any stdout displayed on the terminal screen? Is there any stderr displayed on the terminal screen? Why?

14. At the command prompt, type **cat file2** and press **Enter**. What are the contents of file2 and why?

15. At the command prompt, type **date > file** and press **Enter**.

16. At the command prompt, type **cat file** and press **Enter**. What are the contents of file and why?

17. At the command prompt, type **date >> file** and press **Enter**.

18. At the command prompt, type **cat file** and press **Enter**. What are the contents of file and why? Can you tell when each date command was run?

19. At the command prompt, type **tr o O /etc/hosts** and press **Enter**. What error message do you receive and why?

20. At the command prompt, type **tr o O </etc/hosts** and press **Enter**. What happened and why?

21. Type **exit** and press **Enter** to log out of your shell.

Project 7-2

In this hands-on project, you redirect stdout and stdin using pipe shell metacharacters.

1. Switch to a command-line terminal (tty2) by pressing **Ctrl+Alt+F2** and log in to the terminal using the user name of **root** and the password of **secret**.

2. At the command prompt, type **cat /etc/httpd/conf/httpd.conf** and press **Enter** to view the /etc/httpd/conf/httpd.conf file. Next, type **cat/etc/httpd/conf/ httpd.conf | less** at the command prompt and press **Enter** to perform the same task page-by-page. Explain what the | shell metacharacter does in the previous command. How is this different from the less/etc/httpd/conf/httpd.conf command?

3. At the command prompt, type **cat /etc/httpd/conf/httpd.conf | grep Keep** and press **Enter**. How many lines are displayed? Why did you not need to specify a filename with the **grep** command?

4. At the command prompt, type **cat /etc/httpd/conf/httpd.conf | grep Keep | tr e E** and press **Enter**. Explain the output on the terminal screen.

5. At the command prompt, type **cat /etc/httpd/conf/httpd.conf | grep Keep | tr e E | sort -r** and press **Enter**. Explain the output on the terminal screen.

6. At the command prompt, type **cat /etc/httpd/conf/httpd.conf | grep Keep | tr e E | sort -r | tee file** and press **Enter**. Explain the output on the terminal screen. Next, type **cat file** at the command prompt and press **Enter**. What are the contents? Why? What does the tee command do in the pipe above?

7. At the command prompt, type **cat /etc/httpd/conf/httpd.conf | grep Keep | tr e E | sort -r | tee file | wc -l** and press **Enter**. Explain the output on the terminal screen. Next, type **cat file** at the command prompt and press **Enter**. What are the contents and why?

8. At the command prompt, type **cat /etc/httpd/conf/httpd.conf | grep Keep | sed /#/d | sed /Max/s/100/150/** and press **Enter**. Explain the output on the terminal screen. Can this output be obtained with the grep and tr commands instead of sed? Which is easier?

9. At the command prompt, type **cat /etc/hosts**. Next, type **cat /etc/hosts | awk '/localhost/ {print $1, $3}'** and press **Enter**. Explain the output on the terminal screen.

10. Type **exit** and press **Enter** to log out of your shell.

Project 7-3

In this hands-on project, you create and use an alias, as well as view and change existing shell variables. In addition to this, you export user-defined variables and load variables automatically upon shell startup.

1. Switch to a command-line terminal (tty2) by pressing **Ctrl+Alt+F2** and log in to the terminal using the user name of **root** and the password of **secret**.

2. At the command prompt, type **set | less** and press **Enter** to view the BASH shell environment variables currently loaded into memory. Scroll through this list using the cursor keys on the keyboard. When finished, press **q** to quit the less utility.

3. At the command prompt, type **env | less** and press **Enter** to view the exported BASH shell environment variables currently loaded into memory. Scroll through this list using the cursor keys on the keyboard. Is this list larger or smaller than the list generated in Step 2? Why? When finished, press **q** to quit the less utility.

4. At the command prompt, type **PS1="Hello There:"** and press **Enter**. What happened and why? Next, type **echo $PS1** at the command prompt and press **Enter** to verify the new value of the PS1 variable.

5. At the command prompt, type **exit** and press **Enter** to log out of the shell. Next, log in to the terminal using the user name of **root** and the password of **secret**. What prompt

did you receive and why? How could you ensure that the "Hello There:" prompt occurs at every login?

6. At the command prompt, type **vi .bash_profile** and press **Enter**. At the bottom of the file, add the following lines. When finished, save and quit the vi editor.

```
echo -e "Would you like a hello prompt? (y/n) -->\c"
read ANSWER
if [ $ANSWER = "y" ]
then
PS1="Hello There: "
fi
```

Explain what the preceding lines will perform after each login.

7. At the command prompt, type **exit** and press **Enter** to log out of the shell. Next log in to the terminal using the user name of **root** and the password of **secret**. When prompted for a hello prompt, type **y** and press **Enter**. What prompt did you receive and why?

8. At the command prompt, type **exit** and press **Enter** to log out of the shell. Next, log in to the terminal using the user name of **root** and the password of **secret**. When prompted for a hello prompt, type **n** and press **Enter** to receive the default prompt.

9. At the command prompt, type **MYVAR="My sample variable"** and press **Enter** to create a variable called MYVAR. Verify its creation by typing **echo $MYVAR** at the command prompt and press **Enter**.

10. At the command prompt, type **set | grep MYVAR** and press **Enter**. Is the MYVAR variable listed? Why?

11. At the command prompt, type **env | grep MYVAR** and press **Enter**. Is the MYVAR variable listed? Why?

12. At the command prompt, type **export MYVAR** and press **Enter**. Next, type **env | grep MYVAR** at the command prompt and press **Enter**. Is the MYVAR variable listed now? Why?

13. At the command prompt, type **exit** and press **Enter** to log out of the shell. Next, log in to the terminal using the user name of **root** and the password of **secret**.

14. At the command prompt, type **echo $MYVAR** and press **Enter** to view the contents of the MYVAR variable. What is listed and why?

15. At the command prompt, type **vi .bash_profile** and press **Enter**. At the bottom of the file, add the following line. When finished, save and quit the vi editor.

```
export MYVAR="My sample variable"
```

16. At the command prompt, type **exit** and press **Enter** to log out of the shell. Next, log in to the terminal using the user name of **root** and the password of **secret**.

17. At the command prompt, type **echo $MYVAR** and press **Enter** to list the contents of the MYVAR variable. What is listed and why?

18. At the command prompt, type **alias** and press **Enter**. What aliases are present in your shell?

19. At the command prompt, type **alias asample="cd /etc ; cat hosts ; cd ~ ; ls -F"** and press **Enter**. What does this command do?

20. At the command prompt, type **asample** and press **Enter**. What happened and why? What environment file could you add this alias to so that it is executed each time a new BASH shell is created?

21. Type **exit** and press **Enter** to log out of your shell.

Project 7-4

In this hands-on project, you create a basic shell script and execute it on the system.

1. Switch to a command-line terminal (tty2) by pressing **Ctrl+Alt+F2** and log in to the terminal using the user name of **root** and the password of **secret**.

2. At the command prompt, type **vi myscript** and press **Enter** to open a new file for editing called myscript in your home directory.

3. Enter the following text into the myscript2 file. When finished, save and quit the vi editor.

```
#!/bin/bash
echo -e "This is a sample shell script. \t It displays mounted
  filesystems \a"
mount
```

4. At the command prompt, type **ls -l myscript** and press **Enter**. What permissions does the myscript file have? Next, type **bash myscript** at the command prompt and press **Enter**. Did the shell script execute? What do the \t and \a escape sequences do?

5. Next, type **./myscript** at the command prompt and press **Enter**. What error message did you receive and why?

6. At the command prompt, type **chmod u+x myscript** and press **Enter**. Next, type **./myscript** at the command prompt and press **Enter**. Did the script execute? Why?

7. Type **exit** and press **Enter** to log out of your shell.

Project 7-5

In this hands-on project, you create a shell script that uses decision and loop constructs to analyze user input.

1. Switch to a command-line terminal (tty2) by pressing **Ctrl+Alt+F2** and log in to the terminal using the user name of **root** and the password of **secret**.

2. At the command prompt, type **vi myscript2** and press **Enter** to open a new file for editing called myscript2 in your home directory.

3. Enter the following text into the myscript2 file. When finished, save and quit the vi editor.

```
#!/bin/bash
echo -e "This program adds entries to a family database file.\n"
echo -e "Please enter the name of the family member --> \c"
read NAME
echo -e "Please enter the family member's relation to you
(e.g., mother) --> \c"
```

```
read RELATION
echo -e "Please enter the family member's telephone number --> \c"
read PHONE
echo -e "$NAME\t$RELATION\t$PHONE" >> database
```

4. At the command prompt, type **chmod u+x myscript2** and press **Enter**. Next, type **./myscript2** at the command prompt and press **Enter**. Answer the questions with information regarding one of your family members.

5. At the command prompt, type **cat database** and press **Enter**. Was the entry from Step 4 present? Why?

6. Re-execute the myscript2 script (from Step 4) several times to populate the database file with entries.

7. At the command prompt, type **vi myscript2** and press **Enter**. Edit the text inside the myscript2 shell script so that it reads:

```
#!/bin/bash
echo -e "Would you like to add an entry to the family database file?\n"
read ANSWER1
if [ $ANSWER1 = "y" -o $ANSWER1 = "Y" ]
then
echo -e "Please enter the name of the family member --> \c"
read NAME
echo -e "Please enter the family member's relation to you (i.e. mother)
    --> \c"
read RELATION
echo -e "Please enter the family member's telephone number --> \c"
read PHONE
echo -e "$NAME\t$RELATION\t$PHONE" >> database
fi
echo -e "Would you like to search an entry in the family database
    file?\n"
read ANSWER2
if [ $ANSWER2 = "y" -o $ANSWER2 = "Y" ]
then
echo -e "What word would you like to look for? --> \c"
read WORD
grep "$WORD" database
fi
```

8. At the command prompt, type **./myscript2** and press **Enter**. When prompted to enter an entry into the database, choose **y** and press **Enter**. Answer the questions with information regarding one of your family members. Next, when prompted to search the database, answer **y** and press **Enter**. Search for the name that you just entered a few seconds ago. Is it there?

9. At the command prompt, type **./myscript2** and press **Enter**. When prompted to enter an entry into the database, choose **n** and press **Enter**. Next, when prompted to search the database, answer **y** and press **Enter**. Search for a name that you entered in Step 6. Was it there? Why?

10. At the command prompt, type **vi myscript2** and press **Enter**. Edit the text inside the myscript2 shell script so that it reads:

```
#!/bin/bash
echo -e "What would you like to do?
Add an entry (a)
Search an entry (s)
Enter your choice (a/s)-->\c"
read ANSWER
case $ANSWER in
a|A ) echo -e "Please enter the name of the family member --> \c"
     read NAME
     echo -e "Please enter the family member's relation to you
(i.e. mother)-->\c"
     read RELATION
     echo -e "Please enter the family member's telephone number --> \c"
     read PHONE
     echo -e "$NAME\t$RELATION\t$PHONE" >> database
     ;;
s|S ) echo -e "What word would you like to look for? --> \c"
     read WORD
     grep "$WORD" database
     ;;
  *) echo "You must enter either the letter a or s."
     ;;
esac
```

11. At the command prompt, type **./myscript2** and press **Enter**. Choose **y** and press **Enter**. What error message do you receive and why?

12. At the command prompt, type **./myscript2** and press **Enter**. Choose **a** and press **Enter**. Enter information about another family member. Does it matter whether you entered **a** or **A** at the prompt earlier? Why?

13. At the command prompt, type **./myscript2** and press **Enter**. Choose **s** and press **Enter**. Search for the family member entered in Step 12. Does it matter whether you entered **s** or **S** at the prompt earlier? Why?

14. At the command prompt, type **vi myscript2** and press **Enter**. Edit the text inside the myscript2 shell script so that it reads:

```
#!/bin/bash
while true
do
clear
echo -e "What would you like to do?
Add an entry (a)
Search an entry (s)
Quit (q)
Enter your choice (a/s/q)-->\c"
read ANSWER
```

```
case $ANSWER in
a|A ) echo -e "Please enter the name of the family member --> \c"
    read NAME
    echo -e "Please enter the family member's relation to you
(i.e. mother) -->\c"
    read RELATION
    echo -e "Please enter the family member's telephone number --> \c"
    read PHONE
    echo-e "$NAME\t$RELATION\t$PHONE" >> database
    ;;
s|S ) echo-e "What word would you like to look for? --> \c"
    read WORD
    grep "$WORD" database
    sleep 4
    ;;
q|Q ) exit
    ;;
*)    echo "You must enter either the letter a or s."
    sleep 4
    ;;
esac
done
```

15. At the command prompt, type **./myscript2** and press **Enter**. Choose **a** and press **Enter**. Enter information about another family member. Does the menu appear again after you were finished? Why? Choose **s** and press **Enter**. Search for the family member that you just entered. Choose **q** to quit the shell script.

16. At the command prompt, type **vi myscript3** and press **Enter** to edit a new file called myscript3 in your home directory.

17. Enter the following text into the myscript3 file. When finished, save and quit the vi editor.

```
#!/bin/bash
echo -e "This program copies a file to the /stuff directory.\n"
echo -e "Which file would you like to copy? --> \c"
read FILENAME
mkdir /stuff || echo "The /stuff directory could not be created."
cp -f $FILENAME /stuff && echo "$FILENAME was successfully copied to
    /stuff"
```

18. At the command prompt, type **chmod u+x myscript3** and press **Enter**. Next, type **./myscript3** at the command prompt and press **Enter**. When prompted for a filename, type **/etc/hosts** and press **Enter**. Was the /stuff directory created successfully? Why or why not? Was the /etc/hosts file copied successfully to the /stuff directory? Why or why not?

19. Type **./myscript3** at the command prompt and press **Enter**. When prompted for a filename, type **/etc/inittab** and press **Enter**. Was the /stuff directory created successfully? Why or why not? Was the /etc/inittab file copied successfully to the /stuff directory? Why or why not?

20. At the command prompt, type **vi myscript4** and press **Enter** to edit a new file called myscript4 in your home directory.

21. Enter the following text into the myscript4 file. When finished, save and quit the vi editor.

```
#!/bin/bash
echo "These are the scripts that you have created previously:"
ls -l myscript myscript2 myscript3
sleep 2
echo "This script will now change the permissions on each script
such that the root user has exclusive rights only."
sleep 3
for FILE in myscript myscript2 myscript3
do
chmod 700 $FILE
done

echo "The new permissions are listed below:"
ls -l myscript myscript2 myscript3
```

22. At the command prompt, type **chmod u+x myscript4** and press **Enter**. Next, type **./myscript4** at the command prompt and press **Enter**. Were the permissions changed to rwx------ for myscript, myscript2, and myscript3?

23. Type **exit** and press **Enter** to log out of your shell.

Discovery Exercises

1. Name the command that can be used to:

   a. Create an alias called mm that displays only those filesystems that are mounted and contain an ext2 filesystem.

   b. Create and export a variable called NEWHOME that is equivalent to the value contained in the HOME variable.

   c. Find all files that start with the word "host" starting from the /etc directory and save the stdout to a file called file1 and the stderr to the same file.

   d. Display only the lines from the output of the set command that have the word "bash" in them. This output on the terminal screen should be sorted alphabetically.

   e. Display only the user name (first field) in the colon-delimited /etc/password file and save the output to a file called users in the current directory.

2. What would happen if the user executed the following command?

   ```
   tr a A </etc/hosts | sort -r | pr -d >/etc/hosts
   ```

   Explain the output.

3. Recall that only stdout can be sent across a pipe to another command. Using the information presented in this chapter, how could you send stderr across the pipe in the following command?

   ```
   ls /etc/hosts /etc/h | tr h H
   ```

4. Name the test statement that can be used to test whether:

   a. The user has read permission to the /etc/hosts file

   b. The user has read and execute permission to the /etc directory

   c. The contents of the variable $TEST are equal to the string "success"

   d. The contents of the variable $TEST are numerically equal to the contents of the variable $RESULT

   e. The contents of the variable $TEST are equal to the string "success" and the file /etc/hosts exists

   f. The contents of the variable $TEST are equal to the string "success," or the number 5, or the contents of the variable $RESULT

5. Examine the /root/.bash_profile file shown next. Using the information presented in this chapter, describe what each line of this file does.

```
# .bash_profile
# Get the aliases and functions
if [ -f ~/.bashrc ]; then
        . ~/.bashrc
fi
# User specific environment and startup programs

PATH=$PATH:$HOME/bin
BASH_ENV=$HOME/.bashrc
USERNAME="root"
export USERNAME BASH_ENV PATH
```

6. Write a shell script that contains a hashpling and comments. It should perform the following tasks:

   a. Display a list of currently logged-in users.

   b. Display the system's host name.

   c. Display the time and date.

   d. Display the disk usage.

   e. Display the current working directory.

   f. Display the pathname to the BASH shell.

7. Write a shell script that prompts the user for a grade between 0 and 100. The shell script should calculate the corresponding letter for this grade based on the following criteria:

   0–49 = F

   50–59 = D

   60–69 = C

   70–79 = B

   80–100 = A

   Ensure that the shell script continues to prompt the user for grades until they choose to exit the shell script.

## chapter 8

System Initialization and X Windows

After completing this chapter, you will be able to:

- Summarize the major steps necessary to boot a Linux system
- Configure the GRUB and LILO boot loaders
- Explain how the init daemon initializes the system at boot time into different runlevels
- Configure the system to start daemons upon entering certain runlevels
- Explain the purpose of the major Linux GUI components: X Windows, window manager, and desktop environment
- List common window managers and desktop environments used in Linux
- Configure X Windows settings

Earlier in this book, you installed the GRUB boot loader for the Linux kernel during the Fedora installation program. In this chapter, you investigate the boot process in greater detail. You explore how to configure boot loaders and the process used to start daemons after the kernel has loaded. Additionally, you examine the procedures used to start and stop new daemons. Finally, you examine the various components the Linux GUI comprises and how to configure these components using common Linux utilities.

The Boot Process

When a computer first initializes, the system BIOS performs a **power-on self test** (POST). Following the POST, the BIOS checks its configuration for boot devices to search for and operating systems to execute. Typically, computers first check for an operating system (OS) on floppy disk, CD, DVD, and USB devices because these devices can contain installation media for an OS. If it fails to find an OS on any of these options, the BIOS usually checks the MBR/GPT on the first hard disk inside the computer.

Recall that you can alter the order in which boot devices are checked in the computer BIOS.

Also recall that the MBR/GPT stores the list of all partitions on the hard disk.

The MBR/GPT might contain a **boot loader** that can then locate and execute the kernel of the OS. Alternatively, the MBR/GPT might contain a pointer to a partition on the system that contains a boot loader on the first sector; this partition is referred to as the **active partition.** There can be only one active partition per hard disk.

In addition to storing the list of all partitions on the hard disk, the MBR/GPT also stores the location of the active partition.

Regardless of whether the boot loader is loaded from the MBR/GPT or the first sector of the active partition, the remainder of the boot process is the same. The boot loader then executes the Linux kernel from the partition that contains it.

The Linux kernel is stored in the **/boot** directory and is named **vmlinuz-<kernel version>**.

After the Linux kernel is loaded into memory, the boot loader is no longer active; instead, the Linux kernel continues to initialize the system by loading daemons into memory. A **daemon** is a system process that performs useful tasks, such as printing, scheduling, and OS maintenance. The first daemon process on the system is called the **initialize (init) daemon**; it is responsible for loading all other daemons on the system required to bring the system to a usable state in which users can log in and interact with services. The whole process is depicted in Figure 8-1.

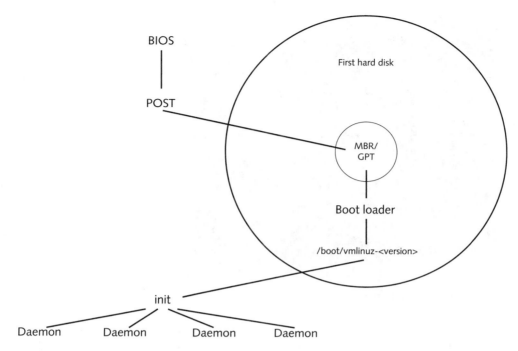

Figure 8-1 The boot process

Source: Course Technology/Cengage Learning

Boot Loaders

As discussed in the previous section, the primary function of boot loaders during the boot process is to load the Linux kernel into memory. However, boot loaders can perform other functions as well, including passing information to the kernel during system startup and booting other OSs that are present on the hard disk. Using one boot loader to boot one of several OSs is known as dual booting; the boot loader simply loads a different OS kernel based on user input.

Normally, only one OS can be active at any one time.

Virtualization software can be used to run multiple OSs at the same time. Many virtualization software packages are available for Linux, including Kernel-based Virtual Machine (KVM), QEMU, Xen, and VirtualBox.

The two most common boot loaders used on Linux systems are GRUB and LILO.

GRUB

GRand Unified Bootloader (GRUB) is the most common boot loader used on modern Linux systems and the only boot loader supported by Fedora 13. The first major part of the GRUB boot loader (called Stage1) typically resides on the MBR/GPT; the remaining parts of the boot loader (called Stage1.5 and Stage2) reside in the /boot/grub directory. GRUB Stage1 simply points to GRUB Stage1.5, which loads filesystem support and proceeds to load

Figure 8-2 The GRUB boot screen

Source: Course Technology/Cengage Learning

GRUB Stage2. GRUB Stage2 performs the actual boot loader functions and displays a graphical boot loader screen similar to that shown in Figure 8-2.

You configure GRUB by editing a configuration file (**/boot/grub/grub.conf**) that is read directly by the Stage2 boot loader. A sample /boot/grub/grub.conf file is shown here:

```
[root@server1 ~]# cat /boot/grub/grub.conf
# grub.conf generated by anaconda
#
# Note that you do not have to rerun grub after making changes
# NOTICE:  You do not have a /boot partition. This means that
#          all kernel and initrd paths are relative to /, eg.
#          root (hd0,0)
#          kernel /boot/vmlinuz-version ro root=/dev/sda1
#          initrd /boot/initrd-[generic-]version.img
boot=/dev/sda
default=0
timeout=5
splashimage=(hd0,0)/boot/grub/splash.xpm.gz
password --md5 $1$•~AŠ†Õ.R$W.uLzTHpvhCchfS0iTTSO0
hiddenmenu

title Fedora (2.6.33.3-85.fc13.i686.PAE)
  root (hd0,0)
  kernel /boot/vmlinuz-2.6.33.3-85.fc13.i686.PAE ro root=/dev/sda1 rhgb
    quiet
  initrd /boot/initramfs-2.6.33.3-85.fc13.i686.PAE.img
[root@server1 ~]# _
```

Alternatively, you can view and edit the /etc/grub.conf file, which is simply a symbolic link to /boot/grub/grub.conf.

Lines can be commented out of /boot/grub/grub.conf by preceding those lines with a # symbol.

Some other Linux distributions use a /boot/grub/menu.lst file in place of /boot/grub/grub.conf to hold GRUB configuration.

To understand the entries in the /boot/grub/grub.conf file, you must first understand how GRUB refers to partitions on hard disks. Hard disks and partitions on those hard disks are identified by numbers in the following format: (hd<drive#>,<partition#>). Thus, the (hd0,0) notation in the preceding /boot/grub/grub.conf file refers to the first hard disk on the system (regardless of whether it is SCSI, SATA, or PATA) and the first partition on that hard disk, respectively. Similarly, the second partition on the first hard disk is referred to as (hd0,1), and the fourth partition on the third hard disk is referred to as (hd2,3).

In addition, GRUB calls the partition that contains Stage2 of the GRUB boot loader the **GRUB root partition**. Normally, the GRUB root partition is the filesystem that contains the /boot directory and should not be confused with the Linux root filesystem. If your system has a separate partition mounted to /boot, GRUB refers to the file /boot/grub/grub.conf as /grub/grub.conf. If your system does not have a separate filesystem for the /boot directory, this file is simply referred to as /boot/grub/grub.conf in GRUB.

Thus, the sample /boot/grub/grub.conf file shown earlier displays a graphical boot screen (splashimage=(hd0,0)/boot/grub/splash.xpm.gz) and boots the default OS kernel on the first hard drive (default=0) in five seconds (timeout=5) without showing any additional menus (hiddenmenu). The default OS kernel is located on the GRUB root filesystem (root (hd0,0)) and is called /boot/vmlinuz-2.6.33.3-85.fc13.i686.PAE.

The kernel then mounts the root filesystem on /dev/sda1 (root=/dev/sda1) initially as read-only (ro) to avoid problems with the fsck command and uses a ramdisk image to load modules into RAM that are needed at boot time (initrd /boot/initramfs-2.6.33.3-85.fc13.i686.PAE.img).

Fedora 13 prefers to use a GUID label (i.e., root=UUID=42c0fce6-bb79-4218-af1a-0b89316bb7d1) in place of root=/dev/sda1 to identify the partition that holds the root filesystem.

All other keywords present on the kernel line within /boot/grub/grub.conf are used to pass information to the kernel from the GRUB boot loader. For example, the keyword rhgb (Red Hat Graphical Boot) tells the Linux kernel to use a graphical boot screen as it is loading daemons, and the keyword quiet tells the Linux kernel to avoid printing errors to the screen during system startup. You can add your own keywords to the kernel line in /boot/grub/grub.conf to control how your Linux kernel is loaded. For example, appending the text nosmp to the kernel line disables Symmetric Multi-Processing (SMP) support within the Linux kernel. Alternatively, appending the text mem=4096M to the kernel line forces your Linux kernel to see 4096MB of physical RAM in the event that your Linux kernel does not detect all of the RAM in your computer properly.

For a list of all keywords that can be appended to the `kernel` line within GRUB, consult the documentation available at *www.gnu.org/ software/grub/*.

Normally, GRUB allows users to manipulate the boot loader during system startup; to prevent this, you can optionally password protect GRUB modifications during boot time. The line `password --md5 $1$●~AŠ†Õ.R$W.uLzTHpvhCchfS0iTTSO0` in the preceding /boot/grub/grub.conf file prompts a user for a password to access the boot loader during system startup. Furthermore, the password specified in this file is encrypted to prevent users from viewing the password when viewing the file.

To create an encrypted password for use in /boot/grub/grub.conf, you can use the **grub-md5-crypt command**.

Recall from the /boot/grub/grub.conf file shown earlier that you have five seconds after the BIOS POST to interact with the GRUB boot screen shown in Figure 8-2. If you press any key within these five seconds, you will be presented with a graphical GRUB boot menu screen similar to Figure 8-3 that you can use to manipulate the boot process. If you have several different Linux kernels installed on your system (from updating your system software), you can select the kernel that you would like to boot, or you can highlight your kernel and press a to append keywords to the `kernel` line, or press e to edit the entire boot configuration for the kernel listed in /boot/grub/grub.conf, as shown in Figure 8-4.

You can also press c to obtain a grub> prompt where you can enter a variety of commands to view system hardware configuration, find and display files, alter the configuration of

Figure 8-3 The GRUB boot menu

Source: Course Technology/Cengage Learning

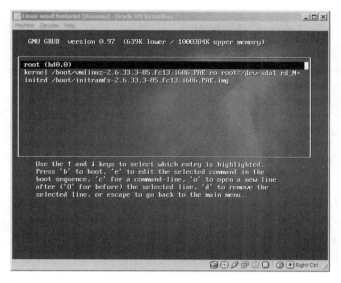

Figure 8-4 Configuring the GRUB boot loader

Source: Course Technology/Cengage Learning

8

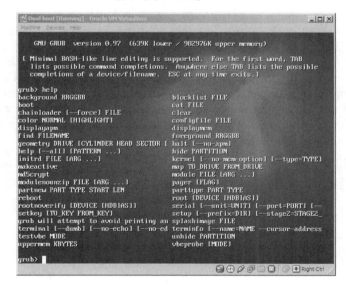

Figure 8-5 Viewing help at the GRUB prompt

Source: Course Technology/Cengage Learning

GRUB, or boot an OS kernel. To view all available commands when at the grub> prompt, simply type help at this screen, as shown in Figure 8-5.

The grub prompt can also be used to boot the system in the same manner as seen in /boot/grub/grub.conf; to boot the Linux OS used in the previous examples, you would simply type the kernel and initrd lines from /boot/grub/grub.conf at the grub> prompt (pressing Enter after each line), followed by the boot command, and press Enter again to continue the boot process.

If the GRUB boot loader becomes damaged, you can reinstall it using the **grub-install command** that is available on the system or within System Rescue. To install GRUB Stage1 on the MBR/GPT of the first SATA hard disk, you can type the following command:

```
[root@server1 ~]# grub-install /dev/sda
Installation finished. No error reported.
This is the contents of the device map /boot/grub/device.map.
Check if this is correct or not. If any of the lines is incorrect,
fix it and re-run the script 'grub-install'.

# this device map was generated by anaconda
(hd0)    /dev/sda
[root@server1 ~]# _
```

Alternatively, you can use the `grub-install /dev/sda1` command to install GRUB Stage1 at the beginning of the first primary partition of the same hard disk.

LILO

Linux Loader (LILO) is the traditional Linux boot loader. Although it is no longer supported by Fedora, it is often found on other Linux distributions that require a smaller boot loader than GRUB, as well as legacy Linux installations, such as Fedora Core 2. Although LILO can reside on the first sector of an active Linux partition, it is typically located on the MBR/ GPT of the hard disk. When the computer completes the POST and locates the LILO boot loader, a LILO boot: prompt appears. You can then press the Tab key to see a list of OSs that you can boot. Following this, you can enter the name of an OS or press Enter to boot the default OS (usually Linux). Alternatively, you can wait five seconds for the system to boot the default OS automatically.

After the OS is fully loaded, you can configure the LILO boot loader by editing the **/etc/lilo.conf** file. An example of this file is as follows:

```
[root@server1 ~]# cat /etc/lilo.conf
prompt
timeout=50
default=linux
boot=/dev/hda
map=/boot/map
install=/boot/boot.b
lba32

image=/boot/vmlinuz-2.6.5-1.358
label=linux
initrd=/boot/initrd-2.6.5-1.358.img
read-only
append="rhgb quiet root=/dev/hda1"
[root@server1 ~]# _
```

Keyword	Description
image=	Specifies the absolute pathname to the Linux kernel.
root=	Specifies the device and partition that contain the Linux root filesystem.
prompt	Displays a LILO boot prompt provided there is no message= keyword specified.
message=	Specifies the absolute pathname to the file that contains a graphical LILO screen that can be used instead of a prompt. You can press Ctrl+x at this graphical screen to switch to the LILO boot: prompt.
timeout=	Specifies the number of 1/10th seconds to wait for user input before loading the default OS kernel.
default=	Specifies the label for the default OS kernel.
label=	Specifies the friendly name used to identify an OS kernel within boot loader screens.
boot=	Specifies where LILO should be installed. If the device specified is a partition on a hard disk, LILO is installed at the beginning of the partition. If the device specified is a disk, LILO is installed to the MBR on that device.
linear	Specifies that LILO uses linear sector addressing.
read-only	Initially mounts the Linux root filesystem as read-only to reduce any errors with running fsck during system startup.
initrd=	Specifies the pathname to a ramdisk image used to load modules into memory needed for the Linux kernel at boot time.
password=	Specifies a password required to boot the Linux kernel.
append=	Specifies parameters that are passed to the Linux kernel when loaded.
map=	Specifies the file that contains the exact location of the Linux kernel on the hard disk.
install=	Specifies the file that contains the physical layout of the disk drive.
lba32	Specifies large block addressing (32-bit) for hard drives that have more than 1,024 cylinders.

Table 8-1   Common /etc/lilo.conf keywords

The preceding /etc/lilo.conf file indicates that LILO boots the Linux kernel /boot/vmlinuz-2.6.5-1.358 provided the user chooses the OS name linux (label=linux). Furthermore, the system continues to boot the default OS (default=linux) if the user does not enter any input for five seconds (timeout=50). Furthermore, the LILO boot loader tells the Linux kernel to use a Red Hat Graphical Boot after it has loaded (rhgb), suppress detailed kernel messages (quiet), and mount the root filesystem on /dev/hda1 (root=/dev/hda1).

Table 8-1 lists some keywords commonly used in /etc/lilo.conf, along with their definitions.

As with /boot/grub/grub.conf, you can transform a line in /etc/lilo.conf to a comment by preceding it with a # symbol.

If the kernel does not detect the correct system information, you can use the append= keyword in /etc/lilo.conf to pass information to the Linux kernel manually at boot time. For example, if the Linux kernel did not detect the RAM or hard disk installed in your system properly, you can add the line append="mem=4096M" to /etc/lilo.conf to allow your Linux kernel to recognize that your system has 4096MB of RAM, as well as the line append= "hd=2100,16,63" to /etc/lilo.conf to tell your Linux kernel that your hard disk has 2,100 cylinders, 16 heads, and 63 sectors.

Unlike with /boot/grub/grub.conf, if you change the /etc/lilo.conf file, LILO must be reinstalled using the new information in /etc/lilo.conf for those changes to take effect. To do this, you can use the **lilo** command:

```
[root@server1 ~]# lilo
Added linux *
[root@server1 ~]# _
```

To uninstall LILO from an active partition or the MBR/GPT, you can use the lilo -U command.

Although LILO is a robust boot loader, it might encounter errors and fail to load properly. In that case, you see an error code indicating the nature of the problem. Table 8-2 lists common LILO error messages and possible solutions.

ELILO is a version of LILO that is available for computers that use Extensible Firmware Interface (EFI). You can download ELILO at *http://sourceforge.net/projects/elilo/*.

Dual Booting Linux

Linux servers are usually dedicated to their role all day long. However, if you use Linux as a workstation, you might only want to use the Linux OS at certain times. At other times, you might use the same computer with a different OS. Because you normally use only one OS at a time, a process must exist that allows you to choose which OS to load at boot time; this process, called **dual boot**, is typically handled by the boot loader.

Using GRUB or LILO to Dual Boot Other OSs
If you are using a Linux boot loader to dual boot an OS in addition to Linux, it is easiest to install Linux after you install

Error Message	Description
L	The first part of the LILO boot loader failed to load, usually as a result of incorrect hard disk parameters. Simply rebooting the machine sometimes fixes this problem. However, you might also need to add the word "linear" to /etc/lilo.conf.
LI	The second part of the LILO boot loader failed to load, or the /boot/boot.b file is missing. Adding the word "linear" to /etc/lilo.conf might fix the problem.
LIL LIL- LIL?	LILO has loaded properly but cannot find certain files required to operate, such as the /boot/map and /boot/boot.b files. Adding the word "linear" to /etc/lilo.conf might fix the problem.

Table 8-2 LILO error messages

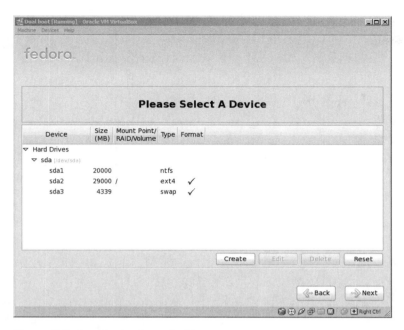

Figure 8-6 Partitioning for a dual-boot system

Source: Course Technology/Cengage Learning

the other OS; this allows the Linux installation program to detect the other OS on the disk and place the appropriate entries in the boot loader configuration file.

Take, for example, an installation of Fedora that creates Linux partitions on the free space of a hard disk containing an NTFS partition (/dev/sda1) with the Microsoft Windows Server 2008 OS installed on it, as shown in Figure 8-6.

During the Fedora installation, you can choose to shrink the size of your Windows partition to allow free space on your hard disk that can be used to create Linux partitions.

If the Windows partition is preserved during partitioning, the boot loader configuration options include a section that allows you to choose to dual boot Linux with a Microsoft Windows OS using GRUB, as shown in Figure 8-7.

The /boot/grub/grub.conf file created by the installation program seen in Figures 8-6 and 8-7 is shown in the following output:

```
[root@server1 ~]# cat /boot/grub/grub.conf
# grub.conf generated by anaconda
#
# Note that you do not have to rerun grub after making changes
# NOTICE:  You do not have a /boot partition. This means that
#          all kernel and initrd paths are relative to /, eg.
#          root (hd0,1)
#          kernel /boot/vmlinuz-version ro root=/dev/sda2
```

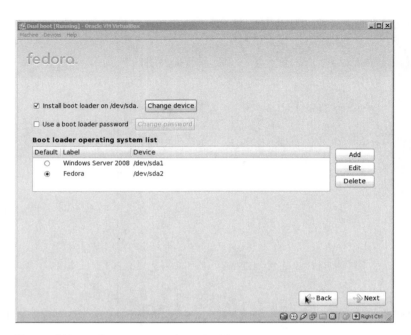

Figure 8-7 Configuring GRUB for a dual-boot system

Source: Course Technology/Cengage Learning

```
#              initrd /boot/initrd-[generic-]version.img
#boot=/dev/sda
default=0
timeout=5
splashimage=(hd0,1)/boot/grub/splash.xpm.gz
hiddenmenu

title Fedora (2.6.33.3-85.fc13.i686.PAE)
     root (hd0,1)
     kernel /boot/vmlinuz-2.6.33.3-85.fc13.i686.PAE ro root=/dev/sda2
        rhgb quiet
     initrd /boot/initramfs-2.6.33.3-85.fc13.i686.PAE.img

title Windows Server 2008
     rootnoverify (hd0,0)
     chainloader +1
[root@server1 ~]# _
```

The `title Windows Server 2008` in the preceding output identifies the new OS. This output is displayed on the GRUB boot menu screen (when you press any key within five seconds of seeing the initial GRUB boot screen), as shown in Figure 8-8.

The `rootnoverify (hd0,0)` line indicates that the OS lies on the first partition on the first hard disk and that it should not be automatically mounted by GRUB (because it might contain a foreign filesystem). Because GRUB cannot load a Windows kernel directly, GRUB must load the Windows boot loader from the Windows partition. This boot loader typically

Figure 8-8 The GRUB boot menu on a dual-boot system

Source: Course Technology/Cengage Learning

8

starts on the first block of the Windows partition. The `chainloader +1` line allows GRUB to load another boot loader starting from the first block of the partition (hd0,0).

The /etc/lilo.conf file that would perform the same function as the /boot/grub/grub.conf file shown earlier is described in the following output:

```
[root@server1 ~]# cat /etc/lilo.conf
prompt
timeout=50
default=linux
boot=/dev/hda
map=/boot/map
install=/boot/boot.b
lba32

image=/boot/vmlinuz-2.6.33.3-85.fc13.i686.PAE
label=linux
initrd=/boot/initramfs-2.6.33.3-85.fc13.i686.PAE.img
read-only
append="rhgb quiet root=/dev/sda2"

other=/dev/sda1
optional
label="Windows Server 2008"
[root@server1 ~]# _
```

LILO cannot boot a Windows kernel directly. Instead, the `other=` keyword in the preceding /etc/lilo.conf loads the boot loader that is present on the /dev/sda1 partition. The `optional` keyword prevents the GRUB boot loader from checking for a Linux system on the /dev/sda1 partition, and the `label` keyword identifies this OS using a name that will be displayed if you press Tab at the `LILO` boot: prompt.

Using a Windows Boot Loader to Dual Boot Linux

If you install the Windows OS after installing Linux, the Windows installation program usually rewrites the MBR/GPT on your first hard disk and, in the process, removes the GRUB boot loader. If that happens, you can use System Rescue to modify the /boot/grub/grub.conf file to allow you to boot the Windows OS and then reinstall the GRUB boot loader.

Alternatively, you can choose to use a Windows boot loader to load the Linux OS. However, because Windows boot loaders are not designed to boot a Linux kernel, you must first modify the Windows boot loader by adding some additional components. To do this, you can take advantage of any one of several free software packages. One popular option is **EasyBCD**, which you can download from *http://neosmart.net*.

To use EasyBCD, follow these steps:

1. Copy your /boot/grub/grub.conf file to removable media, such as a USB flash memory drive.

2. Install Windows.

3. Download the EasyBCD program from *http://neosmart.net* and install it.

4. Open EasyBCD within Windows, click Add New Entry in the left column, and then display the NeoGrub tab, as shown in Figure 8-9.

5. On the NeoGrub tab, click the Install button to modify the Windows boot loader to include Linux support.

6. Click the Configure button. This opens the C:\NST\menu.lst configuration file within Windows Notepad.

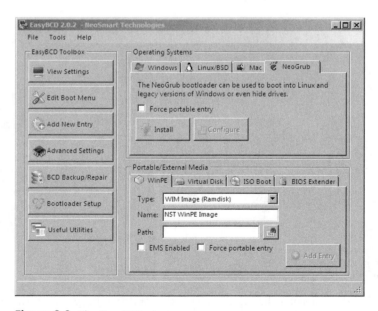

Figure 8-9 The EasyBCD program

Source: Course Technology/Cengage Learning

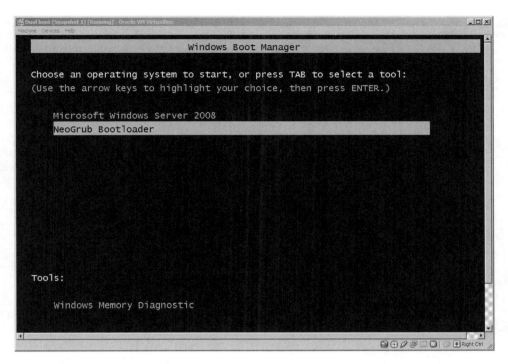

Figure 8-10 Booting Linux from a Windows boot loader

Source: Course Technology/Cengage Learning

7. Copy the contents of the grub.conf file from your removable media into this text file and save your changes to the C:\NST\menu.lst file to complete the configuration.

The next time you boot your system, the Windows boot loader screen will prompt you to choose to boot the default Windows OS, or start the NeoGrub Bootloader that will allow you to boot your Linux OS. See Figure 8-10.

Linux Initialization

Recall that after a boot loader loads the Linux OS kernel into memory, the kernel resumes control and executes the first daemon, called init, on the system. The init daemon then uses its configuration file, **/etc/inittab** (the name is short for "init table"), to determine the number of daemons that need to be loaded on the system to provide system services and ultimately allow users to log in and use the system. Furthermore, the init daemon is responsible for unloading daemons that are loaded in memory when the system is halted or rebooted.

Runlevels

Because the init daemon often has to manage several daemons at once, the init daemon categorizes the system into runlevels. A **runlevel** defines the number and type of daemons that are loaded into memory and executed by the kernel on a particular system. At any one time, a Linux system might be in any of the seven standard runlevels defined in Table 8-3.

Runlevel	Common Name	Description
0	halt	A system that has no daemons active in memory and is ready to be powered off.
1 s S single	single user mode	A system that has only enough daemons to allow one user to log in and perform system maintenance tasks. A user is automatically logged in to the system as the root user when entering single user mode.
2	multiuser mode	A system with most daemons running and that allows multiple users the ability to log in and use system services. Most common network services other than specialized network services are available in this runlevel as well.
3	extended multiuser mode	A system that has the same abilities as multiuser mode, yet with all extra networking services started (for example, SNMP, NFS).
4	not used	Not normally used, but can be customized to suit your needs.
5	graphical mode	A system that has the same abilities as extended multiuser mode, yet with a graphical login program called the **GNOME Display Manager (gdm)** started on tty1 or tty7 that allows for graphical logins.
6	reboot	A special runlevel used to reboot the system.

Table 8-3 Linux runlevels

Because the init daemon is responsible for starting and stopping daemons and, hence, changing runlevels, runlevels are often called **initstates**.

Fedora 13 uses a new version of the init daemon called the **upstart init system.**

To see the current runlevel of the system and the previous runlevel (if runlevels have been changed since system startup), you can use the **runlevel command**, as shown in the following output:

```
[root@server1 ~]# runlevel
N 5
[root@server1 ~]# _
```

The preceding runlevel command indicates that the system is in runlevel 5 and that the most recent runlevel prior to entering this runlevel is nonexistent (N).

To change the runlevel on a running system, you simply need to specify the **init command** followed by the new runlevel; to change from runlevel 5 to runlevel 1 to perform system maintenance tasks, you can use the following commands:

```
[root@server1 ~]# runlevel
N 5
[root@server1 ~]# init 1
```

*A list of daemons that are being stopped by the init
daemon while the system enters single user mode.*

Telling INIT to go to single user mode.

```
[root@server1 /]# _
[root@server1 /]# runlevel
1 S
[root@server1 /]# _
```

The **telinit command** is a shortcut to the init command. Thus, the command `telinit 1` can instead be used to switch to single user mode.

When in single user mode, the `runlevel` command displays S (single user mode) for the current runlevel and 1 (single user mode) for the most recent runlevel. However, when the runlevel is changed back to runlevel 5, as shown in the following output, the `runlevel` command displays the current and most recent runlevels properly.

```
[root@server1 /]# init 5
```

*A list of daemons that are being started by the init
daemon while the system enters runlevel 5. The gdm is started at the end.*

```
[root@server1 ~]# _
[root@server1 ~]# runlevel
S 5
[root@server1 ~]# _
```

You can also pass options from the boot loader to the Linux kernel to force the system to boot to a particular runlevel. If you append the keyword `single` to the kernel line within the GRUB configuration screen, you will boot to single user mode. Similarly, you can boot to single user mode from the `LILO boot:` prompt by typing the name of the Linux image followed by 1, S, s, or `single`.

The /etc/inittab file

Unless you specify otherwise, the init daemon enters the **default runlevel** indicated in the /etc/inittab file. In the past, the /etc/inittab file contained the entire configuration for the init daemon. However, with the new upstart init system in Fedora 13, the /etc/inittab simply contains a single uncommented line, preceded by a series of explanatory comments, as shown here:

```
[root@server1 ~]# cat /etc/inittab
# inittab is only used by upstart for the default runlevel.
#
# ADDING OTHER CONFIGURATION HERE WILL HAVE NO EFFECT ON YOUR SYSTEM.
#
# System initialization is started by /etc/init/rcS.conf
#
# Individual runlevels are started by /etc/init/rc.conf
#
```

```
# Ctrl-Alt-Delete is handled by /etc/init/control-alt-delete.conf
#
# Terminal gettys are handled by /etc/init/tty.conf and
# /etc/init/serial.conf, with configuration in /etc/sysconfig/init.
#
# For information on how to write upstart event handlers, or how
# upstart works, see init(5), init(8), and initctl(8).
#
# Default runlevel. The runlevels used are:
# 0 - halt (Do NOT set initdefault to this)
# 1 - Single user mode
# 2 - Multiuser, without NFS (The same as 3, if networking not used)
# 3 - Full multiuser mode
# 4 - unused
# 5 - X11
# 6 - reboot (Do NOT set initdefault to this)
#
id:5:initdefault:

[root@server1 ~]# _
```

The line id:5:initdefault: in the /etc/inittab file tells the init daemon that runlevel 5 is the default runlevel to boot to when initializing the Linux system at system startup.

Runlevel 5 is the default runlevel in most Linux distributions.

Runtime Configuration Scripts

During the boot process, the init daemon must execute several scripts that prepare the system, start daemons, and eventually bring the system to a usable state. These scripts are called **runtime configuration (rc) scripts.**

At boot time, the upstart Linux system first runs the **/etc/rc.d/rc.sysinit** script to initialize the hardware components of the system, set environment variables such as PATH and HOST-NAME, check filesystems, and perform system tasks required for daemon loading.

The hardware that is detected by the Linux kernel (which is stored in a kernel ring buffer in RAM) as well as the output of the /etc/rc.d/rc.sysinit script are hidden by the graphical startup screen during system initialization. To see this output after the system has booted, simply run the **dmesg command**. To ensure that you capture all of the system startup information in the kernel ring buffer before it is cleared by ongoing system events, you could run the dmesg > boot.messages command immediately after system initialization to save the messages to a file called boot.messages in the current directory for later use.

Next, the init daemon identifies the default runlevel in the /etc/inittab file. Because the default runlevel is 5, the init daemon executes the /etc/rc.d/rc 5 script, which in turn executes all files that start with S or K in the /etc/rc.d/rc5.d directory. Each file in this directory is a symbolic link to a script that can be used to start or stop a certain daemon. Moreover, each of the files in the /etc/rc.d/rc5.d directory is executed in alphabetical order; the S or the K indicates whether to start or kill the daemon upon entering this runlevel, respectively. Some sample contents of the /etc/rc.d/rc5.d directory are shown in the following output:

```
[root@server1 ~]# ls /etc/rc.d/rc5.d
K01smartd           K50netconsole      K87speech-dispatcherd S24avahi-daemon
K01smolt            K50snmpd           K89rdisc              S24nfslock
K05innd             K50snmptrapd       K90network            S24rpcgssd
K10dc_server        K50vsftpd          K91capi               S24rpcidmapd
K10psacct           K60nfs             K95firstboot          S25cups
K10saslauthd        K66gpsd            S02lvm2-monitor       S25netfs
K12dc_client        K69rpcsvcgssd      S07iscsid             S26acpid
K15httpd            K73ypbind          S08ip6tables          S26haldaemon
K20jetty            K74nscd            S08iptables           S26udev-post
K24irda             K74ntpd            S09isdn               S27pcscd
K25squid            K75ntpdate         S11auditd             S50bluetooth
K30spamassassin     K76ipsec           S11portreserve        S55sshd
K35backuppc         K76openvpn         S12rsyslog            S80sendmail
K35dovecot          K80sssd            S13cpuspeed           S82abrtd
K35nmb              K83named           S13irqbalance         S85gpm
K35smb              K84btseed          S13iscsi              S90crond
K35vncserver        K84bttrack         S13rpcbind            S95atd
K36mysqld           K84wpa_supplicant  S15mdmonitor          S99local
K36postgresql       K87multipathd      S22messagebus
K50dnsmasq          K87restorecond     S23NetworkManager
[root@server1 ~]# _
```

From the preceding output, you can see that the init daemon will start the cron daemon (S90crond) upon entering this runlevel and kill the nfs daemon (K60nfs) if it exists in memory upon entering this runlevel. In addition, the files in the preceding directory are executed in alphabetical order; the file K35nmb is executed before the file K35smb.

NOTE   Normally, you would expect most files within the /etc/rc.d/rc5.d directory to start with S because runlevel 5 contains the greatest number of running services compared with other runlevels. However, not all daemons that are added during Linux installation are configured to start at system initialization in order to conserve system resources. As a result, Linux places files for these daemons in the /etc/rc.d/rc5.d directory that start with K. Later in this chapter, you learn how to configure these daemons to start when the system enters runlevel 5.

Recall that runlevel 1 (single user mode) contains only enough daemons for a single user to log in and perform system tasks. If a user tells the init daemon to change to this runlevel using the init 1 command, the init daemon runs the /etc/rc.d/rc 5 script, which then proceeds to execute every file that starts with S or K in the /etc/rc.d/rc1.d directory. Because few daemons are started in single user mode, most files in this directory start with a K:

```
[root@server1 ~]# ls /etc/rc.d/rc1.d
K01smartd          K35dovecot      K74ntpd           K87rpcbind
K01smolt           K35nmb          K75netfs          K87speech-dispatcherd
K02avahi-daemon    K35smb          K75ntpdate        K88auditd
K05atd             K35vncserver    K76ipsec          K88iscsi
K05innd            K36mysqld       K76openvpn        K88rsyslog
K10cups            K36postgresql   K80sssd           K89iscsid
K10dc_server       K50dnsmasq      K83bluetooth      K89portreserve
K10psacct          K50netconsole   K83named          K89rdisc
K10saslauthd       K50snmpd        K83nfslock        K90network
K12dc_client       K50snmptrapd    K83rpcgssd        K91capi
K15gpm             K50vsftpd       K83rpcidmapd      K91isdn
K15httpd           K60crond        K84btseed         K92ip6tables
K16abrtd           K60nfs          K84bttrack        K92iptables
K20jetty           K66gpsd         K84NetworkManager K95firstboot
K24irda            K69rpcsvcgssd   K84wpa_supplicant S02lvm2-monitor
K25squid           K73pcscd        K85mdmonitor      S13cpuspeed
K25sshd            K73ypbind       K85messagebus     S26udev-post
K30sendmail        K74acpid        K87irqbalance     S99single
K30spamassassin    K74haldaemon    K87multipathd
K35backuppc        K74nscd         K87restorecond
[root@server1 ~]# _
```

Most daemons that are loaded upon system startup are executed from scripts that start with an S in the appropriate **/etc/rc.d/rc*.d** directory (where * refers to the default runlevel). After these scripts have been executed, the **/etc/rc.d/rc.local** script is executed to perform tasks that must occur after system startup. The Linux initialization process is summarized in Figure 8-11.

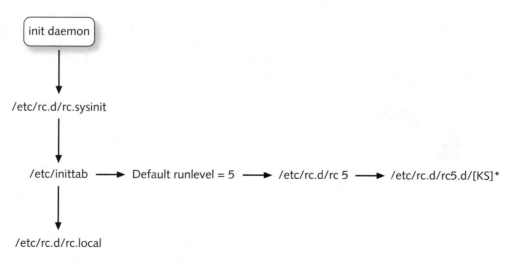

Figure 8-11 The Linux initialization process

Source: Course Technology/Cengage Learning

A message during system initialization indicates whether each runtime configuration script within the /etc/rc.d/rc*.d directories has loaded successfully or unsuccessfully. However, the graphical boot screen that is displayed while the init daemon loads other daemons at system initialization hides these messages. You can press the Esc key during system initialization to remove the graphical boot screen and view these messages, as shown in Figure 8-12.

The output of all runtime configuration scripts within the /etc/rc.d/rc*.d directories is logged to the /var/log/messages file. Thus, to view the information shown in Figure 8-12 after system startup, simply view the entries within the /var/log/messages file that have time stamps that occurred during the previous system startup.

Configuring Daemon Startup

Recall from the preceding section that most daemons are started by the init daemon from symbolic links in the /etc/rc.d/rc*.d directories (/etc/rc.d/rc0.d, /etc/rc.d/rc1.d, /etc/rc.d/rc2.d, /etc/rc.d/rc3.d, /etc/rc.d/rc4.d, /etc/rc.d/rc5.d), depending on the runlevel entered. Most of these links point to the appropriate scripts within the **/etc/rc.d/init.d** directory that can be used to start the actual daemon. A partial listing of the /etc/rc.d/rc5.d directory demonstrates this:

```
[root@server1 ~]# ls -l /etc/rc.d/rc5.d |head
total 0
lrwxrwxrwx. 1 root root 16 Aug  2 09:59 K01smartd -> ../init.d/smartd
lrwxrwxrwx. 1 root root 15 Aug  2 10:01 K01smolt -> ../init.d/smolt
lrwxrwxrwx. 1 root root 14 Aug  2 10:00 K05innd -> ../init.d/innd
lrwxrwxrwx. 1 root root 19 Aug  2 09:58 K10dc_server -> ../init.d/dc_server
lrwxrwxrwx. 1 root root 16 Aug  2 09:46 K10psacct -> ../init.d/psacct
lrwxrwxrwx. 1 root root 19 Aug  2 09:56 K10saslauthd -> ../init.d/saslauthd
lrwxrwxrwx. 1 root root 19 Aug  2 09:58 K12dc_client -> ../init.d/dc_client
lrwxrwxrwx. 1 root root 15 Aug  2 09:55 K15httpd -> ../init.d/httpd
lrwxrwxrwx. 1 root root 15 Aug  2 10:18 K20jetty -> ../init.d/jetty
[root@server1 ~]# _
```

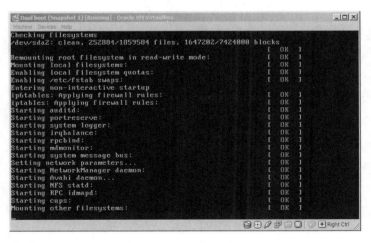

Figure 8-12 Viewing daemon startup

Source: Course Technology/Cengage Learning

In addition, most daemon scripts accept the arguments start, stop, and restart. Thus, to manipulate daemons after system startup, you can execute them directly from the /etc/rc.d/init.d directory, as shown next with the crond daemon:

```
[root@server1 ~]# /etc/rc.d/init.d/crond restart
Stopping crond:                                      [  OK  ]
Starting crond:                                      [  OK  ]
[root@server1 ~]# _
```

The /etc/init.d directory is symbolically linked to the /etc/rc.d/init.d directory; thus, the `/etc/init.d/crond restart` command would perform the same function as the command used in the preceding example.

You can also use the **service command** to start, stop, or restart any daemons listed within the /etc/rc.d/init.d directory. For example, to restart the crond daemon using the following command:

```
[root@server1 ~]# service crond restart
Stopping crond:                                      [  OK  ]
Starting crond:                                      [  OK  ]
[root@server1 ~]# _
```

Because most daemon startup/shutdown script files are centrally stored in the /etc/rc.d/init.d directory, if you want to add a daemon that is automatically started by the init daemon upon entering a certain runlevel at system startup, you can add a daemon startup/shutdown script to this directory and create the appropriate links in each of the /etc/rc.d/rc*.d directories to start or kill the daemon upon entering certain runlevels.

Thus, to configure the init daemon to automatically start a script called testdaemon when entering runlevels 2, 3, and 5 only, you can perform the following commands:

```
[root@server1 ~]# cp testdaemon /etc/rc.d/init.d
[root@server1 ~]# cd /etc/rc.d/init.d
[root@server1 ~]# ln -s testdaemon /etc/rc.d/rc2.d/S99testdaemon
[root@server1 ~]# ln -s testdaemon /etc/rc.d/rc3.d/S99testdaemon
[root@server1 ~]# ln -s testdaemon /etc/rc.d/rc5.d/S99testdaemon
[root@server1 ~]# _
```

You can see whether the script was executed successfully at boot time by checking the contents of the /var/log/messages file after the system has fully initialized, as shown here:

```
[root@server1 ~]# grep testdaemon /var/log/messages
Aug 22 12:44:34 server1 testdaemon: testdaemon startup succeeded
[root@server1 ~]# _
```

For ease of administration, Fedora places a large number of files that start with K in most /etc/rc.d/rc*.d directories, even though the daemons represented by those files are probably not started. This means you can change a filename so that it starts with S, thus ensuring that the daemon starts when the system enters that runlevel. However, manually renaming files can be time consuming. Instead, you can view and modify the daemons that are started in each runlevel by using the **chkconfig command**. The chkconfig command views and manipulates the appropriate runtime configuration files in the /etc/rc.d/rc*.d directories. For example, the following command indicates that the ntpd daemon is not started in any runlevel:

```
[root@server1 ~]# chkconfig --list ntpd
ntpd        0:off 1:off 2:off 3:off 4:off 5:off 6:off
[root@server1 ~]# _
```

To configure the ntpd daemon to start in runlevels 3 and 5, and to verify the results, you could run the following commands:

```
[root@server1 ~]# chkconfig --level 35 ntpd on
[root@server1 ~]# chkconfig --list ntpd
ntpd        0:off 1:off 2:off 3:on  4:off 5:on  6:off
[root@server1 ~]# _
```

Alternatively, you can use the **ntsysv** utility to modify the appropriate runtime configuration files so that they start and stop daemons when entering a particular runlevel. For example, if you type ntsysv –level 5 to modify the daemons that will be started in runlevel 5, you see the screen shown in Figure 8-13.

Perhaps the easiest way to control daemon startup by runlevel is the **Service Configuration utility** shown in Figure 8-14. To start the Service Configuration utility within the GNOME Desktop Environment, navigate to the System menu and then select Administration, Services. If you highlight a daemon listed in Figure 8-14 and click the Customize button, you are prompted to choose the runlevels in which the daemon should start.

Figure 8-13 The ntsysv utility

Source: Course Technology/Cengage Learning

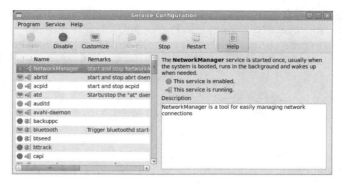

Figure 8-14 The Service Configuration utility

Source: Course Technology/Cengage Learning

The X Windows System

So far in this chapter, we've focused on performing tasks using a BASH shell command-line interface obtained after logging in to a character terminal. Although most administrators favor the command-line interface, some prefer the graphical user interfaces (GUIs) because they simplify certain tasks. In addition, Linux users typically use graphical interfaces for running user programs. Thus, you need to understand the components that make up the Linux GUI. In particular, you need to know how to start, stop, and configure them.

Linux GUI Components

The Linux graphical user interface (GUI) was designed to function consistently, no matter what video adapter card and monitor are installed on the computer system. It is composed of many components, each of which works separately from the video hardware.

A Linux installation usually includes all of the components listed in Figure 8-15. A typical installation of Fedora usually uses 3–6GB of data on the hard disk for the GUI and related programs.

X Windows   The core component of a Linux GUI is **X Windows**, which provides the ability to draw graphical images in windows that are displayed on a terminal screen. The programs that tell X Windows how to draw the graphics and display the results are known as **X clients**. X clients need not run on the same computer as X Windows; you can use X Windows on one computer to send graphical images to an X client on an entirely different computer by changing the DISPLAY environment variable discussed in Chapter 7. Because of this, X Windows is sometimes referred to as the server component of X Windows, or simply the **X server**.

X Windows was jointly developed by Digital Equipment Corporation (DEC) and the Massachusetts Institute of Technology (MIT) in 1984. At that time, it was code-named Project Athena and was released in 1985 as X Windows in hopes that a new name would be found to replace the X. Shortly thereafter, X Windows was sought by many UNIX vendors, and by 1988, MIT released version 11 release 2 of X Windows (X11R2). Since 1988, X Windows has been maintained by The Open Group, which released version 11 release 6 of

Graphical programs (X clients)

Desktop environment

Window manager

X Windows

Video hardware

Figure 8-15 Components of the Linux GUI

Source: Course Technology/Cengage Learning

X Windows (X11R6) in 1995. Since 2004, X Windows has been maintained as Open Source Software by the **X.Org** Foundation.

To find out more about X Windows, visit the X.Org Foundation on the Internet at *www.x.org*.

Until recently, X Windows was governed by a separate license than the GPL, which restricted the usage of X Windows and its source code. As a result, open source developers created an open source version of X Windows in the 1990s. This freely available version of X Windows is used in many Linux distributions and is called **XFree86** because it was originally intended for the Intel x86 platform.

To find out more about XFree86, visit The XFree86 Project on the Internet at *www.xfree86.org*.

Today, Linux distributions offer either X Windows or the XFree86 implementation of X Windows because they are both Open Source Software. Fedora 13 uses X Windows instead of XFree86.

Window Managers and Desktop Environments To modify the look and feel of X Windows, you can use a **window manager**. For example, the dimensions and color of windows that are drawn on a graphical screen, as well as the method used to move windows around on a graphical screen, are functions of a window manager.

Window Manager	Description
compiz	A highly configurable and expandable window manager that utilizes 3D acceleration on modern video cards to produce 3D graphical effects, including 3D window behavior and desktop cube workspaces.
enlightenment	A highly configurable window manager that allows for multiple desktops with different settings. It is commonly used by the GNOME desktop.
fvwm	A window manager based on twm (tab window manager) that uses less computer memory and gives the desktop a 3D look; its full name is "feeble virtual window manager."
kwin	The window manager used for the KDE desktop.
lxde	A window manager specifically designed for use on underpowered systems such as netbooks, mobile devices, and legacy computers; its full name is "Lightweight X Desktop Environment."
metacity	The window manager used for the GNOME desktop in Red Hat Fedora Core 2. It allows the user to configure custom themes that modify the look and feel of the desktop.
mwm	A window manager that allows the user to configure settings using standard X utilities; its full name is "motif window manager."
sawfish	A window manager commonly used for the GNOME desktop. It allows the user to configure most of its settings via tools or scripts.
twm	One of the oldest and most basic window managers; its full name is "tab window manager."
wmaker	A window manager that provides drag-and-drop mouse movement and imitates the NeXTSTEP OS interface made by Apple Computer, Inc.; its full name is "window maker Window Manager."

Table 8-4 Common window managers

Many different window managers are available for Linux, including those listed in Table 8-4.

You can use a window manager alone or in conjunction with a **desktop environment.**

A desktop environment is a standard set of GUI tools designed to be packaged together, including Web browsers, file managers, and drawing programs. Desktop environments also provide sets of development tools, known as toolkits, that speed up the process of creating new software. As discussed earlier in this book, the two most common desktop environments used on Linux are the **K Desktop Environment (KDE)** and the **GNU Object Model Environment (GNOME)**.

KDE is the traditional desktop environment used on Linux systems. First released by Matthias Ettrich in 1996, KDE uses the **K Window Manager (kwin)** and the **Qt toolkit** for the C++ programming language. A typical KDE Desktop Environment is depicted in Figure 8-16.

To learn more about KDE, visit *www.kde.org.*

The Qt toolkit included in KDE was created by a company called Trolltech in Norway in the 1990s. However, Qt was slow in building a following because, at the time, most open source developers preferred to develop in the C programming language instead of C++. Also, the fact that Qt was not released as Open Source Software until 1998 was a drawback, because most developers preferred source code that was freely modifiable.

Figure 8-16 The KDE Desktop Environment

Source: Course Technology/Cengage Learning

As a result of the general dissatisfaction with the Qt toolkit, the GNOME Desktop Environment was created in 1997. GNOME typically uses the **Metacity Window Manager** and the **GTK+ toolkit** for the C programming language. The GTK+ toolkit was originally developed for the **GNU Image Manipulation Program (GIMP)**, and like the GIMP, is open source. GNOME is the default desktop environment in Fedora Linux and can be seen in Figure 8-17.

To learn more about GNOME, visit *www.gnome.org*.

Instead of using the default window manager within the KDE or GNOME desktop environment, you can instead configure KDE or GNOME to use a different window manager. One popular choice is compiz, which requires a modern video card with hardware-based 3D acceleration support. After installing compiz, you need to configure your desktop environment to use the window manager. For example, within the GNOME Desktop Environment, you could navigate to the System menu, Preferences, Desktop Effects, and then select Compiz and the desired 3D effects, as shown in Figure 8-18.

After compiz is enabled, you can drag windows around on your desktop, as well as minimize and maximize them. It offers a number of other ways to alter the desktop. For

Figure 8-17 The GNOME Desktop Environment

Source: Course Technology/Cengage Learning

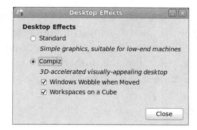

Figure 8-18 Configuring the compiz window manager

Source: Course Technology/Cengage Learning

example, to control window transparency, press and hold Ctrl+Alt while using the scroll button on your mouse. To display four different desktops options in a cube effect, press and hold Ctrl+Alt while using your cursor keys. After you display a desktop cube in this way, you can move it in full 3D space by pressing and holding Ctrl+Alt while dragging the menu bar within the GNOME desktop. See Figure 8-19.

To learn more about compiz, including its graphical effects and additional plug-ins, visit *www.compiz.org*.

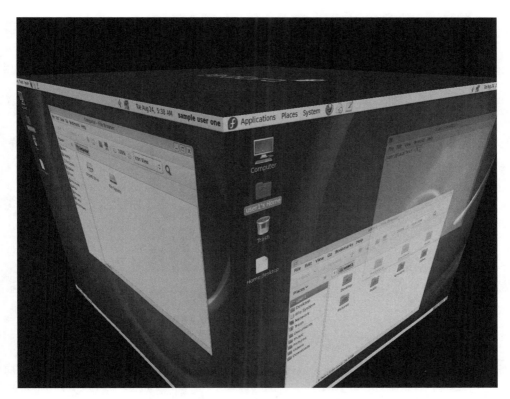

Figure 8-19 The desktop cube effect within the compiz window manager

Source: Course Technology/Cengage Learning

Starting and Stopping X Windows

You need to know how to start and stop X Windows, the window manager, and, if you are using one, the desktop environment. As explained earlier in this chapter, runlevel 5 starts the GNOME Display Manager (gdm), which in turn displays the graphical login screen shown in Figure 8-20. You can use the Session menu in the lower-right corner of this screen to select a desktop environment during the login process.

You can override the default appearance and behavior of the GNOME Display Manager by editing the /etc/gdm/custom.conf file.

The GNOME Display Manager is a variant of the **X Display Manager (xdm)**, which displays a basic graphical login for users. In addition, other Linux distributions might use the **KDE Display Manager (kdm)** to display a KDE-style graphical login for users.

The default desktop environment started by the GNOME Display Manager is GNOME. However, after you log in as a particular user and select KDE using the Session menu shown in Figure 8-20, the GNOME Display Manager will continue to use KDE as the default desktop environment unless you choose otherwise. This is because the GNOME Display Manager writes any desktop environments that you manually select in the Session menu to a **.dmrc (display manager runtime configuration) file** in your home directory. For

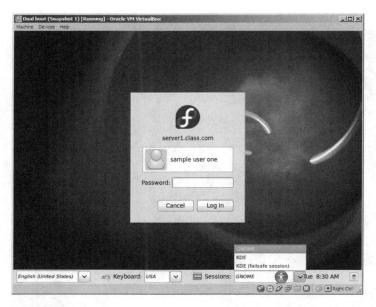

Figure 8-20 Selecting a session within the GNOME Display Manager

Source: Course Technology/Cengage Learning

example, if user1 chooses to log in to a KDE Desktop Environment using the GNOME Display Manager, the GNOME Display Manager will write the following information to the /home/user1/.dmrc file to ensure that KDE is listed as the default desktop environment the next time user1 logs in to the system using the GNOME Display Manager:

```
[user1@server1 ~]# cat .dmrc
[Desktop]
Session=kde
[user1@server1 ~]# _
```

If user1 later chooses the GNOME Desktop Environment from the Session menu within the GNOME Display Manager, the line `Session=gnome` will replace `Session=kde` in the /home/user1/.dmrc file.

By default, the root user is not allowed to log in to the system using the GNOME Display Manager. This prevents any GUI processes that might compromise the system from starting as the root user. However, you can disable this feature and allow root logins via the GNOME Display Manager. To do so, change the following line in the /etc/pam.d/gdm and /etc/pam.d/gdm-password files to a comment by inserting a # symbol at the beginning of the line:

```
auth required pam_succeed_if.so user != root quiet
```

The GNOME Display Manager is the easiest way to log in and access the desktop environments that are available on your system. If, however, you use runlevel 3 instead of runlevel 5, the GNOME Display Manager is not started by default. In this case, you can type gdm at a character terminal to start the GNOME Display Manager manually, or use the `startx` command to start X Windows and the window manager or desktop environment specified in the **.xinitrc** (**X initialization runtime configuration**) file in your home directory. If the

.xinitrc file does not exist, a GNOME Desktop Environment is started. By default, Fedora 13 does not create a .xinitrc file in any user's home directory. However, you can create one manually and add the line exec startkde to it if you would like the startx command to start the KDE Desktop Environment, or the line exec gnome-session if you would like the startx command to start the GNOME Desktop Environment.

Configuring X Windows

X Windows is the component of the GUI that interfaces with the video hardware in the computer. For X Windows to perform its function, it needs information regarding the keyboard, mouse, monitor, and video adapter card. By default, X Windows attempts to automatically detect this information. If the automatic detection fails, you may need to specify the correct hardware information manually.

If your system uses the X.Org implementation of X Windows, the mouse, keyboard, monitor, and video adapter card information is stored in the **/etc/X11/xorg.conf** file in text format. If your system uses the XFree86 implementation of X Windows, this information is stored in the **/etc/X11/XF86Config** file instead. You can edit these files manually or use a program to edit them indirectly.

If you plan to edit X Windows configuration files manually, ensure that you read its associated manual or info page first. For Fedora 13, ensure that you read the xorg.conf manual page.

Because one mistake in the /etc/X11/xorg.conf or /etc/X11/XF86Config files could prevent the GUI from running, it is good practice to use a configuration program to edit these files.

If you performed a graphical installation of Fedora 13, your mouse was automatically detected and configured. However, if you performed a text-based installation, and X Windows was unable to detect the mouse automatically, you may need to run the **mouse-test** command as the root user to detect the mouse in your computer.

Similarly, the keyboard layout is automatically detected during the Fedora 13 installation, and you are prompted to confirm the selection. However, if you change the keyboard and X Windows cannot detect its layout, you can manually run the **system-config-keyboard command** at a terminal prompt within a desktop environment to start the Keyboard tool. See Figure 8-21.

To configure your video card and monitor, you can install the **Display Settings utility** from software repositories on the Internet by executing the yum install system-config-display command as the root user. Next, you can type **system-config-display** at a terminal command prompt within a desktop environment to start the Display Settings utility shown in Figure 8-22.

You can also start the Display Settings utility using the appropriate menus within a desktop environment. For example, you can navigate to the System menu within the GNOME Desktop Environment and select Administration, Display to start the Display Settings utility.

Figure 8-21 Selecting a keyboard layout

Source: Course Technology/Cengage Learning

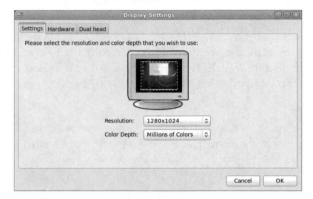

Figure 8-22 The Display Settings utility

Source: Course Technology/Cengage Learning

By default, there is no /etc/X11/xorg.conf file in Fedora 13 because X Windows detects all hardware information automatically. However, if a /etc/X11/xorg.conf file exists, the X Windows System in Fedora 13 will use the information within to configure itself. When you open the Display Settings utility for the first time, it automatically creates a /etc/X11/xorg.conf file.

The Settings tab shown in Figure 8-22 allows you to configure the resolution and color depth that will be used by Linux. You can also use the Hardware tab shown in Figure 8-23 to configure your video card and monitor model, as well as the Dual head tab shown in Figure 8-24 to configure two displays to act as a single large display, provided that you have two monitors that are connected to two separate video cards.

It is important to choose the correct resolution and color depth for your monitor as well as the correct video card model and monitor type. If you do not, X Windows will appear blank or garbled when started, or may fail to start entirely. If this is the case, simply run the `system-config-display` command within a command-line terminal to start an X Windows GUI environment using a basic configuration that all video cards support to allow you to configure the correct settings for your video card and monitor.

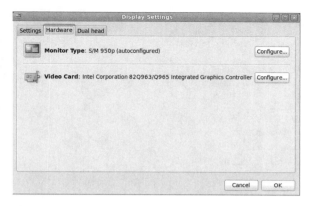

Figure 8-23 Configuring video card and monitor model

Source: Course Technology/Cengage Learning

Figure 8-24 Configuring dual display support

Source: Course Technology/Cengage Learning

After you click OK in the configuration utility, the previous /etc/X11/xorg.conf file is saved as /etc/X11/xorg.conf.backup and the new settings are written to /etc/X11/xorg.conf. You must then restart X Windows for the changes to take effect.

To restart X Windows, you simply need to log out of X Windows and log back in using the gdm, or type `startx` at the command prompt if the gdm is not started.

Another method used to log out of X Windows is the Ctrl+Alt+Backspace key combination.

After configuring X Windows, you can fine-tune the vertical refresh rate (vsync) and horizontal refresh rate (hsync) settings using the **xvidtune** utility within a desktop environment. Simply open a command-line terminal within the desktop environment and type `xvidtune` to start the utility, as shown in Figure 8-25.

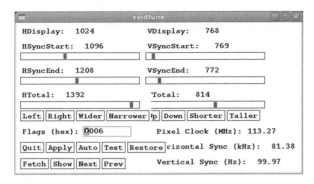

Figure 8-25 The xvidtune utility

Source: Course Technology/Cengage Learning

Although most monitors today support a wide range of hsync and vsync values, choosing too high a value for either might damage the monitor. On the flip side, choosing an hsync or vsync value that is too low is bad for the humans who have to look at the monitors because they can cause headaches.

Chapter Summary

- Boot loaders are typically loaded by the system BIOS from the MBR/GPT or the first sector of the active partition of a hard disk.

- The boot loader is responsible for loading the Linux kernel as well as booting other OSs in a dual-boot configuration.

- The GRUB boot loader uses the /boot/grub/grub.conf configuration file, whereas the LILO boot loader uses the /etc/lilo.conf configuration file.

- Seven standard runlevels are used to categorize a Linux system based on the number and type of daemons loaded in memory. The default runlevel entered at system startup is listed in /etc/inittab.

- The init daemon is responsible for loading and unloading daemons when switching between runlevels, as well as at system startup and shutdown.

- Daemons are typically stored in the /etc/rc.d/init.d directory and loaded at system startup from entries in the /etc/rc.d/rc.d directories.

- The Linux GUI has several interchangeable components, including the X server, X clients, window manager, and optional desktop environment.

- X Windows is the core component of the Linux GUI that draws graphics to the terminal screen. It comes in one of two open source implementations: X.Org and XFree86.

- You can start the Linux GUI from runlevel 3 by typing startx at a command prompt, or from runlevel 5 by using the GNOME Display Manager.

- The hardware information required by X Windows is automatically detected, but can be modified using several utilities, including mouse-test, system-config-keyboard, system-config-display, and xvidtune.

Key Terms

.dmrc (display manager runtime configuration) file   A file that is stored within each user's home directory to list the preferred desktop environment for use by the GNOME Display Manager.

.xinitrc (X initialization runtime configuration) file   A file that is stored within each user's home directory to list the preferred desktop environment for use by the startx command.

/boot   The directory that contains the kernel and boot-related files.

/boot/grub/grub.conf   The GRUB configuration file.

/etc/inittab   The configuration file for the init daemon that specifies the default runlevel.

/etc/lilo.conf   The LILO configuration file.

/etc/rc.d/init.d   The directory in which most daemons', startup/shutdown scripts are located.

/etc/rc.d/rc*.d   The directories used to start and kill daemons in each runlevel.

/etc/rc.d/rc.local   The final script executed during system startup.

/etc/rc.d/rc.sysinit   The first script executed during system startup.

/etc/X11/XF86Config   The configuration file used by the XFree86 implementation of X Windows.

/etc/X11/xorg.conf   The configuration file used by the X.Org implementation of X Windows.

active partition   The partition searched for by an OS after the MBR.

boot loader   A program used to load an OS.

chkconfig command   A command that can be used to configure daemon startup by runlevel.

compiz   A window manager that is commonly used within the KDE and GNOME desktops to provide 3D effects.

daemon   A Linux system process that provides a certain service.

default runlevel   The runlevel that is entered when the Linux system is initialized at boot time.

desktop environment   The software that works with a window manager to provide a standard GUI environment that uses standard programs and development tools.

Display Settings utility   A graphical utility that can be used to configure the video card and monitor settings for use by X Windows.

dmesg command   A command that displays hardware-related messages generated by the Linux kernel.

dual boot   A configuration in which two or more OSs exist on the hard disk of a computer; a boot loader allows the user to choose which OS to load at boot time.

EasyBCD   A free Windows utility that can be used to modify and configure the Windows boot loader so that it can dual boot a Linux OS.

ELILO   A boot loader used with computers that support Intel Extensible Firmware Interface (EFI) technology.

extended multiuser mode   Also called runlevel 3; the mode that provides most daemons and a full set of networking daemons.

GNOME Display Manager (gdm)   A program that provides a graphical login screen.

GNU Image Manipulation Program (GIMP)   An open source graphics manipulation program that uses the GTK+ toolkit.

GNU Object Model Environment (GNOME)   The default desktop environment in Fedora Linux; it was created in 1997.

GRand Unified Bootloader (GRUB)   A common boot loader used on Linux systems.

`grub-install` **command**   The command used to install the GRUB boot loader.

`grub-md5-crypt` **command**   The command used to generate an encrypted password for use in the /etc/grub/grub.conf file.

GRUB root partition   The partition containing the second stage of the GRUB boot loader and the /boot/grub/grub.conf file.

GTK+ toolkit   A development toolkit for C programming; it is used in the GNOME desktop and the GNU Image Manipulation Program (GIMP).

`init` **command**   The command used to change the OS from one runlevel to another.

initialize (init) daemon   The first process started by the Linux kernel; it is responsible for starting and stopping other daemons.

initstate   *See* runlevel.

K Desktop Environment (KDE)   A desktop environment created by Matthias Ettrich in 1996.

K Window Manager (kwin)   The window manager that works under the KDE Desktop Environment.

KDE Display Manager (kdm)   A graphical login screen for users that resembles the KDE desktop.

`lilo` **command**   The command used to reinstall the LILO boot loader based on the configuration information in /etc/lilo.conf.

Linux Loader (LILO)   A common boot loader used on Linux systems.

Metacity Window Manager   The default window manager for the GNOME Desktop Environment in Fedora 13.

`mouse-test` **command**   A command used to detect and configure your mouse.

multiuser mode   Also called runlevel 2; the mode that provides most daemons and a partial set of networking daemons.

ntsysv   A utility that can be used to alter the daemons that are started in each runlevel.

power on-self test (POST)   An initial series of tests run when a computer is powered on to ensure that hardware components are functional.

Qt toolkit   The software toolkit used with the K Desktop Environment.

runlevel   A term that defines a certain type and number of daemons on a Linux system.

`runlevel` **command**   The command used to display the current and most recent (previous) runlevel.

runtime configuration (rc) scripts   Shell scripts that are used by the init daemon to initialize the system at boot time as well as start and stop daemons when entering a particular runlevel.

`service` **command**   A command that can be used to manually start, stop, and restart daemons.

Service Configuration utility   A graphical utility that can be used to start, stop, and restart daemons as well as configure the runlevels that they are automatically started and stopped in.

single user mode   Also called runlevel 1; the mode that provides a single terminal and a limited set of services.

system-config-display command   A command used to configure a video adapter card and monitor for use by X Windows.

system-config-keyboard command   A command used to configure a keyboard for use by X Windows.

telinit command   An alias to the `init` command.

upstart init system   The next-generation init daemon and related files used by modern Linux distributions such as Fedora 13.

virtualization software   Software that can be used to run multiple OSs simultaneously on the same computer.

vmlinuz-<kernel version>   The Linux kernel file.

window manager   The GUI component that is responsible for determining the appearance of the windows drawn on the screen by X Windows.

X client   The component of X Windows that requests graphics to be drawn from the X server and displays them on the terminal screen.

X Display Manager (xdm)   A graphical login screen.

XFree86   A common implementation of X Windows used in Linux distributions.

X.Org   A common implementation of X Windows used in Linux distributions.

X server   The component of X Windows that draws graphics to windows on the terminal screen.

xvidtune   A program used to fine-tune the vsync and hsync video card settings for use in X Windows.

X Windows   The component of the Linux GUI that displays graphics to windows on the terminal screen.

Review Questions

1. Which command can be used to fine-tune the vsync and hsync of a video card for use in X Windows?

   a. `vidtune`

   b. `synctune`

   c. `xvidtune`

   d. `vhtune`

2. Which of the following statements is true?

   a. GRUB needs to be reinstalled after it has been modified.

   b. LILO need not be reinstalled after it has been modified.

   c. GRUB points to LILO.

   d. GRUB need not be reinstalled after it has been modified.

3. Which runtime configuration file is executed last during system initialization?

   a. /etc/rc.d/rc5.d/init

   b. /etc/rc.d/rc.local

   c. /etc/rc.d/rc.sysinit

   d. /etc/inittab

4. Which runlevel halts the system?

   a. 1

   b. 6

   c. 0

   d. 5

5. Which file does init reference on startup to determine the default runlevel?

   a. /etc/initstate

   b. /inittab

   c. /etc/init

   d. /etc/inittab

6. Which two commands entered at a command prompt can be used to start X Windows, the window manager, and the default desktop environment? (Choose two answers.)

   a. `startgui`

   b. `gdm`

   c. `startx`

   d. `winstart`

7. Which of the following statements is true?

   a. The boot loader points to the MBR/GPT.

   b. Either the MBR/GPT or the active partition can contain the boot loader.

   c. Both the MBR/GPT and the active partition point to the boot loader.

   d. The boot loader points to the active partition.

8. Which command is used to reinstall LILO after its configuration has been altered?

   a. `lilo`

   b. `refresh`

   c. `set lilo`

   d. `reset lilo`

9. To make dual booting as easy as possible, Linux should be the second OS installed. True or False?

10. If you want to modify the Windows boot loader to dual boot Linux, you can use the EasyBCD program within Windows. True or False?

11. How many active partitions are allowed per hard disk drive?

   a. 4

   b. 16

c.   1

d.   2

12. Which of the following indicates the second partition on the third hard disk drive to GRUB?

a.   (hd3,2)

b.   (hd4,3)

c.   (hd2,3)

d.   (hd2,1)

13. Which implementations of X Windows are commonly used in Linux? (Choose two answers.)

a.   X.org

b.   XFce

c.   Xconfigurator

d.   XFree86

14. What is the name of the directory that contains the configuration information for runlevel 2?

a.   /etc/rc.d/rc2.d

b.   /rc.d/rc2.d

c.   /etc/rc.d/l2.d

d.   /etc/inittab/rc2/d

15. In what directory is the Linux kernel stored?

a.   /boot

b.   /root

c.   /bin

d.   /

16. If a user enters single user mode, who is she automatically logged in as?

a.   the user name she provided

b.   root

c.   admin

d.   There is no user available in single user mode.

17. The first process generated on a Linux system is _____.

a.   initstate

b.   inittab

c.   init

d.   linux

18. Which utility can be used to configure the video card and monitor used by X Windows in Fedora 13?

   a. X.config

   b. system-config-display

   c. xconfig

   d. xvidtune

19. Which command causes the system to enter single user mode?

   a. `init 0`

   b. `init 1`

   c. `init 6`

   d. `initstate 5`

20. The timeout value in the GRUB configuration file is measured in _____.

   a. seconds

   b. 1/10 of minutes

   c. 1/10 of seconds

   d. 1/100 of seconds

Hands-On Projects

HANDS-ON PROJECTS

These projects should be completed in the order given. The hands-on projects presented in this chapter should take a total of three hours to complete. The requirements for this lab include:

- A computer with Fedora 13 installed according to Hands-On Project 2-2

Project 8-1

In this hands-on project, you use and configure the GRUB boot loader.

1. When your system has booted, switch to a command-line terminal (tty2) by pressing **Ctrl+Alt+F2** and log in to the terminal using the user name of **root** and the password of **secret**.

2. At the command prompt, type **cat /boot/grub/grub.conf** and press **Enter** to view the GRUB configuration file. Can you tell where the boot loader is installed? What does each entry indicate?

3. At the command prompt, type **vi /boot/grub/grub.conf** and press **Enter** to edit the GRUB configuration file. Change the value of **timeout** to **0**. Save your changes and quit the vi editor. How long do you have to interact with the GRUB boot loader after POST before the default OS is booted? Do you need to reinstall GRUB after making changes to the /boot/grub/grub.conf file?

4. Reboot your system by typing **reboot** and press **Enter**. Was the graphical GRUB boot screen shown after POST?

5. When your system has booted, switch to a command-line terminal (tty2) by pressing **Ctrl+Alt+F2** and log in to the terminal using the user name of **root** and the password of **secret**.

6. At the command prompt, type **vi /boot/grub/grub.conf** and press **Enter** to edit the GRUB configuration file. Change the value of **timeout** to **10**. Save your changes and quit the vi editor. How long do you have to interact with the GRUB boot loader after POST before the default OS is booted?

7. Reboot your system by typing **reboot** and pressing **Enter**. After the POST, note the graphical GRUB boot screen. How many seconds do you have to interrupt the automatic boot process? Press any key on your keyboard to interact with the GRUB boot menu.

8. At the GRUB boot menu, type **e** to edit the configuration of GRUB. Do you recognize the entries listed? Next, type **c** at the GRUB boot menu to open a grub> prompt.

9. At the grub> prompt, type **help** and press **Enter** to view a list of commands you can use at the grub> prompt. Next, type **displaymem** at the grub> prompt and press **Enter**. Does GRUB recognize all the memory in your computer correctly?

10. At the grub> prompt, type **cat /boot/grub/grub.conf** and press **Enter** to view the /boot/grub/grub.conf file. Why did you have to specify the full path to grub.conf within the GRUB boot loader?

11. At the grub> prompt, type the kernel line shown in Step 10 and press **Enter**. This loads the kernel into memory.

12. At the grub> prompt, type the initrd line shown in Step 10 and press **Enter**. This loads the initialization ramdisk image into memory.

13. At the grub> prompt, type **boot** and press **Enter** to continue the boot process using the Linux kernel and initialization ramdisk image loaded into memory during the previous two steps. Allow the system to boot normally.

14. After the system has loaded successfully, switch to a command-line terminal (tty2) by pressing **Ctrl+Alt+F2** and log in to the terminal using the user name of **root** and the password of **secret**.

15. At the command prompt, type **grub-md5-crypt** and press **Enter**. When prompted, type **secret** and press **Enter**. Repeat the password when prompted again and press **Enter**. Record the encrypted password returned for future reference.

16. At the command prompt, type **vi /boot/grub/grub.conf** and press **Enter** to edit the GRUB configuration file. While in the vi editor, position the cursor on the line that says splashimage=(hd0,0)/boot/grub/splash.xpm.gz.

17. Next, type **o** to open a line underneath the splashimage line in insert mode, and type the following (where <encrypted password> is the encrypted password you recorded in Step 15):

      password --md5 <encrypted password>

18. Save your changes and quit the vi editor.

19. Reboot your system by typing **reboot** and pressing **Enter**. At the graphical GRUB boot screen, press any key on your keyboard to open the GRUB boot menu. Observe the

legend. Note that you must press the p key to access the configuration of GRUB. Type **p** to edit the configuration of GRUB. Enter the password of **secret** and press **Enter**. Is the GRUB boot menu displayed?

20. Press **Enter** to boot the default OS.

Project 8-2

In this hands-on project, you explore runlevels and the /etc/inittab file used to change runlevels at system startup and afterward.

1. Switch to a command-line terminal (tty2) by pressing **Ctrl+Alt+F2** and log in to the terminal using the user name of **root** and the password of **secret**.

2. At the command prompt, type **runlevel** and press **Enter**. What is your current runlevel? What is the most recent runlevel?

3. At the command prompt, type **cat /etc/inittab** and press **Enter**. Which line in this file determines the default runlevel at boot time? Can this be changed?

4. At the command prompt, type **init 2** and press **Enter**. Press **Enter** again to obtain your command prompt. What was displayed on your terminal screen? Are any daemons started? Are any daemons stopped? Why?

5. Next, type **runlevel** at the command prompt and press **Enter**. What is your current runlevel? What is the most recent runlevel?

6. At the command prompt, type **init 5** and press **Enter**. Were daemons started? Was the gdm started?

7. Switch back to tty2 by pressing **Ctrl+Alt+F2** and press **Enter** to obtain your command prompt.

8. Next, type **runlevel** at the command prompt and press **Enter**. What is your current runlevel? What is the most recent runlevel?

9. At the command prompt, type **init 1** and press **Enter**. What is displayed on your terminal screen? Are most daemons started or stopped? Why?

10. Next, type **runlevel** at the command prompt and press **Enter**. Note that both your current and most recent runlevels refer to single user mode. This is because the process that tracks runlevel is stopped when entering single user mode.

11. At the command prompt, type **init 6** and press **Enter**. What does this command do?

Project 8-3

In this hands-on project, you examine the system runlevel directories, start and stop daemons manually, and configure daemon startup by runlevel.

1. Once your system has booted, switch to a command-line terminal (tty2) by pressing **Ctrl+Alt+F2** and log in to the terminal using the user name of **root** and the password of **secret**.

2. At the command prompt, type **ls /etc/rc.d** and press **Enter**. What directories are listed? What is contained within each directory?

3. At the command prompt, type `ls -F /etc/rc.d/rc0.d` and press **Enter**. What type of files are listed? In which order will these files be executed by the init daemon? How many of these start with K compared to S? Why?

4. At the command prompt, type `ls -F /etc/rc.d/rc5.d` and press **Enter**. What types of files are listed? How many of these start with K compared to S? Why?

5. At the command prompt, type `ls -F /etc/rc.d/init.d` and press **Enter**. What types of files are listed? What happens when you execute a file from this directory?

6. At the command prompt, type `/etc/rc.d/init.d/atd stop` and press **Enter**. What happened?

7. At the command prompt, type `/etc/rc.d/init.d/atd start` and press **Enter**. What happened?

8. At the command prompt, type `/etc/rc.d/init.d/atd restart` and press **Enter**. What happened?

9. At the command prompt, type `service atd stop` and press **Enter** to perform the same action as Step 6.

10. At the command prompt, type `service atd start` and press **Enter** to perform the same action as Step 7.

11. At the command prompt, type `service atd restart` and press **Enter** to perform the same action as Step 8.

12. At the command prompt, type `chkconfig --list httpd` and press **Enter**. In which runlevels are Apache (httpd) daemons started?

13. At the command prompt, type `chkconfig --level 235 httpd on` and press **Enter**. Next, type `chkconfig --list httpd` and press **Enter**. In which runlevels are Apache (httpd) daemons started?

14. At the command prompt, type `chkconfig --level 23 httpd off` and press **Enter**. Next, type `chkconfig --list httpd` and press **Enter**. In which runlevels are Apache (httpd) daemons started?

15. At the command prompt, type `ntsysv --level 5` and press **Enter**. Next, navigate to the httpd daemon listing. Is there an asterisk (*) indicating that the daemon is started upon entering this runlevel? Use your Spacebar to remove the * next to httpd. Press Tab to navigate to the **OK** button and press **Enter** to exit the ntsysv utility. What other graphical utility can be used to perform the same action?

16. Type `exit` and press **Enter** to log out of your shell.

Project 8-4

In this hands-on project, you configure a fake daemon process to execute upon system startup.

1. Once your system has booted, switch to a command-line terminal (tty2) by pressing **Ctrl+Alt+F2** and log in to the terminal using the user name of **root** and the password of **secret**.

2. At the command prompt, type `vi /etc/rc.d/init.d/sample` and press **Enter** to create a fake daemon in the /etc/rc.d/init.d directory.

3. Enter the following information in the vi editor. When finished, save your changes and quit the vi editor. (*Note:* The variable $1 refers to the first argument given when executing the shell script on the command line.)

```
#!/bin/bash
if [ $1="start" ]
then
        echo "The sample daemon has started"
        sleep 2
elif [ $1="stop" ]
then
        echo "The sample daemon has been stopped"
        sleep 2
elif [ $1="restart" ]
then
        echo "The sample daemon has been restarted"
        sleep 2
fi
```

4. At the command prompt, type `ls -l /etc/rc.d/init.d/sample` and press **Enter**. What are the permissions on the file?

5. At the command prompt, type `chmod 755 /etc/rc.d/init.d/sample` and press **Enter** to allow the sample file to be executed.

6. At the command prompt, type `ln -s /etc/rc.d/init.d/sample/etc/rc.d/rc5.d/ S50sample` and press **Enter**. What does this command do? What will happen at system startup?

7. At the command prompt, type **reboot** and press **Enter** to reboot the system. When the graphical boot screen appears, press the Esc key on your keyboard. Pay close attention to the list of daemons as they are started. Does the sample daemon start? Why? Allow the system to boot normally.

8. When the system has booted successfully, switch to a command-line terminal (tty2) by pressing **Ctrl+Alt+F2** and log in to the terminal using the user name of **root** and the password of **secret**.

9. At the command prompt, type **service sample stop** and press **Enter**. What happened?

10. At the command prompt, type **service sample start** and press **Enter**. What happened?

11. At the command prompt, type **service sample restart** and press **Enter**. What happened?

12. Type **exit** and press **Enter** to log out of your shell.

Project 8-5

In this hands-on project, you examine X Windows configuration utilities, start X Windows using various methods, switch desktop environments, and explore the compiz window manager.

1. Switch to a command-line terminal (tty2) by pressing **Ctrl+Alt+F2** and log in to the terminal using the user name of **root** and the password of **secret**.

2. At the command prompt, type `ls /etc/X11` and press **Enter**. Is there an xorg.conf file present in this directory by default? Why?

3. At the command prompt, type `yum install system-config-display` and press **Enter**. Press **y** when prompted to install the necessary packages from the Internet, and press **y** again (if necessary) to confirm the GPG key used for authentication.

4. Switch to the gdm by pressing **Ctrl+Alt+F1** or **Ctrl+Alt+F7** and log in to the GNOME Desktop Environment as user1.

5. Open a Terminal application and type `system-config-display` at the BASH shell prompt. Supply the root password of **secret** when prompted and click **OK**. Navigate the three tabs within this utility and note your default resolution and color depth, as well as your video card and monitor model. Optionally, make a change to your resolution and color depth that are supported by your video card and monitor. Click **OK** when finished, and click **OK** again to close the information dialog window indicating that a new xorg.conf file has been written.

6. Switch back to tty2 by pressing **Ctrl+Alt+F2**, type `ls /etc/X11` at the command prompt, and press **Enter**. Is there an xorg.conf file present in this directory now? Why?

7. At the command prompt, type `less /etc/X11/xorg.conf` and press **Enter**. View the information about your keyboard, video card, and monitor, and press **q** to quit when finished.

8. At the command prompt, type `mouse-test` and press **Enter**. Observe the output and press **Ctrl+c** when finished.

9. Switch to the gdm by pressing **Ctrl+Alt+F1** or **Ctrl+Alt+F7**, and type `system-config-keyboard` at the BASH shell prompt in the Terminal window. Supply the root password of **secret** when prompted and click **OK**. Observe your default keyboard layout and click **OK**.

10. Log out of the GNOME Desktop Environment when finished.

11. At the gdm, click **sample user one** and then choose **KDE** from the Session dialog box. Supply the password of **secret** for user1 and click **Log In** to log in to the KDE Desktop Environment.

12. Click the **f** start button in the lower left of the screen and navigate to **Applications, System, Terminal** to open a BASH shell terminal. At the prompt, type `cat ~/.dmrc` and press **Enter**. Did the gdm record your latest desktop environment preference as KDE?

13. Click the **f** start button again and click **Leave** and then **Logout**. Click **Logout** again to return to the gdm.

14. At the gdm, click **sample user one**. Is KDE listed as the default session in the Session dialog box? Choose **GNOME** from the Session dialog box, supply the password of **secret** for user1, and click **Log In** to log in to the GNOME Desktop Environment.

15. Click the **System** menu and select **Preferences, Desktop Effects**. If your video card has 3D hardware acceleration support, select **Compiz**, click **Use this setting** when prompted, and select the two standard desktop effects. If you instead receive an error message indicating the lack of 3D support on your video card, skip to Step 17.

16. Hold down the **Ctrl** and **Alt** keys on your keyboard. While holding them down, use your cursor keys to move the desktop cube left and right. Next, while holding down the **Ctrl** and **Alt** keys, drag the menu bar using your mouse to view the entire desktop cube. Next, open an application of your choice. Click and hold the upper-left corner of the window and drag it around your desktop to view the window effect. Next, minimize your application and then log out of the GNOME Desktop Environment.

17. Switch back to tty2 by pressing **Ctrl+Alt+F2**, type `init 3` at the command prompt, and press **Enter**. Press **Enter** again to obtain your command.

18. At the command prompt, type `startx` and press **Enter**. Close any root user warning dialog boxes. Why was GNOME started? Log out of the GNOME Desktop Environment.

19. At the command prompt, type `vi .xinitrc` and press **Enter**. Add the line `exec startkde` to the .xinitrc file, save your changes, and quit the vi editor.

20. At the command prompt, type `startx` and press **Enter**. Close any root user warning dialog boxes. Why was KDE started? Log out of the KDE Desktop Environment.

21. At the command prompt, type `gdm` and press **Enter** to start the GNOME Display Manager in runlevel 3. What is another way to start the gdm?

Discovery Exercises

1. Describe what would happen if you edited the /etc/inittab file and changed the line that reads as follows: `id:5:initdefault:` to read as follows: `id:6:initdefault:`.

2. You have created a daemon called mydaemon that performs database management tasks on the system; however, you want to have this daemon start only in runlevel 5. This daemon should not exist in memory when the system is in any other runlevel. In which directory should you place a script that can be used to start, stop, and restart this daemon? What links to this daemon should you create? Write the commands you would use to have this daemon start and stop automatically on the system.

3. Using the Internet, research two boot loaders used for Linux other than LILO and GRUB. What configuration file do they use? What are their benefits and disadvantages compared with LILO and GRUB?

4. Install Microsoft Windows on a hard disk drive, leaving adequate free space outside the Windows partition for the installation of Linux. Next, install Linux and choose to dual boot Linux with the Windows OS using GRUB. Examine the /boot/grub/grub.conf file after the installation has completed.

5. Runlevel 4 is typically not used on most Linux systems. What file defines this runlevel? How could you start daemons in this runlevel if you needed to? Outline the steps required to utilize runlevel 4; it should load all daemons from runlevel 3, plus some special database daemons as well.

6. Examine the /etc/rc.d/rc.sysinit shell script. What does each section do? Why must this file be run before the files in the /etc/rc.d/rc.d directories?

7. Use the Internet, books, or other resources to learn more about three Linux window managers or desktop environments that were not discussed in this chapter. For each, describe its common usage and benefits over other window managers and desktop environments. In addition, list how each was developed.

## chapter 9

Managing Linux Processes

After completing this chapter, you will be able to:

- Categorize the different types of processes on a Linux system
- View processes using standard Linux utilities
- Explain the difference between common kill signals
- Describe how binary programs and shell scripts are executed
- Create and manipulate background processes
- Use standard Linux utilities to modify the priority of a process
- Schedule commands to execute in the future using the at daemon
- Schedule commands to execute repetitively using the cron daemon

A typical Linux system can run thousands of processes simultaneously, including those that you have explored in previous chapters. In this chapter, you focus on viewing and managing processes. In the first part of the chapter, you examine the different types of processes on a Linux system and how to view them and terminate them. You then discover how processes are executed on a system, run in the background, and prioritized. Finally, you examine the various methods used to schedule commands to execute in the future.

Linux Processes

Throughout this book, the terms "program" and "process" are used interchangeably. The same is true in the workplace. However, a fine distinction exists between these two terms. Technically, a **program** is an executable file on the hard disk that can be run when you execute it. A **process**, on the other hand, is a program that is running in memory and on the CPU. In other words, a process is a program in action.

If you start a process while logged in to a terminal, that process runs in that terminal and is labeled a **user process**. Examples of user processes include ls, grep, and find, not to mention most of the other commands that you have executed throughout this book. Recall that a system process that is not associated with a terminal is called a **daemon process**; these processes are typically started on system startup, but you can also start them manually. Most daemon processes provide system services, such as printing, scheduling, and system maintenance, as well as network server services, such as Web servers, database servers, file servers, and print servers.

Every process has a unique **process ID (PID)** that allows the kernel to identify it uniquely. In addition, each process can start an unlimited number of other processes called **child processes**. Conversely, each process must have been started by an existing process called a **parent process**. As a result, each process has a **parent process ID (PPID)**, which identifies the process that started it. An example of the relationship between parent and child processes is depicted in Figure 9-1.

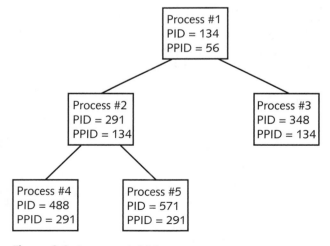

Figure 9-1 Parent and child processes

Source: Course Technology/Cengage Learning

PIDs are not necessarily given to new processes in sequential order; each PID is generated from free entries in a process table used by the Linux kernel.

Remember that although each process can have an unlimited number of child processes, it can only have one parent process.

Recall that the first process started by the Linux kernel is the init daemon, which has a PID of 1 and a PPID of 0 referring to the kernel itself. The init daemon then starts most other daemons, including those that allow for user logins. After you log in to the system, the login program starts a BASH shell. The BASH shell then interprets user commands and starts all user processes. Thus, each process on the Linux system can be traced back to the init daemon by examining the series of PPIDs, as shown in Figure 9-2.

The init daemon is often referred to as the "grandfather of all user processes."

9

Viewing Processes

Although several Linux utilities can view processes, the most versatile and common is the **ps** command. Without arguments, the **ps** command simply displays a list of processes that are

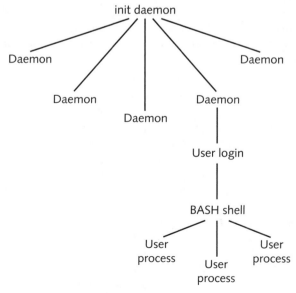

Figure 9-2 Process genealogy

Source: Course Technology/Cengage Learning

running in the current shell. The following example shows the output of this command while the user is logged in to tty2:

```
[root@server1 ~]# ps
  PID TTY              TIME CMD
 2159 tty2        00:00:00 bash
 2233 tty2        00:00:00 ps
[root@server1 ~]# _
```

The preceding output shows that two processes were running in the terminal tty2 when the ps command executed. The command that started each process (CMD) is listed next to the time it has taken on the CPU (TIME), its PID, and terminal (TTY). In this case, the process took less than one second to run, and so the time elapsed reads nothing. To find out more about these processes, you could instead use the -f, or full, option to the ps command, as shown next:

```
[root@server1 ~]# ps -f
UID        PID  PPID  C STIME  TTY         TIME CMD
root      2159  2156  0 16:18  tty2    00:00:00 -bash
root      2233  2159  3 16:28  tty2    00:00:00 ps -f
[root@server1 ~]# _
```

This listing provides more information about each process. It displays the user who started the process (UID), the PPID, the time it was started (STIME), as well as the CPU utilization (C), which starts at zero and is incremented with each processor cycle that the process runs on the CPU.

The most valuable information provided by the ps -f command is each process's PPID and lineage. The bash process (PID = 2159) displays a shell prompt and interprets user input; it started the ps process (PID = 2233) because the ps process had a PPID of 2159.

Because daemon processes are not associated with a terminal, they are not displayed by the ps -f command. To display an entire list of processes across all terminals and including daemons, you can add the -e option to any ps command, as shown in the following output:

```
[root@server1 ~]# ps -ef
UID        PID  PPID  C STIME  TTY         TIME  CMD
root         1     0  0 16:15  ?       00:00:01  /sbin/init
root         2     0  0 16:15  ?       00:00:00  [kthreadd]
root         3     2  0 16:15  ?       00:00:00  [migration/0]
root         4     2  0 16:15  ?       00:00:00  [ksoftirqd/0]
root         8     2  0 16:15  ?       00:00:00  [watchdog/1]
root         9     2  0 16:15  ?       00:00:00  [events/0]
root        11     2  0 16:15  ?       00:00:00  [cpuset]
root        12     2  0 16:15  ?       00:00:00  [khelper]
root        13     2  0 16:15  ?       00:00:00  [netns]
root        14     2  0 16:15  ?       00:00:00  [async/mgr]
root        15     2  0 16:15  ?       00:00:00  [pm]
root        16     2  0 16:15  ?       00:00:00  [sync_supers]
root        17     2  0 16:15  ?       00:00:00  [bdi-default]
root        18     2  0 16:15  ?       00:00:00  [kintegrityd/0]
```

```
root        34      2   0 16:15 ?       00:00:00 [kswapd0]
root        35      2   0 16:15 ?       00:00:00 [ksmd]
root        38      2   0 16:15 ?       00:00:00 [crypto/0]
root        39      2   0 16:15 ?       00:00:00 [crypto/1]
root        45      2   0 16:15 ?       00:00:00 [kpsmoused]
root       133      2   0 16:15 ?       00:00:00 [nouveau/0]
root       134      2   0 16:15 ?       00:00:00 [nouveau/1]
root       135      2   0 16:15 ?       00:00:00 [ttm_swap]
root       297      2   0 16:15 ?       00:00:00 [scsi_eh_0]
root       321      2   0 16:15 ?       00:00:00 [scsi_eh_1]
root       349      2   0 16:15 ?       00:00:00 [jbd2/sda1-8]
root       350      2   0 16:15 ?       00:00:00 [ext4-dio-unwrit]
root       351      2   0 16:15 ?       00:00:00 [ext4-dio-unwrit]
root       908      1   0 16:15 ?       00:00:00 /usr/bin/system-setup
root       950    437   0 16:15 ?       00:00:00 /sbin/udevd -d
root       951    437   0 16:15 ?       00:00:00 /sbin/udevd -d
root      1011      1   0 16:15 ?       00:00:00 auditd
root      1013   1011   0 16:15 ?       00:00:00 /sbin/audispd
root      1017   1013   0 16:15 ?       00:00:00 /usr/sbin/sedispatch
root      1038      1   0 16:15 ?       00:00:00 /sbin/rsyslogd -c 4
root      1073      1   0 16:15 ?       00:00:00 irqbalance
rpc       1088      1   0 16:15 ?       00:00:00 rpcbind
rpcuser   1102      1   0 16:15 ?       00:00:00 rpc.statd
root      1114      1   0 16:15 ?       00:00:00 mdadm --monitor --scan
root      1143      1   0 16:15 ?       00:00:00 rpc.idmapd
dbus      1156      1   0 16:15 ?       00:00:01 dbus-daemon --system
root      1166      1   0 16:15 ?       00:00:00 NetworkManager --pid
root      1171      1   0 16:15 ?       00:00:00 /usr/sbin/modem-manager
avahi     1177      1   0 16:15 ?       00:00:00 avahi-daemon: running
avahi     1178   1177   0 16:15 ?       00:00:00 avahi-daemon: chroot
root      1190      1   0 16:15 ?       00:00:00 cupsd -C
root      1191      1   0 16:15 ?       00:00:00 /usr/sbin/wpa_supplicant
root      1218      1   0 16:15 ?       00:00:00 /usr/sbin/acpid
root      1227   1226   0 16:15 ?       00:00:00 hald-runner
root      1256   1227   0 16:15 ?       00:00:00 hald-addon-input
root      1293      1   0 16:15 ?       00:00:00 pcscd
root      1315      1   0 16:15 ?       00:00:00 /usr/sbin/sshd
ntp       1323      1   0 16:15 ?       00:00:00 ntpd -u ntp:ntp
root      1358      1   0 16:15 ?       00:00:00 /usr/sbin/abrtd
root      1367      1   0 16:15 ?       00:00:00 /usr/sbin/gpm
root      1375      1   0 16:15 ?       00:00:00 crond
root      1386      1   0 16:15 ?       00:00:00 /usr/sbin/atd
root      1394      1   0 16:15 ?       00:00:00 /usr/sbin/gdm-binary
root      1399      1   0 16:15 tty2    00:00:00 /sbin/mingetty /dev/tty2
root      1401      1   0 16:15 tty3    00:00:00 /sbin/mingetty /dev/tty3
root      1405      1   0 16:15 tty4    00:00:00 /sbin/mingetty /dev/tty4
root      1413      1   0 16:15 tty5    00:00:00 /sbin/mingetty /dev/tty5
root      1417      1   0 16:15 tty6    00:00:00 /sbin/mingetty /dev/tty6
```

9

```
root      1437   1394   0 16:15   ?       00:00:00 /usr/libexec/gdm-simple
root      1440   1437   0 16:15   tty1    00:00:04 /usr/bin/Xorg :0 -nr
root      1454      1   0 16:15   ?       00:00:00 /usr/sbin/console-kit
gdm       1524      1   0 16:15   ?       00:00:00 /usr/bin/dbus-launch
root      1529      1   0 16:15   ?       00:00:00 /usr/libexec/upowerd
root      1580   1437   0 16:16   ?       00:00:00 pam: gdm-password
user1     1599   1580   0 16:16   ?       00:00:00 gnome-session
user1     1692      1   0 16:16   ?       00:00:00 /usr/libexec/gconfd-2
user1     1703      1   0 16:16   ?       00:00:00 /usr/libexec/gvfsd
user1     1706   1599   0 16:16   ?       00:00:00 metacity
user1     1712      1   0 16:16   ?       00:00:00 /usr/bin/pulseaudio
user1     1714   1599   0 16:16   ?       00:00:01 gnome-panel
user1     1723   1599   0 16:16   ?       00:00:01 nautilus
user1     1736   1599   0 16:16   ?       00:00:00 nm-applet --sm-disable
user1     1737   1599   0 16:16   ?       00:00:00 /usr/bin/seapplet
user1     1738   1599   0 16:16   ?       00:00:00 gpk-update-icon
user1     1748   1599   0 16:16   ?       00:00:00 deja-dup-monitor
user1     1759   1599   0 16:16   ?       00:00:00 evolution-alarm-notify
user1     1763   1599   0 16:16   ?       00:00:00 abrt-applet
user1     1773   1599   0 16:16   ?       00:00:00 gnome-power-manager
user1     1777   1599   0 16:16   ?       00:00:00 bluetooth-applet
user1     1787      1   0 16:16   ?       00:00:00 gnome-screensaver
smmsp     2120      1   0 16:16   ?       00:00:00 sendmail
root      2122      1   0 16:16   ?       00:00:00 sendmail
root      2156   1315   0 16:18   ?       00:00:00 sshd: root@pts/0
root      2159   2156   0 16:18   pts/0   00:00:00 -bash
root      2236   2159   3 16:30   pts/0   00:00:00 ps -ef
[root@server1 ~]# _
```

As shown in the preceding output, the kernel thread (kthreadd) daemon has a PID of 2 and starts most subprocesses within the actual Linux kernel because those subprocesses have a PPID of 2, whereas the init daemon (PID = 1) starts most other daemons because those daemons have a PPID of 1. In addition, there is a ? in the TTY column for any daemon or kernel subprocess, because they do not run on a terminal.

Because the output of the ps -ef command can be several hundred lines long on a Linux server, you usually pipe its output to the less command to send the output to the terminal screen page-by-page, or to the grep command, which can be used to display lines containing only certain information. For example, to display only the BASH shells in the preceding output, you could use the following command:

```
[root@server1 ~]# ps -ef | grep bash
user1     2094   2008   0 14:29 pts/1   00:00:00 bash
root      2159   2156   0 14:30 tty2    00:00:00 -bash
root      2294   2159   0 14:44 tty2    00:00:00 grep bash
[root@server1 ~]# _
```

Notice that the grep bash command is also displayed alongside the BASH shells in the preceding output because it was running in memory at the time the ps command was executed. This might not always be the case, because the Linux kernel schedules commands to run based on a variety of factors.

The -e and -f options are the most common options used with the ps command; however, many other options are available. The -l option to the ps command lists even more information about each process than the -f option. An example of using this option to view the processes in the terminal tty2 is shown in the following output:

```
[root@server1 ~]# ps -l
F S   UID   PID  PPID  C PRI  NI ADDR SZ  WCHAN  TTY     TIME CMD
4 S     0  2159  2156  0  80   0 -   1238  wait   tty2   00:00:00 bash
4 R     0  2295  2159  2  80   0 -    744  -      tty2   00:00:00 ps
[root@server1 ~]# _
```

The process flag (F) indicates particular features of the process; the flag of 4 in the preceding output indicates that the root user ran the process. The **process state** (S) column is the most valuable to systems administrators, because it indicates what the process is currently doing. If a process is not being run on the processor at the current time, you see an S (sleeping) in the process state column; processes are in this state most of the time, as seen with bash in the preceding output. You will see an R in this column if the process is currently running on the processor, or a T if it has stopped or is being traced by another process. In addition to these, you might also see a Z in this column indicating a **zombie process**. When a process finishes executing, the parent process must check to see if it executed successfully and then release the child process's PID so that it can be used again. While a process is waiting for its parent process to release the PID, the process is said to be in a zombie state, because it has finished but retains a PID. On a busy Linux server, zombie processes can accumulate and prevent new processes from being created; if this occurs, you can simply kill the parent process of the zombies, as discussed in the next section.

Zombie processes are also known as defunct processes.

To view a list of zombie processes on your entire system, you could use the ps -el | grep Z command.

Process priority (PRI) is the priority used by the kernel for the process; it is measured between 0 (high priority) and 127 (low priority). The **nice value** (NI) can be used to affect the process priority indirectly; it is measured between -20 (a greater chance of a high priority) and 19 (a greater chance of a lower priority). The ADDR in the preceding output indicates the memory address of the process, whereas the WCHAN indicates what the process is waiting for while sleeping. In addition, the size of the process in memory (SZ) is also listed and measured in kilobytes; often, it is roughly equivalent to the size of the executable file on the filesystem.

Some options to the ps command are not prefixed by a dash character; these are referred to as Berkeley style options. The two most common of these are the a option, which lists all processes across terminals, and the x option, which lists processes that do not run on a terminal, as shown in the following output for the first 10 processes on the system:

```
[root@server1 ~]# ps ax | head -11
PID TTY      STAT    TIME COMMAND
  1 ?        S       0:01 /sbin/init
  2 ?        S       0:00 [kthreadd]
```

```
   3 ?         S              0:00  [migration/0]
   4 ?         S<             0:00  [ksoftirqd/0]
   5 ?         S              0:00  [watchdog/0]
   6 ?         S              0:00  [migration/1]
   7 ?         S              0:00  [ksoftirqd/1]
   8 ?         S              0:00  [watchdog/1]
   9 ?         S              0:00  [events/0]
  10 ?         S              0:00  [events/1]
[root@server1 ~]# _
```

The columns just listed are equivalent to those discussed earlier; however, the process state column is identified with STAT and might contain additional characters to indicate the full nature of the process state. For example, a W indicates that the process has no contents in memory, a < symbol indicates a high-priority process, and an N indicates a low-priority process.

For a full list of symbols that may appear in the STAT or S columns shown in the prior output, consult the manual page for the `ps` command.

Several dozen options to the `ps` command can be used to display processes and their attributes; the options listed in this section are the most common and are summarized in Table 9-1.

The `ps` command is not the only command that can display process information. The kernel exports all process information subdirectories under the /proc directory. Each subdirectory is named for the PID of the process whose information it contains, as shown in the following output:

```
[root@server1 ~]# ls /proc
1     1218  1417  1723  19    26    6        diskstats    modules
10    1226  1437  1725  1909  27    692      dma          mounts
1011  1227  1440  1732  2     28    699      dri          mtrr
1013  1256  1454  1733  20    29    7        driver       net
1017  1260  15    1735  2019  297   700      execdomains  pagetype
```

Option	Description
-e	Displays all processes running on terminals as well as processes that do not run on a terminal (daemons)
-f	Displays a full list of information about each process, including the UID, PID, PPID, CPU utilization, start time, terminal, processor time, and command name
-l	Displays a long list of information about each process, including the flag, state, UID, PID, PPID, CPU utilization, priority, nice value, address, size, WCHAN, terminal, and command name
a	Displays all processes running on terminals
x	Displays all processes that do not run on terminals

Table 9-1   Common options to the `ps` command

```
1038  1266  1524  1736  2042  3    8      fb             partitions
1061  1271  1529  1737  2048  30   817    filesystems    sched_d
1062  1272  1563  1738  2049  321  825    fs             schedstat
1073  1293  1566  1740  2051  33   858    interrupts     scsi
1084  13    1575  1743  2062  34   859    iomem          self
1088  1315  1580  1748  21    349  860    ioports        slabinfo
11    1323  1592  1750  2120  35   9      irq            softirqs
1102  133   1599  1752  2122  350  906    kallsyms       stat
1114  134   16    1758  2156  351  908    kcore          swaps
1135  135   1609  1759  2159  36   950    keys           sys
1136  1358  1610  1763  22    37   951    key-users      sysrq
1143  1367  1692  1767  2246  38   acpi   kmsg           sysvipc
1156  1375  1699  1769  2247  39   asound kpagecount     timer_list
1166  1386  17    1773  2248  4    buddyinfo kpageflags  timer_stat
1171  1394  1703  1775  2272  437  bus    latency_stats  tty
1177  1399  1706  1777  23    45   cgroups loadavg       uptime
1178  14    1712  1779  2369  46   cmdline locks         version
1190  1401  1714  1782  2370  47   cpuinfo mdstat        vmms
1191  1405  1716  1787  24    48   crypto meminfo        vmstat
12    1413  1722  18    25    5    devices misc          zoneinfo
[root@server1 ~]# _
```

Thus, any program that can read from the /proc directory can display process information. For example, the **pstree command** displays the lineage of a process by tracing its PPIDs until the init daemon. The first 20 lines of this command are shown in the following output:

```
[root@server1 ~]# pstree | head -20
init─┬─NetworkManager─┬─dhclient
     │                └─{NetworkManager}
     ├─abrtd
     ├─acpid
     ├─atd
     ├─auditd─┬─audispd─┬─sedispatch
     │        │         └─{audispd}
     │        └─{auditd}
     ├─avahi-daemon───avahi-daemon
     ├─bonobo-activati───{bonobo-activat}
     ├─clock-applet
     ├─console-kit-dae───63*[{console-kit-da}]
     ├─crond
     ├─cupsd
     ├─2*[dbus-daemon]
     ├─2*[dbus-launch]
     ├─gconf-im-settin
     ├─gconfd-2
     ├─gdm-binary─┬─gdm-simple-slav─┬─Xorg
     │            │                 └─gdm-session-wor─┬─gnome
[root@server1 ~]# _
```

The most common command used to display processes, aside from ps, is the **top command**. The top command displays an interactive screen listing processes organized by processor time. Processes that use the most processor time are listed at the top of the screen. An example of the screen that appears when you type the top command is shown next:

```
top - 17:03:23 up 47 min, 4 users, load average: 0.00, 0.00, 0.02
Tasks: 165 total, 1 running, 164 sleeping, 0 stopped, 0 zombie
Cpu(s): 0.0%us, 0.3%sy, 0.0%ni, 98.3%id, 1.3%wa, 0.0%hi, 0.0%si, 0.0%st
Mem:   961284k total,  638652k used,  322632k free,   34452k buffers
Swap: 4095992k total,       0k used, 4095992k free,  442908k cached

  PID USER      PR  NI  VIRT  RES  SHR S %CPU %MEM    TIME+  COMMAND
 2409 root      20   0  2696 1128  856 R  0.7  0.1  0:00.08 top
  321 root      20   0  3092 1220  324 S  0.3  0.0  0:01.15 Xorg
    1 root      20   0  2828 1344 1144 S  0.0  0.1  0:01.40 init
    2 root      20   0     0    0    0 S  0.0  0.0  0:00.00 kthreadd
    5 root      RT   0     0    0    0 S  0.0  0.0  0:00.00 watchdog/0
    8 root      RT   0     0    0    0 S  0.0  0.0  0:00.00 watchdog/1
    9 root      20   0     0    0    0 S  0.0  0.0  0:00.03 events/0
   10 root      20   0     0    0    0 S  0.0  0.0  0:00.02 events/1
   11 root      20   0     0    0    0 S  0.0  0.0  0:00.00 cpuset
   12 root      20   0     0    0    0 S  0.0  0.0  0:00.00 khelper
   13 root      20   0     0    0    0 S  0.0  0.0  0:00.00 netns
   14 root      20   0     0    0    0 S  0.0  0.0  0:00.00 async/mgr
   15 root      20   0     0    0    0 S  0.0  0.0  0:00.00 pm
```

Note that the top command displays many of the same columns that the ps command does, yet it contains a summary paragraph at the top of the screen and a cursor between the summary paragraph and the process list. From the preceding output, you can see that the top command itself uses the most processor time, followed by X Windows (Xorg) and the init daemon.

You might come across a process that has encountered an error during execution and continuously uses up system resources. These processes are referred to as **rogue processes,** and they appear at the top of the listing produced by the top command. The top command can also be used to change the priority of processes or kill them. Thus, you can stop rogue processes from the top command immediately after they are identified. Process priority and killing processes are discussed later in this chapter.

To get a full listing of the different commands that you can use while in the top utility, simply press h to get a help screen. An example of this help screen is shown next:

```
Help for Interactive Commands - procps version 3.2.8
Window 1:Def: Cumulative mode Off. System: Delay 3.0 secs; Secure mode Off.

Z,B      Global: 'Z' change color mappings; 'B' disable/enable bold
l,t,m    Toggle Summaries: 'l' load avg; 't' task/cpu stats; 'm' mem info
1,I      Toggle SMP view: '1' single/separate states; 'I' Irix/Solaris
         mode
```

```
f,o     . Fields/Columns: 'f' add or remove; 'o' change display order
F or O  . Select sort field
<,>     . Move sort field: '<' nextcol left; '>' next col right
R,H     . Toggle: 'R' normal/reverse sort; 'H' show threads
c,i,S   . Toggle: 'c' cmd name/line; 'i' idle tasks; 'S' cumulative time
x,y     . Toggle highlights: 'x' sort field; 'y' running tasks
z,b     . Toggle: 'z' color/mono; 'b' bold/reverse (only if 'x' or 'y')
u       . Show specific user only
n or #  . Set maximum tasks displayed

k,r       Manipulate tasks: 'k' kill; 'r' renice
d or s    Set update interval
W         Write configuration file
q         Quit
          ( commands shown with '.' require a visible task display window )

Press 'h' or '?' for help with Windows,
any other key to continue
```

Killing Processes

As indicated earlier, a large number of rogue and zombie processes use up system resources. When system performance suffers due to these processes, you should send them a **kill signal**, which terminates a process. The most common command used to send kill signals is the `kill` **command**. All told, the `kill` command can send 64 different kill signals to a process. Each of these kill signals operates in a different manner. To view the different kill signal names and associated numbers, you can use the `-l` option to the `kill` command, as shown in the following output:

```
[root@server1 ~]# kill -l
 1) SIGHUP        2) SIGINT        3) SIGQUIT       4) SIGILL
 5) SIGTRAP       6) SIGABRT       7) SIGBUS        8) SIGFPE
 9) SIGKILL      10) SIGUSR1      11) SIGSEGV      12) SIGUSR2
13) SIGPIPE      14) SIGALRM      15) SIGTERM      17) SIGCHLD
18) SIGCONT      19) SIGSTOP      20) SIGTSTP      21) SIGTTIN
22) SIGTTOU      23) SIGURG       24) SIGXCPU      25) SIGXFSZ
26) SIGVTALRM    27) SIGPROF      28) SIGWINCH     29) SIGIO
30) SIGPWR       31) SIGSYS       33) SIGRTMIN     34) SIGRTMIN+1
35) SIGRTMIN+2   36) SIGRTMIN+3   37) SIGRTMIN+4   38) SIGRTMIN+5
39) SIGRTMIN+6   40) SIGRTMIN+7   41) SIGRTMIN+8   42) SIGRTMIN+9
43) SIGRTMIN+10  44) SIGRTMIN+11  45) SIGRTMIN+12  46) SIGRTMIN+13
47) SIGRTMIN+14  48) SIGRTMIN+15  49) SIGRTMAX-15  50) SIGRTMAX-14
51) SIGRTMAX-13  52) SIGRTMAX-12  53) SIGRTMAX-11  54) SIGRTMAX-10
55) SIGRTMAX-9   56) SIGRTMAX-8   57) SIGRTMAX-7   58) SIGRTMAX-6
59) SIGRTMAX-5   60) SIGRTMAX-4   61) SIGRTMAX-3   62) SIGRTMAX-2
63) SIGRTMAX-1   64) SIGRTMAX
[root@server1 ~]# _
```

Name	Number	Description
SIGHUP	1	Also known as the hang-up signal, it stops a process, then restarts it with the same PID. If you edit the configuration file used by a running daemon, that daemon might be sent a SIGHUP to restart the process; when the daemon starts again, it reads the new configuration file.
SIGINT	2	This signal sends an interrupt signal to a process. Although this signal is one of the weakest kill signals, it works most of the time. When you use the Ctrl+c key combination to kill a currently running process, a SIGINT is actually being sent to the process.
SIGQUIT	3	Also known as a core dump, the quit signal terminates a process by taking the process information in memory and saving it to a file called core on the hard disk in the current working directory. You can use the Ctrl+\ key combination to send a SIGQUIT to a process that is currently running.
SIGTERM	15	The software termination signal is the most common kill signal used by programs to kill other processes. It is the default kill signal used by the `kill` command.
SIGKILL	9	Also known as the absolute kill signal, this forces the Linux kernel to stop executing the process by sending the process's resources to a special device file called /dev/null.

Table 9-2 Common administrative kill signals

Most of the kill signals listed in the preceding output are not useful for systems administrators. The five most common kill signals used for administration are listed in Table 9-2.

To send a kill signal to a process, you specify the kill signal to send as an option to the `kill` command, followed by the appropriate PID of the process. For example, to send a SIGQUIT to a process called sample, you could use the following commands to locate and terminate the process:

```
[root@server1 ~]# ps -ef | grep sample
root     1199    1 0    Jun30 tty3    00:00:00 /sbin/sample
[root@server1 ~]# kill -3 1199
[root@server1 ~]# _
[root@server1 ~]# ps -ef | grep sample
[root@server1 ~]# _
```

 The `kill -SIGQUIT 1199` command does the same thing as the `kill -3 1199` command shown in the preceding output.

 If you do not specify the kill signal when using the `kill` command, the `kill` command uses the default kill signal, the SIGTERM signal.

Some processes have the ability to ignore, or **trap**, certain kill signals that are sent to them. The only kill signal that cannot be trapped by any process is the SIGKILL. Thus, if a SIGINT, SIGQUIT, and SIGTERM do not terminate a stubborn process, you can use a SIGKILL to terminate it. However, you should only use SIGKILL as a last resort, because it prevents a process from closing temporary files and other resources properly.

If you send a kill signal to a process that has children, the parent process terminates all of its child processes before terminating itself. Thus, to kill several related processes, you can simply send a kill signal to their parent process. In addition, to kill a zombie process, it is often necessary to send a kill signal to its parent process.

Another command that can be used to send kill signals to processes is the **killall command**. The killall command works similarly to the kill command in that it takes the kill signal as an option; however, it uses the process name to kill, instead of the PID. This allows multiple processes of the same name to be killed in one command. An example of using the killall command to send a SIGQUIT to multiple sample processes is shown in the following output:

```
[root@server1 ~]# ps -ef | grep sample
root      1729      1    0 Jun30 tty3     00:00:00 /sbin/sample
root     20198      1    0 Jun30 tty4     00:00:00 /sbin/sample
[root@server1 ~]# killall -3 sample
[root@server1 ~]# _
[root@server1 ~]# ps -ef | grep sample
[root@server1 ~]# _
```

Alternatively, you could use the command killall –SIGQUIT sample to do the same as the killall -3 sample command used in the preceding output.

As with the kill command, if you do not specify the kill signal when using the killall command, it sends a SIGTERM signal by default.

In addition to the kill and killall commands, the top command can be used to kill processes. While in the top utility, simply press the k key and supply the appropriate PID and kill signal when prompted.

Process Execution

You can execute three main types of Linux commands:

- Binary programs
- Shell scripts
- Shell functions

Most commands, such as ls, find, and grep, are binary programs that exist on the filesystem until executed. They were written in a certain programming language and compiled into a binary format that only the computer can understand. Other commands, such as cd and exit, are built into the BASH shell running in memory, and they are called shell functions. Shell scripts can also contain a list of binary programs, shell functions, and special constructs for the shell to execute in order.

When executing compiled programs or shell scripts, the BASH shell that interprets the command you typed creates a new BASH shell. This creation of a new subshell is known as **forking**, and it is carried out by the fork function in the BASH shell. The new subshell then executes the binary program or shell script using its exec function. After the binary program or shell script has completed, the new BASH shell uses its exit function to kill itself and return control to the original BASH shell. The original BASH shell uses its wait function to wait for the new BASH shell to carry out the aforementioned tasks before returning a prompt to the user. Figure 9-3 depicts this process when a user types the ls command at the command line.

Running Processes in the Background

As discussed in the previous section, the BASH shell creates, or forks, a subshell to execute most commands on the Linux system. Unfortunately, the original BASH shell must wait for the command in the subshell to finish before displaying a shell prompt to accept new commands. Commands run in this fashion are known as **foreground processes**.

Alternatively, you can omit the wait function shown in Figure 9-3 by appending an ampersand (&) character to the command. Commands run in this fashion are known as **background processes**. When a command is run in the background, the shell immediately returns the shell

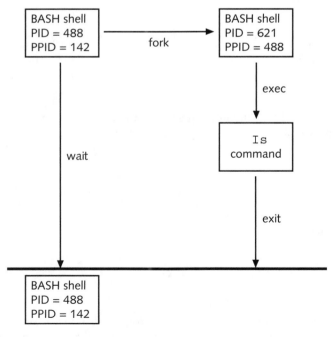

Figure 9-3 Process forking

Source: Course Technology/Cengage Learning

prompt for the user to enter another command. To run the `sample` command in the background, you can enter the following command:

```
[root@server1 ~]# sample &
[1] 2583
[root@server1 ~]# _
```

Space characters between the command and the ampersand (&) are optional. In other words, the command `sample&` is equivalent to the command `sample &`, used in the preceding output.

The shell returns the PID (2583 in the preceding example) and the background job ID (1 in the preceding example) so that you can manipulate the background job after it has been run. After the process has been started, you can use the `ps` command to view the PID or the **jobs** command to view the background job ID, as shown in the following output:

```
[root@server1 ~]# jobs
[1]+  Running                 sample &
[root@server1 ~]# ps | grep sample
2583 tty2     00:00:00 sample
[root@server1 ~]# _
```

To terminate the background process, you can send a kill signal to the PID (as shown earlier in this chapter), or you can send a kill signal to the background job ID. Background job IDs must be prefixed by a % character. To send a SIGINT signal to the `sample` background process created earlier, you could use the following `kill` command:

```
[root@server1 ~]# jobs
[1]+  Running                 sample &
[root@server1 ~]# kill -2 %1
[1]+ Interrupt               sample
[root@server1 ~]# jobs
[root@server1 ~]# _
```

You can also use the `killall -2 sample` command or the top utility to terminate the sample background process used in the preceding example.

After a background process has been started, you can move it to the foreground by using the **foreground (fg) command** followed by the background job ID. Similarly, you can pause a foreground process by using the Ctrl+z key combination. You can then send the process to the background with the **background (bg) command**. The Ctrl+z key combination assigns the foreground process a background job ID that is then used as an argument to the `bg` command. To start a `sample` process in the background and move it to the foreground, then pause it and move it to the background again, you can use the following commands:

```
[root@server1 ~]# sample &
[1] 7519
[root@server1 ~]# fg %1
sample
```

```
Ctrl+z
```

```
[1]+  Stopped                 sample
[root@server1 ~]# bg %1
[1]+ sample &
[root@server1 ~]# jobs
[1]+  Running                 sample &
[root@server1 ~]# _
```

When there are multiple background processes executing in the shell, the jobs command indicates the most recent one with a + symbol and the second most recent one with a – symbol. If you place the % notation in a command without specifying the background job ID, the command operates on the most recent background process. An example of this is shown in the following output, in which four sample processes are started and sent SIGQUIT kill signals using the % notation:

```
[root@server1 ~]# sample &
[1] 7605
[root@server1 ~]# sample2 &
[2] 7613
[root@server1 ~]# sample3 &
[3] 7621
[root@server1 ~]# sample4 &
[4] 7629
[root@server1 ~]# jobs
[1]   Running                 sample &
[2]   Running                 sample2 &
[3]-  Running                 sample3 &
[4]+  Running                 sample4 &
[root@server1 ~]# kill -3 %
[root@server1 ~]# jobs
[1]   Running                 sample &
[2]-  Running                 sample2 &
[3]+  Running                 sample3 &
[root@server1 ~]# kill -3 %
[root@server1 ~]# jobs
[1]-  Running                 sample &
[2]+  Running                 sample2 &
[root@server1 ~]# kill -3 %
[root@server1 ~]# jobs
[1]+  Running                 sample &
[root@server1 ~]# kill -3 %
[root@server1 ~]# jobs
[root@server1 ~]# _
```

Process Priorities

Recall that Linux is a multitasking operating system. That is, it can perform several different tasks at the same time. Because most computers contain only a single CPU, Linux executes small amounts of each process on the processor in series. This makes it seem to the user as if processes are executing simultaneously. The amount of time a process has to use the CPU is called a **time slice**; the more time slices a process has, the more time it has to execute on the CPU and the faster it executes. Time slices are typically measured in milliseconds. Thus, several hundred processes can be executing on the processor in a single second.

The ps –l command lists the Linux kernel priority (PRI) of a process. This value is directly related to the amount of time slices a process has on the CPU. A PRI of 0 is the most likely to get time slices on the CPU, and a PRI of 127 is the least likely to receive time slices on the CPU. An example of this command is shown next:

```
[root@server1 ~]# ps -l
F S   UID   PID  PPID  C  PRI  NI   ADDR  SZ  WCHAN  TTY      TIME  CMD
4 S     0  3194  3192  0   75   0   -    1238  wait4  pts/1  00:00:00  bash
4 S     0  3896  3194  0   76   0   -     953  -      pts/1  00:00:00  sleep
4 S     0  3939  3194 13   75   0   -    7015  -      pts/1  00:00:01  gedit
4 R     0  3940  3194  0   77   0   -     632  -      pts/1  00:00:00  ps
[root@server1 ~]# _
```

The bash, sleep, gedit, and ps processes all have different PRI values because the kernel automatically assigns time slices based on several factors. You cannot change the PRI directly, but you can influence it indirectly by assigning a certain nice value to a process. A negative nice value increases the likelihood that the process will receive more time slices, whereas a positive nice value does the opposite. The range of nice values is depicted in Figure 9-4.

All users can be "nice" to other users of the same computer by lowering the priority of their own processes by increasing their nice value. However, only the root user has the ability to increase the priority of a process by lowering its nice value.

Processes are started with a nice value of 0 by default, as shown in the NI column of the ps –l output previously. To start a process with a nice value of +19 (low priority), you can use the **nice command** and specify the nice value using the –n option and the command to start. If the –n option is omitted, a nice value of +10 is assumed. To start the ps –l command with a nice value of +19, you can issue the following command:

```
[root@server1 ~]# nice -n 19 ps -l
F S   UID   PID  PPID  C  PRI  NI   ADDR  SZ  WCHAN  TTY      TIME  CMD
4 S     0  3194  3192  0   75   0   -    1238  wait4  pts/1  00:00:00  bash
```

–20	0	+19
Most likely to receive time slices; the PRI will be closer to zero	The default nice value for new processes	Least likely to receive time slices; the PRI will be closer to 127

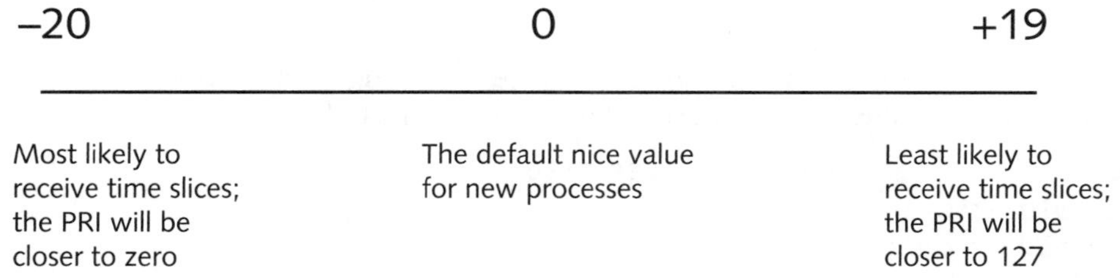

Figure 9-4 The nice value scale

Source: Course Technology/Cengage Learning

```
4 S    0  3896  3194   0  76   0   -    953  -       pts/1     00:00:00 sleep
4 S    0  3939  3194   0  76   0   -   7015  -       pts/1     00:00:02 gedit
4 R    0  3946  3194   0  99  19   -    703  -       pts/1     00:00:00 ps
[root@server1 ~]# _
```

Notice from the preceding output that NI is 19 for the ps command, as compared with 0 for the bash, sleep, and bash commands. Furthermore, the PRI of 99 for the ps command results in fewer time slices than the PRI of 76 for the sleep and gedit commands and the PRI of 75 for the bash shell.

Conversely, to increase the priority of the ps -l command, you can use the following command:

```
[root@server1 ~]# nice –n -20 ps -l
F S UID   PID  PPID  C PRI  NI   ADDR SZ  WCHAN  TTY        TIME  CMD
4 S   0  3194  3192  0  75   0    -   1238  wait4  pts/1     00:00:00 bash
4 S   0  3896  3194  0  76   0    -    953  -      pts/1     00:00:00 sleep
4 S   0  3939  3194  0  76   0    -   7015  -      pts/1     00:00:02 gedit
4 R   0  3947  3194  0  60 -20    -    687  -      pts/1     00:00:00 ps
[root@server1 ~]# _
```

Note from the preceding output that the nice value of -20 for the ps command resulted in a PRI of 60, which is more likely to receive time slices than the PRI of 76 for the sleep and gedit commands and the PRI of 75 for the bash shell.

On some Linux systems, background processes are given a nice value of 4 by default to lower the chance that they will receive time slices.

After a process has been started, you can change its priority by using the **renice command** and specifying the change to the nice value as well as the PID of the processes to change. Suppose, for example, three sample processes are currently executing on a terminal:

```
[root@server1 ~]# ps -l
F S UID   PID  PPID  C PRI  NI   ADDR  SZ  WCHAN  TTY          TIME  CMD
4 S   0  1229  1228  0  71   0    -   617  wait4  pts/0     00:00:00 bash
4 S   0  1990  1229  0  69   0    -   483  nanosl pts/0     00:00:00 sample
4 S   0  2180  1229  0  70   0    -   483  nanosl pts/0     00:00:00 sample
4 S   0  2181  1229  0  71   0    -   483  nanosl pts/0     00:00:00 sample
4 R   0  2196  1229  0  75   0    -   768  -      pts/0     00:00:00 ps
[root@server1 ~]# _
```

To lower priority of the first two sample processes by changing the nice value from 0 to +15 and view the new values, you can use the following commands:

```
[root@server1 ~]# renice +15 1990 2180
1990: old priority 0, new priority 15
2180: old priority 0, new priority 15
[root@server1 ~]# ps -l
```

```
F S UID   PID  PPID C PRI NI  ADDR  SZ WCHAN  TTY            TIME CMD
4 S   0  1229  1228 0  71  0    -   617 wait4  pts/0      00:00:00 bash
4 S   0  1990  1229 0  93 15    -   483 nanosl pts/0      00:00:00 sample
4 S   0  2180  1229 0  96 15    -   483 nanosl pts/0      00:00:00 sample
4 S   0  2181  1229 0  71  0    -   483 nanosl pts/0      00:00:00 sample
4 R   0  2196  1229 0  75  0    -   768 -      pts/0      00:00:00 ps
[root@server1 ~]# _
```

You can also use the top utility to change the nice value of a running process. Simply press the r key, then supply the PID and the nice value when prompted.

As with the nice command, only the root user can change the nice value to a negative value using the renice command.

The root user can use the renice command to change the priority of all processes that are owned by a certain user or group. To change the nice value to +15 for all processes owned by the users mary and bob, you could execute the command renice +15 -u mary bob at the command prompt. Similarly, to change the nice value to +15 for all processes started by members of the group sys, you could execute the command renice +15 -g sys at the command prompt.

Scheduling Commands

Although most processes are begun by users executing commands while logged in to a terminal, at times you might want to schedule a command to execute at some point in the future. For example, scheduling system maintenance commands to run during nonworking hours is good practice, as it does not disrupt normal business activities.

You can use two different daemons to schedule commands: the **at daemon** (**atd**) and the **cron daemon** (**crond**). The at daemon can be used to schedule a command to execute once in the future, whereas the cron daemon is used to schedule a command to execute repeatedly in the future.

Scheduling Commands with atd

To schedule a command or set of commands for execution at a later time by the at daemon, you can specify the time as an argument to the **at command**; some common time formats used with the at command are listed in Table 9-3.

After being invoked, the at command displays an at> prompt allowing you to type commands to be executed, one per line. After the commands have been entered, use the Crtl+d key combination to schedule the commands using atd.

Command	Description
at 10:15pm	Schedules commands to run at 10:15 p.m. on the current date
at 10:15pm July 15	Schedules commands to run at 10:15 p.m. on July 15
at midnight	Schedules commands to run at midnight on the current date
at noon July 15	Schedules commands to run at noon on July 15
at teatime	Schedules commands to run at 4:00 p.m. on the current date
at tomorrow	Schedules commands to run the next day
at now + 5 minutes	Schedules commands to run in five minutes
at now + 10 hours	Schedules commands to run in 10 hours
at now + 4 days	Schedules commands to run in four days
at now + 2 weeks	Schedules commands to run in two weeks
at now at batch	Schedules commands to run immediately
at 9:00am 01/03/2015 at 9:00am 01032015 at 9:00am 03.01.2015	Schedules commands to run at 9:00 a.m. on January 3, 2015

Table 9-3 Common **at** commands

The at daemon uses the current shell's environment when executing scheduled commands. The shell environment and scheduled commands are stored in the **/var/spool/at** directory.

If the standard output of any command scheduled using atd has not been redirected to a file, it is mailed to the user. You can check your local mail by typing mail at a command prompt. More information about the mail utility can be found in its manual page or info page.

To schedule the commands date and who to run at 10:15 p.m. on July 15th, you can use the following commands:

```
[root@server1 ~]# at 10:15pm July 15
at> date > /root/atfile
at> who >> /root/atfile
at>
job 1 at Thurs July 15 22:15:00 2015
[root@server1 ~]# _
```

As shown in the preceding output, the at command returns an at job ID. You can use this ID to query or remove the scheduled command. To display a list of at Job IDs, you can specify the −1 option to the at command:

```
[root@server1 ~]# at -l
1          Thurs July 15 22:15:00 2015 a root
[root@server1 ~]# _
```

Alternatively, you can use the `atq` command to see scheduled at jobs. The `atq` command is simply a shortcut to the `at -l` command.

When running the `at -l` command, a regular user only sees his own scheduled at jobs; however, the root user sees all scheduled at jobs.

To see the contents of the at job listed in the previous output alongside the shell environment at the time the at job was scheduled, you can use the `-c` option to the `at` command and specify the appropriate at Job ID:

```
[root@server1 ~]# at -c 1
#!/bin/sh
# atrunuid=0 gid=0
# mail      root 0
umask 22
SSH_AGENT_PID=2964; export SSH_AGENT_PID
HOSTNAME=server1; export HOSTNAME
DESKTOP_STARTUP_ID=; export DESKTOP_STARTUP_ID
HISTSIZE=1000; export HISTSIZE
GTK_RC_FILES=/etc/gtk/gtkrc:/root/.gtkrc-1.2-gnome2; export
GTK_RC_FILES
WINDOWID=33554952; export WINDOWID
QTDIR=/usr/lib/qt-3.3; export QTDIR
USER=root; export USER
GNOME_KEYRING_SOCKET=/tmp/keyring-lZSvC3/socket; export GNOME_KEYRING_
SOCKET
SSH_AUTH_SOCK=/tmp/ssh-sece2901/agent.2901; export SSH_AUTH_SOCK
KDEDIR=/usr; export KDEDIR
SESSION_MANAGER=local/server1:/tmp/.ICE-unix/2901; export SESSION_
MANAGER
USERNAME=root; export USERNAME
PATH=/usr/kerberos/sbin:/usr/kerberos/bin:/usr/local/sbin:/usr/local/
bin:/sbin:/bin:/usr/sbin:/usr/bin:/usr/X11R6/bin:/usr/java/
j2sdk1.4.2_04/bin/::/root/bin; export PATH
DESKTOP_SESSION=default; export DESKTOP_SESSION
MAIL=/var/spool/mail/root; export MAIL
PWD=/root; export PWD
INPUTRC=/etc/inputrc; export INPUTRC
LANG=en_US.UTF-8; export LANG
GDMSESSION=default; export GDMSESSION
SSH_ASKPASS=/usr/libexec/openssh/gnome-ssh-askpass; export SSH_ASKPASS
```

9

```
SHLVL=2; export SHLVL
HOME=/root; export HOME
GNOME_DESKTOP_SESSION_ID=Default; export GNOME_DESKTOP_SESSION_ID
BASH_ENV=/root/.bashrc; export BASH_ENV
LOGNAME=root; export LOGNAME
LESSOPEN=\|/usr/bin/lesspipe.sh\ %s; export LESSOPEN
G_BROKEN_FILENAMES=1; export G_BROKEN_FILENAMES
COLORTERM=gnome-terminal; export COLORTERM
XAUTHORITY=/root/.Xauthority; export XAUTHORITY
cd /root || {
echo 'Execution directory inaccessible' >&2
exit 1
}
${SHELL:-/bin/sh} << 'marcinDELIMITER46b6765b'

date > /root/atfile
who >> /root/atfile
[root@server1 ~]# _
```

To remove the at job used in the preceding example, simply specify the −d option to the at command, followed by the appropriate at Job ID, as shown in the following output:

```
[root@server1 ~]# at -d 1
[root@server1 ~]# at -l
[root@server1 ~]# _
```

Alternatively, you can use the atrm 1 command to remove the first at job. The atrm command is simply a shortcut to the at −d command.

If there are many commands to be scheduled using the at daemon, you can place these commands in a shell script and then schedule the shell script to execute at a later time using the −f option to the at command. An example of scheduling a shell script called myscript using the at command is shown next:

```
[root@server1 ~]# cat myscript
#this is a sample shell script
date > /root/atfile
who >> /root/atfile
[root@server1 ~]# at 10:15pm July 16 -f myscript
job 2 at Thurs July 15 22:15:00 2015
[root@server1 ~]# _
```

If the **/etc/at.allow** and **/etc/at.deny** files do not exist, only the root user is allowed to schedule tasks using the at daemon. To give this ability to other users, simply create an /etc/at.allow file and add the names of users allowed to use the at daemon, one per line. Conversely, you can use the /etc/at.deny file to deny certain users access to the at daemon; any user not listed in this file is then allowed to use the at daemon. If both files exist, the system checks the /etc/at.allow file and does not process the entries in the /etc/at.deny file.

 On Fedora Linux systems, only an /etc/at.deny file exists by default. Because this file is initially left blank, all users are allowed to use the at daemon after a Fedora Linux installation.

Scheduling Commands with the Cron Daemon

The at daemon is useful for scheduling tasks that occur on a certain date in the future, yet is ill suited for scheduling repetitive tasks, because each task requires its own at job ID. The cron daemon is better suited for repetitive tasks, because it uses configuration files called **cron tables** to specify when a command should be executed.

A cron table includes six fields separated by space or tab characters. The first five fields specify the times to run the command, and the sixth field is the absolute pathname to the command to be executed. As with the at command, you can place commands in a shell script and schedule the shell script to run repetitively; in this case, the sixth field is the absolute pathname to the shell script. Each of the fields in a cron table is depicted in Figure 9-5.

Thus, to execute the /root/myscript shell script at 5:20 p.m. and 5:40 p.m. Monday to Friday regardless of the day of the month or month of the year, you could use the cron table depicted in Figure 9-6.

1	2	3	4	5	command

```
1 = Minute past the hour (0–59)
2 = Hour (0–23)
3 = Day of month (1–31)
4 = Month of year (1–12)
5 = Day of week
        0 = Sun (or 7 = Sun)
        1 = Mon
        2 = Tues
        3 = Wed
        4 = Thurs
        5 = Fri
        6 = Sat
```

Figure 9-5 User cron table format

Source: Course Technology/Cengage Learning

1	2	3	4	5	command
20,40	17	*	*	1–5	/root/myscript

Figure 9-6 Sample user cron table entry

Source: Course Technology/Cengage Learning

9

The first field in Figure 9-6 specifies the minute past the hour. Because the command must be run at 20 minutes and 40 minutes past the hour, this field has two values, separated by a comma. The second field specifies the time in 24-hour format, with 5:00 p.m. being the 17th hour. The third and fourth fields specify the day of month and month of year, respectively, to run the command. Because the command might run during any month regardless of the day of month, both fields use the * wildcard shell metacharacter to match all values. The final field indicates the day of the week to run the command; as with the first field, the command must be run on multiple days, but a range of days was specified (day 1 to day 5).

Two different types of cron tables are used by the cron daemon. User cron tables exist in **/var/spool/cron** and represent tasks that individual users schedule, whereas the system cron tables contain system tasks and exist in the **/etc/crontab** file as well as the **/etc/cron.d** directory.

User Cron Tables On a newly installed Fedora Linux system, all users have the ability to schedule tasks using the cron daemon because there is only a single blank line within the **/etc/cron.deny** file. However, if you create an **/etc/cron.allow** file and add a list of users to it, only those users will be able to schedule tasks using the cron daemon. All other users are denied. Conversely, you can modify the /etc/cron.deny file to list those users who are denied the ability to schedule tasks. Thus, any users not listed in this file are allowed to schedule tasks only. If both files exist, only the /etc/cron.allow file is processed.

To create or edit a user cron table, you can use the −e option to the **crontab command**, which opens the vi editor. You can then enter the appropriate cron table entries. Suppose, for example, that the root user executed the crontab −e command. To schedule /bin/command1 to run at 4:30 a.m. every Friday and /bin/command2 to run at 2:00 p.m. on the first day of every month, you can add the following lines while in the vi editor:

```
30 4 * * 5 /bin/command1
0 14 1 * * /bin/command2
~
~
~
~
~
~
~
~
~
~
~
~
~
~
~
"/tmp/crontab.4101"   2L 41C
```

When the user saves the changes and quits the vi editor, the information is stored in the file /var/spool/cron/*username* where *username* is the name of the user who executed the crontab −e command. In the preceding example, the file would be named /var/spool/cron/root.

To list your user cron table, you can use the -l option to the `crontab` command. The following output lists the cron table created earlier:

```
[root@server1 ~]# crontab -l
30 4 * * 5 /bin/command1
0 14 1 * * /bin/command2
[root@server1 ~]# _
```

Furthermore, to remove a cron table and all scheduled jobs, you can use the -r option to the `crontab` command, as illustrated next:

```
[root@server1 ~]# crontab -r
[root@server1 ~]# crontab -l
no crontab for root
[root@server1 ~]# _
```

The root user can edit, list, or remove any other user's cron table by using the -u option to the `crontab` command followed by the user name. For example, to edit the cron table for the user mary, the root user could use the command `crontab -e -u mary` at the command prompt. Similarly, to list and remove mary's cron table, the root user could execute the commands `crontab -l -u mary` and `crontab -r -u mary`, respectively.

System Cron Tables
Linux systems are typically scheduled to run many commands during nonbusiness hours. These commands might perform system maintenance, back up data, or run CPU-intensive programs. Most of these commands are scheduled by the cron daemon from entries in the system cron table /etc/crontab, which can only be edited by the root user. The default /etc/crontab file is shown in the following output:

```
[root@server1 ~]# cat /etc/crontab
SHELL=/bin/bash
PATH=/sbin:/bin:/usr/sbin:/usr/bin
MAILTO=root
HOME=/

# For details see man 4 crontabs

# Example of job definition:
# .---------------- minute (0 - 59)
# |  .------------- hour (0 - 23)
# |  |  .---------- day of month (1 - 31)
# |  |  |  .------- month (1 - 12) OR jan,feb,mar,apr ...
# |  |  |  |  .---- day of week (0 - 6) (Sunday=0 or 7) OR
# |  |  |  |  |           sun,mon,tue,wed,thu,fri,sat
# |  |  |  |  |
# *  *  *  *  * command to be executed

[root@server1 ~]# _
```

The initial section of the cron table specifies the environment used while executing commands. The remainder of the file contains comments that identify the format of a cron table entry. If you add your own cron table entries to the bottom of this file, they will be executed as the root user.

You can also place a cron table with the same information in the /etc/cron.d directory. Any cron tables found in this directory can have the same format as /etc/crontab and are run by the system as a user of your choice. For example, if the sysstat package is installed on your system, the sa1 command is run every 10 minutes as the root user by the cron daemon from the file /etc/cron.d/sysstat, as shown next:

```
[root@server1 ~]# cat /etc/cron.d/sysstat
# Run system activity accounting tool every 10 minutes
*/10 * * * * root /usr/lib/sa/sa1 -S DISK 1 1
# 0 * * * * root /usr/lib/sa/sa1 -S DISK 600 6 &
# Generate a daily summary of process accounting at 23:53
53 23 * * * root /usr/lib/sa/sa2 -A
[root@server1 ~]# _
```

Notice in the preceding output that the second uncommented line runs at 11:53 p.m. as the root user.

Many administrative tasks are performed on an hourly, daily, weekly, or monthly basis. If you have a task of this type, you don't need to create a system cron table. Instead, you can place a shell script that runs the appropriate commands in one of the following directories:

- Scripts that should be executed hourly in the /etc/cron.hourly/ directory
- Scripts that should be executed daily in the /etc/cron.daily/ directory
- Scripts that should be executed weekly in the /etc/cron.weekly/ directory
- Scripts that should be executed monthly in the /etc/cron.monthly/ directory

The cron daemon runs the /etc/cron.d/0hourly script, which executes the contents of the /etc/cron.hourly/ directory one minute past the hour, every hour on the hour. The /etc/cron.hourly/0anacron file starts the anacron daemon, which then executes the contents of the /etc/cron.daily/, /etc/cron.weekly/, and /etc/cron.monthy/ directories at the times specified in /etc/anacrontab.

Chapter Summary

- Processes are programs that are executing on the system.
- User processes are run in the same terminal as the user who executed them, whereas daemon processes are system processes that do not run on a terminal.
- Every process has a parent process associated with it and, optionally, several child processes.
- Process information is stored in the /proc filesystem. You can use the ps, pstree, and top commands to view this information.
- Zombie and rogue processes that exist for long periods of time use up system resources and should be killed to improve system performance.
- You can send kill signals to a process using the kill, killall, and top commands.
- The BASH shell creates, or forks, a subshell to execute most commands.

- Processes can be run in the background by appending an & to the command name. The BASH shell assigns each background process a background job ID so that it can be manipulated afterward.

- The priority of a process can be affected indirectly by altering its nice value; nice values range from -20 (high priority) to +19 (low priority). Only the root user can increase the priority of a process.

- You can use the at and cron daemons to schedule commands to run at a later time. The at daemon schedules tasks to occur once at a later time, whereas the cron daemon uses cron tables to schedule tasks to occur repetitively in the future.

Key Terms

/etc/at.allow   A file listing all users who can use the at command.

/etc/at.deny   A file listing all users who cannot access the at command.

/etc/cron.allow   A file listing all users who can use the cron command.

/etc/cron.d   A directory that contains additional system cron tables.

/etc/cron.deny   A file listing all users who cannot access the cron command.

/etc/crontab   The default system cron table.

/var/spool/at   A directory that stores the information used to schedule commands using the at daemon.

/var/spool/cron   A directory that stores user cron tables.

at command   The command used to schedule commands and tasks to run at a preset time in the future.

at daemon (atd)   The system daemon that executes tasks at a future time; it is configured with the at command.

background (bg) command   The command used to run a foreground process in the background.

background process   A process that does not require the BASH shell to wait for its termination. Upon execution, the user receives the BASH shell prompt immediately.

child process   A process that was started by another process (parent process).

cron daemon (crond)   The system daemon that executes tasks repetitively in the future and that is configured using cron tables.

crontab command   The command used to view and edit user cron tables.

cron table   A file specifying tasks to be run by the cron daemon; there are user cron tables and system cron tables.

daemon process   A system process that is not associated with a terminal.

foreground (fg) command   The command used to run a background process in the foreground.

foreground process   A process for which the BASH shell that executed it must wait for its termination.

forking   The act of creating a new BASH shell child process from a parent BASH shell process.

jobs command   The command used to see the list of background processes running in the current shell.

`killall` **command**   The command that kills all instances of a process by command name.

`kill` **command**   The command used to kill or terminate a process.

kill signal   The type of signal sent to a process by the `kill` command; different kill signals affect processes in different ways.

`nice` **command**   The command used to change the priority of a process as it is started.

nice value   The value that indirectly represents the priority of a process; the higher the value, the lower the priority.

parent process   A process that has started other processes (child processes).

parent process ID (PPID)   The PID of the parent process that created the current process.

process   A program currently loaded into physical memory and running on the system.

process ID (PID)   A unique identifier assigned to every process as it begins.

process priority   A number assigned to a process, used to determine how many time slices on the processor that process will receive; the higher the number, the lower the priority.

process state   The current state of the process on the processor; most processes are in the sleeping or running state.

program   A structured set of commands stored in an executable file on a filesystem. A program can be executed to create a process.

`ps` **command**   The command used to obtain information about processes currently running on the system.

`pstree` **command**   A command that displays processes according to their lineage, starting from the init daemon.

`renice` **command**   The command used to alter the nice value of a process currently running on the system.

rogue process   A process that has become faulty in some way and continues to consume far more system resources than it should.

time slice   The amount of time a process is given on a CPU in a multiprocessing operating system.

`top` **command**   The command used to give real-time information about the most active processes on the system; it can also be used to renice or kill processes.

trapping   The process of ignoring a kill signal.

user process   A process begun by a user and which runs on a terminal.

zombie process   A process that has finished executing, but whose parent has not yet released its PID; the zombie retains a spot in the kernel's process table.

Review Questions

1. Which command entered without arguments is used to display a list of processes running in the current shell?

   a. `ppid`

   b. `list`

   c. `pid`

   d. `ps`

2. Which of the following statements is true? (Choose all that apply.)

 a. If /etc/at.allow exists, only users listed in it can use the `at` command.

 b. If /etc/cron.allow exists, only users listed in it can use the `cron` command.

 c. If /etc/cron.deny exists and /etc/cron.allow does not exist, any user not listed in /etc/cron.deny can use the `cron` command.

 d. If /etc/cron.allow and /etc/cron.deny exist, only users listed in the former can use the `cron` command, and any users listed in the latter are denied access to the `cron` command.

 e. If a user is listed in both /etc/cron.allow and /etc/cron.deny, then /etc/cron.deny takes precedence and the user cannot access the `crontab` command.

3. Where are individual user tasks scheduled to run with the cron daemon stored?

 a. /etc/crontab

 b. /etc/cron/(the user's login name)

 c. /var/spool/cron

 d. /var/spool/cron/(the user's login name)

4. Which process will always have a PID of 1 and a PPID of 0?

 a. the kernel itself

 b. ps

 c. init

 d. top

5. A process spawning or initiating another process is referred to as _____.

 a. a child process

 b. forking

 c. branching

 d. parenting

6. As daemon processes are not associated with terminals, you must use the −e switch with the `ps` command to view them. True or False?

7. Which of the following commands will most likely increase the chance of a process receiving more time slices?

 a. `renice 0`

 b. `renice 15`

 c. `renice -12`

 d. `renice 19`

8. How can you bypass the wait function and send a user process to the background?

   a. This cannot happen once a process is executing; it can be done only when the command is started by placing an ampersand (&) after it.

   b. This cannot happen; only daemon processes can run in the background.

   c. You can use the ps command.

   d. You can use the Ctrl+z key combination and the bg command.

9. The at command is used to _____.

   a. schedule processes to run periodically in the background

   b. schedule processes to run periodically on a recurring basis in the future

   c. schedule processes to run at a single instance in the future

   d. schedule processes to run in the foreground

10. What command is used to view and modify user jobs scheduled to run with cron?

    a. crontab

    b. cron

    c. ps

    d. sched

11. Every process has a process ID and a _____.

    a. fork process

    b. daemon

    c. child process

    d. parent process ID

12. The killall command terminates _____.

    a. all instances of a process with the same PPID

    b. all instances of a process with the same PID

    c. all instances of a process with the same priority

    d. all instances of a process with the same name

13. Nice values are used to affect process priorities using a range between _____.

    a. 0 and 20

    b. 0 and -19

    c. -19 and 20

    d. -20 and 19

14. What is the name given to a process not associated with a terminal?

    a. child process

    b. parent process

    c. user process

    d. daemon process

15. To kill a process running in the background, you must place a % character before its process ID. True or False?

16. What kill level signal cannot be trapped?

    a. 1

    b. 9

    c. 3

    d. 15

17. A runaway process that is faulty and consuming mass amounts of system resources _____.

    a. is a zombie process

    b. is an orphaned process

    c. has a PPID of Z

    d. is a rogue process

18. When you run the `ps` command, how are daemon processes recognized?

    a. The terminal is listed as tty0.

    b. There is a question mark in the TTY column.

    c. There is an asterisk in the STIME column.

    d. There is a "d" for daemon in the terminal identification column.

19. Which command is used to gain real-time information about processes running on the system, with the most processor-intensive processes listed at the beginning of the list?

    a. `ps`

    b. `ps -elf`

    c. `top`

    d. `top -l`

20. Which command can be used to see processes running in the background?

    a. `bg`

    b. `jobs`

    c. `ps -%`

    d. `fg`

Hands-On Projects

These projects should be completed in the order given. The hands-on projects presented in this chapter should take a total of three hours to complete. The requirements for this lab include:

- A computer with Fedora 13 installed according to Hands-On Project 2-2

Project 9-1

In this hands-on project, you view characteristics of processes using the ps command.

1. Turn on your computer. After your Linux system has loaded, switch to a command-line terminal (tty2) by pressing **Ctrl+Alt+F2** and log in to the terminal using the user name of **root** and the password of **secret**.

2. At the command prompt, type **ps –ef | more** and press **Enter** to view the first processes started on the entire Linux system.

3. Fill in the following information from the data displayed on the terminal screen after typing the command:

   a. Which process has a Process ID of 1? (PID=1)_____

   b. What character do most processes have in the terminal column (tty)? _____

   c. What does this character in the terminal column indicate?_____

   d. Which user started most of these processes? _____

   e. Most processes that are displayed on the screen are started by a certain parent process indicated in the Parent Process ID column (PPID). Which process is the parent to most processes? _____

   Type **q** at the MORE prompt to quit.

4. At the command prompt, type **ps –el | more** and press **Enter** to view the process states for the first processes started on the entire Linux system.

5. Fill in the following information from the data displayed on the terminal screen after typing the command:

   a. What character exists in the State (S) column for most processes, and what does this character indicate? _____

   b. What range of numbers is it possible to have in the Nice (NI) column? _____

   c. Which processes have the number 4 in the Flag (F) column, and what does this number indicate? _____

   Type **q** at the MORE prompt to quit.

6. At the command prompt, type **ps –el | grep Z** and press **Enter** to display zombie processes on your Linux system. Are there any zombie processes indicated in the State (S) column?

7. Type **exit** and press **Enter** to log out of your shell.

Project 9-2

In this hands-on project, you use kill signals to terminate processes on your system.

1. Switch to a command-line terminal (tty2) by pressing **Ctrl+Alt+F2** and log in to the terminal using the user name of **root** and the password of **secret**.

2. At the command prompt, type **ps –ef | grep bash** and press **Enter** to view the BASH shells that are running in memory on your computer. Record the PID of the BASH shell running in your terminal (tty2): _____.

3. At the command prompt, type **kill –l** and press **Enter** to list the available kill signals that you can send to a process.

4. At the command prompt, type **kill -2 PID** (where PID is the PID that you recorded in Step 2) and press **Enter**. Did your shell terminate?

5. At the command prompt, type **kill -3 PID** (where PID is the PID that you recorded in Step 2) and press **Enter**. Did your shell terminate?

6. At the command prompt, type **kill -15 PID** (where PID is the PID that you recorded in Step 2) and press **Enter**. Did your shell terminate?

7. At the command prompt, type **kill -9 PID** (where PID is the PID that you recorded in Step 2), and press **Enter**. Did your shell terminate? Why did this command work when the others did not?

Project 9-3

In this hands-on project, you run processes in the background, kill them using the kill and killall commands, and change their priorities using the nice and renice commands.

1. Switch to a command-line terminal (tty2) by pressing **Ctrl+Alt+F2** and log in to the terminal using the user name of **root** and the password of **secret**.

2. At the command prompt, type **sleep 6000** and press **Enter** to start the sleep command, which waits 6,000 seconds in the foreground. Do you get your prompt back after you enter this command? Why? Send the process an INT signal by typing the **Ctrl+c** key combination.

3. At the command prompt, type **sleep 6000&** and press **Enter** to start the sleep command, which waits 6,000 seconds in the background. Observe the background Job ID and PID that is returned.

4. Bring the background sleep process to the foreground by typing **fg %1** at the command prompt, and press **Enter**. Send the process an INT signal by typing the **Ctrl+c** key combination.

5. Place another sleep command in memory by typing **sleep 6000&** and pressing **Enter**. Repeat this command three more times to place a total of four sleep commands in memory.

6. At the command prompt, type **jobs** and press **Enter** to view the jobs running in the background. What does the + symbol indicate?

7. At the command prompt, type **kill %** and press **Enter** to terminate the most recent process and view the output.

8. At the command prompt, type **kill %1** and press **Enter** to terminate background job #1 and view the output.

9. At the command prompt, type **killall sleep** and press **Enter** to terminate the remaining sleep processes in memory. Verify that there are no more sleep processes in memory by typing the **jobs** command, and press **Enter**.

10. Place a sleep command in memory by typing **sleep 6000&** at a command prompt and pressing **Enter**.

11. Place a sleep command in memory with a lower priority by typing **nice -n 19 sleep 6000&** at a command prompt and pressing **Enter**.

12. Verify that these two processes have different nice values by typing the command **ps -el | grep sleep** at the command prompt and pressing **Enter**. Record the PID of the process with a nice value of 0: _____.

13. At the command prompt, type **renice +10 PID** (where PID is the PID you recorded in the previous step) to change the priority of the process. Type the command **ps-el | grep sleep** and press **Enter** to verify the new priority.

14. Type **exit** and press **Enter** to log out of your shell.

Project 9-4

In this hands-on project, you view and manage processes using the top command-line utility.

1. Switch to a command-line terminal (tty2) by pressing **Ctrl+Alt+F2** and log in to the terminal using the user name of **root** and the password of **secret**.

2. At the command prompt, type **top** and press **Enter**.

3. From the output on the terminal screen, record the following information:

   a. Number of processes: _____

   b. Number of sleeping processes: _____

   c. Amount of total memory (K): _____

   d. Amount of total swap memory (K): _____

4. While in the top utility, press the **h** key and observe the output. When finished, press any key to return to the previous top output.

5. By observing the output under the COMMAND column on your terminal screen, identify the PID of the top command in the output and record it: _____.

6. Type **r** in the top utility to change the priority of a running process. When asked which process to change (renice), type the PID from the previous question. When asked which value to use, type **10** to lower the priority of the top process to 10. Does this new priority take effect immediately?

7. Type **k** in the top utility to send a kill signal to a process. When asked which process, type the **PID** used in the previous question. When asked which signal to send, type **2** to send an INT signal. Did the top utility terminate?

8. At the command prompt, type **top** and press **Enter**.

9. By observing the output under the COMMAND column on your terminal screen, identify the PID of the top command in the output and record it: _____.

10. Type **k** in the top utility to send a kill signal to a process. When asked which process, type the **PID** from the previous question. When asked which signal to send, type **15** to send a TERM signal. Did the TERM signal allow top to exit cleanly?

11. At the command prompt, type **clear** and press **Enter** to clear the screen.

12. Type **exit** and press **Enter** to log out of your shell.

Project 9-5

In this hands-on project, you schedule processes by using the at and crontab utilities.

1. Switch to a command-line terminal (tty2) by pressing **Ctrl+Alt+F2** and log in to the terminal using the user name of **root** and the password of **secret**.

2. Schedule processes to run one minute in the future by typing the command **at now + 1 minute** at a command prompt, and press **Enter**.

3. When the at> prompt appears, type the word **date** and press **Enter**.

4. When the second at> prompt appears, type the word **who** and press **Enter**.

5. When the third at> prompt appears, press the **Ctrl+d** key combination to finish the scheduling and observe the output. When will your job run? Where will the output of the date and who commands be sent?

6. In approximately one minute, you will receive mail from the at daemon. Check your mail by typing **mail** at the command line and pressing **Enter**. Look for the e-mail with the subject "Output from your job" and record the number: _____.

7. At the & prompt, type the number that corresponds to the e-mail in the previous step, press **Enter**, and observe the output. When finished, type **q** at the & prompt, and press **Enter** to exit the mail program.

8. At the command prompt, type **crontab -l** and press **Enter** to list your cron table. Do you have one?

9. At the command prompt, type **crontab -e** and press **Enter** to edit a new cron table for the root user. When the vi editor appears, add the line:

   30 20 * * 5 /bin/false

10. When you finish typing, save and quit the vi editor and observe the output on the terminal screen.

11. At the command prompt, type **crontab -l** and press **Enter** to list your cron table. When will the /bin/false command run?

12. At the command prompt, type **cat /var/spool/cron/root** and press **Enter** to list your cron table from the cron directory. Is it the same as the output from the previous command?

13. At the command prompt, type **crontab -r** and press **Enter** to remove your cron table.

14. Type **exit** and press **Enter** to log out of your shell.

Project 9-6

In this hands-on project, you view information that is exported by the Linux kernel to the /proc directory.

1. Switch to a command-line terminal (tty2) by pressing **Ctrl+Alt+F2** and log in to the terminal using the user name of **root** and the password of **secret**.

2. At the command prompt, type **cd /proc** and press **Enter** to change your current directory to /proc. Next, type **ls** to list the directory contents and examine the output on the terminal screen. Why are the subdirectories named using numbers?

3. At the command prompt, type **cat meminfo | less** and press **Enter** to list information about total and available memory. How does the value for total memory (MemTotal) compare with the information from Step 3 in Project 9-4?

4. At the command prompt, type **cat swaps** and press **Enter** to list information about total and available swap memory. How does the value for total swap memory (Size) compare with the information from Step 3 in Project 9-4?

5. At the command prompt, type **cd 1** and press **Enter** to enter the subdirectory that contains information about the init daemon (PID = 1).

6. At the command prompt, type **ls** and press **Enter** to list the files in the /proc/1 directory. Next, type **cat status | less** and press **Enter**. What is the state of the init daemon? Does it list the correct PID and PPID?

7. Type **exit** and press **Enter** to log out of your shell.

Discovery Exercises

1. Type the command **sleep 5** at a command prompt and press **Enter**. When did you receive your shell prompt? Explain the events that occurred by referencing Figure 9-3. Next, type **exec sleep 5** at a command prompt and press **Enter**. What happened? Can you explain the results using Figure 9-3? Redraw Figure 9-3 to indicate what happens when a command is directly executed.

2. Using the man or info pages, research four more options to the ps command. What processes does each option display? What information is given about each process?

3. Log in to the GNOME desktop and open a command-line terminal. At a shell prompt, type **xeyes** to execute the Xeyes program. Does the terminal window stay open? Click the terminal window to bring it to the foreground. Do you see your shell prompt? Why? Close your terminal window by clicking the X symbol in the upper-right corner. What happened to the Xeyes program? Why?

   Next, open another command-line terminal and type **xeyes&** at the command prompt to execute the Xeyes program in the background. Click the terminal window to bring it to the foreground. Do you see your shell prompt? Why? Close your terminal window by clicking the X symbol in the upper-right corner. What happened to the Xeyes program? Why?

4. You are the systems administrator for a large trust company. Most of the Linux servers in the company host databases that are accessed frequently by company employees. One particular Linux server has been reported as being very slow today. Upon further investigation using the top utility, you found a rogue process that is wasting a great deal of system resources. Unfortunately, the rogue process is a database maintenance program and should be killed with caution. Which kill signal would you send this process and why? If the rogue process traps this signal, which other kill signals would you try? Which command could you use as a last resort to kill the rogue process?

5. Write the lines that you could use in your user cron table to schedule the /bin/ myscript command to run:

   a. Every Wednesday afternoon at 2:15 p.m.

   b. Every hour on the hour every day of the week

   c. Every 15 minutes on the first of every month

   d. Only on February 25th at 6:00 p.m.

   e. On the first Monday of every month at 12:10 p.m.

## chapter 10

Common Administrative Tasks

After completing this chapter, you will be able to:

- Set up, manage, and print to printers on a Linux system
- Understand the purpose of log files and how they are administered
- Create, modify, manage, and delete user and group accounts

In previous chapters, you learned how to administer filesystems, X Windows, system startup, and processes. In this chapter, you examine other essential areas of Linux administration. First, you learn about the print process and how to administer and set up printers, followed by a discussion on managing log files using the System Log Daemon and the logrotate utility. Finally, you examine system databases that store user and group information and the utilities that can be used to create, modify, and delete user and group accounts on a Linux system.

Printer Administration

Printing work files is commonly required by most users on a Linux system, and printing log files and system configuration information is good procedure in case of a system failure. Thus, a firm understanding of how to set up, manage, and print to printers is vital for those who set up and administer Linux servers.

The Common UNIX Printing System

Today, the most common printing system used on Linux computers is the **Common Unix Printing System (CUPS)**. Fundamental to using CUPS on a Linux system is an understanding of the process by which information is sent to a printer. A set of information that is sent to a printer at the same time is called a **print job**. Print jobs can consist of a file, several files, or the output of a command. To send a print job to a printer, you must first use the **lp** command and specify what to print.

Next, the **cups daemon (cupsd)** assigns the print job a unique **print job ID** and places a copy of the print job into a temporary directory on the filesystem called the **print queue**, provided the printer is **accepting** requests. If the printer is **rejecting** requests, the cups daemon prints an error message stating that the printer is not accepting print jobs.

Accepting print jobs into a print queue is commonly called **spooling** or **queuing.**

The print queue for a printer is typically /var/spool/cups. Regardless of how many printers you have on your Linux system, all print jobs are sent to the same directory.

After a print job is in the print queue, it is ready to be printed. If the printer is **enabled**, and ready to accept the print job, the cups daemon then sends the print job from the print queue to the printer and removes the copy of the print job in the print queue. Conversely, if the printer is **disabled**, the print job remains in the print queue.

Sending print jobs from a print queue to a printer is commonly called **printing**.

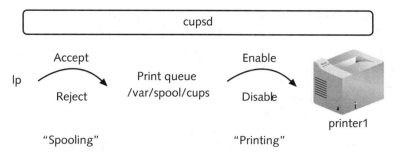

Figure 10-1 The print process

Source: Course Technology/Cengage Learning

An example of this process for a printer called printer1 is illustrated in Figure 10-1.

To see a list of all printers on the system and their status, you can use the −t (total) option to the **lpstat command**, as shown in the following output:

```
[root@server1 ~]# lpstat -t
scheduler is running
system default destination: printer1
device for printer1: parallel:/dev/lp0
printer1 accepting requests since Thu 26 Aug 2010 08:34:30 AM EDT
printer printer1 is idle. enabled since Thu 26 Aug 2010 08:42:23 AM EDT
[root@server1 ~]# _
```

The preceding output indicates that there is only one printer on the system, called printer1, which prints to a printer connected to the first parallel port on the computer (parallel:/dev/lp0). The output also tells you that there are no print jobs in its print queue and that the cups daemon (scheduler) is running and accepting jobs into the print queue for this printer. Also, the cups daemon sends print jobs from the print queue to the printer because the printer is enabled.

You can manipulate the status of a printer using either the **cupsaccept, cupsreject, cupsenable,** or **cupsdisable** command followed by the printer name. Thus, to enable spooling and disable printing for the printer called printer1, you can use the following commands:

```
[root@server1 ~]# cupsaccept printer1
[root@server1 ~]# cupsdisable printer1
[root@server1 ~]# lpstat -t
scheduler is running
system default destination: printer1
device for printer1: parallel:/dev/lp0
printer1 accepting requests since Thu 26 Aug 2010 08:51:21 AM EDT
printer printer1 disabled since Thu 26 Aug 2010 08:51:21 AM EDT -
        Paused
[root@server1 ~]# _
```

Any print jobs now sent to the printer called *printer1* are sent to the print queue but remain in the print queue until the printer is started again.

10

You can also use the −r option to the cupsdisable and cupsreject commands to specify a reason for the action, as shown in the following output:

```
[root@server1 ~]# cupsdisable -r "Changing toner cartridge" printer1
[root@server1 ~]# lpstat -t
scheduler is running
system default destination: printer1
device for printer1: parallel:/dev/lp0
printer1 accepting requests since Thu 26 Aug 2010 08:51:21 AM EDT
printer printer1 disabled since Thu 26 Aug 2010 08:51:21 AM EDT –
        Changing toner cartridge
[root@server1 ~]# _
```

Managing Print Jobs

Recall that you create a print job by using the lp command. To print a copy of the /etc/inittab file to the printer called printer1 shown in earlier examples, you can use the following command, which returns a print job ID that you can use to manipulate the print job afterward:

```
[root@server1 ~]# lp -d printer1 /etc/inittab
request id is printer1-1 (1 file(s))
[root@server1 ~]# _
```

The lp command uses the −d option to specify the destination printer name. If this option is omitted, the lp command assumes the default printer on the system. Because printer1 is the only printer on the system and, hence, is the default printer, the command lp /etc/inittab is equivalent to the one used in the preceding output.

You can set the default printer for all users on your system by using the lpoptions −d *printername* command, where *printername* is the name of the default printer. This information is stored in the /etc/cups/lpoptions file.

Alternatively, each user on a Linux system can specify his own default printer by adding the line default *printername* to the .lpoptions file in his home directory, where *printername* is the name of the default printer. Alternatively, you can use the PRINTER or LPDEST variable to set the default printer. For example, to specify printer2 as the default printer, you can add either the line export PRINTER=printer2 or the line export LPDEST=printer2 to an environment file in your home directory such as .bash_profile.

Table 10-1 lists some common options to the lp command.

You can also specify several files to be printed using a single lp command by specifying the files as arguments. In this case, only one print job is created to print all of the files. To print the files /etc/hosts and /etc/issue to the printer printer1, you can execute the following command:

```
[root@server1 ~]# lp -d printer1 /etc/hosts /etc/issue
request id is printer1-2 (2 file(s))
[root@server1 ~]# _
```

Option	Description
-d *printername*	Specifies the name of the printer to send the print job to
-i *print job ID*	Specifies a certain print job ID to modify
-n *number*	Prints a certain number of copies, where *number* can be any number
-m	Mails you confirmation of print job completion
-o *option*	Specifies certain printing options. Common printing options include the following: cpi=*number*—Specifies the number of characters per inch, where *number* is the number of characters landscape—Prints in landscape orientation number-up=number—Prints the number of pages on a single page, where *number* is 1, 2, or 4 sides=*string*—Sets double-sided printing, where *string* is either "two-sided-short-edge" or "two-sided-long-edge"
-q *priority*	Specifies a print job priority from 1 (low priority) to 100 (high priority); by default, all print jobs have a priority of 50

Table 10-1 Common options to the lp command

The lp command accepts information from standard input; thus, you can place the lp command at the end of a pipe to print information. To print a list of logged-in users, you can use the following pipe:

```
[root@server1 ~]# who | lp -d printer1
request id is printer1-3 (1 file(s))
[root@server1 ~]# _
```

To see a list of print jobs in the queue for printer1, you can use the lpstat command. Without arguments, this command displays all jobs in the print queue that you have printed:

```
[root@server1 ~]# lpstat
printer1-1        root         2048     Thu 26 Aug 2010 08:54:18 AM EDT
printer1-2        root         3072     Thu 26 Aug 2010 08:54:33 AM EDT
printer1-3        root         1024     Thu 26 Aug 2010 08:54:49 AM EDT
[root@server1 ~]# _
```

Table 10-2 lists common options to the lpstat command.

To remove a print job that is in the print queue, you can use the **cancel command** followed by the print job IDs of the jobs to remove. To remove the print job IDs printer1-1 and printer1-2 created earlier, you can use the following command:

```
[root@server1 ~]# cancel printer1-1 printer1-2
[root@server1 ~]# lpstat
printer1-3        root         3072     Thu 26 Aug 2010 08:54:49 AM EDT
[root@server1 ~]# _
```

Option	Description
-a	Displays a list of printers that are accepting print jobs
-d	Displays the default destination printer
-o *printername*	Displays the print jobs in the print queue for `printername` only
-p	Displays a list of printers that are enabled
-r	Shows whether the cups daemon (scheduler) is running
-t	Shows all information about printers and their print jobs

Table 10-2 Common options to the `lpstat` command

You can instead remove all jobs started by a certain user; simply specify the -u option to the `cancel` command followed by the user name. To remove all jobs in a print queue, you can use the -a option to the `cancel` command, as shown in the following example:

```
[root@server1 ~]# cancel -a
[root@server1 ~]# lpstat
[root@server1 ~]# _
```

Not all users might be allowed access to a certain printer. As a result, you can restrict access to certain printers by using the **lpadmin command**. For example, to deny all users other than root and user1 the ability to print to the printer1 printer created earlier, you can use the following command:

```
[root@server1 ~]# lpadmin –u allow:root,user1 –u deny:all –d printer1
[root@server1 ~]# _
```

The LPD Printing System

Although CUPS is the preferred printing system for Linux computers today, many older Linux computers use the traditional **Line Printer Daemon (LPD)** printing system. In this printing system, the **lpr command** is used to print documents to the print queue much like the `lp` command; the **lpc command** can be used to view the status of printers; the **lpq command** can be used to view print jobs in the print queue, much like the `lpstat` command; and the **lprm command** can be used to remove print jobs, much like the `cancel` command.

For those users who are used to using the LPD printing system, CUPS contains versions of the `lpr`, `lpc`, `lpq`, and `lprm` commands. The following output displays the status of all printers on the system, prints two copies of /etc/inittab to printer1, views the print job in the queue, and removes the print job:

```
[root@server1 ~]# lpc status
printer1:
        printing is enabled
        queuing is enabled
```

```
        no entries
        daemon present
[root@server1 ~]# lpr -#2 -P printer1 /etc/inittab
[root@server1 ~]# lpq
printer1 is ready and printing
Rank    Owner   Job   File(s)                  Total Size
1st     root    1     inittab                  2048 bytes
[root@server1 ~]# lprm 1
[root@server1 ~]# lpq
printer1 is ready
no entries
[root@server1 ~]# _
```

Configuring Printers

Recall that the core component of printing is the cups daemon (cupsd), which accepts print jobs into a queue and sends them to the printer. The file that contains settings for cupsd is **/etc/cups/cupsd.conf**, and the file that contains the configuration information for each printer installed on the system is **/etc/cups/printers.conf**. Instead of editing these files manually, you can use the **Printer Configuration tool**, as shown in Figure 10-2. To access this tool, you can type `system-config-printer` in a terminal screen in a desktop environment or navigate to the System menu, Administration, Printing within the GNOME Desktop Environment.

The Printer Configuration tool depicted in Figure 10-2 indicates that there are no configured printers on the system. To add a printer, you can click the Add button and specify the printer device, as shown in Figure 10-3.

The Printer Configuration tool prompts you to supply the root user password whenever you attempt to perform an operation that requires special privileges, such as accessing device files or printer configuration.

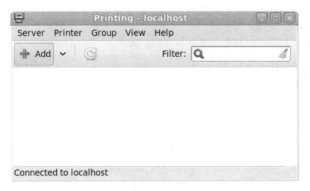

Figure 10-2 The Printer Configuration tool

Source: Course Technology/Cengage Learning

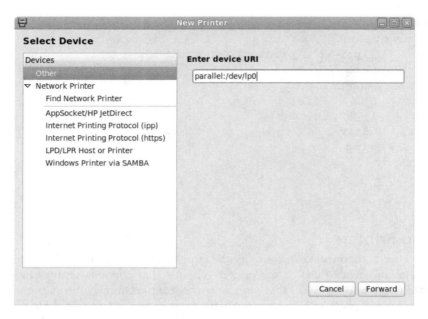

Figure 10-3 Specifying the printer device

Source: Course Technology/Cengage Learning

 Most printers are **Plug and Play (PnP)** compatible and are automatically configured with a default name when they are plugged into the system. As a result, you do not need to add these printers within the Printer Configuration tool. Instead, you can use the Printer Configuration tool to modify their settings if required.

As shown in Figure 10-3, you can choose to print to a printer that is connected to the network using Hewlett-Packard JetDirect technology, or to a printer that is shared on a remote computer across a network with the **Internet Printing Protocol (IPP)**, the Line Printer Daemon (LPD), or the Windows (SAMBA) printing service. If you want to print to a local printer that does not support PnP, you must select Other in Figure 10-3 and specify the **Uniform Resource Identifier (URI)** for the device. The URI identifies the type and path of a device; in Figure 10-3, the URI `parallel:/dev/lp0` specifies the parallel printer port device file /dev/lp0.

After you click Forward in Figure 10-3, the device you select is queried to determine the printer model so that CUPS can locate the appropriate print driver. If the printer model cannot be determined, you are prompted to manually select the manufacturer and model of your printer, as shown in Figures 10-4 and 10-5.

Regardless of whether your printer driver was automatically or manually selected, you will then see the screen shown in Figure 10-6, where you can select a name for your printer that can be used to identify it within programs and commands. In addition, you can optionally specify a description and location that will appear next to the printer name when you search for a printer or display its properties. After you have made your selections, click Apply. At this point, you are prompted to optionally print a test page. Next, your printer is added to the system, ready for use, as shown in Figure 10-7.

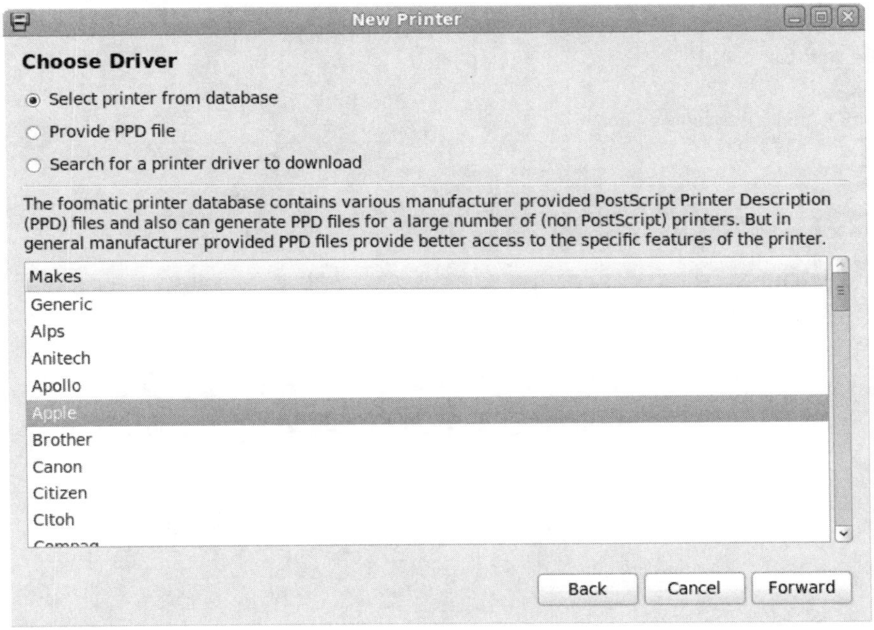

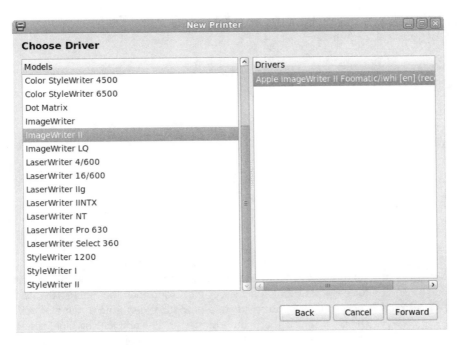

Figure 10-4 Selecting a printer manufacturer

Source: Course Technology/Cengage Learning

Figure 10-5 Selecting a printer model

Source: Course Technology/Cengage Learning

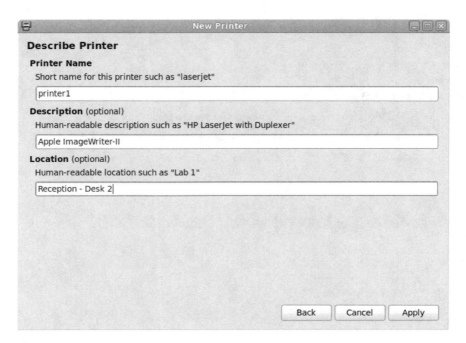

Figure 10-6 Completing the creation of a new printer

Source: Course Technology/Cengage Learning

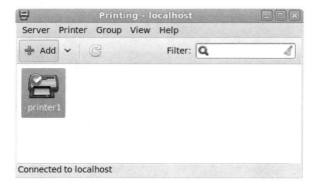

Figure 10-7 Viewing installed printers

Source: Course Technology/Cengage Learning

If you have a large number of installed printers on your system, you can group them into subfolders within the Printer Configuration tool for easy viewing. Simply select the Group menu in Figure 10-7 and choose New Group to create a new subfolder using a name of your choice. You can then add a printer to the subfolder by highlighting your printer in Figure 10-7, selecting the Printer menu, and choosing Add to Group followed by the desired subfolder name.

After you have added a printer to the system, you can modify its properties by highlighting the printer in Figure 10-7, selecting the Printer menu, and clicking Properties. This opens the Printer Properties window shown in Figure 10-8, which allows you to modify the general information regarding the printer, change the print device, and perform tests.

To manage the status of the printer (enable/disable, accept/reject), share the printer using IPP, choose an error action, and configure banner pages (cover pages printed at the beginning of each print job), click Policies in the Printer Properties window shown in Figure 10-8. This displays the options shown in Figure 10-9. By default, all users on your system have the

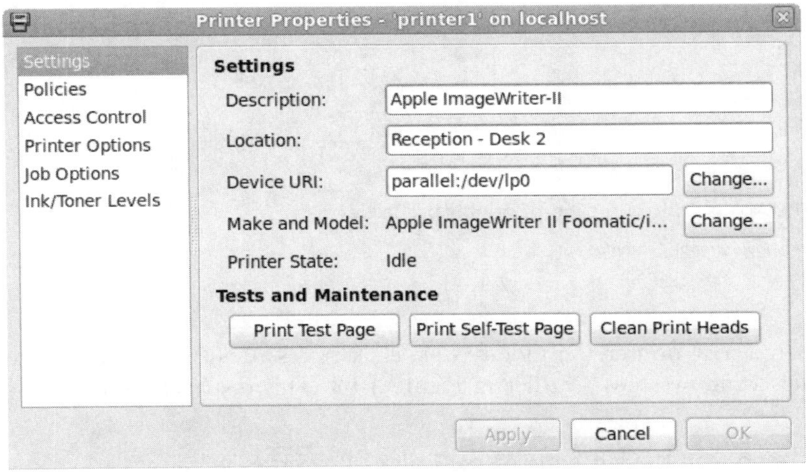

Figure 10-8 Modifying printer properties

Source: Course Technology/Cengage Learning

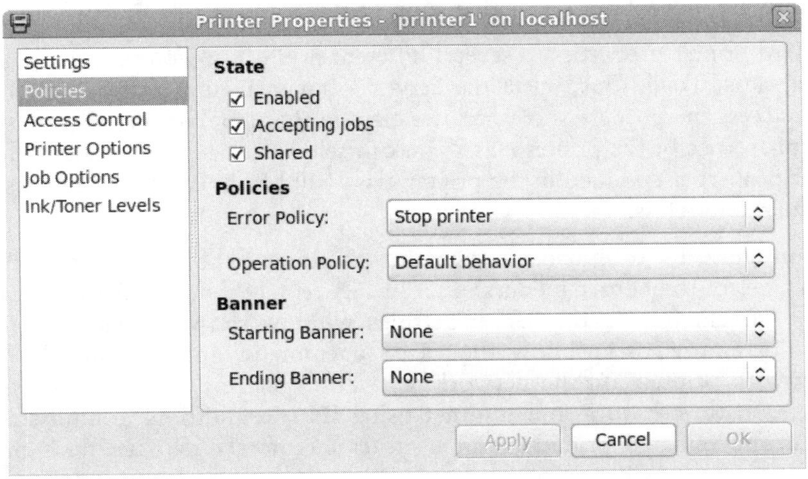

Figure 10-9 The Policies section of printer properties

Source: Course Technology/Cengage Learning

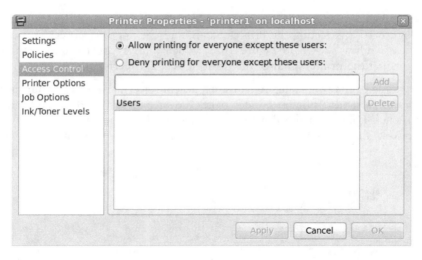

Figure 10-10 The Access Control section of printer properties

Source: Course Technology/Cengage Learning

ability to print to a new printer. To modify this, click Access Control in the left pane of the Printer Properties window shown earlier in Figure 10-8. This displays the options shown in Figure 10-10.

The remaining options in the left pane of the Printer Properties window vary, depending on the printer model; different printer models have different configurable features. You can use Printer Options to configure page size and resolution for your printer model, and Job Options to set the default options submitted with each print job. Finally, you can use Ink/Toner Levels to display detailed information regarding the remaining ink or toner within your printer; however, not all printer models support this feature.

To apply standard printer properties to several different printers on your system, you need to create a **printer class**. To do this, select the Server menu in Figure 10-7 and choose New, Class. You can access the properties of a printer class in the same manner that you would a printer. In the properties of the printer class, you can select the Members node to add members. Any other properties specified in the printer class will be applied to all printers that are a member of the printer class.

The Printer Configuration tool also allows you to configure the properties of the CUPS daemon. Simply select the Server menu shown in Figure 10-7, choose Settings, and enter the appropriate information in the Server Settings window shown in Figure 10-11. The options shown in Figure 10-11 allow the CUPS daemon to automatically browse and add shared network printers on the network, as well as share printers on the system to other computers on the network and Internet using IPP. In addition, administrators can remotely create and manage printers, and users can remotely manage their print jobs using a Web browser on TCP port 631 by navigating to *http://servername:631*, as shown in Figure 10-12. At this site, click the Administration tab, and then provide the root username and password to begin creating and managing printers. This site is also useful for users, who can use the Jobs tab to log in, then view and manage their own print jobs.

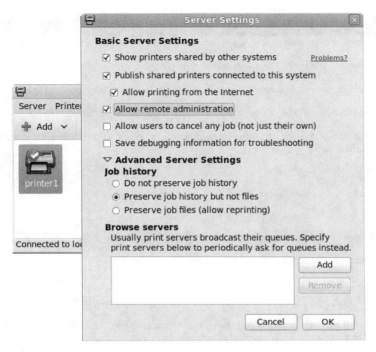

Figure 10-11 Configuring CUPS settings

Source: Course Technology/Cengage Learning

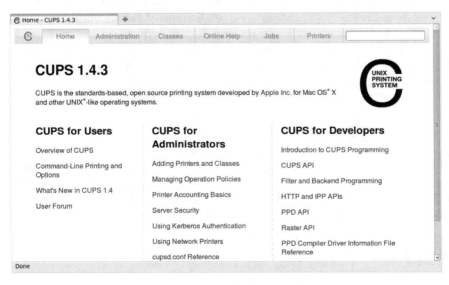

Figure 10-12 The CUPS remote administration Web page

Source: Course Technology/Cengage Learning

Log File	Description
boot.log	Contains basic information regarding daemon startup obtained during system initialization
cron	Contains information and error messages generated by the cron and at daemons
dmesg	Contains detected hardware information obtained during system startup
maillog	Contains information and error messages generated by the sendmail daemon
secure	Contains information and error messages regarding network access generated by daemons such as sshd and xinetd
wtmp	Contains a history of all login sessions
rpmpkgs yum.log	Contains a list of packages installed by the Red Hat Package Manager and related error messages
xferlog	Contains information and error messages generated by the FTP daemon
Xorg.0.log XFree86	Contains information and error messages generated by X Windows
lastlog	Contains a list of users and their last login time; must be viewed using the lastlog command
messages	Contains detailed information regarding daemon startup obtained at system initialization as well as important system messages produced after system initialization

Table 10-3 Common Linux log files found in /var/log

Log File Administration

To identify and troubleshoot problems on a Linux system, you must view the events that occur over time. Because administrators cannot observe all events that take place on a Linux system, most daemons record information and error messages to files stored on the filesystem. These files are referred to as **log files** and are typically stored in the **/var/log** directory. Many programs store their log files in subdirectories of the /var/log directory. For example, the /var/log/samba directory contains the log files created by the samba file-sharing daemons. Table 10-3 lists some common log files found in the /var/log directory and their descriptions.

The System Log Daemon

The logging of most events is handled centrally in Linux via the **System Log Daemon (rsyslogd)**. When this daemon is loaded upon system startup, it creates a socket (/dev/log) for other system processes to write to. It then reads any information written to this socket and saves the information in the appropriate log file according to entries in the **/etc/rsyslog.conf** file. A sample /etc/rsyslog.conf file is shown in the following output:

```
[root@server1 ~]# cat /etc/rsyslog.conf
#rsyslog v3 config file

# if you experience problems, check
# http://www.rsyslog.com/troubleshoot for assistance
```

```
#### MODULES ####

$ModLoad imuxsock.so    # provides support for local system logging
(e.g. via logger command)
$ModLoad imklog.so      # provides kernel logging support (previously done
by rklogd)
#$ModLoad immark.so     # provides --MARK-- message capability

# Provides UDP syslog reception
#$ModLoad imudp.so
#$UDPServerRun 514

# Provides TCP syslog reception
#$ModLoad imtcp.so
#$InputTCPServerRun 514

#### GLOBAL DIRECTIVES ####

# Use default timestamp format
$ActionFileDefaultTemplate RSYSLOG_TraditionalFileFormat
# File syncing capability is disabled by default. This feature is usually
not required,
# not useful and an extreme performance hit
#$ActionFileEnableSync on

#### RULES ####
# Log all kernel messages to the console.
# Logging much else clutters up the screen.
#kern.*                                          /dev/console

# Log anything (except mail) of level info or higher.
# Don't log private authentication messages!
*.info;mail.none;news.none;authpriv.none;cron.none    /var/log/messages

# The authpriv file has restricted access.
authpriv.*                                       /var/log/secure

# Log all the mail messages in one place.
mail.*                                           -/var/log/maillog

# Log cron stuff
cron.*                                           /var/log/cron

# Everybody gets emergency messages
*.emerg                                          *
```

10

```
# Save news errors of level crit and higher in a special file.
uucp,news.crit                                  /var/log/spooler

# Save boot messages also to boot.log
local7.*                                        /var/log/boot.log

# ### begin forwarding rule ###
# The statement between the begin ... end define a SINGLE forwarding
# rule. They belong together, do NOT split them. If you create multiple
# forwarding rules, duplicate the whole block!
# Remote Logging (we use TCP for reliable delivery)

#
# An on-disk queue is created for this action. If the remote host is
# down, messages are spooled to disk and sent when it is up again.
#$WorkDirectory /var/spppl/rsyslog # where to place spool files
#$ActionQueueFileName fwdRule1 # unique name prefix for spool files
#$ActionQueueMaxDiskSpace 1g   # 1gb space limit
#$ActionQueueSaveOnShutdown on # save messages to disk on shutdown
#$ActionQueueType LinkedList   # run asynchronously
#$ActionResumeRetryCount -1    # infinite retries if host is down
# remote host is: name/ip:port, e.g. 192.168.0.1:514, port optional
#*.* @@remote-host:514
# ### end of the forwarding rule ###

#
# INN
#
news.=crit                                  /var/log/news/news.crit
news.=err                                   /var/log/news/news.err
news.notice                                 /var/log/news/news.notice
news.=debug                                 /var/log/news/news.debug
[root@server1 ~]# _
```

 On legacy Linux systems, the System Log Daemon is represented by syslogd and configured using the /etc/syslog.conf file.

Any line that starts with a # character is a comment in the /etc/rsyslog.conf file. All other entries have the following format:

```
facility.priority     /var/log/logfile
```

The **facility** is the area of the system to listen to, whereas the **priority** refers to the importance of the information. For example, a facility of kern and a priority of warning indicates that the System Log Daemon should listen for kernel messages with a priority of warning, as well as kernel messages with more serious priorities. When found, the System Log Daemon places these messages in the /var/log/logfile file. The aforementioned entry would read:

```
kern.warning        /var/log/logfile
```

To only log warning messages from the kernel to the /var/log/logfile, you can use the following entry instead:

```
kern.=warning        /var/log/logfile
```

Alternatively, you can log all error messages from the kernel to /var/log/logfile by using the * wildcard, as shown in the following entry:

```
kern.*        /var/log/logfile
```

In addition, you can specify multiple facilities and priorities; to log all error messages except warnings from the kernel to the /var/log/logfile, you can use the following entry:

```
kern.*;kern.!=warn        /var/log/logfile
```

To log all error messages from the kernel and news daemons, you can use the following entry:

```
kern,news.*        /var/log/logfile
```

To log all warnings from all facilities except for the kernel, you can use the "none" keyword, as shown in the following entry:

```
*.=warn;kern.none        /var/log/logfile
```

Table 10-4 describes the different facilities available and their descriptions.

Facility	Description
auth or security	Specifies messages from the login system, such as the login program, the getty program, and the su command
authpriv	Specifies messages from the login system when authenticating users across the network or to system databases
cron	Specifies messages from the cron and at daemons
daemon	Specifies messages from system daemons, such as the FTP daemon
kern	Specifies messages from the Linux kernel
lpr	Specifies messages from the printing system (lpd)
mail	Specifies messages from the e-mail system (sendmail)
mark	Specifies time stamps used by syslogd; used internally only
news	Specifies messages from the Inter Network News daemon and other USENET daemons
syslog	Specifies messages from the syslog daemon
user	Specifies messages from user processes
uucp	Specifies messages from the uucp (UNIX to UNIX copy) daemon
local0-7	Specifies local messages; these are not used by default but can be defined for custom use

Table 10-4 Facilities used by the System Log Daemon

Priority	Description
debug	Indicates all information from a certain facility
info	Indicates normal information messages as a result of system operations
notice	Indicates information that should be noted for future reference, yet does not indicate a problem
warning or warn	Indicates messages that might be the result of an error but are not critical to system operations
error or err	Indicates all other error messages not described by other priorities
crit	Indicates system critical errors such as hard disk failure
alert	Indicates an error that should be rectified immediately, such as a corrupt system database
emerg or panic	Indicates very serious system conditions that would normally be broadcast to all users

Table 10-5   Priorities used by the System Log Daemon

Table 10-5 displays the different priorities available listed in ascending order.

The /etc/rsyslog.conf file may also send logging information to another computer using the format `facility.priority @hostname:portnumber`; however, the remote computer must have the modules that listen on either the TCP or UDP protocol uncommented in the /etc/rsyslog.conf file. For example, by uncommenting the $ModLoad, $UDPServerRun, and $InputTCPServerRun lines shown below in the /etc/rsyslog.conf file, you allow your system to accept incoming requests from another System Log Daemon on TCP and UDP port 514 (the default System Log Daemon port):

```
# Provides UDP syslog reception
#$ModLoad imudp.so
#$UDPServerRun 514

# Provides TCP syslog reception
#$ModLoad imtcp.so
#$InputTCPServerRun 514
```

Managing Log Files

Although log files can contain important system information, they might take up unnecessary space on the filesystem over time. Thus, it is important to clear the contents of log files over time.

Do not remove log files, because the permissions and ownership will be removed as well.

Before clearing log files, it is good form to print them and store them in a safe place for future reference. To clear a log file, recall that you can use a > redirection symbol. The following commands display the size of the /var/log/messages log file before and after it has been printed and cleared:

```
[root@server1 ~]# ls -l /var/log/messages
-rw-------    1 root     root     21705 Aug 27 10:52 /var/log/messages
[root@server1 ~]# lp -d printer1 /var/log/messages
[root@server1 ~]# >/var/log/messages
[root@server1 ~]# ls -l /var/log/messages
-rw-------    1 root     root         0 Aug 27 10:52 /var/log/messages
[root@server1 ~]# _
```

You can also schedule commands to print and clear log files on a repetitive basis using the cron daemon.

Alternatively, you can schedule the **logrotate command** to back up and clear log files from entries stored in the **/etc/logrotate.conf** file and files stored in the /etc/logrotate.d directory. The logrotate command typically renames (or rotates) log files on a cyclic basis; a log file called test.log is renamed test.log.YYYYMMDD, where YYYY is the year, MM is the month, and DD is the day. Next, a new test.log is created to accept system information. You can specify the number of log files that logrotate keeps. If logrotate is configured to keep only two copies of old log files, then after two log rotations, the oldest log file will automatically be removed.

An example of the /etc/logrotate.conf file is shown in the following output:

```
[root@server1 ~]# cat /etc/logrotate.conf
# see "man logrotate" for details
# rotate log files weekly
weekly

# keep 4 weeks worth of backlogs
rotate 4

# create new (empty) log files after rotating old ones
create

# use date as a suffix of the rotated file
dateext

# uncomment this if you want your log files compressed
#compress

# RPM packages drop log rotation information into this directory
include /etc/logrotate.d

# no packages own wtmp and btmp -- we'll rotate them here
/var/log/wtmp {
    monthly
    create 0664 root utmp
    minsize 1M
```

10

```
        rotate  1
}

/var/log/btmp {
    missingok
    monthly
    create 0600 root utmp
    rotate 1
}

# system-specific logs may be also be configured here.
[root@server1 ~]# _
```

In the preceding output, any # character indicates a comment and is ignored. The other lines indicate that log files contained in this file and all other files in the /etc/logrotate.d directory (include /etc/logrotate.d) are rotated on a weekly basis unless otherwise specified (weekly) using a date extension (dateext), and up to four weeks of log files will be kept (rotate 4).

The bottom of the /etc/logrotate.conf file has two entries that override these values. For the file /var/log/wtmp, this rotation occurs monthly instead of weekly, only if the size of the log file is greater than 1MB. Only one old log file is kept, and the new log file created has the permissions 0664(rw-rw-r--), the owner root, and the group utmp. For the file /var/log/btmp, this rotation occurs monthly instead of weekly, and no errors are reported if the log file is missing. Only one old log file is kept, and the new log file created has the permissions 0600 (rw-------), the owner root, and the group utmp.

Most rotation information within /etc/logrotate.conf is overridden from files stored in the /etc/logrotate.d directory. Take the file /etc/logrotate.d/psacct as an example:

```
[root@server1 ~]# cat /etc/logrotate.d/psacct
# Logrotate file for psacct RPM

/var/account/pacct {
    compress
    delaycompress
    notifempty
    daily
    rotate 31
    create 0600 root root
    postrotate
        if /etc/init.d/psacct status >/dev/null 2>&1; then
            /usr/sbin/accton /var/account/pacct
        fi
    endscript
}
[root@server1 ~]# _
```

This file indicates that the /var/account/pacct file should be rotated daily if it is not empty, and that new log files will be owned by the root user/group and have the permissions

0600 (rw-------). Up to 31 old log files will be kept and compressed, but only on the next rotation (delaycompress). In addition, the /usr/sbin/accton /var/account/pacct command is run after each rotation if the /etc/init.d/psacct status command returns true.

On most Linux systems, the logrotate utility is automatically scheduled to run daily via the file /etc/cron.daily/logrotate; however, you might choose to run it manually by typing the command logrotate /etc/logrotate.conf at a command prompt.

Over time, the logrotate command generates several copies of each log file, as shown in the following listing of the /var/log directory:

```
[root@server1 ~]# ls /var/log
anaconda.log           dmesg                  ppp                    wtmp
anaconda.program.log   dmesg.old              prelink                Xorg.0.log
anaconda.storage.log   gdm                    sa                     Xorg.0.log.old
anaconda.syslog        httpd                  samba                  Xorg.1.log
anaconda.xlog          jetty                  sa-update.log          Xorg.1.log.old
anaconda.yum.log       lastlog                secure                 Xorg.2.log
audit                  mail                   secure-20100808        Xorg.2.log.old
BackupPC               maillog                secure-20100818        Xorg.3.log
bittorrent             maillog-20100808       secure-20100823        Xorg.3.log.old
boot.log               maillog-20100818       setroubleshoot         Xorg.4.log
boot.log-20100808      maillog-20100823       speech-dispatcher      Xorg.4.log.old
boot.log-20100818      messages               spooler                Xorg.5.log
boot.log-20100823      messages-20100808      spooler-20100808       Xorg.5.log.old
btmp                   messages-20100818      spooler-20100818       Xorg.9.log
ConsoleKit             messages-20100823      spooler-20100823       Xorg.9.log.old
cron                   mysqld.log             squid                  Xorg.setup.log
cron-20100808          news                   sssd                   yum.log
cron-20100818          ntpstats               tallylog
cron-20100823          pm-powersave.log       vbox
cups                   pm-suspend.log         wpa_supplicant.log
[root@server1 ~]# _
```

Given the preceding output, the most recent events for the cron daemon are recorded in the cron.log file, followed by the cron.log.20100823 file, followed by the cron.log.20100818 file, and the cron-20100808 file.

Administering Users and Groups

You must log in to a Linux system with a valid user name and password before a BASH shell is granted. This process is called **authentication** because the user name and password are authenticated against a system database that contains all **user account** information. Authenticated users are then granted access to files, directories, and other resources on the system based on their user accounts.

The system database that contains user account information typically consists of two files: **/etc/passwd** and **/etc/shadow**. Every user typically has a line that describes the user account in /etc/passwd and a line that contains the encrypted password and expiration information in /etc/shadow.

Older Linux systems stored the encrypted password in the /etc/passwd file and did not use an /etc/shadow file at all. This is considered poor security today because processes often require access to the user information in /etc/passwd. Storing the encrypted password in a separate file that cannot be accessed by processes prevents a process from obtaining all user account information. By default, Fedora 13 configures passwords using an /etc/shadow file. However, you can use the **dfdffpwunconv command** to revert to using an /etc/passwd file only. Also, you can use the **pwconv command** to configure the system again using an /etc/shadow file for password storage.

Each line of the /etc/passwd file has the following colon-delimited format:

```
name:password:UID:GID:GECOS:homedirectory:shell
```

The name in the preceding output refers to the name of the user. If an /etc/shadow is not used, the password field contains the encrypted password for the user; otherwise, it just contains an x character as a placeholder for the password stored in /etc/shadow.

The **User Identifier (UID)** specifies the unique User ID that is assigned to each user. Typically, UIDs that are less than 500 refer to user accounts that are used by daemons when logging in to the system. The root user always has a UID of zero.

The **Group Identifier (GID)** is the primary Group ID for the user. Each user can be a member of several groups, but only one of those groups can be the primary group. The **primary group** of a user is the group that is made the group owner of any file or directory that the user creates. Similarly, when a user creates a file or directory, that user becomes the owner of that file or directory.

GECOS represents a text description of the user and is typically left blank; this information was originally used in the **General Electric Comprehensive Operating System (GECOS)**. The last two fields represent the absolute pathname to the user's home directory and the shell, respectively.

An example of an /etc/passwd file is shown next:

```
[root@server1 ~]# cat /etc/passwd
root:x:0:0:root:/root:/bin/bash
bin:x:1:1:bin:/bin:/sbin/nologin
daemon:x:2:2:daemon:/sbin:/sbin/nologin
adm:x:3:4:adm:/var/adm:/sbin/nologin
lp:x:4:7:lp:/var/spool/lpd:/sbin/nologin
sync:x:5:0:sync:/sbin:/bin/sync
shutdown:x:6:0:shutdown:/sbin:/sbin/shutdown
halt:x:7:0:halt:/sbin:/sbin/halt
mail:x:8:12:mail:/var/spool/mail:/sbin/nologin
uucp:x:10:14:uucp:/var/spool/uucp:/sbin/nologin
operator:x:11:0:operator:/root:/sbin/nologin
games:x:12:100:games:/usr/games:/sbin/nologin
gopher:x:13:30:gopher:/var/gopher:/sbin/nologin
ftp:x:14:50:FTP User:/var/ftp:/sbin/nologin
```

```
nobody:x:99:99:Nobody:/:/sbin/nologin
dbus:x:81:81:System message bus:/:/sbin/nologin
usbmuxd:x:113:113:usbmuxd user:/:/sbin/nologin
avahi-autoipd:x:499:499:avahi-autoipd:/var/lib/avahi-autoipd:/sbin/
nologin
vcsa:x:69:498:virtual console memory owner:/dev:/sbin/nologin
oprofile:x:16:16:Special user account to be used by OProfile:/home/
oprofile:/sbin/nologin
rpc:x:32:32:Rpcbind Daemon:/var/lib/rpcbind:/sbin/nologin
rpcuser:x:29:496:RPC Service User:/var/lib/nfs:/sbin/nologin
nfsnobody:x:65534:65534:Anonymous NFS User:/var/lib/nfs:/sbin/nologin
named:x:25:25:Named:/var/named:/sbin/nologin
rtkit:x:498:495:RealtimeKit:/proc:/sbin/nologin
nscd:x:28:494:NSCD Daemon:/:/sbin/nologin
abrt:x:497:493::/etc/abrt:/sbin/nologin
tcpdump:x:72:72::/:/sbin/nologin
torrent:x:496:488:BitTorrent Seed/Tracker:/var/lib/bittorrent:/sbin/
nologin
avahi:x:495:487:avahi-daemon:/var/run/avahi-daemon:/sbin/nologin
apache:x:48:486:Apache:/var/www:/sbin/nologin
saslauth:x:494:485:"Saslauthd user":/var/empty/saslauth:/sbin/nologin
mailnull:x:47:484::/var/spool/mqueue:/sbin/nologin
smmsp:x:51:483::/var/spool/mqueue:/sbin/nologin
haldaemon:x:68:482:HAL daemon:/:/sbin/nologin
openvpn:x:493:481:OpenVPN:/etc/openvpn:/sbin/nologin
mysql:x:27:480:MySQL Server:/var/lib/mysql:/bin/bash
distcache:x:94:479:Distcache:/:/sbin/nologin
ntp:x:38:38::/etc/ntp:/sbin/nologin
nm-openconnect:x:492:478:NetworkManager user for OpenConnect:/:/sbin/
nologin
postgres:x:26:26:PostgreSQL Server:/var/lib/pgsql:/bin/bash
webalizer:x:67:477:Webalizer:/var/www/usage:/sbin/nologin
sshd:x:74:476:Privilege-separated SSH:/var/empty/sshd:/sbin/nologin
dovecot:x:491:475:Dovecot IMAP server:/usr/libexec/dovecot:/sbin/
nologin
squid:x:23:23::/var/spool/squid:/sbin/nologin
news:x:9:13:News server user:/etc/news:/sbin/nologin
smolt:x:490:474:Smolt:/usr/share/smolt:/sbin/nologin
backuppc:x:489:473::/var/lib/BackupPC:/sbin/nologin
pulse:x:488:472:PulseAudio System Daemon:/var/run/pulse:/sbin/nologin
gdm:x:42:468::/var/lib/gdm:/sbin/nologin
hsqldb:x:96:96::/var/lib/hsqldb:/sbin/nologin
jetty:x:487:467::/usr/share/jetty:/bin/sh
user1:x:500:500:sample user one:/home/user1:/bin/bash
[root@server1 ~]# _
```

The root user is usually listed at the top of the /etc/passwd file as just shown, followed by user accounts used by daemons when logging in to the system, followed by regular user accounts.

The final line of the preceding output indicates that the user user1 has a UID of 500, a primary GID of 500, a GECOS of "sample user one," the home directory /home/user1, and uses the BASH shell.

Like /etc/passwd, the /etc/shadow file is colon-delimited, yet has the following format:

```
name:password:lastchange:min:max:warn:disable1:disable2:
```

Although the first two fields in the /etc/shadow file are the same as those in /etc/passwd, the contents of the password field are different; the password field in the /etc/shadow file contains the encrypted password, whereas the password field in /etc/passwd contains an x character, because it is not used.

The lastchange field represents the date of the most recent password change; it is measured in the number of days since January 1, 1970. For example, the number 10957 represents January 1, 2000, because January 1, 2000, is 10957 days after January 1, 1970.

Traditionally, a calendar date was represented by a number indicating the number of days since January 1, 1970. Many calendar dates found in configuration files follow the same convention.

To prevent unauthorized access to a Linux system, it is good form to change passwords for user accounts regularly. To ensure that passwords are changed, you can set them to expire at certain intervals. The next three fields of the /etc/shadow file indicate information about password expiration: min represents the number of days a user must wait before she changes her password after receiving a new one, max represents the number of days a user can use the same password without changing it, and warn represents the number of days before a password expires that a user is warned to change her password.

By default on Red Hat Fedora Linux systems, min is equal to zero days, max is equal to 99,999 days, and warn is equal to seven days. This means you can change your password immediately after receiving a new one, your password expires in 99,999 days, and you are warned seven days in advance before your password needs to be changed.

When a password has expired, the user is still allowed to log in to the system for a certain period of time, after which point the user is disabled from logging in. The number of days after a password expires that a user account is disabled is represented by the disable1 field in /etc/shadow. In addition, you can choose to disable a user from logging in at a certain date, such as the end of an employment contract. The disable2 field in /etc/shadow represents the number of days since January 1, 1970, that a user account will be disabled.

A sample /etc/shadow file is shown next:

```
[root@server1 ~]# cat /etc/shadow
root:$6$vIoletCT$E5zaz6q.5UTH/SriWiFlh9.OgHMFvSH3R515uyxyj9pjezZb8m
WG8p
KpIwvfUatNzCw3tiaXU1bqDYQeeBTK2.:14841:0:99999:7:::
bin:*:14715:0:99999:7:::
daemon:*:14715:0:99999:7:::
adm:*:14715:0:99999:7:::
lp:*:14715:0:99999:7:::
```

```
sync:*:14715:0:99999:7:::
shutdown:*:14715:0:99999:7:::
halt:*:14715:0:99999:7:::
mail:*:14715:0:99999:7:::
uucp:*:14715:0:99999:7:::
operator:*:14715:0:99999:7:::
games:*:14715:0:99999:7:::
gopher:*:14715:0:99999:7:::
ftp:*:14715:0:99999:7:::
nobody:*:14715:0:99999:7:::
dbus:!!:14823::::::
usbmuxd:!!:14823::::::
avahi-autoipd:!!:14823::::::
vcsa:!!:14823::::::
oprofile:!!:14823::::::
rpc:!!:14823:0:99999:7:::
rpcuser:!!:14823::::::
nfsnobody:!!:14823::::::
named:!!:14823::::::
rtkit:!!:14823::::::
nscd:!!:14823::::::
abrt:!!:14823::::::
tcpdump:!!:14823::::::
torrent:!!:14823::::::
avahi:!!:14823::::::
apache:!!:14823::::::
saslauth:!!:14823::::::
mailnull:!!:14823::::::
smmsp:!!:14823::::::
haldaemon:!!:14823::::::
openvpn:!!:14823::::::
mysql:!!:14823::::::
distcache:!!:14823::::::
ntp:!!:14823::::::
nm-openconnect:!!:14823::::::
postgres:!!:14823::::::
webalizer:!!:14823::::::
sshd:!!:14823::::::
dovecot:!!:14823::::::
squid:!!:14823::::::
news:!!:14823::::::
smolt:!!:14823::::::
backuppc:!!:14823::::::
pulse:!!:14823::::::
gdm:!!:14823::::::
hsqldb:!!:14823::::::
jetty:!!:14823::::::
```

```
user1:$6$PVyl5FBX$nK5DvuCfTaFX0U3.h38n.doqSc824YzuINXdBjQ/nEUREPQlpqr
Z3qxPg3eWlS84fYtJoDPvDUdumcT.dNIWF1:14827:0:99999:7:::
[root@server1 ~]# _
```

Note from the preceding output that most user accounts used by daemons do not receive an encrypted password.

Although every user must have a primary group listed in the /etc/passwd file, each user can be a member of multiple groups. All groups and their members are listed in the **/etc/group** file. The /etc/group file has the following colon-delimited fields:

```
name:password:GID:members
```

The first field is the name of the group, followed by a group password.

The `password` field usually contains an `x`, because group passwords are rarely used. If group passwords are used on your system, you need to specify a password to change your primary group membership using the `newgrp` command discussed later in this chapter. These passwords are set using the `gpasswd` command and can be stored in the /etc/gshadow file for added security. Refer to the gpasswd manual or info page for more information.

The GID represents the unique Group ID for the group, and the members field indicates the list of group members. A sample /etc/group file is shown next:

```
[root@server1 ~]# cat /etc/group
root:x:0:root
bin:x:1:root,bin,daemon
daemon:x:2:root,bin,daemon
sys:x:3:root,bin,adm
adm:x:4:root,adm,daemon
tty:x:5:
disk:x:6:root
lp:x:7:daemon,lp
mem:x:8:
kmem:x:9:
wheel:x:10:root
mail:x:12:mail
uucp:x:14:uucp
man:x:15:
games:x:20:
gopher:x:30:
video:x:39:
dip:x:40:
ftp:x:50:
lock:x:54:
audio:x:63:
nobody:x:99:
users:x:100:
dbus:x:81:
```

```
utmp:x:22:
utempter:x:35:
usbmuxd:x:113:
avahi-autoipd:x:499:
floppy:x:19:
vcsa:x:498:
oprofile:x:16:
jackuser:x:497:
rpc:x:32:
rpcuser:x:496:
nfsnobody:x:65534:
named:x:25:
rtkit:x:495:
nscd:x:494:
abrt:x:493:
tcpdump:x:72:
screen:x:84:
ccache:x:492:
slocate:x:21:
mock:x:491:
desktop_admin_r:x:490:
desktop_user_r:x:489:
torrent:x:488:
cdrom:x:11:
tape:x:33:
dialout:x:18:
avahi:x:487:
apache:x:486:
saslauth:x:485:
mailnull:x:484:
smmsp:x:483:
haldaemon:x:482:
openvpn:x:481:
mysql:x:480:
distcache:x:479:
ntp:x:38:
nm-openconnect:x:478:
postgres:x:26:
webalizer:x:477:
sshd:x:476:
dovecot:x:475:
squid:x:23:
news:x:13:
smolt:x:474:
backuppc:x:473:apache
pulse:x:472:
pulse-access:x:471:
stapdev:x:470:
```

10

```
stapusr:x:469:
stap-server:x:155:
gdm:x:468:
hsqldb:x:96:
jetty:x:467:
user1:x:500:
[root@server1 ~]# _
```

From the preceding output, the "bin" group has a GID of 1, and three users as members: root, bin, and daemon.

Creating User Accounts

You can create user accounts on the Linux system by using the **useradd command**, specifying the user name as an argument, as shown next:

```
[root@server1 ~]# useradd bobg
[root@server1 ~]# _
```

In this case, all other information, such as the UID, shell, and home directory locations, are taken from two files that contain user account creation default values.

The first file, **/etc/login.defs**, contains parameters that set the default location for e-mail, password expiration information, minimum password length, and the range of UIDs and GIDs available for use. In addition, it determines whether home directories will be automatically made during user creation, as well as the password hash algorithm used to store passwords within /etc/shadow.

A sample /etc/login.defs file is shown next:

```
[root@server1 ~]# cat /etc/login.defs
# *REQUIRED*
# Directory where mailboxes reside, _or_ name of file, relative to the
# home directory. If you _do_ define both, MAIL_DIR takes precedence.
# QMAIL_DIR is for Qmail
#
#QMAIL_DIR      Maildir
MAIL_DIR        /var/spool/mail
#MAIL_FILE      .mail

# Password aging controls:
#
# PASS_MAX_DAYS      Maximum days a password may be used.
# PASS_MIN_DAYS      Minimum days allowed between password changes.
# PASS_MIN_LEN       Minimum acceptable password length.
# PASS_WARN_AGE      Number of days warning given before password expiry.
#
PASS_MAX_DAYS   99999
PASS_MIN_DAYS   0
PASS_MIN_LEN    5
PASS_WARN_AGE   7
```

```
#
# Min/max values for automatic uid selection in useradd
#
UID_MIN                    500
UID_MAX                    60000


#
# Min/max values for automatic gid selection in groupadd
#
GID_MIN                    500
GID_MAX                    60000


#
# If defined, this command is run when removing a user.
# It should remove any at/cron/print jobs etc. owned by
# the user to be removed (passed as the first argument).
#
#USERDEL_CMD    /usr/sbin/userdel_local


#
# If useradd should create home directories for users by default
# On RH systems, we do. This option is overridden with the -m flag on
# useradd command line.
#
CREATE_HOME    yes

# The permission mask is initialized to this value. If not specified,
# the permission mask will be initialized to 022.
UMASK          077

# This enables userdel to remove user groups if no members exist.
#
USERGROUPS_ENAB yes

# Use SHA512 to encrypt password.
ENCRYPT_METHOD SHA512

[root@server1 ~]# _
```

The second file, **/etc/default/useradd**, contains information regarding the default primary group, the location of home directories, the default number of days to disable accounts with expired passwords, the date to disable user accounts, the shell used, and the skeleton directory used. The **skeleton directory**, **/etc/skel** on most Linux systems, contains files that are copied to all new users' home directories when the home directory is created. Most of these files are environment files, such as .bash_profile and .bashrc.

A sample /etc/default/useradd file is shown in the following output:

```
[root@server1 ~]# cat /etc/default/useradd
```

```
# useradd defaults file
GROUP=100
HOME=/home
INACTIVE=-1
EXPIRE=
SHELL=/bin/bash
SKEL=/etc/skel
CREATE_MAIL_SPOOL=yes
[root@server1 ~]# _
```

To override any of the default parameters for a user in the /etc/login.defs and /etc/default/ useradd files, you can specify options to the useradd command when creating user accounts. For example, to create a user named maryj with a UID of 762, you can use the -u option to the useradd command, as shown in the following example:

```
[root@server1 ~]# useradd -u 762 maryj
[root@server1 ~]# _
```

Table 10-6 lists some common options available to the useradd command and their descriptions.

After a user account has been added, the password field in the /etc/shadow file contains two ! characters, indicating that no password has been set for the user account. To set the password, simply type the **passwd command**, type the name of the new user account at a

Option	Description
-c "description"	Adds a description for the user to the GECOS field of /etc/passwd.
-d homedirectory	Specifies the absolute pathname to the user's home directory.
-e expirydate	Specifies a date to disable the account from logging in.
-f days	Specifies the number of days until a user account with an expired password is disabled.
-g group	Specifies the primary group for the user account. By default in Fedora Linux, a group is created with the same name as the user and made the primary group for that user.
-G group1, group2, etc.	Specifies all other group memberships for the user account.
-m	Specifies that a home directory should be created for the user account. By default in Fedora Linux, home directories are created for all users via an entry in the /etc/login.defs file.
-k directory	Specifies the skeleton directory used when copying files to a new home directory.
-s shell	Specifies the absolute pathname to the shell used for the user account.
-u UID	Specifies the UID of the user account.

Table 10-6 Common options to the useradd command

command prompt, and then supply the appropriate password when prompted. An example of setting the password for the bobg user is shown in the following:

```
[root@server1 ~]# passwd bobg
Changing password for user bobg.
New UNIX password:
Retype new UNIX password:
passwd: all authentication tokens updated successfully.
[root@server1 ~]# _
```

Without arguments, the `passwd` command changes the password for the current user.

All user accounts must have a password set before they are used to log in to the system.

The root user can set the password on any user account using the `passwd` command; however, regular users can change their passwords only using this command.

Passwords should be difficult to guess and contain a combination of uppercase, lowercase, and special characters to increase system security. An example of a good password is C2Jr1;Pwr.

Modifying User Accounts

To modify the information regarding a user account after creation, you can edit the /etc/passwd or /etc/shadow file. This is not recommended, however, because typographical errors in these files might prevent the system from functioning. Instead, it's better to use the **usermod command**, which you can use to modify most information regarding user accounts. For example, to change the login name of the user bobg to barbg, you can use the -l option to the usermod command:

```
[root@server1 ~]# usermod -l barbg bobg
[root@server1 ~]# _
```

Table 10-7 displays a list of options used with the usermod command to modify user accounts.

Recall from Chapter 2 that the `finger` command can be used to view information about users. This information is stored in the GECOS field of /etc/passwd. As a result, instead of using the -c option to the usermod command, users can change their own GECOS, or finger information, using the **chfn command**.

Option	Description
`-c "description"`	Specifies a new description for the user in the GECOS field of /etc/passwd
`-d homedirectory`	Specifies the absolute pathname to a new home directory
`-e expirydate`	Specifies a date to disable the account from logging in
`-f days`	Specifies the number of days until a user account with an expired password is disabled
`-g group`	Specifies a new primary group for the user account
`-G group1, group2, etc.`	Specifies all other group memberships for the user account
`-l name`	Specifies a new login name
`-s shell`	Specifies the absolute pathname to a new shell used for the user account
`-u UID`	Specifies a new UID for the user account

Table 10-7   Common options to the `usermod` command

The only user account information that the `usermod` command cannot modify is the password expiration information stored in /etc/shadow (`min`, `max`, `warn`) discussed earlier. To change this information, you can use the **chage command** with the appropriate option. For example, to specify that the user bobg must wait two days before changing his password after receiving a new password, as well as to specify that his password expires every 50 days with seven days of warning prior to expiration, you can use the following options to the chage command:

```
[root@server1 ~]# chage -m 2 -M 50 -W 7 bobg
[root@server1 ~]# _
```

Sometimes, it's necessary to **lock an account**—that is, to temporarily prevent a user from logging in. To lock an account, you can use the command usermod -L *username* at the command prompt. This places a ! character at the beginning of the encrypted password field in the /etc/shadow file. To unlock the account, simply type usermod -U *username* at the command prompt, which removes the ! character from the password field in the /etc/shadow file.

Alternatively, you can use the passwd -l *username* command to lock a user account, and the passwd -u *username* command to unlock a user account. These commands place and remove two ! characters at the beginning of the encrypted password field in the /etc/shadow file respectively.

Yet another method commonly used to lock a user account is to change the shell specified in /etc/passwd for a user account from /bin/bash to an invalid shell such as /bin/false. Without a valid shell, a user cannot use the system. To lock a user account this way, you can edit the /etc/passwd file and make the appropriate change, use the -s option to the `usermod` command, or use the **chsh command**. The following example uses the chsh command to change the shell to /bin/false for the user bobg:

```
[root@server1 ~]# chsh -s /bin/false bobg
Changing shell for bobg.
```

```
Warning: "/bin/false" is not listed in /etc/shells
Shell changed.
[root@server1 ~]# _
```

Deleting User Accounts

To delete a user account, you can use the **userdel command** and specify the user name as an argument. This removes entries from the /etc/passwd and /etc/shadow files corresponding to the user account. Furthermore, you can specify the −r option to the userdel command to remove the home directory for the user and all of its contents.

When a user account is deleted, any files that were previously owned by the user become owned by a number that represents the UID of the deleted user. Any future user account that is given the same UID then becomes the owner of those files.

Suppose, for example, that the user bobg leaves the company. To delete bobg's user account and display the ownership of his old files, you can use the following commands:

```
[root@server1 ~]# userdel bobg
[root@server1 ~]# ls -la /home/bobg
total 52
drwx------     4 502        502          4096 Jul 17 15:37 .
drwxr-xr-x     5 root       root         4096 Jul 17 15:37 ..
-rw-r--r--     1 502        502            24 Jul 17 15:37 .bash_logout
-rw-r--r--     1 502        502           191 Jul 17 15:37 .bash_profile
-rw-r--r--     1 502        502           124 Jul 17 15:37 .bashrc
-rw-r--r--     1 502        502          5542 Jul 17 15:37 .canna
-rw-r--r--     1 502        502           820 Jul 17 15:37 .emacs
-rw-r--r--     1 502        502           118 Jul 17 15:37 .gtkrc
-rw-r--r--     3 502        502          4096 Jul 17 15:37 .kde
drwxr-xr-x     2 502        502          4096 Jul 17 15:37 .xemacs
-rw-r--r--     1 502        502          3511 Jul 17 15:37 .zshrc
[root@server1 ~]# _
```

From the preceding output, you can see that the UID of the bobg user was 502. Now suppose the company hires Sue—that is, the user sueb—to replace bobg. You can then assign the UID of 502 to Sue's user account. Although she will have her own home directory (/home/sueb), she will also own all of bobg's old files within /home/bobg and otherwise. She can then copy the files that she needs to her own home directory and remove any files that she doesn't need as part of her job function.

To create the user sueb with a UID of 502 and list the ownership of the files in bobg's home directory, you can use the following commands:

```
[root@server1 ~]# useradd -u 502 sueb
[root@server1 ~]# ls -la /home/bobg
total 52
drwx------     4 sueb       sueb         4096 Jul 17 15:37 .
drwxr-xr-x     5 root       root         4096 Jul 17 18:56 ..
-rw-r--r--     1 sueb       sueb           24 Jul 17 15:37 .bash_logout
-rw-r--r--     1 sueb       sueb          191 Jul 17 15:37 .bash_profile
```

```
-rw-r--r--    1 sueb      sueb          124 Jul 17 15:37 .bashrc
-rw-r--r--    1 sueb      sueb         5542 Jul 17 15:37 .canna
-rw-r--r--    1 sueb      sueb          820 Jul 17 15:37 .emacs
-rw-r--r--    1 sueb      sueb          118 Jul 17 15:37 .gtkrc
-rw-r--r--    3 sueb      sueb         4096 Jul 17 15:37 .kde
drwxr-xr-x    2 sueb      sueb         4096 Jul 17 15:37 .xemacs
-rw-r--r--    1 sueb      sueb         3511 Jul 17 15:37 .zshrc
[root@server1 ~]# _
```

Managing Groups

By far, the easiest way to add groups to a system is to edit the /etc/group file using a text editor. Another method is to use the **groupadd command**. To add a group called group1 to the system and assign it a GID of 492, you can use the following command:

```
[root@server1 ~]# groupadd –g 492 group1
[root@server1 ~]# _
```

Then, you can use the -G option to the usermod command to add members to the group. To add the user maryj to this group and view the addition, you can use the following usermod command:

```
[root@server1 ~]# usermod –G group1 maryj
[root@server1 ~]# tail -1 /etc/group
group1:x:492:maryj
[root@server1 ~]# _
```

There also exists a **groupmod command** that can be used to modify the group name and GID, as well as a **groupdel command**, which can be used to remove groups from the system.

To see a list of groups of which you are a member, simply run the **groups command**; to see the GIDs for each group, simply run the **id command**. The primary group is always listed first by each command. The following output shows the output of these commands when executed by the root user:

```
[root@server1 ~]# groups
root bin daemon sys adm disk wheel
[root@server1 ~]# id
uid=0(root)     gid=0(root)       groups=0(root),1(bin),2(daemon),3(sys),
4(adm),6(disk),10(wheel)
[root@server1 ~]# _
```

You can see from the preceding output that the primary group for the root user is the root group. This group is attached as the group owner for all files that are created by the root user, as shown in the following output:

```
[root@server1 ~]# touch samplefile1
[root@server1 ~]# ls -l samplefile1
-rw-r--r--    1 root      root           0 Aug 27 19:22 samplefile1
[root@server1 ~]# _
```

Figure 10-13 Configuring users and groups within a desktop environment

Source: Course Technology/Cengage Learning

To change the primary group temporarily to another group that is listed in the output of the `groups` and `id` commands, you can use the `newgrp` command. Any new files created afterward will then have the new group owner. The following output demonstrates how changing the primary group for the root user affects file ownership:

```
[root@server1 ~]# newgrp sys
[root@server1 root]# id
uid=0(root) gid=3(sys) groups=0(root),1(bin),2(daemon),3(sys),4(adm),
6(disk),10(wheel)
[root@server1 ~]# touch samplefile2
[root@server1 ~]# ls -l samplefile2
-rw-r--r--   1 root    sys          0 Aug 27 19:28 samplefile2
[root@server1 ~]# _
```

If you use group passwords as described earlier in this section, you can use the **newgrp command** to change your primary group to a group of which you are not a member, provided you supply the appropriate password when prompted.

Although command-line utilities are commonly used to administer users and groups, you can instead use a graphical utility to create, modify, and delete user and group accounts on the system. These utilities run the appropriate command-line utility in the background. To create and manage users and groups in Fedora 13 from within a desktop environment, you can navigate to the System menu, select Administration, Users, and Groups, and use the utility shown in Figure 10-13.

Alternatively, you can use the `system-config-users` command at a terminal within a desktop environment to display the window shown in Figure 10-13.

Chapter Summary

- Print jobs are spooled to a print queue before being printed to a printer.
- You can configure spooling or printing for a printer by using the `cupsaccept`, `cupsreject`, `cupsenable`, and `cupsdisable` commands.
- Print jobs are created using the `lp` command, can be viewed in the print queue using the `lpstat` command, and are removed from the print queue using the `cancel` command.
- You can create local and remote printers using the Printer Configuration tool or by modifying the /etc/cups/printers.conf file.
- Most log files on a Linux system are stored in the /var/log directory.
- System events are typically logged to files by the System Log Daemon.
- Log files should be cleared or rotated over time to save disk space; the logrotate utility can be used to rotate log files.
- User and group account information is typically stored in the /etc/passwd, /etc/shadow, and /etc/group files.
- You can use the `useradd` command to create users and the `groupadd` command to create groups.
- All users must have a valid password before logging in to a Linux system.
- Users can be modified with the `usermod`, `chage`, `chfn`, `chsh`, and `passwd` commands, and groups can be modified using the `groupmod` command.
- The `userdel` and `groupdel` commands can be used to remove users and groups from the system, respectively.

Key Terms

/etc/cups/cupsd.conf   A file that holds daemon configuration for the cups daemon.

/etc/cups/printers.conf   A file that holds printer configuration for the cups daemon.

/etc/default/useradd   A file that contains default values for user creation.

/etc/group   The file that contains group definitions and memberships.

/etc/login.defs   A file that contains default values for user creation.

/etc/logrotate.conf   The file used by the logrotate utility to specify rotation parameters for log files.

/etc/passwd   The file that contains user account information.

/etc/shadow   The file that contains the encrypted password as well as password and account expiry parameters for each user account.

/etc/skel   A directory that contains files that are copied to all new users' home directories upon creation.

/etc/syslog.conf   The file that specifies the events for which the System Log Daemon listens and the log files to which it saves the events.

/var/log   A directory that contains most log files on a Linux system.

accepting printer   A printer that accepts print jobs into the print queue.

authentication   The act of verifying a user's identity by comparing a user name and password with a system database (/etc/passwd and /etc/shadow).

`cancel` **command**   The command used to remove print jobs from the print queue in the CUPS print system.

`chage` **command**   The command used to modify password expiry information for user accounts.

`chfn` **command**   The command used to change the GECOS for a user.

`chsh` **command**   The command used to change a valid shell to an invalid shell.

Common Unix Printing System (CUPS)   The printing system commonly used on Linux computers.

`cupsaccept` **command**   The command used to allow a printer to accept jobs into the print queue.

cups daemon (cupsd)   The daemon responsible for printing in the CUPS printing system.

`cupsdisable` **command**   The command used to prevent print jobs from leaving the print queue.

`cupsenable` **command**   The command used to allow print jobs to leave the print queue.

`cupsreject` **command**   The command used to force a printer to reject jobs from entering the print queue.

disabled printer   A printer that does not send print jobs from the print queue to a printer.

enabled printer   A printer that sends print jobs from the print queue to a printer.

facility   The area of the system from which information is gathered when logging system events.

General Electric Comprehensive Operating System (GECOS)   The field in the /etc/passwd file that contains a description of the user account.

`groupadd` **command**   The command used to add a group to the system.

`groupdel` **command**   The command used to delete a group from the system.

Group Identifier (GID)   A unique number given to each group.

`groupmod` **command**   The command used to modify the name or GID of a group on the system.

`groups` **command**   The command that lists group membership for a user.

`id` **command**   The command that lists UIDs for a user and the GIDs for the groups that the same user belongs to.

Internet Printing Protocol (IPP)   A printing protocol that can be used to send print jobs across a TCP/IP network, such as the Internet, using HTTP or HTTPS.

Line Printer Daemon (LPD)   A printing system typically used on legacy Linux computers.

lock an account   To make an account temporarily unusable by altering the password information for it stored on the system.

log file   A file containing information about the Linux system.

`logrotate` **command**   The command used to rotate log files; it typically uses the configuration information stored in /etc/logrotate.conf.

`lpadmin` **command**   The command used to perform printer administration in the CUPS printing system.

lpc command   The command used to view the status of and control printers in the LPD printing system.

lp command   The command used to create print jobs in the print queue in the CUPS printing system.

lpq command   The command used to view the contents of print queues in the LPD printing system.

lpr command   The command used to create print jobs in the print queue in the LPD printing system.

lprm command   The command used to remove print jobs from the print queue in the LPD printing system.

lpstat command   The command used to view the contents of print queues and printer information in the CUPS printing system.

newgrp command   The command used to change temporarily the primary group of a user.

passwd command   The command used to modify the password associated with a user account.

Plug and Play (PnP)   A technology that allows users to add hardware to a computer without having to configure the hardware to work with the system.

primary group   The group that is specified for a user in the /etc/passwd file and that is specified as group owner for all files created by a user.

printing   The process by which print jobs are sent from a print queue to a printer.

print job   The information sent to a printer for printing.

print job ID   A unique numeric identifier used to mark and distinguish each print job.

print queue   A directory on the filesystem that holds print jobs that are waiting to be printed.

printer class   A template that can be used to apply settings to printers on a CUPS system.

Printer Configuration tool   A graphical utility used to configure printers on the system.

priority   The importance of system information when logging system events.

pwconv command   The command used to enable the use of the /etc/shadow file.

pwunconv command   The command used to disable the use of the /etc/shadow file.

queuing   *See* spooling.

rejecting printer   A printer that does not accept print jobs into the print queue.

skeleton directory   A directory that contains files that are copied to all new users' home directories upon creation; the default skeleton directory on Linux systems is /etc/skel.

spooling   The process of accepting a print job into a print queue.

System Log Daemon (rsyslogd)   The daemon that logs system events to various log files via information stored in /etc/rsyslog.conf.

Uniform Resource Identifier (URI)   A naming convention that identifies hardware and software components using a two-part name that consists of a type followed by an identifier.

user account   The information regarding a user that is stored in a system database (/etc/passwd and /etc/shadow), which can be used to log in to the system and gain access to system resources.

useradd command   The command used to add a user account to the system.

userdel command   The command used to remove a user account from the system.

User Identifier (UID)   A unique number assigned to each user account.

`usermod` **command**   The command used to modify the properties of a user account on the system.

Review Questions

1. The process of sending print jobs from the print queue to the printer is called _____.

   a. spooling

   b. queuing

   c. redirecting

   d. printing

2. You can clear a log file simply by redirecting nothing into it. True or False?

3. When a printer is disabled, _____.

   a. the print queue does not accept jobs and sends a message to the user noting that the printer is unavailable

   b. the print queue accepts jobs into the print queue and holds them there until the printer is enabled again

   c. the printer appears as off-line when an lp request is sent

   d. the print queue redirects all print jobs sent to it to /dev/null

4. What is the name used to describe a user providing a user name and password to log in to a system?

   a. validation

   b. authorization

   c. login

   d. authentication

5. Which command can you use to lock a user account?

   a. `lock username`

   b. `secure username`

   c. `usermod -L username`

   d. `useradd -L username`

6. Which command can be used to alter the primary group associated with a given user temporarily?

   a. `usermod`

   b. `chggrp`

   c. `gpasswd`

   d. `newgrp`

7. Which command can be used to send a print job to the default printer named Printer1? (Choose all that apply.)

   a. `lp -d Printer1 file`

   b. `lp Printer1 file`

   c. `lp file`

   d. `lp -m Printer1 file`

8. What is the name of the file that contains a listing of all users on the system and their home directories?

   a. /etc/passwd

   b. /etc/users

   c. /etc/shadow

   d. /etc/password

9. UIDs and GIDs are unique to the system and, once used, can never be reused. True or False?

10. What is the name of the utility used to rotate log files?

    a. syslog

    b. jetpack

    c. logrotate

    d. logbackup

11. You can lock a user account by changing the default login shell to an invalid shell in /etc/passwd. True or False?

12. When a printer is rejecting requests, _____.

    a. the print queue does not accept jobs and sends a message to the user noting that the printer is unavailable

    b. the print queue accepts jobs into the print queue and holds them there until the printer is accepting requests again

    c. the printer appears as off-line when an lp request is sent

    d. the print queue redirects all print jobs sent to it to /dev/null

13. When referring to the /etc/rsyslog.conf file, _____ specifies information from a certain area of the system, whereas _____ is the level of importance of that information.

    a. section, priority

    b. service, precedents

    c. process, degree

    d. facility, priority

14. Most log files on the system are found in which directory?

    a. /etc/logfiles

    b. /etc/log

    c. /var/log

    d. /dev/log

15. Which file contains default information such as UID and GID ranges and minimum password length to be used at user creation?

    a. /etc/skel

    b. /etc/passwd

    c. /etc/login.defs

    d. /etc/default/useradd

16. What is the background process responsible for printing on Fedora Linux?

    a. lp

    b. cupsd

    c. lpd

    d. lpstat

17. Which command would you use to unlock a user account?

    a. `unlock username`

    b. `open username`

    c. `usermod -U username`

    d. `useradd -U username`

18. Along with a listing of user accounts, the /etc/passwd file contains information on account expiry. True or False?

19. You use `lpstat` and determine that a user named User1 has placed two large print jobs in the queue for Printer1 that have yet to start printing. They have print job IDs of Printer1-17 and Printer1-21, respectively. Which command would you use to remove these two jobs from the print queue?

    a. `cancel Printer1-17 Printer1-21`

    b. `cancel -u Printer1-17 Printer1-21`

    c. `cancel -a Printer1-17 Printer1-21`

    d. `cancel 17 21`

20. Which command is used to delete a user account?

    a. `usermod -d username`

    b. `del username`

    c. `userdel username`

    d. `rm username`

Hands-On Projects

These projects should be completed in the order given. The hands-on projects presented in this chapter should take a total of three hours to complete. The requirements for this lab include:

- A computer with Fedora 13 installed according to Hands-On Project 2-2

Project 10-1

In this hands-on project, you create a local printer using the Printer Configuration tool.

1. Turn on your computer. After your Linux system has been loaded, log in to the GNOME Desktop Environment as user1.

2. After the GNOME desktop has loaded, navigate to the **System** menu, **Administration**, **Printing**.

3. Create a new printer by clicking the **Add** button. Supply the root user password of **secret** when prompted and click **Authenticate** (you will be prompted twice).

4. Click **Forward** at the Add a new print queue screen.

5. Ensure that **Other** is selected in the left pane, type **parallel:/dev/null** in the Enter Device URI dialog box, and click **Forward**.

The special device /dev/null represents nothing; any print jobs sent to this device will be discarded.

6. At the Choose Driver screen, ensure that **Generic** is selected and click **Forward**. Ensure that **text-only printer** is highlighted in the left pane and click **Forward**.

7. At the Describe Printer screen, type **p1** in the Printer Name dialog box and click **Apply**. Supply the root user password of **secret** when prompted and click **Authenticate**. If prompted for the root password again, type **secret** and click **OK**. If prompted to print a test page, click **NO**.

8. Close the Printer Configuration tool and log out of the GNOME desktop.

Project 10-2

In this hands-on project, you view your printer configuration, control the print process, create print jobs, and manage jobs in the print queue.

1. Switch to a command-line terminal (tty2) by pressing **Ctrl+Alt+F2** and log in to the terminal using the user name of **root** and the password of **secret**.

2. At the terminal screen prompt, type **cat /etc/cups/printers.conf** and press **Enter**. Compare the entries in this file for your printer with the settings you specified in Project 10-1.

3. At the command prompt, type **lpstat -t** and press **Enter**. Is the cups daemon running? Is spooling and printing enabled for p1?

4. At the command prompt, type **cupsdisable -r "To pause print jobs in the print queue" p1** and press **Enter** to prevent printing for the p1 printer.

5. At the command prompt, type **lpstat -t** and press **Enter**. Verify that spooling is enabled but printing is disabled for p1.

6. Next, type **lp –n 2 –d p1 /etc/hosts** at the command prompt and press **Enter** to print two copies of /etc/hosts to p1. What print job ID do you receive?

7. At the command prompt, type **lpstat** and press **Enter**. Is your print job in the queue?

8. At the command prompt, type **sort /etc/hosts | lp** and press **Enter** to sort the file /etc/hosts and send the output to p1. Note that you did not need the –d option to the lp command because it was the default printer. What print job ID did you receive?

9. At the command prompt, type **lpstat** and press **Enter**. Verify that both print jobs are in the print queue.

10. At the command prompt, type **cancel p1-1 p1-2** (or the numbers of the print jobs on your screen if they are different) to remove both print jobs from the queue. Type **lpstat** and press **Enter** to verify that they were removed.

11. At the command prompt, type **lpadmin –u allow:all –u deny:user1 –d p1** and press **Enter** to allow all users to print to p1 except user1.

12. Press **Ctrl+Alt+F3** to switch to tty3 and log in as **user1** using the password **secret**. Type **lp –d p1 /etc/hosts**. Was user1 allowed to print to p1? Type **exit** to log out of the tty3 terminal.

13. Press **Ctrl+Alt+F2** to switch back to tty2, type **cancel -a** and press **Enter** to remove any print jobs from the queue.

14. Type **exit** and press **Enter** to log out of your shell.

Project 10-3

In this hands-on project, you view the configuration of the System Log Daemon and the logrotate utility.

1. Switch to a command-line terminal (tty2) by pressing **Ctrl+Alt+F2** and log in to the terminal using the user name of **root** and the password of **secret**.

2. At the command prompt, type **ls –l /dev/log** and press **Enter**. What is the file type? Which daemon uses this file, and what is its purpose?

3. At the command prompt, type **less /etc/rsyslog.conf** and press **Enter** to view the configuration file for the System Log Daemon. Observe the entries. To which file does all information from the cron daemon get logged? Why? Press **q** when finished to quit the less utility.

4. At the command prompt, type **tail /var/log/cron** and observe the entries. Write down the last few entries that you see in this file.

5. At the command prompt, type **killall -9 crond** and press **Enter** to stop the cron daemon.

6. At the command prompt, type **crond** and press **Enter** to start the cron daemon.

7. At the command prompt, type **tail /var/log/cron** and observe the entries. Compare the output from Step 4 with the output on your terminal screen. What are the last few entries? Why?

8. At the command prompt, type **cat /etc/cron.daily/logrotate** and press **Enter** to observe the logrotate command that is run each day.

9. At the command prompt, type **less /etc/logrotate.conf** and press **Enter** to view the configuration file for the logrotate command. When are log files rotated by default? How many copies of old log files are kept by default? When finished, press **q** to quit the less utility.

10. At the command prompt, type **ls /etc/logrotate.d** and press **Enter**. How many files are in this directory? Will entries in these files override the same entries in /etc/logrotate.conf?

11. At the command prompt, type **cat /etc/logrotate.d/psacct** and press **Enter**. How many copies of old log files are kept for this log file?

12. At the command prompt, type **ls /var/log** and press **Enter**. How many log files are present? What do the subdirectories represent? Are there any old log files?

13. Type **exit** and press **Enter** to log out of your shell.

Project 10-4

In this hands-on project, you observe user account databases and create a user account using command-line utilities.

1. Switch to a command-line terminal (tty2) by pressing **Ctrl+Alt+F2** and log in to the terminal using the user name of **root** and the password of **secret**.

2. At the command prompt, type **less /etc/passwd** and press **Enter**. Where is the line that describes the root user located in this file? Where is the line that describes the user1 user in this file? How many daemon accounts are present? What is in the password field for all accounts? When finished, press the **q** key to quit the less utility.

3. At the command prompt, type **ls -l /etc/passwd** and press **Enter**. Who is the owner and group owner of this file? Who has permission to read this file?

4. At the command prompt, type **less /etc/shadow** and press **Enter**. What is in the password field for the root user and user1 user accounts? What is in the password field for most daemon accounts? Press the **q** key to quit the less utility.

5. At the command prompt, type **ls -l /etc/shadow** and press **Enter**. Who is the owner and group owner of this file? Who has permission to read this file? Compare the permissions for /etc/shadow with those of /etc/passwd obtained in Step 3 and explain the difference.

6. At the command prompt, type **pwunconv** and press **Enter**. Next, type **less /etc/shadow** at the command prompt and press **Enter**. What error message do you receive? Why?

7. At the command prompt, type **less /etc/passwd** and press **Enter**. What is in the password field for all accounts? Why? When finished, press the **q** key to quit the less utility.

8. At the command prompt, type **pwconv** and press **Enter**. What does the pwconv command do?

9. Next, type **less /etc/shadow** at the command prompt and press **Enter**. Verify that the file has contents, and press **q** when finished. Next, type **less /etc/passwd** at the command prompt and press **Enter**. Verify that the file has contents, and press **q** when finished.

10. At the command prompt, type **cat /etc/default/useradd** and press **Enter**. What is the default shell used when creating users? What is the default location of the skel directory used when creating users? Where are user home directories created by default?

11. At the command prompt, type **ls –a /etc/skel** and press **Enter**. What files are stored in this directory? What is the purpose of this directory when creating users?

12. At the command prompt, type **cp /etc/inittab /etc/skel** and press **Enter** to create a copy of the init table in the /etc/skel directory.

13. At the command prompt, type **useradd –m bozo** and press **Enter**. What does the –m option specify? From where is the default shell, home directory information taken?

14. At the command prompt, type **less /etc/login.defs** and press **Enter**. Observe the entries and descriptive comments. Did you need to specify the –m option to the useradd command in Step 13? Explain. Press the **q** key to quit the less utility.

15. At the command prompt, type **cat /etc/passwd** and press **Enter**. What shell and home directory does bozo have? What is bozo's UID?

16. At the command prompt, type **cat /etc/shadow** and press **Enter**. Does bozo have a password? Can bozo log in to the system?

17. At the command prompt, type **passwd bozo** and press **Enter**. Enter the password of **secret** and press **Enter**. Enter the password of **secret** again to confirm and press **Enter**.

18. At the command prompt, type **ls -a /home/bozo** and press **Enter**. How many files are in this directory? Compare this list with the one obtained in Step 11. Is the **inittab** file present?

19. Type **exit** and press **Enter** to log out of your shell.

Project 10-5

In this hands-on project, you modify user accounts using command-line utilities.

1. Switch to a command-line terminal (tty2) by pressing **Ctrl+Alt+F2** and log in to the terminal using the user name of **root** and the password of **secret**.

2. At the command prompt, type **cat /etc/passwd** and press **Enter**. Record the line used to describe the user bozo.

3. At the command prompt, type **cat /etc/shadow** and press **Enter**. Record the line used to describe the user bozo.

4. At the command prompt, type **usermod –l bozo2 bozo** and press **Enter** to change the login name for the user bozo to bozo2. Next, type **cat /etc/passwd** at the command prompt and press **Enter**. Was the login name changed from bozo to bozo2? Was the UID changed? Was the home directory changed?

5. At the command prompt, type **usermod –l bozo bozo2** and press **Enter** to change the login name for the user bozo2 back to bozo.

6. At the command prompt, type **usermod –u 666 bozo** and press **Enter** to change the UID of the user bozo to 666. Next, type **cat /etc/passwd** at the command prompt and press **Enter**. Was the UID changed?

7. At the command prompt, type **usermod –f 14 bozo** and press **Enter** to disable bozo's user account 14 days after the password expires. Next, type **cat /etc/shadow** at the command prompt and press **Enter**. Which field was changed?

8. At the command prompt, type **usermod -e "01/01/2020" bozo** and press **Enter** to expire bozo's user account on January 1, 2020. Next type **cat /etc/shadow** at the command prompt and press **Enter**. Which field was changed? What does the number represent in this field?

9. At the command prompt, type **chage -m 2 bozo** and press **Enter** to require that the user bozo wait at least two days before making password changes. Next, type **cat /etc/shadow** at the command prompt and press **Enter**. Which field was changed?

10. At the command prompt, type **chage -M 40 bozo** and press **Enter** to require that the user bozo change passwords every 40 days. Next, type **cat /etc/shadow** at the command prompt and press **Enter**. Which field was changed?

11. At the command prompt, type **chage -W 5 bozo** and press **Enter** to warn the user bozo five days in advance that a password change is required. Next, type **cat /etc/shadow** at the command prompt and press **Enter**. Which field was changed?

12. Type **exit** and press **Enter** to log out of your shell.

Project 10-6

In this hands-on project, you lock and unlock user accounts using command-line utilities.

1. Switch to a command-line terminal (tty2) by pressing **Ctrl+Alt+F2** and log in to the terminal using the user name of **root** and the password of **secret**.

2. At the command prompt, type **cat /etc/shadow** and press **Enter**. Record the encrypted password for bozo's user account.

3. At the command prompt, type **passwd -l bozo** and press **Enter** to lock bozo's user account.

4. At the command prompt, type **cat /etc/shadow** and press **Enter**. What has been changed regarding the original encrypted password recorded in Step 2?

5. Switch to a command-line terminal (tty5) by pressing **Ctrl+Alt+F5** and attempt to log in to the terminal using the user name of **bozo** and the password of **secret**. Were you successful?

6. Switch back to the command-line terminal (tty2) by pressing **Ctrl+Alt+F2**.

7. At the command prompt, type **passwd -u bozo** and press **Enter** to unlock bozo's user account.

8. At the command prompt, type **cat /etc/shadow** and press **Enter**. Compare the encrypted password for bozo's user account with the one recorded in Step 2.

9. Switch to a command-line terminal (tty5) by pressing **Ctrl+Alt+F5** and attempt to log in to the terminal using the user name of **bozo** and the password of **secret**. Were you successful?

10. Type **exit** and press **Enter** to log out of your shell.

11. Switch back to the command-line terminal (tty2) by pressing **Ctrl+Alt+F2**.

12. At the command prompt, type **chsh -s /bin/false bozo** and press **Enter** to change bozo's shell to /bin/false. What message did you receive? Was the shell changed? Type **cat /etc/passwd** at a command prompt to verify that the shell was changed to /bin/false for bozo's user account.

13. Switch to a command-line terminal (tty5) by pressing **Ctrl+Alt+F5** and attempt to log in to the terminal using the user name of **bozo** and the password of **secret**. Were you successful?

14. Switch back to the command-line terminal (tty2) by pressing **Ctrl+Alt+F2**.

15. At the command prompt, type **chsh -s /bin/bash bozo** and press **Enter** to change bozo's shell to /bin/bash.

16. Switch to a command-line terminal (tty5) by pressing **Ctrl+Alt+F5** and attempt to log in to the terminal using the user name of **bozo** and the password of **secret**. Were you successful?

17. Type **exit** and press **Enter** to log out of your shell.

18. Switch back to the command-line terminal (tty2) by pressing **Ctrl+Alt+F2**.

19. Type **exit** and press **Enter** to log out of your shell.

Project 10-7

In this hands-on project, you remove a user account and create a new user account in its place using command-line utilities.

1. Switch to a command-line terminal (tty2) by pressing **Ctrl+Alt+F2** and log in to the terminal using the user name of **root** and the password of **secret**.

2. At the command prompt, type **ls -la /home/bozo** and press **Enter**. Who owns most files in this directory? Why?

3. At the command prompt, type **userdel bozo** and press **Enter**. Was the home directory removed for bozo as well?

4. At the command prompt, type **ls -la /home/bozo** and press **Enter**. Who owns most files in this directory? Why?

5. At the command prompt, type **useradd -m -u 666 bozoette** and press **Enter**. What do the -m and the -u options do in this command?

6. At the command prompt, type **passwd bozoette** and press **Enter**. Enter the password of **secret** and press **Enter**. Enter the password of **secret** again to confirm, and press **Enter**.

7. At the command prompt, type **cat /etc/passwd** and press **Enter**. What is bozoette's home directory? What is bozoette's UID?

8. At the command prompt, type **ls -la /home/bozo** and press **Enter**. Who owns most files in this directory? Why? Can bozoette manage these files?

9. Type **exit** and press **Enter** to log out of your shell.

Project 10-8

In this hands-on project, you create, use, and delete groups using command-line utilities.

1. Switch to a command-line terminal (tty2) by pressing **Ctrl+Alt+F2** and log in to the terminal using the user name of **root** and the password of **secret**.

2. At the command prompt, type **vi /etc/group** and press **Enter** to open the /etc/group file in the vi editor. Add a line to the bottom of this file that reads:

```
groupies:x:1234:root,bozoette
```

This adds a group to the system with a GID of 1234 and the members root and bozoette. When finished, save and quit the vi editor.

3. Switch to a command-line terminal (tty5) by pressing **Ctrl+Alt+F5** and log in to the terminal using the user name of **bozoette** and the password of **secret**.

4. At the command prompt, type **groups** and press **Enter**. Of which groups is bozoette a member?

5. At the command prompt, type **id** and press **Enter**. Which group is the primary group for the user bozoette?

6. At the command prompt, type **touch file1** and press **Enter** to create a new file called file1 in the current directory.

7. At the command prompt, type **ls -l** and press **Enter**. Who is the owner and group owner of the file called file1? Why?

8. At the command prompt, type **newgrp groupies** and press **Enter** to temporarily change bozoette's primary group to groupies.

9. At the command prompt, type **touch file2** and press **Enter** to create a new file called file2 in the current directory.

10. At the command prompt, type **ls -l** and press **Enter**. Who is the owner and group owner of the file called file2? Why?

11. Type **exit** and press **Enter** to log out of your shell.

12. Switch back to the command-line terminal (tty2) by pressing **Ctrl+Alt+F2**.

13. At the command prompt, type **groupdel groupies** and press **Enter** to remove the group called groupies from the system. Which file is edited by the groupdel command?

14. Type **exit** and press **Enter** to log out of your shell.

Discovery Exercises

1. Which entry could you add to /etc/rsyslog.conf to _____?

   a. log all critical messages from the kernel to /var/log/alert

   b. log all messages from the user processes to /var/log/userlog

   c. log all debug messages, as well as more serious ones, from the printing daemon to /var/log/printer

   d. log all messages except notices from the mail daemon to /var/log/mailman

   e. log all alerts and critical error messages to /var/log/serious

   f. log all warnings and errors from the kernel and the printing daemon to /var/log/shared

2. Use the man or info pages to find a description of the -D option to the useradd command. What does this option do? What file does it edit? Use this option with the useradd command to set the date that all new user accounts will be disabled to March 5, 2055. What command did you use?

3. Configure the System Log Daemon on your Linux system to log all warnings and more serious messages to the /var/log/sample.log file. Next, configure the `logrotate` command to rotate this log file each day, keeping up to six old log files that should be compressed. Which files did you change? What entries did you add?

4. Create a user called testuser using the system-config-users utility that has a GECOS of "Test User Account," password of "secret," and home directory of /home/test. Passwords for this user should expire every 60 days, with 10 days of warning beforehand. After a password has been changed, the user must wait five days to change it again. The user account should expire on April 1, 2028, and be a member of the sys and adm groups.

5. Enable the remote administration option within the Printer Configuration tool. Next, access your CUPS administration Web site using the Web browser on your computer (*http://server1.class.com:631*). Use this Web site to create a printer called p2 that prints to /dev/null. Send some print jobs to p2 and then use the CUPS administration Web site to view and remove your print jobs.

6. When adding several user accounts, you might want to use the newusers utility, which can process a text file full of entries to add user accounts. Use the man or info page to find out how to use this utility, and use it to add three users. When finished, view the /etc/passwd, /etc/shadow, and /etc/group files to verify that the users were added successfully.

7. Write commands to accomplish the following (use the manual or info pages if necessary):

   a. Create a user with a login name of bsmith, a UID of 733, a GECOS field entry of "accounting manager," and a password of Gxj234.

   b. Delete the user jdoe, but leave the home directory intact.

   c. Change the properties of the existing user wjones so that the user has a new comment field of "shipping" and an account expiry of March 23, 2022.

   d. Lock the account of wjenkins.

   e. Change the password of bsmith to We34Rt.

   f. Change the properties of the existing user tbanks such that the user is a member of the managers group and has a login name of artbanks.

   g. Create a user with the same UID and primary group as root and a login name of wjones.

   h. Create a new user with a login name of jdoe who has a password of he789R and no home directory.

   i. Change the primary group of the user wsmith to root.

   j. Add the users tbanks and jdoe to the group acctg.

Compression, System Backup, and Software Installation

After completing this chapter, you will be able to:

- Outline the features of common compression utilities
- Compress and decompress files using common compression utilities
- Perform system backups using the `tar`, `cpio`, and `dump` commands
- View and extract archives using the `tar`, `cpio`, and `restore` commands
- Use burning software to back up files to CD and DVD
- Describe common types of Linux software
- Compile and install software packages from source code
- Use the Red Hat Package Manager to install, manage, and remove software packages
- Use the `yum` command to obtain software from Internet software repositories

In the preceding chapter, you examined common administrative tasks that are performed on a regular basis. In this chapter, you also learn about tasks that are performed frequently, but you focus on file- and software-related administration. You begin this chapter learning about utilities commonly used to compress files on filesystems, followed by a discussion of system backup and archiving utilities. Finally, you learn about the different forms of software available for Linux systems, how to compile source code into functional programs, and the features and usage of the Red Hat Package Manager.

Compression

At times, you might want to reduce the size of a file or set of files due to limited disk space. You might also want to compress files that are sent across the Internet or other computer network to decrease transfer time. In either case, you can choose from several utilities that reduce a file's size by stripping out characters via a process known as **compression**. The standard set of instructions used to compress a file is known as a **compression algorithm**. To decompress a file, you run the compression algorithm in reverse.

Because compression utilities use different compression algorithms, they achieve different rates of compression, or **compression ratios**, for similar file types. To calculate the compression ratio for a utility, you subtract the compressed percentage from 100. For example, if a compression utility compresses a file to 52 percent of its original size, it has a compression ratio of 48 percent.

Many compression utilities are available to Linux users; this section examines the three most common:

- compress
- gzip
- bzip2

The compress Utility

The compress utility is one of the oldest compression utilities common to most UNIX and Linux systems. Its compression algorithm, which is called Adaptive Lempel-Ziv coding (LZW), has an average compression ratio of 40 to 50 percent.

To compress a file using the compress utility, you specify the files to compress as arguments to the **compress command**. Each file is renamed with a .z filename extension to indicate that it is compressed. In addition, you can use the –v (verbose) option to the compress command to display the compression ratio during compression. The following output displays the filenames and sizes of the samplefile and samplefile2 files before and after compression:

```
[root@server1 ~]# ls -l
total 28
drwx------    3 root      root      4096 Jul 21 08:15 Desktop
-rw-r--r--    1 root      root     20239 Jul 21 08:15 samplefile
-rw-rw-r--    1 root      root       574 Jul 21 08:18 samplefile2
[root@server1 ~]# compress -v samplefile samplefile2
samplefile: -- replaced with samplefile.Z Compression: 48.06%
samplefile2: -- replaced with samplefile2.Z Compression: 26.13%
```

```
[root@server1 root]# ls -l
total 20
drwx------      3 root        root        4096 Jul 21 08:15 Desktop
-rw-rw-r--      1 root        root         424 Jul 21 08:18 samplefile2.Z
-rw-r--r--      1 root        root       10512 Jul 21 08:15 samplefile.Z
[root@server1 ~]# _
```

The compress utility is not installed on Fedora 13 by default. To install the compress utility from a software repository on the Internet, you can execute the `yum install ncompress` command as the root user.

The compress utility preserves the original ownership, modification, and access time for each file that it compresses.

By default, the compress utility does not compress symbolic links or very small files; to force the compress utility to compress these files, you must use the −f option. You can compress all of the files in a certain directory by using the −r option and specifying the directory name as an argument to the compress command.

After compression, the **zcat command** can be used to display the contents of a compressed file, as shown in the following output:

```
[root@server1 ~]# zcat samplefile2.Z
Hi there, I hope this day finds you well.

Unfortunately we were not able to make it to your dining
room this year while vacationing in Algonquin Park - I
especially wished to see the model of the Highland Inn
and the train station in the dining room.

I have been reading on the history of Algonquin Park but
no where could I find a description of where the Highland
Inn was originally located on Cache lake.

If it is no trouble, could you kindly let me know such that
I need not wait until next year when I visit your lodge?

Regards,
Mackenzie Elizabeth


[root@server1 ~]# _
```

You can use the **zmore** and **zless** commands to view the contents of a compressed file page-by-page.

To decompress files that have been compressed with the compress utility, simply use the **uncompress command** followed by the names of the files to be decompressed. This restores the original filename. The following output decompresses and displays the filenames for the samplefile.Z and samplefile2.Z files created earlier:

```
[root@server1 ~]# uncompress -v samplefile.Z samplefile2.Z
samplefile.Z:   -- replaced with samplefile
samplefile2.Z:  -- replaced with samplefile2
[root@server1 ~]# ls -l
total 28
drwx------    3 root       root          4096 Jul 21 08:15 Desktop
-rw-r--r--    1 root       root         20239 Jul 21 08:15 samplefile
-rw-rw-r--    1 root       root           574 Jul 21 08:18 samplefile2
[root@server1 ~]# _
```

The uncompress command prompts you for confirmation if any existing files will be overwritten during decompression. To prevent this confirmation, you can use the -f option to the uncompress command.

You can omit the .Z extension when using the uncompress command. The command uncompress -v samplefile samplefile2 would achieve the same results as the command shown in the preceding output.

Furthermore, the compress utility is a filter command that can take information from standard input (stdin) and send it to standard output (stdout). For example, to send the output of the who command to the compress utility and save the compressed information to a file called file.Z, you can execute the following command:

```
[root@server1 ~]# who | compress -v >file.Z
Compression: 21.35%
[root@server1 ~]# _
```

Following this, you can display the contents of file.Z using the zcat command, or decompress it using the uncompress command, as shown in the following output:

```
[root@server1 ~]# zcat file.Z
root        pts/1     Jul 20 19:22 (3.0.0.2)
root        tty5      Jul 15 19:03
root        pts/1     Jul 17 19:58
[root@server1 root]# uncompress -v file.Z
file.Z:   -- replaced with file
[root@server1 ~]# _
```

Table 11-1 provides a summary of options commonly used with the compress utility.

The gzip Utility

The **GNU zip (gzip)** utility uses a Lempel-Ziv compression algorithm (LZ77) that varies slightly from the one used by the compress utility. Typically, this algorithm yields better

Option	Description
-c	When used with the uncompress command, it displays the contents of the compressed file to SO (same function as the zcat command).
-f	When used with the compress command, it can be used to compress symbolic links. When used with the uncompress command, it overwrites any existing files without prompting the user.
-r	This option Specifies to compress or decompress all files recursively within a specified directory.
-v	This option Displays verbose output (compression ratio and filenames) during compression and decompression.

Table 11-1 **Common options used with the compress utility**

compression than the one used by compress. The average compression ratio for gzip is 60 to 70 percent.

Like the compress utility, symbolic links are not compressed by the gzip utility unless the −f option is given, and the −r option can be used to compress all files in a certain directory. In addition, the ownership, modification, and access times of compressed files are preserved by default, and the −v option to the gzip command can be used to display the compression ratio and filename. However, gzip uses the .gz filename extension by default.

To compress the samplefile and samplefile2 files shown earlier and view the compression ratio, you can use the following command:

```
[root@server1 ~]# gzip –v samplefile samplefile2
samplefile:                    56.8% -- replaced with samplefile.gz
samplefile2:                   40.7% -- replaced with samplefile2.gz
[root@server1 ~]# _
```

You can also use the zcat and zmore commands to send the contents of a compressed file to SO. Along the same lines, the gzip command can accept information via SI. Thus, to compress the output of the date command to a file called file.gz and view its contents afterward, you can use the following commands:

```
[root@server1 ~]# date | gzip -v >file.gz
- 6.8%
[root@server1 ~]# zcat file.gz
Sun Jul 25 19:24:56 EDT 2010
[root@server1 ~]# _
```

To decompress the file.gz file in the preceding output, you can use the −d option to the gzip command, or the **gunzip command**, as shown in the following output:

```
[root@server1 ~]# gunzip -v file.gz
file.gz:              - 6.8% -- replaced with file
[root@server1 ~]# _
```

Like the uncompress command, the gunzip command prompts you to overwrite existing files unless the −f option is specified. Furthermore, you can omit the .gz extension when decompressing files, as shown in the following example:

11

```
[root@server1 ~]# ls -l
total 20
drwx------    3 root    root     4096 Jul 21 08:15 Desktop
-rw-rw-r--    1 root    root      370 Jul 21 08:18 samplefile2.gz
-rw-r--r--    1 root    root     8763 Jul 21 08:15 samplefile.gz
[root@server1 ~]# gunzip -v samplefile samplefile2
samplefile.gz:          56.8% -- replaced with samplefile
samplefile2.gz:         40.7% -- replaced with samplefile2
[root@server1 ~]# ls -l
total 28
drwx------    3 root    root     4096 Jul 21 08:15 Desktop
-rw-r--r--    1 root    root    20239 Jul 21 08:15 samplefile
-rw-rw-r--    1 root    root      574 Jul 21 08:18 samplefile2
[root@server1 ~]# _
```

One of the largest advantages the gzip utility has over the compress utility is its ability to control the level of compression via a numeric option. The -1 option is also known as fast compression and results in a lower compression ratio. Alternatively, the -9 option is known as best compression and results in the highest compression ratio at the expense of time. If no level of compression is specified, the gzip command assumes the number 6.

The following command compresses the samplefile file shown earlier using fast compression and displays the compression ratio:

```
[root@server1 ~]# gzip -v -1 samplefile
samplefile:             51.3% -- replaced with samplefile.gz
[root@server1 ~]# _
```

Notice from the preceding output that samplefile was compressed with a compression ratio of 51.3 percent, which is much lower than the compression ratio of 56.8 percent obtained earlier when samplefile was compressed with the default level of 6.

You need not specify the level of compression when decompressing files, as it is built in to the compressed file itself.

Many more options are available to the gzip utility than to the compress utility, and many of these options have a POSIX option equivalent. Table 11-2 shows a list of these options.

The bzip2 Utility

The **bzip2** utility differs from the compress and gzip utilities previously discussed in that it uses the Burrows-Wheeler Block Sorting Huffman Coding algorithm when compressing files. In addition, the bzip2 utility cannot be used to compress a directory full of files, the zcat and zmore commands cannot be used to view files compressed with bzip2, and the compression ratio is 50 to 75 percent on average.

Like the compress and gzip utilities, symbolic links are only compressed if the -f option is used, and the -v option can be used to display compression ratios. Also, file ownership, modification, and access time are preserved during compression.

Option	Description
-#	Specifies how thorough the compression will be, where # can be any number between 1 and 9. The option -1 represents fast compression, which takes less time to compress but results in a lower compression ratio. The option -9 represents thorough compression, which takes more time but results in a higher compression ratio.
--best	Results in a higher compression ratio; same as the -9 option.
-c --stdout -to-stdout	Displays the contents of the compress file to SO (same function as the zcat command) when used with the gunzip command.
-d --decompress --uncompress	Decompresses the files specified (same as the gunzip command) when used with the gzip command.
-f --force	Compresses symbolic links when used with the gzip command. When used with the gunzip command, it overwrites any existing files without prompting the user.
--fast	Results in a lower compression ratio; same as the -1 option.
-h --help	Displays the syntax and available options for the gzip and gunzip commands.
-l --list	Lists the compression ratio for files that have been compressed with gzip.
-n --no-name	Does not allow gzip and gunzip to preserve the original modification and access time for files.
-q --quiet	Suppresses all warning messages.
-r --recursive	Specifies to compress or decompress all files recursively within a specified directory.
-S .suffix --suffix .suffix	Specifies a file suffix other than .gz when compressing or decompressing files.
-t --test	Performs a test decompression such that a user can view any error messages before decompression, when used with the gunzip command; it does not decompress files.
-v --verbose	Displays verbose output (compression ratio and filenames) during compression and decompression.

Table 11-2 Common options used with the gzip utility

The filename extension given to files compressed with bzip2 is .bz2. To compress the samplefile and samplefile2 files and view their compression ratios and filenames, you can use the following commands:

```
[root@server1 ~]# bzip2 -v samplefile samplefile2
samplefile: 2.637:1, 3.034 bits/byte, 62.08% saved, 20239 in, 7675 out.
samplefile2: 1.483:1, 5.394 bits/byte, 32.58% saved, 574 in, 387 out.
[root@server1 ~]# ls -l
total 16
drwx------    3 root      root        4096 Jul 21 08:15 Desktop
-rw-rw-r--    1 root      root         387 Jul 21 08:18 samplefile2.bz2
-rw-r--r--    1 root      root        7675 Jul 21 08:15 samplefile.bz2
[root@server1 ~]# _
```

Because the compression algorithm is different than the one used by the compress and gzip utilities, you must use the **bzcat command** to display the contents of compressed files to SO, as shown in the following example:

```
[root@server1 ~]# bzcat samplefile2.bz2
Hi there, I hope this day finds you well.

Unfortunately we were not able to make it to your dining
room this year while vacationing in Algonquin Park - I
especially wished to see the model of the Highland Inn
and the train station in the dining room.

I have been reading on the history of Algonquin Park but
no where could I find a description of where the Highland
Inn was originally located on Cache lake.

If it is no trouble, could you kindly let me know such that
I need not wait until next year when I visit your lodge?

Regards,
Mackenzie Elizabeth

[root@server1 ~]# _
```

 You can also use the **bzmore** and **bzless** commands to view the contents of a bzip2-compressed file page-by-page.

To decompress files, you can use the **bunzip2 command** followed by the filename(s) to decompress; unlike with compress and gzip, you must include the filename extension when decompressing files. To decompress the samplefile and samplefile2 files created earlier and view the results, you can use the following command:

```
[root@server1 ~]# bunzip2 -v samplefile.bz2 samplefile2.bz2
 samplefile.bz2: done
 samplefile2.bz2: done
[root@server1 ~]# _
```

Option	Description
`-#`	Specifies the block size used during compression; `-1` indicates a block size of 100K, whereas `-9` indicates a block size of 900K.
`-c` `--stdout`	Displays the contents of the compressed file to SO when used with the `bunzip2` command.
`-d` `--decompress`	Decompresses the files specified (same as the `bunzip2` command) when used with the `bzip2` command.
`-f` `--force`	Compresses symbolic links when used with the `bzip2` command. When used with the `bunzip2` command, it overwrites any existing files without prompting the user.
`-k` `--keep`	Keeps the original file during compression; a new file is created with the extension `.bz2`.
`-q` `--quiet`	Suppresses all warning messages.
`-s` `--small`	Minimizes memory usage during compression.
`-t` `--test`	Performs a test decompression such that a user can view any error messages before decompression, when used with the `bunzip2` command; it does not decompress files.
`-v` `--verbose`	Displays verbose output (compression ratio) during compression and decompression.

Table 11-3 **Common options used with the bzip2 utility**

If any files are about to be overwritten, the `bunzip2` command prompts the user for confirmation. To skip this confirmation, you can include the `-f` option. Table 11-3 lists other common options used with the bzip2 utility.

System Backup

It's a good idea to create backup copies of files and directories regularly and store them at an alternate location. You can then distribute these backup copies to other computers or use them to restore files lost as a result of a system failure. This entire process is known as **system backup**, and the backup copies of files and directories are called **archives**.

You can create archives on many different types of media, such as tapes, Zip disks, floppy disks, CDs, DVDs, or hard disks. Traditionally, tapes were used to back up data. Today, large backups are typically performed using separate hard disks. Smaller backups are performed using CDs or DVDs, which require special burning software described later in this chapter.

Table 11-4 shows a list of some common device files for use with different tape devices.

Device File	Description
/dev/st0	First SCSI tape device (rewinding)
/dev/st1	Second SCSI tape device (rewinding)
/dev/st2	Third SCSI tape device (rewinding)
/dev/nst0	First SCSI tape device (nonrewinding)
/dev/ht0	First ATAPI IDE tape device (rewinding)
/dev/nht0	First ATAPI IDE tape device (nonrewinding)
/dev/ftape	First floppy tape device

Table 11-4 Common tape device files

A typical Linux system can include hundreds of thousands of files, but you don't have to include all of them in an archive. For example, you don't have to include temporary files in the /tmp and /var/tmp directories, nor do you need to include any cached Internet content found in the .mozilla directory (if you use the Mozilla Firefox Web browser) under each user's home directory.

As a rule of thumb, you should back up user files from home directories and any important system configuration files such as /etc/passwd. In addition to this, you might want to back up files used by system services. For example, you need to back up Web site files if the Linux computer is used as a Web server. Programs such as grep and vi need not be backed up because they can be restored from the original installation media in the event of a system failure.

After files have been selected for system backup, you can use a backup utility to copy the files to the appropriate media. Several backup utilities are available to Linux administrators. The most common are the following:

- tar
- cpio
- dump/restore
- Disk-burning software

The tar Utility

The **tape archive (tar)** utility is one of the oldest and most widely used backup utilities. It can create an archive in a file on a filesystem or directly on a device.

Like the compression utilities discussed earlier, the tar utility accepts options to determine the location of the archive and the action to perform on the archive. Any arguments specified to the `tar` command list the file(s) to place in the archive. Table 11-5 depicts a list of common options used with the `tar` command.

Because tar is a widely used utility, the options shown in Table 11-5 are often used in other similar utilities. One example is the jar utility, which archives reusable class files used by the Java programming language.

Option	Description

`-A`
`--catenate`
`--concatenate`
	Appends whole archives to another archive

`-c` `--create`	Creates a new archive
`--exclude FILENAME`	Excludes *FILENAME* when creating an archive
`-f FILENAME` `--file FILENAME`	Specifies the location of the archive (*FILENAME*); it can be a file on a filesystem or a device file
`-h` `--dereference`	Prevents tar from backing up symbolic links; instead, *tar* backs up the target files of symbolic links
`-j` `--bzip`	Compresses/decompresses the archive using the bzip2 utility
`-P` `--absolute-paths`	Stores filenames in an archive using absolute pathnames
`-r` `--append`	Appends files to an existing archive
`--remove-files`	Removes files after adding them to an archive
`-t` `--list`	Lists the filename contents (table of contents) of an existing archive
`-u` `--update`	Appends files to an existing archive only if they are newer than the same filename inside the archive
`-v` `--verbose`	Displays verbose output (file and directory information) when manipulating archives

`-w`
`--interactive`
`--confirmation`
	Prompts the user for confirmation of each action

`-W` `--verify`	Verifies the contents of each archive after creation

`-x`
`--extract`
`--get`
	Extracts the contents of an archive

`-z`
`--gzip`
`--ungzip`
	Compresses/decompresses the archive using the gzip utility

`-Z`
`--compress`
`--uncompress`
	Compresses/decompresses the archive using the compress utility

Table 11-5 Common options used with the tar utility

To create an archive called /backup.tar that contains the contents of the current directory and view the results, you can use the following commands:

```
[root@server1 ~]# tar -cvf /backup.tar *
Desktop/
Desktop/Home.desktop
Desktop/trash.desktop
samplefile
samplefile2
[root@server1 ~]# ls -l /backup.tar
-rw-r--r--        1 root      root           40960 Jul 27 10:49 /backup.tar
[root@server1 ~]# _
```

Note from the preceding command that the -f option is followed by the pathname of the archive and that the * metacharacter indicates that all files in the current directory will be added to this archive. Also note that files are backed up recursively by default and stored using relative pathnames; to force the use of absolute pathnames when creating archives, simply use the -P option to the tar command.

The filename used for an archive need not have an extension. However, it is good practice to name archive files with an extension to identify their contents, as with /backup.tar in the preceding example.

The tar utility cannot back up device files or files with filenames longer than 255 characters.

After creating an archive, you can view its detailed contents by specifying the -t (table of contents) option to the tar command and the archive to view. For example, to view the detailed contents of the /backup.tar archive created earlier, you can use the following command:

```
[root@server1 ~]# tar -tvf /backup.tar
drwx------ root/root          0 2010-07-21 08:15  Desktop/
-rw-r--r-- root/root       3595 2010-06-21 20:32  Desktop/Home.desktop
-rw-r--r-- root/root       3595 2010-06-21 20:32  Desktop/trash.desktop
-rw-r--r-- root/root      20239 2010-07-21 08:15  samplefile
-rw-rw-r-- root/root        574 2010-07-21 08:18  samplefile2
[root@server1 ~]# _
```

You can use the -x option with the tar command to extract a specified archive. To extract the contents of the /backup.tar file to a new directory called /tartest and view the results, you can use the following commands:

```
[root@server1 ~]# mkdir /tartest
[root@server1 ~]# cd /tartest
[root@server1 tartest]# tar -xvf /backup.tar
Desktop/
```

```
Desktop/Home.desktop
Desktop/trash.desktop
samplefile
samplefile2
[root@server1 tartest]# ls -F
Desktop/  samplefile  samplefile2
[root@server1 tartest]# _
```

After an archive has been created in a file on a filesystem, that file can be sent to other computers across a network or the Internet. This is the most common form of backup today and a common method used to distribute software across the Internet. Unfortunately, the tar utility does not compress files inside the archive. Thus, the time needed to transfer the archive across a network is high. To reduce transfer times, you can compress the archive using a compression utility before transmission. Because this is a common task, the tar command accepts options that allow you to compress an archive immediately after creation using the compress, gzip, or bzip2 utilities.

To create a gzip-compressed archive called /backup.tar.gz that contains the contents of the current directory and view the results, you can use the following commands:

```
[root@server1 ~]# tar -zcvf /backup.tar.gz *
Desktop/
Desktop/Home.desktop
Desktop/trash.desktop
samplefile
samplefile2
[root@server1 ~]# ls -l /backup.tar*
-rw-r--r--   1 root      root        40960 Jul 27 10:49 /backup.tar
-rw-r--r--   1 root      root        12207 Jul 27 11:18 /backup.tar.gz
[root@server1 ~]# _
```

Note in the preceding output that the −z option indicated compression using the gzip utility, and that we chose to end the filename with the .tar.gz extension. In addition, the size of the /backup.tar.gz file is much less than the /backup.tar file created earlier.

Filenames that end with the .tar.gz or .tgz extensions are commonly called **tarballs** because they represent compressed tar archives.

To view the contents of a gzip-compressed archive, you must use the −z option in addition to the −t option followed by the archive to view. The detailed contents of the /backup.tar.gz file can be viewed using the following command:

```
[root@server1 ~]# tar -ztvf /backup.tar.gz
drwx------ root/root         0 2010-07-21 08:15  Desktop/
-rw-r--r-- root/root      3595 2010-06-21 20:32  Desktop/Home.desktop
-rw-r--r-- root/root      3595 2010-06-21 20:32  Desktop/trash.desktop
-rw-r--r-- root/root     20239 2010-07-21 08:15  samplefile
-rw-rw-r-- root/root       574 2010-07-21 08:18  samplefile2
[root@server1 ~]# _
```

Similarly, when extracting a gzip-compressed archive, you must supply the -z option to the tar command. To extract the contents of the /backup.tar.gz file to a new directory called /tartest2 and view the results, you can use the following commands:

```
[root@server1 ~]# mkdir /tartest2
[root@server1 ~]# cd /tartest2
[root@server1 tartest2]# tar -zxvf /backup.tar.gz
Desktop/
Desktop/Home.desktop
Desktop/trash.desktop
samplefile
samplefile2
[root@server1 tartest2]# ls -F
Desktop/  samplefile  samplefile2
[root@server1 tartest2]# _
```

Backing up files to a compressed archive on a filesystem is useful when you plan to transfer the archived data across a network. However, you can use tar to back up data directly to a device such as a tape. To back up files to a device, you can use the -f option to the tar command to specify the pathname to the appropriate device file. Files are then transferred directly to the device, overwriting any other data or filesystems that might be present.

For example, to create an archive on the first rewinding SCSI tape device containing the contents of the current directory, you can use the following command:

```
[root@server1 ~]# tar -cvf /dev/st0 *
Desktop/
Desktop/Home.desktop
Desktop/trash.desktop
samplefile
samplefile2
[root@server1 ~]#
```

You can then view the contents of the archive on the tape device used in the preceding example using the command tar -tvf /dev/st0, or you can extract the contents of the archive on the tape device using the command tar -xvf /dev/st0 in a similar fashion to the examples shown earlier.

Because tape devices can hold large amounts of information, you might want to add to a tar archive that already exists on the tape device. To do this, simply replace the -c option with the -r option when using the tar utility. For example, to append a file called samplefile3 to the archive created in the previous output and view the results, you can use the following commands:

```
[root@server1 ~]# tar -rvf /dev/st0 samplefile3
samplefile3
[root@server1 ~]# tar -tvf /dev/st0
drwx------ root/root        0 2010-07-21 08:15  Desktop/
-rw-r--r-- root/root     3595 2010-06-21 20:32  Desktop/Home.desktop
-rw-r--r-- root/root     3595 2010-06-21 20:32  Desktop/trash.desktop
-rw-r--r-- root/root    20239 2010-07-21 08:15  samplefile
-rw-rw-r-- root/root      574 2010-07-21 08:18  samplefile2
-rw-r--r-- root/root      147 2010-07-27 16:15  samplefile3
[root@server1 ~]# _
```

The cpio Utility

Another common backup utility is **copy in/out (cpio)**. Although this utility uses options similar to the `tar` utility, `cpio` has some added features, including long filenames and the ability to back up device files.

Because its primary use is to back up files in case of system failure, `cpio` uses absolute pathnames by default when archiving. In addition, `cpio` normally takes a list of files to archive from SI and sends the files "out" to the archive specified by the –O option. Conversely, when extracting an archive, you must include the –I option to indicate the archive from which to read "in" files.

Table 11-6 provides a list of commonly used options to the `cpio` command and their descriptions.

Option	Description
-A --append	Appends files to an existing archive
-B	Changes the default block size from 512 bytes to 5KB, thus speeding up the transfer of information
-c	Uses a storage format (SVR4) that is widely recognized by different versions of cpio for UNIX and Linux
-d --make-directories	Creates directories as needed during extraction
-i --extract	Reads files from an archive
-I FILENAME	Represents the input archive; it is the file or device file of the archive used when viewing or extracting files
-L --dereference	Prevents cpio from backing up symbolic links; instead, cpio backs up the target files of symbolic links
--no-absolute-filenames	Stores filenames in an archive using relative pathnames
-o --create	Creates a new archive
-O FILENAME	Represents the output archive; it is the file or device file of the target archive when backing up files
-t --list	Lists the filename contents (table of contents) of an existing archive
-u --unconditional	Overwrites existing files during extraction without prompting for user confirmation
-v --verbose	Displays verbose output (file and directory information) when manipulating archives

Table 11-6 Common options used with the `cpio` command

To create an archive using cpio, you must first generate a list of filenames. You can do this using the find command. To list all filenames underneath the /root/sample directory, you can use the following command:

```
[root@server1 ~]# find /root/sample
/root/sample
/root/sample/samplefile
/root/sample/samplefile2
[root@server1 ~]# _
```

Next, you can send this list via SI to the cpio command. For example, to verbosely back up all files in /root/sample to the first SCSI tape device using a block size of 5KB and a common format, you can use the following command:

```
[root@server1 ~]# find /root/sample | cpio -vocB -O /dev/st0
/root/sample
/root/sample/samplefile
/root/sample/samplefile2
5 blocks
[root@server1 ~]# _
```

To view the verbose table of contents of this archive, you can use the following command:

```
[root@server1 ~]# cpio -vitB -I /dev/st0
drwxr-xr-x   2 root   root       0 Jul 27 13:40 /root/sample
-rw-r--r--   1 root   root   20239 Jul 21 08:15 /root/sample/samplefile
-rw-rw-r--   1 root   root     574 Jul 21 08:18 /root/sample/samplefile2
5 blocks
[root@server1 ~]# _
```

Following this, you can extract the archive on /dev/st0, creating directories and overwriting files as needed by using the following command:

```
[root@server1 ~]# cpio -vicduB -I /dev/st0
/root/sample
/root/sample/samplefile
/root/sample/samplefile2
5 blocks
[root@server1 ~]# _
```

Like tar, the cpio command can be used to create an archive on a file on the filesystem; to do this, specify the filename after the –O option. To create an archive called /root/sample.cpio that contains the files from the directory /root/sample, using a block size of 5KB as well as a common header, and view the results, you can issue the following commands:

```
[root@server1 ~]# find /root/sample | cpio -vocB –O /root/sample.cpio
/root/sample
/root/sample/samplefile
/root/sample/samplefile2
5 blocks
[root@server1 ~]# ls -l sample.cpio
```

```
-rw-rw-rw-    1 root    root    25600 Jul 27 13:45 sample.cpio
[root@server1 ~]# _
```

As with the tar utility, cpio archive filenames need not have an extension to identify their contents. However, it is good practice to use extensions, as shown with /root/sample.cpio in the preceding example.

The dump/restore Utility

Like the tar and cpio utilities, the **dump/restore** utility can be used to back up files and directories to a device or to a file on the filesystem. However, the dump/restore utility can only work with files on ext2 and ext3 filesystems.

Although the dump/restore utility can be used to back up only certain files and directories, it was designed to back up entire filesystems to an archive and keep track of these filesystems in a file called **/etc/dumpdates**. Because archiving all data on a filesystem (known as a **full backup**) might take a long time, you can choose to perform a full backup only on weekends and incremental backups each evening during the week. An **incremental backup** backs up only the data that has been changed since the last backup. In the case of a system failure, you can restore the information from the full backup and then restore the information from all subsequent incremental backups in sequential order. You can perform up to nine different incremental backups using the dump/restore utility; number 0 represents a full backup, whereas numbers 1 through 9 represent incremental backups.

Suppose, for example, that you perform a full backup of the /dev/sda3 filesystem on Sunday, perform incremental backups from Monday to Wednesday, and on Thursday the /dev/sda3 filesystem becomes corrupted, as depicted in Figure 11-1.

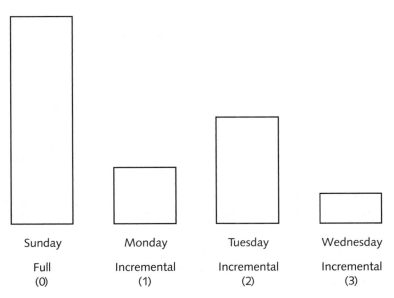

Sunday	Monday	Tuesday	Wednesday
Full	Incremental	Incremental	Incremental
(0)	(1)	(2)	(3)

Figure 11-1 A sample backup strategy

Source: Course Technology/Cengage Learning

Option	Description
-#	Specifies the type of backup when used with the dump command; if # is 0, a full backup is performed. If # is 1 through 9, the appropriate incremental backup is performed.
-b NUM	Specifies a certain block size to use in Kilobytes; the default block size is 10KB.
-f FILENAME	Specifies the pathname to the archive; the FILENAME can be a file on a filesystem or a device file.
-u	Specifies to update the /etc/dumpdates file after a successful backup.
-n	Notifies the user if any errors occur and when the backup has completed.
-r	Extracts an entire archive when used with the restore command.
-x FILENAME	Extracts a certain file or files represented by FILENAME when used with the restore command.
-i	Restores files interactively, prompting the user for confirmation for all actions, when used with the restore command.
-t	Lists the filename contents (table of contents) of an existing archive when used with the restore command.
-v	Displays verbose output (file and directory information) when manipulating archives.

Table 11-7 Common options used with the dump/restore utility

After the filesystem has been re-created, you should restore the full backup (0) followed by the first incremental backup (1), the second incremental backup (2), and the third incremental backup (3) to ensure that data has been properly recovered.

The dump/restore utility has many options available to it, as do the tar and cpio utilities. Table 11-7 provides a list of these options.

Take, for example, the output from the following df command:

```
[root@server1 ~]# df
Filesystem          1K-blocks        Used  Available  Use%  Mounted on
/dev/sda1            30237648     6885728   21815920   24%  /
tmpfs                  480640         272     480368    1%  /dev/shm
/dev/sda3            15481840      169484   14525924    2%  /data
[root@server1 ~]# _
```

To perform a full backup of the /data partition (/dev/sda3) to the first rewinding SCSI tape device and update the /etc/dumpdates file when completed, you can issue the following command:

```
[root@server1 ~]# dump -0uf /dev/st0 /dev/sda3
DUMP: Date of this level 0 dump: Sat Aug 28 10:39:12 2010
DUMP: Dumping /dev/sda3 (/data) to /dev/st0
DUMP: Label: none
DUMP: Writing 10 Kilobyte records
DUMP: mapping (Pass I) [regular files]
DUMP: mapping (Pass II) [directories]
```

```
DUMP: estimated 300 blocks.
DUMP: Volume 1 started with block 1 at: Sat Aug 28 10:39:12 2010
DUMP: dumping (Pass III) [directories]
DUMP: dumping (Pass IV) [regular files]
DUMP: Closing /dev/sda3
DUMP: Volume 1 completed at: Sat Aug 28 10:39:12 2010
DUMP: Volume 1 290 blocks (0.28MB)
DUMP: 290 blocks (0.28MB) on 1 volume(s)
DUMP: finished in less than a second
DUMP: Date of this level 0 dump: Sat Aug 28 10:39:12 2010
DUMP: Date this dump completed: Sat Aug 28 10:39:12 2010
DUMP: Average transfer rate: 0 kB/s
DUMP: DUMP IS DONE
[root@server1 ~]# _
```

Alternatively, you can specify the filesystem mount point when using the dump command. The command dump -0uf /dev/st0 /data is equivalent to the one used in the preceding example.

The contents of the /etc/dumpdates file now indicate that a full backup has taken place:

```
[root@server1 ~]# cat /etc/dumpdates
/dev/sda3 0 Sat Aug 28 10:39:12 2010 -0400
[root@server1 ~]# _
```

To perform the first incremental backup and view the contents of the /etc/dumpdates file, you can place a new tape into the SCSI tape drive and use the following commands:

```
[root@server1 ~]# dump -1uf /dev/st0 /dev/hda2
DUMP: Date of this level 1 dump: Sat Aug 28 10:41:09 2010
DUMP: Date of last level 0 dump: Sat Aug 28 10:39:12 2010
DUMP: Dumping /dev/sda3 (/data) to /dev/st0
DUMP: Label: none
DUMP: Writing 10 Kilobyte records
DUMP: mapping (Pass I) [regular files]
DUMP: mapping (Pass II) [directories]
DUMP: estimated 255 blocks.
DUMP: Volume 1 started with block 1 at: Sat Aug 28 10:41:10 2010
DUMP: dumping (Pass III) [directories]
DUMP: dumping (Pass IV) [regular files]
DUMP: Closing /dev/sda3
DUMP: Volume 1 completed at: Sat Aug 28 10:41:10 2010
DUMP: Volume 1 250 blocks (0.24MB)
DUMP: 250 blocks (0.24MB) on 1 volume(s)
DUMP: finished in less than a second
DUMP: Date of this level 1 dump: Sat Aug 28 10:41:09 2010
DUMP: Date this dump completed: Sat Aug 28 10:41:10 2010
DUMP: Average transfer rate: 0 kB/s
DUMP: DUMP IS DONE
```

```
[root@server1 ~]# cat /etc/dumpdates
/dev/sda3 0 Sat Aug 28 10:39:12 2010 -0400
/dev/sda3 1 Sat Aug 28 10:41:09 2010 -0400
[root@server1 ~]# _
```

To view the contents of an archive, you can specify the -t option to the restore command followed by the archive information. To view the contents of the full backup performed earlier, you can place the appropriate tape into the tape drive and execute the following command:

```
[root@server1 ~]# restore -tf /dev/st0
Dump date: Sat Aug 28 10:39:12 2010
Dumped from: the epoch
Level 0 dump of /data on server1.class.com:/dev/sda3
Label: none
        2       .
       11       ./lost+found
       12       ./inittab
       13       ./hosts
       14       ./issue
       17       ./aquota.user
       15       ./aquota.group
[root@server1 ~]# _
```

To extract the full backup shown in the preceding output, you can specify the -r option to the restore command followed by the archive information. In addition, you can specify the -v option to list the filenames restored, as shown in the following example:

```
[root@server1 ~]# restore -vrf /dev/st0
Verify tape and initialize maps
Input is from a local file/pipe
Input block size is 32
Dump date: Sat Aug 28 10:39:12 2010
Dumped from: the epoch
Level 0 dump of /data on server1.class.com:/dev/sda3
Label: none
Begin level 0 restore
Initialize symbol table.
Extract directories from tape
Calculate extraction list.
Make node ./lost+found
Extract new leaves.
Check pointing the restore
extract file ./inittab
extract file ./hosts
extract file ./issue
extract file ./aquota.group
extract file ./aquota.user
Add links
Set directory mode, owner, and times.
```

Figure 11-2 The Brasero Disc Burner program

Source: Course Technology/Cengage Learning

```
Check the symbol table.
Check pointing the restore
[root@server1 ~]# _
```

Burning Software

The tar, cpio, and dump utilities copy data to a backup medium in a character-by-character or block-by-block format. As a result, they are typically used to create backup copies of files on tape, floppy, and hard disk media because those media accept data in that format. To write files to CD and DVD media, you must use a program that allows you to select the data to copy, organize that data, build a CD or DVD filesystem, and write the entire filesystem (including the data) to the CD or DVD. Recall from Chapter 5 that the programs that can be used to do this are collectively called disc-burning software. Fedora 13 comes with the Brasero Disc Burner burning software, as shown in Figure 11-2. You can access the Brasero Disc Burner program by navigating to Applications, Sound & Video, Brasero Disc Burner within the GNOME Desktop Environment.

Software Installation

Primary responsibilities of most Linux administrators typically include installing and maintaining software packages. Software for Linux can consist of binary files that have been precompiled to run on certain hardware architectures such as 32-bit Intel (x86), or as source code, which must be compiled on the local architecture before use. The largest advantage to obtaining and compiling source code is that the source code is not created for a particular hardware architecture. After being compiled, the program executes natively on the architecture from which it was compiled.

The most common method for obtaining software for Linux is via the Internet. Appendix C lists some common Web sites that host Linux Open Source Software for download.

When downloading software files from the Internet, you might notice that the Internet site lists a **checksum** value for the file, which was calculated from the exact file contents. To ensure that the file was received in its entirety after you download it, you should verify that the checksum value hasn't changed. You can use one of several ***sum commands**, depending on the algorithm used to create the checksum. For example, you can use the `md5sum programfile` command to check an MD5 checksum, the `sha1sum program-file` command to check an SHA-1 checksum, the `sha256sum programfile` command to check an SHA-256 checksum, or the `sha512sum programfile` command to check an SHA-512 checksum.

Program source code is typically distributed as a format, which you can uncompress. After you have uncompressed it, you can extract the source code and compile it. Precompiled binary programs can also be distributed in tarball format, but are typically distributed in a format for use with a package manager.

Recall from Chapter 1 that a **package manager** provides a standard format for distributing programs as well as a central database to store information about software packages installed on the system; this allows software packages to be queried and easily uninstalled. Most Linux distributions today, including Fedora, use the **Red Hat Package Manager** (**RPM**). However, Debian and Debian-based Linux distributions, such as Ubuntu Linux, use the **Debian Package Manager** (**DPM**). Because the DPM is not supported on Fedora, we focus on the RPM in this chapter.

Compiling Source Code into Programs

The procedure for compiling source code into binary programs is standardized today among most Open Source Software (OSS) developers. Because most source code comes in tarball format, you must uncompress and extract the files. This creates a subdirectory under the current directory containing the source code. In addition, this directory typically contains a README file with information about the program and an INSTALL file with instructions for installation.

While inside the source code directory, the first step to installation is to run the configure program. This performs a preliminary check for system requirements and creates a list of what to compile inside a file called Makefile in the current directory.

Next, you can type the `make` command, which looks for the Makefile file and uses the information in it to compile the source code into binary programs using the appropriate compiler program for the local hardware architecture. For example, software written in the C programming language is compiled using the **GNU C Compiler** (**gcc**). After compilation, the binary files the program comprises remain in the source code directory. To copy the files to the appropriate location on the filesystem, such as a directory listed in the PATH variable, you must type `make install`.

 Most Linux programs are installed to a subdirectory of the /usr/local directory after compilation.

After the program has been compiled and copied to the correct location on the filesystem, you can remove the source code directory and its contents from the system.

Suppose, for example, that you download the source code for rdesktop (Remote Desktop Protocol client) version 1.6.0 from the Internet at *www.sourceforge.net*:

```
[root@server1 ~]# ls -F
Desktop/   rdesktop-1.6.0.tar.gz
[root@server1 ~]# _
```

The first step to installing this program is to uncompress and extract the tarball, as shown in the following output. This creates a directory called rdesktop-1.6.0 containing the source code and supporting files.

```
[root@server1 ~]# tar -zxvf rdesktop-1.6.0.tar.gz
rdesktop-1.6.0/COPYING
rdesktop-1.6.0/README
rdesktop-1.6.0/configure
rdesktop-1.6.0/configure.ac
rdesktop-1.6.0/config.sub
rdesktop-1.6.0/config.guess
rdesktop-1.6.0/bootstrap
rdesktop-1.6.0/install-sh
rdesktop-1.6.0/Makefile.in
rdesktop-1.6.0/rdesktop.spec
rdesktop-1.6.0/bitmap.c
rdesktop-1.6.0/cache.c
rdesktop-1.6.0/channels.c
rdesktop-1.6.0/cliprdr.c
rdesktop-1.6.0/disk.c
rdesktop-1.6.0/ewmhints.c
rdesktop-1.6.0/iso.c
rdesktop-1.6.0/licence.c
rdesktop-1.6.0/lspci.c
rdesktop-1.6.0/mcs.c
rdesktop-1.6.0/mppc.c
rdesktop-1.6.0/orders.c
rdesktop-1.6.0/parallel.c
rdesktop-1.6.0/printer.c
rdesktop-1.6.0/printercache.c
rdesktop-1.6.0/pstcache.c
rdesktop-1.6.0/rdesktop.c
rdesktop-1.6.0/rdp.c
rdesktop-1.6.0/rdp5.c
rdesktop-1.6.0/rdpdr.c
```

```
rdesktop-1.6.0/rdpsnd.c
rdesktop-1.6.0/rdpsnd_alsa.c
rdesktop-1.6.0/rdpsnd_dsp.c
rdesktop-1.6.0/rdpsnd_libao.c
rdesktop-1.6.0/rdpsnd_oss.c
rdesktop-1.6.0/rdpsnd_sgi.c
rdesktop-1.6.0/rdpsnd_sun.c
rdesktop-1.6.0/scard.c
rdesktop-1.6.0/seamless.c
rdesktop-1.6.0/secure.c
rdesktop-1.6.0/serial.c
rdesktop-1.6.0/ssl.c
rdesktop-1.6.0/tcp.c
rdesktop-1.6.0/xclip.c
rdesktop-1.6.0/xkeymap.c
rdesktop-1.6.0/xwin.c
rdesktop-1.6.0/constants.h
rdesktop-1.6.0/disk.h
rdesktop-1.6.0/orders.h
rdesktop-1.6.0/parse.h
rdesktop-1.6.0/proto.h
rdesktop-1.6.0/rdesktop.h
rdesktop-1.6.0/rdpsnd.h
rdesktop-1.6.0/rdpsnd_dsp.h
rdesktop-1.6.0/scancodes.h
rdesktop-1.6.0/scard.h
rdesktop-1.6.0/seamless.h
rdesktop-1.6.0/ssl.h
rdesktop-1.6.0/types.h
rdesktop-1.6.0/xproto.h
rdesktop-1.6.0/proto.head
rdesktop-1.6.0/proto.tail
rdesktop-1.6.0/keymaps/common
rdesktop-1.6.0/keymaps/modifiers
rdesktop-1.6.0/keymaps/convert-map
rdesktop-1.6.0/doc/HACKING
rdesktop-1.6.0/doc/AUTHORS
rdesktop-1.6.0/doc/TODO
rdesktop-1.6.0/doc/ChangeLog
rdesktop-1.6.0/doc/keymapping.txt
rdesktop-1.6.0/doc/keymap-names.txt
rdesktop-1.6.0/doc/ipv6.txt
rdesktop-1.6.0/doc/licensing.txt
rdesktop-1.6.0/doc/patches.txt
rdesktop-1.6.0/doc/redirection.txt
rdesktop-1.6.0/doc/rdesktop.1
[root@server1 ~]# _
```

Next, you can move to this directory and view the file contents, as shown in the following output:

```
[root@server1 ~]# cd rdesktop-1.6.0
[root@server1 rdesktop-1.6.0]# ls -F
bitmap.c        doc/           parse.h         rdpsnd_alsa.c   seamless.c
bootstrap*      ewmhints.c     printer.c       rdpsnd.c        seamless.h
cache.c         install-sh*    printercache.c  rdpsnd_dsp.c    secure.c
channels.c      iso.c          proto.h         rdpsnd_dsp.h    serial.c
cliprdr.c       keymaps/       proto.head      rdpsnd.h        ssl.c
config.guess*   licence.c      proto.tail      rdpsnd_libao.c  ssl.h
config.sub*     lspci.c        pstcache.c      rdpsnd_oss.c    tcp.c
configure*      Makefile.in    rdesktop.c      rdpsnd_sgi.c    types.h
configure.ac    mcs.c          rdesktop.h      rdpsnd_sun.c    xclip.c
constants.h     mppc.c         rdesktop.spec   README          xkeymap.c
COPYING         orders.c       rdp5.c          scancodes.h     xproto.h
disk.c          orders.h       rdp.c           scard.c         xwin.c
disk.h          parallel.c     rdpdr.c         scard.h
[root@server1 rdesktop-1.6.0]# _
```

In the preceding output, you can see that a README and configure file exist and that the configure file is executable. To execute the configure file without using the PATH variable, you can use the following command:

```
[root@server1 rdesktop-1.6.0]# ./configure
checking for gcc... gcc
checking for C compiler default output file name... a.out
checking whether the C compiler works... yes
checking whether we are cross compiling... no
checking for suffix of executables...
checking for suffix of object files... o
checking whether we are using the GNU C compiler... yes
checking whether gcc accepts -g... yes
checking for gcc option to accept ISO C89... none needed
checking for a BSD-compatible install... /usr/bin/install -c
checking how to run the C preprocessor... gcc -E
checking for grep that handles long lines and -e... /bin/grep
checking for egrep... /bin/grep -E
checking for ANSI C header files... yes
checking for sys/types.h... yes
checking for sys/stat.h... yes
checking whether byte ordering is bigendian... no
checking for X... libraries , headers
checking for gethostbyname... yes
checking for connect... yes
checking for remove... yes
checking for shmat... yes
checking for IceConnectionNumber in -lICE... yes
checking for pkg-config... /usr/bin/pkg-config
```

```
checking for library containing socket... none required
checking for library containing inet_aton... none required
checking sys/select.h usability... yes
checking sys/select.h presence... yes
checking for sys/strtio.h... no
checking locale.h usability... yes
checking locale.h presence... yes
checking for locale.h... yes
checking langinfo.h usability... yes
checking langinfo.h presence... yes
checking for langinfo.h... yes
checking for strip... strip
checking for OpenSSL directory... /usr
checking pkg-config is at least version 0.9.0... yes
checking if architecture needs alignment... no
checking for LIBSAMPLERATE... no
checking for dirent.h that defines DIR... yes
checking for library containing opendir... none required
checking for dirfd... yes
checking whether dirfd is declared... yes
checking whether dirfd is a macro... no
checking iconv.h usability... yes
checking iconv.h presence... yes
checking for iconv.h... yes
checking for iconv... yes
checking for iconv declaration...
          extern size_t iconv (iconv_t cd, char * *inbuf, size_t *inbytesleft,
             char * *outbuf, size_t *outbytesleft);
checking for socklen_t... yes
checking sys/vfs.h usability... yes
checking sys/vfs.h presence... yes
checking for sys/vfs.h... yes
configure: checking how to get filesystem space usage...
checking statvfs64 function (SVR4)... no
checking statvfs function (SVR4)... yes
checking for struct statfs.f_namemax... no
checking for struct statvfs.f_namemax... yes
checking for struct statfs.f_namelen... yes
checking for struct statvfs.f_namelen... no
checking for special C compiler options needed for large files... no
checking for _FILE_OFFSET_BITS value needed for large files... 64
checking mntent.h usability... yes
checking build system type... i686-redhat-linux-gnu
checking host system type... i686-redhat-linux-gnu
configure: creating ./config.status
config.status: creating Makefile
[root@server1 rdesktop-1.6.0]# _
```

After the configure script has run, a Makefile exists in the current directory, as shown in the following output:

```
[root@server1 rdesktop-1.6.0]# head Makefile
#
# rdesktop: A Remote Desktop Protocol client
# Makefile.in
# Copyright (C) Matthew Chapman 1999-2007
#

prefix      = /usr/local
exec_prefix = ${prefix}
bindir      = ${exec_prefix}/bin
mandir      = ${datarootdir}/man
[root@server1 rdesktop-1.6.0]# _
```

This Makefile contains most of the information and commands necessary to compile the program. Some program source code that you download might contain commented lines that you need to uncomment to enable certain features of the program or to allow the program to compile on your computer architecture. Instructions for these commented areas are documented in the Makefile itself; thus, it is good form to read the Makefile after you run the configure script. You can also edit the Makefile if you want to change the location to which the program is installed. For rdesktop, simply change the line prefix=/usr/local shown in the preceding output to reflect the new directory.

Next, you must compile the program according to the settings stored in the Makefile by typing the make command while in the source code directory. This uses the gcc program to compile the source code files, as shown in the following output:

```
[root@server1 rdesktop-1.6.0]# make
gcc -g -O2 -Wall -I/usr/include -I/usr/include/alsa -
DPACKAGE_NAME=\"rdesktop\" -DPACKAGE_TARNAME=\"rdesktop\" -
DPACKAGE_VERSION=\"1.6.0\" -DPACKAGE_STRING=\"rdesktop\ 1.6.0\" -
DPACKAGE_BUGREPORT=\"\" -DSTDC_HEADERS=1 -DHAVE_SYS_TYPES_H=1 -
DHAVE_SYS_STAT_H=1 -DHAVE_STDLIB_H=1 -DHAVE_STRING_H=1 -
DHAVE_MEMORY_H=1 -DHAVE_STRINGS_H=1 -DHAVE_INTTYPES_H=1 -
DHAVE_STDINT_H=1 -DHAVE_UNISTD_H=1 -DL_ENDIAN=1 -DHAVE_SYS_SELECT_H=1 -
DHAVE_LOCALE_H=1 -DHAVE_LANGINFO_H=1 -Dssldir=\"/usr\" -
DEGD_SOCKET=\"/var/run/egd-pool\" -DWITH_RDPSND=1 -DRDPSND_OSS=1 -
DRDPSND_ALSA=1 -DHAVE_DIRENT_H=1 -DHAVE_DIRFD=1 -DHAVE_DECL_DIRFD=1 -
DHAVE_ICONV_H=1 -DHAVE_ICONV=1 -DICONV_CONST= -DHAVE_SYS_VFS_H=1 -
DHAVE_SYS_STATVFS_H=1 -DHAVE_SYS_STATFS_H=1 -DHAVE_SYS_PARAM_H=1 -
DHAVE_SYS_MOUNT_H=1 -DSTAT_STATVFS=1 -DHAVE_STRUCT_STATVFS_F_NAMEMAX=1
-DHAVE_STRUCT_STATFS_F_NAMELEN=1 -D_FILE_OFFSET_BITS=64 -
DHAVE_MNTENT_H=1 -DHAVE_SETMNTENT=1 -
DKEYMAP_PATH=\"/usr/local/share/rdesktop/keymaps/\" -o rdesktop.
o - crdesktop.c
gcc -g -O2 -Wall -I/usr/include -I/usr/include/alsa -
DPACKAGE_NAME=\"rdesktop\" -DPACKAGE_TARNAME=\"rdesktop\" -
DPACKAGE_VERSION=\"1.6.0\" -DPACKAGE_STRING=\"rdesktop\ 1.6.0\" -
DPACKAGE_BUGREPORT=\"\" -DSTDC_HEADERS=1 -DHAVE_SYS_TYPES_H=1 -
```

11

```
DHAVE_SYS_STAT_H=1 -DHAVE_STDLIB_H=1 -DHAVE_STRING_H=1 -
DHAVE_MEMORY_H=1 -DHAVE_STRINGS_H=1 -DHAVE_INTTYPES_H=1 -
DHAVE_STDINT_H=1 -DHAVE_UNISTD_H=1 -DL_ENDIAN=1 -DHAVE_SYS_SELECT_H=1 -
DHAVE_LOCALE_H=1 -DHAVE_LANGINFO_H=1 -Dssldir=\"/usr\" -
DEGD_SOCKET=\"/var/run/egd-pool\" -DWITH_RDPSND=1 -DRDPSND_OSS=1 -
DRDPSND_ALSA=1 -DHAVE_DIRENT_H=1 -DHAVE_DIRFD=1 -DHAVE_DECL_DIRFD=1 -
DHAVE_ICONV_H=1 -DHAVE_ICONV=1 -DICONV_CONST= -DHAVE_SYS_VFS_H=1 -
DHAVE_SYS_STATVFS_H=1 -DHAVE_SYS_STATFS_H=1 -DHAVE_SYS_PARAM_H=1 -
DHAVE_SYS_MOUNT_H=1 -DSTAT_STATVFS=1 -DHAVE_STRUCT_STATVFS_F_NAMEMAX=1
-DHAVE_STRUCT_STATFS_F_NAMELEN=1 -D_FILE_OFFSET_BITS=64 -
DHAVE_MNTENT_H=1 -DHAVE_SETMNTENT=1 -
DKEYMAP_PATH=\"/usr/local/share/rdesktop/keymaps/\" -o xwin.o -c xwin.c
```

<Additional gcc commands omitted here>

```
DKEYMAP_PATH=\"/usr/local/share/rdesktop/keymaps/\" -o rdesktop
rdesktop.o xwin.o xkeymap.o ewmhints.o xclip.o cliprdr.o rdpsnd.o
rdpsnd_dsp.o rdpsnd_oss.o rdpsnd_alsa.o tcp.o iso.o mcs.o secure.o
licence.o rdp.o orders.o bitmap.o cache.o rdp5.o channels.o rdpdr.o
serial.o printer.o disk.o parallel.o printercache.o mppc.o pstcache.o
lspci.o seamless.o ssl.o -L/usr/lib -lcrypto -lasound    -lX11
[root@server1 rdesktop-1.6.0]# _
```

After you compile the source code files, you can copy the compiled executable programs to the correct location on the filesystem by typing the following command:

```
[root@server1 rdesktop-1.6.0]# make install
mkdir -p /usr/local/bin
/usr/bin/install -c rdesktop /usr/local/bin
strip /usr/local/bin/rdesktop
chmod 755 /usr/local/bin/rdesktop
mkdir -p /usr/local/share/rdesktop/keymaps/
cp keymaps/?? keymaps/??-?? /usr/local/share/rdesktop/keymaps/
cp keymaps/common /usr/local/share/rdesktop/keymaps/
cp keymaps/modifiers /usr/local/share/rdesktop/keymaps/
chmod 644 /usr/local/share/rdesktop/keymaps//*
mkdir -p /usr/local/share/man/man1
cp doc/rdesktop.1 /usr/local/share/man/man1
chmod 644 /usr/local/share/man/man1/rdesktop.1
[root@server1 rdesktop-1.6.0]# _
```

After you copy the executable program files to the appropriate directory, you can remove the source code and tarball and locate the main binary file for the program, as shown in the following example:

```
[root@server1 rdesktop-1.6.0]# cd ..
[root@server1 ~]# rm -Rf rdesktop-1.6.0
[root@server1 ~]# rm -f rdesktop-1.6.0.tar.gz
[root@server1 ~]# which rdesktop
/usr/local/bin/rdesktop
[root@server1 ~]# _
```

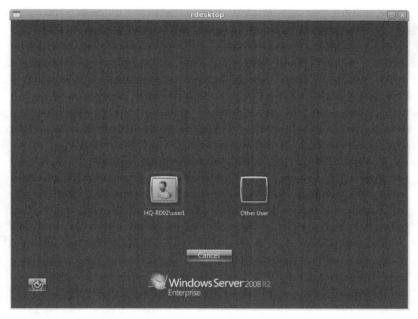

Figure 11-3 The rdesktop program

Source: Course Technology/Cengage Learning

Finally, you can view the rdesktop manual page, then switch to a desktop environment and run the command rdesktop remote_server_name to connect to a remote Windows server that runs the Remote Desktop Protocol (RDP), as shown in Figure 11-3.

Installing Programs Using RPM

The Red Hat Package Manager (RPM) format is the most widely used format for Linux software distributed via the Internet. Packages in this format have filenames that indicate the hardware architecture for which the software was compiled, and end with the .rpm extension. The following output indicates that the bluefish RPM package (a Web page editor) version 2.0.1-2 was compiled for Fedora 13 (fc13) on the Intel i686 (x86) platform:

```
[root@server1 ~]# ls -F
Desktop/    bluefish-2.0.1-2.fc13.i686.rpm
[root@server1 ~]# _
```

To install an RPM package, you can use the –i option to the **rpm command**. In addition, you can use the –v and –h options to print the verbose information and hash marks, respectively, during installation. The following command installs the bluefish RPM package using these options:

```
[root@server1 ~]# rpm -ivh bluefish-2.0.1-2.fc13.i686.rpm
Preparing... ################################### [100%]
   1:bluefish      ################################### [100%]
[root@server1 ~]# _
```

 Some RPM packages require that other RPM packages be installed on your system first. This type of relationship is known as a **package dependency**. If you attempt to install an RPM package that has package dependencies, you receive an error message that indicates the RPM packages that need to be installed first. After installing these prerequisite packages, you can successfully install your desired RPM package.

After you install an RPM package, the RPM database (stored within files in the /var/lib/rpm directory) is updated to contain information about the package and the files contained within. To query the full package name after installation, you can use the –q (query) option to the rpm command followed by the common name of the package:

```
[root@server1 ~]# rpm -q bluefish
bluefish-2.0.1-2.fc13.i686.rpm
[root@server1 ~]# _
```

In addition, you can add the –i (info) option to the preceding command to display the detailed package information for the bluefish package:

```
[root@server1 ~]# rpm -qi bluefish
Name         : bluefish          Relocations: (not relocatable)
Version      : 2.0.1             Vendor: endur
Release      : 2.fc13            Build Date: Sat 19 Jun 2010 05:44:09 AM EDT
Install Date: Sun 29 Aug 2010 07:42:07 AM EDT
Build Host   : bennew01
Group        : Development/Tools
Source RPM   : bluefish-2.0.1-2.fc13.src.rpm
Size         : 6532379
License      : GPLv2+
Signature    : DSA/SHA1, Sat 19 Jun 2010 05:44:16 AM EDT, Key ID d5e9afe6e8d479fc
Packager     : Matthias Haase <matthias_haase@bennewitz.com>
URL          : http://bluefish.openoffice.nl/
Summary      : A GTK2 web development application for experienced users
Description :
Bluefish is a powerful editor for experienced web designers and programmers.
Bluefish supports many programming and markup languages, but it focuses on
editing dynamic and interactive websites
[root@server1 ~]# _
```

Because the RPM keeps track of all installed files, you can find the executable file for the bluefish program by using the –q and –l (list) options followed by the package name to list all files contained within the package. The following command lists the first 10 files in the bluefish package:

```
[root@server1 ~]# rpm -ql bluefish | head
/usr/bin/bluefish
/usr/lib/bluefish
/usr/lib/bluefish/about.so
/usr/lib/bluefish/charmap.so
/usr/lib/bluefish/entities.so
/usr/lib/bluefish/htmlbar.so
/usr/lib/bluefish/infbrowser.so
/usr/lib/bluefish/snippets.so
```

```
/usr/share/applications/fedora-bluefish.desktop
/usr/share/bluefish
[root@server1 ~]# _
```

From the preceding output, you can see that the pathname to the executable file is /usr/bin/bluefish, which resides in a directory that is in our PATH variable. Upon execution in a desktop environment, you see the screen depicted in Figure 11-4.

Conversely, you can find out to which package a certain file belongs by using the –q and –f (file) options with the rpm command, followed by the filename:

```
[root@server1 ~]# rpm -qf /usr/bin/bluefish
bluefish-2.0.1-2.fc13.i686
[root@server1 ~]# _
```

To remove a package from the system, you can use the –e option to the rpm command; all files that belong to the package will be removed as well. To remove the bluefish package and verify its deletion, you can use the following commands:

```
[root@server1 ~]# rpm -e bluefish
[root@server1 ~]# rpm -q bluefish
package bluefish is not installed
[root@server1 ~]# _
```

Table 11-8 displays a list of common options used with the rpm utility.

Most RPM packages are located on Internet servers, called **software repositories**, for free download. You can use the **yum** (**Yellowdog Updater Modified**) **command** to search Internet software repositories for RPM packages and automatically install or upgrade those packages

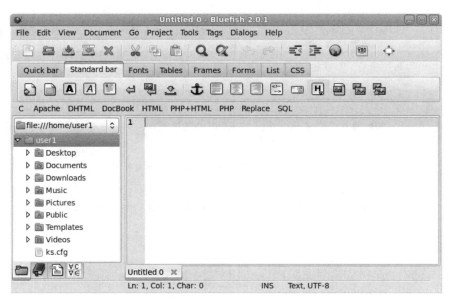

Figure 11-4 The bluefish program

Source: Course Technology/Cengage Learning

Option	Description
-a --all	Displays all package names installed on the system (when used with the -q option)
-c --configfiles	Displays the locations of the configuration files for a package installed on the system (when used with the -q option)
--dump	Displays detailed information regarding configuration files for a package installed on the system (when used following the -q and -c options)
-e --erase	Removes a specified package from the system
-F --freshen	Upgrades a specified package only if an older version exists on the system
-f --file	Displays the package to which the specified file belongs (when used with the -q option)
-h --hash	Prints hash marks on the screen to indicate installation progress (when used with the -i option)
-i --install	Installs a specified package (provided the -q option is not used)
-i --info	Displays full information about the specified package (when used with the -q option)
-K	Validates the checksum listed within the RPM file (when used before a filename argument)
-l --list	Lists the filenames the specified package comprises (when used with the -q option)
--nodeps	Forces the RPM to avoid checking for dependencies before installing packages (when used following the -i option)
-q --query	Queries information about packages on the system
--test	Performs a test installation only (when used with the -i option)
-U --upgrade	Upgrades a specified package; the package is installed even if no older version exists on the system
-V --verify	Verifies the location of all files that belong to the specified package
-v	Prints verbose information when installing or manipulating packages

Table 11-8 Common options used with the rpm utility

on your system. Prior to installing the desired RPM package, the yum command also downloads and installs any dependent packages.

Yum, which is installed by default on Fedora, uses the /etc/yum.conf and /etc/yum.repos.d/* files to specify the locations of Internet software repositories. During Fedora installation, files are added to the /etc/yum.repos.d directory that list standard software repositories on the Internet that contain RPM packages. Some of these RPM packages are also included within the Fedora Linux installation media. Thus, if you forgot to choose a particular software package during the Fedora installation, you can easily install it afterward using the yum install packagename command.

You used the yum command in previous chapters to install the Emacs program and the ncompress command.

Because newer versions of RPM packages are frequently added to software repositories, you can also upgrade an installed package to the latest version using the yum update packagename command. For example, to upgrade your Firefox Web browser to the latest version, you could use the following command and press y when prompted to download and install the latest packages:

```
[root@server1 ~]# yum update firefox
Loaded plugins: presto, refresh-packagekit
Setting up Update Process
Resolving Dependencies
---> Running transaction check
---> Package firefox.i686 0:3.6.7-1.fc13 set to be updated
---> Processing Dependency: xulrunner >= 1.9.2.7-1 for package: firefox-
3.6.7-1.fc13.i686
---> Running transaction check
---> Processing Dependency: xulrunner=1.9.2.3-1.fc13 for package:
xulrunner-devel-1.9.2.3-1.fc13.i686
---> Package xulrunner.i686 0:1.9.2.7-2.fc13 set to be updated
---> Running transaction check
---> Package xulrunner-devel.i686 0:1.9.2.7-2.fc13 set to be updated
---> Finished Dependency Resolution


Dependencies Resolved

================================================================================
 Package                Arch     Version          Repository       Size
================================================================================
Updating:
 firefox                i686     3.6.7-1.fc13     updates          14 M
Updating for dependencies:
 xulrunner              i686     1.9.2.7-2.fc13   updates          9.3 M
 xulrunner-devel        i686     1.9.2.7-2.fc13   updates          3.6 M

Transaction Summary
================================================================================
Install       0 Package(s)
Upgrade       3 Package(s)

Total download size: 27 M
```

11

```
Is this ok [y/N]: y
Downloading Packages:
Setting up and reading Presto delta metadata
http://www.muug.mb.ca/pub/fedora/linux/updates/13/i386/repodata/
b26993476f7ed2bb2d288c74f46f715d383f6f7bdd95e89d5027ecc61c130af5-
prestodelta.xml.gz: [Errno 14] HTTP Error 404 :
http://www.muug.mb.ca/pub/fedora/linux/updates/13/i386/repodata/
b26993476f7ed2bb2d288c74f46f715d383f6f7bdd95e89d5027ecc61c130af5-
prestodelta.xml.gz
Trying other mirror.
ftp://ftp.muug.mb.ca/pub/fedora/linux/updates/13/i386/repodata/
b26993476f7ed2bb2d288c74f46f715d383f6f7bdd95e89d5027ecc61c130af5-
prestodelta.xml.gz: [Errno 14] FTP Error 550 :
ftp://ftp.muug.mb.ca/pub/fedora/linux/updates/13/i386/repodata/
b26993476f7ed2bb2d288c74f46f715d383f6f7bdd95e89d5027ecc61c130af5-
prestodelta.xml.gz
Trying other mirror.
 updates/prestodelta                              | 192 kB     00:00
 Processing delta metadata
 Package(s) data still to download: 27 M
 (1/3): firefox-3.6.7-1.fc13.i686.rpm             |  14 MB     00:38
 (2/3): xulrunner-1.9.2.7-2.fc13.i686.rpm         | 9.3 MB     00:24
 (3/3): xulrunner-devel-1.9.2.7-2.fc13.i686.rpm   | 3.6 MB     00:08
 ----------------------------------------------------------------
 Total                              382 kB/s | 27 MB     01:11
Running rpm_check_debug
Running Transaction Test
Transaction Test Succeeded
Running Transaction
 Updating   : xulrunner-1.9.2.7-2.fc13.i686            1/6
 Updating   : xulrunner-devel-1.9.2.7-2.fc13.i686      2/6
 Updating   : firefox-3.6.7-1.fc13.i686                3/6
 Cleanup    : firefox-3.6.3-4.fc13.i686                4/6
 Cleanup    : xulrunner-devel-1.9.2.3-1.fc13.i686      5/6
 Cleanup    : xulrunner-1.9.2.3-1.fc13.i686            6/6

Updated:
  firefox.i686 0:3.6.7-1.fc13

Dependency Updated:
  xulrunner.i686 0:1.9.2.7-2.fc13
  xulrunner-devel.i686 0:1.9.2.7-2.fc13

Complete!
[root@server1 ~]# _
```

Note from the previous output that the yum command found two dependent packages that it installed prior to installing Firefox: xulrunner and xulrunner-devel. Also note that the yum command tried two different software repositories that contained the necessary software (called **software mirrors**) before finding one that accepted a connection. This is common, because software repositories limit their concurrent download connections to allow for fast download. When a software repository reaches its concurrent connection limit, it returns a negative response to the yum command and the yum command searches for the software on the next software mirror listed in the yum configuration files.

The GNOME and KDE desktop environments contain a Software Update utility that periodically checks for updated RPM packages for the software installed on your system. If you select the Install Updates option in the notification window, this utility notifies you of any newer packages and automatically downloads and installs them using the yum command. You can also run the Software Update utility manually. To start the Software Update utility within the GNOME Desktop Environment, open the System menu and navigate to Administration, Software Update.

Software packages that are not hosted on the default Fedora software repositories can still be downloaded and installed using the yum command. Many software authors host their software packages on private software repositories and include instructions on their Web site that guide you through the process of adding the private software repository to your yum configuration files (usually by installing a special RPM) and installing the packages using the yum command. For example, if you want to install the VideoLAN VLC media player, you can access these instructions for Fedora 13 from *www.videolan.org/vlc/down load-fedora.html*. Because the VideoLAN VLC media player is hosted on the private RPM Fusion software repository, the VideoLAN Web site instructs you to run the following command to update your yum configuration files with the location of the RPM Fusion software repository:

```
[root@server1 ~]# rpm -ivh
   http://download1.rpmfusion.org/free/fedora/rpmfusion-free-release-
   stable.noarch.rpm
Retrieving   http://download1.rpmfusion.org/free/fedora/rpmfusion-free-
release-stable.noarch.rpm
Preparing...                      ################################### [100%]
1:rpmfusion-free-release          ################################### [100%]
[root@server1 ~]# _
```

Next, the VideoLAN Web site instructs you to run the yum install vlc mozilla-vlc command to install the VLC media player and the VLC Firefox plug-in.

You can choose from many graphical utilities to update or install packages using the yum command. Fedora 13 comes with the **KPackageKit utility**, as shown in Figure 11-5. You can start the KPackageKit utility within the GNOME Desktop Environment by opening the Applications menu and navigating to System Tools, KPackageKit.

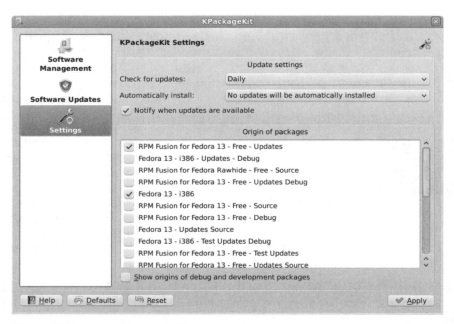

Figure 11-5 The KPackageKit utility

Source: Course Technology/Cengage Learning

The DPM is similar to the RPM. However, it uses the .deb extension for its packages. The dpkg command can be used to install DPM packages that have been downloaded locally (for example, dpkg -i packagename). Similarly, to query installed DPM packages, you can use various options to the dpkg-query command. In addition, the apt-get command can be used to download and install DPM packages from software repositories on the Internet and is analogous to the yum command for the RPM.

Chapter Summary

- Many compression utilities are available for Linux systems; each of them uses a different compression algorithm and produces a different compression ratio.

- Files can be backed up to an archive using a backup utility. To back up files to CD-RW or DVD-RW, you must use burning software instead of a backup utility.

- The tar utility is the most common backup utility used today; it is typically used to create compressed archives called tarballs.

- The source code for Linux software can be obtained and compiled afterward using the GNU C Compiler; most source code is available in tarball format via the Internet.

- Package Managers install and manage compiled software of the same format. The Red Hat Package Manager is the most common package manager available for Linux systems today.

■ You can install or upgrade RPM packages using the yum command. The yum command obtains RPM packages from software repositories on the Internet.

Key Terms

*sum commands   Commands that can be used to verify the checksum on a file where * represents the checksum algorithm. For example, to verify a SHA-1 checksum, you could use the sha1sum command.

/etc/dumpdates   The file used to store information about incremental and full backups for use by the dump/restore utility.

archive   The location (file or device) that contains a copy of files; it is typically created by a backup utility.

bunzip2 command   The command used to decompress files compressed by the bzip2 command.

bzcat command   A command used to view the contents of an archive created with bzip2 to SO.

bzip2 command   The command used to compress files using a Burrows-Wheeler Block Sorting Huffman Coding compression algorithm.

bzless command   A command used to view the contents of an archive created with bzip2 to SO in a page-by-page fashion.

bzmore command   A command used to view the contents of an archive created with bzip2 to SO in a page-by-page fashion.

checksum   A calculated value that is unique to a file's size and contents.

compress command   The command used to compress files using a Lempel-Ziv compression algorithm.

compression   The process in which files are reduced in size by a compression algorithm.

compression algorithm   The set of instructions used to reduce the contents of a file systematically.

compression ratio   The amount of compression that occurred during compression.

cpio (copy in/out) command   A command used to run a common backup utility.

Debian Package Manager (DPM)   A package manager used on Debian and Debian-based Linux distributions.

dump command   A command used to run a utility that creates full and incremental backups.

full backup   An archive of an entire filesystem.

GNU C Compiler (gcc) command   The command used to compile source code written in the C programming language into binary programs.

GNU zip (gzip) command   A command used to compress files using a Lempel-Ziv compression algorithm.

gunzip command   The command used to decompress files compressed by the gzip command.

incremental backup   An archive of a filesystem that contains only files that were modified since the last archive was created.

KPackageKit utility   A program that can be used to install, update, and remove RPM packages within a desktop environment.

package dependencies   A list of packages that are prerequisite to the current package being installed on the system.

package manager   A system that defines a standard package format and can be used to install, query, and remove packages.

Red Hat Package Manager (RPM)   The most commonly used package manager for Linux.

`restore` **command**   The command used to extract archives created with the `dump` command.

`rpm` **command**   The command used to install, query, and remove RPM packages.

software mirrors   Software repositories that host the same RPM or DPM packages as other software repositories for fault tolerance and load balancing of download requests.

software repositories   Servers on the Internet that host RPM or DPM packages for download.

system backup   The process whereby files are copied to an archive.

`tape archive (tar)` **command**   The most common command for creating archives.

tarball   A gzip-compressed tar archive.

`uncompress` **command**   The command used to decompress files compressed by the `compress` command.

`yum (Yellowdog Updater Modified)` **command**   A program used to install and upgrade software packages.

`zcat` **command**   A command used to view the contents of an archive created with `compress` or `gzip` to SO.

`zless` **command**   A command used to view the contents of an archive created with `compress` or `gzip` to SO in a page-by-page fashion.

`zmore` **command**   A command used to view the contents of an archive created with `compress` or `gzip` to SO in a page-by-page fashion.

Review Questions

1. Most source code is available on the Internet in tarball format. True or False?

2. Which dump level indicates a full backup?

   a.   0
   b.   9
   c.   1
   d.   f

3. Which filename extension indicates a tarball?

   a.   `.tar.gz`
   b.   `.cpio`
   c.   `.dump`
   d.   `.tar`

4. Files that have been compressed using the compress utility typically have the _____ extension.

   a. `.tar.gz`

   b. `.gz`

   c. `.Z`

   d. `.bz2`

5. The bzip2 and gzip utilities use similar compression algorithms. True or False?

6. When compiling source code into a binary program, which command performs compilation by running the GNU C Compiler?

   a. `tar`

   b. `./configure`

   c. `make`

   d. `make install`

7. The -9 option to the gzip utility results in a higher compression ratio. True or False?

8. You have created a full backup and four incremental backups. In which order must you restore these backups?

   a. 0, 1, 2, 3, 4

   b. 0, 4, 3, 2, 1

   c. 4, 3, 2, 1, 0

   d. 1, 2, 3, 4, 0

9. Which of the following commands extracts an archive?

   a. `cpio -vocBL /dev/fd0`

   b. `cpio -vicdu -I /dev/fd0`

   c. `cpio -vicdu -O /dev/fd0`

   d. `cpio -vti -I /dev/fd0`

10. The Debian Package Manager (DPM) is the default package manager used by Fedora 13. True or False?

11. Which of the following commands can be used to list the files contained within an installed RPM package?

   a. `rpm -qa packagename`

   b. `rpm -qi packagename`

   c. `rpm -ql packagename`

   d. `rpm -q packagename`

12. When compiling source code into a binary program, which command copies compiled binary files to the correct location on the filesystem?

    a. `tar`

    b. `./configure`

    c. `make`

    d. `make install`

13. To install a new program from RPM software repositories on the Internet, you can use the `yum update programname` command. True or False?

14. Which file contains full and incremental backup information for use with the dump/restore utility?

    a. /etc/dumps

    b. /etc/dumpdates

    c. /etc/dumpfile

    d. /etc/dump.conf

15. Which of the following represents the first nonrewinding SCSI tape device on a system?

    a. /dev/st0

    b. /dev/ht0

    c. /dev/nht0

    d. /dev/nst0

16. What is the most common method for obtaining Linux software?

    a. CD-ROM

    b. floppy disk

    c. Internet download

    d. e-mail

17. Which option to the `rpm` command can be used to remove a package from the system?

    a. `-r`

    b. `-e`

    c. `-u`

    d. `-U`

18. Which of the following commands creates an archive?

    a. `tar -cvf /dev/fd0`

    b. `tar -xvf /dev/fd0`

    c. `tar -tvf /dev/fd0`

    d. `tar -zcvf /dev/fd0*`

19. When compiling source code into a binary program, which command performs a system check and creates the Makefile?

    a. `tar`

    b. `./configure`

    c. `make`

    d. `make install`

20. Which of the following commands can be used to list detailed information about a package, such as its installation date and license?

    a. `rpm –qa packagename`

    b. `rpm –qi packagename`

    c. `rpm –ql packagename`

    d. `rpm –q packagename`

Hands-On Projects

These projects should be completed in the order given. The hands-on projects presented in this chapter should take a total of three hours to complete. The requirements for this lab include:

- A computer with Fedora 13 installed according to Hands-On Project 2-2
- A floppy disk

Project 11-1

In this hands-on project, you use common compression utilities to compress and uncompress information.

1. Turn on your computer. After your Linux system has been loaded, switch to a command-line terminal (tty2) by pressing **Ctrl+Alt+F2** and log in to the terminal using the user name of **root** and the password of **secret**.

2. At the command prompt, type **cp /etc/services ~** and press **Enter** to make a copy of the /etc/services file in your current directory. Next, type **ls –l** at the command prompt and press **Enter**. How large is the services file?

3. At the command prompt, type **compress5 -v services** and press **Enter** to compress the services file. (The compress utility is not installed by default. You can install it by running the `yum install ncompress` command, as shown earlier in this chapter.) What was the compression ratio? Next, type **ls –l** at the command prompt and press **Enter**. What extension does the services file have and how large is it?

4. At the command prompt, type **uncompress -v services.Z** and press **Enter** to decompress the services file.

5. At the command prompt, type **compress -vr Desktop** and press **Enter** to compress the contents of the Desktop subdirectory. Next, type **ls –lR Desktop** at the command prompt and press **Enter** to view the contents of the Desktop directory.

Which files were compressed? If there were symbolic links in this directory, how could you force the compress utility to compress these files as well?

6. At the command prompt, type **uncompress -vr Desktop** and press **Enter** to decompress the contents of the Desktop subdirectory. Next, type **ls –1R Desktop** at the command prompt and press **Enter** to verify that these files were uncompressed.

7. At the command prompt, type **ps –ef | compress –v >psfile.Z** and press **Enter** to compress the output of the ps –ef command to a file called psfile.Z. What was the compression ratio?

8. At the command prompt, type **zmore psfile.Z** and press **Enter** to view the compressed contents of the psfile.Z file. When finished, press **q** to quit the zmore utility.

9. At the command prompt, type **gzip -v services** and press **Enter** to compress the services file. What was the compression ratio? How does this ratio compare with the one obtained in Step 3? Why? Next, type **ls –1** at the command prompt and press **Enter**. What extension does the services file have and how large is it?

10. At the command prompt, type **gunzip -v services.gz** and press **Enter** to decompress the services file.

11. At the command prompt, type **gzip -v -9 services** and press **Enter** to compress the services file. What was the compression ratio? Why?

12. At the command prompt, type **gunzip -v services.gz** and press **Enter** to decompress the services file.

13. At the command prompt, type **gzip -v -1 services** and press **Enter** to compress the services file. What was the compression ratio? Why?

14. At the command prompt, type **gunzip -v services.gz** and press **Enter** to decompress the services file.

15. At the command prompt, type **bzip2 -v services** and press **Enter** to compress the services file. What was the compression ratio? How does this compare with the ratios from Step 3 and Step 9? Why? Next, type **ls –1** at the command prompt and press **Enter**. What extension does the services file have and how large is it?

16. At the command prompt, type **bunzip2 -v services.bz2** and press **Enter** to decompress the services file.

17. Type **exit** and press **Enter** to log out of your shell.

Project 11-2

In this hands-on project, you create, view, and extract archives using the tar utility.

1. Switch to a command-line terminal (tty2) by pressing **Ctrl+Alt+F2** and log in to the terminal using the user name of **root** and the password of **secret**.

2. At the command prompt, type **tar –cvf test1.tar /etc/samba** and press **Enter** to create an archive called test1.tar in the current directory that contains the /etc/samba directory and its contents. Next, type **ls –1** at the command prompt and press **Enter**. How large is the test1.tar file?

3. At the command prompt, type **tar –tvf test1.tar** and press **Enter**. What is displayed?

4. At the command prompt, type **mkdir /new1** and press **Enter**. Next, type **cd /new1** at the command prompt and press **Enter** to change the current directory to the /new1 directory.

5. At the command prompt, type **tar –xvf /root/test1.tar** and press **Enter** to extract the contents of the test1.tar archive. Next, type **ls –F** at the command prompt and press **Enter** to view the contents of the /new1 directory. Was the extraction successful?

6. At the command prompt, type **cd** and press **Enter** to return to your home directory.

7. At the command prompt, type **tar –zcvf test2.tar.gz /etc/samba** and press **Enter** to create a gzip-compressed archive called test2.tar.gz in the current directory that contains the /etc/samba directory and its contents. Next, type **ls –l** at the command prompt and press **Enter**. How large is the test2.tar.gz file? How does this compare with the size obtained for test1.tar in Step 2? Why?

8. At the command prompt, type **tar –ztvf test2.tar.gz** and press **Enter**. What is displayed?

9. At the command prompt, type **mkdir /new2** and press **Enter**. Next, type **cd /new2** at the command prompt and press **Enter** to change the current directory to the /new2 directory.

10. At the command prompt, type **tar –zxvf /root/test2.tar.gz** and press **Enter** to uncompress and extract the contents of the test2.tar.gz archive. Next, type **ls –F** at the command prompt and press **Enter** to view the contents of the /new2 directory. Was the extraction successful?

11. At the command prompt, type **cd** and press **Enter** to return to your home directory.

12. Insert a floppy disk into the floppy disk drive of your computer, type **modprobe floppy** at the command prompt, and press **Enter**.

13. At the command prompt, type **tar –cvf /dev/fd0 /etc/samba** and press **Enter** to create an archive on the device /dev/fd0 that contains the /etc/samba directory and its contents.

14. At the command prompt, type **tar –tvf /dev/fd0** and press **Enter**. What is displayed?

15. At the command prompt, type **mkdir /new3** and press **Enter**. Next, type **cd /new3** at the command prompt and press **Enter** to change the current directory to the /new3 directory.

16. At the command prompt, type **tar –xvf /dev/fd0** and press **Enter** to extract the contents of the archive stored on the first floppy disk. Next, type **ls –F** at the command prompt and press **Enter** to view the contents of the /new3 directory. Was the extraction successful?

17. At the command prompt, type **mount /dev/fd0** and press **Enter** to mount the floppy from the appropriate entry in /etc/fstab. What error message do you receive and why? Why was the filesystem type not automatically detected? Can this floppy be mounted?

18. At the command prompt, type **rm –Rf /new[123]** and press **Enter** to remove the directories created in this hands-on project.

19. At the command prompt, type **rm –f /root/test*** and press **Enter** to remove the tar archives created in this hands-on project.

20. Remove the floppy disk from your floppy disk drive, type **exit,** and press **Enter** to log out of your shell.

Project 11-3

In this hands-on project, you create, view, and extract archives using the cpio and dump utilities.

1. Switch to a command-line terminal (tty2) by pressing **Ctrl+Alt+F2** and log in to the terminal using the user name of **root** and the password of **secret**.

2. At the command prompt, type **find /etc/samba | cpio -ovcBL –O test.cpio** and press **Enter** to create an archive in the file test.cpio that contains the /etc/samba directory and its contents. What does each option indicate in the aforementioned command?

3. At the command prompt, type **cpio -ivtB –I test.cpio** and press **Enter**. What is displayed? What does each option indicate in the aforementioned command?

4. At the command prompt, type **cpio -ivcdumB –I test.cpio** and press **Enter** to extract the contents of the archive in the test.cpio file. To what location were the files extracted? Were any files overwritten? What does each option indicate in the aforementioned command?

5. At the command prompt, type **dump -of test.dump /etc/samba** and press **Enter** to create an archive of the /etc/samba directory in the archive file test.dump. What type of backup was performed? Will the /etc/dumpdates file be updated?

6. At the command prompt, type **mkdir /new** and press **Enter**. Next, type **cd /new** at the command prompt and press **Enter** to change the current directory to the /new directory.

7. At the command prompt, type **restore -tf /root/test.dump** and press **Enter**. What was displayed? Are absolute or relative pathnames used?

8. Type **ls –F** at the command prompt and press **Enter** to view the contents of the /new directory. What is displayed? Next, type **ls –RF** at the command prompt and press **Enter** to view the contents of the /new directory recursively. What is displayed?

9. At the command prompt, type **cd** and press **Enter** to return to your home directory.

10. At the command prompt, type **rm –Rf /new** and press **Enter** to remove the directory created in this hands-on project.

11. At the command prompt, type **rm –f /root/test*** and press **Enter** to remove the archives created in this hands-on project.

12. Type **exit** and press **Enter** to log out of your shell.

Project 11-4

In this hands-on project, you compile and install a program from source code.

1. Switch to the gdm by pressing **Ctrl+Alt+F1** or **Ctrl+Alt+F7** and log in to the GNOME Desktop Environment using the user name of **sample user one** and the password of **secret**.

2. Start the Firefox Web browser and download the gzipped source code tarball for Bluefish 2.0.1 or later from *http://sourceforge.net* to the /home/user1/Downloads folder. The file should be called bluefish-2.0.1.tar.gz. (If you downloaded a version of Bluefish later than 2.0.1, make sure you modify the commands used in this section to reflect the version you have downloaded.)

3. Switch to a command-line terminal (tty2) by pressing **Ctrl+Alt+F2** and log in to the terminal using the user name of **root** and the password of **secret**.

4. At the command prompt, type **cp ~user1/Downloads/bluefish-2.0.1.tar.gz ~** and press **Enter** to copy the bluefish source code tarball to your home directory. Does the filename of the bluefish tarball indicate the architecture for which the source code was designed? Explain.

5. At the command prompt, type **tar –zxvf bluefish-2.0.1.tar.gz** and press **Enter** to uncompress and extract the contents of the tarball. Next, type **ls -F** at the command prompt and press **Enter**. What directory was created?

6. At the command prompt, type **cd bluefish-2.0.1** and press **Enter**. Next, type **ls -F** at the command prompt and press **Enter**. Is there an executable configure program? Are there README and INSTALL files present?

7. At the command prompt, type **less README** and press **Enter**. Scroll through the output on the terminal screen. What does the bluefish program do? When finished, press **q** to quit the less utility.

8. At the command prompt, type **less INSTALL** and press **Enter**. Scroll through the output on the terminal screen. What does this file contain? When finished, press **q** to quit the less utility.

9. At the command prompt, type **./configure** and press **Enter**. What does this program do? Near the bottom of the output, can you see whether the Makefile was created successfully?

10. At the command prompt, type **make** and press **Enter**. This step should take about five minutes, depending on the speed of your computer. What does the make program do? Which program compiles the different parts of the program?

11. At the command prompt, type **make install** and press **Enter**. What does the make install command do?

12. At the command prompt, type **cd** and press **Enter** to return to your home directory. Next, type **rm –Rf bluefish-2.0.1** to remove the source code directory for bluefish.

13. At the command prompt, type **which bluefish** and press Enter. Which directory contains the bluefish executable program? Is a central database updated with this information as it was when the bluefish RPM was installed in this chapter?

14. Type **exit** and press **Enter** to log out of your shell.

15. Switch back to your GNOME Desktop Environment by pressing **Ctrl+Alt+F1 or Ctrl+Alt+F7** and open a BASH terminal.

16. Type **bluefish &** at the command prompt and press **Enter**. Observe the bluefish interface. When finished, close the bluefish program, close the terminal shell, and log out of the GNOME Desktop Environment.

Project 11-5

In this hands-on project, you use the rpm and yum commands to install, view, and remove an RPM package on your system.

1. Switch to a command-line terminal (tty2) by pressing **Ctrl+Alt+F2** and log in to the terminal using the user name of **root** and the password of **secret**.

2. At the command prompt, type **rpm –qa | less** and press **Enter** to view the RPM packages installed on your computer. Are there many of them? Briefly scroll through the list and press **q** when finished to exit the less utility.

3. At the command prompt, type **rpm –q tripwire** and press **Enter**. Is Tripwire installed on your computer?

4. At the command prompt, type **yum install tripwire** and press **Enter**. What architecture is indicated in the filename for this RPM? Press **y** when prompted to continue the installation.

5. At the command prompt, type **rpm –q tripwire** and press **Enter**. Has the Tripwire package been installed successfully?

6. At the command prompt, type **rpm –qi tripwire** and press **Enter** to view the information about the Tripwire package. What does the Tripwire program do? What license does this package use?

7. At the command prompt, type **rpm –ql tripwire** and press **Enter** to view the locations of all files that belong to the Tripwire package. Which file is the executable program itself?

8. At the command prompt, type **rpm –qc tripwire** and press **Enter** to view the configuration files for the Tripwire package. How many configuration files does the Tripwire package have?

9. At the command prompt, type **rpm –e tripwire** and press **Enter**. What does this option to the rpm command do?

10. At the command prompt, type **rpm –q tripwire** and press **Enter**. Is Tripwire installed?

11. Type **exit** and press **Enter** to log out of your shell.

Discovery Exercises

1. Go to *www.sourceforge.net* and *www.freshmeat.net* and obtain software of your choice to install. Are most packages available as source code in tarball format and as compiled binaries in RPM format? Download two RPM files for your architecture. Execute both programs.

2. Write the command that can be used to perform the following:

   a. Compress the symbolic link /root/sfile using the compress utility and display the compression ratio.

   b. Compress the contents of the directory /root/dir1 using the gzip utility and display the compression ratio.

   c. Decompress the file /root/letter.bz2.

   d. Compress the file /root/letter using gzip fast compression.

   e. Find the compression ratio of the file /root/letter.gz.

   f. Perform a test compression of the file /root/sample using the bzip2 utility.

   g. Compress the file /root/sample using the bzip2 utility while minimizing memory usage during the compression.

3. Write the command that can be used to perform the following:

   a. Back up the contents of the /var directory (which contains symbolically linked files) to the second nonrewinding SCSI tape device on the system using the tar utility.

   b. Append the file /etc/inittab to the archive created in Exercise 3a.

   c. Create a tarball called /stuff.tar.gz that contains all files in the /root/stuff directory.

   d. Use the cpio utility to back up all files in the /var directory (which contains symbolically linked files) to the first rewinding IDE tape device that has a block size of 5KB.

   e. Perform a full filesystem backup of the /var filesystem using the dump utility and record the event in the /etc/dumpdates file.

   f. View the contents of the archives created in Exercises 3a, 3c, 3d, and 3e.

   g. Extract the contents of the archives created in Exercises 3a and 3c to the /root directory.

   h. Extract the contents of the archives created in Exercises 3d and 3e to their original locations.

4. Use the Internet, library, or other resources to research two other package managers available for Linux systems. For each package manager, list the commands and options required to install, query, and remove packages. Also list the benefits that the package manager offers to Linux users and from where it can be downloaded on the Internet.

11

## chapter 12

Network Configuration

After completing this chapter, you will be able to:

- Describe the purpose and types of networks, protocols, and media access methods
- Explain the basic configuration of TCP/IP
- Configure a network interface to use TCP/IP
- Configure a modem, ISDN, and DSL interface
- Describe the purpose of host names and how they are resolved to IP addresses
- Configure TCP/IP routing
- Identify common network services
- Use command-line and graphical utilities to perform remote administration

Throughout this book, you have examined the installation and administration of local Linux services. This chapter focuses on configuring Linux to participate on a network. First, you become acquainted with some common network terminology, then you learn about TCP/IP and the procedure for configuring a network interface. Next, you learn about the domain name space and the processes by which host names are resolved to IP addresses. Finally, you learn how to configure TCP/IP routing, as well as set up and use various utilities to perform remote administration of a Linux system.

Networks

Most functions that computers perform today involve the sharing of information between computers. Information is usually transmitted from computer to computer via media such as fiber optic, telephone, coaxial, or unshielded twisted pair (UTP) cable, but it can also be transmitted via wireless media such as radio, micro, or infrared waves. This media typically interacts directly with a peripheral card on the computer, such as a network interface card (NIC) or modem device.

Two or more computers connected via media that can exchange information are called a **network**. Networks that connect computers within close proximity are called **local area networks (LANs)**, whereas networks that connect computers separated by large distances are called **wide area networks (WANs)**.

Many companies use LANs to allow employees to connect to databases and other shared resources, such as printers. Home users can also use LANs to connect several home computers. Alternatively, home users can use a WAN to connect home computers to an **Internet service provider (ISP)** to gain access to resources such as Web sites on the worldwide public network called the Internet.

 The Internet (the name is short for "internetwork") is merely several interconnected public networks. Both home and company networks can be part of the Internet. Special computers called **routers** transfer information from one network to another.

Network media serve as the conduit for information as it travels across a network. But simply sending information through this conduit is not enough. For devices on the network to make sense of this information, it must be organized according to a set of rules, or protocols. A network **protocol** breaks information down into **packets** that can be recognized by workstations, routers, and other devices on a network.

You can configure many different network protocols in Linux, including but not limited to the following:

- TCP/IP (Transmission Control Protocol/Internet Protocol)
- UDP/IP (User Datagram Protocol/Internet Protocol)
- IPX/SPX (Internetwork Packet Exchange/Sequenced Packet Exchange)
- AppleTalk
- DLC (Data Link Control)
- DECnet (Digital Equipment Corporation network)

The most common LAN protocol used today is TCP/IP. It is the standard protocol used to transmit information across the Internet and the one discussed in this chapter.

When transmitting information across a WAN, you might also use a WAN protocol in addition to a specific LAN protocol to format packets for safer transmission. The two most common WAN protocols are Serial Line Internet Protocol (SLIP) and Point-to-Point Protocol (PPP).

Another important part of the puzzle, the **media access method,** is a set of rules that governs how the various devices on the network share the network media. The media access method is usually contained within the hardware on the NIC or modem. Although many media access methods are available, the one most commonly used to send TCP/IP packets onto network media is called **Ethernet**. It ensures that any TCP/IP packets are retransmitted onto the network if a network error occurs. Another popular media access method, **Token Ring**, controls which computer has the ability to transmit information by passing a special packet of information, called a token, around the network. Only the computer that currently has the token can transmit information.

The TCP/IP Protocol

The TCP/IP protocol is actually a set, or suite, of protocols, with two core components—TCP and IP. Together, these two protocols ensure that information packets travel across a network as quickly as possible, without getting lost or mislabeled.

When you transfer information across a network, such as the Internet, that information is often divided into many thousands of small packets. Each of these packets may take a different physical route when reaching its destination because routers can transfer information to multiple interconnected networks. TCP ensures that packets can be assembled in the correct order at their destination regardless of the order in which they arrive. Additionally, TCP ensures that any lost packets are retransmitted.

IP is responsible for labeling each packet with the destination address. As a result, each computer that participates on a TCP/IP network must have a valid **Internet Protocol (IP) address** that identifies itself to the IP protocol. Nearly all computers on the Internet use a version of the IP protocol called **IP version 4 (IPv4)**. However, a small number of computers use a next-generation IP protocol called **IP version 6 (IPv6)**. We examine the structure and configuration of IPv4 and IPv6 in this chapter.

The IPv4 Protocol

To participate on an IPv4 network, your computer must have a valid IP address as well as a **subnet mask**. Optionally, you can configure a **default gateway** to participate on larger networks such as the Internet.

IPv4 Addresses
An IP address is a unique number assigned to the computer that identifies itself on the network, similar to a unique postal address that identifies your location in

the world. If any two computers on the same network have the same IP address, it is impossible for information to be correctly delivered to them. Directed communication from one computer to another single computer using TCP/IP is referred to as a **unicast**.

The most common format for IPv4 addresses is an **octet**, which is four numbers separated by periods. Each octet represents an 8-bit binary number (0–255). An example of an IP address in this notation is 192.168.5.69.

You can convert between decimal and binary by recognizing that an 8-bit binary number represents the decimal binary powers of two in the following order:

128 64 32 16 8 4 2 1

Thus, the number 255 is 11111111 (128+64+32+16+8+4+2+1) in binary, and the number 69 is 01000101 (64+4+1) in binary. When the computer looks at an IP address, the numbers are converted to binary. To learn more about binary-decimal number conversion, visit *www.wikihow.com/Convert-from-Decimal-to-Binary*.

All IPv4 addresses are composed of two parts: the network ID and the host ID. The **network ID** represents the network on which the computer is located, whereas the **host ID** represents a single computer on that network. Athough no two computers on the same network can have the same host, two computers on different networks can have the same host ID.

The network ID and the host ID are similar to a postal mailing address, which is made up of a street name and a house number. The street name is similar to a network ID. No two streets can have the same name, just as no two networks can have the same network ID. The host ID is like the house number. Two houses can have the same house number as long as they are on different streets, just as two computers can have the same host ID as long as they are on different networks.

Only computers with the same network ID can communicate with each other without the use of a router. This allows administrators to logically separate computers on a network. For example, computers in the Accounting Department could use one network ID, whereas computers in the Sales Department could use a different network number. If the two departments are connected by a router, computers in the Accounting Department can communicate with computers in the Sales Department, and vice versa.

If your TCP/IP network is not connected to the Internet, the choice of IP address is entirely up to you. However, if your network is connected to the Internet, you might need to use preselected IP addresses for the computers on your network. IP addresses that can be used on the Internet are assigned by your Internet service provider.

The IP address 127.0.0.1 is called the loopback IP address. It always refers to the local computer. In other words, on your computer, 127.0.0.1 refers to your computer. On your coworker's computer, 127.0.0.1 refers to your coworker's computer.

Subnet Masks   Each computer with an IPv4 address must also be configured with a subnet mask to define which part of its IP address is the network ID and which part is the host ID. Subnet masks are composed of four octets, just like an IP address. The simplest subnet masks use only the values 0 and 255. An octet in a subnet mask containing 255 is part of the network ID. An octet in a subnet mask containing 0 is part of the host ID. Your computer uses the binary process called **ANDing** to find the network ID. ANDing is a mathematical operation that compares two binary digits and gives a result of 1 or 0. If both binary digits being compared have a value of 1, the result is 1. If one digit is 0 and the other is 1, or if both digits are 0, the result is 0.

When an IP address is ANDed with a subnet mask, the result is the network ID. Figure 12-1 shows an example of how the network ID and host ID of an IP address can be calculated using the subnet mask.

Thus, the IP address shown in Figure 12-1 identifies the first computer (host portion 0.1) on the 192.168 network (network portion 192.168).

IP addresses and their subnet masks are often written using the **Classless Interdomain Routing (CIDR) notation**. For example, the notation 172.11.4.66/16 refers to the IP address 172.11.4.66 with a 16-bit subnet mask (255.255.0.0).

The IP addresses 0.0.0.0 and 255.255.255.255 cannot be assigned to a host computer because they refer to all networks and all computers on all networks, respectively. Similarly, using the number 255 (all 1s in binary format) in an IP address can specify many hosts. For example, the IP address 192.168.255.255 refers to all hosts on the 192.168.0.0 network; this IP address is also called the **broadcast** address for the 192.168 network.

A computer uses its IP address and subnet mask to determine what network it is on. If two computers are on the same network, they can deliver packets directly to each other. If two computers are on different networks, they must use a router to communicate.

12

IP address   192 . 168 . 0 . 1
         11000000.10101000.00000000.00000001

Subnet mask
         255   255   0   0
         11111111.11111111.00000000.00000000

         Network portion   Host portion

Figure 12-1 A sample IP address and subnet mask

Source: Course Technology/Cengage Learning

Default Gateway Typically, all computers on a LAN are configured with the same network ID and different host IDs. A LAN can connect to another LAN by means of a router, which has IP addresses for both LANs and can forward packets to and from each network. Each computer on a LAN can contain the IP address of a router in its TCP/IP configuration, and any packets that are not destined for the local LAN are then sent to the router, which can then forward the packet to the appropriate network or to another router. The IP address of the network interface on the router to which you send packets is called the default gateway.

A router is often a dedicated hardware device from a vendor such as Cisco, D-Link, or Linksys. Other times, a router is actually a computer with multiple network cards. The one consistent feature of routers, regardless of the manufacturer, is that they can distinguish between different networks and move (or route) packets between them. A router has an IP address on every network to which it is attached. When a computer sends a packet to the default gateway for further delivery, the address of the router must be on the same network as the computer, as computers can send packets directly to devices only on their own network.

IPv4 Classes and Subnetting IPv4 addresses are divided into classes to make them easier to manage. The class of an IP address defines the default subnet mask of the device using that address. All of the IP address classes can be identified by the first octet of the address, as shown in Table 12-1.

Class A addresses use 8 bits for the network ID and 24 bits for the host ID. You can see this is true by looking at the subnet mask, 255.0.0.0. The value of the first octet will always be somewhere in the range 1 to 127. This means there are only 127 potential Class A networks available for the entire Internet. Class A networks are only assigned to very large companies and Internet providers.

Class B addresses, which are identified by the subnet mask 255.255.0.0, use 16 bits for the network ID and 16 bits for the host ID. The value of the first octet ranges from 128 to 191. There are 16,384 Class B networks with 65,534 hosts on each network. Class B networks are assigned to many larger organizations, such as governments, universities, and companies with several thousand users.

Class C addresses, which are identified by the subnet mask 255.255.255.0, use 24 bits for the network ID and 8 bits for the host ID. The value of the first octet ranges from 192 to 223. There are 2,097,152 Class C networks with 254 hosts on each network. Although

Class	Subnet Mask	First Octet	Maximum Number of Networks	Maximum Number of Hosts	Sample IP Address
A	255.0.0.0	1–127	127	16,777,214	3.4.1.99
B	255.255.0.0	128–191	16,384	65,534	144.129.188.1
C	255.255.255.0	192–223	2,097,152	254	192.168.1.1
D	N/A	224–239	N/A	N/A	224.0.2.1
E	N/A	240–254	N/A	N/A	N/A

Table 12-1 IP address classes

there are very many Class C networks, they have a relatively small number of hosts and are thus suited only for smaller organizations.

Class D addresses are not divided into networks and cannot be assigned to computers as IP addresses; instead, they are used for multicasting. **Multicast** addresses are used by groups of computers. A packet addressed to a multicast address is delivered to each computer in the multicast group. This is better than a broadcast message because routers can be configured to allow multicast traffic to move from one network to another. In addition, all computers on the network process broadcasts, whereas only computers that are part of that multicast group process multicasts. Streaming media and network conferencing software often use multicasting to communicate to several computers at once.

Like Class D addresses, Class E addresses are not typically assigned to a computer. Class E addresses are considered experimental and are reserved for future use.

Notice from Table 12-1 that Class A and Class B networks can have many thousands or millions of hosts on a single network. Because this is not practically manageable, Class A and Class B networks are typically subnetted. **Subnetting** is the process in which a single large network is subdivided into several smaller networks to control traffic flow and improve manageability. After a network has been subnetted, a router is required to move packets from one subnet to another.

You can subnet any Class A, B, or C network.

To subnet a network, you take some bits from the host ID and give them to the network ID. Suppose, for example, that you want to divide the 3.0.0.0/8 network into 17 subnets. The binary representation of this network is:

```
3.0.0.0 = 00000011.00000000.00000000.00000000
255.0.0.0 = 11111111.00000000.00000000.00000000
```

You then borrow some bits from the host portion of the subnet mask. Because the number of combinations of binary numbers can be represented in binary powers of two and valid subnet masks do not contain all 0s or 1s, you can use the equation $2^n - 2$ to represent the minimum number of subnets required, where n is the number of binary bits that are borrowed from the host portion of the subnet mask. For our example, this is represented as:

$$2^n - 2 \geq 15$$
$$2^n \geq 17$$

Thus, n = 5 (because $2^4 = 16$, which is less than 17, but $2^5 = 32$ is greater than 17). Following this, our subnet mask borrows five bits from the default Class A subnet mask:

```
255.248.0.0 = 11111111.11111000.00000000.00000000
```

Similarly, because there are 19 zeros in the preceding subnet mask, you can use the $2^n - 2$ equation referred to previously to identify the number of hosts per subnet:

```
2^19 - 2 = number of hosts per subnet
         = 524,286 hosts per subnet
```

You can then work out the IP address ranges for each of the network ranges. Because three bits in the second octet were not borrowed during subnetting, the ranges of IP addresses that can be given to each subnet must be in ranges of 23 = 8. Thus, the first five ranges that can be given to different subnets on the 3.0.0.0/8 network that use the subnet mask 255.248.0.0 are as follows:

```
3.0.0.1-3.7.255.254
3.8.0.1-3.15.255.254
3.16.0.1-3.23.255.254
3.24.0.1-3.31.255.254
3.32.0.1-3.39.255.254
```

From the preceding ranges, a computer with the IP address 3.34.0.6/13 cannot communicate with the computer 3.31.0.99/13, because they are on different subnets. To communicate, there must be a router between them.

When subnetting a Class C network, ensure that you discard the first and last IP address in each range to account for the broadcast and network address for the subnet.

The IPv6 Protocol

As the Internet grew in the 1990s, ISPs realized that the number of IP addresses available using IPv4 was inadequate to accommodate future growth. As a result, the IPv6 protocol was designed in 1998 to accommodate far more IP addresses. IPv6 uses 128 bits to identify computers, whereas IPv4 only uses 32 bits (4 octets). This allows IPv6 to address up to 340,282,366,920,938,463,463,374,607,431,768,211,456 (or 340 trillion trillion trillion) unique computers.

Due to the large address space, subnetting is not necessary using IPv6.

IPv6 IP addresses are written using eight colon-delimited 16-bit hexadecimal numbers—for example, 2001:0db8:3c4d:0015:0000:0000:adb6:ef12. If an IPv6 IP address contains 0000 segments, they are often omitted in most notation; thus, 2001:0db8:3c4d:0015::: adb6:ef12 is equivalent to 2001:0db8:3c4d:0015:0000:0000:adb6:ef12. The IPv6 loopback address is 0000:0000:0000:0000:0000:0000:0000:0001, but is often referred to as ::1 for simplicity.

Unlike our traditional decimal numbering scheme, hexadecimal uses an expanded numbering system that includes the letters A through F in addition to the numbers 0–9. Thus, the number 10 is called A in hexadecimal, the number 11 is called B in hexadecimal, the number 12 is called C in hexadecimal, the number 13 is called D in hexadecimal, the number 14 is called E in hexadecimal, and the number 15 is called F in hexadecimal.

Although IPv6 addresses can be expressed several different ways, the first half of an IPv6 address is assigned by your ISP and typically identifies your network. The last half of an IPv6 address is called the **link local** portion and is used to uniquely identify the computers in your LAN.

Although most operating systems today support IPv6, very few networks and computers on the Internet have adopted it. In early 2009, Google reported that less than 1 percent of all computers in any country have adopted IPv6. This slow adoption of IPv6 is primarily the result of two technologies that allow IPv4 to address many more computers than was previously possible: **proxy servers** and **Network Address Translation (NAT)** routers.

Proxy servers and NAT routers are computers or hardware devices that have an IP address and access to a network such as the Internet. Other computers on the network can use a proxy server or NAT router to obtain network or Internet resources on their behalf. Moreover, there are three reserved ranges of IPv4 addresses that are not distributed to computers on the Internet and intended only for use behind a proxy server or NAT router:

- The entire 10.0.0.0 Class A network (10.0.0.0/8)
- The 172.16 through 172.31 Class B networks (172.16–31.0.0/16)
- The 192.168 Class C networks (192.168.0–255.0/24)

Thus, a computer behind a proxy server in Iceland and a computer behind a NAT router in Seattle could use the same IPv4 address, 10.0.5.4, without problems because each of these computers only requests Internet resources using its proxy server or NAT router. A company may use a Cisco NAT router, for example, to allow other networks and computers in the company to gain access to the Internet. Similarly, a high-speed home Internet modem typically functions as a NAT router to allow multiple computers in a home to access the Internet.

Most computers in the world today obtain Internet access via a proxy server or NAT router. Because these computers share IPv4 addresses on a reserved network range rather than use a unique IP address, the number of available IPv4 addresses has remained high and slowed the adoption of IPv6.

Configuring a Network Interface

Linux computers in a business environment typically connect to the company network via a wired or wireless NIC. At home, more and more people are connecting to the Internet by means of a NIC, using technologies such as fiber optic, WiMAX, digital subscriber line (DSL), and Broadband Cable Networks (BCNs).

If the NIC was detected during installation, Fedora Linux automatically configures the appropriate driver to allow the Linux kernel to work with the NIC driver. However, some NICs are not detected upon installation because an appropriate Linux driver for the NIC is not included in the installation media.

NIC drivers are usually contained within modules that can be inserted into the Linux kernel. Modules end with the .ko (kernel object) extension and are typically stored in the /lib/modules directory. They can be manually loaded into the Linux kernel using the **insmod** or **modprobe command**. To see a list of modules that are currently loaded into the Linux kernel, you can use the **lsmod command.** You can remove a module from the Linux kernel using the **rmmod command.**

Modules can be automatically loaded at boot time from entries within the files in the /etc/modprobe.d directory. Although hardware vendors can add files to this directory to load their module device drivers, most modules for your Linux distribution are loaded from the dist.conf file. For example, to load the module for the DEC tulip-wired NIC into memory at boot time and give it the alias eth0, simply add the line alias eth0 tulip to the /etc/modprobe.d/dist.conf file. The tulip module will then be located from subdirectories of /lib/modules and loaded into the Linux kernel and called eth0.

Alternatively, by adding modules to the /etc/modprobe.d/blacklist.conf file, you will prevent a module from loading, regardless of whether it is also listed in another file within the /etc/modprobe.d directory.

The first wired NIC in your system is typically called eth0, the second wired NIC in your system is typically called eth1, and so on. Similarly, the first wireless NIC in your system is called wlan0, the second wireless NIC in your system is called wlan1, and so on.

Older Linux kernels used the /etc/modprobe.conf or /etc/modules.conf file in place of entries within files under the /etc/modprobe.d directory; the syntax of lines in these files is identical to those within files under the /etc/modprobe.d directory.

If your Linux system does not detect your NIC using the network utilities described later in this section, you will need to search for and install the appropriate driver module on your system. Most driver modules are packaged in RPM format. When you install the RPM, it adds the appropriate driver module to the /lib/modules directory and a file to the /etc/modprobe.d directory that allows your system to load the driver module at boot time.

After a driver module for the NIC has been loaded into the Linux kernel, you can configure it to use TCP/IP. The **ifconfig (interface configuration) command** can be used to assign a TCP/IP configuration to a NIC as well as view the configuration of all network interfaces in the computer. To assign eth0 the IP address of 3.4.5.6 with a subnet mask of 255.0.0.0 and broadcast address of 3.255.255.255, you can use the following command at the command prompt:

ifconfig eth0 3.4.5.6 netmask 255.0.0.0 broadcast 3.255.255.255

Alternatively, you can receive TCP/IP configuration from a Dynamic Host Configuration Protocol (DHCP) or Boot Protocol (BOOTP) server on the network. To obtain and configure TCP/IP information from a server on the network for the first Ethernet adapter, you can use the command dhclient eth0 at the command prompt.

The process of obtaining an IP address for your NIC varies, depending on whether your computer is on an IPv4 or IPv6 network. If you attempt to obtain IPv4 configuration for your NIC from a DHCP or BOOTP server and no DHCP or BOOTP server exists on your network, your system will assign an IPv4 address of 169.254.$x.x$ where $.x.x$ is a randomly generated host ID. This automatic assignment feature is called **Automatic Private IP Addressing (APIPA).** If your network has IPv6-configured routers, an IPv6 address is automatically assigned to each NIC. This is because NICs use **Internet Control Message Protocol version 6**

(**ICMPv6**) router discovery messages to probe their networks for IPv6 configuration information. Alternatively, you can obtain your IPv6 configuration from a DHCP server on the network. If there are no IPv6-configured routers or DHCP servers on your network from which you can obtain an IPv6 configuration for your NIC, your system will assign an IPv6 link local address that begins with the hexadecimal equivalent of your IPv4 address and ends with the last half of your NIC's hardware address.

A single NIC can have both an IPv4 and an IPv6 address. Each address can be used to access the Internet using the IPv4 and IPv6 protocols, respectively.

To view the configuration of all interfaces, you can use the `ifconfig` command without any arguments, as shown in the following output:

```
[root@server1 ~]# ifconfig
eth0      Link encap:Ethernet HWaddr 00:80:C6:F9:1B:8C
          inet addr:3.4.5.6 Bcast:3.255.255.255 Mask:255.0.0.0
          inet6addr: fe80::280:c6ff:fef9:1b8c/64 Scope:Link
          UP BROADCAST RUNNING MULTICAST MTU:1500 Metric:1
          RX packets:47 errors:0 dropped:0 overruns:0 frame:0
          TX packets:13 errors:5 dropped:0 overruns:0 carrier:5
          collisions:0 txqueuelen:1000
          RX bytes:5560 (5.4 Kb) TX bytes:770 (770.0 b)
          Interrupt:10 Base address:0x8000

lo        Link encap:Local Loopback
          inet6 addr: ::1/128 Scope:Host
          UP LOOPBACK RUNNING MTU:16436 Metric:1
          RX packets:3142 errors:0 dropped:0 overruns:0 frame:0
          TX packets:3142 errors:0 dropped:0 overruns:0 carrier:0
          collisions:0 txqueuelen:0
          RX bytes:3443414 (3.2 Mb) TX bytes:3443414 (3.2 Mb)

[root@server1 ~]# _
```

The output of the `ifconfig` command shows that the eth0 NIC has an IPv4 address of `3.4.5.6` and an IPv6 address of `fe80::280:c6ff:fef9:1b8c` that was automatically configured by the system because the end of the IPv6 is identical to the last half of the hardware address (`EthernetHWaddr 00:80:C6:F9:1B:8C`). It also shows interface statistics and the special loopback adapter (`lo`) with the IP address 127.0.0.1; this IP address represents the local computer and is required on all computers that use TCP/IP.

The `netstat -i` command can also be used to show interface statistics.

If you restart the computer, the TCP/IP information configured for eth0 will be lost. To allow the system to activate and configure the TCP/IP information for an interface at each boot time, simply place entries in the /etc/sysconfig/network-scripts/ifcfg-*interface* file, where *interface* is the name of the network interface. An example of the configuration file for the first Ethernet interface (eth0) is shown in the following output:

```
[root@server1 ~]# cat /etc/sysconfig/network-scripts/ifcfg-eth0
DEVICE=eth0
BOOTPROTO=none
HWADDR=00:80:C6:F9:1B:8C
IPADDR=3.4.5.6
NETMASK=255.0.0.0
GATEWAY=3.0.0.1
ONBOOT=yes
TYPE=Ethernet
IPV6INIT=yes
USERCTL=no
DEFROUTE=yes
IPV4_FAILURE_FATAL=yes
NAME="System eth0"
UUID=5fb06bd0-0bb0-7ffb-45f1-d6edd65f3e03
PEERDNS=yes
PEERROUTES=yes
IPV6_AUTOCONF=yes
IPV6_DEFROUTE=yes
IPV6_PEERDNS=yes
IPV6_PEERROUTES=yes
IPV6_FAILURE_FATAL=no
[root@server1 ~]# _
```

The entries in the preceding output indicate that the TCP/IP configuration for the first Ethernet adapter (eth0) will be activated at boot time (ONBOOT=yes) and IPv6 will be automatically configured using ICMPv6 if an IPv6-configured router is available (IPV6_AUTOCONF=yes). The NIC does not obtain information from a DHCP or BOOTP server (BOOTPROTO=none). IPv4 is instead configured using the IP address 3.4.5.6, a subnet mask of 255.0.0.0, and a default gateway of 3.0.0.1. Also, you can change the BOOTPROTO=none line to BOOTPROTO=dhcp or BOOTPROTO=bootp to gain all TCP/IP configuration information from a DHCP or BOOTP server on the network, respectively.

The /etc/sysconfig/network-scripts/ifcfg-eth0 file can also contain information regarding the configuration of other network protocols, such as IPX/SPX.

After editing the /etc/sysconfig/network-scripts/ifcfg-eth0 file, you do not need to reboot your system to have the new TCP/IP configuration take effect. Instead, simply run the command ifdown eth0 to unconfigure the eth0 network interface, followed by ifup eth0 to configure the eth0 network interface using the settings in the /etc/sysconfig/network-scripts/ifcfg-eth0 file. Alternatively, you can use the ifconfig eth0 down and ifconfig eth0 up commands to deactivate and activate the eth0 network interface.

After a NIC has been configured to use TCP/IP, you should test the configuration by using the **ping (Packet Internet Groper) command**. The ping command sends a small

TCP/IP packet to another IP address and awaits a response. By default, the `ping` command sends packets continuously every second until the Ctrl+c key combination is pressed. To send only five ping requests to the loopback interface, simply use the -c option to the `ping` command, as shown in the following example:

```
[root@server1 ~]# ping -c 5 127.0.0.1
PING 127.0.0.1 (127.0.0.1)  56(84) bytes of data.
64 bytes from 127.0.0.1: icmp_seq=0 ttl=64 time=0.154 ms
64 bytes from 127.0.0.1: icmp_seq=1 ttl=64 time=0.109 ms
64 bytes from 127.0.0.1: icmp_seq=2 ttl=64 time=0.110 ms
64 bytes from 127.0.0.1: icmp_seq=3 ttl=64 time=0.119 ms
64 bytes from 127.0.0.1: icmp_seq=4 ttl=64 time=0.111 ms

--- 127.0.0.1 ping statistics ---
5 packets transmitted, 5 received, 0% packet loss, time 3999ms
rtt min/avg/max/mdev = 0.109/0.120/0.154/0.020 ms
[root@server1 ~]# _
```

If the `ping` command fails to receive any responses from the loopback interface, there is a problem with TCP/IP itself.

In addition, to send five ping requests to the IP address configured earlier, you can use the following command:

```
[root@server1 ~]# ping -c 5 3.4.5.6
PING 3.4.5.6 (3.4.5.6)  56(84) bytes of data.
64 bytes from 3.4.5.6: icmp_seq=0 ttl=64 time=0.157 ms
64 bytes from 3.4.5.6: icmp_seq=1 ttl=64 time=0.113 ms
64 bytes from 3.4.5.6: icmp_seq=2 ttl=64 time=0.106 ms
64 bytes from 3.4.5.6: icmp_seq=3 ttl=64 time=0.107 ms
64 bytes from 3.4.5.6: icmp_seq=4 ttl=64 time=0.115 ms

--- 3.4.5.6 ping statistics ---
5 packets transmitted, 5 received, 0% packet loss, time 4000ms
rtt min/avg/max/mdev = 0.106/0.119/0.157/0.022 ms
[root@server1 ~]# _
```

If the `ping` command fails to receive any responses from the newly configured IP address, there is a problem with the TCP/IP configuration for the NIC.

Next, you need to test whether the Linux computer can ping other computers on the same network. The following command can be used to send five ping requests to the computer that has the IP address 3.0.0.2 configured:

```
[root@server1 ~]# ping -c 5 3.0.0.2
PING 3.0.0.2 (3.0.0.2)  56(84) bytes of data.
64 bytes from 3.0.0.2: icmp_seq=0 ttl=128 time=0.448 ms
```

```
64 bytes from 3.0.0.2:  icmp_seq=1 ttl=128 time=0.401 ms
64 bytes from 3.0.0.2:  icmp_seq=2 ttl=128 time=0.403 ms
64 bytes from 3.0.0.2:  icmp_seq=3 ttl=128 time=0.419 ms
64 bytes from 3.0.0.2:  icmp_seq=4 ttl=128 time=0.439 ms

--- 3.0.0.2 ping statistics ---
5 packets transmitted, 5 received, 0% packet loss, time 4001ms
rtt min/avg/max/mdev = 0.401/0.422/0.448/0.018 ms
[root@server1 ~]# _
```

If the `ping` command fails to receive any responses from other computers on the network, there is a problem with the network media.

You can also configure a network interface from a desktop environment using the **Network Configuration tool** shown in Figure 12-2. To start the Network Configuration tool from within the GNOME Desktop Environment, open the System menu and navigate to Administration, Network.

Next, highlight your network interface and click the Edit button shown in Figure 12-2. This displays the window shown in Figure 12-3, where you can supply the appropriate IP configuration.

By default, all network interfaces are configured to obtain their IP configurations from a DHCP server, as shown in Figure 12-3, where Automatically obtain IP address settings with dhcp is selected. However, you can instead select Statically set IP addresses and supply the appropriate IP address, subnet mask, and default gateway IP address.

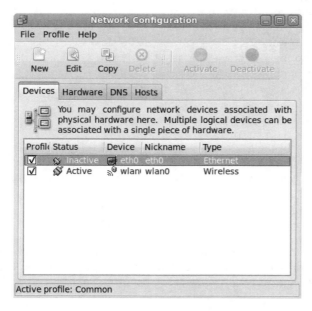

Figure 12-2 Configuring network interfaces

Source: Course Technology/Cengage Learning

Ethernet Device ☒

| General | Route | Hardware Device |

Nickname: [etho]

☑ Controlled by NetworkManager

☑ Activate device when computer starts

☐ Allow all users to enable and disable the device

☑ Enable IPv6 configuration for this interface

◉ Automatically obtain IP address settings with: [dhcp ◇]

DHCP Settings

Hostname (optional): [   ]

☑ Automatically obtain DNS information from provider

◯ Statically set IP addresses:

Manual IP Address Settings

Address: [3.4.5.6]

Subnet mask: [255.0.0.0]

Default gateway address: [3.0.0.254]

Primary DNS: [|]

Secondary DNS: [   ]

☐ Set MTU to: [1500   ⬍]

[Cancel]   [OK]

Figure 12-3 Configuring TCP/IP information for a network interface

Source: Course Technology/Cengage Learning

12

After you have edited your IP configuration and clicked OK, be certain to click Save from the File menu shown in Figure 12-2 to save your changes to the appropriate file in the /etc/sysconfig/network-scripts directory. Next, to activate your changes without rebooting, you need to click the Activate button shown in Figure 12-2.

You can also view the hardware information for your NIC by accessing the Hardware tab within the Network Configuration tool. If your NIC is not listed on this tab, you might need to install the appropriate Linux driver module for your NIC.

Mobile computers, such as laptops and netbooks, often have both wired and wireless NICs. In addition, users typically configure their mobile computer to connect to different wired and wireless networks as they travel. As a result, the **Network Manager** daemon is started by default in Fedora 13. This daemon allows users to quickly connect to wired and wireless networks from their desktop environments. For example, you can select the Network Manager icon in the upper-right corner of the GNOME Desktop Environment to display the menu shown in Figure 12-4, which allows you to choose from the available networks in your proximity and configure their options. The Network Manager menu shown in Figure 12-4

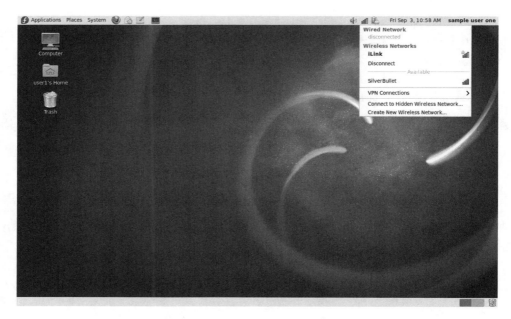

Figure 12-4 Using Network Manager within GNOME

Source: Course Technology/Cengage Learning

indicates that the system is currently connected to the wireless network called iLink, but that another wireless network called SilverBullet is also available. The fact that the Wired Network is listed as disconnected in Figure 12-4 tells you that no functional cable is plugged into the wired NIC.

You can prevent Network Manager from configuring a NIC by deselecting Controlled by NetworkManager within the properties of the network interface in the Network Configuration tool, as shown earlier in Figure 12-3.

Configuring a PPP Interface

Instead of configuring TCP/IP to run on a NIC to gain network access, you can instead run TCP/IP over serial lines (such as telephone lines) using a WAN protocol, such as SLIP or PPP. PPP is a newer technology than SLIP and incorporates all of SLIP's features; thus, PPP is the standard protocol for connecting to remote networks over serial lines.

Three common technologies use PPP to connect computers to the Internet or other networks:

- Modems
- ISDN
- DSL

Modem (modulator-demodulator) devices use PPP to send TCP/IP information across normal telephone lines. They were the most common method for home users to gain Internet access in the 1990s. Modem connections are considered slow today compared with most other technologies; most modems can only transmit data at 56KB/s. Because modems transmit information on a serial port, the system typically makes a symbolic link called /dev/modem that points to the correct serial port device, such as /dev/ttyS0 for COM1.

Integrated Services Digital Network (ISDN) is a set of standards designed for transmitting voice, video, and data over normal copper telephone lines. It allows data to be transferred at 128KB/s. ISDN uses an ISDN modem device to connect to a different type of media than regular phone lines. Although ISDN is popular in Europe, it does not have a large presence in North America.

One of the most popular connection technologies in North America is DSL. DSL has many variants, such as Asynchronous DSL (ADSL), which is the most common DSL used in homes across North America, and High bit-rate DSL (HDSL), which is common in business environments; for simplification, all variants of DSL are referred to as xDSL. You use an Ethernet NIC to connect to a DSL modem using TCP/IP and PPP; the DSL modem then transmits information across normal telephone lines at speeds that can exceed 20MB/s.

Because modem, ISDN, and DSL connections require additional configuration information that is specific to the ISP, they are not normally configured during the Linux installation and must be configured manually.

Configuring a PPP connection requires support for PPP compiled into the kernel or available as a module, the PPP daemon (pppd), and a series of supporting utilities such as the chat program, which is used to communicate with a modem. PPP configuration in the past was tedious at best. You needed to create a chat script that contained the necessary information to establish a PPP connection (user name, password, and so on) and a connection script that contained device parameters used by the PPP daemon. In addition, you needed to use a program such as minicom to initiate network communication. Because the TCP/IP configuration is typically assigned by the ISP to which you connect, it rarely needs to be configured during the process.

Today, a wide variety of graphical programs can configure the necessary files and start the necessary utilities to allow PPP network communication. To get started in Fedora 13, start the Network Configuration tool shown earlier in Figure 12-2, then click the New button. This displays the window shown in Figure 12-5, where you can specify which type of device to add.

If you choose to configure a Modem connection or ISDN connection, you need to select your modem or ISDN device, ISP configuration, and an ISP account user name and password. Alternatively, if you choose to set up an xDSL connection, you are prompted to choose the Ethernet interface that is connected to the DSL modem as well as an ISP account user name and password.

Just like when you configure a NIC, when you configure one of these alternative devices, information about each PPP device is stored in files named ifcfg-*InternetServiceProviderName* underneath the /etc/sysconfig/network-scripts directory. For example, the information

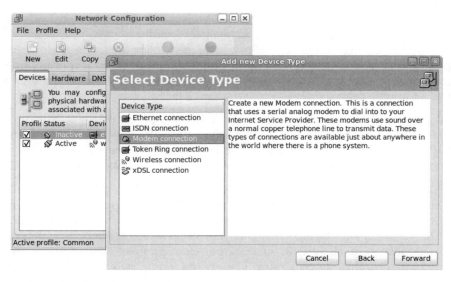

Figure 12-5 Adding a network interface

Source: Course Technology/Cengage Learning

configured earlier for the xDSL connection is stored in the /etc/sysconfig/network-scripts/ifcfg-isp file, as shown in the following output:

```
[root@server1 ~]# cat /etc/sysconfig/network-scripts/ifcfg-isp
DEVICE=ppp0
BOOTPROTO=dialup
TYPE=Modem
ONBOOT=no
USERCTL=yes
PEERDNS=yes
AC=off
BSDCOMP=off
VJCCOMP=off
CCP=off
PC=off
VJ=off
LINESPEED=115200
MODEMPORT=/dev/ttyS0
IDLETIMEOUT=600
PROVIDER=Sympatico
DEFROUTE=yes
PERSIST=no
PPPOPTIONS=
PAPNAME=sampleuser
WVDIALSECT=Sympatico
MODEMNAME=Modem0
DEMAND=no
[root@server1 ~]# _
```

Other configurations used by the PPP daemon are stored in the /etc/ppp and /etc/isdn directories. It is good form to double-check the passwords used to connect to the ISP, because incorrect passwords represent the most common problem with PPP connections. These passwords are stored in two files: /etc/ppp/pap-secrets (Password Authentication Protocol secrets) and /etc/ppp/chap-secrets (Challenge Handshake Authentication Protocol secrets). If the ISP accepts passwords sent across the network in text form, the /etc/ppp/pap-secrets file is consulted for the correct password. However, if the ISP requires a more secure method for validating the identity of a user, the passwords in the /etc/ppp/chap-secrets file are used. When you configure a PPP connection, this information is automatically added to both files, as shown in the following output:

```
[root@server1 ~]# cat /etc/ppp/pap-secrets
# Secrets for authentication using PAP
# client       server     secret                    IP addresses
####### system-config-network will overwrite this part!!! (begin) ####
"user1"        "isp"      "secret"
####### system-config-network will overwrite this part!!! (end) ######
[root@server1 ~]# cat /etc/ppp/chap-secrets
# Secrets for authentication using CHAP
# client       server     secret                    IP addresses
####### system-config-network will overwrite this part!!! (begin) ####
"user1"        "isp"      "secret"
####### system-config-network will overwrite this part!!! (end) ######
[root@server1 ~]# _
```

After a PPP device has been configured, you must activate it by connecting to (that is, dialing) the ISP. You can do this by using the command ifup InternetServiceProviderName at a command prompt, or by clicking the Activate button within the Network Configuration tool.

After the device is activated, the ifconfig command indicates the interface using the appropriate names such as ppp0 (for the first modem or xDSL device) or ippp0 (for the first ISDN device) as well as the IP configuration obtained from the ISP. The following output depicts the output of the ifconfig command when the xDSL interface is activated:

```
[root@server1 ~]# ifconfig
eth0      Link encap:Ethernet HWaddr 00:80:C6:F9:1B:8C
          inet addr:3.4.5.6 Bcast:3.255.255.255 Mask:255.0.0.0
          inet6 addr: fe80::280:c6ff:fef9:1b8c/64 Scope:Link
          UP BROADCAST RUNNING MULTICAST MTU:1500 Metric:1
          RX packets:47 errors:0 dropped:0 overruns:0 frame:0
          TX packets:13 errors:5 dropped:0 overruns:0 carrier:5
          collisions:0 txqueuelen:1000
          RX bytes:5560 (5.4 Kb) TX bytes:770 (770.0 b)
          Interrupt:10 Base address:0x8000

lo        Link encap:Local Loopback
          inet6 addr: ::1/128 Scope:Host
          UP LOOPBACK RUNNING MTU:16436 Metric:1
          RX packets:3142 errors:0 dropped:0 overruns:0 frame:0
          TX packets:3142 errors:0 dropped:0 overruns:0 carrier:0
```

12

```
            collisions:0 txqueuelen:0
            RX bytes:3443414 (3.2 Mb) TX bytes:3443414 (3.2 Mb)

ppp0        Link encap:Point-to-Point Protocol
            inet addr:65.95.13.217 P-t-P:65.95.13.1 Mask:255.255.255.255
            UP POINTOPOINT RUNNING NOARP MULTICAST MTU:1492 Metric:1
            RX packets:15 errors:0 dropped:0 overruns:0 frame:0
            TX packets:31 errors:0 dropped:0 overruns:0 carrier:0
            collisions:0 txqueuelen:3
            RX bytes:1448 (1.4 Kb) TX bytes:3088 (3.0 Kb)

[root@server1 ~]# _
```

Name Resolution

Computers that communicate on a TCP/IP network identify themselves using unique IP addresses. However, this identification scheme is impractical for human use because it is difficult to remember IP addresses. As a result, every computer on a network is identified by a name that makes sense to humans, such as "Accounting1" or "Reception." Because each computer on a network is called a host, the name assigned to an individual computer is its **host name**.

For computers that require a presence on the Internet, simple host names are rarely used. Instead, they are given a host name called a **fully qualified domain name (FQDN)** according to a hierarchical naming scheme called **domain name space (DNS)**. At the top of the domain name space is the root domain, which is really just a theoretical starting point for the branching, tree like structure. Below the root domain are the top-level domain names, which identify the type of organization in which a network is located. For example, the com domain is primarily used for business, or commercial, networks. Several second-level domains exist underneath each top-level domain name to identify the name of the organization, and simple host names are listed underneath the second-level domains. Figure 12-6 shows a portion of the domain name space.

For simplicity, FQDNs are often referred to as host names.

Thus, the host computer shown in Figure 12-6 has an FQDN of *www.linux.org*.

The host name www (World Wide Web) is often used by servers that host Web pages.

Second-level domains must be purchased and registered with an ISP to be recognized by other computers on the Internet. You can use the **whois command** to obtain registration information about any domain within the domain name space. For example, to obtain information

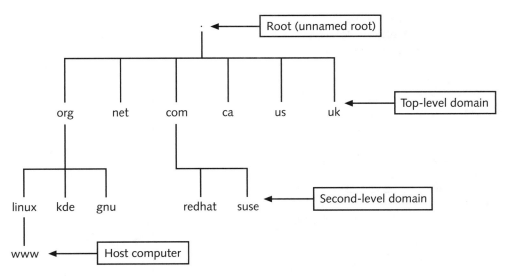

Figure 12-6 The domain name space

Source: Course Technology/Cengage Learning

about the organization responsible for maintaining the linux.org domain, you can use the following command:

```
[root@server1 ~]# whois linux.org
[Querying whois.publicinterestregistry.net]
[whois.publicinterestregistry.net]
Domain ID:D2338975-LROR
Domain Name:LINUX.ORG
Created On:10-May-1994 04:00:00 UTC
Last Updated On:19-Oct-2004 00:24:17 UTC
Expiration Date:11-May-2013 04:00:00 UTC
Sponsoring Registrar:Network Solutions LLC (R63-LROR)
Status:CLIENT TRANSFER PROHIBITED
Registrant ID:22275688-NSI
Registrant Name:Linux Online, Inc
Registrant Organization:Linux Online, Inc
Registrant Street1:59 E. River St, #2
Registrant Street2:
Registrant Street3:
Registrant City:Ogdensburg
Registrant State/Province:NY
Registrant Postal Code:13669
Registrant Country:US
Registrant Phone:+1.3153931202
Registrant Phone Ext.:
Registrant FAX:
Registrant FAX Ext.:
Registrant Email:mmclagan@INVLOGIC.COM
```

12

```
Admin ID:15412138-NSI
Admin Name:Michael McLagan
Admin Street1:59 E RIVER ST # 2
Admin Street2:
Admin Street3:
Admin City:OGDENSBURG
Admin State/Province:NY
Admin Postal Code:13669-1307
Admin Country:US
Admin Phone:+1.3153931202
Admin Phone Ext.:
Admin FAX:+1.231231234
Admin FAX Ext.:
Admin Email:mmclagan@INVLOGIC.COM
Tech ID:15412138-NSI
Tech Name:Michael McLagan
Tech Street1:59 E RIVER ST # 2
Tech Street2:
Tech Street3:
Tech City:OGDENSBURG
Tech State/Province:NY
Tech Postal Code:13669-1307
Tech Country:US
Tech Phone:+1.3153931202
Tech Phone Ext.:
Tech FAX:+1.231231234
Tech FAX Ext.:
Tech Email:mmclagan@INVLOGIC.COM
Name Server:NS.INVLOGIC.COM
Name Server:NS0.AITCOM.NET
DNSSEC:Unsigned
[root@server1 ~]# _
```

You can view or set the host name for a Linux computer using the **hostname command,** as shown in the following output:

```
[root@server1 ~]# hostname
server1.class.com
[root@server1 ~]# hostname computer1.sampledomain.com
[root@server1 ~]# hostname
computer1.sampledomain.com
[root@server1 ~]# _
```

To configure the host name shown in the preceding output at every boot time, simply modify the "HOSTNAME" line in the /etc/sysconfig/network file, as shown in the following example:

```
[root@server1 ~]# cat /etc/sysconfig/network
NETWORKING=yes
HOSTNAME=server1.class.com
[root@server1 ~]# _
```

Planning an appropriate host name prior to installation is good practice because many applications record this host name in their configuration files during installation. You might need to change these files if you change the host name after installation.

Although host names are easier to use when specifying computers on the network, TCP/IP cannot use them to identify computers. Thus, you must map host names to their associated IP addresses so that applications that contact other computers across the network can find the appropriate IP address for a host name.

The simplest method for mapping host names to IP addresses is by placing entries into the /etc/hosts file, as shown in the following example:

```
[root@server1 ~]# cat /etc/hosts
127.0.0.1    server1 server1.class.com localhost localhost.localdomain
::1          server1 server1.class.com localhost localhost.localdomain
3.0.0.2      ftp.sampledomain.com fileserver
192.168.0.1 alpha
[root@server1 ~]# _
```

The entries in the preceding output identify the local computer, 127.0.0.1, by the host names server1, server1.class.com, localhost, and localhost.localdomain. Similarly, you can use the host name ftp.sampledomain.com or fileserver to refer to the computer with the IP address 3.0.0.2. Also, the computer with the IP address 192.168.0.1 can be referred to using the name alpha.

You can also edit the /etc/hosts file by accessing the Hosts tab within the Network Configuration tool.

12

You can use the Network Information Service (NIS) to share the /etc/hosts configuration file among several Linux computers on the network. NIS is discussed in Chapter 13.

Because it would be cumbersome to list names for all hosts on the Internet in the /etc/hosts file, ISPs can list FQDNs in DNS servers on the Internet. Applications can then ask DNS servers for the IP address associated with a certain FQDN. To configure your system to resolve names to IP addresses by contacting a DNS server, simply specify the IP address of the DNS server in the /etc/resolv.conf file. This file can contain up to three DNS servers. If the first DNS server is unavailable, the system attempts to contact the second DNS server, followed by the third DNS server listed in the file. A sample /etc/resolv.conf file is shown in the following output:

```
[root@server1 ~]# cat /etc/resolv.conf
nameserver 209.121.197.2
nameserver 192.139.188.144
nameserver 6.0.4.211
[root@server1 ~]# _
```

You can also edit the /etc/resolv.conf file by accessing the DNS tab within the Network Configuration tool.

To test the DNS configuration by resolving a name to an IP address, you can type `nslookup name`, `dig name`, or `host name` at a command prompt, where *name* is the host *name* or FQDN of a remote host.

When you specify a host name while using a certain application, that application must then resolve that host name to the appropriate IP address by searching either the local /etc/hosts file, a DNS server, or an NIS server. The method that applications use to resolve host names is determined by the "hosts" line in the /etc/nsswitch.conf file. An example of this file is shown in the following output:

```
[root@server1 ~]# grep hosts /etc/nsswitch.conf
#hosts:    db files nisplus nis dns
hosts:     files dns nis
[root@server1 ~]# _
```

The preceding output indicates that applications first try to resolve host names using the /etc/hosts file (`files`). If unsuccessful, applications contact the DNS servers listed in /etc/resolv.conf (`dns`), followed by an NIS server (`nis`) if one is configured.

On older Linux computers, the /etc/host.conf file was used instead of /etc/nsswitch.conf. The /etc/host.conf file still exists today to support older application programs and should contain the same name resolution order as /etc/nsswitch.conf. A sample /etc/host.conf file that tells applications to search the /etc/hosts file (`hosts`), followed by DNS servers (`bind`) and NIS servers (`nis`) is shown in the following output:

```
[root@server1 ~]# cat /etc/host.conf
multi on
order hosts,bind,nis
[root@server1 ~]# _
```

Routing

Every computer on a network maintains a list of TCP/IP networks so that packets are sent to the appropriate location. This list is called a **route table** and is stored in system memory. To see the route table, you can simply use the **route command**, as shown in the following output:

```
[root@server1 ~]# route
Kernel IP routing table
Destination     Gateway         Genmask         Flags Metric Ref    Use Iface
10.0.0.0        *               255.255.0.0     U     2      0      0   wlan0
192.168.0.0     *               255.255.0.0     U     0      0      0   eth0
127.0.0.0       *               255.0.0.0       U     0      0      0   lo
default         192.168.0.1     0.0.0.0         UG    0      0      0   eth0
[root@server1 ~]# _
```

The `netstat -r` command is equivalent to the `route` command.

The route table shown in the preceding output indicates that all packets destined for the 10.0.0.0 network will be sent to the device wlan0. Similarly, all packets destined for the 192.168.0.0 network will be sent to the device eth0, and packets destined for the 127.0.0.0 network will be sent to the loopback adapter (`lo`). Packets that must be sent to any other network will be sent to the default gateway. The final line in the preceding output indicates that the default gateway is a computer with the IP address 192.168.0.1, via the eth0 device.

If your computer has more than one network interface configured, the route table will have more entries that define the available TCP/IP networks. Computers that have more than one network interface are called **multihomed hosts**. Multihomed hosts can be configured to forward packets from one interface to another to aid a packet in reaching its destination; this process is commonly called **routing** or **IP forwarding**. To enable routing on your Linux computer, simply place the number 1 in the file /proc/sys/net/ipv4/ip_forward for IPv4 or /proc/sys/net/ipv6/conf/all/forwarding for IPv6, as shown in the following output:

```
[root@server1 ~]# cat /proc/sys/net/ipv4/ip_forward
0
[root@server1 ~]# cat /proc/sys/net/ipv6/conf/all/forwarding
0
[root@server1 ~]# echo 1 > /proc/sys/net/ipv4/ip_forward
[root@server1 ~]# echo 1 > /proc/sys/net/ipv6/conf/all/forwarding
[root@server1 ~]# cat /proc/sys/net/ipv4/ip_forward
1
[root@server1 ~]# cat /proc/sys/net/ipv6/conf/all/forwarding
1
[root@server1 ~]# _
```

To enable IPv4 routing at every boot, ensure that the line `net.ipv4.ip_forward = 1` exists in the /etc/sysctl.conf file. To enable IPv6 routing at every boot, ensure that the line `net.ipv6.conf.default.forwarding = 1` exists in the /etc/sysctl.conf file.

If your computer has more than one network interface and routing is enabled, your computer will route packets only to networks for which it has a network interface. On larger networks, however, you might have several routers, in which case packets might have to travel through several routers to reach their destination. Because routers only know the networks to which they are directly connected, you might need to add entries to the route table on a router so that it knows where to send packets that are destined for a remote network. Suppose, for example, your organization has three TCP/IP networks (1.0.0.0/8, 2.0.0.0/8, and 3.0.0.0/8) divided by two routers, as shown in Figure 12-7.

RouterA has an entry in its route table that says it is connected to (1) the 1.0.0.0/8 network via the network interface that has the IP address 1.0.0.1 and (2) the 2.0.0.0/8 network via the network interface that has the IP address 2.0.0.1. These two routes are automatically established when TCP/IP is configured. If RouterA receives a packet that is destined for the 3.0.0.0/8 network, it does not know where to forward it, because it does not have a route

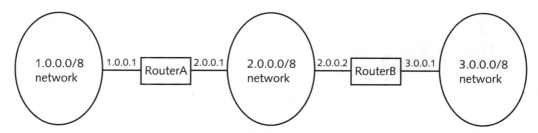

Figure 12-7 A sample routed network

Source: Course Technology/Cengage Learning

for the 3.0.0.0/8 network in its routing table. To add the appropriate route to the 3.0.0.0/8 network on RouterA, you can run the following command on RouterA:

```
[root@server1 ~]# route add -net 3.0.0.0 netmask 255.0.0.0 gw 2.0.0.2
[root@server1 ~]# _
```

Now, RouterA sends any packets destined for the 3.0.0.0/8 network to the computer 2.0.0.2 (RouterB). RouterB then forwards the packets to the 3.0.0.0/8 network because it has a route in its route table that says it is connected to the 3.0.0.0/8 network via the network interface that has the IP address 3.0.0.1.

Similarly, for RouterB to forward packets it receives destined for the 1.0.0.0/8 network, it must have a route that sends those packets to RouterA via the interface 2.0.0.1:

```
[root@server1 ~]# route add -net 1.0.0.0 netmask 255.0.0.0 gw 2.0.0.1
[root@server1 ~]# _
```

You can use the `route del <route>` command to remove entries from the route table.

The **ip command** can also be used to manipulate the route table. For example, the command `ip route add 1.0.0.0/8 via 2.0.0.1` can be used to add the route shown in the previous output to the route table.

The contents of the route table are lost when the computer is powered off. To load routes to remote networks to the route table at every boot time, simply place the appropriate `route` or `ip` command in the /etc/rc.d/rc.local file. Alternatively, you can add routes on the Route tab of a network interface within the Network Configuration tool, as shown earlier in Figure 12-3. These routes are stored alongside the network interface configuration within the /etc/sysconfig/network-scripts directory and are added to the route table when the network interface is activated at boot time.

You can also use a routing protocol on routers within your network to automate the addition of routes to the routing table. Two common routing protocols are Routing Information Protocol (RIP) and Open Shortest Path First (OSPF). If you install the Quagga package using the `yum install quagga` command, you can configure the RIP and OSPF routing protocols using the `zebra` command.

Because the list of all routes on large networks, such as the Internet, is too large to be stored in a route table on a router, most routers are configured with a default gateway. Any packets that are addressed to a destination that is not listed in the route table are sent to the default gateway, which is a router that can forward the packet to the appropriate network or to the router's own default gateway and so on until the packets reach their destination.

If computers on your network are unable to connect to other computers on a remote network, the problem is likely routing-related. A common utility used to troubleshoot routing is the **traceroute command**. It displays all routers between the current computer and a remote computer. To trace the path from the local computer to the computer with the IP address 3.4.5.6, you can use the following command:

```
[root@server1 ~]# traceroute 3.4.5.6
traceroute to 3.4.5.6 (3.4.5.6), 30 hops max, 38 byte packets
1   linksys (192.168.0.1)   2.048 ms   0.560 ms   0.489 ms
2   apban.pso.com (7.43.111.2)   2.560 ms   0.660 ms   0.429 ms
3   tfs.ihtfcid.net (3.0.0.1)   3.521 ms   0.513 ms   0.499 ms
4   srl.lala.com (3.4.5.6)   5.028 ms   0.710 ms   0.554 ms
[root@server1 ~]# _
```

Network Services

Recall from Chapter 1 that Linux provides a wide variety of services that are available to users across a network. Before you are able to configure the appropriate network services to meet your organization's needs, you must first identify the types and features of network services.

Network services are processes that run on your computer and provide some type of valuable service for client computers on the network. They are often represented by a series of daemon processes that listen for certain requests on the network. Daemons identify the packets to which they should respond using a **port** number that uniquely identifies each network service. Different daemons listen for different port numbers. A port number is like an apartment number for the delivery of mail. The network ID of the IP address ensures that the packet is delivered to the correct street (network); the host ID ensures that the packet is delivered to the correct building (host); and the Transport-layer protocol and port number ensure that the packet is delivered to the proper apartment (service).

Ports and their associated protocols are defined in the /etc/services file. To see to which port the telnet daemon listens, you can use the following command:

```
[root@server1 ~]# grep telnet /etc/services
telnet              23/tcp
telnet              23/udp
rtelnet             107/tcp         # Remote Telnet
rtelnet             107/udp
telnets             992/tcp
telnets             992/udp
skytelnet           1618/tcp        # skytelnet
skytelnet           1618/udp        # skytelnet
hp-3000-telnet      2564/tcp        # HP 3000 NS/VT block mode telnet
tl1-telnet          3083/tcp        # TL1-TELNET
tl1-telnet          3083/udp        # TL1-TELNET
telnetcpcd          3696/tcp        # Telnet Com Port Control
telnetcpcd          3696/udp        # Telnet Com Port Control
scpi-telnet         5024/tcp        # SCPI-TELNET
scpi-telnet         5024/udp        # SCPI-TELNET
ktelnet             6623/tcp        # Kerberos V5 Telnet
ktelnet             6623/udp        # Kerberos V5 Telnet
[root@server1 ~]# _
```

The preceding output indicates that the telnet daemon listens on port 23 using both TCP/IP and UDP/IP.

The **User Datagram Protocol/Internet Protocol (UDP/IP)** is a faster and consequently less-reliable version of TCP/IP.

Ports range in number from 0 to 65534. The ports 0–1023 are called **well-known ports** because they represent commonly used services. Table 12-2 provides a list of common well-known ports.

Service	Port
FTP	TCP 20, 21
Secure Shell (SSH)	TCP 22
Telnet	TCP 23
SMTP	TCP 25
HTTP / HTTPS	TCP 80 / TCP 443
rlogin	TCP 513
DNS	TCP 53, UDP 53
Trivial FTP (TFTP)	UDP 69
POP3 / POP3S	TCP 110 / TCP 995
NNTP / NNTPS	TCP 119 / TCP 563
IMAP4 / IMAP4S	TCP 143 / TCP 993

Table 12-2 Common well-known ports

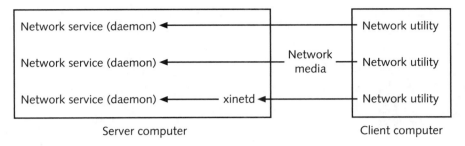

Figure 12-8 Interacting with network services

Source: Course Technology/Cengage Learning

 Many protocols have a secure version that uses encrypted communication. For example, secure HTTP is called HTTPS and uses a different port number as a result.

Network utilities can connect to daemons that provide network services directly; these daemons are called **stand-alone daemons**. Alternatively, network utilities can connect to network services via the **Internet Super Daemon** (**xinetd**), which starts the appropriate daemon to provide the network service as needed. This structure is shown in Figure 12-8.

The Internet Super Daemon is typically used to start and manage connections for smaller network daemons, such as telnet and rlogin, and is not installed in Fedora 13 by default. To install the Internet Super Daemon, you can execute the yum install xinetd command. Next, you can edit the /etc/xinetd.conf file to configure the Internet Super Daemon. Normally, this file incorporates all of the files in the /etc/xinetd.d directory as well. Most daemons that are managed by the Internet Super Daemon are configured by files in the /etc/xinetd.d directory named after the daemons. For example, if you install the telnet daemon, you can configure it to be started by the Internet Super Daemon via the /etc/xinetd.d/telnet file, as shown in the following output:

```
[root@server1 ~]# cat /etc/xinetd.d/telnet
# default: on
# description: The telnet server serves telnet sessions; it uses \
#       unencrypted username/password pairs for authentication.
service telnet
{
  flags            = REUSE
  socket_type      = stream
  wait             = no
  user             = root
  server           = /usr/sbin/in.telnetd
  log_on_failure   += USERID
  disable          = yes
}
[root@server1 ~]# _
```

The preceding output displays the full path to the telnet daemon (/usr/sbin/in.telnetd). In addition, the disable = yes line in the /etc/xinetd.d/telnet file indicates that the telnet daemon is currently disabled.

Older Linux systems use a version of the Internet Super Daemon called inetd, which uses the configuration file /etc/inetd.conf.

Large network daemons are rarely started by the Internet Super Daemon. Instead, they are stand-alone daemons that are started at boot time from files in the /etc/rc.d/rc*.d directories. The chkconfig command or the ntsysv utility discussed in Chapter 8 can be used to configure stand-alone daemons to start in various runlevels. In addition, most stand-alone daemons can be started manually from files in the /etc/init.d or /etc/rc.d/init.d directory.

Many stand-alone and xinetd-managed daemons also have configuration files that control how they operate and indicate the pathname to other important files used by the daemon. For simplicity, many of these daemons store all information in only one configuration file that contains comments that indicate the syntax and purpose of each line. As a result, these configuration files can be very large; the configuration file used by the Apache Web server is over 1,000 lines long. In addition to this, most stand-alone network daemons do not use the rsyslog daemon to log information related to their operation. Instead, they log this information themselves to subdirectories of the same name underneath the /var/log directory. For example, log files for the Samba daemon are located in the /var/log/samba directory.

Table 12-3 lists the names and features of network services that are commonly found on Linux computers that participate in a network environment. You'll learn how to configure many of these network services in Chapters 13 and 14.

Network Service	Type	Port	Description
Apache Web server (httpd)	Stand-alone	TCP 80 TCP 443	Serves Web pages using HTTP/HTTPS to other computers on the network that have a Web browser. Configuration file: /etc/httpd/conf/httpd.conf
BIND/DNS server (named)	Stand-alone	TCP 53 UDP 53	Resolves fully qualified domain names to IP addresses for a certain namespace on the Internet. Configuration file: /etc/named.conf
DHCP server (dhcpd)	Stand-alone	UDP 67 UDP 68	Provides IP configuration for computers on a network. Configuration file: /etc/dhcp/dhcpd.conf
Washington University FTP Server (in.ftpd)	xinetd	TCP 20 TCP 21 UDP 69	Transfers files to and accepts files from other computers on the network with an FTP utility. Configuration file: /etc/ftpaccess Hosts denied FTP access: /etc/ftphosts Users denied FTP access: /etc/ftpusers FTP data compression: /etc/ftpconversions

Table 12-3 Common network services

Network Service	Type	Port	Description
Very Secure FTP Server (vsftpd)	Stand-alone	TCP 20 TCP 21 UDP 69	Transfers files to and accepts files from other computers on the network with an FTP utility. Configuration file: /etc/vsftpd/vsftpd.conf Users denied FTP access: /etc/vsftpd.ftpusers and /etc/vsftpd.user_list
Internetwork News Server (innd)	Stand-alone	TCP 119 TCP 563	Accepts and manages newsgroup postings and transfers them to other news servers. Configuration file: /etc/news/inn.conf
NFS Server (rpc.nfsd)	Stand-alone	TCP 2049	Shares files to other computers on the network that have an NFS client utility. Configuration file: /etc/exports
NIS Server (ypserv & ypbind)	Stand-alone	TCP 111	Shares configuration information to NIS clients that are members of an NIS domain. Configuration file: /etc/ypserv.conf
POP3 Server (ipop3d)	Stand-alone	TCP 110 TCP 995	Allows users with an e-mail reader to obtain e-mail from the server using the Post Office Protocol version 3.
IMAP4 Server (imapd)	Stand-alone	TCP 143 TCP 993	Allows users with an e-mail reader to obtain e-mail from the server using the Internet Message Access Protocol.
Sendmail Email Server (sendmail)	Stand-alone	TCP 25	Accepts and sends e-mail to users or other e-mail servers on the Internet using the Simple Mail Transfer Protocol (SMTP). Configuration file: /etc/sendmail.cf
Postfix Email Server (postfix)	Stand-alone	TCP 25	Accepts and sends e-mail to users or other e-mail servers on the Internet using the Simple Mail Transfer Protocol (SMTP). Configuration file: /etc/postfix/main.cf
rlogin Daemon (in.rlogind)	xinetd	TCP 513	Allows users who use the rlogin and rcp utilities to copy files and obtain shells on other computers on the network using trusted access.
rsh Daemon (in.rshd)	xinetd	TCP 514	Allows users who use the rsh utility to run commands on other computers on the network using trusted access.
Samba Server (smbd & nmbd)	Stand-alone	TCP 137 TCP 138 TCP 139 TCP 445	Allows Windows users to view shared files and printers on a Linux server. Configuration file: /etc/samba/smb.conf
Secure Shell Daemon (sshd)	Stand-alone	TCP 22	Provides a secure alternative to the telnet, rlogin, and rsh utilities by using encrypted communication. Configuration file: /etc/ssh/sshd_config
Squid Proxy Server (squid)	Stand-alone	TCP 3128	Allows computers on a network to share one connection to the Internet. It is also known as a proxy server. Configuration file: /etc/squid/squid.conf
telnet Daemon (in.telnetd)	xinetd	TCP 23	Allows users who have a telnet utility to log in to the system from across the network and obtain a shell.
X Server	Stand-alone	TCP 0	Generates graphics that will be displayed on a computer on the network that has an X client using the DISPLAY variable on the X server.

12

Table 12-3   Common network services (continued)

Remote Administration

In most organizations, servers are typically stored within a server room and administered remotely. There are several ways to perform command-line and graphical administration of remote Linux servers, including telnet, remote commands, Secure Shell (SSH), X Windows, and Virtual Network Computing (VNC).

Telnet

The easiest way to perform administration on a remote Linux computer is via a command-line interface. The **telnet command** has traditionally been used to obtain a command-line shell on remote UNIX and Linux servers across the network that run a telnet server daemon. Nearly all operating systems today, such as Windows, Macintosh, and UNIX, come with a telnet command.

The telnet server daemon (in.telnetd) is managed by xinetd and is not installed by default in Fedora 13. To install the telnet server daemon, you can execute the yum install telnet-server command. Next, you can configure xinetd to allow telnet connections by changing the line disable = yes to disable = no in the /etc/xinetd.d/telnet file, and restart the xinetd daemon using the service xinetd restart command.

By default, you are prevented from logging in and obtaining a shell as the root user to certain network services, such as telnet, due to entries in the /etc/securetty file. Removing or renaming this file allows the root user to log in and receive a shell across the network using the telnet command.

Once the telnet daemon has been configured, you can connect to it from a remote computer. Simply specify the host name or IP address of the target computer to the telnet command and log in as the appropriate user and password. A shell obtained during a telnet session runs on a pseudoterminal (a terminal that does not obtain input directly from the computer keyboard) rather than a local terminal and works much the same way a normal shell does. You can execute commands and use the exit command to kill the BASH shell and end the session. A sample telnet session is shown in the following output using a computer with a host name of appserver:

```
[root@server1 ~]# telnet appserver
Trying 192.168.0.1. . .
Connected to appserver (192.168.0.1).
Escape character is '^]'.
Fedora release 13 (Goddard)
Kernel 2.6.33.3-85.fc13.i686.PAE on an i686 (3)
login: root
Password:
Last login: Tue Aug 10 14:14:27 from server1
[root@server1 ~]# who
user1      tty1          2010-09-01 07:41  (:0)
user1      pts/0         2010-09-01 08:04  (:0.0)
root       pts/1         2010-09-02 13:52  (server1)
[root@server1 ~]# exit
```

```
logout
Connection closed by foreign host.
[root@server1 ~]# _
```

Remote Commands

The **remote commands** (commonly called the **r commands**) are a set of commands that can be used to execute commands on remote systems, obtain remote shells, and copy files between systems. To install the remote command services on Fedora 13, you can execute the `yum install rsh-server` command. Next, you can configure xinetd to allow remote command connections by changing the line `disable = yes` to `disable = no` in the /etc/xinetd.d/rlogin and /etc/xinetd.d/rsh files, and then restart the xinetd daemon using the `service xinetd restart` command.

Next, you can use the remote commands to perform administration tasks on your Linux system from across the network. The `rlogin` command can obtain a shell on a remote system, the `rcp` command can be used to copy files between computers, and the `rsh` command can be used to execute a command on a remote computer.

The r commands allow access to remote computers without a password, provided the remote computer has **trusted access**—in other words, permission to do so. One method of setting up trusted access is to add the host names of computers to the /etc/hosts.equiv file on the remote computer. The following /etc/hosts.equiv file gives users who have logged in to the computers *www.sampledomain.com* and *www.sampledomain2.com* the ability to use the `rlogin`, `rcp`, and `rsh` commands to connect to the computer as the same user without specifying a password:

```
[root@server1 ~]# cat /etc/hosts.equiv
www.sampledomain.com
www.sampledomain2.com
[root@server1 ~]# _
```

Thus, if the user mary logs in to the computer *www.sampledomain.com* and uses an r command to connect to the local computer, she is automatically logged in to the system using the local mary user account without having to specify a password. The only user that cannot be trusted using the /etc/hosts.equiv file is the root user. Trusted access is common in companies that have several Linux servers that have the same user accounts. Setting up trusted access allows users who log in to one Linux computer to access other computers without having to reenter their password.

Another method for setting trusted access is to create an .rhosts file in the home directory of each user who wants to connect using trusted access. Consider the following /home/mary/.rhosts file:

```
[root@server1 ~]# cat /home/mary/.rhosts
www.sampledomain.com
www.sampledomain2.com
[root@server1 ~]# _
```

This gives the user mary on the computers *www.sampledomain.com* and *www.sampledomain2.com* the ability to use the r commands to connect to the local Linux computer as the user mary without specifying a password. In addition, the /root/.rhosts file can be used to give the root user on other trusted computers the ability to use r commands to connect to the local computer without specifying a password.

 Newer versions of the r commands attempt to validate trusted users using the Kerberos protocol, which prevents other network users from viewing the traffic generated by the r command. To use Kerberos with r commands, you must have a .k5login file in your home directory or an /etc/krb.equiv file that lists the users and Kerberos realms that are allowed. If these files do not exist, the /etc/hosts.equiv and ~/.rhosts files are examined, as discussed earlier.

Suppose that a remote computer called remoteserver has trusted access set up; you can use the following command to obtain a shell:

```
[root@server1 ~]# rlogin remoteserver
Last login: Thu Sep 2 14:20:50 from 10.0.1.3
[root@server1 ~]# _
```

Similarly, you can copy the /etc/hosts file from the computer remoteserver to the /root directory of the local computer by using the following command:

```
[root@server1 ~]# rcp remoteserver:/etc/hosts localhost:/root
[root@server1 ~]# ls -F /root
Desktop/ hosts
[root@server1 ~]# _
```

In addition, to run the who command on the computer remoteserver and display the results to the local terminal, you can use the following command:

```
[root@server1 ~]# rsh remoteserver who
user1    tty1        2010-09-01 07:41 (:0)
user1    pts/0       2010-09-01 08:04 (:0.0)
root     pts/1       2010-09-02 14:24 (10.0.1.3)
user1    pts/2       2010-09-02 07:58 (:0.0)
[root@server1 ~]# _
```

Secure Shell (SSH)

Although the telnet, rlogin, rcp, and rsh commands can be quickly used to perform remote administration, they do not encrypt the information that passes between computers. **Secure Shell (SSH)** was designed as a secure replacement for these commands that encrypts information that passes across the network. As a result, the SSH daemon (sshd) is installed by default on Fedora 13 and configured to start during runlevel 5. To connect to a remote Linux computer running sshd, you can use the **ssh command** followed by the host name or IP address of the target computer. For example, you can connect to a computer with the host name of appserver using the ssh appserver command. Your local user name will be passed to the server automatically during the SSH request, and you will be prompted to supply the password for the same user on the target computer. If you need to log in using a different user name on the remote appserver computer, you can instead use the ssh -l username appserver command or the ssh username@appserver command. A sample ssh session is shown in the following output:

```
[root@server1 ~]# ssh root@appserver
root@appserver's password:
Last login: Thu Sep 2 14:29:06 2010 from 10.0.1.3
[root@server1 ~]# who
root        :0              Aug 10 14:13
root        pts/8           Aug 10 14:14 (:0.0)
root        pts/9           Aug 10 14:14 (10.0.1.3)
[root@server1 root]# exit
Connection to appserver closed.
[root@server1 ~]# _
```

When you connect to a new computer for the first time using SSH, you will be prompted to accept the RSA encryption fingerprint for the target computer, which is stored in ~/.ssh/known_hosts for subsequent connections. If the target computer's encryption keys are regenerated, you will need to remove the old key from the ~/.ssh/known_hosts file before you connect again.

You can regenerate the keys used by sshd using the `ssh-keygen` command.

SSH can also be used to transfer files between computers. For example, to transfer the /root/ sample file on a remote computer called appserver to the /var directory on the local computer, you could run the following command:

```
[root@server1 ~]# ssh root@appserver cat /root/sample > /var/sample
root@appserver's password:
[root@server1 ~]# _
```

Alternatively, to transfer the /root/sample file on the local computer to the /var directory on a remote computer called appserver, you could run the following command:

```
[root@server1 ~]# ssh root@appserver cat </root/sample "> " /var/sample
root@appserver's password:
[root@server1 ~]# _
```

Because SSH is typically used to perform remote administration, sshd allows root logins and a wide range of encryption algorithms by default. However, you can configure the functionality of sshd by editing the /etc/ssh/sshd_config file. Most of this file is commented and should only be edited to change the default settings that sshd uses when servicing SSH clients. The most commonly changed options in this file are those that deal with authentication and encryption. By default, sshd uses a secure challenge-response authentication method that ensures that the password is not transmitted on the network, but this can be changed to Kerberos authentication or authentication that allows uses based on the ~/.rhosts or /etc/hosts.equiv files.

Organizations use many types of encryption to secure communication on the network. Each type of encryption differs in its method of encryption and the cryptography key length used to encrypt data; the longer the key length, the more difficult it is for malicious users to decode the data. The main types of encryption supported by sshd are as follows:

- Triple Data Encryption Standard (3DES), which encrypts blocks of data in three stages using a 168-bit key length
- Advanced Encryption Standard (AES), which is an improvement on 3DES encryption and is available in 128-, 192-, and 256-bit key lengths
- Blowfish, which is an encryption algorithm that is much faster than 3DES and can use keys up to 448 bits in length
- Carlisle Adams Stafford Tavares (CAST), which is a general-purpose encryption similar to 3DES and is commonly available using a 128-bit key length
- ARCfour, which is a fast encryption algorithm that operates on streams of data instead of blocks of data and uses variable-length keys up to 2048 bits in length

In addition, all of the aforementioned types of encryption except ARCfour typically use Cipher Block Chaining (CBC), which can encrypt larger amounts of data.

Client computers can use an /etc/ssh/ssh_config or ~/ssh/ssh_config file to set SSH options for use with the `ssh` command. The authentication and encryption settings on the client computer must match those in the server configuration file (/etc/ssh/sshd_config) for a connection to be successful.

Remote X Windows

Since its creation, X Windows has always been a network application. X Windows clients listen on port 0 for graphics generated by the server portion of X Windows. You can use this feature of X Windows to obtain graphical utilities from a remote Linux computer in order to perform system administration.

To obtain graphical utilities from another Linux computer using X Windows, you must first add the line `DisallowTCP=false` to /etc/gdm/custom.conf (under the `[security]` section) on both the local and remote computers. Next, you can start X Windows on the local computer and run the `xhost +` command at a command prompt within a graphical terminal to allow other computers to write to the X Windows client on your computer.

Following this, you can connect to the target computer using `telnet` or `ssh` and obtain a remote shell. At this remote shell, you can type `export DISPLAY='IP_Address:0.0'` where IP_Address is the IP address of your local computer. The DISPLAY variable on the remote computer redirects the output of X Windows on the remote computer during your telnet or ssh session to your local computer's X Windows.

The `:0.0` in the previous command refers to port 0 (`:0`) and the first display (`.0`).

Finally, you can execute any graphical utility within your remote shell, such as `system-config-network`, to open the remote graphical utility on your local computer.

Virtual Network Computing (VNC)

Virtual Network Computing (VNC) is another graphical option for administrating a Linux system remotely. After you install a VNC server daemon on a computer, other computers that run a VNC client can connect to the VNC server daemon across a network to obtain a desktop environment. VNC uses a special platform-independent protocol called Remote FrameBuffer (RFB) to transfer graphics, mouse movements, and keystrokes across the network.

VNC server software and client software exist for Linux, UNIX, Mac, and Windows systems. You can use a single system to obtain the desktop of all of the Linux, UNIX, Mac, and Windows systems on your network.

Although a VNC client is installed on Fedora 13 by default, to allow remote connections you must install a VNC server by running the `yum install vnc-server` command. Next, you must configure the VNC server by editing the /etc/sysconfig/vncservers file. The following lines in the /etc/sysconfig/vncservers file create a shared VNC server instance on display number 2 as the root user using 1024 x 768 resolution at a 16-bit color depth. You can have multiple VNC server instances listed in /etc/sysconfig/vncservers, provided that the servers use different display numbers.

```
[root@localhost ~]# tail -2 /etc/sysconfig/vncservers
VNCSERVERS= "2:root"
VNCSERVERARGS[2]= "-geometry 1024x768 -depth 16"
[root@localhost ~]# _
```

The port number to which the VNC server listens is 5900 plus the display number listed in the /etc/sysconfig/vncservers file. The VNC server listed in the preceding output would be listed on port 5902.

Next, you must configure a password for the connection(s) listed in the /etc/sysconfig/vncservers file using the **vncpasswd command** and start the VNC server. The VNC password is stored in the ~/.vnc/passwd file. For the root user listed in the /etc/sysconfig/vncservers file shown earlier, the VNC password will be stored in the /root/.vnc/passwd file.

Next, other computers can connect to the VNC server using the **vncviewer command**. To use the vncviewer command, you must use the syntax vncviewer *IPaddress:Port: Display#*. For example, to connect to the VNC server that uses display number 2 on the computer server1.class.com, you could use the following command: vncviewer server1.class.com:5902:2 After supplying the appropriate VNC password, you will then obtain a desktop session on the remote computer, as shown in Figure 12-9.

12

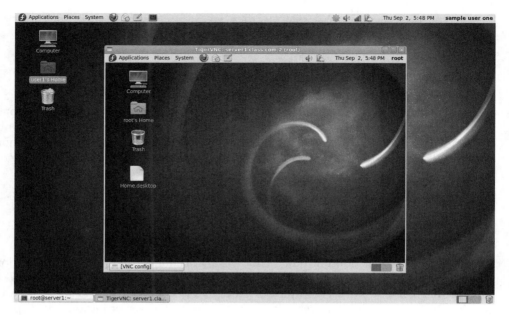

Figure 12-9 A remote VNC session

Source: Course Technology/Cengage Learning

Chapter Summary

- A network is a collection of connected computers that shares information.

- A protocol is a set of rules that defines the format of information that is transmitted across a network. The protocol suite used by the Internet and most networks is TCP/IP.

- Each computer on a TCP/IP network must have a valid IPv4 or IPv6 address.

- The IPv4 configuration of a network interface can be specified manually, obtained automatically from a DHCP or BOOTP server, or autoconfigured by the system.

- The IPv6 configuration of a network interface can be obtained from a router using ICMPv6, from a DHCP server, or autoconfigured by the system.

- The /etc/sysconfig/network-scripts directory contains the configuration for NIC and PPP interfaces.

- Host names are computer names that, unlike IP names, are easy for humans to remember. Host names that are generated by the hierarchical domain name space are called FQDNs.

- Host names must be resolved to an IP address before network communication can take place.

- Routers are devices that forward TCP/IP packets from one network to another. Each computer and router has a route table that it uses to determine how TCP/IP packets are forwarded.

- Network services are started by the Internet Super Daemon or by a stand-alone daemon. In either case, they listen for requests on a certain port.

- There are many ways to remotely administer a Linux system. You can perform command-line administration remotely via the telnet, rsh, rcp, rlogin, and ssh commands. For graphical remote administration, you can use X Windows and VNC.

Key Terms

ANDing   The process by which binary bits are compared to calculate the network and host IDs from an IP address and subnet mask.

Automatic Private IP Addressing (APIPA)   A feature that automatically configures a network interface using an IPv4 address on the 169.254.0.0 network.

broadcast   The TCP/IP communication destined for all computers on a network.

Classless Interdomain Routing (CIDR) notation   A notation that is often used to represent an IP address and its subnet mask.

default gateway   The IP address of the router on the network used to send packets to remote networks.

domain name space (DNS)   A hierarchical namespace used for host names.

Ethernet   The most common media access method used in networks today.

fully qualified domain name (FQDN)   A host name that follows DNS convention.

host ID   The portion of an IP address that denotes the host.

host name   A user-friendly name assigned to a computer.

hostname command   A command used to display and change the host name of a computer.

ifconfig command   A command used to display and modify the TCP/IP configuration information for a network interface.

insmod command   A command used to insert a module into the Linux kernel.

Internet Control Message Protocol version 6 (ICMPv6)   A protocol used by computers to obtain an IPv6 configuration from a router on the network.

Internet Protocol (IP) address   A series of four 8-bit numbers that represents a computer on a network.

Internet service provider (ISP)   A company that provides Internet access.

Internet Super Daemon (xinetd)   A network daemon that is used to start other network daemons on demand.

ip command   A command that can be used to manipulate the route table.

IP forwarding   The act of forwarding TCP/IP packets from one network to another. *See also* Routing.

IP version 4 (IPv4)   The most common version of IP used on the Internet. It uses a 32-bit addressing scheme organized into different classes.

IP version 6 (IPv6)   A recent version of IP that is used by some hosts on the Internet. It uses a 128-bit addressing scheme.

link local   The portion of an IPv6 address that refers to a unique computer. It is analogous to the host portion of an IPv4 address.

12

local area networks (LANs)   The networks in which the computers are all in close physical proximity.

lsmod command   A command used to list the modules that are currently used by the Linux kernel.

media access method   A system that defines how computers on a network share access to the physical medium.

modprobe command   A command used to insert a module into the Linux kernel.

multicast   The TCP/IP communication destined for a certain group of computers.

multihomed hosts   The computers that have more than one network interface.

network   Two or more computers joined together via network media and able to exchange information.

Network Address Translation (NAT)   A technology used on routers that allows computers on a network to obtain Internet resources via a single network interface on the router itself.

Network Configuration tool   A graphical utility in Fedora Linux that can be used to configure network settings for the NICs on the system.

network ID   The portion of an IP address that denotes the network.

Network Manager   A daemon that allows multiple network interfaces to be easily configured by users on the system.

network service   A process that responds to network requests.

octet   A portion of an IP address that represents eight binary bits.

packets   The packages of data formatted by a network protocol.

ping (Packet Internet Groper) command   A command used to check TCP/IP connectivity on a network.

port   A number that uniquely identifies a network service.

protocol   A set of rules of communication used between computers on a network.

proxy server   A network server that accepts Internet requests from other computers on the same LAN and obtains the desired resource on their behalf.

r commands   *See* remote commands.

remote commands   A set of commands (rsh, rlogin, and rcp) that can be used to perform remote administration on Linux and UNIX systems.

rmmod command   A command used to remove a module from the Linux kernel.

route command   A command that can be used to manipulate the route table.

routers   The devices capable of transferring packets from one network to another.

route table   A table of information used to indicate which networks are connected to network interfaces.

routing   The act of forwarding data packets from one network to another.

Secure Shell (SSH)   A technology that can be used to run remote applications on a Linux computer; it encrypts all client/server traffic.

ssh command   A command that connects to a remote SSH daemon to perform remote administration.

stand-alone daemons   The daemons that configure themselves at boot time without assistance from the Internet Super Daemon.

subnet mask   A series of four 8-bit numbers that determines the network and host portions of an IP address.

subnetting   The process in which a single large network is subdivided into several smaller networks to control traffic flow.

`telnet` **command**   A command that can be used to run remote applications on a Linux computer.

Token Ring   A popular media access method.

`traceroute` **command**   A command used to trace the path a packet takes through routers to a destination host.

trusted access   A configuration in which computers are allowed to access a given computer without having to provide a password first.

unicast   The TCP/IP communication destined for a single computer.

User Datagram Protocol/Internet Protocol (UDP/IP)   A faster but unreliable version of TCP/IP.

`vncpasswd` **command**   A command used to set a VNC password for a user.

`vncviewer` **command**   A client utility used to connect to a remote VNC server.

well-known ports   Of the 65,535 possible ports, the ports from 0 to 1024 used by common networking services.

`whois` **command**   A command used to obtain information about the organization that maintains a DNS domain.

wide area networks (WANs)   The networks in which computers are separated geographically by large distances.

Review Questions

1. A subnet mask is used to differentiate the host portion from the network portion in a TCP/IP address. True or False?

2. Which networking service allows you to share files with other computers on the network?

   a. NIS

   b. NFS

   c. POP3

   d. BIND

3. Stand-alone daemons are started on demand using the Internet Super Daemon (xinetd). True or False?

4. Which file stores the TCP/IP addresses of the DNS servers used to resolve host names?

   a. /etc/hosts

   b. /etc/host.conf

   c. /etc/resolve

   d. /etc/resolv.conf

5. To test DNS configuration by resolving a host name to an IP address, which command or commands can you use? (Choose all that apply.)

    a. `nslookup` *hostname*

    b. `dig` *hostname*

    c. `host` *hostname*

    d. `resolve` *hostname*

6. Which two commands can be used to modify the route table on a Linux computer? (Choose two answers.)

    a. `route`

    b. `ipconfig`

    c. `ip`

    d. `traceroute`

7. Which file holds the methods to be used and the order in which they will be applied for host name resolution?

    a. /etc/nsswitch.conf

    b. /etc/resolve.conf

    c. /etc/hosts

    d. /etc/dns.conf

8. What are two means available to resolve a host name to the appropriate TCP/IP address? (Choose two answers.)

    a. DHCP

    b. DNS

    c. /etc/hosts

    d. /etc/resolve.conf

9. SSH encrypts all traffic that passes across the network, whereas telnet and rlogin do not. True or False?

10. What devices are used to transfer information from one network to another?

    a. routers

    b. LANs

    c. DNS servers

    d. DHCP servers

11. Which of the following are graphical remote administration technologies? (Choose all that apply.)

    a. telnet

    b. X Windows

    c. rlogin

    d. VNC

12. The daemons associated with network services listen for network traffic associated with a particular _____.

    a. station

    b. port

    c. TCP/IP address

    d. allocation number

13. The TCP/IP address 127.0.0.1 is also referred to as the _____.

    a. local address

    b. lookup address

    c. local host

    d. loopback address

14. The line that configures the host name for the computer at boot time can be found in /etc/sysconfig/network. True or False?

15. Which command would be used to activate the NIC aliased as eth0?

    a. `ifup`

    b. `ifup eth0`

    c. `ipup eth0`

    d. `ifdown eth0`

16. Which of the following port numbers is associated with telnet?

    a. 20

    b. 137

    c. 49

    d. 23

17. Which file would you modify to change the TCP/IP address of the first wired NIC on the system the next time the system is booted or the card is brought up?

    a. /etc/sysconfig/network-scripts/ifcfg-eth1

    b. /etc/sysconfig/network-scripts/ifcfg-eth0

    c. /etc/sysconfig/network-scripts/ipcfg-eth0

    d. /etc/sysconfig/network-scripts/ipcfg-eth1

18. Before a computer can use a router, what configuration information must it be provided?

    a. routing table

    b. subnet mask

    c. default gateway

    d. default router

12

19. Which of the following are stand-alone daemons? (Choose all that apply.)

   a. Apache (httpd)

   b. Washington University FTP (in.ftpd)

   c. telnet (in.telnetd)

   d. DNS (named)

20. Which of the following utilities can be used to check TCP/IP configuration and test network connectivity? (Choose all that apply.)

   a. ifconfig

   b. ipconfig

   c. ping

   d. netstat –i

Hands-On Projects

These projects should be completed in the order given. The hands-on projects presented in this chapter should take a total of three hours to complete. The requirements for this lab include:

- A computer with Fedora 13 installed according to Hands-On Project 2-2

Project 12-1

In this hands-on project, you view and modify the TCP/IP configuration of your network interface.

1. Turn on your computer. After your Linux system has been loaded, log in to the GNOME Desktop Environment using the user name of **sample user one** and the password of **secret**.

2. Navigate to the **System** menu, **Administration**, **Network**. Supply the root password of **secret** when prompted and click **OK**.

3. View the network interfaces listed on the Devices tab. How many wired or wireless NICs do you have? Click the **Hardware** tab. What drivers are listed for your NICs?

4. Click the **Devices** tab again. Highlight the network interface that you use to gain access to your network and click the **Edit** button. When the Ethernet Device screen appears, observe the current TCP/IP settings. When were these configured? Ensure that **Enable IPv6 configuration for this interface** is selected and click **OK**.

5. Click the **File** menu and choose **Save**. Click **OK** when the information message appears, close the Network Configuration window, and log out of the GNOME Desktop Environment.

6. Switch to a command-line terminal (tty2) by pressing **Ctrl+Alt+F2** and log in to the terminal using the user name of **root** and the password of **secret**.

7. At the command prompt, type **service network restart** and press **Enter** to restart your network after making changes to your TCP/IP configuration. Next, type **ifconfig** and press **Enter**. What IPv4 and IPv6 configuration do you see?

8. Using an editor such as vi, edit the **/etc/sysconfig/network-scripts/ifcfg-*interface*** file, where ***interface*** is the network interface that you use to connect to your network. Do the entries contain the correct information? Change the fourth number in your IPv4 address so that it is incremented by 1. Save your changes and quit the editor to return to the command prompt.

9. At the command prompt, type **ifdown *interface*; ifup *interface*** and press **Enter**, where ***interface*** is the network interface that you use to connect to your network.

10. At the command prompt, type **ifconfig** and press **Enter**. Was your IPv4 address changed?

11. Using an editor such as vi, edit the **/etc/sysconfig/network-scripts/ifcfg-*interface*** file where ***interface*** is the network interface that you use to connect to your network. Change your IPv4 address back to its original value. Save your changes and quit the editor to return to the command prompt.

12. At the command prompt, type **ifdown *interface*; ifup *interface*** and press **Enter**, where ***interface*** is the network interface that you use to connect to your network.

13. At the command prompt, type **ifconfig** and press **Enter**. What configuration do you see? Why?

14. At the command prompt, type **ping *interfaceIP*** and press **Enter**, where ***interfaceIP*** is the IPv4 address of the network interface that you use to connect to your network. Do you receive ping responses from your network interface? Press **Ctrl+c** when finished to quit the ping command.

15. At the command prompt, type **netstat -i** and press **Enter**. View the statistics for your network interfaces. If necessary, consult the netstat manual page to determine the meaning of each column displayed.

16. Type **exit** and press **Enter** to log out of your shell.

Project 12-2

In this hands-on project, you view your host name as well as resolve host names and configure host name resolution.

1. Switch to a command-line terminal (tty2) by pressing **Ctrl+Alt+F2** and log in to the terminal using the user name of **root** and the password of **secret**.

2. At the command prompt, type **hostname** and press **Enter**. What is your host name? Next, type **cat /etc/sysconfig/network** at the command prompt and press **Enter**. What host name is listed here? Why?

3. At the command prompt, type **cat /etc/resolv.conf** and press **Enter**. Do you have a DNS server configured?

4. At the command prompt, type **less /etc/nsswitch.conf** and press **Enter**. What method will applications use to resolve host names first? Second? Press **q** to quit the less utility.

5. Edit the **/etc/hosts** file with a text editor such as vi. Add a line to the bottom of the file that reads:

   1.2.3.4 fakehost.fakedomain.com sample

   When finished, save your changes and quit the editor.

6. At the command prompt, type **ping –c 5 server1** and press **Enter**. Was the name resolved correctly?

7. At the command prompt, type **ping –c 5 localhost** and press **Enter**. Was the name resolved correctly?

8. At the command prompt, type **ping –c 5 fakehost.fakedomain.com** and press **Enter**. Was the name resolved correctly? Was the ping command able to contact the host?

9. At the command prompt, type **ping –c 5 sample** and press **Enter**. Was the name resolved correctly? Was the ping command able to contact the host?

10. Type **exit** and press **Enter** to log out of your shell.

Project 12-3

In this hands-on project, you test name resolution using your ISP's DNS server.

1. Switch to a command-line terminal (tty2) by pressing **Ctrl+Alt+F2** and log in to the terminal using the user name of **root** and the password of **secret**.

2. At the command prompt, type **host ftp.kernel.org** and press **Enter**. What IP address was returned for ftp.kernel.org? Is there another name for ftp.kernel.org?

3. At the command prompt, type **nslookup ftp.kernel.org** and press **Enter**. How do you know that this information came from your ISP's DNS server?

4. At the command prompt, type the command **dig ftp.kernel.org** and press **Enter**. What additional information does dig provide compared with the nslookup and host utilities?

5. Type **exit** and press **Enter** to log out of your shell.

Project 12-4

In this hands-on project, you view and configure your computer's route table as well as view and test your routing configuration.

1. Switch to a command-line terminal (tty2) by pressing **Ctrl+Alt+F2** and log in to the terminal using the user name of **root** and the password of **secret**.

2. At the command prompt, type **route** and press **Enter**. What entries are listed? What does each entry represent? What IPv4 address is listed as your default gateway?

3. At the command prompt, type **ip route add 1.0.0.0/8 via** *gwIP* and press **Enter**, where *gwIP* is the IPv4 address of your default gateway.

4. At the command prompt, type **route** and press **Enter**. Is the route added in Step 3 visible? Will this route interfere with traffic that is sent to the 1.0.0.0 network? Explain.

5. At the command prompt, type **traceroute ftp.kernel.org** and press **Enter**. How many routers are used to pass your packet to the ftp.kernel.org computer?

6. At the command prompt, type the command **cat /proc/sys/net/ipv4/ip_forward** and press **Enter**. Is your system configured as an IPv4 router? Next, type the command **cat /proc/sys/net/ipv6/conf/all/forwarding** and press **Enter**. Is your system configured as an IPv6 router? How many network interfaces at minimum must you have in order to be a router?

7. Type **exit** and press **Enter** to log out of your shell.

Project 12-5

In this hands-on project, you install and configure the Internet Super Daemon as well as the telnet and r command daemons. Next, you perform remote administration on your local computer using telnet and the r commands.

1. Switch to a command-line terminal (tty2) by pressing **Ctrl+Alt+F2** and log in to the terminal using the user name of **root** and the password of **secret**.

2. At the command prompt, type **telnet localhost** and press **Enter**. What error did you receive? Why?

3. At the command prompt, type **yum install xinetd telnet-server rsh-server** and press **Enter**. Type **y** and press **Enter** when prompted to confirm the downloads.

4. Edit the **/etc/xinetd.d/telnet** file with a text editor such as vi and change the line that reads:

disable = yes

to

disable = no

When finished, save your changes and quit the editor. Repeat this step for the /etc/xinetd.d/rlogin and /etc/xinetd.d/rsh files.

5. At the command prompt, type **service xinetd start** and press **Enter** to start the Internet Super Daemon. Next, type **chkconfig --level 5 xinetd on** to ensure that the Internet Super Daemon is started in runlevel 5.

6. At the command prompt, type **telnet localhost** and press **Enter**. Why were you successful? Next, log in to the system using the user name of **root** and the password of **secret** when prompted. Were you successful? What error message did you receive? Wait one minute for the telnet utility to close.

7. At the command prompt, type **rm -f /etc/securetty** and press **Enter**.

8. At the command prompt, type **telnet localhost** and press **Enter**. Next, log in to the system using the user name of **root** and the password of **secret** when prompted. Were you successful? Why?

12

9. At the command prompt, type **date** and press **Enter**. Next, type **who** at the command prompt and press **Enter**. Given the output of these commands, can you tell which terminal you are using?

10. Type **exit** and press **Enter** to log out of your shell. Which shell were you logged out of? Next, type **who** at the command prompt and press **Enter**. How can you tell that the telnet session has been closed?

11. At the command prompt, type **echo localhost >> .rhosts** and press **Enter**. What does this command do?

12. At the command prompt, type **rlogin localhost** and press **Enter**. Why were you not prompted to log in to the system before obtaining a remote shell?

13. At the command prompt, type **who** and press **Enter**. What remote terminal are you using?

14. Type **exit** and press **Enter** to log out of your remote shell.

15. At the command prompt, type **rsh localhost mount** and press **Enter** to run the mount command on localhost.

16. At the command prompt, type **rcp localhost:/etc/issue localhost:/var/issue** and press **Enter** to copy the /etc/issue file on localhost to the /var directory on localhost.

17. Type **exit** and press **Enter** to log out of your shell.

Project 12-6

In this hands-on project, you use SSH to perform remote administration on your local computer and a partner's computer.

1. Switch to a command-line terminal (tty2) by pressing **Ctrl+Alt+F2** and log in to the terminal using the user name of **root** and the password of **secret**.

2. At the command prompt, type **chkconfig --list sshd** and press **Enter**. What runlevel is the SSH daemon started in by default?

3. At the command prompt, type **ssh root@localhost** and press **Enter**. When prompted to connect to the remote system, type **yes** and press **Enter**. Next, supply the root user's password of **secret** and press **Enter**.

4. At the command prompt, type **who** and press **Enter**. Can you tell whether you received a BASH shell via SSH?

5. At the command prompt, type **exit** and press **Enter**. What did this do?

6. At the command prompt, type **who** and press **Enter**. Compare this with the output from Step 4.

7. At the command prompt, type **ssh IP_address** and press **Enter**, where **IP_address** is the IPv4 address of your partner's computer. When prompted to continue connecting, type **yes** and press **Enter**. Next, supply the root user's password of **secret** and press **Enter**.

8. At the command prompt, type **ps -elf | grep Z** and press **Enter**. Are there any zombie processes on your partner's computer? Could you monitor your partner's computer using other commands remotely?

9. At the command prompt, type **ifconfig** and press **Enter**. Is your computer's IP configuration listed? Why?

10. At the command prompt, type **exit** and press **Enter**.

11. At the command prompt, type **ifconfig** and press **Enter**. Is your computer's IP configuration listed? Why?

12. At the command prompt, type **ssh** *IP_address* **cat /etc/issue > /root/ partner_issue** and press **Enter**, where *IP_address* is the IPv4 address of your partner's computer. Next, supply the root user's password of **secret** and press **Enter**.

13. At the command prompt, type **ifconfig** and press **Enter**. Is your computer's IP configuration listed? Why?

14. At the command prompt, type **cat partner_issue** and press **Enter**. Was your partner's issue file transferred successfully?

15. At the command prompt, type **less /etc/ssh/ssh_config** and press **Enter**. Examine the SSH client options available. Note the encryption algorithms supported in the commented Ciphers line. Press **q** when finished.

16. At the command prompt, type **less /etc/ssh/sshd_config** and press **Enter**. Examine the SSH daemon options available. What line would allow root connections to the SSH daemon if they were not allowed by default? Press **q** when finished.

17. At the command prompt, type **cat /root/.ssh/known_hosts** and press **Enter**. What two hosts are listed in this file and why?

18. Type **exit** and press **Enter** to log out of your shell.

Project 12-7

In this hands-on project, you remotely administer a partner's computer using X Windows.

1. Switch to a command-line terminal (tty2) by pressing **Ctrl+Alt+F2** and log in to the terminal using the user name of **root** and the password of **secret**.

2. Edit the **/etc/gdm/custom.conf** file with a text editor such as vi and add the following line under the [Security] section:

DisallowTCP=false

When finished, save your changes and quit the editor.

3. At the command prompt, type **reboot** and press **Enter** to reboot your system.

4. Once your system has rebooted, log into the GNOME Desktop Environment as **sample user one** with the password **secret**.

5. Perform Steps 1, 2, 3, and 4 on your partner's computer.

6. Open a BASH shell terminal within the GNOME Desktop Environment on your computer.

7. At the command prompt, type **xhost +** and press **Enter**.

8. At the command prompt, type **ssh root@***IP_address* and press **Enter**, where *IP_address* is the IPv4 address of your partner's computer. Supply the root user password of **secret** when prompted.

12

9. At the remote shell prompt, type **export DISPLAY='*IP_address*:0.0'** and press **Enter**, where **_IP_address_** is the IPv4 address of your computer.

10. At the remote shell prompt, type **system-config-network&** and press **Enter**. Examine the configuration of the network interfaces on the Devices tab. Can you confirm that you are using the Network Configuration tool from your partner's computer?

11. Close all windows and log out of the GNOME Desktop Environment.

Project 12-8

In this hands-on project, you configure and test VNC for remote administration.

1. Switch to a command-line terminal (tty2) by pressing **Ctrl+Alt+F2** and log in to the terminal using the user name of **root** and the password of **secret**.

2. At the command prompt, type **yum install vnc-server** and press **Enter** to install the Tiger VNC server on your system. Type y and press **Enter** when prompted to install the program.

3. Edit the **/etc/sysconfig/vncservers** file with a text editor such as vi and add the following lines to the end of the file:

   VNCSERVERS="2:root"
   VNCSERVERARGS[2]="-geometry 800x600"

   When finished, save your changes and quit the editor.

4. At the command prompt, type **vncpasswd** and press **Enter**. Type **secret** and press **Enter** when prompted both times to change the VNC password for the root user.

5. At the command prompt, type **service vncserver start** and press **Enter** to start the VNC server daemon.

6. At the command prompt, type **chkconfig --level 5 vncserver on** and press **Enter** to ensure that the VNC server daemon is started when entering runlevel 5.

7. Switch to the gdm by pressing **Ctrl+Alt+F1** or **Ctrl+Alt+F7** and log in to the GNOME Desktop Environment as **sample user one** with the password **secret**.

8. Open a BASH shell terminal in the GNOME Desktop Environment.

9. At the command prompt, type **vncviewer localhost:5902:2** and press **Enter**. Supply the root user's password of **secret** when prompted and press **Enter**. Examine your graphical desktop. What user name is listed in the upper-right corner? Why?

10. Close all windows and log out of the GNOME Desktop Environment.

Discovery Exercises

1. Assuming that your company uses the Class A network 100.0.0.0/8, with what subnet mask would you need to configure all computers on the network to divide this network 11 times to match the company's 11 departments? How many hosts can you have per network? What are the first five ranges of addresses that you can assign to different departments?

2. In Project 12-6, you used the following method to transfer a file from a remote system to your local computer:

   `ssh remotecomputer cat remotefile > localfile`

   Using your knowledge of redirection, briefly describe how this command achieves this transfer. Can this command be used to transfer a binary file? Explain.

3. Use the Internet, books, or other resources to find out how to register an FQDN on a DNS server for use on the Internet. Describe the procedure and cost involved. Also, find three domain names that would be available for you to register if you wanted to.

4. Use the Internet, books, or other resources to research the history of domain name space (DNS). How and where did it start? Are there different versions of DNS? If so, what are their differences?

5. Use the Internet, books, or other resources to research PPP and SLIP. What are the differences between the two? Briefly list the benefits and disadvantages of each.

6. Use the Internet, books, or other resources to research other remote access technologies available for Linux that were not discussed in this chapter. Briefly explain the features and configuration of each in a short report.

12

## chapter 13

Configuring Network Services

After completing this chapter, you will be able to:

- Configure infrastructure network services, including DHCP, DNS, NTP, and NIS
- Configure Web services using the Apache Web server
- Configure file sharing services, including Samba, NFS, and FTP
- Configure e-mail services, including Sendmail and Postfix
- Configure database services using PostgreSQL

In the previous chapter, you examined the concepts and procedures that allow Linux to participate on a network. You also learned about the network services that are commonly used on a Linux system. In this chapter, you examine the configuration of network services that provide infrastructure, Web, file sharing, e-mail, and database services to users across a network.

Infrastructure Services

Some networking services provide network configuration and support for other computers on a network in the form of TCP/IP configuration, name resolution, time management, and centralized authentication. These services, which are collectively called **infrastructure services**, include DHCP, DNS, NTP, and NIS.

DHCP

Recall from the previous chapter that your network interface can be configured manually or automatically using Dynamic Host Configuration Protocol (DHCP). If your network interface is configured using DHCP, it sends a DHCP broadcast on the network requesting IP configuration information. If a DHCP server on the network has a range of IP addresses, it leases an IP address to the client computer for a certain period of time; after this lease has expired, the client computer must send another DHCP request. Because DHCP servers keep track of the IP addresses they lease to client computers, they can ensure that no two computers receive the same IP address. If two computers are accidentally configured manually with the same IP address, neither would be able to communicate using the IP protocol.

DHCP servers can also send client computers other IP configuration information, such as the default gateway and the DNS server they should use.

The DHCP Lease Process The process by which a DHCP client requests IP configuration from a DHCP server involves several stages. First, the client sends a request (DHCPDISCOVER packet) to all hosts on the network. In reply, a DHCP server sends an offer (DHCPOFFER packet) that contains a potential IP configuration. The DHCP client then selects (accepts) the offer by sending a DHCPREQUEST packet to the associated DHCP server. Next, the DHCP server sends to the client an acknowledgment indicating the amount of time the client can use the IP configuration (DHCPACK packet). Finally, the client configures itself with the IP configuration. This process is illustrated in Figure 13-1.

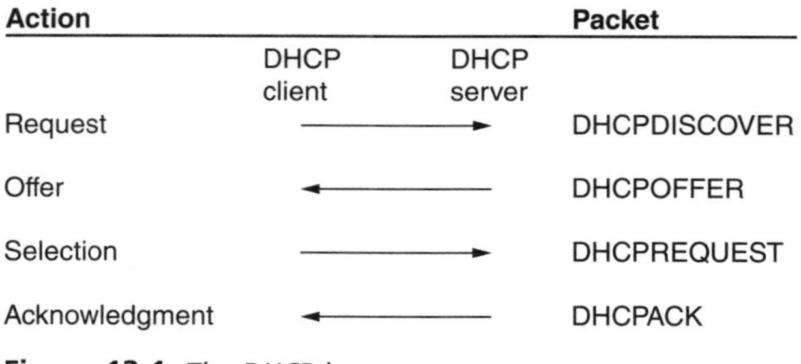

Action			Packet
	DHCP client	DHCP server	
Request	——————▶		DHCPDISCOVER
Offer	◀——————		DHCPOFFER
Selection	——————▶		DHCPREQUEST
Acknowledgment	◀——————		DHCPACK

Figure 13-1 The DHCP lease process

Source: Course Technology/Cengage Learning

If there are multiple DHCP servers on your network, DHCP clients will accept the first offer that they receive and decline all other offers by sending a DHCPDECLINE packet to the other DHCP servers.

Halfway through the time period specified by its lease (in other words, at 50 percent of its lease), the DHCP client will send another DHCPREQUEST packet to its DHCP server to renew its IP configuration. If its DHCP server is unreachable, it will try to renew its IP configuration again at 87.5 percent of its lease by sending a DHCPDISCOVER packet to all hosts on the network to allow any DHCP server on the network to respond with an offer. Once the lease is up, the DHCP client discards its IP configuration obtained from the DHCP server and automatically configures the network interface using APIPA (the IPv4 169.254.0.0 network).

Configuring a Linux DHCP Server   To configure your Fedora 13 computer as a DHCP server, you must first install the DHCP daemon using the command yum install dhcp. Next, you must add lines to the appropriate DHCP daemon configuration files to list the appropriate IP address range for your network, as well as lease information and other IP configuration options. The daemon configuration files for IPv4 and IPv6 are as follows:

- /etc/dhcp/dhcpd.conf stores IPv4 configuration
- /etc/dhcp/dhcpd6.conf stores IPv6 configuration

You don't need to configure the /etc/dhcp/dhcpd.conf file unless you want to configure IPv4 clients. Similarly, you don't need to configure the /etc/dhcp/dhcpd6.conf file unless you want to configure IPv6 clients.

You can refer to the manual page for the dhcpd.conf file to obtain a complete list of parameters that can be configured within the /etc/dhcp/dhcpd.conf and /etc/dhcp/dhcpd6.conf files.

An example of an /etc/dhcp/dhcpd.conf file that leases IPv4 addresses on the 192.168.1.0/24 network is shown in the following output:

```
[root@server1 ~]# cat /etc/dhcp/dhcpd.conf
default-lease-time 36000;
option routers 192.168.1.254;
option domain-name-servers 192.168.1.200;
subnet 192.168.1.0 netmask 255.255.255.0 {
range 192.168.1.1 192.168.1.100;
}
[root@server1 ~]# _
```

Note from the preceding output that the DHCP server leases clients an IP address between 192.168.1.1 and 192.168.1.100 for 36,000 seconds. In addition, the DHCP server configures the client with a default gateway of 192.168.1.254 and a DNS server of 192.168.1.200.

After the /etc/dhcp/dhcpd.conf file has been configured with the appropriate information, you can start the DHCP daemon using the `service dhcpd start` command, as well as configure the DHCP daemon to start when the system enters runlevel 5 using the `chkconfig --level 5 dhcpd on` command.

To view current DHCP leases, you can examine the /var/lib/dhcp/dhcpd.leases file for IPv4 leases and the /var/lib/dhcp/dhcpd6.leases file for IPv6 leases.

 After changing the /etc/dhcp/dhcpd.conf configuration file, you must restart the DHCP daemon for the changes to take effect.

DNS

Recall that DNS is a hierarchical namespace used to identify computers on large TCP/IP networks such as the Internet. Each part of this namespace is called a **zone,** and DNS servers contain all host name information for a zone. DNS servers typically resolve FQDNs to IP addresses (called a **forward lookup**), but they can also resolve IP addresses to FQDNs (called a **reverse lookup**).

The DNS Lookup Process When you contact a Web server on the Internet using a Web browser, the Web browser performs a forward lookup of the FQDN so that it can contact the IP address of the Web server. This forward lookup can be performed by a DNS server or a series of DNS servers. The whole process used to resolve the FQDN *www.linux. org* is illustrated in Figure 13-2.

In the first step from Figure 13-2, the Linux computer sends a forward lookup request for *www.linux.org* to the DNS server that is configured in /etc/resolv.conf; this is typically the

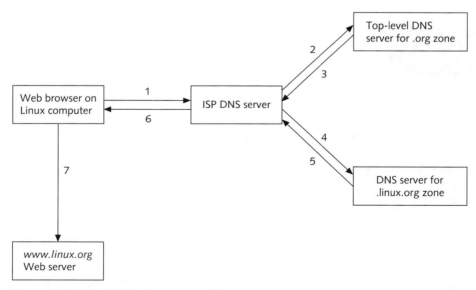

Figure 13-2 The DNS lookup process

Source: Course Technology/Cengage Learning

DNS server at your ISP. If the ISP DNS server has recently resolved the FQDN and placed the result in its local DNS cache, you receive the response immediately. (A DNS lookup query that generates a reply from a DNS cache is called an **iterative query**.) If it has not, the ISP DNS server normally contacts the DNS server for the .org top-level zone (Step 2) and repeats the forward lookup request for *www.linux.org* (called a **recursive query**). The .org DNS server will not contain the IP address for the *www.linux.org* computer in its zone but will reply with the IP address of the DNS server for the linux.org zone (Step 3).

All DNS servers contain a **DNS cache file** that contains the IP addresses of DNS servers that hold top-level DNS zones.

Your ISP DNS server then contacts the DNS server for the linux.org zone (Step 4) and repeats the forward lookup request for *www.linux.org* (another recursive query). The DNS server for the linux.org domain contains a record that lists the IP address for the *www.linux.org* computer and returns this IP address to the ISP DNS server (Step 5). The local DNS server then returns the result to the client Web browser (Step 6), which then uses the IP address to connect to the Web server (Step 7).

Each zone typically has more than one DNS server to ensure that names can be resolved if one server is unavailable. The first DNS server in a zone is called the **master** or **primary DNS server**, and all additional DNS servers are called **slave** or **secondary DNS servers**. New zone information is added to the master DNS server; slave DNS servers periodically copy the new records from the master DNS server in a process known as a **zone transfer**.

Configuring a Linux DNS Server

Configuring a Linux DNS Server To configure your Linux computer as a DNS server, you must configure the DNS name daemon (called "named") for a specific zone and add resource records that list FQDNs for computers in that zone as well as their associated IP addresses. Table 13-1 lists the files that can be used to configure this zone information.

13

On some Linux distributions, including Fedora 13, the DNS name daemon runs in a restricted shell for additional security. In this case, the files and paths listed in Table 13-1 are contained under the /var/named/chroot directory. For example, the /etc/named.conf file would be /var/named/chroot/etc/named.conf.

The files listed in Table 13-1 have a standard format called **Berkeley Internet Name Daemon (BIND)** and are difficult to create manually. As a result, it is best to use a graphical utility to create these files. You can install a graphical **BIND configuration utility** within Fedora 13 using the `yum install system-config-bind` command. Next, you can run the `system-config-bind &` command at a BASH terminal prompt within a desktop environment and configure the appropriate zones, as shown in Figure 13-3.

After you configure the appropriate zones within the graphical BIND utility shown in Figure 13-3, you must click the Save button to save your configuration to the /etc/named.conf file and the appropriate files within the /var/named directory.

File	Description
/etc/named.conf	Contains the list of DNS zones and their type (master/slave) that the name daemon will manage.
/var/named/ *zone_name*.db or /var/named/ *zone_name*.zone	Contains **resource records** used to perform forward lookups for a particular *zone_name*. Lines in this file have a type that determines the type of resource record: • A (add host) records map FQDNs to IPv4 addresses. • AAAA (add host) records map FQDNs to IPv6 addresses. • CNAME (canonical name) records provide additional aliases for A records. • NS (name server) records provide the names of DNS servers for the zone. • MX (mail exchanger) records provide the IP address for the e-mail server for a zone. • SOA (start of authority) determines the parameters used for zone transfers as well as how long information can be cached by the computer performing the forward or reverse lookup (called the **Time to Live**, or **TTL**).
/var/named/ *reverse_network_ID*.in-addr.arpa or /var/named/ *network_ID*.db or /var/named/ *network_ID*.zone	Contains resource records of type PTR (pointer), which list names used for reverse lookups for a particular network. The network is incorporated into the filename itself; for example, the filename that contains PTR records for the 192.168.1.0 IPv4 network would be called 1.168.192.in-addr.arpa or 192.168.1.db or 192.168.1.zone.
/var/named/named.local & /var/named/named.ip6.local or /var/named/named.localhost or /var/named/named.loopback	Contains PTR records used to identify the loopback adapter (127.0.0.1 for IPv4, ::1 for IPv6).
/var/named/named.ca or /var/named/named.root	Contains the IP addresses of top-level DNS servers; commonly called the DNS cache file.

Table 13-1 Common zone configuration files

After the files that contain the zone information have been created, you can start the DNS name daemon to provide DNS services on the network using the `service named start` command. You can also configure the DNS name daemon to start when the system enters runlevel 5 using the `chkconfig --level 5 named on` command.

 If you modify any files associated with the name daemon (for example, to add additional resource records), you must restart the name daemon for those changes to take effect.

Recall from Chapter 12 that you can use the `dig` command to test name resolution. The `dig` command can also query the records that exist on a specific DNS server using the format `dig @server record type` where *server* is the name or IP address of the DNS server, *record* is the name of the resource record or domain, and *type* is the *type* of record (A, CNAME, PTR, MX, NS, SOA, ANY, etc.). This is especially useful if you

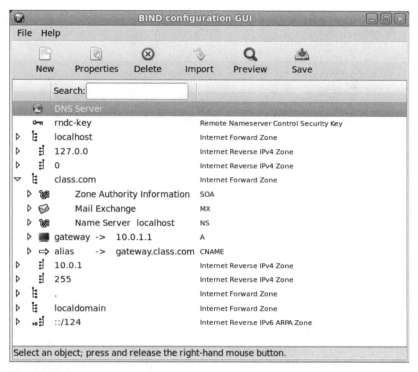

Figure 13-3 The BIND configuration utility

Source: Course Technology/Cengage Learning

want to see whether a zone transfer from a primary (master) DNS server to a secondary (slave) DNS server was successful. Simply query the secondary DNS server to find out whether the new records have been added.

NTP

Most system components and network services require the correct date and time to function properly. The BIOS on each computer contains a system clock that stores the current date and time. Operating systems can choose to use the time from this system clock or obtain time information from other servers on the network using the **Network Time Protocol (NTP)**.

You can view and modify the date and time within the BIOS using the BIOS configuration utility on your computer or by using the `hwclock` **command**.

NTP is one of the oldest Internet protocols still commonly used on the Internet. It is designed to simplify the setting of time and date information on computers across the Internet using UDP port 123.

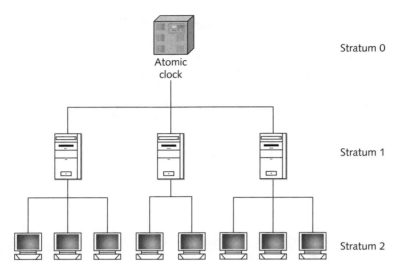

Figure 13-4 A sample strata structure

Source: Course Technology/Cengage Learning

Understanding NTP Strata NTP uses a hierarchical series of time sources called **strata**. Stratum 0 is at the top of this hierarchy and consists of atomic devices or GPS clocks. Stratum 1 devices obtain their time directly from Stratum 0 devices. Stratum 2 devices obtain their time from Stratum 1 devices, and so on. This organization is shown in Figure 13-4.

The stratum is not an indication of quality or reliability because NTP servers typically obtain time information from multiple time sources (NTP servers) and use an algorithm to determine the most reliable time information. As a result, it is common to find a Stratum 3 device that is more accurate than a Stratum 2 device.

NTP supports up to 256 strata.

Most Internet time servers, such as time.apple.com, are Stratum 1 devices.

Configuring a Linux NTP Client The NTP daemon (ntpd) is installed and started by default in most Linux distributions and can act as both an NTP client to obtain time from an Internet time server or an NTP server that other computers can query for time information.

To configure Fedora 13 as an NTP client, you can modify the /etc/ntp.conf file and add lines for different NTP servers the client can query. These servers could be any stratum or combinations of different strata.

For example, the following lines in /etc/ntp.conf query three time servers: ntp.research.gov, ntp.redhat.com, and 0.fedora.pool.ntp.org.

```
server ntp.research.gov
server ntp.redhat.com
server 0.fedora.pool.ntp.org
```

 **NOTE** Each of the FQDNs listed may point to multiple servers because NTP servers typically have several A (host) records in DNS that list the name FQDN for different IP addresses. This allows NTP requests to be spread across all servers to reduce server load.

If your time differs significantly from the time on these time servers, you must first stop ntpd and then run the **ntpdate command** to manually synchronize the time. You might need to run the ntpdate command several times until the time difference (or **offset**) is far less than 1 second. After manually synchronizing the time in this way, you can start the ntpd daemon again. This process is shown in the following output:

```
[root@server1 ~]# service ntpd stop
Shutting down ntpd:                                    [  OK  ]
[root@server1 ~]# ntpdate -u 0.fedora.pool.ntp.org
4 Sep 15:03:43 ntpdate[2908]: adjust time server 206.248.190.142 offset
0.977783 sec
[root@server1 ~]# ntpdate -u 0.fedora.pool.ntp.org
4 Sep 15:03:53 ntpdate[2909]: adjust time server 206.248.190.142 offset
0.001751 sec
[root@server1 ~]# ntpdate -u 0.fedora.pool.ntp.org
4 Sep 15:04:01 ntpdate[2910]: adjust time server 206.248.190.142 offset
0.001291 sec
[root@server1 ~]# service ntpd start
Starting ntpd:                                         [  OK  ]
[root@server1 ~]# _
```

After restarting the ntpd daemon, you can use the **ntpq command** to see what actual time servers you are synchronizing with. Because time varies greatly by location, NTP uses a **jitter** buffer to store the difference between the same time measurements from different NTP servers. The jitter information is used by NTP when determining the most reliable time when several NTP servers are queried for time information. The ntpq –p command displays the offset and jitter in milliseconds, as follows:

```
[root@server1 ~]# ntpq -p
remote          refid          st t when poll reach   delay offset jitter
==============================================================================
ox.eicat.ca     139.78.135.14  2  u   6   64    3     28.662 11.138  0.046
adelaide.ph     142.3.100.15   3  u   2   64    3     62.211 30.870  0.574
one.trx.com     209.51.161.238 2  u   3   64    3     43.329 22.867  0.190
[root@server1 ~]# _
```

Alternatively, you can configure an NTP client using a desktop environment. Within the GNOME Desktop Environment, navigate to the System menu, Administration, Date & Time to open the Date/Time Properties dialog box shown in Figure 13-5.

13

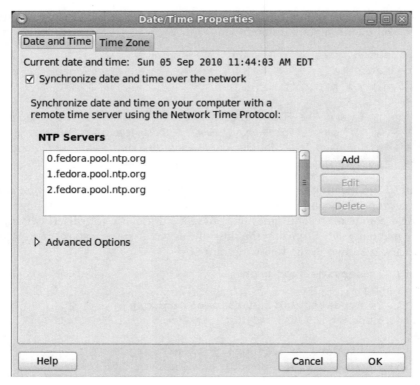

Figure 13-5 The Date/Time Properties dialog box

Source: Course Technology/Cengage Learning

Fedora 13 is configured as an NTP client by default using the NTP servers listed in Figure 13-5, but you can modify the list to include any NTP server.

All system date information is calculated relative to the time zone you selected during Linux installation. The configuration of each time zone is stored in the /usr/share/zoneinfo directory. If you need to change the time zone following installation, you could select the correct time zone on the Time Zone tab shown in Figure 13-5 or by using the **tzselect command**.

Configuring a Linux NTP Server

By default in Fedora 13, the NTP daemon is not configured as an NTP server because there is only a single NTP `restrict` line within the /etc/ntp.conf file:

```
restrict 127.0.0.1
```

This line allows your local client to query the NTP daemon for time information with no restrictions. If you want to allow other computers to query your NTP daemon (ntpd) for time information, simply edit the /etc/ntp.conf file again and add a line that identifies the specific computers or networks that are allowed to query your NTP daemon. For example, the following line within /etc/ntp.conf allows all computers on the 192.168.1.0 network to query your NTP daemon for time information but prevents other computers from modifying your NTP server configuration (nomodify notrap):

```
restrict 192.168.1.0 mask 255.255.255.0 nomodify notrap
```

 If you modify the /etc/ntp.conf file, you must restart the NTP daemon for those changes to take effect.

NIS

You can use the **Network Information Service (NIS)** to coordinate common configuration files, such as /etc/passwd and /etc/hosts, across several Linux computers within an organization. Each computer that participates in NIS belongs to an **NIS domain** and uses an **NIS map** for accessing certain information rather than using the local configuration file. Furthermore, you can configure an **NIS master server** to send all NIS map configurations to **NIS slave servers**, which then distribute these NIS maps to all other Linux computers, known as **NIS clients**. Alternatively, a master NIS server can send NIS map configuration directly to NIS clients.

Configuring an NIS Server The most common configuration files that companies use NIS to coordinate across multiple systems are password databases (/etc/passwd and /etc/shadow). These allow users to log in to several different Linux servers using the same user name and password. The steps required to set up an NIS server for this purpose are as follows:

1. Install the NIS server daemons by running the command yum install ypserv at a command prompt.

2. Define the NIS domain name by typing the command domainname NIS_domain_ name at a command prompt.

3. Add the following line to /etc/sysconfig/network to configure the NIS domain from Step 1 at every boot time:

   ```
   NISDOMAIN="NIS_domain"
   ```

4. Edit the file /var/yp/Makefile, navigate to the line that starts with all:, and edit the list of files to be made into maps. If you have no slave servers, also ensure that NOPUSH=true is in this file. If you have slave servers, they must be listed in the /var/yp/ ypservers file.

5. Add the names or IP addresses of allowed clients to the /var/yp/securenets file.

6. Allow the clients from Step 5 access to the appropriate maps in the /etc/ypserv.conf file.

7. Start the NIS server daemon by typing service ypserv start at the command prompt.

8. Ensure that the NIS server daemon is started when the system enters runlevel 5 by typing chkconfig --level 5 ypserv on at the command prompt.

13

9. Start the NIS password server daemon by typing `service yppasswdd start` at the command prompt.

10. Ensure that the NIS password server daemon is started when the system enters runlevel 5 by typing `chkconfig --level 5 yppasswdd on` at the command prompt.

11. Generate the configuration file maps by typing `/usr/lib/yp/ypinit -m` at a command prompt.

12. Allow clients to connect by typing `service ypbind start` at a command prompt.

13. Ensure that the NIS binding server daemon is started when the system enters runlevel 5 by typing `chkconfig --level 5 ypbind on` at the command prompt.

Configuring an NIS Client After configuring an NIS server, you must configure NIS clients to obtain their configuration information from the NIS server. To set up an NIS client to obtain user and password information from an NIS server, you can perform the following steps:

1. Define the NIS domain name by typing the command `domainname NIS_domain_name` at a command prompt.

2. Add the following line to /etc/sysconfig/network to configure the NIS domain from Step 1 at every boot time:

   `NISDOMAIN="NIS_domain"`

3. Edit the /etc/yp.conf file and add the following line to query a specific NIS server:

   `domain NIS_domain server NIS_server`

   Alternatively, you can add the following line to listen for NIS broadcasts on the network:

   `domain NIS_domain broadcast`

4. Start the NIS client program by typing `service ypbind start` at a command prompt.

5. Ensure that the NIS binding server daemon is started when the system enters runlevel 5 by typing `chkconfig --level 5 ypbind on` at the command prompt.

6. Locate the NIS server by typing the command `ypwhich` at a command prompt.

7. Add the following line to /etc/passwd to redirect all requests to the NIS server:

   `+:*:0:0:::`

After the NIS server and client have been set up, ensure that all users on NIS clients use the `yppasswd` command to change their NIS password; using only the `passwd` command modifies the local password database.

NIS was originally called Yellow Pages; as a result, many configuration commands and files are prefixed with the letters yp.

Directive	What It Specifies
`Listen 80`	Apache daemon will listen for HTTP requests on port 80.
`ServerName server1.class.com`	Name of the local server is server1.class.com.
`DocumentRoot "/var/www/html"`	Document root directory is /var/www/html on the local computer.
`DirectoryIndex index.html`	Index.html file in the document root directory will be sent to clients who request an HTML document.
`ServerRoot /etc/httpd`	All paths listed within the /etc/httpd/conf/httpd.conf file are relative to the /etc/httpd directory.
`ErrorLog logs/error_log`	All Apache daemon messages will be written to the /etc/httpd/logs/error_log file.
`CustomLog logs/access_log combined`	All Web requests will be written to the /etc/httpd/logs/access_log file using a combined log format.
`MaxClients 150`	Maximum number of simultaneous connections is 150.
`User apache`	Apache daemon will run as the "apache" local user account.
`Group apache`	Apache daemon will run as the "apache" local group account.

`<Directory /var/www/html>`
`Order allow,deny`
`Allow from all`
`Deny from 192.168.1.51`
`</Directory>`
	All hosts are allowed to access HTML files and other Web content from the /var/www/html directory, except for the computer with the IP address 192.168.1.51.

Table 13-2   Common httpd.conf directives

Web Services

Apache is the world's most common Web server. It started as the HTTP Daemon (httpd), developed by Rob McCool for the NCSA (National Center for Supercomputing Applications) at the University of Illinois. In the early 1990s, McCool became too busy to continue the project single-handedly, so he released the source code for httpd under the GPL. Open Source Software developers then made patches to this code, with each patch improving one component of the system. These patches gave rise to the name Apache server (a patchy server). After these early days, the Apache Group of Open Source Developers took over development of Apache. (To learn more about this group, go to *www.apache.org*.)

Recall that Web servers hand out HTML files and other Web content using the Hypertext Transfer Protocol (HTTP) from a specific directory in the directory tree. This directory is called the **document root** directory and contains the default Web site that is used on the server. The default document root directory on Fedora 13 is /var/www/html, and the default document that is handed out from this directory is index.html. Nearly all configuration options for Apache are set in a single large configuration file. By default, this configuration file is /etc/httpd/conf/httpd.conf. Each line in the httpd.conf file is called a **directive**. Table 13-2 lists some common directives.

The default settings in the httpd.conf file are sufficient for most simple Web servers. Thus, you simply need to copy the appropriate HTML files to the /var/www/html directory, including the index.html file, and start Apache (`service httpd start`) to host Web content on your network. To ensure that Apache is started when entering runlevel 5, you should run the `chkconfig --level 5 httpd on` command. Client computers can then enter the location *http://servername_or_IPaddress* in their Web browser to obtain the default Web page. Each time a client request is received by the Apache Web server (called a **Web page hit**), a separate httpd daemon is started to service the request.

You can also use the **curl command** at a BASH command prompt to obtain a Web page. For example, the `curl http://127.0.0.1/` command can be used to test your local Apache Web server to ensure that it is sending the correct Web page to clients.

On a busy Web server, there may be several hundred httpd daemons running on the system responding to client requests. The first httpd daemon is started as the root user and is used to start all other httpd daemons. These non-root httpd daemons are started as the Apache user to prevent privileged access to the system. As a result, any Web content must have Linux permissions that allow it to be readable by the Apache user. When you restart Apache, the root httpd daemon is restarted, which in turn restarts all other httpd daemons. If you change the HTML content inside the document root directory, you do not need to restart Apache. However, if you change the contents of httpd.conf, you need to restart Apache to activate those changes.

The **apachectl command** is useful when managing Apache. The `apachectl graceful` command can be used to restart Apache without dropping any client connections, whereas the `apachectl configtest` command checks the syntax of lines within /etc/httpd/conf/httpd.conf and notes any errors.

The **ab (Apache benchmark) command** can be used to monitor the performance of the Apache Web server by sending null requests to it. To send 1,000 requests to the local Apache Web server (100 at a time), you could use the `ab -n1000 -c100 http://127.0.0.1/` command.

File Sharing Services

There are many different file sharing services available on Linux systems. Each is tailored for a specific purpose and has a different configuration method. Among the most common are Samba, NFS, and FTP.

Samba

Microsoft Windows is the most commonly used client computer operating system, so you need to know how to configure your Linux system to communicate with Windows computers. Windows computers format TCP/IP data using the **Server Message Block (SMB)** protocol. To share information with Windows client computers, you can use the Samba daemon, which emulates the SMB protocol. In addition, Windows computers advertise their computer names using the **NetBIOS** protocol. To create and advertise a NetBIOS name that Windows computers can use to connect to your Linux server, you can use the NetBIOS name daemon.

NetBIOS names can be up to 15 characters long and are normally resolved on the network using a WINS (Windows Internet Naming Service) server or NetBIOS broadcasts. All NetBIOS names that are successfully resolved are placed in a NetBIOS name cache to speed future access to the same servers. The **nmblookup command** can be used to test NetBIOS name resolution in Linux.

Because of the widespread popularity of SMB, nearly all operating systems, including UNIX, Linux, Macintosh OS X, and Microsoft Windows, can connect to shared directories using the SMB protocol.

Configuring a Samba Server When a Windows client computer accesses a shared directory using SMB, the Windows user name and password are transmitted alongside the request, in case the shared directory allows access to certain users only. As a result, you should first create local Linux user accounts for each Windows user and create a Samba password for all of them using the **smbpasswd command** that matches the password that they use on their Windows computers, as shown in the following output:

```
[root@server1 ~]# useradd mary
[root@server1 ~]# passwd mary
Changing password for user mary.
New UNIX password:
Retype new UNIX password:
passwd: all authentication tokens updated successfully.
[root@server1 ~]# smbpasswd -a mary
New SMB password:
Retype new SMB password:
Added user mary.
[root@server1 ~]# _
```

Following this, you can edit the main configuration file for Samba. On Fedora 13, this file is /etc/samba/smb.conf by default. Like the httpd.conf file for Apache, the smb.conf contains directives that can be used to set your NetBIOS name, server settings, shared directories, and shared printers. By default, the smb.conf file shares all printers and home directories (for recognized Windows users). However, you need to add a line under the [global] section of this file to set your NetBIOS name. For example, to set your NetBIOS name to server1, you could add the directive netbios name = server1 to the smb.conf file.

You can use the testparm command to ensure that there are no syntax errors in the /etc/samba/smb.conf file. As a result, it is good practice to run this command after you edit the /etc/samba/smb.conf file.

Finally, you can start the Samba and NetBIOS name daemons using the service smb start ; service nmb start command. To ensure that the Samba and NetBIOS name

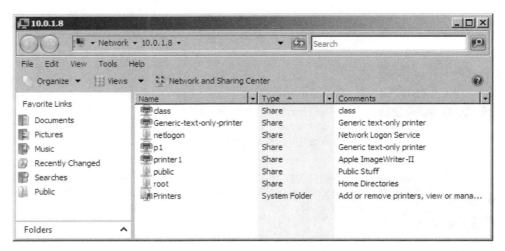

Figure 13-6 Accessing a Samba server from a Windows client

Source: Course Technology/Cengage Learning

daemons are started when the system enters runlevel 5, you can use the chkconfig --level 5 smb on ; chkconfig --level 5 nmb on command. As with Apache, if you change the smb.conf file, you must restart the Samba and NetBIOS name daemons.

Connecting to a Samba Server After configuring Samba, you should test its functionality to ensure that it is functioning normally. To do this, you could log in to a Windows client and enter *Samba_server* in the Run dialog box, where *Samba_server* is the NetBIOS name or IP address of your Samba server. If successful, the Windows operating system will open a new window that displays your home directory, shared printers, and other shared directories that you have permission to, as shown in Figure 13-6.

Alternatively, you could connect to your Samba server using the **smbclient command** on your Linux computer. Simply log in to a BASH terminal using the login information for an established Windows user account. Then run the smbclient -L *Samba_server* command, where *Samba_server* is the NetBIOS name or IP address of your Samba server. This connects your computer to the Samba server using your current user account credentials and lists the shared directories and available printers, as shown in the following sample output:

```
[root@server1 ~]# smbclient -L server1
Enter root's password:
Domain=[MYGROUP] OS=[Unix] Server=[Samba 3.5.2-60.fc13]
    Sharename       Type          Comment
    ---------       ----          -------
    IPC$            IPC           IPC Service (Samba Server
                                  Version 3.5.2)
    printer1        Printer       Apple ImageWriter-II
    root            Disk          Home Directories
    stuff           Disk          Homework Assignments

Domain=[MYGROUP] OS=[Unix] Server=[Samba 3.5.2-60.fc13]
```

```
Server                          Comment
---------                       -------
SERVER1                         Samba Server Version
                                3.5.2-60.fc13
---------                       -------
Workgroup                       Master
---------                       -------
MYGROUP

[root@server1 ~]# _
```

 You can use the `smbclient` command to connect to both Samba and Windows servers.

Additionally, you can use the `smbclient` command to display an FTP-like interface for transferring files to and from shared directories on Samba or Windows servers. The following output shows how to connect to the stuff shared directory, seen earlier, using an FTP-like interface:

```
[root@server1 root]# smbclient //server1/stuff
Enter root's password:
Domain=[MYGROUP] OS=[Unix] Server=[Samba 3.5.2-60.fc13]
smb: \> dir
  .                      D        0      Mon Sep  6 22:28:12 2010
  ..                     D        0      Mon Sep  6 22:28:12 2010
  Final Exam.doc         A    26624      Mon Sep  6 23:17:30 2010
  homework               A    46080      Mon Sep  6 23:33:03 2010
  questions.doc
  Part 0.DOC             A    13312      Mon Sep  6 23:27:51 2010
  Part 1.DOC             A    35328      Mon Sep  6 23:24:44 2010
  Part 2.doc             A    70656      Mon Sep  6 23:25:28 2010
  Part 3.DOC             A    38912      Mon Sep  6 23:26:07 2010
  Part 4.doc             A    75776      Mon Sep  6 23:26:57 2010
  Part 5.DOC             A    26624      Mon Sep  6 23:27:23 2010
  Part 6.doc             A    59904      Mon Sep  6 23:05:32 2010
  TOC.doc                A    58880      Mon Sep  6 23:09:16 2010
  39032 blocks of size 262144. 14180 blocks available

smb: \> help
?               allinfo         altname         archive         blocksize
cancel          case_sensitive  cd              chmod           chown
close           del             dir             du              echo
exit            get             getfacl         hardlink        help
history         iosize          lcd             link            lock
lowercase       ls              l               mask            md
mget            mkdir           more            mput            newer
open            posix           posix_encrypt   posix_open      posix_mkdir
```

```
posix_rmdir     posix_unlink    print       prompt      put
pwd             q               queue       quit        readlink
rd              recurse         reget       rename      reput
rm              rmdir           showacls    setmode     stat
symlink         tar             tarmode     translate   unlock
volume          vuid            wdel        logon       listconnect
showconnect     ..              !
smb: \> get TOC.doc
getting file \TOC.doc of size 58880 as TOC.doc (16.0 KiloBytes/sec)
(average 16.0 KiloBytes/sec)
smb: \> exit
[root@server1 root]# _
```

NFS

Network File System (NFS) allows UNIX, Linux, and Macintosh OS X computers to share files transparently. In NFS, one computer shares (or **exports**) a directory in the directory tree by placing the name of that directory in the /etc/exports file. The other computer can then access that directory across the network by using the mount command to mount the remote directory on the local computer.

Configuring a Linux NFS Server To configure an NFS server in Linux, perform the following steps:

1. Create a directory that contains the information that is to be shared to client computers. Although you can use an existing directory, try to avoid doing so because you might accidentally give client computers the ability to view or modify existing system files.

2. Edit the /etc/exports file and add a line that lists the directory to be shared and the appropriate options. For example, the following lines in the /etc/exports file share the /source directory to the computer server1, allowing users to read and write data and ensuring that the root user is treated as an anonymous user on the NFS server. These lines also share the /admin directory to all users, allowing users to read and write data:

```
/source server1(rw,root_squash)
/admin_*(rw)
```

3. Save your changes to the /etc/exports file and return to the command prompt.

4. Run the exportfs -a command to update the list of exported filesystems in memory from the /etc/exports file.

5. Run the service nfs start and service nfslock start commands to start the NFS daemons.

Connecting to a Linux NFS Server To access files using NFS, you mount a directory from a remote NFS server on the network to a directory on your local computer. That is, you specify the NFS filesystem type, server name or IP address, remote directory, and local directory as arguments to the mount command. For example, to mount the /var directory on the remote computer named nfs.sampledomain.com (IP address 192.168.0.1) to the /mnt directory on the local computer using NFS and view the results, you can use the following commands:

```
[root@server1 ~]# mount -t nfs nfs.sampledomain.com:/var /mnt
[root@server1 ~]# mount
```

```
/dev/sda1 on / type ext4 (rw)
proc on /proc type proc (rw)
sysfs on /sys type sysfs (rw)
devpts on /dev/pts type devpts (rw,gid=5,mode=620)
tmpfs on /dev/shm type tmpfs (rw)
/dev/mapper/vg00-data on /data type ext4 (rw,usrquota,grpquota)
none on /proc/sys/fs/binfmt_misc type binfmt_misc (rw)
sunrpc on /var/lib/nfs/rpc_pipefs type rpc_pipefs (rw)
192.168.0.1:/var on /mnt type nfs (rw,vers=4,clientaddr=192.168.0.1)
[root@server1 ~]# ls /mnt
arpwatch        ftpkerberos   lock    mailman    nis       run      tux
cachegdm        lib           log     mars_nwe   opt       spool    www
dbiptraf        local         mail    named      preserve  tmpyp
[root@server1 ~]# _
```

After running these commands, you can use the /mnt directory as any other local directory, with all file operations performed in the /var directory on the remote computer. You can then dismount the NFS filesystem using the umount command.

FTP

The protocol most commonly used to transfer files on public networks is the **File Transfer Protocol (FTP)**. FTP hosts files differently than NFS. In anonymous access, a special directory is available to any user who wants to connect to the FTP server. Alternatively, users can log in, via an FTP client program, to a home directory on the FTP server.

Configuring a Linux FTP Server The traditional FTP server program is the Washington University FTP daemon (wu-ftpd). However, most Linux systems today, including Fedora 13, use the **Very Secure FTP daemon (vsftpd)**. This stand-alone daemon is much easier to configure than wu-ftpd. The following steps show how to configure vsftpd to host files that can be downloaded from a client computer by user1 after user1 logs in with a valid password:

1. Create a directory underneath user1's home directory and ensure that user1 owns this directory. This directory will be used to host the files.

2. Edit the /etc/vsftpd/vsftpd.conf file and modify the appropriate commented options to control what actions the vsftpd daemon will allow from FTP clients. This includes:

    a. Whether to allow anonymous connections

    b. Whether to allow local user connections

    c. Whether to allow users to upload files

    d. Whether to prevent users from accessing files outside their home directory (called a "chroot jail")

3. At the command prompt, run the `service vsftpd start` command to start the vsftpd daemon.

4. At the command prompt, run the `chkconfig --level 5 vsftpd on` command to ensure that the vsftpd daemon is started upon entering runlevel 5.

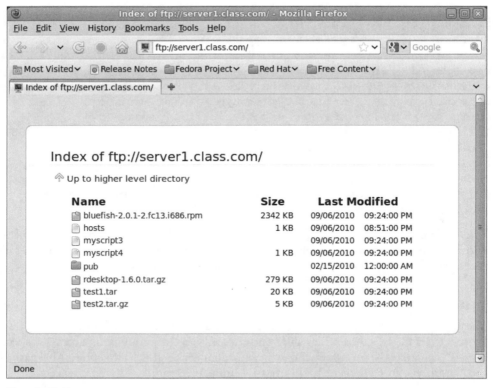

Figure 13-7 Using a Web browser FTP client

Source: Course Technology/Cengage

When you connect to the vsftpd daemon using an FTP client utility, you are prompted to log in. If you log in as the user "anonymous," you will be placed in the /var/ftp directory. Alternatively, if you log in as a valid user account on the system, you will be placed in that user's home directory.

The root user is not allowed to connect to vsftpd by default. To log in as the root user to vsftpd, you must remove the line root from the /etc/vsftpd/ftpusers and /etc/vsftpd/user_list files.

Connecting to a Linux FTP Server Most Web browsers have a built-in FTP utility that allows you to access files and directories on a remote computer. To connect to an FTP server using a Web browser, simply specify the location *ftp://servername_or_IPaddress* in your Web browser for anonymous access or the location *ftp://user:password@servername_or_IPaddress* to log in as a particular user account and password. A sample FTP session within a Web browser is shown in Figure 13-7.

Command	Description
Help	Displays a list of commands
Pwd	Displays the current directory on the remote computer
dir ls	Displays a directory listing from the remote computer
cd *directory*	Changes the current directory to *directory* on the remote computer
lcd *directory*	Changes the current directory to *directory* on the local computer
get *filename*	Downloads the *filename* to the current directory on the local computer
ascii	Specifies text file downloads (default)
binary	Specifies binary file downloads
mget *filename*	Downloads the file named *filename* to the current directory on the local computer; it also allows the use of wildcard metacharacters to specify the *filename*
put *filename*	Uploads the *filename* from the current directory on the local computer to the current directory on the remote computer
mput *filename*	Uploads the *filename* from the current directory on the local computer to the current directory on the remote computer; it also allows the use of wildcard metacharacters to specify the *filename*
!	Runs a shell on the local computer
close	Closes the FTP connection to the remote computer
open *hostname or IP*	Opens an FTP connection to the hostname or *IP* address specified
bye quit	Quits the FTP utility

Table 13-3 Common FTP commands

Clicking a file displayed in Figure 13-7 opens a dialog box that allows you to save the file to the appropriate location on a local filesystem.

Most operating systems also come with a command-line FTP utility that can connect to an FTP server. To use such a utility, you specify the host name or IP address of an FTP server as an argument to the **ftp command**. This opens a connection that allows the transfer of files to and from that computer. You can then log in as a valid user on that computer, in which case you are automatically placed in your home directory. Alternatively, you can log in as the user "anonymous" and be placed in the /var/ftp directory. After you are logged in, you receive an ftp> prompt that accepts FTP commands. A list of common FTP commands is depicted in Table 13-3.

Most FTP servers require the user to enter a password when logging in as the anonymous user via a command-line FTP utility; this password is typically the user's e-mail address.

The exact output displayed during an FTP session varies slightly depending on the version of the FTP software used on the FTP server. The following output is an example of using the ftp command to connect to an FTP server named ftp.sampledomain.com as the root user:

```
[root@server1 ~]# ftp ftp.sampledomain.com
Connected to ftp.sampledomain.com.
220 (vsFTPd 2.2.2)
Name (ftp.sampledomain.com:root): root
331 Please specify the password.
Password:
230 Login successful.
Remote system type is UNIX.
Using binary mode to transfer files.
ftp>
```

The current directory on the remote computer is the home directory for the root user in the preceding output. To verify this and see a list of files to download, you can use the following commands at the ftp> prompt:

```
ftp> pwd
257 "/root"
ftp> ls
227 Entering Passive Mode (192,168,0,1,56,88).
150 Here comes the directory listing.
total 2064
-rw-r--r--    1 root      root            1756  Aug 14 08:48  file1
-rw-r--r--    1 root      root             160  Aug 14 08:48  file2
-rw-r--r--    1 root      root         1039996  Aug 14 08:39  file3
drwxr-xr-x    2 root      root            4096  Aug 14 08:50  stuff
226 Directory send OK.
ftp>
```

The preceding output shows three files and one subdirectory. To download file3 to the current directory on the local computer, you can use the following command:

```
ftp> get file3
local: file3 remote: file3
227 Entering Passive Mode (192,168,0,1,137,37)
150 Opening BINARY mode data connection for file3 (1039996 bytes).
226 Transfer complete.
ftp>
```

Similarly, to change the current directory on the remote computer to /root/stuff and upload a copy of file4 from the current directory on the local computer to it, as well as view the results and then exit the FTP utility, you can use the following commands at the ftp> prompt:

```
ftp> cd stuff
250 Directory successfully changed.
ftp> pwd
```

```
257 "/root/stuff"
ftp> mput file4
mput file4? y
227 Entering Passive Mode (192,168,0,1,70,109)
150 Opening BINARY mode data connection for file4.
226 Transfer complete.
929 bytes sent in 0.00019 seconds (4.8e+03 Kbytes/s)
ftp> ls
227 Entering Passive Mode (192,168,0,1,235,35)
150 Opening ASCII mode data connection for directory listing.
total 8
-rw-r--r--   1 root        root              929 Aug 14 09:26 file4
226 Transfer complete.
ftp> bye
221 Goodbye.
[root@server1 ~]# _
```

In addition to using the FTP client included with your computer's operating system, you can use a Web browser as an FTP client program, or you can choose from many third-party graphical FTP client programs.

E-Mail Services

E-mail servers typically accept e-mail and route it over the Internet using Simple Mail Transfer Protocol (SMTP) or Enhanced Simple Mail Transfer Protocol (ESMTP) on TCP port 25. Additionally, client computers can retrieve e-mail from e-mail servers using a variety of protocols, such as Post Office Protocol (POP) or Internet Message Access Protocol (IMAP). Client computers can also send e-mail to e-mail servers using SMTP/ESMTP for later relay on the Internet.

Most e-mail servers provide the functions of the mail transfer agent (MTA) and mail delivery agent (MDA) described in Chapter 1.

13

To relay e-mail to other servers on the Internet, an e-mail server must look up the name of the target e-mail server in the domain's MX (mail exchanger) records, which are stored on a public DNS server. For example, if your local e-mail server needs to send e-mail to jason.eckert@trios.com, the e-mail server locates the name of the target e-mail server by looking up the MX record for the trios.com domain. It then resolves the target e-mail server name to the appropriate IP address using the A (host) record for the server on the public DNS server.

Daemons and other system components on Linux systems rely on e-mail to send important information to the root user. Most Linux distributions, including Fedora 13, use the Sendmail e-mail daemon by default to accept and redirect e-mail for local Linux users.

Working with Sendmail

Sendmail, one of the oldest and most complex e-mail daemons, has its roots in the Internet's predecessor, ARPANET. The Sendmail daemon on Fedora 13 is configured by default to accept e-mail on TCP port 25 and route it to the appropriate user on the Linux system. To test this, you can use the `telnet` command with port 25 as an argument. This displays a Welcome banner that identifies the e-mail server, as shown in the following output. Additionally, you can use the `EHLO` command to test ESMTP support and the `HELO` command to test SMTP support, as shown in the following output:

```
[root@server1 ~]# telnet localhost 25
Connected to localhost.
Escape character is '^]'.
220 server1.class.com ESMTP Sendmail 8.14.4/8.14.4; Wed, 29 Sep 2010
15:50:59 -0400
EHLO server1.class.com
250-server1.class.com Hello server1.class.com [127.0.0.1], pleased to
meet you
250-ENHANCEDSTATUSCODES
250-PIPELINING
250-8BITMIME
250-SIZE
250-DSN
250-ETRN
250-AUTH DIGEST-MD5 CRAM-MD5
250-DELIVERBY
250 HELP
HELO server1.class.com
250 server1.class.com Hello server1.class.com [127.0.0.1], pleased to meet
you
quit
221 2.0.0 server1.class.com closing connection
Connection closed by foreign host.
[root@server1 ~]# _
```

You can also interact with the Sendmail daemon using telnet to send a new e-mail to a user on the Linux server, as follows:

```
[root@server1 ~]# telnet localhost 25
Connected to localhost.
Escape character is '^]'.
220 server1.class.com ESMTP Sendmail 8.14.4/8.14.4; Wed, 29 Sep 2010
15:50:59 -0400
EHLO server1.class.com
250-server1.class.com Hello server1.class.com [127.0.0.1], pleased to
meet you
250-ENHANCEDSTATUSCODES
250-PIPELINING
250-8BITMIME
250-SIZE
```

```
250-DSN
250-ETRN
250-AUTH DIGEST-MD5 CRAM-MD5
250-DELIVERBY
250 HELP
mail from: jason.eckert@trios.com
250 2.1.0 jason.eckert@trios.com … Sender ok
rcpt to: root@server1.class.com
250 2.1.5 root@server1.class.com … Recipient ok
data
354 Enter mail, end with "." on a line by itself
Hey dude
.
250 2.0.0 n9TJox5e003083 Message accepted for delivery
quit
221 2.0.0 server1.class.com closing connection
Connection closed by foreign host.
[root@server1 ~]# _
```

To check your local e-mail, you can then use the **mail command**, as follows:

```
[root@server1 ~]# mail
Heirloom Mail version 12.4 7/29/08. Type ? for help.
"/var/spool/mail/root": 13 messages 6 new 10 unread
 U  1   Cron Daemon          Sat Jul 11 07:01    26/981      "Cron"
 U  2   logwatch@localhost.l Mon Jul 20 11:43    42/1528     "Logwatch"
 U  3   logwatch@localhost.l Tue Jul 21 12:32    151/4669
 N  4   jason.eckert@trios.c Wed Sep 29 15:53    11/430
& 4
Message 4:
From jason.eckert@trios.com Wed Sep 29 15:53:25 2009
Return-Path: <jason.eckert@trios.com>
Date: Wed, 29 Sep 2010 15:52:36 -0400
From: jason.eckert@trios.com
Status: R

Hey dude

& q
[root@server1 ~]# _
```

The mail command is an example of a mail user agent (MUA), as described in Chapter 1.

The /etc/aliases file contains other e-mail names that are used to identify the different users on the system. For example, the entries in the /etc/aliases file shown next, tell you that you can use the names mailer-daemon, postmaster, bin, daemon, or adm to refer to the root user:

```
[root@server1 ~]# head -17 /etc/aliases
#
# Aliases in this file will NOT be expanded in the header from
# Mail, but WILL be visible over networks or from /bin/mail.
#
#      >>>>>>>>>> The program "newaliases" must be run after
#       >> NOTE >> this file is updated for any changes to
#      >>>>>>>>>> show through to sendmail.
#

# Basic system aliases -- these MUST be present.
mailer-daemon: postmaster
postmaster: root

# General redirections for pseudo accounts.
bin:        root
daemon:     root
adm:        root
[root@server1 ~]# _
```

If you modify the /etc/aliases file, you need to run the **newaliases command** to rebuild the aliases database (/etc/aliases.db) based on the entries in the /etc/aliases file. Only the aliases database is used by the Sendmail daemon.

Although Sendmail is configured by default to accept and route local e-mail, you can also configure it to relay e-mail to other servers on the Internet as well as accept connections from e-mail clients on your network using POP and IMAP. To do this, you must modify the /etc/mail/sendmail.mc file and then recompile it to create the /etc/mail/sendmail.cf file. The easiest way to recompile the /etc/mail/sendmail.mc file is to run the make -C/etc/mail command and then restart the Sendmail daemon. Sendmail is a very complex daemon to configure, so you should spend some time familiarizing yourself with the Sendmail documentation at *http://sendmail.org*.

Working with Postfix

Although Sendmail is the default e-mail daemon on most Linux systems, **Postfix** is a far easier e-mail daemon to configure. After installing Postfix (yum install postfix), you can edit its well-commented configuration file, /etc/postfix/main.cf. At minimum, you need to uncomment or add the lines listed in Table 13-4.

Next, you can run the service sendmail stop ; service postfix start command to stop the Sendmail daemon and start the Postfix daemon. Next, you can query the Postfix e-mail server on port 25 using telnet, as follows:

Line	Change
mydomain = sample.com	Sets the e-mail domain name; change to desired name
myorigin = $mydomain	Sets local access to the domain name
inet_interfaces = all	Configures Postfix to listen for e-mail on all interfaces
mydestination = $myhostname, localhost.$mydomain, localhost, $mydomain	Configures destination domain for e-mail
mynetworks_style = class	Trusts e-mail from computers on the local network

Table 13-4   Lines in /etc/postfix/main.cf to uncomment or add when configuring Postfix

```
[root@server1 ~]# telnet localhost 25
Connected to localhost.
Escape character is '^]'.
220 server1.class.com ESMTP Postfix
EHLO sample.com
250-server1.class.com
250-PIPELINING
250-SIZE 10240000
250-VRFY
250-ETRN
250-ENHANCEDSTATUSCODES
250-8BITMIME
250 DSN
HELO sample.com
250 server1.class.com
quit
221 2.0.0 Bye
Connection closed by foreign host.
[root@server1 ~]# _
```

To make the change permanent, you will need to run the chkconfig --level 5 sendmail off ; chkconfig --level 5 postfix on command to disable auto starting of the Sendmail daemon in runlevel 5, as well as automatically register and set the Postfix daemon to start in runlevel 5.

Existing daemons and system components will now use the Postfix daemon to send e-mail to the root user instead of Sendmail. Regardless of whether you use Sendmail or Postfix, e-mail will still be stored within the same mailbox for each user (/var/spool/mail/username), and e-mail-related information will be logged to /var/log/maillog.

Database Services

Databases are large files that store important information in the form of **tables**. A table organizes information into a list. Within the list, the set of information about a particular item is called a **record**. For example, in a list of customer mailing addresses, a single record would contain a customer's first name, last name, street address, city, state, and zip code. The various categories of information within a record are called **fields**. For example, in our customer mailing address example, one field contains the city information, one contains the state information, and so on.

Most databases consist of dozens or hundreds of tables that store information used by applications. For example, accounting software typically stores financial data within a database. In large databases, information within certain tables can be related to information within other tables in the same database. These databases are called **relational databases**, and the tables within are usually linked by a common field. Figure 13-8 shows a simple relational database that consists of two tables with a related EmployeeID field.

Structured Query Language (SQL) is a special programming language used to store and access the data in databases. The database server programs that allow users to access and update the data stored within a database are called **SQL servers**. Table 13-5 lists common SQL statements that are used to manipulate data on SQL servers.

SQL servers usually offer advanced backup, repair, replication, and recovery utilities for the data within the database. In addition, SQL servers can store multiple databases and allow programs to access these databases from across the network. Thus, a single SQL server can store the data needed by all programs that exist on servers and client computers within the network. Although there are several SQL servers available for Linux, PostgreSQL is one of the most widely used.

EmployeeID	FirstName	LastName	Address	ZIP	Home Phone	Mobile Phone
A518	Bob	Smith	14 Wallington St.	49288	555-123-1399	555-144-2039
A827	Jill	Sagan	51 York Ave. N.	49282	555-123-1039	
A988	Frank	Kertz	623 Queen St.	44922	555-209-1039	555-199-2938
A472	Bethany	Weber	82 Shepherd Ave.	49100	555-299-0199	555-203-1000
A381	John	Lauer	55 Rooshill Ave.	49288	555-123-2883	555-203-2811

Common field

EmployeeID	Week	Hours	MgroK
A518	08/20/10	37	Yes
A827	08/20/10	40	Yes
A988	08/20/10	40	Yes
A472	08/20/10	40	Yes
A381	08/20/10	22	Yes
A518	08/27/10	40	Yes
A827	08/27/10	35	Yes
A988	08/27/10	0	Yes
A472	08/27/10	40	Yes
A381	08/27/10	22	Yes

Field names

Record

Figure 13-8 A simple relational database structure

Source: Course Technology/Cengage Learning

Command	Description
CREATE DATABASE *database_name*	Creates a database
DROP DATABASE *database_name*	Deletes a database
CREATE TABLE *table_name field_definitions*	Creates a table within a database
DROP TABLE *table_name*	Deletes a table within a database
INSERT INTO *table_name VALUES record*	Inserts a new record within a table
UPDATE *table_name SET record_modifications*	Modifies records within a table
DELETE FROM *table_name record*	Deletes a record within a table
SELECT * FROM *table_name*	Displays all records within a table
SELECT *fields* FROM *table_name* WHERE *criteria*	Displays one or more fields for records within a table that meet a specific criteria
SELECT *fields* FROM *table_name* GROUP BY *field*	Displays one or more fields for records within a table and groups the results according to the values within a common field
SELECT *fields* FROM *table_name* ORDER BY *field* [ASC/DESC]	Displays one or more fields for records within a table and sorts the results in ascending or descending order according to the values within a common field
SELECT *fields* FROM *table1* INNER JOIN *table2* ON *table1.common_field* = *table2.common_field*	Displays one or more fields for records within two related tables (*table1* and *table2*) that have a common field; only records that have matching information within the common field in both tables are displayed
SELECT *fields* FROM *table1_name* LEFT OUTER JOIN *table2_name* ON *table1_name.common_field* = *table2_name.common_field*	Displays one or more fields for all records within *table1* and any records within *table2* that have matching information within a common field
SELECT *fields* FROM *table1_name* RIGHT OUTER JOIN *table2_name* ON *table1_name.common_field* = *table2_name.common_field*	Displays one or more fields for all records within *table2* and any records within *table1* that have matching information within a common field
CREATE USER *user_name* WITH PASSWORD *password*	Creates a user that can access the SQL server
GRANT *permissions* ON *table1* TO *user_name*	Assigns permissions to a user that give the user the ability to work with the table, where *permissions* can include INSERT, UPDATE, SELECT, or DELETE

Table 13-5 Common SQL statements

Configuring PostgreSQL

PostgreSQL is a powerful SQL server that provides a large number of features. You can choose to install the PostgreSQL SQL server when installing Linux, or you can install it afterward using the `yum install postgresql` command. During installation, the PostgreSQL installation creates a postgres user within the /etc/passwd and /etc/shadow files that has a home directory of /var/lib/pgsql and a shell of /bin/bash.

Next, you can prepare PostgreSQL for use by following these steps:

1. Assign the postgres user a password using the `passwd postgres` command.
2. Initialize the internal PostgreSQL databases and configuration structure under the /var/lib/pgsql/ directory using the `service postgresql initdb` command.
3. Modify the PostgreSQL configuration files:
   - /var/lib/pgsql/data/postgresql.conf stores configuration information for the PostgreSQL daemon.
   - /var/lib/pgsql/data/pg_hba.conf contains information regarding the hosts that are allowed to connect to PostgreSQL.
   - /var/lib/pgsql/data/pg_ident.conf contains authentication information for use by PostgreSQL.
4. Start the PostgreSQL engine using the `service postgresql start` command.
5. Configure PostgreSQL to start upon entering runlevel 5 using the `chkconfig --level 5 postgresql on` command.

Configuring PostgreSQL Databases

To configure PostgreSQL databases, you must first log in as the postgres user. Next, you can execute one of several PostgreSQL command-line utilities to create and manage databases. These commands are summarized in Table 13-6.

For example, to create a database called sampledb, you could use the following command:

```
-bash-4.1$ createdb sampledb
-bash-4.1$
```

Next, you can connect to the employee database using the interactive **PostgreSQL utility**, where you can obtain information about the SQL and psql commands that can perform most database administration.

```
-bash-4.1$ psql sampledb
psql (8.4.3)
Type "help" for help.

sampledb=# help
You are using psql, the command-line interface to PostgreSQL.
Type: \copyright for distribution terms
      \h for help with SQL commands
      \? for help with psql commands
      \g or terminate with semicolon to execute query
      \q to quit
sampledb=# _
```

You can create tables and add records within the PostgreSQL utility using the appropriate SQL statements. The following output shows how to (1) create a table called "employee"

Command	Description
clusterdb	Associates a PostgreSQL database with another database on a different server
createdb	Creates a PostgreSQL database
createlang	Allows a new programming language to be used with PostgreSQL
createuser	Creates a PostgreSQL user
dropdb	Deletes a PostgreSQL database
droplang	Removes support for a programming language within PostgreSQL
dropuser	Deletes a PostgreSQL user
pg_dump	Backs up PostgreSQL database settings
pg_dumpall	Backs up PostgreSQL database cluster settings
pg_restore	Restores PostgreSQL database settings
psql	The PostgreSQL utility
reindexdb	Reindexes a PostgreSQL database
vacuumdb	Analyzes and regenerates internal PostgreSQL database statistics

Table 13-6 PostgreSQL command-line utilities

with three fields (Name, Dept, Title) that each allow 20 characters of information; (2) add three employee records; and (3) display the results.

```
sampledb=# CREATE TABLE employee (Name char(20), Dept char(20), Title
char(20));
CREATE TABLE
sampledb=# INSERT INTO employee VALUES ('Jeff
Smith', 'Research','Analyst');
INSERT 0 1
sampledb=# INSERT INTO employee VALUES ('Mary
Wong','Accounting','Manager');
INSERT 0 1
sampledb=# INSERT INTO employee VALUES ('Pat
Clarke','Marketing','Coordinator');
INSERT 0 1
sampledb=# SELECT * from employee;
        name         |        dept        |        title
---------------------+--------------------+--------------------
 Jeff Smith          | Research           | Analyst
 Mary Wong           | Accounting         | Manager
 Pat Clarke          | Marketing          | Coordinator
(3 rows)

sampledb=# _
```

13

Command	Description
\l	Lists available databases
\c *database_name*	Connects to a different database
\d	Lists the tables within the current database
\d *table_name*	Lists the fields within a table
\q	Exits the PostgreSQL utility

Table 13-7 Common built-in PostgreSQL utility commands

 Each SQL statement that is entered within the PostgreSQL utility must end with a ; metacharacter.

In addition to SQL statements, the PostgreSQL utility has many built-in commands. These commands, which are prefixed with a \ character, can be used to obtain database information or perform functions within the PostgreSQL utility. The most common of these built-in commands are listed in Table 13-7.

Chapter Summary

- DHCP, DNS, NTP, and NIS are called infrastructure services because they provide network-related services to other computers on the network.

- DHCP servers lease other computers an IPv4 or IPv6 configuration.

- DNS servers provide name resolution services for other computers on the network. Each DNS server can contain several zones that store resource records for names that can be resolved.

- Linux computers can use the system time stored within the computer BIOS or obtain their time from an NTP server across the network. NTP servers obtain their time from other NTP servers in a hierarchical organization that consists of several strata.

- NIS servers provide key configuration files such as /etc/passwd and /etc/shadow to other Linux computers that are configured as NIS clients.

- The Apache server shares Web pages from its document root directory to computers on the network using the HTTP protocol.

- Samba can be used to share files to Linux, UNIX, Macintosh, and Windows computers using the SMB protocol.

- NFS can be used to natively share files among Linux, UNIX, and Macintosh systems. NFS clients access these files by mounting shared directories on an NFS server.

- FTP can be used to share files to any computer that has an FTP client utility and is the most common method for file sharing on the Internet. The default FTP daemon in Fedora 13 is vsftpd.

- E-mail servers deliver e-mail to users. They also accept new e-mail from users and relay it to other e-mail servers on the Internet for delivery. The most common e-mail servers used on Linux systems are Sendmail and Postfix.

- Many large applications store their data within databases on a database server. These applications use SQL statements to add, manipulate, and retrieve information within a database across the network.

- PostgreSQL, a common database server often used on Linux systems, provides advanced configuration and utilities.

Key Terms

`ab (Apache benchmark)` **command**   A command that can be used to obtain performance benchmarks for a Web server such as Apache.

`apachectl` **command**   A command that can be used to start, stop, and restart the Apache Web server as well as check for syntax errors within the Apache configuration file.

Berkeley Internet Name Daemon (BIND)   The standard that all DNS servers and DNS configuration files adhere to.

BIND configuration utility   A graphical utility that can be used to generate and modify the files that are used by the DNS name daemon.

`curl` **command**   A command that can be used to obtain a Web page from a Web server.

database   A file that contains data that is organized into tables.

directive   A line within a configuration file.

DNS cache file   A file that contains the IP addresses of top-level DNS servers.

document root   The directory on a Web server that stores Web content for distribution to Web browsers.

exporting   The process used to describe the sharing of a directory using NFS to other computers.

field   An attribute within a record in a database table.

File Transfer Protocol (FTP)   The most common protocol used to transfer files across networks such as the Internet.

forward lookup   A DNS name resolution request whereby an FQDN is resolved to an IP address.

`ftp` **command**   A command-line FTP client that is found in most operating systems.

`hwclock` **command**   A command that can be used to view and modify the system clock within the computer BIOS.

infrastructure services   Network services that provide network and operating system-specific functionality to other computers on the network.

iterative query   A DNS resolution request that was resolved without the use of top-level DNS servers.

jitter   The difference between time measurements from several different NTP servers.

`mail` **command**   A common e-mail client on UNIX, Linux, and Macintosh systems.

master DNS server   The DNS server that contains a read/write copy of the zone. *See also* primary DNS server.

NetBIOS A protocol used by Windows computers that adds a unique 15-character name to file- and printer-sharing traffic.

Network File System (NFS) A set of software components that can be used to share files natively between UNIX, Linux, and Macintosh computers on a network.

Network Information Service (NIS) A set of software components that can be used to standardize the configuration files across several different Linux and UNIX computers.

Network Time Protocol (NTP) A protocol that can be used to obtain time information from other computers on the Internet.

`newaliases` **command** A command that can be used to rebuild the e-mail alias database based on the entries within the /etc/aliases file.

NIS client A computer in an NIS domain that receives its configuration from an NIS master server or NIS slave server.

NIS domain A group of computers that share the same NIS configuration.

NIS map A system configuration that is shared by the computers within an NIS domain.

NIS master server The computer in an NIS domain that contains the master copy of all NIS maps.

NIS slave server A computer in an NIS domain that receives a read-only copy of all NIS maps from an NIS master server.

`nmblookup` **command** A command that can test NetBIOS name resolution on a Linux system.

`ntpdate` **command** A command that can view the current system time as well as synchronize the system time with an NTP server.

`ntpq` **command** A command that can query the state of an NTP server or client.

offset The difference in time between two computers that use the NTP protocol.

Postfix A common e-mail server daemon used on Linux systems that is easy to configure.

PostgreSQL A common SQL server used on Linux computers.

PostgreSQL utility The program used to perform most database management on a PostgreSQL server.

primary DNS server The DNS server that contains a read/write copy of the zone.

record A line within a database table that represents a particular object.

recursive query A DNS resolution request that was resolved with the use of top-level DNS servers.

relational database A database that contains multiple tables that are linked by common fields.

resource records The records within a zone on a DNS server that provide name resolution for individual computers.

reverse lookup A DNS name resolution request whereby an IP address is resolved to an FQDN.

secondary DNS server A DNS server that contains a read-only copy of the zone. *See also* slave DNS server.

Sendmail The default e-mail server daemon used in Fedora 13.

Server Message Block (SMB) The protocol that Windows computers use to format file and printer sharing traffic on TCP/IP networks.

slave DNS server A DNS server that contains a read-only copy of the zone.

`smbclient` **command** A command that can be used to connect to a remote Windows or Samba server and transfer files.

`smbpasswd` **command**   A command used to generate a Samba password for a user.

SQL server   A server service that provides other programs and computers the ability to access a database.

strata   The levels used within an NTP hierarchy that describe the relative position of a server to an original time source such as an atomic clock.

Structured Query Language (SQL)   A language used by database servers to query, add, and modify the data within a database.

table   A database structure that organizes data using records and fields.

Time to Live (TTL)   The amount of time that a computer is allowed to cache name resolution information obtained from a DNS server.

`tzselect` **command**   A command that can be used to change the time zone of a Linux computer.

Very Secure FTP daemon (vsftpd)   The default FTP server program used in modern Linux distributions, including Fedora 13.

Web page hit   A single HTTP request that is sent from a Web browser to a Web server.

zone   A portion of the domain name space that is administered by one or more DNS servers.

zone transfer   The process of copying resource records for a zone from a master to a slave DNS server.

Review Questions

1. NFS can be used to share files natively with computers running the Microsoft Windows operating system. True or False?

2. Which file stores the Apache configuration in Fedora 13?

    a. /etc/apache/httpd.conf

    b. /etc/apache.conf

    c. /etc/httpd.conf

    d. /etc/httpd/conf/httpd.conf

3. Which DNS resource record is an alias to other records?

    a. A

    b. AAAA

    c. CNAME

    d. NS

4. NIS clients use NIS records to access their configuration information. True or False?

5. Which command can be used to connect to check the /etc/samba/smb.conf file for syntax errors?

    a. `apachectl`

    b. `sambactl`

    c. `testparm`

    d. `psql`

6. You have modified the /etc/aliases file to include a new e-mail alias. However, when you send e-mail to the alias, it cannot be delivered. What should you do?

   a. Add the line to the /etc/aliases.db file instead.

   b. Run the `newaliases` command.

   c. Restart the Sendmail daemon.

   d. Log out of the system and then log back in to the system and resend the e-mail.

7. Which command within the command-line FTP utility can be used to change the current directory on the local computer?

   a. `cd`

   b. `dir`

   c. `lcd`

   d. `get`

8. You have opened a telnet session on port 25 with your e-mail server. What command can you type within your telnet session to start an e-mail session? (Choose all that apply.)

   a. `START`

   b. `HELO`

   c. `EHLO`

   d. `WAZUP`

9. Which of the following must you perform to share a directory using NFS? (Choose all that apply.)

   a. Edit the /etc/exports file.

   b. Mount the directory to the /etc/exports directory using the `mount` command.

   c. Run the `exportfs -a` command.

   d. Start or restart the NFS daemons.

10. DHCP clients send a DHCPREQUEST packet when they require a new IP configuration. True or False?

11. Which command can be used to connect to a remote Windows share called data on the server called fileserver?

    a. `smbclient -L fileserver:data`

    b. `smbclient -L //fileserver/data`

    c. `smbclient //fileserver/data`

    d. `smbclient \\fileserver\data`

12. The lines within the Apache configuration file that modify the functionality of the Apache are called directives. True or False?

13. Which of the following can be used to create a database within PostgreSQL? (Choose all that apply.)

    a. the CREATE DATABASE statement within the PostgreSQL utility

    b. the ADD DATABASE statement within the PostgreSQL utility

    c. the `adddb` command

    d. the `createdb` command

14. Stratum 1 NTP servers do not obtain time information from other NTP servers. True or False?

15. What must you do to transform your computer into a DNS server? (Choose all that apply.)

    a. Create zone files.

    b. Create resource records for DNS lookups.

    c. Create NIS maps.

    d. Run the name daemon (named).

16. What directory are you placed in when you log in as the anonymous user to a Fedora 13 FTP server?

    a. /var/ftp

    b. /var/www/ftp

    c. /home/anonymous

    d. /var/ftp/pub

17. Postfix is an e-mail server daemon that is easier to configure compared with the Sendmail e-mail daemon. True or False?

18. Which SQL statement key word can be used to delete a record within a table?

    a. DELETE

    b. DROP

    c. REMOVE

    d. CLEAR

19. Which command can you use to synchronize your computer with an NTP time source?

    a. `ntp`

    b. `ntpquery`

    c. `ntpq`

    d. `hwclock`

20. Mary is a system administrator in your organization. She has recently made changes to the DHCP configuration file, but the DHCP daemon does not seem to recognize the new changes. What should she do?

    a. Log in as the root user and reedit the configuration file.

    b. Run the `dhcpconf` command to edit the configuration file.

    c. Restart the DHCP daemon.

    d. Restart the xinetd daemon.

13

Hands-On Projects

These projects should be completed in the order given. The hands-on projects presented in this chapter should take a total of three hours to complete. The requirements for this lab include:

- A computer with Fedora 13 installed according to Hands-On Project 2-2
- A wired Ethernet NIC and crossover cable

Project 13-1

In this hands-on project, you configure and test the DHCP daemon.

1. Turn on your computer. After your Linux system has been loaded, switch to a command-line terminal (tty2) by pressing **Ctrl+Alt+F2** and log in to the terminal using the user name of **root** and the password of **secret**.

2. At the command prompt, type **yum install dhcp** and press **Enter** to install the DHCP server daemon. Type **y** and press **Enter** when prompted to continue the installation.

3. Edit the **/etc/dhcp/dhcpd.conf** file with a text editor and add the following lines:

   ```
   default-lease-time 72000;
   option routers IP_address_of_your_class_default_gateway;
   option domain-name-servers IP_address_of_your_class_DNS_server;
   subnet class_network netmask subnet_mask {
       range class_network.50 class_network.100;
   }
   ```

   For example, if your class uses the 192.168.1 network (subnet mask 255.255.255.0) and a default gateway and DNS server of 192.168.1.254, you would add the following lines:

   ```
   default-lease-time 72000;
   option routers 192.168.1.254;
   option domain-name-servers 192.168.1.254;
   subnet 192.168.1.0 netmask 255.255.255.0 {
       range 192.168.1.50 192.168.1.100;
   }
   ```

   When finished, save your changes and quit the editor.

4. At the command prompt, type **service dhcpd start** and press **Enter** to start the DHCP daemon.

5. Connect a crossover cable to the Ethernet port on your computer's NIC. Connect the other end of the cable to the Ethernet port on the NIC of your partner's computer.

6. At the command prompt on your partner's computer, type **dhclient eth0** and press **Enter** to request a DHCP address.

7. At the command prompt on your computer, type **cat /var/lib/dhcpd/dhcpd .leases** and press **Enter**. Note the line that details the lease information.

8. At the command prompt, type **service dhcpd stop** and press **Enter** to stop the DHCP daemon.

9. Remove the crossover cable from your computer and your partner's computer.

10. Type **exit** and press **Enter** to log out of your shell.

Project 13-2

In this hands-on project, you configure and test the DNS daemon.

1. Switch to a command-line terminal (tty2) by pressing **Ctrl+Alt+F2** and log in to the terminal using the user name of **root** and the password of **secret**.

2. At the command prompt, type **yum install system-config-bind** and press **Enter** to install the graphical BIND configuration utility. Type **y** and press **Enter** when prompted to continue the installation.

3. Switch to the gdm by pressing **Ctrl+Alt+F2** or **Ctrl+Alt+F7** and log in to the GNOME Desktop Environment as **sample user one**, with the password of **secret**.

4. Once the GNOME Desktop Environment has started, open a BASH shell terminal, type **system-config-bind&** and press **Enter**. When prompted to supply the root user's password, type **secret** and click **OK**.

5. Highlight **DNS Server** and click **Properties**. Add the **forwarders** option to the Current Options box. Highlight **IPV4 Address** and supply the IPv4 address of your classroom DNS server for this option and click **OK** when finished. Click **OK** to close the DNS server property window. This configures your DNS server to forward requests to the classroom DNS server if it cannot resolve the destination address using the information within its own zone files.

6. Click **New, Zone** and accept the default zone scope of **Internet** by clicking **OK** underneath the Class drop-down box. Next, accept the default zone type of **Forward** by clicking **OK** below the Origin Type drop-down box and type the zone name **class.com.** (taking care to include the trailing . in the zone name). Accept the default DNS server zone role of **Master** (Primary) by clicking **OK**.

7. Examine the default SOA record parameters. What is the default minimum TTL? Briefly explain what this setting does. Click **OK** to return to the BIND configuration utility window.

8. Expand your **class.com** zone. What default records are created in this new zone?

9. Highlight the **class.com** zone and click **New, A IPv4 Address**. Type **gateway.class.com.** in the Domain Name dialog box (taking care to include the trailing . in the FQDN) and supply the IPv4 address of your classroom's default gateway. Click **OK** to create the A record.

10. Highlight the **class.com** zone and click **New, A IPv4 Address**. Type **server1.class.com.** in the Domain Name dialog box (taking care to include the trailing . in the FQDN) and supply your computer's IPv4 address. Click **OK** to create the A record.

11. Highlight the **class.com** zone and click **New, CNAME Alias**. Type **alias.class.com.** in the Domain Name dialog box and type **server1.class.com.** in the Canonical Name dialog box (taking care to include the trailing . in both FQDNs). Click **OK** to create the CNAME record.

12. Highlight the **class.com** zone and click **New, MX Mail Exchange**. Note the default domain of class.com. in the Domain Name dialog box and type **server1.class.com.** in

13

the Mail Server Name dialog box (taking care to include the trailing . in the FQDN). Click **OK** to create the MX record.

13. Expand your **class.com** zone. Are the new records visible?

14. Expand the zone that represents your classroom network. Are PTR records available for reverse lookups?

15. Click **Save**. Click **OK** when prompted to save your changes to the configuration files on the hard drive. Log out of the GNOME Desktop Environment.

16. Close the BIND configuration utility and switch back to tty2 by pressing **Ctrl+Alt+F2**.

17. At the command prompt, type **service named start** and press **Enter** to start the DNS name daemon.

18. At the command prompt, type **chkconfig --level 5 named on** and press **Enter** to ensure that the DNS name daemon is started when the system enters runlevel 5.

19. Edit the /etc/resolv.conf file with a text editor and remove any existing nameserver lines. Add the line **nameserver 127.0.0.1** to ensure that your Linux computer uses the local DNS server daemon for name resolution. Save your changes and quit the editor when finished.

20. At the command prompt, type **ping –c 4 gateway.class.com** and press **Enter**. Was the name resolved successfully? Explain.

21. At the command prompt, type **ping –c 4 server1.class.com** and press **Enter**. Was the name resolved successfully? Explain.

22. At the command prompt, type **ping –c 4 alias.class.com** and press **Enter**. Was the name resolved successfully? Explain.

23. At the command prompt, type **ping –c 4 www.yahoo.com** and press **Enter**. Was the name resolved successfully? Explain.

24. At the command prompt, type **dig @localhost class.com ANY** and press **Enter**. Are your resource records returned successfully?

25. At the command prompt, type **less /var/named/chroot/etc/named.conf** and press **Enter**. View the entries. Is class.com a master zone? Do you see a line that forwards unknown requests to your classroom DNS server? Press q when finished.

26. At the command prompt, type **cat /var/named/chroot/var/named/class.com .db** and press **Enter**. View the entries. Are your resource records present?

27. At the command prompt, type **cat /var/named/chroot/var/named/network_ ID.db** and press **Enter** where network_ID is your classroom network ID. View the entries. Are PTR resource records present?

28. At the command prompt, type **less /var/named/chroot/var/named/named.root** and press **Enter**. View the entries. What do these entries represent?

29. Type **exit** and press **Enter** to log out of your shell.

Project 13-3

In this hands-on project, you configure and update your NTP daemon.

1. Switch to a command-line terminal (tty2) by pressing **Ctrl+Alt+F2** and log in to the terminal using the user name of **root** and the password of **secret**.

2. At the command prompt, type **chkconfig --list ntpd** and press **Enter**. Note the runlevels that the NTP daemon is started in.

3. Edit the **/etc/ntp.conf** file with a text editor. Note the default NTP servers that are queried for time information. Next, add the following line (where *network* is your classroom network and *subnet_mask* is the associated subnet mask):

   restrict *network* mask *subnet_mask* nomodify notrap

   When finished, save your changes and quit the editor.

4. At the command prompt, type **service ntpd stop** and press **Enter** to stop the NTP daemon.

5. At the command prompt, type **ntpdate -u 0.fedora.pool.ntp.org** and press **Enter** to synchronize your clock with the first time server listed in /etc/ntp.conf. Repeat this command several times until the offset is very low.

6. At the command prompt, type **service ntpd start** and press **Enter** to start the NTP daemon.

7. At the command prompt, type **ntpq -p** and press **Enter** to view information about the time servers that you are synchronizing with (peers).

8. Type **exit** and press **Enter** to log out of your shell.

Project 13-4

In this hands-on project, you configure the Apache Web server and test daemon permissions to files on the system.

1. Switch to a command-line terminal (tty2) by pressing **Ctrl+Alt+F2** and log in to the terminal using the user name of **root** and the password of **secret**.

2. At the command prompt, type **grep DocumentRoot/etc/httpd/conf/httpd. conf** and press **Enter**. What is the document root directory?

3. At the command prompt, type **grep DirectoryIndex /etc/httpd/conf/httpd. conf** and press **Enter**. What file(s) will automatically be handed out by the Apache daemon from the document root directory?

4. At the command prompt, type **grep "User" /etc/httpd/conf/httpd.conf** and press **Enter**. What user does the Apache daemon run as locally?

5. At the command prompt, type **grep "Group" /etc/httpd/conf/httpd.conf** and press **Enter**. What user does the Apache daemon run as locally?

6. At the command prompt, type **apachectl configtest** and press **Enter**. Are there any syntax errors within your /etc/httpd/conf/httpd.conf file?

7. Edit the **/var/www/html/index.html** file with a text editor such as vi. Are there any entries? Add the following lines:

   <html>
   <body>
   <h1>My sample website</h1>
   </body>
   </html>

   When finished, save your changes and quit the editor.

8. At the command prompt, type **service httpd start** and press **Enter** to start Apache.

9. At the command prompt, type **chkconfig --level 5 httpd on** and press **Enter** to ensure that Apache is started when the system enters runlevel 5.

10. At the command prompt, type **curl http://server1.class.com/** and press **Enter**. Was your Web page successfully returned by Apache?

11. At the command prompt, type **ab -n 1000 http://server1.class.com/** and press **Enter**. How long did Apache take to respond to 1,000 requests?

12. At the command prompt, type **less /etc/httpd/logs/access_log** and press **Enter**. How many Web page hits are shown? Explain.

13. Switch to the gdm by pressing **Ctrl+Alt+F2** or **Ctrl+Alt+F7** and log in to the GNOME Desktop Environment as **sample user one** using the password of **secret**.

14. Open the Firefox Web browser. Enter **http://server1.class.com** as the location. Is your Web page displayed?

15. Switch back to your command-line terminal (tty2) by pressing **Ctrl+Alt+F2**.

16. At the command prompt, type **ls -l/var/www/html/index.html** and press **Enter**. Who owns the file? What is the group owner? What category do the Apache daemons use when they run as the user apache and group apache?

17. At the command prompt, type **chmod 640 /var/www/html/index.html** and press **Enter**.

18. Switch to the graphical terminal by pressing **Ctrl+Alt+F1** or **Ctrl+Alt+F7** and refresh the Web page in your Firefox Web browser. What error message do you receive?

19. Switch back to your command-line terminal (tty2) by pressing **Ctrl+Alt+F2**.

20. At the command prompt, type **chmod 644 /var/www/html/index.html** and press **Enter**.

21. Switch to the graphical terminal by pressing **Ctrl+Alt+F1** or **Ctrl+Alt+F7** and refresh the Web page in your Firefox Web browser. Was the Apache daemon able to read the index.html file? Log out of the GNOME Desktop Environment.

22. Switch back to your command-line terminal (tty2) by pressing **Ctrl+Alt+F2**.

23. Type **exit** and press **Enter** to log out of your shell.

Project 13-5

In this hands-on project, you configure and test Samba file sharing.

1. Switch to a command-line terminal (tty2) by pressing **Ctrl+Alt+F2** and log in to the terminal using the user name of **root** and the password of **secret**.

2. Edit the **/etc/samba/smb.conf** file with a text editor such as vi. Add the following line underneath the [global] line in this file:

netbios name = server1X

where X is a unique number assigned to you by your instructor. When finished, save your changes and quit the editor.

3. At the command prompt, type **smbpasswd -a root** and press **Enter**. When prompted, supply the password of **secret**. Repeat the same password when prompted a second time.

4. At the command prompt, type **service smb start ; service nmb start** and press **Enter**. What daemons were started?

5. At the command prompt, type **smbclient -L server1X** and press **Enter** where X is the unique number assigned to you by your instructor. Supply your Samba password of **secret** when prompted. Do you see your shared home directory? Do you see any printer shares?

6. At the command prompt, type **smbclient //server1X/root** and press **Enter** where X is the unique number assigned to you by your instructor. Supply your Samba password of **secret** when prompted.

7. At the smb:\> prompt, type **dir** and press **Enter**. Are you in your home directory?

8. At the smb:\> prompt, type **exit** and press **Enter**.

9. Edit the **/etc/samba/smb.conf** file again with a text editor such as vi. Add the following lines to the end of the file:

```
[newshare]
comment = Web Content
path = /var/www/html
public = yes
read only = no
```

When finished, save your changes and quit the editor.

10. At the command prompt, type **testparm** and press **Enter**. Were any syntax errors reported within /etc/samba/smb.conf? Press **Enter** to view your Samba configuration.

11. At the command prompt, type **service smb restart ; service nmb restart** and press **Enter**.

12. At the command prompt, type **smbclient -L server1X** and press **Enter** where X is the unique number assigned to you by your instructor. Supply your Samba password of **secret** when prompted. Do you see your new shared directory?

13. At the command prompt, type **smbclient //server1X/newshare** and press **Enter** where X is the unique number assigned to you by your instructor. Supply your Samba password of **secret** when prompted.

14. At the smb:\> prompt, type **dir** and press **Enter**. Are you in the /var/www/html directory?

15. At the smb:\> prompt, type **exit** and press **Enter**.

16. Type **exit** and press **Enter** to log out of your shell.

Project 13-6

In this hands-on project, you export the /etc directory using NFS and access it across the network using the mount command.

1. Switch to a command-line terminal (tty2) by pressing **Ctrl+Alt+F2** and log in to the terminal using the user name of **root** and the password of **secret**.

2. Edit the **/etc/exports** file with a text editor such as vi. Are there any entries? Add a line that reads:

/etc * (rw,root_squash)

When finished, save your changes and quit the editor.

3. At the command prompt, type **exportfs -a** and press **Enter**.

4. At the command prompt, type **service nfs start ; service nfslock start** and press **Enter** to start the NFS daemons.

5. At the command prompt, type **mount -t nfs localhost:/etc /mnt** and press **Enter**.

6. At the command prompt, type **mount** and press **Enter**. What is mounted to the /mnt directory?

7. At the command prompt, type **cd /mnt** and press **Enter**. Next, type **ls -F** at the command prompt and press **Enter**. What directory are you observing? Type **ls -F /etc** at the command prompt and press **Enter**. Is the output on the terminal screen identical?

8. At the command prompt, type **cd** and press **Enter** to return to your home directory. Next, type **umount /mnt** at the command prompt and press **Enter** to unmount the NFS filesystem.

9. Type **exit** and press **Enter** to log out of your shell.

Project 13-7

In this hands-on project, you configure and use the Very Secure FTP daemon.

1. Switch to a command-line terminal (tty2) by pressing **Ctrl+Alt+F2** and log in to the terminal using the user name of **root** and the password of **secret**.

2. At the command prompt, type **cp /etc/hosts /var/ftp ; chmod 444 /var/ftp/ hosts** and press **Enter** to copy the file /etc/hosts to the /var/ftp directory and ensure that everyone has read permission to it.

3. At the command prompt, type **service vsftpd start** and press **Enter** to start the Very Secure FTP daemon.

4. At the command prompt, type **chkconfig --level 5 vsftpd on** and press **Enter** to ensure that the Very Secure FTP daemon is started when the system enters runlevel 5.

5. At the command prompt, type **ftp localhost** and press **Enter**. Log in as **user1** using the password of **secret** when prompted.

6. At the ftp> prompt, type **dir** and press **Enter** to list the contents of the /home/user1 directory.

7. At the ftp> prompt, type **lcd /etc** and press **Enter** to change the current working directory on the FTP client to /etc.

8. At the ftp> prompt, type **put inittab** and press **Enter** to upload the inittab file to the remote FTP server.

9. At the ftp> prompt, type **dir** and press **Enter** to list the contents of the /home/user1 directory. Was the inittab file uploaded successfully?

10. At the ftp> prompt, type **lcd /** and press **Enter** to change the current working directory on the FTP client to /.

11. At the ftp> prompt, type **get inittab** and press **Enter** to download the inittab file to the / directory on the local computer.

12. At the ftp> prompt, type **help** and press **Enter** to list the commands available within the FTP client program.

13. At the ftp> prompt, type **bye** and press **Enter** to exit the FTP client program.

14. At the command prompt, type **ls /** and press **Enter**. Was the inittab file downloaded to the / directory successfully?

15. At the command prompt, type **ftp localhost** and press **Enter**. Log in as **anonymous** using the password of **nothing** when prompted (the actual password is not relevant for the anonymous user; you could use any password).

16. At the ftp> prompt, type **dir** and press **Enter** to list the contents of the /var/ftp directory.

17. At the ftp> prompt, type **lcd /** and press **Enter** to change the current working directory on the FTP client to /.

18. At the ftp> prompt, type **get hosts** and press **Enter** to download the hosts file to the / directory on the local computer.

19. At the ftp> prompt, type **bye** and press **Enter** to exit the FTP client program.

20. At the command prompt, type **ls /** and press **Enter**. Was the hosts file downloaded to the / directory successfully?

21. At the command prompt, type **ftp localhost** and press **Enter**. Log in as the **root** user with the password of **secret** when prompted. What error did you receive?

22. At the ftp> prompt, type **bye** and press **Enter** to exit the FTP client program.

23. Edit the **/etc/vsftpd/ftpusers** and **/etc/vsftpd/user_list** files with a text editor and remove the following line:

    root

    When finished, save your changes and quit the editor.

24. At the command prompt, type **service vsftpd restart** and press **Enter** to restart the Very Secure FTP daemon.

25. At the command prompt, type **ftp localhost** and press **Enter**. Log in as the **root** user with the password of **secret** when prompted.

26. At the ftp> prompt, type **dir** and press **Enter** to list the contents of the /root directory.

27. At the ftp> prompt, type **bye** and press **Enter** to exit the FTP client program.

28. Type **exit** and press **Enter** to log out of your shell.

29. Switch to the gdm by pressing **Ctrl+Alt+F2** or **Ctrl+Alt+F7** and log in to the GNOME Desktop Environment as **sample user one** with the password of **secret**.

30. Open the Firefox Web browser, enter the location **ftp://server1.class.com**, and press **Enter**. What directory are you placed in and why?

31. Enter the location **ftp://root:secret@server1.class.com** in the Firefox Web browser and press **Enter**. What directory are you placed in and why?

32. Close the Firefox Web browser and log out of the GNOME Desktop Environment.

Project 13-8

In this hands-on project, you view and send e-mail using the Sendmail e-mail daemon.

1. Switch to a command-line terminal (tty2) by pressing **Ctrl+Alt+F2** and log in to the terminal using the user name of **root** and the password of **secret**.

2. At the command prompt, type **ps -ef | grep sendmail** and press **Enter**. Is the Sendmail daemon running?

3. Edit the **/etc/aliases** file with a text editor and add the following line:

   admin: root

   When finished, save your changes and quit the editor.

4. At the command prompt, type **newaliases** and press **Enter** to update the aliases database using the information within the /etc/aliases file.

5. At the command prompt, type **mail admin user1** and press **Enter** to compose a new e-mail to the users admin and user1. When prompted for a subject, type **Test email** and press **Enter**. Next, type **This is a test email that will be delivered using the Sendmail daemon** and press **Enter**. Next, type **.** (a period) and press **Enter** to complete and send the e-mail.

6. At the command prompt, type **mail** to check your mailbox for e-mail messages. The last e-mail should have a subject line of Test e-mail. If you don't see this message, type **z** to advance to the next screen of messages. Note the number of the e-mail message that has the subject line of Test e-mail and type this number at the & prompt to read your e-mail message. Type **q** when finished to exit the mail program.

7. At the command prompt, type **telnet localhost 25** and press **Enter**. Can you tell that you are interacting with the Sendmail daemon?

8. Type **EHLO server1.class.com** and press **Enter**. Does your Sendmail daemon support ESMTP? Type **quit** and press **Enter** to quit the telnet session.

9. Type **exit** and press **Enter** to log out of your shell.

Project 13-9

In this hands-on project, you create, query, and manage a database using PostgreSQL.

1. Switch to a command-line terminal (tty2) by pressing **Ctrl+Alt+F2** and log in to the terminal using the user name of **root** and the password of **secret**.

2. At the command prompt, type **rpm -qi postgresql** and press **Enter**. Is the PostgreSQL server installed?

3. At the command prompt, type **passwd postgres** and press **Enter**. Type a password of **secret** and press **Enter** at both prompts to set a password of secret for the postgres user account.

4. At the command prompt, type **service postgresql initdb** and press **Enter** to initialize the PostgreSQL system databases.

5. At the command prompt, type **service postgresql start** and press **Enter** to start the PostgreSQL server.

6. Switch to a different command-line terminal (tty3) by pressing **Ctrl+Alt+F3** and log in to the terminal using the user name of **postgres** and the password of **secret**.

7. At the command prompt, type **createdb sales** and press **Enter**.

8. At the command prompt, type **psql sales** and press **Enter** to start the PostgreSQL utility.

9. At the sales=# prompt, type **\l** and press **Enter** to view the databases on your PostgreSQL server. The postgres database stores all information used internally by the PostgreSQL server, and the template databases are used when creating new databases. Note that your sales database is listed and uses the UTF-8 character set for information.

10. At the sales=# prompt, type **CREATE TABLE customer (Name char(20),Address char(40),Balance char(10));** and press **Enter** to create a customer table that has three fields (Name, Address, Balance).

11. At the sales=# prompt, type **\d** and press **Enter** to view the tables within your database. Is the customer database listed?

12. At the sales=# prompt, type **\d customer** and press **Enter** to view the fields within the customer table. How many characters are allowed in each of the three fields?

13. At the sales=# prompt, type **INSERT INTO customer VALUES ('Lily Bopeep','123 Rutherford Lane','526.80');** and press **Enter** to add a record to your table.

14. At the sales=# prompt, type **INSERT INTO customer VALUES ('Harvey Lipshitz', '51 King Street','122.19');** and press **Enter** to add a record to your table.

15. At the sales=# prompt, type **INSERT INTO customer VALUES ('John Escobar','14-6919 Franklin Drive','709.66');** and press **Enter** to add a record to your table.

16. At the sales=# prompt, type **SELECT * from customer;** and press **Enter** to view all records within your table.

17. At the sales=# prompt, type **SELECT * from customter ORDER BY Balance DESC;** and press **Enter** to view all records within your table in descending order by balance.

18. At the sales=# prompt, type **SELECT * from customer WHERE Name = 'Harvey Lipshitz';** and press **Enter** to view the record for Harvey Lipshitz.

19. At the sales=# prompt, type **CREATE USER bob WITH PASSWORD 'supersecret';** and press **Enter** to create a user account within PostgreSQL that can access the customer database.

20. At the sales=# prompt, type **GRANT ALL PRIVILEGES ON customer TO bob** and press **Enter** to grant SELECT, UPDATE, DELETE, and INSERT permission on the customer table to the bob user.

21. At the sales=# prompt, type **\q** and press **Enter** to quit the PostgreSQL utility.

22. Type **exit** and press **Enter** to log out of your shell.

13

Discovery Exercises

1. In Project 13-3, you configured your NTP daemon to share time information to other computers on your classroom network. Edit the /etc/ntp.conf on your partner's computer to obtain time information from your computer and test the results using the **ntpq** command. Next, restore your original configuration.

2. Use the steps outlined in this chapter to configure your system as an NIS master server and configure NIS maps for the /etc/passwd and /etc/shadow files. Next, configure your partner's computer as an NIS client that obtains its /etc/passwd and /etc/shadow configuration from your NIS master server. Test your configuration using the **yppasswd** command. When finished, restore your original configuration.

3. The Samba Web Administration Tool (SWAT) is a Web-based graphical administration tool that can be used to perform advanced Samba configuration. Install SWAT using the **yum install samba-swat** command. Next, remove the **disable = yes** line from the /etc/xinetd.d/swat file and restart the xinetd daemon. Following this, enter the location **http://server1.class.com:901** in the Firefox Web browser and log in as the **root** user with the password **secret**. Navigate the available sections of the SWAT tool. Finally, use the SWAT tool to share a new directory of your choice and test your results.

4. Using the procedures outlined in this chapter, download and install the Postfix e-mail server. Next, configure the Postfix e-mail server to use the class.com domain, stop the Sendmail daemon, and start the Postfix daemon. Finally, use the **telnet** and **mail** programs to test the functionality of the Postfix daemon.

## chapter 14

Troubleshooting, Performance, and Security

After completing this chapter, you will be able to:

- Describe and outline good troubleshooting practices
- Effectively troubleshoot common hardware- and software-related problems
- Monitor system performance using command-line and graphical utilities
- Identify and fix common performance problems
- Describe the different facets of Linux security
- Increase the security of a Linux computer
- Outline measures and utilities that can be used to detect a Linux security breach

Throughout this textbook, you have examined various elements of a Linux system. In this chapter, you focus on fixing common problems that affect these elements. First, you explore system maintenance, troubleshooting procedures, common system problems, and performance utilities. Next, you learn security concepts, good security practices, as well as the utilities that you can use to prevent and detect both local and network-related security breaches.

Troubleshooting Methodology

After you have successfully installed Linux, configured services on the system, and documented settings, you must maintain the system's integrity over time. This includes monitoring, proactive maintenance, and reactive maintenance, as illustrated in Figure 14-1.

Monitoring, the activity on which Linux administrators spend the most time, involves examining log files and running performance utilities periodically to identify problems and their causes. **Proactive maintenance** involves taking the necessary steps to minimize the chance of future problems or their impact. Performing regular system backups and identifying potential problem areas are examples of proactive maintenance. All proactive maintenance tasks should be documented for future reference. This information, along with any data backups, is vital to the reconstruction of your system, should it suffer catastrophic failure.

Reactive maintenance involves correcting problems when they arise during monitoring. When a problem is solved, it needs to be documented and the system adjusted proactively to reduce the likelihood that the same problem will occur in the future. Furthermore, documenting the solution to problems creates a template for action, allowing subsequent or similar problems to be remedied faster.

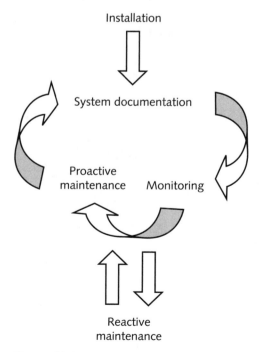

Figure 14-1 The maintenance cycle

Source: Course Technology/Cengage Learning

Any system **documentation** should be printed and kept in a log book, because this information might be lost during a system failure if kept on the Linux system itself.

Reactive maintenance is further composed of many procedures known as **troubleshooting procedures**, which can be used to efficiently solve a problem in a systematic manner.

When a problem occurs, you need to gather as much information about the problem as possible. This might include examining system log files and viewing the contents of the /proc filesystem as well as running information utilities, such as ps or mount. In addition, you might research the symptoms of the problem on the Internet; Web sites and newsgroups often list log files and commands that can be used to check for certain problems.

The `tail -f /path/to/logfile` command opens a specific log file for continuous viewing. This allows you to see entries as they are added, which is useful when gathering information about system problems.

Following this, you need to try to isolate the problem by examining the information gathered. Determine whether the problem is persistent or intermittent, and whether it affects all users or just one.

Given this information, you might then generate a list of possible causes and solutions organized by placing the most probable solution at the top of the list and the least probable solution at the bottom of the list. Using the Internet at this stage is beneficial because solutions for many Linux problems are posted on Web sites or newsgroups. In addition, posing the problem at a local Linux Users Group will likely generate many possible solutions.

Next, you need to implement and test each possible solution for results until the problem is resolved. When implementing possible solutions, it is very important that you only apply one change at a time. If you make multiple modifications, it will be unclear as to what worked and why.

After the problem has been solved, document the solution for future reference and proceed to take proactive maintenance measures to reduce the chance of the same problem recurring in the future. These troubleshooting procedures are outlined in Figure 14-2.

The troubleshooting procedures listed in Figure 14-2 serve as a guideline only. You might need to alter your approach for certain problems. Remember, troubleshooting is an art that you will begin to master only with practice. There are, however, two golden rules that should guide you during any troubleshooting process:

- *Prioritize problems*—If you need to solve multiple problems, prioritize the problems according to severity and spend the most time on the most severe problems. Becoming fixated on a small problem and ignoring larger issues results in much lower productivity. If a problem is too difficult to solve in a given period of time, it is good practice to ask for help.

- *Try to solve the root of the problem*—Some solutions might appear successful in the short term yet fail over the long term because of an underlying problem. Effective troubleshooting requires good instincts, which in turn come from a solid knowledge of

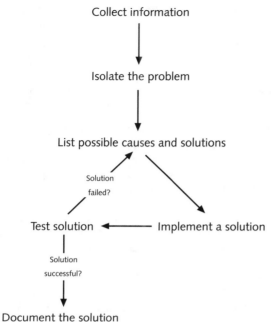

Figure 14-2 Common troubleshooting procedures

Source: Course Technology/Cengage Learning

the system hardware and configuration. To avoid missing the underlying cause of any problem, try to justify why a certain solution was successful. If it is unclear why a certain solution was successful, it is likely that you have missed an underlying cause of the problem that might need to be remedied in the future to prevent the same problem from recurring.

Resolving Common System Problems

The possible problems that can arise on Linux systems are too numerous to list here. However, as a troubleshooter, you'll most often face a set of the common problems described in this section. All Linux problems can be divided into three categories: hardware-related, software-related, and user interface-related.

Hardware-Related Problems

Although hardware problems might be the result of damaged hardware, many hardware-related problems involve improper hardware or software configuration. This is most likely the case if the hardware problem presents itself immediately after Linux installation.

As discussed in earlier chapters, ensuring that all Parallel SCSI drives are properly terminated, that the video card and monitor settings have been configured properly, and that all hardware is on the Hardware Compatibility List minimizes problems later. In addition, if the POST does not complete or alerts the user with two or more beeps at system startup, there is likely a peripheral card, cable, or memory stick that is loose or connected improperly inside the computer.

Some hardware-related problems prevent the use of hardware with the Linux operating system. These problems are typically specific to the type of hardware. Viewing the output of the dmesg command or the contents of the /var/log/boot.log and /var/log/messages log files can isolate most hardware problems.

The absence of a device driver also prevents the operating system from using the associated hardware device. Normally, the Linux kernel detects new hardware devices at boot time and configures the device driver module for them automatically. However, if the Linux kernel doesn't have access to the appropriate driver module for a certain hardware device, the device cannot be used. You can view the hardware that is detected by the Linux kernel by viewing the output of the dmesg command. To only view the USB devices detected by the Linux kernel, you could instead use the **lsusb command**, as follows:

```
[root@server1 ~]# lsusb
Bus 002 Device 002: ID 05ac:0302 Apple, Inc. Optical Mouse [Fujitsu]
Bus 002 Device 001: ID 1d6b:0001 Linux Foundation 1.1 root hub
Bus 001 Device 001: ID 1d6b:0002 Linux Foundation 2.0 root hub
[root@server1 ~]# _
```

Similarly, to only view PCI devices detected by the Linux kernel, you could use the **lspci command**, as shown in the following output:

```
[root@server1 ~]# lspci
00:00.0 RAM memory: nVidia Corporation C51 Host Bridge (rev a2)
00:00.1 RAM memory: nVidia Corporation C51 Memory Controller 0 (rev a2)
00:00.2 RAM memory: nVidia Corporation C51 Memory Controller 1 (rev a2)
00:00.3 RAM memory: nVidia Corporation C51 Memory Controller 5 (rev a2)
00:00.4 RAM memory: nVidia Corporation C51 Memory Controller 4 (rev a2)
00:00.5 RAM memory: nVidia Corporation C51 Host Bridge (rev a2)
00:00.6 RAM memory: nVidia Corporation C51 Memory Controller 3 (rev a2)
00:00.7 RAM memory: nVidia Corporation C51 Memory Controller 2 (rev a2)
00:03.0 PCI bridge: nVidia Corporation C51 PCI Express Bridge (rev a1)
00:05.0 VGA compatible controller: nVidia Corporation C51 [GeForce Go
6100] (rev a2)
00:09.0 RAM memory: nVidia Corporation MCP51 Host Bridge (rev a2)
00:0a.0 ISA bridge: nVidia Corporation MCP51 LPC Bridge (rev a3)
00:0a.1 SMBus: nVidia Corporation MCP51 SMBus (rev a3)
00:0a.3 Co-processor: nVidia Corporation MCP51 PMU (rev a3)
00:0b.0 USB Controller: nVidia Corporation MCP51 USB Controller (rev a3)
00:0b.1 USB Controller: nVidia Corporation MCP51 USB Controller (rev a3)
00:0d.0 IDE interface: nVidia Corporation MCP51 IDE (rev f1)
00:10.0 PCI bridge: nVidia Corporation MCP51 PCI Bridge (rev a2)
00:10.1 Audio device: nVidia Corporation MCP51 High Definition Audio
(rev a2)
00:14.0 Bridge: nVidia Corporation MCP51 Ethernet Controller (rev a3)
00:18.0 Host bridge: Advanced Micro Devices [AMD] K8 [Athlon64/Opteron]
HyperTransport Technology Configuration
```

14

```
00:18.1 Host bridge: Advanced Micro Devices [AMD] K8 [Athlon64/Opteron]
Address Map
00:18.2 Host bridge: Advanced Micro Devices [AMD] K8 [Athlon64/Opteron]
DRAM Controller
00:18.3 Host bridge: Advanced Micro Devices [AMD] K8 [Athlon64/Opteron]
Miscellaneous Control
06:09.0 Ethernet controller: Realtek Semiconductor Co., Ltd. RTL-8185 IEEE
802.11a/b/g Wireless LAN Controller (rev 20)
[root@server1 ~]# _
```

Recall from Chapter 13 that the lsmod command lists the driver modules loaded into the Linux kernel. By comparing the output of the dmesg, lsusb, and lspci commands with the output of the lsmod command, you can determine whether a driver module is missing for a hardware device in your system. By searching Linux forums on the Internet or the hardware vendor's Web site, you will likely find an RPM package that you can add to your system that provides a driver module for this hardware device. After installing this package, simply reboot to allow the Linux kernel to detect your hardware, then load the appropriate driver module.

Although less common than other hardware problems, hardware failure can also render a device unusable. In this case, you must replace the hardware and allow the Linux kernel to detect it and load the appropriate driver module, or obtain the appropriate driver module from the Internet as described earlier. Because hard disks are used frequently and consist of moving parts, they are the most common hardware component to fail on Linux systems. If the Linux system uses hardware RAID level 1 or 5, the data on the hard disk can be regenerated using the RAID configuration utility after you replace the failed hard disk.

If, however, the Linux system does not use hardware RAID and the hard disk that failed contained partitions that were mounted on noncritical directories, such as /home or /var, then you can perform the following steps:

1. Power down the computer and replace the failed hard disk.
2. Boot the Linux system.
3. Use fdisk to create partitions on the replaced hard disk.
4. Optionally configure LVM logical volumes from the partitions created in Step 3.
5. Use mkfs to create filesystems on the partitions or LVM logical volumes.
6. Restore the original data using a backup utility.
7. Ensure that /etc/fstab has the appropriate entries to mount the filesystems at system startup.

Alternatively, if the hard disk that contains the / filesystem fails, you can perform the following steps:

1. Power down the computer and replace the failed hard disk.
2. Reinstall Linux on the new hard disk (remembering to re-create the original partition and volume structure during installation).
3. Restore the original configuration and data files using a backup utility.

Software-Related Problems

Software-related problems are typically more difficult to identify and resolve than hardware-related problems. As a result, you should identify whether the software-related problem is related to application software or operating system (OS) software.

Application-Related Problems Applications can fail during execution for a number of reasons, including missing program libraries and files, process restrictions, or conflicting applications.

As discussed in Chapter 11, when RPM software is installed, the rpm command does a preliminary check to ensure that all shared program libraries and prerequisite packages (package dependencies) required for the application to work properly have been installed. If these are missing, the rpm command prints an error message to the screen and quits the installation. Similarly, uninstalling software using the rpm command fails if the software being uninstalled is a package dependency for another package. Also, when compiling source code, the configure script checks for the presence of any required shared program libraries and programs and fails to create the Makefile if they are absent. Thus, you must download and install the necessary shared libraries and/or packages before installing software packages using these methods.

The yum command also checks for package dependencies. However, if package dependencies exist, they are downloaded and installed by the yum command prior to installing the desired package.

Some programs, however, might fail to check for dependencies during installation, or files that belong to a package dependency might be accidentally removed from the system over time. If this is the case, certain programs fail to execute properly.

To identify any missing files in a package or package dependency, recall that you can use the -V option to the rpm command, followed by the name of the package. The following output indicates that there are two missing files in the bash package:

```
[root@server1 ~]# rpm -V bash
missing     d /usr/share/doc/bash-4.1.2/COPYING
missing     d /usr/share/doc/bash-4.1.2/README
 [root@server1 ~]# _
```

To identify which shared libraries are required by a certain program, you can use the **ldd command**. For example, the following output displays the shared libraries required by the /bin/bash program:

```
[root@server1 ~]# ldd /bin/bash
      linux-gate.so.1 => (0x00591000)
      libtinfo.so.5 => /lib/libtinfo.so.5 (0x0078d000)
      libdl.so.2 => /lib/libdl.so.2 (0x002db000)
      libc.so.6 => /lib/libc.so.6 (0x0014d000)
      /lib/ld-linux.so.2 (0x0012b000)
[root@server1 ~]# _
```

If any shared libraries listed by the ldd command are missing, you can download the appropriate library from the Internet and install it to the correct location, which is typically

14

underneath the /lib or /usr/lib directories. After downloading and installing any shared libraries, it is good practice to run the **ldconfig command** to ensure that the list of shared library directories (**/etc/ld.so.conf**) and the list of shared libraries (**/etc/ld.so.cache**) are updated. Alternatively, you can create a variable in your BASH shell called LD_LIBRARY_ PATH that lists the directories that contain the shared libraries.

Processes come with a number of constraints that can also prevent them from executing properly. Recall that all processes require a PID from the system process table. Too many processes running on the system can use all available PIDs in the process table; this is typically the result of a large number of zombie processes. Killing the parent process of the zombie processes then frees several entries in the process table.

In addition, processes can initiate numerous connections to files on the filesystem in addition to standard input, standard output, and standard error. These connections are called **file handles**. The shell restricts the number of file handles that programs can open to 1,024 by default; to increase the maximum number of file handles to 5,000, you can run the command ulimit -n 5000. The **ulimit command** can also be used to increase the number of processes that users can start in a shell; this might be required for programs that start a great deal of child processes. For example, to increase the maximum number of user processes to 8,000, you can use the command ulimit -u 8000.

To isolate application problems that are not related to missing dependencies or restrictions, you should first check the log file produced by the application. Most application log files are stored in the /var/log directory or subdirectories of the /var/log directory named for the application. Even if an application stores its log files elsewhere, it usually hard links its log files to files within the /var/log directory. For example, to view the errors for the Apache Web server daemon, you can view the file /var/log/httpd/error_log, which is hard linked to the /etc/httpd/logs/error_log file.

Applications might run into difficulties gaining resources during execution and stop functioning. Often, restarting the process using a SIGHUP solves this problem. This condition might also be caused by another process on the system that attempts to use the same resources. To determine if this is the case, attempt to start the application when fewer processes are loaded, such as in single user mode. If resource conflict seems to be the cause of the problem, check the Internet for a newer version of the application or an application fix.

Operating System-Related Problems Many software-related problems are related to the operating system itself. These typically include problems with X Windows, boot loaders, and filesystems.

There are many different video card and monitor models today. As a result, some video cards and monitors may not be detected properly by the kernel, or an updated device driver may be required to properly use them with the Linux kernel. If you configure your display settings using the system-config-display utility discussed in Chapter 8, and your X Windows or gdm fails to start, you can usually isolate the problems by viewing the /var/log/Xorg.0.log file or by executing the xwininfo command or xdpyinfo command.

As discussed in Chapter 8, boot loaders can encounter problems while attempting to load the operating system kernel. For the LILO boot loader, placing the word "linear" and removing the word "compact" from the /etc/lilo.conf file usually remedies the problem. For the GRUB boot loader, errors are typically the result of a missing file in the /boot directory.

Also, ensuring that the Linux kernel resides before the 1024th cylinder of the hard disk and that the 32-bit large block addressing (`lba32`) keyword is specified in the boot loader configuration file typically eliminates BIOS problems with large hard disks.

Because the operating system transfers data to and from the hard disk frequently, the filesystem can become corrupted over time. A corrupted filesystem can be identified by very slow write requests, errors printed to the console, or failure to mount. If the filesystem on a partition mounted to a noncritical directory, such as /home or /var, becomes corrupted, you should perform the following troubleshooting steps:

1. Unmount the filesystem, if mounted.
2. Run the `fsck` command with the `-f` (`full`) option on the filesystem device.
3. If the `fsck` command cannot repair the filesystem, use the `mkfs` command to re-create the filesystem.
4. Restore the original data for the filesystem using a backup utility.

 Do not restore data onto a damaged filesystem. Ensure that the filesystem has been re-created first.

If the **/** filesystem becomes corrupted, the system is unstable and must be turned off. Following this, you can perform the following troubleshooting steps:

1. Boot your system from your Fedora 13 installation media and enter System Rescue, as described in Chapter 6.
2. At the BASH shell prompt within System Rescue, use the `mkfs` command to re-create the filesystem on the appropriate partition or volume that originally hosted the **/** filesystem.
3. At the BASH shell prompt within System Rescue, use a backup utility such as tar, dump, or cpio, to restore the original data to the re-created **/** filesystem.
4. Exit System Rescue and boot your system.

Some Linux administrators prefer to download a bootable CD, DVD, or USB flash drive-based Linux distribution that contains more filesystem repair utilities than the Fedora installation media. Many small Linux distributions are available on the Internet that are designed for this purpose; two examples are **Knoppix Linux** (*www.knoppix.net*) and **BBC Linux** (*www.lnx-bbc.com*). Simply download the ISO image for the Linux distribution and write the image to a CD, DVD, or USB flash drive. Following this, you can boot your computer using this CD, DVD, or USB flash drive, and use the utilities on it to repair your **/** filesystem and restore the files from backup.

User Interface-Related Problems

Because of the large number of open source productivity software applications available, Linux desktop environments are fast becoming popular within organizations as an alternative to the Windows operating system.

To use productivity software properly, Linux users need to understand how to use their desktop environment as well as modify it to suit their needs. As a Linux administrator, you might need to assist users with desktop problems. The tools that users can use to modify their

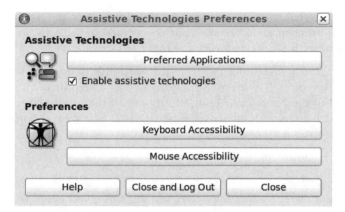

Figure 14-3 The Assistive Technologies Preferences utility

Source: Course Technology/Cengage Learning

desktop experience are collectively called **assistive technologies**. You can configure assistive technologies within Fedora 13 using the Assistive Technologies Preferences utility, as shown in Figure 14-3. To start this utility within the GNOME Desktop Environment, open the System menu and navigate to Preferences, Assistive Technologies.

If you click Preferred Applications within Figure 14-3, you can configure the default Web browser, multimedia player, and terminal application that the desktop environment will open automatically when an associated file type is double-clicked. In addition, you can use this button to configure an on-screen keyboard, as well as voice dictation, screen magnification, and Braille translation using the open source **Orca** program.

If you click Mouse Accessibility in Figure 14-3, you can configure the speed and click behavior for the mice and trackpads on your system. Alternatively, if you click Keyboard Accessibility in Figure 14-3, you can configure the following keyboard-related assistive technologies:

- Repeat keys, which simulate multiple key presses when a key is held down
- Sticky keys, which simulate simultaneous key presses when two keys are pressed in sequence
- Slow keys, which only accept long key presses
- Bounce keys, which ignore fast duplicate key presses
- Mouse keys, which allow the user to control the mouse using the cursor keys on the keyboard

Performance Monitoring

Some problems that you will encounter on a Linux system are not as noticeable as those discussed in the previous section. Such problems affect the overall performance of the Linux system. Like the problems discussed earlier, performance problems can be caused by software or hardware or a combination of the two.

Hardware that is improperly configured might still work, but at a slower speed. In addition, when hardware ages, it might start to malfunction by sending large amounts of information to the CPU when not in use. This process, known as **jabbering**, can slow down a CPU and, hence, the rest of the Linux system. To avoid this hardware malfunction, most companies retire computer equipment after two to five years of use.

Software can also affect the overall performance of a system. Software that requires too many system resources monopolizes the CPU, memory, and peripheral devices. Poor performance can also be the result of too many processes running on a computer, processes that make a great deal of read/write requests to the hard disk (such as databases), or rogue processes. To remedy most software performance issues, you can remove software from the system to free up system resources. If the software is needed for business activity, you can choose to move the software to another Linux system that has more free system resources.

Software performance problems can also sometimes be remedied by altering the hardware. Upgrading or adding another CPU allows the Linux system to execute processes faster and reduce the number of processes running concurrently on the CPU. Alternatively, some peripheral devices can perform a great deal of processing that is normally performed by the CPU; this is known as **bus mastering**. Using bus mastering peripheral components reduces the amount of processing the CPU must perform and, hence, increases system speed.

Adding RAM to the computer also increases system speed because it gives processes more working space in memory and the system will swap much less information to and from the hard disk. Because the operating system, peripheral components, and all processes use RAM constantly, adding RAM to any system often has a profound impact on system performance.

In addition, replacing slower hard disk drives with faster ones or using disk striping RAID improves the performance of programs that require frequent access to filesystems. SCSI hard disks typically have faster rotational speeds and, hence, faster access speeds than other hard disks; many Linux servers use SCSI hard disks for this reason. In addition, CD and DVD drives have a slower access speed than hard disks. Thus, keeping CD and DVD drives on a separate hard disk controller also improves hard disk performance.

To make it easier to identify performance problems, you should run performance utilities on a healthy Linux system on a regular basis during normal business hours and record the results in a system log book. The average results of these performance utilities are known as **baseline** values because they represent normal system activity. When performance issues arise, you can compare the output of performance utilities with the baseline values recorded in the system log book. Values that have changed dramatically from the baseline can help you pinpoint the source of the performance problem.

Although many performance utilities are available to Linux administrators, the most common of these belong to the sysstat package, described next.

Monitoring Performance with sysstat Utilities

The **System Statistics (sysstat) package** contains a wide range of utilities that monitor the system using information from the /proc directory and system devices. You can use the yum install sysstat command to install the sysstat package within Fedora 13.

To monitor CPU performance, you can use the **mpstat (multiple processor statistics) command**. Without arguments, the mpstat command gives average CPU statistics for all processors on the system since the most previous system boot, as shown in the following output:

```
[root@server1 ~]# mpstat
Linux 2.6.33.3-85.fc13.i686.PAE (server1) 09/07/2010 _i686_ (2 CPU)

06:38:42 PM CPU %usr %nice %sys %iowait %irq %soft %steal %guest %idle
06:38:42 PM all 17.53 1.48  6.21 11.73   0.19 0.00  0.00   0.00  62.85
[root@server1 ~]# _
```

If your system has multiple CPUs, you can measure the performance of a single CPU by specifying the −P # option to the mpstat command, where # represents the number of the processor starting from zero. Thus, the command mpstat −P 0 displays statistics for the first processor on the system.

The %usr value shown in the preceding output indicates the percentage of time the processor spent executing user programs and daemons, whereas the %nice value indicates the percentage of time the processor spent executing user programs and daemons that had nondefault nice values. These numbers combined should be greater than the value of %sys, which indicates the amount of time the system spent maintaining itself such that it can execute user programs and daemons.

A system that has a high %sys compared with %usr and %nice is likely executing too many resource-intensive programs.

The %iowait value indicates the percentage of time the CPU was idle when an outstanding disk I/O request existed. The %irq and %soft values indicate the percentage of time the CPU is using to respond to normal interrupts and interrupts that span multiple CPUs, respectively. If these three values rapidly increase over time, the CPU cannot keep up with the number of requests it receives from software. If you have virtualization software installed, the %guest value indicates the percentage of time the CPU is executing another virtual CPU, and the %steal indicates the percentage of time the CPU is waiting to respond to virtual CPU requests.

The %idle value indicates the percentage of time the CPU did not spend executing tasks. Although it might be zero for short periods of time, %idle should be greater than 25 percent over a long period of time.

A system that has a %idle less than 25 percent over a long period of time might require faster or additional CPUs.

Although the average values given by the mpstat command are very useful in determining the CPU health of a Linux system, you might choose to take current measurements using mpstat. To do this, simply specify the interval in seconds and number of measurements as arguments to the mpstat command. For example, the following command takes five current measurements, one per second:

```
[root@server1 ~]# mpstat 1 5
```

```
Linux 2.6.33.3-85.fc13.i686.PAE (server1) 09/08/2010 _i686_ (2 CPU)
```

07:05:10 AM	CPU	%usr	%nice	%sys	%iowait	%irq	%soft	%steal	%guest	%idle
07:05:11 AM	all	8.91	1.98	0.00	0.00	0.99	0.00	0.00	0.00	88.12
07:05:12 AM	all	7.07	2.02	0.00	0.00	0.00	0.00	0.00	0.00	90.91
07:05:13 AM	all	7.92	1.98	0.99	0.00	0.00	0.00	0.00	0.00	89.11
07:05:14 AM	all	7.07	2.02	0.00	0.00	0.00	0.00	0.00	0.00	90.91
07:05:15 AM	all	6.93	2.97	0.99	0.00	0.00	0.00	0.00	0.00	89.11
Average:	all	7.58	2.20	0.40	0.00	0.20	0.00	0.00	0.00	89.62

```
[root@server1 ~]# _
```

The preceding output must be used with caution because it was taken over a short period of time. If, for example, the %idle values are under 25 percent on average, they are not necessarily abnormal because the system might be performing a CPU-intensive task during the short time the statistics were taken.

Another utility in the sysstat package, **iostat (input/output statistics)**, measures the flow of information to and from disk devices. Without any arguments, the iostat command displays CPU statistics similar to mpstat, followed by statistics for each disk device on the system. If your Linux system has one SATA hard disk drive (/dev/sda), the iostat command produces output similar to the following:

```
[root@server1 ~]# iostat
Linux 2.6.33.3-85.fc13.i686.PAE (server1)09/08/2010 _i686_(2 CPU)
```

avg-cpu:	%user	%nice	%system	%iowait	%steal	%idle
	0.10	0.01	0.15	0.39	0.00	99.35

Device:	tps	Blk_read/s	Blk_wrtn/s	Blk_read	Blk_wrtn
sda	0.76	20.94	5.51	1619316	426256
dm-0	0.00	0.01	0.00	890	8
dm-1	0.00	0.01	0.00	472	0

```
[root@server1 ~]# _
```

The output from iostat displays the number of transfers per second (tps) as well as the number of blocks read per second (Blk_read/s) and written per second (Blk_wrtn/s), followed by the total number of blocks read (Blk_read) and written (Blk_wrtn) for the device since the last boot. An increase over time in these values indicates an increase in disk usage by processes. If this increase results in slow performance, the hard disks should be replaced with faster ones or a RAID striping configuration. Like mpstat, the iostat command can take current measurements of the system. Simply specify the interval in seconds followed by the number of measurements as arguments to the iostat command.

Although iostat and mpstat can be used to get quick information about system status, they are limited in their abilities. The **sar (system activity reporter) command** that is contained in the sysstat package can be used to display far more information than iostat and mpstat. As such, it is the most widely used performance monitoring tool on UNIX and Linux systems.

By default, sar commands are scheduled using the cron daemon to run every 10 minutes in Fedora 13. All performance information obtained is logged to a file in the /var/log/sa directory called sa#, where # represents the day of the month. If today were the 14th day of the month, the output from the sar command that is run every 10 minutes would be logged to the file /var/log/sa/sa14. Next month, this file will be overwritten on the 14th day. In other words, only one month of records is kept at any one time in the /var/log/sa directory.

14

You can change the `sar` logging interval by editing the cron table /etc/cron.d/sysstat.

Without arguments, the `sar` command displays the CPU statistics taken every 10 minutes for the current day, as shown in the following output:

```
[root@server1 ~]# sar
Linux 2.6.33.3-85.fc13.i686.PAE (server1) 09/08/2010 _i686_ (2 CPU)
```

03:40:01 AM	CPU	%user	%nice	%system	%iowait	%steal	%idle
03:50:01 AM	all	0.06	0.00	0.13	0.27	0.00	99.54
04:00:01 AM	all	0.06	0.00	0.12	0.23	0.00	99.58
04:10:01 AM	all	0.08	0.00	0.14	0.19	0.00	99.60
04:20:01 AM	all	0.06	0.00	0.13	0.38	0.00	99.43
04:30:01 AM	all	0.06	0.00	0.12	0.20	0.00	99.61
04:40:01 AM	all	0.05	0.00	0.12	0.24	0.00	99.59
04:50:01 AM	all	0.06	0.00	0.12	0.21	0.00	99.61
05:00:01 AM	all	0.07	0.00	0.12	0.22	0.00	99.59
05:10:01 AM	all	0.08	0.00	0.13	0.19	0.00	99.59
05:20:01 AM	all	0.06	0.00	0.12	0.37	0.00	99.45
05:30:01 AM	all	0.07	0.00	0.12	0.20	0.00	99.61
05:40:01 AM	all	0.06	0.00	0.13	0.28	0.00	99.53
05:50:01 AM	all	0.06	0.00	0.12	0.22	0.00	99.60
06:00:01 AM	all	0.07	0.00	0.12	0.22	0.00	99.59
06:10:01 AM	all	0.08	0.00	0.14	0.18	0.00	99.60
06:20:01 AM	all	0.06	0.00	0.12	0.36	0.00	99.46
06:30:01 AM	all	0.07	0.00	0.13	0.20	0.00	99.60
06:40:01 AM	all	0.07	0.00	0.13	0.24	0.00	99.57
06:50:01 AM	all	0.06	0.00	0.13	0.26	0.00	99.56
07:00:01 AM	all	0.10	0.00	0.15	0.27	0.00	99.49
07:10:01 AM	all	0.09	0.00	0.15	0.31	0.00	99.45
07:20:01 AM	all	1.79	0.00	0.99	4.19	0.00	93.04
Average:	all	0.11	0.05	0.15	0.35	0.00	99.34

```
[root@server1 ~]# _
```

To view the CPU statistics for the sixth of the month, you can specify the pathname to the file using the `-f` option to the `sar` command:

```
[root@server1 ~]# sar -f /var/log/sa/sa06 | head
Linux 2.6.33.3-85.fc13.i686.PAE (server1) 09/06/2010 _i686_ (2 CPU)
```

12:00:01 AM	CPU	%user	%nice	%system	%iowait	%steal	%idle
12:10:01 AM	all	0.07	0.00	0.14	0.56	0.00	99.22
12:20:01 AM	all	0.07	0.00	0.14	0.51	0.00	99.28
12:30:01 AM	all	0.07	0.00	0.13	0.53	0.00	99.28
12:40:01 AM	all	0.06	0.00	0.13	0.58	0.00	99.22
12:50:01 AM	all	0.07	0.00	0.13	0.54	0.00	99.26
01:00:01 AM	all	0.07	0.00	0.13	0.58	0.00	99.22
01:10:01 AM	all	0.07	0.00	0.14	0.60	0.00	99.19

```
[root@server1 ~]# _
```

You must use the -f option to the sar command to view files in the /var/log/sa directory with the aforementioned filenames because they contain binary information. A sar text report is also written to the /var/log/sa/sar# file at the end of each day, where # represents the day of the month. To view a sar report file, you can use any text command, such as less.

As with the iostat and mpstat commands, the sar command can be used to take current system measurements. To take four CPU statistics every two seconds, you can use the following command:

```
[root@server1 ~]# sar 2 4
Linux 2.6.33.3-85.fc13.i686.PAE (server1) 09/08/2010 _i686_ (2 CPU)

08:24:41 AM    CPU   %user   %nice   %system   %iowait   %steal   %idle
08:24:43 AM    all   0.00    0.00    0.50      0.00      0.00     99.50
08:24:45 AM    all   0.00    0.00    0.25      0.00      0.00     99.75
08:24:47 AM    all   0.25    0.00    0.76      0.00      0.00     98.99
08:24:49 AM    all   0.00    0.00    0.27      0.00      0.00     99.73
Average:       all   0.06    0.00    0.45      0.00      0.00     99.49
[root@server1 ~]# _
```

Although the sar command displays CPU statistics by default, you can display different statistics by specifying options to the sar command. Table 14-1 lists common options used with the sar command.

From Table 14-1, you can see that the -b and -d options to the sar command display information similar to the output of the iostat command. In addition, the -u option displays CPU statistics equivalent to the output of the mpstat command.

Option	Description
-A	Displays the most information; this option is equivalent to all options
-b	Displays input/output statistics
-B	Displays swap statistics
-d	Displays input/output statistics for each block device on the system
-f file_name	Displays information from the specified file; these files typically reside in the /var/log/sa directory
-n ALL	Reports all network statistics
-o file_name	Saves the output to a file in binary format
-P CPU#	Specifies statistics for a single CPU (the first CPU is 0, the second CPU is 1, and so on)
-q	Displays statistics for the processor queue
-r	Displays memory and swap statistics
-R	Displays memory statistics
-u	Displays CPU statistics; this is the default action when no options are specified
-v	Displays kernel-related filesystem statistics
-W	Displays swapping statistics

Table 14-1 Common options to the sar command

Another important option to the sar command is –q, which shows processor queue statistics. A processor queue is an area of RAM that stores information temporarily for quick retrieval by the CPU. To view processor queue statistics every five seconds, you can execute the following command:

```
[root@server1 ~]# sar -q 1 5
Linux 2.6.33.3-85.fc13.i686.PAE (server1) 09/08/2010 _i686_ (2 CPU)

08:34:36 AM   runq-sz     plist-sz     ldavg-1      ldavg-5      ldavg-15
08:34:37 AM         0          252        0.00         0.00         0.00
08:34:38 AM         0          252        0.00         0.00         0.00
08:34:39 AM         0          252        0.00         0.00         0.00
08:34:40 AM         0          252        0.00         0.00         0.00
08:34:41 AM         0          252        0.00         0.00         0.00
Average:            0          252        0.00         0.00         0.00
[root@server1 ~]# _
```

The runq-sz (run queue size) indicates the number of processes that are waiting for execution on the processor run queue. For most Intel architectures, this number is typically 2 or less.

NOTE

A runq-sz much greater than 2 for long periods of time indicates that the CPU is too slow to respond to system requests.

The plist-sz (process list size) value indicates the number of processes currently running in memory, and the ldavg-1 (load average – 1 minute), ldavg-5 (load average – 5 minutes), and ldavg-15 (load average – 15 minutes) values represent an average CPU load for the last 1 minute, 5 minutes, and 15 minutes, respectively. These four statistics display an overall picture of processor activity. A rapid increase in these values is typically caused by CPU-intensive software that is running on the system.

Recall that all Linux systems use a swap partition to store information that cannot fit into physical memory; this information is sent to and from the swap partition in units called pages. The number of pages that are sent to the swap partition (pswpin/s) and the pages that are taken from the swap partition (pswpout/s) can be viewed using the –W option to the sar command, as shown in the following output:

```
[root@server1 ~]# sar -W 1 5
Linux 2.6.33.3-85.fc13.i686.PAE (server1) 09/08/2010 _i686_ (2 CPU)

08:37:01 AM      pswpin/s      pswpout/s
08:37:02 AM         0.00           0.00
08:37:03 AM         0.00           0.00
08:37:04 AM         0.00           0.00
08:37:05 AM         0.00           0.00
08:37:06 AM         0.00           0.00
Average:            0.00           0.00
[root@server1 ~]# _
```

If a large number of pages is being sent to and taken from the swap partition, the system will suffer from slower performance. To remedy this, you can add more physical memory (RAM) to the system.

Other Performance Monitoring Utilities

The sysstat package utilities are not the only performance monitoring utilities available in Fedora 13. The top utility discussed in Chapter 9 also displays CPU statistics, memory usage, swap usage, and average CPU load at the top of the screen, as shown next:

```
top - 08:40:07 up 22:43, 3 users, load average: 0.00, 0.00, 0.00
Tasks: 166 total, 1 running, 165 sleeping, 0 stopped, 0 zombie
Cpu(s): 0.5%us, 0.3%sy, 0.0%ni, 99.2%id, 0.0%wa, 0.0%hi, 0.0%si, 0.0%st
Mem:    961284k  total, 814576k used,  146708k free, 126036k buffers
Swap: 4095992k  total,    212k used, 4095780k free, 480740k cached

  PID   USER  PR NI  VIRT  RES  SHR S %CPU %MEM    TIME+  COMMAND
 5693   root  20  0  2696 1120  852 R  1.0  0.1  0:00.08  top
    1   root  20  0  2828 1312 1144 S  0.0  0.1  0:01.43  init
    2   root  20  0     0    0    0 S  0.0  0.0  0:00.00  kthreadd
    3   root  RT  0     0    0    0 S  0.0  0.0  0:00.01  migration/0
    4   root  20  0     0    0    0 S  0.0  0.0  0:00.11  ksoftirqd/0
    5   root  RT  0     0    0    0 S  0.0  0.0  0:00.00  watchdog/0
    6   root  RT  0     0    0    0 S  0.0  0.0  0:00.01  migration/1
    7   root  20  0     0    0    0 S  0.0  0.0  0:00.45  ksoftirqd/1
    8   root  RT  0     0    0    0 S  0.0  0.0  0:00.00  watchdog/1
    9   root  20  0     0    0    0 S  0.0  0.0  0:00.66  events/0
   10   root  20  0     0    0    0 S  0.0  0.0  0:00.57  events/1
   11   root  20  0     0    0    0 S  0.0  0.0  0:00.00  cpuset
   12   root  20  0     0    0    0 S  0.0  0.0  0:00.00  khelper
```

Furthermore, the **free command** can be used to display the total amounts of physical and swap memory (in Kilobytes) and their utilizations, as shown in the following output:

```
[root@server1 ~]# free
             total     used     free   shared  buffers    cached
Mem:        961284   814820   146464        0   126120    480740
-/+ buffers/cache:   207960   753324
Swap:      4095992      212  4095780
[root@server1 ~]# _
```

The Linux kernel reserves some memory for its own use (cached) to hold requests from hardware devices (buffers); the total memory in the preceding output is calculated with and without these values to indicate how much memory the system has reserved. The output from the preceding free command indicates that there is sufficient memory in the system because little swap is used and a great deal of free physical memory is available.

14

Like the free utility, the vmstat utility can be used to indicate whether more physical memory is required by measuring swap performance:

```
[root@server1 ~]#vmstat
procs --------- memory---------- -swap- --io--  system ----- cpu-----
 r b  swpd     free    buff   cache si so bi bo in cs us sy id wa st
 1 0   212   146496  126144  480752  0  0  5  2 49 51  0  0 99  0  0
[root@server1 ~]# _
```

The **vmstat command** shown previously indicates more information than the free command used earlier, including the following:

- The number of processes waiting to be run (r)
- The number of sleeping processes (b)
- The amount of swap memory used, in Kilobytes (swpd)
- The amount of free physical memory (free)
- The amount of memory used by buffers, in Kilobytes (buff)
- The amount of memory used as cache (cache)
- The amount of memory, in Kilobytes per second, swapped in to the disk (si)
- The amount of memory, in Kilobytes per second, swapped out to the disk (so)
- The number of blocks per second sent to block devices (bi)
- The number of blocks per second received from block devices (bo)
- The number of interrupts sent to the CPU per second (in)
- The number of context changes sent to the CPU per second (cs)
- The CPU user time (us)
- The CPU system time (sy)
- The CPU idle time (id)
- The time spent waiting for I/O (wa)
- The time stolen from a virtual machine (st)

Thus, the output from vmstat shown previously indicates that little swap memory is being used because swpd is 212KB, and si and so are both zero. However, it also indicates that the reason for this is that the system is not running many processes at the current time (r=1, id=99).

Security

In the past decade, hundreds of new services have been made available to Linux systems, and the number of Linux users has risen to tens of millions. In addition, Linux systems today are typically made available across networks such as the Internet. As a result, Linux is more prone today to security loopholes and attacks both locally and from across networks. To protect your Linux computer, you should take steps to improve local and network security as well as understand how to detect intruders who manage to breach your Linux system.

Securing the Local Computer

One of the most important security-related practices is to limit access to the physical Linux computer itself. If a malicious user has access to the Linux computer, that user could boot the computer using a floppy disk, USB flash drive, CD, or DVD that contains a small operating system and use it to access files on the partitions on the hard disk of the Linux computer without having to log in to the operating system installed on the hard disk. To prevent this, you should lock important computers, such as Linux servers, in a specific room to which only Linux administrators or trusted users have key access. This room is commonly called a **server closet**. Unfortunately, some Linux computers, such as Linux workstations, must be located in public areas. For these computers, you should remove the floppy, CD, and DVD drives from the computer. In addition, you should ensure that the boot order listed in the computer BIOS prevents booting from the USB ports, as well as ensure that a system BIOS password is set to prevent other users from changing the boot order.

Along these same lines, anyone who has access to the physical Linux computer could boot the computer and interact with the boot loader. This could allow a user to specify options that would boot the system in single user mode and gain root access to the system without specifying a password. To prevent this, simply ensure that you set a boot loader password in the LILO or GRUB configuration files, as discussed in Chapter 8.

Another important security consideration for Linux computers is to limit access to graphical desktops and shells. If you walk away from your workstation for a few minutes and leave yourself logged in to the system, another person can use your computer while you are away. To avoid such security breaches, it is good security practice to lock your desktop environment or exit your command-line shell before leaving the computer.

Both the GNOME and KDE desktop environments allow you to lock your screen. For the GNOME desktop, you can click the System menu and choose Lock Screen. To use your desktop again, you need to enter your password.

Although it is good practice to exit a command-line shell before leaving your workstation, doing so necessarily ends any background processes because the parent of those processes is your shell. If you run background processes that take a long time to complete, you can avoid problems associated with exiting the command-line shell by running the processes using the **nohup command**. This allows you to exit your command-line shell without ending any background processes. For example, to run the updatedb command and then exit your system (so that you can leave your workstation), perform the following commands:

```
[root@server1 ~]# nohup updatedb &
[1] 3773
nohup: ignoring input and appending output to 'nohup.out'
[root@server1 ~]# exit

Fedora release 13 (Goddard)
Kernel 2.6.33.3-85.fc13.i686.PAE on an i686 (tty2)

server1 login:
```

If you have root access to a Linux system, it is important to minimize the time that you are logged in as the root user to reduce the chance that another user can access your terminal if you accidentally leave your system without locking your desktop or exiting your shell. It is best practice to create a regular user account that you can use to check e-mails and perform other day-to-day tasks. You can then use the **su (switch user) command** to obtain root access only when you need to perform an administrative task. When you are finished, you can use the exit command to return to your previous shell where you are logged in as a regular user account, as shown in the following output:

```
[user1@server1 ~]$ su - root
Password: ******
[root@server1 ~]# _
[root@server1 ~]# rm -f /etc/securetty
[root@server1 ~]# exit
[user1@server1 ~]$ _
```

The – option to the su command shown in the preceding output loads the root user's environment variables. Also, you can omit the root user's name in the preceding output; if a name is not specified as an argument to the su command, the root user is assumed by default.

If you only intend to run one command as the root user, you can instead choose to use the –c option to the su command; this returns you to your current shell automatically. The following demonstrates how to run the root command shown in the previous output using the –c option to the su command:

```
[user1@server1 ~]$ su –c "rm –f /etc/securetty" root
Password: ******
[user1@server1 ~]$ _
```

The root user can use the su command to switch to any other user account without specifying the user account password.

Still, some users, such as software developers, need to run certain commands as the root user in certain situations. Instead of giving them the root password, it is best to give them the ability to run certain commands as the root user via the **sudo command**. The sudo command checks the /etc/sudoers file to see if you have rights to run a certain command as a different user. The following /etc/sudoers file gives two software developers, mary and bob, the ability to run the kill and killall commands as the root user on the computers server1 and server2:

```
[root@server1 ~]# cat /etc/sudoers
User_Alias SD = mary, bob
Cmnd_Alias KILL = /bin/kill, /usr/bin/killall
Host_Alias SERVERS = server1, server2

SD  SERVERS = (root) KILL
[root@server1 ~]# _
```

Now, if mary needs to kill the cron daemon on server1 (which was started as the root user) to test a program that she wrote, she needs to use the sudo command, as shown in the following output, and supply her own password:

```
[mary@server1 ~]$ ps –ef |grep crond
root  2281  1 0 21:20 ?  00:00:00 crond
[mary@server1 ~]$ kill -9 2281
-bash: kill: (2281) - Operation not permitted
```

```
[mary@server1 ~]$ sudo kill -9 2281
[sudo] password for mary: ******
[mary@server1 ~]$ _
```

Protecting Against Network Attacks

Recall from earlier in this chapter that network services listen for network traffic on a certain port number and interact with that traffic. As long as network services exist on a computer, there is always the possibility that hackers can manipulate the network service by interacting with it in unusual ways. One example of this type of network attack is a **buffer overrun**, which can replace program information used by the network service in memory with new program information, consequently altering how the network service operates.

Network Security Essentials The first step to securing your computer against network attacks such as buffer overruns is to minimize the number of network services running. If you run only the minimum number of network services necessary for your organization, you greatly reduce the chance of network attacks. To see what network services are running on your network, you can run the **nmap (network mapper) command. The following output demonstrates how** nmap **can be used to determine the number of services running on the server1 computer:**

```
[root@server1 ~]# nmap -sT server1.class.com

Starting Nmap 5.21 ( http://nmap.org ) at 2010-09-08 09:16 EDT
Nmap scan report for server1.class.com (127.0.0.1)
Host is up (0.00086s latency).
Not shown: 988 closed ports
PORT        STATE      SERVICE
22/tcp      open       ssh
23/tcp      open       telnet
25/tcp      open       smtp
111/tcp     open       rpcbind
139/tcp     open       netbios-ssn
445/tcp     open       microsoft-ds
513/tcp     open       login
514/tcp     open       shell
631/tcp     open       ipp
873/tcp     open       rsync
901/tcp     open       samba-swat
6000/tcp    open       X11
Nmap done: 1 IP address (1 host up) scanned in 0.20 seconds
[root@server1 ~]# _
```

From the preceding output, you can determine which services are running on your computer by viewing the service name or by searching the descriptions for the port numbers in the /etc/services file or on the Internet. For services that are not needed, ensure that they are not started automatically when entering your runlevel. For daemons started by the Internet Super Daemon, simply add the `disable = yes` to the appropriate file within the /etc/xinetd.d directory and restart the Internet Super Daemon. For stand-alone daemons, use the `chkconfig` or `ntsysv` command to prevent the daemon from starting in the runlevel.

For services that must be used because they are essential to your organization, you can take certain steps to ensure that they are as secure as possible. You should ensure that network service daemons are not run as the root user on the system when possible. If a hacker gains access to your system via a network service daemon run as the root user, the hacker has root access as well. Many network daemons, such as Apache, set the user account by which they execute in their configuration files.

Similarly, for daemons such as Apache that run as a non-root user, you should ensure that the shell listed in /etc/passwd for the daemon is set to /sbin/nologin. If a hacker attempted to remotely log in to the system using a well-known daemon account, the hacker would not be able to get a BASH shell. Instead, the /sbin/nologin simply prints the warning listed in the /etc/nologin.txt file to the screen and exits. If the /etc/nologin.txt file doesn't exist, the /sbin/nologin program prints a standard warning.

In addition, because network attacks are reported in the open source community, new versions of network services usually include fixes for known network attacks. As such, these new versions are more resilient to network attacks. Because of this, it is good form to periodically check for new versions of network services, install them, and check the associated documentation for new security-related parameters that can be set in the configuration file.

If you use network services that are started by the Internet Super Daemon, you can use TCP wrappers to provide extra security. A **TCP wrapper** is a program (/usr/sbin/tcpd) that can start a network daemon. To enable TCP wrappers, you must modify the appropriate file in the /etc/xinetd.d directory and start the network daemon as an argument to the TCP wrapper. For the telnet daemon, you modify the /etc/xinetd.d/telnet file, as shown in the following example:

```
[root@server1 ~]# cat /etc/xinetd.d/telnet
# default: on
# description: The telnet server serves telnet sessions; it uses \
#         unencrypted username/password pairs for authentication.
service telnet
{
        flags                = REUSE
        socket_type          = stream
        wait                 = no
        user                 = root
        server               = /usr/sbin/tcpd
        server_args          = /usr/sbin/in.telnetd
        log_on_failure       += USERID
        disable              = no
}
[root@server1 ~]# _
```

Now, the telnet daemon (/usr/sbin/in.telnetd) will be started by the TCP wrapper (/usr/sbin/tcpd). Before a TCP wrapper starts a network daemon, it first checks the /etc/hosts.allow and /etc/hosts.deny files. This allows you to restrict the network service such that it can only be accessed by certain hosts within your organization. The following /etc/hosts.allow and /etc/hosts.deny files only give the computers client1 and client2 the ability to use the tel-net utility to connect to your telnet server.

```
[root@server1 ~]# cat /etc/hosts.deny
in.telnetd: ALL
[root@server1 ~]# _
[root@server1 ~]# cat /etc/hosts.allow
in.telnetd: client1, client2
[root@server1 ~]# _
```

Another important component of network security involves local file permissions. If every-one had read permission on the /etc/shadow file, any user could read the encrypted pass-words for all user accounts, including the root user, and possibly decrypt the password using a decryption program. Fortunately, the default permissions on the /etc/shadow file allow read permission for the root user only to minimize this possibility. However, similar permission problems exist with many other important files, and hackers typically exploit these files as a result. Thus, you need to carefully examine the permissions on files and direc-tories associated with system and network services.

Take, for example, the Apache Web server discussed earlier in this chapter. Apache daemons are run as the user apache and the group apache by default. These daemons read HTML files from the document root directory such that they can give the information to client Web browsers. The following directory listing from a sample document root directory shows that the Apache daemons also have write permission because they own the index.html file:

```
[root@server1 ~]# ls -l /var/www/html
total 64
-rw-r- - r- - 1 apache apache 61156 Sep 5 08:36 index.html
[root@server1 ~]# _
```

Thus, if a hacker was able to manipulate an Apache daemon, the hacker would have write access to the index.html file and would be able to modify it. It is secure practice to ensure that the index.html is owned by the Web developer (who needs to modify the file), and that the Apache daemons are given read access only through membership in the other category. If your Web developer logs in to the system as the user account webdev, you could perform the following commands to change the permissions on the Web content and verify the results:

```
[root@server1 ~]# chown webma:webma /var/www/html/index.html
[root@server1 root]# ls -l /var/www/html
total 64
-rw-r- - r- - 1 webmawebma  61156 Sep 5 08:36 index.html
[root@server1 ~]# _
```

Configuring a Firewall Another method that you can use to ensure that network ser-vices are as secure as possible is to configure a firewall on your Linux computer using **netfilter/iptables**. Recall from Chapter 1 that firewalls can be used in your organization to block unwanted network traffic; as a result, firewalls are typically enabled on router interfaces.

Netfilter/iptables discards certain network packets according to **chains** of **rules** that are stored in your computer's memory. By default, you can specify firewall rules for three types of chains:

- INPUT chain, for network packets destined for your computer
- FORWARD chain, for network packets that must pass through your computer (if you are a router)
- OUTPUT chain, for network packets that originate from your computer

Netfilter/iptables can also be used to configure a Linux computer with two or more NICs as a NAT router. To do this, you would use the PREROUTING, OUTPUT, and POSTROUTING chains. Consult the iptables manual page for more information.

By default, no rules exist for the INPUT, FORWARD, or OUTPUT chains after a Fedora 13 installation. To create rules that are used for each chain, you must use the **iptables** command. Rules can be based on the source IP address, destination IP address, protocol used (TCP, UDP, ICMP), or packet status. For example, to flush all previous rules from memory, to specify that forwarded packets are dropped by default, and to specify that packets are to be forwarded only if they originate from the 192.168.1.0 network, you can use the following commands:

```
[root@server1 ~]# iptables -F
[root@server1 ~]# iptables -P FORWARD DROP
[root@server1 ~]# iptables -A FORWARD -s 192.168.1.0/24 -j ACCEPT
[root@server1 ~]# _
```

You can then verify the list of rules for each chain in memory by using the following command:

```
[root@server1 ~]# iptables -L
Chain INPUT (policy ACCEPT)
Target      prot opt source           destination

Chain FORWARD (policy DROP)
target      prot opt source           destination
ACCEPT      all  --  192.168.1.0/24   anywhere

Chain OUTPUT (policy ACCEPT)
Target      prot opt source           destination
[root@server1 ~]# _
```

The previous firewall example uses static packet filtering rules. Most technologies today start by using a specific port and then switch to a random port above 30000. A good example of this is SSH. The first SSH packet is addressed to port 22, but the port number is changed in the return packet to a random port above 30000 for subsequent traffic. In a static filter, you would need to allow traffic for all ports above 30000 in order to use SSH.

Instead of doing this, you can use a dynamic (or stateful) packet filter rule by specifying the -m state option to the iptables command. **Stateful packet filters** remember traffic that was originally allowed in an existing session and adjust their rules appropriately. For example, to take all packets from your internal interface eth1 that are addressed to port 22 and

Option	Description
-s address	Specifies the source address of packets for a rule.
-d address	Specifies the destination address of packets for a rule.
-sport port#	Specifies the source port number for a rule.
-dport port#	Specifies the destination port number for a rule.
-p protocol	Specifies the protocol type for a rule.
-i interface	Specifies the input network interface.
-o interface	Specifies the output network interface.
-j action	Specifies the action that is taken for a rule.
-m match	Specifies a match parameter that should be used within the rule. The most common match used is state, which creates a stateful packet filtering firewall.
-A chain	Specifies the chain used.
-L chain	Lists rules for a certain chain. If no chain is given, all chains are listed.
-P policy	Specifies the default policy for a certain chain type.
-D number	Deletes a rule for a chain specified by additional arguments. Rules start at number 1.
-R number	Replaces a rule for a chain specified by additional arguments. Rules start at number 1.
-F chain	Removes all rules for a certain chain. If no chain is specified, it removes all rules for all chains.

Table 14-2   Common iptables options

forward them to your external interface eth0 on your Linux router, you could use the following command:

```
[root@server1 ~]# iptables –A FORWARD –i eth1 –o eth0 –m state
   -state NEW -dport 22 –j ACCEPT
[root@server1 ~]# _
```

Next, you can allow all subsequent packets that are part of an allowed existing session, as shown in the following output. (Remember that only SSH is allowed.)

```
[root@server1 ~]# iptables –A FORWARD –i eth1 –o eth0 –m state
   -state ESTABLISHED,RELATED –j ACCEPT
[root@server1 ~]# _
```

 **NOTE** Because chains and rules are stored in memory, they are lost when your computer is shut down. To ensure that they are loaded on each boot, simply run the service iptables save command to save all current chains and rules to the /etc/sysconfig/iptables file. All entries in this file are loaded by netfilter/iptables at boot time.

Table 14-2 provides a list of common options to the iptables command.

Because firewall rules can quickly become complex, it is often easier to use a graphical utility to configure them. The Firewall Configuration utility shown in Figure 14-4 automatically

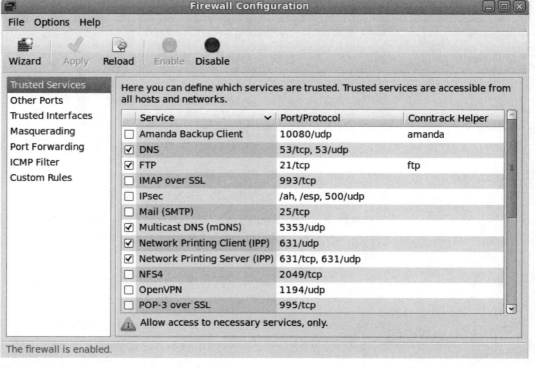

Figure 14-4 The Firewall Configuration utility

Source: Course Technology/Cengage Learning

creates netfilter/iptables rules based on your selections and saves them to /etc/sysconfig/iptables so that they are loaded at each boot. You can start the Firewall Configuration utility within the GNOME Desktop Environment by opening the System menu and navigating to Administration, Firewall.

Older Linux kernels (version 2.2.36 and earlier) used the `ipchains` command to provide firewall services. This utility is not supported by the Linux kernel in Fedora 13.

Configuring SELinux   By default, **Security Enhanced Linux (SELinux)** is configured and enabled during a Fedora 13 installation. SELinux is a series of kernel patches and utilities created by the National Security Agency (NSA) that enforces role-based security on your system using security profiles and policies that prevent applications from being used to access resources and system components in insecure ways.

To learn more about SELinux, visit *www.nsa.gov/research/selinux/index.shtml.*

To enable SELinux, you can edit the /etc/selinux/config file and set one of the following SELINUX options:

- SELINUX = enforcing (policy settings are enforced by SELinux)
- SELINUX = permissive (SELinux generates warnings only and logs events)
- SELINUX = disabled (SELinux is disabled)

Next, you can select a SELinux policy by configuring one of the following SELINUXTYPE options within the /etc/selinux/config file:

- SELINUXTYPE = targeted (only targeted network daemons are protected)
- SELINUXTYPE = strict (all daemons are protected)

By default, Fedora 13 has definitions for the targeted policy that protect the system from malicious applications that can damage system files or compromise security. After modifying the /etc/selinux/config file to enable SELinux, you must reboot to relabel the system for the changes to take effect. Once enabled, you can modify the SELinux targeted policy settings by modifying the files within the /etc/selinux/targeted directory.

To configure SELinux within a desktop environment, you can use the SELinux Administration utility. To start this utility within the GNOME Desktop Dnvironment, open the System menu and navigate to Administration, SELinux Management.

You can also create your own custom SELinux policies using the SELinux Policy Generator Tool utility. To start this utility within the GNOME Desktop Environment, simply open the Applications menu and navigate to System Tools, SELinux Policy Generation Tool.

You can use the **sestatus command** to view your current SELinux status:

```
[root@server1 ~]# sestatus -v
SELinux status:             enabled
SELinuxfs mount:            /selinux
Current mode:               enforcing
Mode from config file:      enforcing
Policy version:             24
Policy from config file:    targeted

Process contexts:
Current context:            unconfined_u:unconfined_r:unconfined_t:s0-s0:
                            c0.c1023
Init context:               system_u:system_r:init_t:s0
/sbin/mingetty              system_u:system_r:getty_t:s0
/usr/sbin/sshd              system_u:system_r:sshd_t:s0-s0:c0.c1023

File contexts:
Controlling term:           unconfined_u:object_r:user_devpts_t:s0
/etc/passwd                 system_u:object_r:etc_t:s0
/etc/shadow                 system_u:object_r:shadow_t:s0
```

14

```
/bin/bash                 system_u:object_r:shell_exec_t:s0
/bin/login                system_u:object_r:login_exec_t:s0
/bin/sh                   system_u:object_r:bin_t:s0 -> system_u:
                          object_r:shell_exec_t:s0

/sbin/agetty              system_u:object_r:getty_exec_t:s0
/sbin/init                system_u:object_r:init_exec_t:s0
/sbin/mingetty            system_u:object_r:getty_exec_t:s0
/usr/sbin/sshd            system_u:object_r:sshd_exec_t:s0
/lib/libc.so.6            system_u:object_r:lib_t:s0 -> system_u:
                          object_r:lib_t:s0

/lib/ld-linux.so.2        system_u:object_r:lib_t:s0 -> system_u:
                          object_r:ld_so_t:s0

[root@server1 ~]# _
```

To view any warnings or alerts generated by SELinux regarding unsafe application access, you can use the SELinux Troubleshooter utility within a desktop environment. To start this utility within the GNOME Desktop Environment, open the Applications menu and navigate to System Tools, SELinux Troubleshooter.

Using Encryption to Protect Network Data

Because network packets pass through many different computers and network devices, the data within them could easily be intercepted and read by hackers. To prevent this, many technologies use an encryption algorithm to protect the data before it is transmitted on the network. An encryption algorithm uses a series of mathematical steps in sequence to scramble data. Because the steps within encryption algorithms are widely known, nearly all encryption algorithms use a random component called a **key** to modify the steps within the algorithm.

Network technologies typically use **asymmetric encryption** to protect the data that travels across the network. Asymmetric encryption uses a pair of keys that are uniquely generated on each system: a **public key** and a **private key**. You can think of a public key as the opposite of a private key. If you encrypt data using a public key, that data can only be decrypted using the matching private key. Alternatively, if you encrypt data using a private key, that data can only be decrypted using the matching public key. Each system must contain at least one public/private key pair. The public key is freely distributed to any other host on the network, whereas the private key is used only by the system and never distributed.

Say, for example, that you want to send an encrypted message from your computer (host A) to another computer (host B). Your computer would first obtain the public key from host B and use it to encrypt the message. Next, your computer will send the encrypted message across the network to host B, at which point host B uses its private key to decrypt the message. Because host B is the only computer on the network that possesses the private key that matches the public key that you used to encrypt the message, host B is the only computer on the network that can decrypt the message.

You can also use private keys to authenticate a message. If host A encrypts a message using its private key and sends that message to host B, host B (and any other host on the network) can easily obtain the matching public key from host A to decrypt the message. By successfully decrypting the message, host B has proved that it must have been encrypted using host A's private key. Because host A is the only computer on the network that possesses this private key, host B has proven that the message was sent by host A and not another computer that has impersonated the message.

A message that has been encrypted using a private key is called a **digital signature**.

The two most common technologies that provide asymmetric encryption on Linux systems are Secure Shell (SSH) and **GNU Privacy Guard (GPG)**.

Working with SSH   Recall from Chapter 12 that SSH allows you to securely administer a remote Linux system by encrypting all traffic that passes between the two computers. By default, SSH uses the **Rivest Shamir Adleman (RSA)** asymmetric algorithm to encrypt data and the **Digital Signature Algorithm (DSA)** asymmetric algorithm to digitally sign data.

System wide RSA and DSA public/private key pairs are generated the first time the SSH daemon is started. These key pairs are stored in the /etc/ssh directory for all future sessions:

- ssh_host_dsa_key contains the DSA private key.
- ssh_host_rsa_key contains the RSA private key.
- ssh_host_dsa_key.pub contains the DSA public key.
- ssh_host_rsa_key.pub contains the RSA public key.

For remote administration, the system wide keys are sufficient, but SSH can also be used to protect the network traffic used by other network services by enclosing the network traffic within encrypted SSH packets (a process called **tunneling**). SSH tunnels are used by a wide variety of programs today.

The most basic type of SSH tunnel involves sending X Windows traffic over an SSH session. To do this, you can simply add the –X option to the ssh command when connecting to a remote computer. Any graphical utilities that you execute during the SSH session will be tunneled to X Windows on your computer.

14

Most programs that use SSH tunnels require that all users have their own SSH keys. Recall from Chapter 12 that the ssh-keygen command can generate or regenerate SSH keys. If you run the ssh-keygen –t rsa command, the following files will be created in the ~/.ssh directory:

- id_rsa contains the user's RSA private key.
- id_rsa.pub contains the user's RSA public key.

Alternatively, if you run the ssh-keygen –t dsa command, the following files will be created in the ~/.ssh directory:

- id_dsa contains the user's DSA private key.
- id_dsa.pub contains the user's DSA public key.

The `ssh-keygen` command prompts you to choose an optional passphrase that protects the private key. If you set a passphrase, you will need to enter the passphrase each time that the private key is used.

These keys can then be used to secure communication to other computers. However, each user will need to authenticate to other computers before SSH is used to encrypt the data. Because private keys can also be used as a form of authentication, you can create an **SSH identity** (using the **ssh-add command**) for your user account and use the **SSH agent** (`ssh-agent`) to automatically authenticate to other computers using digital signatures. In Fedora 13, the SSH agent and SSH identities are provided by the GNOME keyring daemon (`gnome-keyring-daemon`) and managed by the Passwords and Encryption Keys utility shown in Figure 14-5. You can start this utility within the GNOME Desktop Environment by opening the Applications menu and navigating to Accessories, Passwords and Encryption Keys.

Working with GPG   GPG is an open source version of the Pretty Good Privacy (PGP) system, which was popular in the 1990s for encrypting e-mail and e-mail attachments prior to sending them to other hosts on the Internet. Each GPG user has a public/private key pair, which is used for encryption as well as authentication. GPG authentication uses a trust model that involves users digitally signing other users' public keys with their private keys. Say, for example, that UserA has digitally signed UserB's public key and vice versa. This allows UserA and UserB to send and receive e-mail without requiring authentication. If UserB digitally signs UserC's public key and vice versa, then UserA, UserB, and UserC can send and receive e-mail without requiring authentication.

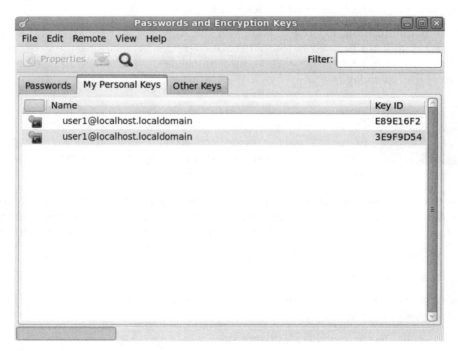

Figure 14-5 The Passwords and Encryption Keys utility

Source: Course Technology/Cengage Learning

Like SSH, GPG typically uses RSA and DSA key pairs for asymmetric encryption and digital signing, respectively. These keys and associated GPG configuration options are stored within the ~/.gnupg directory for each user.

Although you can manage keys, encrypt data, and digitally sign other users' public keys using the **gpg command**, it is much easier to use a graphical utility such as the Passwords and Encryption Keys utility within Fedora 13. Additionally, many graphical e-mail programs for Linux, such as Evolution and Thunderbird, have built-in GPG management tools and wizards that allow you to easily configure GPG keys.

Detecting Intrusion

Although you can take many security precautions on your Linux computers, there is always the chance that someone will gain access to your system either locally or from across a network. Fortunately, log files contain information or irregularities that can indicate if an intrusion has indeed occurred. To get the full benefit of the information stored in log files, you should regularly analyze the log files in the /var/log directory associated with the network services that are run on your computer.

At minimum, you should review system log files associated with authentication to detect whether unauthorized users have logged in to the system. Network applications that authenticate users typically do so via **Pluggable Authentication Modules (PAM)**. PAM logs information to the /var/log/secure file; thus, you should regularly check this file for PAM errors and alerts. You should also check the /var/log/wtmp log file, which lists users who logged in to the system and received a BASH shell. Because this file is in binary format, you must use the who /var/log/wtmp command to view it, as shown in the following output:

```
[root@server1 ~]# who /var/log/wtmp
user1          pts/0             2010-09-05 11:21 (:0.0)
root           pts/1             2010-09-05 11:40 (10.0.1.3)
root           pts/1             2010-09-05 16:41 (10.0.1.3)
root           pts/1             2010-09-06 09:19 (10.0.1.3)
root           tty2              2010-09-06 10:16
postgres       tty2              2010-09-06 10:17
user1          tty1              2010-09-06 15:11 (:0)
root           pts/0             2010-09-06 15:23 (10.0.1.3)
user1          pts/1             2010-09-06 17:21 (:0.0)
user1          tty1              2010-09-07 09:58 (:0)
root           pts/0             2010-09-07 09:58 (10.0.1.3)
root           tty2              2010-09-07 10:01
root           pts/0             2010-09-07 18:06 (10.0.1.3)
root           pts/0             2010-09-08 06:58 (10.0.1.3)
root           pts/0             2010-09-08 11:51 (10.0.1.3)
user1          tty1              2010-09-08 15:05 (:0)
root           pts/0             2010-09-08 15:08 (10.0.1.3)
user1          pts/1             2010-09-08 15:11 (:0.0)
user1          tty1              2010-09-08 15:22 (:0)
root           pts/0             2010-09-08 15:23 (10.0.1.3)
root           tty3              2010-09-08 15:25
user1          pts/1             2010-09-08 15:25 (:0.0)
[root@server1 ~]# _
```

14

If a hacker has gained access to your system, the hacker has likely changed certain files on the hard disk to gain more access, modify sensitive data, or vandalize services. The **lsof (list open files) command** can be used to list files that are currently being edited by users and system processes. Thus, you could use the lsof | grep root command to list the files that are currently open on the system by the root user. If there are key configuration files listed in the output that you are not currently editing, a hacker may have compromised your system.

Hackers often use a buffer overrun exploit to attempt to create executable files within the filesystem that are owned by the root user and have the SUID bit set. This allows the executable program to be run as the root user and gain access to the entire Linux system. As a result, you should periodically search for files on the filesystem that have the SUID bit set using the find / -type f –perm +4000 command.

Not all exploits need to be performed as the root user. For example, hackers may use a malicious program that a user downloads to create a .forward file in the user's home directory. Any e-mail that the user receives will then be forwarded to the e-mail address listed in the ~/.forward file, which is usually an e-mail server that contains a script that records the user's e-mail address and sends unwanted e-mail on that user's behalf. To prevent this type of attack, you can create an empty .forward file in each user's home directory that is owned by the root user and has a mode of 000 to prevent users from modifying it.

If you create and run custom shell scripts to perform security checks, you can use the **logger command** to create entries in system log files via the rsyslog daemon that alert you to potential problems.

Because the list of potential files that hackers can modify on a system is large, many Linux administrators use a program, such as **tripwire**, to check the integrity of important files and directories. To configure tripwire to check for altered files and directories, you can perform the following steps:

1. Install tripwire using the yum install tripwire command if it was not installed during the Fedora 13 installation.

2. Edit the /etc/tripwire/twpol.txt file and change the line HOSTNAME=localhost. localdomain; to HOSTNAME=yourhostname;.

3. Run the tripwire-setup-keyfiles command and enter both a local and a site passphrase when prompted. A passphrase is a password used to administer tripwire later on and will be required when running any tripwire-related program. The /etc/tripwire/tw.cfg binary file will be created with default tripwire settings for monitoring your system. You'll find the same settings exist in the /etc/tripwire/twcfg.txt text file. You can choose to modify those settings and then use the twadmin command to save the modified settings to the /etc/tripwire/tw.cfg file.

4. Run the tripwire --init command to create a tripwire database with settings from the files and directories specified in /etc/tripwire/tw.cfg.

5. Run the tripwire --check command periodically in the future to analyze the files and directories in the /etc/tripwire/tw.cfg file against the settings in the tripwire database to see if any files were modified.

Name	Description
Advanced Intrusion Detection Environment (AIDE)	An alternative to tripwire that has added functionality for checking the integrity of files and directories.
Integrity Checking Utility (ICU)	A PERL-based program that is designed to work with AIDE to check the integrity of Linux computers remotely across a network.
PortSentry	An IDS that monitors traffic on ports and allows you to detect whether hackers are probing your ports using port scanning utilities such as nmap.
Snort Airsnort	A complex IDS that can be used to capture and monitor network packets. It can be used to detect a wide range of network attacks and port probing.
Linux Intrusion Detection System (LIDS)	An IDS that involves modifying the Linux kernel to increase process and file security as well as detect security breaches.
Simple WATCHer (SWATCH)	An IDS that monitors log files and alerts administrators when an intrusion is detected.

Table 14-3   **Common Linux Intrusion Detection Systems**

Because tripwire can be used to detect intruders on a Linux system, it is referred to as an **intrusion detection system (IDS)**. Several IDS programs are available for Linux that can be used to detect hackers who are trying to gain access to your system or have done so already. Table 14-3 lists some common IDS programs.

Chapter Summary

- After installation, Linux administrators monitor the system, perform proactive and reactive maintenance, and document important system information.

- Common troubleshooting procedures involve collecting data to isolate and determine the cause of system problems, as well as implementing and testing solutions that can be documented for future use.

- Invalid hardware settings, absence of device drivers, and hard disk failure are common hardware-related problems on Linux systems.

- Software-related problems can be further categorized as application-related or operating system-related.

- Program limits and absence of program dependencies or shared libraries are common application-related problems, whereas X Windows, boot failure, and filesystem corruption are common operating system-related problems.

- Users can use assistive technologies to modify their desktop experience to suit their needs.

- System performance is affected by a variety of hardware and software factors, including the amount of RAM, CPU speed, and process load.

- Using performance monitoring utilities to create a baseline is helpful when diagnosing performance problems in the future. The sysstat package contains many useful performance monitoring commands.

14

- Securing a Linux computer involves improving local and network security as well as monitoring to detect intruders.

- By restricting access to your Linux computer and using the root account only when required via the su and sudo commands, you greatly improve local Linux security.

- Reducing the number of network services, implementing firewalls, enabling SELinux, performing service updates, using encryption, preventing services from running as the root user, restricting permissions on key files, and using TCP wrappers can greatly reduce the chance of network attacks.

- Analyzing log files and key system files as well as running IDS applications such as tripwire can be used to detect intruders.

Key Terms

/etc/ld.so.cache   The file that contains the location of shared library files.

/etc/ld.so.conf   The file that contains a list of directories that contain shared libraries.

assistive technologies   Software programs that cater to specific user needs.

asymmetric encryption   A type of encryption that uses a key pair to encrypt and decrypt data.

baseline   A measure of normal system activity.

BBC Linux   A small CD/DVD-based Linux distribution.

buffer overrun   An attack in which a network service is altered in memory.

bus mastering   The process by which peripheral components perform tasks normally executed by the CPU.

chains   The components of a firewall that specify the general type of network traffic to which rules apply.

digital signature   Information that has been encrypted using a private key.

Digital Signature Algorithm (DSA)   A common asymmetric encryption algorithm that is primarily used for creating digital signatures.

documentation   The system information that is stored in a log book for future reference.

file handles   The connections that a program makes to files on a filesystem.

`free` **command**   A command used to display memory and swap statistics.

`gpg` **command**   A command used to create and manage GPG keys.

GNU Privacy Guard (GPG)   An open source asymmetric encryption technology that is primarily used by e-mail programs.

Intrusion Detection System (IDS)   A program that can be used to detect unauthorized access to a Linux system.

`iostat (input/output statistics)` **command**   A command that displays input/output statistics for block devices.

`iptables` **command**   The command used to configure a firewall in Fedora Linux.

jabbering   The process by which failing hardware components send large amounts of information to the CPU.

key   A unique piece of information that is used within an encryption algorithm.

Knoppix Linux   A CD/DVD-based Linux distribution.

`ldconfig` **command**   The command that updates the /etc/ld.so.conf and /etc/ld.so.cache files.

`ldd` **command**   The command used to display the shared libraries used by a certain program.

`logger` **command**   A command that can be used to write system log events via the System Log Daemon (rsyslogd).

`lsof (list open files)` **command**   The command that lists the files that are currently being viewed or modified by software programs and users.

`lspci` **command**   The command that lists the hardware devices that are currently attached to the PCI bus on the system.

`lsusb` **command**   The command that lists the USB devices that are currently plugged into the system.

monitoring   The process by which system areas are observed for problems or irregularities.

`mpstat (multiple processor statistics)` **command**   A command that displays CPU statistics.

netfilter/iptables   The Linux kernel components and related software subsystem that provide firewall and NAT capability on modern Linux systems.

`nmap (network mapper)` **command**   A command that can be used to scan ports on network computers.

`nohup` **command**   A command that prevents other commands from exiting when the parent process is killed.

Orca   A Linux software program that provides several assistive technologies to desktop environment users.

Pluggable Authentication Modules (PAM)   The component that handles authentication requests by daemons on a Linux system.

private key   An asymmetric encryption key that is used to decrypt data and create digital signatures.

proactive maintenance   The measures taken to reduce future system problems.

public key   An asymmetric encryption key that is used to encrypt data and decrypt digital signatures.

reactive maintenance   The measures taken when system problems arise.

Rivest Shamir Adleman (RSA)   A common asymmetric encryption algorithm.

rules   The components of a firewall that match specific network traffic that is to be allowed or dropped.

`sar (system activity reporter)` **command**   The command that displays various system statistics.

Security Enhanced Linux (SELinux)   A set of Linux kernel components and related software packages that prevent malicious software from executing on a Linux system.

server closet   A secured room that stores servers within an organization.

`sestatus` **command**   The command that displays the current status and functionality of the SELinux subsystem.

`ssh-add` **command**   The command that users can use to add an SSH identity to their user account.

SSH agent   A software program that can be used to automatically authenticate users using their private key.

14

SSH identity A unique configuration for a user account that is associated with user-specific SSH keys.

stateful packet filter A packet filter that applies rules to related packets within the same network session.

su (switch user) command A command that can be used to switch your current user account to another.

sudo command A command that is used to perform commands as another user via entries in the /etc/sudoers file.

System Statistics (sysstat) package A software package that contains common performance monitoring utilities, such as mpstat, iostat, and sar.

TCP wrapper A program that can be used to run a network daemon with additional security via the /etc/hosts.allow and /etc/hosts.deny files.

tripwire A common IDS for Linux that monitors files and directories.

troubleshooting procedures The tasks performed when solving system problems.

tunneling The process of embedding network packets within other network packets.

ulimit command The command used to modify process limit parameters in the current shell.

vmstat command The command used to display memory, CPU, and swap statistics.

Review Questions

1. On which part of the maintenance cycle do Linux administrators spend the most time?

    a. monitoring

    b. proactive maintenance

    c. reactive maintenance

    d. documentation

2. Which of the following files is likely to be found in the /var/log/sa directory over time?

    a. 15

    b. sa39

    c. sa19

    d. 00

3. The lspci command can be used to isolate problems with X Windows. True or False?

4. Which of the following commands can be used to display memory statistics? (Choose all that apply.)

    a. free

    b. sar

    c. vmstat

    d. iostat

5. Which command indicates the shared libraries required by a certain executable program?

   a. `ldconfig`

   b. `ldd`

   c. `rpm -V`

   d. `slconfig`

6. RSA is a common symmetric encryption algorithm used by SSH and GPG. True or False?

7. What type of netfilter/iptables chain targets traffic that is destined for the local computer?

   a. INPUT

   b. ROUTE

   c. FORWARD

   d. OUTPUT

8. Which of the following steps is not a common troubleshooting procedure?

   a. Test the solution.

   b. Isolate the problem.

   c. Delegate responsibility.

   d. Collect information.

9. Which of the following Linux intrusion detection systems can be used to detect port scans? (Choose all that apply.)

   a. ICU

   b. PortSentry

   c. tripwire

   d. Snort

10. Which file contains information regarding the users, computers, and commands used by the `sudo` command?

   a. /etc/sudo

   b. /etc/su.cfg

   c. /etc/sudo.cfg

   d. /etc/sudoers

14

11. Which command can increase the number of file handles that programs can open in a shell?

   a. `ldd`

   b. `ulimit`

   c. `lba32`

   d. `top`

12. The private key is used when creating a digital signature. True or False?

13. Which of the following actions should you first take to secure your Linux computer against network attacks?

    a. Change permissions on key system files.

    b. Ensure that only necessary services are running.

    c. Run a checksum for each file used by network services.

    d. Configure entries in the /etc/sudoers file.

14. What will the command sar -W 3 50 do?

    a. Take 3 swap statistics every 50 seconds.

    b. Take 50 swap statistics every 3 seconds.

    c. Take 3 CPU statistics every 50 seconds.

    d. Take 50 CPU statistics every 3 seconds.

15. Which of the following commands can be used to scan the available ports on computers within your organization?

    a. traceroute

    b. tracert

    c. nmap

    d. sudo

16. Which of the following are common assistive technologies? (Choose all that apply.)

    a. mouse keys

    b. Orca

    c. sticky keys

    d. on-screen keyboard

17. Which of the following Linux intrusion detection systems can be used to detect altered files and directories? (Choose all that apply.)

    a. AIDE

    b. SWATCH

    c. tripwire

    d. Snort

18. When the fsck command cannot repair a non-root filesystem, you should immediately restore all data from tape backup. True or False?

19. When performing a sar -u command, you notice that %idle is consistently 10 percent. Is this good or bad?

    a. good, because the processor should be idle more than 5 percent of the time

    b. good, because the processor is idle 90 percent of the time

    c. bad, because the processor is idle 10 percent of the time and perhaps a faster CPU is required

    d. bad, because the processor is idle 10 percent of the time and perhaps a new hard disk is required

20. What are best practices for securing a local Linux server? (Choose all that apply.)

   a. Lock the server in a server closet.

   b. Ensure that you are logged in as the root user to the server at all times.

   c. Set a BIOS password on the server.

   d. Set the default run level to 1 (single user mode).

Hands-On Projects

HANDS-ON PROJECTS

These projects should be completed in the order given. The hands-on projects presented in this chapter should take a total of three hours to complete. The requirements for this lab include:

   • A computer with Fedora 13 installed according to Hands-On Project 2-2

Project 14-1

In this hands-on project, you detect modified package contents and observe shared libraries used by programs.

1. Turn on your computer. After your Linux system has been loaded, switch to a command-line terminal (tty2) by pressing **Ctrl+Alt+F2** and log in to the terminal using the user name of **root** and the password of **secret**.

2. At the command prompt, type **rpm -ql grep | less** and press **Enter** to view the file contents of the grep package on the system. When finished, press **q** to quit the less utility. Next, type **rpm -V grep** at the command prompt and press **Enter** to verify the existence of these files on the filesystem. Were any errors reported? Why?

3. At the command prompt, type **rm -f /usr/share/doc/grep-2.6.3/AUTHORS** and press **Enter** to remove a file that belongs to the grep package. Next, type **rpm -V grep** at the command prompt and press **Enter** to verify the existence of all files in the grep package. Were any errors reported? Why? If critical files were missing from this package, how could they be recovered?

4. Next, type **ldd /bin/grep** at the command prompt and press **Enter** to determine the shared libraries used by the grep command.

5. At the command prompt, type **ls -l /lib/linux-gate.so.1 /lib/libpcre.so.0 /lib/libc.so.6 /lib/ld-linux.so.2** and press **Enter** to verify that these shared library files are available. If these libraries are missing, what should you do to regain them?

6. Type **exit** and press **Enter** to log out of your shell.

Project 14-2

In this hands-on project, you monitor system performance using command-line utilities included in the sysstat package.

1. Switch to a command-line terminal (tty2) by pressing **Ctrl+Alt+F2** and log in to the terminal using the user name of **root** and the password of **secret**.

14

2. At the command prompt, type **mpstat** and press **Enter** to view average CPU statistics for your system since the last boot time. (If you do not have the sysstat package installed, simply run the yum install sysstat command.) What is the value for %user? Is this higher, lower, or the same as %system? Why? What is the value for %idle? What should this value be over?

3. At the command prompt, type **mpstat 1 5** and press **Enter** to view five CPU statistic measurements, one per second. How do these values compare with the ones seen in Step 2? Why?

4. Switch to the gdm by pressing **Ctrl+Alt+F1** or **Ctrl+Alt+F7**, and log in to the GNOME Desktop Environment as **sample user one** with a password of **secret**.

5. Open several applications of your choice.

6. Switch back to your command-line terminal (tty2) by pressing **Ctrl+Alt+F2**. Type **mpstat 1 5** at the command prompt and press **Enter** to view five CPU statistic measurements, one per second. How do these values compare with the ones seen in Step 3? Why?

7. Switch back to the GNOME Desktop Environment by pressing **Ctrl+Alt+F1** or **Ctrl+Alt+F7** and close all programs.

8. Switch back to your command-line terminal (tty2) by pressing **Ctrl+Alt+F2**. Type **iostat** at the command prompt and press **Enter** to view average device I/O statistics since the last boot time. What devices are displayed? How many blocks were read and written to your hard disk since the last boot time, on average?

9. At the command prompt, type **iostat 1 5** and press **Enter** to view five I/O statistic measurements, one per second. How do these values compare with the ones seen in Step 8? Why?

10. Switch to your GNOME Desktop Environment by pressing **Ctrl+Alt+F1** or **Ctrl+Alt+F7**, and open several applications of your choice.

11. Switch back to your command-line terminal (tty2) by pressing **Ctrl+Alt+F2**, type **iostat 1 5** at the command prompt, and press **Enter** to view five I/O statistic measurements, one per second. How do these values compare with the ones seen in Step 9? Were there any significant changes? Why?

12. Switch back to the GNOME Desktop Environment by pressing **Ctrl+Alt+F1** or **Ctrl+Alt+F7** and close all programs.

13. Switch back to your command-line terminal (tty2) by pressing **Ctrl+Alt+F2**, type **sar** at the command prompt, and press **Enter**. What statistics are displayed by default? What times were the statistics taken?

14. At the command prompt, type **sar -q** and press **Enter** to view queue statistics. What times were the statistics taken? How does this compare with what you found in Step 13? What is the queue size? What is the average load for the last minute? What is the average load for the last five minutes?

15. At the command prompt, type **sar -q 1 5** and press **Enter** to view five queue statistics, one per second. How do these values compare with those taken in Step 14? Why?

16. Switch to your GNOME Desktop Environment by pressing **Ctrl+Alt+F1** or **Ctrl+Alt+F7** and open several applications of your choice.

17. Switch back to your command-line terminal (tty2) by pressing **Ctrl+Alt+F2**, type **sar -q 1 5** at the command prompt, and press **Enter** to view five queue statistic measurements, one per second. How do these values compare with the ones seen in Step 15? Why?

18. Switch back to the GNOME Desktop Environment by pressing **Ctrl+Alt+F1** or **Ctrl+Alt+F7** and close all programs.

19. Switch back to your command-line terminal (tty2) by pressing **Ctrl+Alt+F2**, type `sar -W` at the command prompt, and press **Enter**. How many pages were swapped to and from the swap partition today, on average?

20. At the command prompt, type `sar -W 1 5` and press **Enter** to view five swap statistics, one per second. How do these values compare with those taken in Step 19? Why?

21. Switch to your GNOME Desktop Environment by pressing **Ctrl+Alt+F1** or **Ctrl+Alt+F7** and open several applications of your choice.

22. Switch back to your command-line terminal (tty2) by pressing **Ctrl+Alt+F2**, type `sar -W 1 5` at the command prompt, and press **Enter** to view five swap statistic measurements, one per second. How do these values compare with the ones seen in Step 20? Why?

23. Switch back to the GNOME Desktop Environment by pressing **Ctrl+Alt+F1** or **Ctrl+Alt+F7**. Close all programs and log out of the GNOME Desktop Environment.

24. Switch back to your command-line terminal (tty2) by pressing **Ctrl+Alt+F2**.

25. Type `exit` and press **Enter** to log out of your shell.

Project 14-3

In this hands-on project, you monitor system performance statistics taken from previous days using the sar utility included in the sysstat package.

1. Switch to a command-line terminal (tty2) by pressing **Ctrl+Alt+F2** and log in to the terminal using the user name of **root** and the password of **secret**.

2. At the command prompt, type `cd /var/log/sa` and press **Enter** to change to the directory that contains recorded performance statistics.

3. Next, type `ls` at the command prompt and press **Enter**. What files are available? What are their filenames? Which files in this directory are safe to view using a text utility? Which file contains binary system statistics for the current day? Use a piece of paper to record the name of a file that contains binary system statistics for a previous day.

4. At the command prompt, type `sar -q -f FILE1 | less` and press Enter, where **FILE1** is the first filename recorded in Step 3. Scroll through the output. How many measurements were taken and when? Was your computer rebooted during that day? How can you tell? When finished, press q to quit the less utility.

5. Type `exit` and press **Enter** to log out of your shell.

Project 14-4

In this hands-on project, you monitor memory and swap performance using the top, free, and vmstat commands.

1. Switch to a command-line terminal (tty2) by pressing **Ctrl+Alt+F2** and log in to the terminal using the user name of **root** and the password of **secret**.

2. At the command prompt, type `top` and press **Enter**. From the information displayed, write the answers to the following questions on a piece of paper:

   a. How many processes are currently running?

   b. How much memory does your system have in total?

c. How much memory is being used?

d. How much memory is used by buffers?

e. How much swap memory does your system have in total?

f. How much swap is being used?

3. Type **q** to quit the top utility.

4. At the command prompt, type **free** and press **Enter**. Does this utility give more or less information regarding memory and swap memory than the top utility? How do the values shown by the free command compare with those from Step 2?

5. At the command prompt, type **vmstat** and press **Enter**. Does this utility give more or less information regarding memory and swap memory than the top and free utilities? How do the values shown by the vmstat command compare with those from Step 2? What other information is provided by the vmstat command?

6. Type **exit** and press **Enter** to log out of your shell.

Project 14-5

In this hands-on project, you examine the services running on your local computer using the nmap utility and /etc/services file.

1. Switch to a command-line terminal (tty2) by pressing **Ctrl+Alt+F2** and log in to the terminal using the user name of **root** and the password of **secret**.

2. At the command prompt, type **service httpd stop** and press **Enter**.

3. At the command prompt, type **service xinetd stop** and press **Enter**.

4. At the command prompt, type **nmap –sT 127.0.0.1** and press **Enter**. What ports are listed that you recognize? Are there any unknown ports? Where could you find information regarding the unknown ports? What is the service associated with port 631/tcp?

5. At the command prompt, type **grep 631 /etc/services** and press **Enter**. What is the full name for the service running on port 631?

6. At the command prompt, type **service httpd start** and press **Enter**.

7. At the command prompt, type **service xinetd start** and press **Enter**.

8. At the command prompt, type **nmap –sT 127.0.0.1** and press **Enter**. What additional ports were opened by the Apache Web server and Internet Super Daemon?

9. Type **exit** and press **Enter** to log out of your shell.

Project 14-6

In this hands-on project, you use the su and sudo utilities to gain root access to your system.

1. Switch to a command-line terminal (tty2) by pressing **Ctrl+Alt+F2** and log in to the terminal using the user name of **root** and the password of **secret**.

2. At the command prompt, type **useradd dailyuser** and press **Enter**.

3. At the command prompt, type **passwd dailyuser** and press **Enter**. Supply the password **secret** when prompted both times.

4. At the command prompt, type **su - dailyuser** and press **Enter**. Were you required to enter a password? At the command prompt, type **whoami** and press **Enter** to ensure that you are now logged in as the user dailyuser.

5. At the command prompt, type **su - root** and press **Enter**. Enter the root password of **secret** when prompted. At the command prompt, type **whoami** and press **Enter** to ensure that you are now logged in as the user root.

6. Type **exit** at the command prompt and press **Enter** to end your root session.

7. Type **exit** at the command prompt and press **Enter** to end your dailyuser session.

8. Run the command **vi /etc/sudoers**. Add the following line to the end of the file:

dailyuser server1 = (root) /bin/touch

When finished, save your changes (you must use **:w!**) and quit the vi editor.

9. At the command prompt, type **su - dailyuser** and press **Enter**.

10. At the command prompt, type **touch /testfile** and press **Enter**. Were you able to create a file under the / directory?

11. At the command prompt, type **sudo touch /testfile** and press **Enter**, then enter the password **secret** when prompted. Were you able to create a file under the / directory?

12. At the command prompt, type **ls –l /testfile** and press **Enter**. Who is the owner and group owner for this file? Why?

13. Type **exit** and press **Enter** to end your dailyuser session.

14. Type **exit** and press **Enter** to log out of your shell.

Project 14-7

In this hands-on project, you configure and test the netfilter/iptables utility.

1. Switch to a command-line terminal (tty2) by pressing **Ctrl+Alt+F2** and log in to the terminal using the user name of **root** and the password of **secret**.

2. At the command prompt, type **iptables -L** and press **Enter**. What is the default action for the three chains?

3. At the command prompt, type **service httpd start** and press **Enter** to ensure that the Apache Web server is running.

4. Switch to the gdm by pressing **Ctrl+Alt+F1** or **Ctrl+Alt+F7** and log in to the GNOME Desktop Environment as **sample user one** with a password of **secret**.

5. Open the Firefox Web browser, type in the location **127.0.0.1** and press **Enter**. Was your Web page displayed?

6. Switch back to your command-line terminal (tty2) by pressing **Ctrl+Alt+F2**.

7. At the command prompt, type **iptables –P INPUT DROP** and press **Enter**. What does this command do?

8. At the command prompt, type **iptables -L** and press **Enter**. What is the default action for the three chains?

9. Switch back to the GNOME Desktop Environment by pressing **Ctrl+Alt+F1** or **Ctrl+Alt+F7** and click the **Reload** button in Firefox. What message is displayed at the bottom of the Mozilla screen? Click the **Stop** button.

10. Switch back to your command-line terminal (tty2) by pressing **Ctrl+Alt+F2**.

11. At the command prompt, type **iptables –A INPUT –s 127.0.0.1 –j ACCEPT** and press **Enter**. What does this command do?

12. At the command prompt, type **iptables -L** and press **Enter**. Do you see your rule underneath the INPUT chain?

13. Switch back to the GNOME Desktop Environment by pressing **Ctrl+Alt+F1** or **Ctrl+Alt+F7** and click the **Reload** button in Firefox. Were you successful? Why? Log out of the GNOME Desktop Environment.

14. Switch back to your command-line terminal (tty2) by pressing **Ctrl+Alt+F2**.

15. At the command prompt, type **iptables -F** and press **Enter**. Next, type **iptables –P INPUT ACCEPT** at the command prompt and press **Enter**. What do these commands do? At the command prompt, type **iptables -L** and press **Enter** to verify that the default chains have been restored.

16. Type **exit** and press **Enter** to log out of your shell.

Project 14-8

In this hands-on project, you create an SSH tunnel using X Windows.

1. Switch to the gdm by pressing **Ctrl+Alt+F1** or **Ctrl+Alt+F7** and log in to the GNOME Desktop Environment as **sample user one** with a password of **secret**.

2. Open a BASH terminal.

3. At the command prompt, type **ssh –X root@localhost** and press **Enter**. Supply the root user password of **secret** when prompted.

4. At the command prompt, type **whoami** and press **Enter**. Are you the root user on the remote computer?

5. At the command prompt, type **xeyes** and press **Enter**. Was the root user's X Windows program redirected to user1's X Windows program?

6. Close your terminal window and log out of the GNOME Desktop Environment.

Discovery Exercises

1. Given the following situations, list any log files or commands that you would use when collecting information during the troubleshooting process.

   a. A CD-ROM device that worked previously with Linux does not respond to the mount command.

   b. The system was unable to mount the /home filesystem (/dev/sda6).

   c. A new database application fails to start successfully.

   d. The Network Configuration utility that you have installed cannot recognize any modems on the system.

   e. You have installed a new sound card in the Linux system, but it is not listed within any sound utility.

2. For each problem in Exercise 1, list as many possible causes and solutions that you can think of, given the material presented throughout this book. Next, research other possible causes using resources such as the Internet, books, local HOWTOs, magazines, or LUGs.

3. You are the administrator of a Linux system that provides file and print services to over 100 clients in your company. The system uses several SCSI hard disks and has a Pentium IV processor with 4096MB of RAM. Since its installation, you have installed database software that is used by only a few users. Unfortunately, you have rarely monitored and documented performance information of this system in the past. Recently, users complain that the performance of the server is very poor. What commands could you use to narrow down the problem? Are there any other troubleshooting methods that might be useful when solving this problem?

4. Briefly describe the purpose of a baseline. What areas of the system would you include in a baseline for your Linux system? Which commands would you use to obtain the information about these areas? Use these commands to generate baseline information for your system (for the current day only) and place this information in a system log book (small binder) for later use. Next, monitor the normal activity of your system for three consecutive days and compare the results with the baseline that you have printed. Are there any differences? Incorporate this new information into your baseline by averaging the results. Are these new values a more accurate indication of normal activity? Why or why not?

5. Use the Assistive Technologies Preference utility to explore the different assistive technologies available within Fedora 13. Note the ones that you find useful.

6. You are a network administrator for your organization and are required to plan and deploy a new file and print server that will service Windows, Linux, and Macintosh client computers. In addition, the server will provide DHCP services on the network and host a small Web site listing company information. In a brief document, draft the services that you plan to implement for this server and the methods that you will use to maximize the security of the system.

7. Using the steps provided in this chapter, configure the tripwire IDS on your Linux computer using the default options. Observe the policy text file to find out the areas of your system that tripwire monitors. Next, make a modification to a key file and run the tripwire program to analyze your system. Observe the information on the report generated by tripwire and note your change. Next, write a memo that outlines the possible uses of tripwire within an organization that uses Linux servers across the Internet.

8. Most hackers attempt to gain access to a system as the root user. As a result, SELinux prevents the root user from interacting with most network services. Enable SELinux by setting the `SELINUX = enforcing` and `SELINUXTYPE = targeted` parameters within the /etc/selinux/config file and reboot your system. Next, perform the Chapter 13 projects again and note any differences that result from steps that involve testing network service connectivity as the root user.

9. Many more security-related tools are available for Linux systems than those discussed in this chapter. One example is NESSUS (*www.nessus.org*), which can test for security vulnerabilities on your system. Use the Internet to research the installation, features, and usage of the NESSUS tool and summarize your findings in a short document. If time permits, download, install, and run NESSUS on your computer.

Certification

As technology advances, so does the need for educated people to manage technology. One of the principal challenges that companies face is the hiring of qualified people to administer, use, or develop programs for Linux. To help meet this challenge, companies seek people who have demonstrated proficiency in certain technical areas. Although this proficiency can be demonstrated in the form of practical experience, it alone is often not enough for companies when hiring for certain technical positions. Certification tests have become a standard benchmark of technical ability and are a requirement of many companies. They can vary based on the technical certification, but they usually involve a multiple-choice computer test administered by an approved testing center. Hundreds of thousands of computer-related certification tests are written worldwide each year, and the certification process is likely to increase in importance in the future as technology advances.

It is important to recognize that certification does not replace ability; rather, it demonstrates ability. An employer might get 30 qualified applicants, and part of the hiring process will likely be a demonstration of ability. It is unlikely the employer will be willing to incur the cost and time it would take to test all 30. It is more likely the employer will look for benchmark certifications, which indicate a base ability, then test this smaller subgroup.

Furthermore, certifications are an internationally administered and recognized standard. Although an employer might not be familiar with the criteria involved in achieving a computer science degree from a particular university in Canada or a certain college in Texas, certification exam criteria are well published on Web sites and are, hence, well known. In addition, it does not matter in which country the certification exam is taken because the tests are standardized and administered by the same authenticating authority using common rules.

Certifications come in two broad categories, vendor-specific and vendor-neutral. Vendor-specific certifications are ones in which the vendor of a particular operating system or program sets the standards to be met and creates the exams. Obtaining one of these certifications demonstrates knowledge of, or on, a particular product or operating system. Microsoft, Novell, and Oracle, for example, all have vendor-specific certifications for their products. Vendor-neutral exams, such as those offered by CompTIA, demonstrate knowledge in a particular area, but not on any specific product or brand of product. In either case, the organizations that create the certification exams and set the standards strive to ensure that they are of the highest quality and integrity and, therefore, worthy of being used as a true benchmark worldwide. One globally recognized and vendor-neutral Linux certification used by the industry is CompTIA's Linux+ Powered by LPI certification.

Linux+ Certification

Linux is a general category of operating system software that shares a common operating system kernel and utilities. What differentiates one Linux distribution from another are the various accompanying software applications, which modify the look and feel of the operating system. Vendor-neutral certification suits Linux particularly well because there is no one specific vendor; Linux distributions can have different brands attached to them, but they essentially work in the same fashion. To certify on one particular distribution might well indicate the ability to port to and work well on another distribution; but with the varied number of distributions, it is probably best to show proficiency on the most common features of Linux that the majority of distributions share. The CompTIA Linux+ Powered by LPI certification achieves this well and tests a wide body of knowledge on the various ways Linux is distributed and installed, as well as common commands, procedures, and user interfaces. There are two exams that make up the ComptTIA Linux+ Powered by LPI certification: LX0-101 and LX0-102. Both exams can be taken at any participating VUE or Sylvan Prometric testing center worldwide, and each exam involves 60 questions to be answered within a 90-minute time frame.

To find out more about the Linux+ Powered by LPI certification exams and how to register for one, visit the CompTIA Web site on the Internet at *www.comptia.org/certifications/listed/linux.aspx*.

Linux+ Certification Objectives

The following tables identify where these topics are covered in this book. Each table represents a separate domain, or skill set, measured by the exam. Domains 101 through 104 are tested on the LX0-101 certification exam, whereas domains 105 through 110 are tested on the LX0-102 certification exam.

Domain 101: System Architecture

Objective	Chapter
101.1 Determine and configure hardware settings	2, 5, 6, 12, 14
101.2 Boot the system	8
101.3 Change runlevels and shut down or reboot system	8

Domain 102: Linux Installation and Package Management

Objective	Chapter
102.1 Design hard disk layout	2, 5, 6
102.2 Install a boot manager	2, 8
102.3 Manage shared libraries	14
102.4 Use Debian package management	11
102.5 Use RPM and YUM package management	11

Domain 103: GNU and UNIX Commands

Objective	Chapter
103.1 Work on the command line	2, 3, 7
103.2 Process text streams using filters	3, 7
103.3 Perform basic file management	4, 11
103.4 Use streams, pipes, and redirects	7
103.5 Create, monitor, and kill processes	9
103.6 Modify process execution priorities	9
103.7 Search text files using regular expressions	3, 7
103.8 Perform basic file editing operations using vi	3

Domain 104: Linux Filesystems, Filesystem Hierarchy Standard

Objective	Chapter
104.1 Create partitions and filesystems	5
104.2 Maintain the integrity of filesystems	5
104.3 Control mounting and unmounting of filesystems	5
104.4 Manage disk quotas	5
104.5 Manage file permissions and ownership	4
104.6 Create and change hard and symbolic links	4
104.7 Find system files and place files in the correct location	4

Domain 105: Shells, Scripting and Data Management

Objective	Chapter
105.1 Customize and use the shell environment	7
105.2 Customize or write simple scripts	7
105.3 SQL data management	13

Domain 106: User Interfaces and Desktops

Objective	Chapter
106.1 Install and configure X11	2, 6, 8, 14
106.2 Set up a display manager	8
106.3 Accessibility	14

Domain 107: Administrative Tasks

Objective	Chapter
107.1 Manage user and group accounts and related system files	10
107.2 Automate system administration tasks by scheduling jobs	9
107.3 Localization and internationalization	2, 13

Domain 108: Essential System Services

Objective	Chapter
108.1 Maintain system time	2, 13
108.2 System logging	10, 14
108.3 Mail transfer agent (MTA) basics	1, 13
108.4 Manage printers and printing	10

Domain 109: Networking Fundamentals

Objective	Chapter
109.1 Fundamentals of Internet protocols	12
109.2 Basic network configuration	12
109.3 Basic network troubleshooting	12
109.4 Configure client-side DNS	12

Domain 110: Security

Objective	Chapter
110.1 Perform security administration tasks	4, 10, 12, 14
110.2 Set up host security	10, 12, 14
110.3 Securing data with encryption	12, 14

GNU General Public License

A copy of the original GNU General Public License referred to in Chapter 1 is shown here in Figure B-1. This license and its revisions can be found on the Internet at *www.gnu.org*.

```
GNU GENERAL PUBLIC LICENSE
                    Version 2, June 1991

Copyright (C) 1989, 1991 Free Software Foundation, Inc.
59 Temple Place, Suite 330, Boston, MA  02111-1307  USA
Everyone is permitted to copy and distribute verbatim copies
of this license document, but changing it is not allowed.

                         Preamble

  The licenses for most software are designed to take away your
freedom to share and change it.  By contrast, the GNU General Public
License is intended to guarantee your freedom to share and change free
software--to make sure the software is free for all its users.  This
General Public License applies to most of the Free Software
Foundation's software and to any other program whose authors commit to
using it.  (Some other Free Software Foundation software is covered by
the GNU Library General Public License instead.)  You can apply it to
your programs, too.

  When we speak of free software, we are referring to freedom, not
price.  Our General Public Licenses are designed to make sure that you
have the freedom to distribute copies of free software (and charge for
this service if you wish), that you receive source code or can get it
if you want it, that you can change the software or use pieces of it
in new free programs; and that you know you can do these things.

  To protect your rights, we need to make restrictions that forbid
anyone to deny you these rights or to ask you to surrender the rights.
These restrictions translate to certain responsibilities for you if you
distribute copies of the software, or if you modify it.

  For example, if you distribute copies of such a program, whether
gratis or for a fee, you must give the recipients all the rights that
you have.  You must make sure that they, too, receive or can get the
source code.  And you must show them these terms so they know their
rights.

  We protect your rights with two steps: (1) copyright the software, and
(2) offer you this license which gives you legal permission to copy,
distribute and/or modify the software.

  Also, for each author's protection and ours, we want to make certain
that everyone understands that there is no warranty for this free
software.  If the software is modified by someone else and passed on, we
want its recipients to know that what they have is not the original, so
that any problems introduced by others will not reflect on the original
authors' reputations.

  Finally, any free program is threatened constantly by software
patents.  We wish to avoid the danger that redistributors of a free
program will individually obtain patent licenses, in effect making the
program proprietary.  To prevent this, we have made it clear that any
patent must be licensed for everyone's free use or not licensed at all.

  The precise terms and conditions for copying, distribution and
modification follow.
                    GNU GENERAL PUBLIC LICENSE
   TERMS AND CONDITIONS FOR COPYING, DISTRIBUTION AND MODIFICATION

  0. This License applies to any program or other work which contains
a notice placed by the copyright holder saying it may be distributed
under the terms of this General Public License.  The "Program", below,
refers to any such program or work, and a "work based on the Program"
means either the Program or any derivative work under copyright law:
that is to say, a work containing the Program or a portion of it,
either verbatim or with modifications and/or translated into another
language.  (Hereinafter, translation is included without limitation in
the term "modification".)  Each licensee is addressed as "you".
```

Figure B-1 GNU General Public License

Source: Course Technology/Cengage Learning

Activities other than copying, distribution and modification are not
covered by this License; they are outside its scope. The act of
running the Program is not restricted, and the output from the Program
is covered only if its contents constitute a work based on the
Program (independent of having been made by running the Program).
Whether that is true depends on what the Program does.

  1. You may copy and distribute verbatim copies of the Program's
source code as you receive it, in any medium, provided that you
conspicuously and appropriately publish on each copy an appropriate
copyright notice and disclaimer of warranty; keep intact all the
notices that refer to this License and to the absence of any warranty;
and give any other recipients of the Program a copy of this License
along with the Program.

You may charge a fee for the physical act of transferring a copy, and
you may at your option offer warranty protection in exchange for a fee.

  2. You may modify your copy or copies of the Program or any portion
of it, thus forming a work based on the Program, and copy and
distribute such modifications or work under the terms of Section 1
above, provided that you also meet all of these conditions:

    a) You must cause the modified files to carry prominent notices
    stating that you changed the files and the date of any change.

    b) You must cause any work that you distribute or publish, that in
    whole or in part contains or is derived from the Program or any
    part thereof, to be licensed as a whole at no charge to all third
    parties under the terms of this License.

    c) If the modified program normally reads commands interactively
    when run, you must cause it, when started running for such
    interactive use in the most ordinary way, to print or display an
    announcement including an appropriate copyright notice and a
    notice that there is no warranty (or else, saying that you provide
    a warranty) and that users may redistribute the program under
    these conditions, and telling the user how to view a copy of this
    License. (Exception: if the Program itself is interactive but
    does not normally print such an announcement, your work based on
    the Program is not required to print an announcement.)

These requirements apply to the modified work as a whole. If
identifiable sections of that work are not derived from the Program,
and can be reasonably considered independent and separate works in
themselves, then this License, and its terms, do not apply to those
sections when you distribute them as separate works. But when you
distribute the same sections as part of a whole which is a work based
on the Program, the distribution of the whole must be on the terms of
this License, whose permissions for other licensees extend to the
entire whole, and thus to each and every part regardless of who wrote it.

Thus, it is not the intent of this section to claim rights or contest
your rights to work written entirely by you; rather, the intent is to
exercise the right to control the distribution of derivative or
collective works based on the Program.

In addition, mere aggregation of another work not based on the Program
with the Program (or with a work based on the Program) on a volume of
a storage or distribution medium does not bring the other work under
the scope of this License.

  3. You may copy and distribute the Program (or a work based on it,
under Section 2) in object code or executable form under the terms of
Sections 1 and 2 above provided that you also do one of the following:

    a) Accompany it with the complete corresponding machine-readable
    source code, which must be distributed under the terms of Sections
    1 and 2 above on a medium customarily used for software interchange; or,

    b) Accompany it with a written offer, valid for at least three

Figure B-1 GNU General Public License (continued)

Source: Course Technology/Cengage Learning

years, to give any third party, for a charge no more than your cost of physically performing source distribution, a complete machine-readable copy of the corresponding source code, to be distributed under the terms of Sections 1 and 2 above on a medium customarily used for software interchange; or,

c) Accompany it with the information you received as to the offer to distribute corresponding source code. (This alternative is allowed only for noncommercial distribution and only if you received the program in object code or executable form with such an offer, in accord with Subsection b above.)

The source code for a work means the preferred form of the work for making modifications to it. For an executable work, complete source code means all the source code for all modules it contains, plus any associated interface definition files, plus the scripts used to control compilation and installation of the executable. However, as a special exception, the source code distributed need not include anything that is normally distributed (in either source or binary form) with the major components (compiler, kernel, and so on) of the operating system on which the executable runs, unless that component itself accompanies the executable.

If distribution of executable or object code is made by offering access to copy from a designated place, then offering equivalent access to copy the source code from the same place counts as distribution of the source code, even though third parties are not compelled to copy the source along with the object code.

4. You may not copy, modify, sublicense, or distribute the Program except as expressly provided under this License. Any attempt otherwise to copy, modify, sublicense or distribute the Program is void, and will automatically terminate your rights under this License. However, parties who have received copies, or rights, from you under this License will not have their licenses terminated so long as such parties remain in full compliance.

5. You are not required to accept this License, since you have not signed it. However, nothing else grants you permission to modify or distribute the Program or its derivative works. These actions are prohibited by law if you do not accept this License. Therefore, by modifying or distributing the Program (or any work based on the Program), you indicate your acceptance of this License to do so, and all its terms and conditions for copying, distributing or modifying the Program or works based on it.

6. Each time you redistribute the Program (or any work based on the Program), the recipient automatically receives a license from the original licensor to copy, distribute or modify the Program subject to these terms and conditions. You may not impose any further restrictions on the recipients' exercise of the rights granted herein. You are not responsible for enforcing compliance by third parties to this License.

7. If, as a consequence of a court judgment or allegation of patent infringement or for any other reason (not limited to patent issues), conditions are imposed on you (whether by court order, agreement or otherwise) that contradict the conditions of this License, they do not excuse you from the conditions of this License. If you cannot distribute so as to satisfy simultaneously your obligations under this License and any other pertinent obligations, then as a consequence you may not distribute the Program at all. For example, if a patent license would not permit royalty-free redistribution of the Program by all those who receive copies directly or indirectly through you, then the only way you could satisfy both it and this License would be to refrain entirely from distribution of the Program.

If any portion of this section is held invalid or unenforceable under any particular circumstance, the balance of the section is intended to apply and the section as a whole is intended to apply in other circumstances.

Figure B-1 GNU General Public License (continued)

Source: Course Technology/Cengage Learning

It is not the purpose of this section to induce you to infringe any patents or other property right claims or to contest validity of any such claims; this section has the sole purpose of protecting the integrity of the free software distribution system, which is implemented by public license practices. Many people have made generous contributions to the wide range of software distributed through that system in reliance on consistent application of that system; it is up to the author/donor to decide if he or she is willing to distribute software through any other system and a licensee cannot impose that choice.

This section is intended to make thoroughly clear what is believed to be a consequence of the rest of this License.

8. If the distribution and/or use of the Program is restricted in certain countries either by patents or by copyrighted interfaces, the original copyright holder who places the Program under this License may add an explicit geographical distribution limitation excluding those countries, so that distribution is permitted only in or among countries not thus excluded. In such case, this License incorporates the limitation as if written in the body of this License.

9. The Free Software Foundation may publish revised and/or new versions of the General Public License from time to time. Such new versions will be similar in spirit to the present version, but may differ in detail to address new problems or concerns.

Each version is given a distinguishing version number. If the Program specifies a version number of this License which applies to it and "any later version", you have the option of following the terms and conditions either of that version or of any later version published by the Free Software Foundation. If the Program does not specify a version number of this License, you may choose any version ever published by the Free Software Foundation.

10. If you wish to incorporate parts of the Program into other free programs whose distribution conditions are different, write to the author to ask for permission. For software which is copyrighted by the Free Software Foundation, write to the Free Software Foundation; we sometimes make exceptions for this. Our decision will be guided by the two goals of preserving the free status of all derivatives of our free software and of promoting the sharing and reuse of software generally.

NO WARRANTY

11. BECAUSE THE PROGRAM IS LICENSED FREE OF CHARGE, THERE IS NO WARRANTY FOR THE PROGRAM, TO THE EXTENT PERMITTED BY APPLICABLE LAW. EXCEPT WHEN OTHERWISE STATED IN WRITING THE COPYRIGHT HOLDERS AND/OR OTHER PARTIES PROVIDE THE PROGRAM "AS IS" WITHOUT WARRANTY OF ANY KIND, EITHER EXPRESSED OR IMPLIED, INCLUDING, BUT NOT LIMITED TO, THE IMPLIED WARRANTIES OF MERCHANTABILITY AND FITNESS FOR A PARTICULAR PURPOSE. THE ENTIRE RISK AS TO THE QUALITY AND PERFORMANCE OF THE PROGRAM IS WITH YOU. SHOULD THE PROGRAM PROVE DEFECTIVE, YOU ASSUME THE COST OF ALL NECESSARY SERVICING, REPAIR OR CORRECTION.

12. IN NO EVENT UNLESS REQUIRED BY APPLICABLE LAW OR AGREED TO IN WRITING WILL ANY COPYRIGHT HOLDER, OR ANY OTHER PARTY WHO MAY MODIFY AND/OR REDISTRIBUTE THE PROGRAM AS PERMITTED ABOVE, BE LIABLE TO YOU FOR DAMAGES, INCLUDING ANY GENERAL, SPECIAL, INCIDENTAL OR CONSEQUENTIAL DAMAGES ARISING OUT OF THE USE OR INABILITY TO USE THE PROGRAM (INCLUDING BUT NOT LIMITED TO LOSS OF DATA OR DATA BEING RENDERED INACCURATE OR LOSSES SUSTAINED BY YOU OR THIRD PARTIES OR A FAILURE OF THE PROGRAM TO OPERATE WITH ANY OTHER PROGRAMS), EVEN IF SUCH HOLDER OR OTHER PARTY HAS BEEN ADVISED OF THE POSSIBILITY OF SUCH DAMAGES.

END OF TERMS AND CONDITIONS

How to Apply These Terms to Your New Programs

If you develop a new program, and you want it to be of the greatest

Figure B-1 GNU General Public License (continued)

Source: Course Technology/Cengage Learning

```
possible use to the public, the best way to achieve this is to make it
free software which everyone can redistribute and change under these terms.

   To do so, attach the following notices to the program.  It is safest
to attach them to the start of each source file to most effectively
convey the exclusion of warranty; and each file should have at least
the "copyright" line and a pointer to where the full notice is found.

   , 1 April 1989
  Ty Coon, President of Vice

This General Public License does not permit incorporating your program into
proprietary programs.  If your program is a subroutine library, you may
consider it more useful to permit linking proprietary applications with the
library.  If this is what you want to do, use the GNU Library General
Public License instead of this License.
```

Figure B-1 GNU General Public License (continued)

Source: Course Technology/Cengage Learning

Finding Linux Resources on the Internet

Open source development has made Linux a powerful and versatile operating system. However, this development has also increased the complexity of Linux and Linux resources available on the Internet. Newcomers to Linux might find this bounty of resources intimidating, but there are some simple rules that make finding particular types of Linux resources easier. Understanding how to navigate the Internet to find these resources is a valuable skill to develop.

By far, the easiest way to locate resources on any topic is by using a search engine such as Google. However, because a plethora of Linux-related Web sites is available on the Internet, a search of the word "Linux" yields thousands of results. You might find that you need to be more specific in your request to a search engine to obtain a list of Web sites that likely contain the information you desire. Thus, it is very important to approach Linux documentation by topic; otherwise, you might be searching for hours through several Web sites to find the resources you need.

Many Web sites describe the features of Linux and Open Source Software. Many of these Web sites contain links to other Linux resources organized by topic and, hence, are a good place for people to start if they are new to Linux and desire some background or terminology. Unfortunately, many of the sites do not follow a common naming scheme. Table C-1 is a partial list of some valuable Web sites offering general Linux information.

Description	Web Site
Linux Online	*www.linux.org*
Linux International	*www.li.org*
The Jargon File (Terminology)	*www.catb.org/~esr/jargon/html/*
The Cathedral and the Bazaar (History of Open Source)	*www.catb.org/~esr/writings/cathedral-bazaar/*
Free Software Foundation	*www.fsf.org*
GNU Operating System	*www.gnu.org*

Table C-1   General Linux and open source Web sites

Other important sources of information, for inexperienced and expert Linux users alike, are Linux news sites. Some of these Web sites are hosted by organizations that publish trade magazines and, as a result, share the same name as the magazine, only with a ".com" suffix, making the Web site easier to find. One example is the *Linux Journal*, which can be found at *www.linuxjournal.com*. Often, these sites contain more than just Linux news; they also contain tutorials, FAQs (frequently asked questions), and links to other Linux resources. Table C-2 lists some common Linux news Web sites.

Description	Web Site
Linux Journal (magazine)	*www.linuxjournal.com*
Slashdot	*www.slashdot.org*
Linux Weekly News	*www.lwn.net*
LinuxFocus	*www.linuxfocus.org*
Linux Magazine (magazine)	*www.linux-mag.com*

Table C-2 **Common Linux news Web sites**

Although many Web sites offer general information and news regarding Linux and Open Source Software, the most important resources the Internet offers are help files and product documentation. These resources take many forms, including instructions for completing tasks (HOWTO documents), frequently asked questions (FAQs), supporting documentation (text files and HTML files), and newsgroup postings (Usenet). Almost every Web site containing Linux information of some type provides at least one of these resources; however, many centralized Web sites make finding this information easier. Table C-3 lists some common Web sites that make locating documentation and help files easier.

Description	Web Site
The Linux Documentation Project (HOWTOs)	*www.tldp.org*
Linux Help	*www.linuxhelp.net*
Google groups (formerly Deja News)	*www.groups.google.com*

Table C-3 **Common Linux documentation and help resources**

In many cases, you can find help on a particular Open Source Software component for Linux by visiting its development Web site. Most large Open Source Software projects, such as the KDE project, have their own Web site where information and news regarding the software is available and the latest release can be downloaded. These Web sites usually follow the naming convention www.*projectname*.org, where "*projectname*" is the name of the project; thus, these Web sites are easy to locate without using a search engine. Table C-4 is a partial list of common Open Source Software project Web sites available on the Internet.

Description	Web Site
The Apache Web Server	*www.apache.org*
The KDE Desktop	*www.kde.org*
The GNOME Desktop	*www.gnome.org*
The XFree86 Project, Inc. (X Windows)	*www.xfree86.org*
X.Org Project (X Windows)	*www.x.org*
Linux Kernel Archives	*www.kernel.org*

Table C-4 Open Source Software project Web sites

Smaller Open Source Software packages and projects rarely have Web sites hosting the development. Instead, they are listed on Open Source Software repository Web sites, also known as Open Source Software archives, which contain thousands of software packages available for download. Often, these Web sites offer several different distributions of Linux as well, conveniently saving a visit to a distribution Web site in order to obtain one. There are many repository Web sites, a sampling of which is listed in Table C-5.

Description	Web Site
Freshmeat	*www.freshmeat.net*
SourceForge	*www.sourceforge.net*
Tucows	*http://linux.tucows.com*
Linux Online	*www.linux.org/apps/*
Ibiblio	*www.ibiblio.org/pub/Linux/*

Table C-5 Common Open Source Software archives

Glossary

*sum commands Commands that can be used to verify the checksum on a file where * represents the checksum algorithm. For example, to verify a SHA-1 checksum, you could use the `sha1sum` command.

.dmrc (display manager runtime configuration) file A file that is stored within each user's home directory to list the preferred desktop environment for use by the GNOME Display Manager.

.xinitrc (X initialization runtime configuration) file A file that is stored within each user's home directory to list the preferred desktop environment for use by the `startx` command.

/bin directory The directory that contains binary commands for use by all users.

/boot directory The directory that contains the Linux kernel and files used by the boot loader data block.

/boot The directory that contains the kernel and boot-related files.

/boot/grub/grub.conf The GRUB configuration file.

/dev directory The directory that contains device files.

/dev/MAKEDEV command The command used to re-create a device file if one or more of the following pieces of device information is unknown: major number, minor number, or type (character or block).

/etc directory The directory that contains system-specific configuration files.

/etc/at.allow A file listing all users who can use the `at` command.

/etc/at.deny A file listing all users who cannot access the `at` command.

/etc/cron.allow A file listing all users who can use the `cron` command.

/etc/cron.d A directory that contains additional system cron tables.

/etc/cron.deny A file listing all users who cannot access the `cron` command.

/etc/crontab The default system cron table.

/etc/cups/cupsd.conf A file that holds daemon configuration for the cups daemon.

/etc/cups/printers.conf A file that holds printer configuration for the cups daemon.

/etc/default/useradd A file that contains default values for user creation.

/etc/dumpdates The file used to store information about incremental and full backups for use by the dump/restore utility.

/etc/fstab A file used to specify which filesystems to mount automatically at boot time and queried by the `mount` command if an insufficient number of arguments is specified.

/etc/group The file that contains group definitions and memberships.

/etc/inittab The configuration file for the init daemon that specifies the default runlevel.

/etc/ld.so.cache file The file that contains the location of shared library files.

/etc/ld.so.conf file The file that contains a list of directories that contain shared libraries.

/etc/lilo.conf The LILO configuration file.

/etc/login.defs A file that contains default values for user creation.

/etc/logrotate.conf The file used by the logrotate utility to specify rotation parameters for log files.

/etc/mtab A file that stores a list of currently mounted filesystems.

/etc/passwd The file that contains user account information.

/etc/rc.d/init.d The directory in which most daemons', startup/shutdown scripts are located.

/etc/rc.d/rc*.d The directories used to start and kill daemons in each runlevel.

/etc/rc.d/rc.local The final script executed during system startup.

/etc/rc.d/rc.sysinit The first script executed during system startup.

/etc/shadow The file that contains the encrypted password as well as password and account expiry parameters for each user account.

/etc/skel A directory that contains files that are copied to all new users' home directories upon creation.

/etc/syslog.conf The file that specifies the events for which the System Log Daemon listens and the log files to which it saves the events.

/etc/X11/XF86Config The configuration file used by the XFree86 implementation of X Windows.

/etc/X11/xorg.conf The configuration file used by the X.Org implementation of X Windows.

/home directory The default location for user home directories.

/lib directory The directory that contains shared program libraries (used by the commands in /bin and /sbin) as well as kernel modules.

/media directory A directory typically used for mounting removable media devices.

/mnt directory An empty directory used for temporarily mounting media.

/opt directory The directory that stores additional software programs.

/proc directory The directory that contains process and kernel information.

/proc/devices A file that contains currently used device information.

/root directory The root user's home directory.

/sbin directory The directory that contains system binary commands (used for administration).

/tmp directory The directory that holds temporary files created by programs.

/usr directory The directory that contains most system commands and utilities.

/usr/local directory The location for most additional programs.

/var directory The directory that contains log files and spools.

/var/log A directory that contains most log files on a Linux system.

/var/spool/at A directory that stores the information used to schedule commands using the at daemon.

/var/spool/cron A directory that stores user cron tables.

| A shell metacharacter used to pipe the stdout from one command to the stdin of another command.

; A shell metacharacter used to chain multiple commands together for execution.

< A shell metacharacter used to obtain stdin from a file.

> A shell metacharacter used to redirect stdout and stderr to a file.

~ A metacharacter used to represent a user's home directory.

ab (Apache benchmark) command A command that can be used to obtain performance benchmarks for a Web server such as Apache.

absolute pathname The full pathname to a certain file or directory, starting from the root directory.

accepting printer A printer that accepts print jobs into the print queue.

active partition The partition searched for by an OS after the MBR.

Advanced Technology Attachment (ATA) *See also* Parallel Advanced Technology Attachment.

AIX A version of UNIX developed by IBM.

alias command A command used to create special variables that are shortcuts to longer command strings.

ANDing The process by which binary bits are compared to calculate the network and host IDs from an IP address and subnet mask.

apachectl command A command that can be used to start, stop, and restart the Apache Web server as well as check for syntax errors within the Apache configuration file.

application The software that runs on an operating system and provides the user with specific functionality (such as word processing or financial calculation).

archive The location (file or device) that contains a copy of files; it is typically created by a backup utility.

arguments The text that appears after a command name, does not start with a dash "-" character, and specifies information the command requires to work properly.

artistic license An open source license that allows source code to be distributed freely but changed only at the discretion of the original author.

assistive technologies Software programs that cater to specific user needs.

asymmetric encryption A type of encryption that uses a key pair to encrypt and decrypt data.

at command The command used to schedule commands and tasks to run at a preset time in the future.

at daemon (atd) The system daemon that executes tasks at a future time; it is configured with the at command.

authentication The act of verifying a user's identity by comparing a user name and password with a system database (/etc/passwd and /etc/shadow).

Automatic Private IP Addressing (APIPA) A feature that automatically configures a network interface using an IPv4 address on the 169.254.0.0 network.

awk command A filter command used to search for and display text.

background (bg) command The command used to run a foreground process in the background.

background process A process that does not require the BASH shell to wait for its termination. Upon execution, the user receives the BASH shell prompt immediately.

bad blocks The areas of a storage medium unable to store data properly.

baseline A measure of normal system activity.

BASH shell The Bourne Again Shell; it is the default command-line interface in Linux.

BBC Linux A small CD/DVD-based Linux distribution.

Beowulf clustering A popular and widespread method of clustering computers together to perform useful tasks using Linux.

Berkeley Internet Name Domain (BIND) The standard that all DNS servers and DNS configuration files adhere to.

binary data file A file that contains machine language (binary 1s and 0s) and stores information (such as common functions and graphics) used by binary compiled programs.

BIND configuration utility A graphical utility that can be used to generate and modify the files that are used by the DNS name daemon.

BIOS (Basic Input/Output System) The part of a computer system that contains the programs used to initialize hardware components at boot time.

block The unit of data commonly used by filesystem commands; a block can contain several sectors.

block devices The storage devices that transfer data to and from the system in chunks of many data bits by caching the information in RAM; they are represented by block device files.

boot loader A program used to load an OS.

broadcast The TCP/IP communication destined for all computers on a network.

BSD (Berkeley Software Distribution) A version of UNIX developed out of the original UNIX source code and given free to the University of California at Berkeley by AT&T.

buffer overrun An attack in which a network service is altered in memory.

`bunzip2` **command** The command used to decompress files compressed by the `bzip2` command.

bus mastering The process by which peripheral components perform tasks normally executed by the CPU.

`bzcat` **command** A command used to view the contents of an archive created with bzip2 to SO.

`bzip2` **command** The command used to compress files using a Burrows-Wheeler Block Sorting Huffman Coding compression algorithm.

`bzless` **command** A command used to view the contents of an archive created with bzip2 to SO in a page-by-page fashion.

`bzmore` **command** A command used to view the contents of an archive created with bzip2 to SO in a page-by-page fashion.

`cancel` **command** The command used to remove print jobs from the print queue in the CUPS print system.

`cat` **command** A Linux command used to display (or concatenate) the entire contents of a text file to the screen.

`cd` (`change directory`) **command** A Linux command used to change the current directory in the directory tree.

`cfdisk` **command** A command used to partition hard disks; it displays a graphical interface in which the user can select partitioning options.

`chage` **command** The command used to modify password expiry information for user accounts.

chains The components of a firewall that specify the general type of network traffic to which rules apply.

character devices The storage devices that transfer data to and from the system one data bit at a time; they are represented by character device files.

checksum A calculated value that is unique to a file's size and contents.

`chfn` **command** The command used to change the GECOS for a user.

`chgrp` (`change group`) **command** The command used to change the group owner of a file or directory.

child process A process that was started by another process (parent process).

`chkconfig` **command** A command that can be used to configure daemon startup by runlevel.

`chmod` (`change mode`) **command** The command used to change the mode (permissions) of a file or directory.

`chown` (`change owner`) **command** The command used to change the owner and group owner of a file or directory.

`chsh` **command** The command used to change a valid shell to an invalid shell.

classless interdomain routing (CIDR) notation A notation that is often used to represent an IP address and its subnet mask.

closed source software The software whose source code is not freely available from the original author; Windows 7, for example.

cluster A grouping of several smaller computers that function as one large supercomputer.

clustering The act of making a cluster; *see also* cluster.

command A program that exists on the hard disk and is executed when typed on the command line.

command mode One of the two modes in vi; it allows a user to perform any available text editing task that is not related to inserting text into the document.

Common Unix Printing System (CUPS) The printing system commonly used on Linux computers.

compiz A window manager that is commonly used within the KDE and GNOME desktops to provide 3D effects.

compress command The command used to compress files using a Lempel-Ziv compression algorithm.

compression The process in which files are reduced in size by a compression algorithm.

compression algorithm The set of instructions used to reduce the contents of a file systematically.

compression ratio The amount of compression that occurred during compression.

concatenation The joining of text to make one larger whole. In Linux, words and strings of text are joined together to form a displayed file.

counter variable A variable that is altered by loop constructs to ensure that commands are not executed indefinitely.

cp (copy) command The command used to create copies of files and directories.

cpio (copy in/out) command A command used to run a common backup utility.

cracker A person who uses computer software maliciously for personal profit.

cron daemon (crond) The system daemon that executes tasks repetitively in the future and that is configured using cron tables.

cron table A file specifying tasks to be run by the cron daemon; there are user cron tables and system cron tables.

crontab command The command used to view and edit user cron tables.

cups daemon (cupsd) The daemon responsible for printing in the CUPS printing system.

cupsaccept command The command used to allow a printer to accept jobs into the print queue.

cupsdisable command The command used to prevent print jobs from leaving the print queue.

cupsenable command The command used to allow print jobs to leave the print queue.

cupsreject command The command used to force a printer to reject jobs from entering the print queue.

curl command A command that can be used to obtain a Web page from a Web server.

cylinder A series of tracks on a hard disk that are written to simultaneously by the magnetic heads in a hard disk drive.

daemon A Linux system process that provides a certain service.

daemon process A system process that is not associated with a terminal.

data blocks A filesystem allocation unit in which the data that makes up the contents of the file as well as the filename are stored.

database A file that contains data that is organized into tables.

database management system (DBMS) Software that manages databases.

dd command A Linux command that can be used to write image files to a device such as a USB flash memory drive or hard disk.

Debian Package Manager (DPM) A package manager used on Debian and Debian-based Linux distributions.

decision construct A special construct used in a shell script to alter the flow of the program based on the outcome of a command or contents of a variable. Common decision constructs include if, case, &&, and ||.

default gateway The IP address of the router on the network used to send packets to remote networks.

default runlevel The runlevel that is entered when the Linux system is initialized at boot time.

desktop environment The software that works with a window manager to provide a standard GUI environment that uses standard programs and development tools.

developmental kernel A Linux kernel whose minor number is odd and has been recently developed yet not thoroughly tested.

device driver A piece of software containing instructions that the kernel of an operating system uses to control and interact with a specific type of computer hardware.

device file A file used by Linux commands that represents a specific device on the system; these files do not have a data section and use major and minor numbers to reference the proper driver and specific device on the system, respectively.

df (disk free space) command A command that displays disk free space by filesystem.

digital signature Information that has been encrypted using a private key.

Digital Signature Algorithm (DSA) A common asymmetric encryption algorithm that is primarily used for creating digital signatures.

directive A line within a configuration file.

directory A special file on the filesystem used to organize other files into a logical tree structure.

disabled printer A printer that does not send print jobs from the print queue to a printer.

disk imaging software Software used to copy sectors between devices. For example, you can use disk imaging software to copy an ISO image to a disk device sector-by-sector, preserving the image's boot sector. An ISO image copied in this way can be used to start the system BIOS.

disk mirroring A RAID configuration consisting of two identical hard disks to which identical data is written in parallel, thus ensuring fault tolerance. Also known as RAID 1.

disk striping A RAID configuration in which a single file is divided into sections, which are then written to different hard disks concurrently to speed up access time; this type of RAID is not fault tolerant. Also known as RAID 0.

disk striping with parity A RAID configuration that incorporates disk striping for faster file access, as well as parity information to ensure fault tolerance. Also known as RAID 5.

disk-burning software Software that can be used to record data to CD-RW or DVD-RW media.

Display Settings utility A graphical utility that can be used to configure the video card and monitor settings for use by X Windows.

distribution A complete set of operating system software, including the Linux kernel, supporting function libraries and a variety of OSS packages that can be downloaded from the Internet free of charge. These OSS packages are what differentiate the various distributions of Linux.

dmesg command A command that displays hardware-related messages generated by the Linux kernel.

DNS cache file A file that contains the IP addresses of top-level DNS servers.

document root The directory on a Web server that stores Web content for distribution to Web browsers.

documentation The system information that is stored in a log book for future reference.

domain name space (DNS) A hierarchical namespace used for host names.

du (directory usage) command A command that displays directory usage.

dual boot A configuration in which two or more OSs exist on the hard disk of a computer; a boot loader allows the user to choose which OS to load at boot time.

dual booting The process of installing more than one operating system on a computer. The user can then choose the operating system to load at system startup.

dump command A command used to run a utility that creates full and incremental backups.

EasyBCD A free Windows utility that can be used to modify and configure the Windows boot loader so that it can dual boot a Linux OS.

echo command A command used to display or echo output to the terminal screen. It might utilize escape sequences.

edquota command A command used to specify quota limits for users and groups.

egrep command A variant of the grep command, used to search files for patterns using extended regular expressions.

ELILO A boot loader used with computers that support Intel Extensible Firmware Interface (EFI) technology.

Emacs (Editor MACroS) editor A popular and widespread text editor more conducive to word processing than vi. It was originally developed by Richard Stallman.

enabled printer A printer that sends print jobs from the print queue to a printer.

env command A command used to display a list of exported variables present in the current shell, except special variables.

environment files The files used immediately after login to execute commands; they are typically used to load variables into memory.

environment variables The variables that store information commonly accessed by the system or programs executing on the system—together, these variables form the user environment.

escape sequences The character sequences that have special meaning inside the echo command. They are prefixed by the \ character.

Ethernet The most common media access method used in networks today.

executable program A file that can be executed by the Linux operating system to run in memory as a process and perform a useful function.

export command A command used to send variables to subshells.

exporting The process used to describe the sharing of a directory using NFS to other computers.

ext2 A nonjournaling Linux filesystem.

ext3 A journaling Linux filesystem.

ext4 An improved version of the ext3 filesystem with an extended feature set and better performance.

extended multiuser mode Also called runlevel 3; the mode that provides most daemons and a full set of networking daemons.

extended partition A partition on a hard disk that can be further subdivided into components called logical drives.

facility The area of the system from which information is gathered when logging system events.

fault tolerant Term used to describe a device that exhibits a minimum of downtime in the event of a failure.

`fdisk` **command** A command used to create, delete, and manipulate partitions on hard disks.

`fgrep` **command** A variant of the `grep` command that does not allow the use of regular expressions.

field An attribute within a record in a database table.

`file` **command** A Linux command that displays the file type of a specified filename.

file descriptors The numeric labels used to define command input and command output.

file handles The connections that a program makes to files on a filesystem.

File Transfer Protocol (FTP) The most common protocol used to transfer files across networks such as the Internet.

filename The user-friendly identifier given to a file.

filename extension At the end of a filename, a dot followed by a series of identifiers that denotes the file type; the filename extension .txt denotes a text file.

filesystem The organization imposed on a physical storage medium that is used to manage the storage and retrieval of data.

filesystem corruption The errors in a filesystem structure that prevent the retrieval of stored data.

Filesystem Hierarchy Standard (FHS) A standard outlining the location of set files and directories on a Linux system.

`filter` **command** A command that can take from stdin and send to stdout. In other words, a filter is a command that can exist in the middle of a pipe.

`find` **command** The command used to find files on the filesystem using various criteria.

firmware RAID A RAID system controlled by the computer's BIOS.

firstboot wizard A configuration utility that is run at system startup immediately following a Fedora Linux installation.

flavor A specific type of UNIX operating system. For example, Solaris and BSD are two flavors of UNIX.

`foreground (fg)` **command** The command used to run a background process in the foreground.

foreground process A process for which the BASH shell that executed it must wait for its termination.

forking The act of creating a new BASH shell child process from a parent BASH shell process.

formatting The process in which a filesystem is placed on a disk device.

forward lookup A DNS name resolution request whereby a FQDN is resolved to an IP address.

`free` **command** A command used to display memory and swap statistics.

Free Identity, Policy, and Audit (FreeIPA) A set of security software that provides secure authentication across a network using several technologies that work together, including LDAP, Kerberos, NTP, and DNS.

Free Software Foundation (FSF) An organization, started by Richard Stallman, that promotes and encourages the collaboration of software developers worldwide to allow the free sharing of source code and software programs.

freeware Software distributed by the developer at no cost to the user.

frequently asked questions (FAQs) An area on a Web site where answers to commonly posed questions can be found.

`fsck (filesystem check)` **command** A command used to check the integrity of a filesystem and repair damaged files.

`ftp` **command** A command-line FTP client that is found in most operating systems.

full backup An archive of an entire filesystem.

fully qualified domain name (FQDN) A string of words identifying a server on the Internet.

`fuser` **command** A command used to identify any users or processes using a particular file or directory.

gedit editor A common text editor used within GUI environments.

General Electric Comprehensive Operating System (GECOS) The field in the /etc/passwd file that contains a description of the user account.

GNOME Display Manager (gdm) A program that provides a graphical login screen.

GNU An acronym that stands for "GNU's not UNIX."

`GNU C Compiler (gcc)` **command** The command used to compile source code written in the C programming language into binary programs.

GNU General Public License (GPL) A software license ensuring that the source code for any OSS will remain freely available to anyone who wants to examine, build on, or improve upon it.

GNU Image Manipulation Program (GIMP) An open source graphics manipulation program that uses the GTK+ toolkit.

GNU Network Object Model Environment (GNOME) One of the two competing graphical user interface (GUI) environments for Linux.

GNU Object Model Environment (GNOME) The default desktop environment in Fedora Linux; it was created in 1997.

`gpg` **command** A command used to create and manage GPG keys.

GNU Privacy Guard (GPG) An open source asymmetric encryption technology that is primarily used by email programs.

GNU Project A free operating system project started by Richard Stallman.

`GNU zip (gzip)` **command** A command used to compress files using a Lempel-Ziv compression algorithm.

GRand Unified Bootloader (GRUB) A common boot loader used on Linux systems.

graphical user interface (GUI) The component of an operating system that provides a userfriendly interface comprising graphics or icons to represent desired tasks. Users can point and click to execute a command rather than having to know and use proper command-line syntax.

`grep (Global Regular Expression Print)` **command** A program used to search one or more text files for a desired string of characters.

Group Identifier (GID) A unique number given to each group.

group When used in the mode of a certain file or directory, the collection of users who have ownership of that file or directory.

`groupadd` **command** The command used to add a group to the system.

`groupdel` **command** The command used to delete a group from the system.

`groupmod` **command** The command used to modify the name or GID of a group on the system.

`groups` **command** The command that lists group membership for a user.

GRUB root partition The partition containing the second stage of the GRUB boot loader and the /boot/grub/grub.conf file.

`grub-install` **command** The command used to install the GRUB boot loader.

`grub-md5-crypt` **command** The command used to generate an encrypted password for use in the /etc/grub/grub.conf file.

GTK+ toolkit A development toolkit for C programming; it is used in the GNOME desktop and the GNU Image Manipulation Program (GIMP).

GUI environment A GUI core component such as X Windows, combined with a window manager and desktop

environment that provides the look and feel of the GUI. Although functionality might be similar among GUI environments, users might prefer one environment to another due to its ease of use.

GUID Partition Table (GPT) The area of a large hard disk (> 2TB) outside a partition that stores partition information and boot loaders.

`gunzip` **command** The command used to decompress files compressed by the `gzip` command.

hacker A person who explores computer science to gain knowledge. It should not be confused with the term cracker.

hard disk quotas The limits on the number of files, or total storage space on a hard disk drive, available to a user.

hard limit A hard disk quota that the user cannot exceed.

hard link A file joined to other files on the same filesystem that shares the same inode.

Hardware Compatibility List (HCL) A list of hardware components that have been tested and deemed compatible with a given operating system.

hardware platform A particular configuration and grouping of computer hardware, normally centered on and determined by processor type and architecture.

hardware RAID A RAID system controlled by hardware located on a disk controller card within the computer.

hardware The tangible parts of a computer, such as the network boards, video card, hard disk drives, printers, and keyboards.

hashpling The first line in a shell script, which defines the shell that will be used to interpret the commands in the script file.

`head` **command** A Linux command that displays the first set of lines of a text file; by default, the `head` command displays the first 10 lines.

home directory A directory on the filesystem set aside for users to store personal files and information.

host ID The portion of an IP address that denotes the host.

host name A user-friendly name assigned to a computer.

`hostname` **command** A command used to display and change the host name of a computer.

hot fix A solution made by a closed source vendor that fixes a software bug.

HOWTO A task-specific instruction guide to performing any of a wide variety of tasks; freely available from the Linux Documentation Project at http://tldp.org/.

HP-UX A version of UNIX developed by Hewlett-Packard.

`hwclock` **command** A command that can be used to view and modify the system clock within the computer BIOS.

Hypertext Transfer Protocol (HTTP) The protocol used to transfer information over the Internet.

id command The command that lists UIDs for a user and the GIDs for the groups that the same user belongs to.

ifconfig command A command used to display and modify the TCP/IP configuration information for a network interface.

incremental backup An archive of a filesystem that contains only files that were modified since the last archive was created.

info pages A set of local, easy-to-read command syntax documentation available by typing the info command.

infrastructure services Network services that provide network and operating system specific functionality to other computers on the network.

init command The command used to change the OS from one runlevel to another.

initialize (init) daemon The first process started by the Linux kernel; it is responsible for starting and stopping other daemons.

initstate *See* runlevel.

inode The portion of a file that stores information on the file's attributes, access permissions, location, ownership, and file type.

inode table The collection of inodes for all files and directories on a filesystem.

insert mode One of the two modes in vi; it allows the user to insert text into the document but does not allow any other functionality.

insmod command A command used to insert a module into the Linux kernel.

installation log files The files created at installation to record actions that occurred or failed during the installation process.

Integrated Drive Electronics (IDE) *See also* Parallel Advanced Technology Attachment.

interactive mode The mode that file management commands use when a file can be overwritten; the system interacts with a user, asking the user to confirm the action.

Internet Control Message Protocol version 6 (ICMPv6) A protocol used by computers to obtain an IPv6 configuration from a router on the network.

Internet Printing Protocol (IPP) A printing protocol that can be used to send print jobs across a TCP/IP network, such as the Internet, using HTTP or HTTPS.

Internet Protocol (IP) address A series of four 8-bit numbers that represents a computer on a network.

Internet SCSI (iSCSI) A SCSI technology that transfers data via TCP/IP networks.

Internet service provider (ISP) A company that provides Internet access.

Internet Super Daemon (xinetd) A network daemon that is used to start other network daemons on demand.

Intrusion Detection System (IDS) A program that can be used to detect unauthorized access to a Linux system.

iostat (input/output statistics) command A command that displays Input/Output statistics for block devices.

ip command A command that can be used to manipulate the route table.

IP forwarding The act of forwarding TCP/IP packets from one network to another. *See also* Routing.

IP version 4 (IPv4) The most common version of IP used on the Internet. It uses a 32-bit addressing scheme organized into different classes.

IP version 6 (IPv6) A recent version of IP that is used by some hosts on the Internet. It uses a 128-bit addressing scheme.

iptables command The command used to configure a firewall in Fedora Linux.

iSCSI initiator The software and hardware components that can be used to transfer files to and from an iSCSI target.

iSCSI target An external iSCSI storage device that hosts one or more hard disks.

ISO image A file that contains an ISO filesystem.

iterative query A DNS resolution request that was resolved without the use of top-level DNS servers.

jabbering The process by which failing hardware components send large amounts of information to the CPU.

jitter The difference between time measurements from several different NTP servers.

jobs command The command used to see the list of background processes running in the current shell.

journaling A filesystem function that keeps a journal of the information that needs to be written to the hard disk; common Linux journaling filesystems include ext3, ext4, and REISER.

K Desktop Environment (KDE) A desktop environment created by Matthias Ettrich in 1996.

K Window Manager (kwin) The window manager that works under the KDE Desktop Environment.

KDE Display Manager (kdm) A graphical login screen for users that resembles the KDE desktop.

kernel The central, core program of the operating system. The shared commonality of the kernel is what defines Linux; the differing OSS applications that can interact with the common kernel are what differentiate Linux distributions.

key A unique piece of information that is used within an encryption algorithm.

Kickstart Configurator A graphical utility that can be used to create a kickstart file.

kickstart file A file that can be specified at the beginning of a Fedora Linux installation to automate the installation process.

kill command The command used to kill or terminate a process.

kill signal The type of signal sent to a process by the `kill` command; different kill signals affect processes in different ways.

killall command The command that kills all instances of a process by command name.

Knoppix Linux A CD/DVD-based Linux distribution.

KPackageKit utility A program that can be used to install, update, and remove RPM packages within a desktop environment.

ldconfig command The command that updates the /etc/ld. so.conf and /etc/ld.so.cache files.

ldd command The command used to display the shared libraries used by a certain program.

less command A Linux command used to display a text file page-by-page on the terminal screen; users can then use the cursor keys to navigate the file.

Lightweight Directory Access Protocol (LDAP) A protocol that is used by services to query directory databases for purposes of authentication.

lilo command The command used to reinstall the LILO boot loader based on the configuration information in /etc/lilo.conf.

Line Printer Daemon (LPD) A printing system typically used on legacy Linux computers.

link local The portion of an IPv6 address that refers to a unique computer. It is analogous to the host portion of an IPv4 address.

linked file The files that represent the same data as other files.

Linus Torvalds A Finnish graduate student who coded and created the first version of Linux and subsequently distributed it under the GNU Public License.

Linux A software operating system originated by Linus Torvalds. The common core, or kernel, continues to evolve and be revised. Differing OSS bundled with the Linux kernel is what defines the wide variety of distributions now available.

Linux Documentation Project (LDP) A large collection of Linux resources, information, and help files supplied free of charge and maintained by the Linux community.

Linux Loader (LILO) A common boot loader used on Linux systems.

Linux User Group (LUG) An open forum of Linux users who discuss and assist each other in using and modifying the Linux operating system and the OSS run on it. There are LUGs worldwide.

ll command An alias for the `ls -l` command; it gives a long file listing.

ln (link) command The command used to create hard and symbolic links.

local area networks (LANs) The networks in which the computers are all in close physical proximity.

locate command The command used to locate files from a file database.

lock an account To make an account temporarily unusable by altering the password information for it stored on the system.

log file A file that contains past system events.

logger command A command that can be used to write system log events via the System Log Daemon (rsyslogd).

logical drives The smaller partitions contained within an extended partition on a hard disk.

Logical Unit Number (LUN) A unique identifier for each device attached to any given node in a SCSI chain.

logical volume (LV) A volume that is managed by the LVM and composed of free space within a VG.

Logical Volume Manager (LVM) A set of software components within Linux that can be used to manage the storage of information across several different hard disks on a Linux system.

logrotate command The command used to rotate log files; it typically uses the configuration information stored in /etc/logrotate.conf.

loop construct A special construct used in a shell script to execute commands repetitively. Common loop constructs include for and while.

lp command The command used to create print jobs in the print queue in the CUPS printing system.

lpadmin command The command used to perform printer administration in the CUPS printing system.

lpc command The command used to view the status of and control printers in the LPD printing system.

lpq command The command used to view the contents of print queues in the LPD printing system.

lpr command The command used to create print jobs in the print queue in the LPD printing system.

lprm command The command used to remove print jobs from the print queue in the LPD printing system.

lpstat command The command used to view the contents of print queues and printer information in the CUPS printing system.

ls command A Linux command used to list the files in a given directory.

lsmod command A command used to list the modules that are currently used by the Linux kernel.

lsof (list open files) command The command that lists the files that are currently being viewed or modified by software programs and users.

lspci command The command that lists the hardware devices that are currently attached to the PCI bus on the system.

lsusb command The command that lists the USB devices that are currently plugged into the system.

lvcreate command A command used to create LVM logical volumes.

lvdisplay command A command used to view LVM logical volumes.

lvextend command A command used to add additional space from volume groups to existing LVM logical volumes.

lvscan command A command used to view LVM logical volumes.

mail command A common e-mail client on UNIX, Linux, and Macintosh systems.

mail delivery agent (MDA) The service that downloads e-mail from a mail transfer agent.

mail transfer agent (MTA) An e-mail server.

mail user agent (MUA) A program that allows e-mail to be read by a user.

major number For a Linux kernel version, the major number is the number preceding the first dot in the number. For a device file, the major number identifies the hardware device type within the Linux kernel.

man pages *See* manual pages.

manual pages The most common set of local command syntax documentation, available by typing the man command. Also known as man pages.

Master Boot Record (MBR) The area of a typical hard disk (< 2TB) outside a partition that stores partition information and boot loaders.

master DNS server The DNS server that contains a read/write copy of the zone. *See also* Primary DNS server.

media access method A system that defines how computers on a network share access to the physical medium.

memtest86 A common RAM-checking utility.

metacharacters The key combinations that have special meaning in the Linux operating system.

Metacity Window Manager The default window manager for the GNOME Desktop Environment in Fedora 13.

MINIX Mini-UNIX created by Andrew Tannenbaum. Instructions on how to code the kernel for this version of the UNIX operating system were publicly available. Using this as a starting point, Linus Torvalds improved this version of UNIX for the Intel platform and created the first version of Linux.

minor number For a Linux kernel version, the minor number is the number following the first dot in the number. An odd minor number in a Linux kernel version denotes a kernel that is currently in development. For a device file, the minor number identifies the hardware device driver used within the Linux kernel.

mkdir (make directory) command The command used to create directories.

mkfs (make filesystem) command A command used to format or create filesystems.

mkisofs command A command used to create an ISO image from one or more files on the filesystem.

mknod command A command used to re-create a device file, provided the major number, minor number, and type (character or block) are known.

mkswap command A command used to prepare newly created swap partitions for use by the Linux system.

mode The part of the inode that stores information on access permissions.

modprobe command A command used to insert a module into the Linux kernel.

monitoring The process by which system areas are observed for problems or irregularities.

more command A Linux command used to display a text file page-by-page and line-by-line on the terminal screen.

mount command A command used to mount filesystems on devices to mount point directories.

mount point The directory in a file structure to which something is mounted.

mounting A process used to associate a device with a directory in the logical directory tree such that users can store data on that device.

mouse-test command A command used to detect and configure your mouse.

mpstat (multiple processor statistics) command A command that displays CPU statistics.

multicast The TCP/IP communication destined for a certain group of computers.

multihomed hosts The computers that have more than one network interface.

Multiplexed Information and Computing Service (MULTICS) A prototype time-sharing operating system that was developed in the late-1960s by AT&T Bell Laboratories.

multitasking A type of operating system that has the capability to manage multiple tasks simultaneously.

multiuser A type of operating system that has the capability to provide access to multiple users simultaneously.

multiuser mode Also called runlevel 2; the mode that provides most daemons and a partial set of networking daemons.

mv (move) command The command used to move/rename files and directories.

named pipe file A temporary connection that sends information from one command or process in memory to another; it can also be represented by a file on the filesystem.

nano editor A user-friendly terminal text editor that uses Ctrl key combinations to perform basic functions.

NetBIOS A protocol used by Windows computers that adds a unique 15-character name to file and printer sharing traffic.

netfilter/iptables The Linux kernel components and related software subsystem that provide firewall and NAT capability on modern Linux systems.

network Two or more computers joined together via network media and able to exchange information.

Network Address Translation (NAT) A technology used on routers that allows computers on a network to obtain Internet resources via a single network interface on the router itself.

Network Configuration tool A graphical utility in Fedora Linux that can be used to configure network settings for the NICs on the system.

Network File System (NFS) A set of software components that can be used to share files natively between UNIX, Linux- and Macintosh computers on a network.

network ID The portion of an IP address that denotes the network.

Network Information Service (NIS) A set of software components that can be used to standardize the configuration files across several different Linux and UNIX computers.

Network Manager A daemon that allows multiple network interfaces to be easily configured by users on the system.

network service A process that responds to network requests.

Network Time Protocol (NTP) A protocol that is used to synchronize the time on a computer from across a network such as the Internet.

newaliases command A command that can be used to rebuild the e-mail alias database based on the entries within the /etc/aliases file.

newgrp command The command used to change temporarily the primary group of a user.

newsgroup An Internet protocol service accessed via an application program called a newsreader. This service allows access to postings (e-mails in a central place accessible by all newsgroup users) normally organized along specific themes. Users with questions on specific topics can post messages, which can be answered by other users.

nice command The command used to change the priority of a process as it is started.

nice value The value that indirectly represents the priority of a process; the higher the value, the lower the priority.

NIS client A computer in an NIS domain that receives its configuration from an NIS master server or NIS slave server.

NIS domain A group of computers that share the same NIS configuration.

NIS map A system configuration that is shared by the computers within an NIS domain.

NIS master server The computer in an NIS domain that contains the master copy of all NIS maps.

NIS slave server A computer in an NIS domain that receives a read-only copy of all NIS maps from an NIS master server.

nmap (network mapper) command A command that can be used to scan ports on network computers.

nmblookup command A command that can test NetBIOS name resolution on a Linux system.

nohup command A command that prevents other commands from exiting when the parent process is killed.

ntpdate command A command that can view the current system time as well as synchronize the system time with an NTP server.

ntpq command A command that can query the state of an NTP server or client.

ntsysv A utility that can be used to alter the daemons that are started in each runlevel.

octet A portion of an IP address that represents eight binary bits.

od command A Linux command used to display the contents of a file in octal format.

offset The difference in time between two computers that use the NTP protocol.

Open Source Software (OSS) The programs distributed and licensed so that the source code making up the program is freely available to anyone who wants to examine, utilize, or improve upon it.

operating system (OS) The software used to control and directly interact with the computer hardware components.

options The specific letters that start with a dash "-" or two and appear after the command name to alter the way the command works.

Orca A Linux software program that provides several assistive technologies to desktop environment users.

other When used in the mode of a certain file or directory, refers to all users on the Linux system.

overclocked Term used to describe a CPU that runs faster than the clock speed for which it has been rated.

owner The user whose name appears in a long listing of a file or directory and who has the ability to change permissions on that file or directory.

package dependencies A list of packages that are prerequisite to the current package being installed on the system.

package manager A system that defines a standard package format and can be used to install, query, and remove packages.

packets The packages of data formatted by a network protocol.

Parallel Advanced Technology Attachment (PATA) A legacy hard disk technology that uses ribbon cables to typically attach up to four hard disk devices to a single computer.

Parallel SCSI The traditional SCSI technology that transfers data across parallel cables.

parent directory The directory that is one level closer to the root directory in the directory tree relative to your current directory.

parent process A process that has started other processes (child processes).

parent process ID (PPID) The PID of the parent process that created the current process.

partition A physical division of a hard disk drive.

passwd command The command used to modify the password associated with a user account.

PATH variable A variable that stores a list of directories that will be searched in order when commands are executed without an absolute or relative pathname.

permissions A list that identifies who can access a file or folder and their level of access.

physical extent (PE) size The block size used by the LVM when storing data on a volume group.

physical volume (PV) A hard disk partition that is used by the LVM.

ping (Packet Internet Groper) command A command used to check TCP/IP connectivity on a network.

pipe A string of commands connected by | shell metacharacters.

Plug and Play (PnP) A technology that allows users to add hardware to a computer without having to configure the hardware to work with the system.

Pluggable Authentication Modules (PAM) The component that handles authentication requests by daemons on a Linux system.

port A number that uniquely identifies a network service.

Postfix A common e-mail server daemon used on Linux systems that is easy to configure.

PostgreSQL A common SQL server used on Linux computers.

PostgreSQL utility The program used to perform most database management on a

power on-self test (POST) An initial series of tests run when a computer is powered on to ensure that hardware components are functional.

primary DNS server The DNS server that contains a read/write copy of the zone.

primary group The group that is specified for a user in the /etc/passwd file and that is specified as group owner for all files created by a user.

primary partitions The separate divisions into which a hard disk can be divided (up to four are allowed per hard disk).

print job The information sent to a printer for printing.

print job ID A unique numeric identifier used to mark and distinguish each print job.

print queue A directory on the filesystem that holds print jobs that are waiting to be printed.

printer class A template that can be used to apply settings to printers on a CUPS system.

Printer Configuration tool A graphical utility used to configure printers on the system.

printing The process by which print jobs are sent from a print queue to a printer.

priority The importance of system information when logging system events.

private key An asymmetric encryption key that is used to decrypt data and create digital signatures.

proactive maintenance The measures taken to reduce future system problems.

process A program loaded into memory and running on the processor, performing a specific task.

process ID (PID) A unique identifier assigned to every process as it begins.

process priority A number assigned to a process, used to determine how many time slices on the processor that process will receive; the higher the number, the lower the priority.

process state The current state of the process on the processor; most processes are in the sleeping or running state.

production kernel A Linux kernel whose minor number (the number after the dot in the version number) is even and which is, therefore, deemed stable for use after widespread testing.

program A structured set of commands stored in an executable file on a filesystem. A program can be executed to create a process.

programming language The syntax used for developing a program. Different programming languages use different syntaxes.

protocol A set of rules of communication used between computers on a network.

proxy server A server or hardware device that requests Internet resources on behalf of other computers.

ps command The command used to obtain information about processes currently running on the system.

pstree command A command that displays processes according to their lineage, starting from the init daemon.

public key An asymmetric encryption key that is used to encrypt data and decrypt digital signatures.

pvcreate command A command used to create LVM physical volumes.

pvdisplay command A command used to view LVM physical volumes.

pvscan command A command used to view LVM physical volumes.

pwconv command The command used to enable the use of the /etc/shadow file.

pwd (print working directory) command A Linux command used to display the current directory in the directory tree.

pwunconv command The command used to disable the use of the /etc/shadow file.

Qt toolkit The software toolkit used with the K Desktop Environment.

queuing *See* spooling.

quota command A command used to view disk quotas imposed on a user.

quotaoff command A command used to deactivate disk quotas.

quotaon command A command used to activate disk quotas.

quotas The limits that can be imposed on users and groups for filesystem usage.

r commands *See* remote commands.

reactive maintenance The measures taken when system problems arise.

read command A command used to read stdin from a user into a variable.

record A line within a database table that represents a particular object.

recursive A term referring to itself and its own contents; a recursive search includes all subdirectories in a directory and their contents.

recursive query A DNS resolution request that was resolved with the use of top-level DNS servers.

Red Hat One of the most popular and prevalent distributions of Linux in North America, distributed and supported by Red Hat Inc. Fedora is a Red Hat-based Linux distribution.

Red Hat Package Manager (RPM) The most commonly used package manager for Linux.

redirection The process of changing the default locations of stdin, stdout, and stderr.

redundant array of inexpensive disks (RAID) A type of storage that can be used to combine hard disks together for performance and/or fault tolerance.

regexp *See* regular expressions.

regular expressions The special metacharacters used to match patterns of text within text files; they are commonly used by text tool commands, including grep.

REISER A journaling filesystem used in Linux.

rejecting printer A printer that does not accept print jobs into the print queue.

relational database A database that contains multiple tables that are linked by common fields.

relative pathname The pathname of a target directory relative to your current directory in the tree.

remote commands A set of commands (rsh, rlogin, and rcp) that can be used to perform remote administration on Linux and UNIX systems.

renice command The command used to alter the nice value of a process currently running on the system.

repquota command A command used to produce a report on quotas for a particular filesystem.

resource records The records within a zone on a DNS server that provide name resolution for individual computers.

restore command The command used to extract archives created with the dump command.

reverse lookup A DNS name resolution request whereby an IP address is resolved to a FQDN.

revision number The number after the second dot in the version number of a Linux kernel, which identifies the certain release number of a kernel.

Rivest Shamir Adleman (RSA) A common asymmetric encryption algorithm.

rm (remove) command The command used to remove files and directories.

rmdir (remove directory) command The command used to remove empty directories.

rmmod command A command used to remove a module from the Linux kernel.

rogue process A process that has become faulty in some way and continues to consume far more system resources than it should.

root filesystem The filesystem that contains most files that make up the operating system; it should have enough free space to prevent errors and slow performance.

route command A command that can be used to manipulate the route table.

route table A table of information used to indicate which networks are connected to network interfaces.

routers The devices capable of transferring packets from one network to another.

routing The act of forwarding data packets from one network to another.

rpm command The command used to install, query, and remove RPM packages.

rules The components of a firewall that match specific network traffic that is to be allowed or dropped.

runlevel A term that defines a certain type and number of daemons on a Linux system.

runlevel command The command used to display the current and most recent (previous) runlevel.

runtime configuration (rc) scripts Shell scripts that are used by the init daemon to initialize the system at boot time as well as start and stop daemons when entering a particular runlevel.

sar (system activity reporter) command The command that displays various system statistics.

scalability The capability of computers to increase workload as the number of processors increases.

SCSI ID A number that uniquely identifies and prioritizes devices attached to a SCSI controller.

search engine An Internet Web site, such as www.google. com, where you simply enter a phrase representing your search item and receive a list of Web sites that contain relevant material.

secondary DNS server A DNS server that contains a read-only copy of the zone. *See also* Slave DNS server.

sector The smallest unit of data storage on a hard disk; sectors are arranged into concentric circles called tracks and can be grouped into blocks for use by the system.

Secure Shell (SSH) A technology that can be used to run remote applications on a Linux computer; it encrypts all client-server traffic.

Security Enhanced Linux (SELinux) A set of Linux kernel components and related software packages that prevent malicious software from executing on a Linux system.

sed command A filter command used to search for and manipulate text.

segmentation fault An error that software encounters when it cannot locate the information needed to complete its task.

Sendmail The default e-mail server daemon used in Fedora 13.

Serial Advanced Technology Attachment (SATA) A hard disk technology that allows for fast data transfer along a serial cable. It is commonly used in newer workstation and serverclass computers.

Serial Attached SCSI (SAS) A SCSI technology that transfers information in serial mode rather than the traditional parallel mode.

server A computer configured to allow other computers to connect to it from across a network.

server closet A secured room that stores servers within an organization.

Server Message Blocks (SMB) The protocol that Windows computers use to format file and printer sharing traffic on TCP/IP networks.

server services The services that are made available for other computers across a network.

service command A command that can be used to manually start, stop, and restart daemons.

Service Configuration utility A graphical utility that can be used to start, stop, and restart daemons as well as configure the runlevels that they are automatically started and stopped in.

sestatus command The command that displays the current status and functionality of the SELinux subsystem.

set command A command used to view all variables in the shell, except special variables.

shareware The programs developed and provided at minimal cost to the end user. These programs are initially free but require payment after a period of time or a certain amount of usage.

shell A user interface that accepts input from the user and passes the input to the kernel for processing.

shell scripts The text files that contain a list of commands or constructs for the shell to execute in order.

single user mode Also called runlevel 1; the mode that provides a single terminal and a limited set of services.

skeleton directory A directory that contains files that are copied to all new users' home directories upon creation; the default skeleton directory on Linux systems is /etc/skel.

slave DNS server A DNS server that contains a read-only copy of the zone.

Small Computer Systems Interface (SCSI) A high-performance hard disk technology that is commonly used in server-class computers.

smbclient command A command that can be used to connect to a remote Windows or Samba server and transfer files.

smbpasswd command A command used to generate a Samba password for a user.

socket file A named pipe connecting processes on two different computers; it can also be represented by a file on the filesystem.

soft limit A hard disk quota that the user can exceed for a certain period of time.

software The programs stored on a storage device in a computer that provide a certain function when executed.

software mirrors Software repositories that host the same RPM or DPM packages as other software repositories for fault tolerance and load balancing of download requests.

software RAID A RAID system that is controlled by software running within the operating system.

software repositories Servers on the Internet that host RPM or DPM packages for download.

Solaris A version of UNIX developed by Sun Microsystems from AT&T source code.

Solid-State Drives (SSDs) Hard disk devices that use flash memory chips for storage instead of electromagnetic platters.

sort command A command used to sort lines in a file.

source code The sets of organized instructions on how to function and perform tasks that define or constitute a program.

source file/directory The portion of a command that refers to the file or directory from which information is taken.

spanning A type of RAID level 0 that allows two or more devices to be represented as a single large volume.

special device file A file used to identify hardware devices such as hard disks and serial ports.

spooling The process of accepting a print job into a print queue.

SQL server A server service that provides other programs and computers the ability to access a database.

SSH agent A software program that can be used to automatically authenticate users using their private key.

ssh command A command that connects to a remote SSH daemon to perform remote administration.

SSH identity A unique configuration for a user account that is associated with user-specific SSH keys.

ssh-add command The command that users can use to add an SSH identity to their user account.

stand-alone daemons The daemons that configure themselves at boot time without assistance from the Internet Super Daemon.

standard error (stderr) A file descriptor that represents any error messages generated by a command.

standard input (stdin) A file descriptor that represents information input to a command during execution.

standard output (stdout) A file descriptor that represents the desired output from a command.

stateful packet filter A packet filter that applies rules to related packets within the same network session.

Storage Area Network (SAN) A group of computers that access the same storage device across a fast network.

strata The levels used within an NTP hierarchy that describe the relative position of a server to an original time source such as an atomic clock.

strings command A Linux command used to search for and display text characters in a binary file.

Structured Query Language (SQL) A language used by database servers to query, add, and modify the data within a database.

su (switch user) command A command that can be used to switch your current user account to another.

subdirectory A directory that resides within another directory in the directory tree.

subnet mask A series of four 8-bit numbers that determines the network and host portions of an IP address.

subnetting The process in which a single large network is subdivided into several smaller networks to control traffic flow.

subshell A shell started by the current shell.

sudo command A command that is used to perform commands as another user via entries in the /etc/sudoers file.

superblock The portion of a filesystem that stores critical information, such as the inode table and block size.

SuSE One of the most popular and prevalent distributions of Linux in Europe.

swap memory *See also* virtual memory.

swapoff command A command used to disable a partition for use as virtual memory on the Linux system.

swapon command A command used to enable a partition for use as virtual memory on the Linux system.

symbolic link A pointer to another file on the same or another filesystem; commonly referred to as a shortcut.

syncing The process of writing data to the hard disk drive that was stored in RAM.

system backup The process whereby files are copied to an archive.

System Log Daemon (rsyslogd) The daemon that logs system events to various log files via information stored in /etc/rsyslog.conf.

System Rescue A feature that allows you to boot a small Linux system from DVD to repair a Linux system that resides on the hard disk.

system service The additional functionality provided by a program that has been incorporated into and started as part of the operating system.

System Statistics (sysstat) package A software package that contains common performance monitoring utilities, such as mpstat, iostat, and sar.

system-config-display command A command used to configure a video adapter card and monitor for use by X Windows.

system-config-keyboard command A command used to configure a keyboard for use by X Windows.

Tab-completion feature A feature of the BASH shell that fills in the remaining characters of a unique filename or directory name when the user presses Tab.

table A database structure that organizes data using records and fields.

tac command A Linux command that displays a file on the screen, beginning with the last line of the file and ending with the first line of the file.

tail command A Linux command used to display lines of text at the end of a file; by default, the tail command displays the last 10 lines of the file.

tape archive (tar) command The most common command for creating archives.

tarball A gzip-compressed tar archive.

target file/directory The portion of a command that refers to the file or directory to which information is directed.

target ID *See also* SCSI ID.

TCP wrapper A program that can be used to run a network daemon with additional security via the /etc/hosts.allow and /etc/hosts.deny files.

tee command A command used to take from stdin and send to both stdout and a specified file.

telinit command An alias to the init command.

telnet command A command that can be used to run remote applications on a Linux computer.

terminal The channel that allows a certain user to log in and communicate with the kernel via a user interface.

terminator A device used to terminate an electrical conduction medium to absorb the transmitted signal and prevent signal bounce.

test statement A statement used to test a certain condition and generate a True/False value.

text file A file that stores information in a readable text format.

text tools The programs that allow for the creation, modification, and searching of text files.

time slice The amount of time a process is given on a CPU in a multiprocessing operating system.

Time-To-Live (TTL) The amount of time that a computer is allowed to cache name resolution information obtained from a DNS server.

Token Ring A popular media access method.

`top` **command** The command used to give real-time information about the most active processes on the system; it can also be used to renice or kill processes.

total cost of ownership (TCO) The full sum of all accumulated costs, over and above the simple purchase price of utilizing a product. Includes training, maintenance, additional hardware, and downtime.

`touch` **command** The command used to create new files. It was originally used to update the time stamp on a file.

`tr` **command** A command used to transform or change characters received from stdin.

`traceroute` **command** A command used to trace the path a packet takes through routers to a destination host.

track The area on a hard disk that forms a concentric circle of sectors.

trapping The process of ignoring a kill signal.

tripwire A common IDS for Linux that monitors files and directories.

troubleshooting procedures The tasks performed when solving system problems.

trusted access A configuration in which computers are allowed to access a given computer without having to provide a password first.

`tune2fs` **command** A command used to modify ext2 and ext3 filesystem parameters.

tunneling The process of embedding network packets within other network packets.

`tzselect` **command** A command that can be used to change the time zone of a Linux computer.

`ulimit` **command** The command used to modify process limit parameters in the current shell.

umask A special variable used to alter the permissions on all new files and directories by taking away select default file and directory permissions.

`umask` **command** The command used to view and change the umask variable.

`umount` **command** A command used to break the association between a device and a directory in the logical directory tree.

uncompress **command** The command used to decompress files compressed by the `compress` command.

unicast The TCP/IP communication destined for a single computer.

Uniform Resource Identifier (URI) A naming convention that identifies hardware and software components using a two-part name that consists of a type followed by an identifier.

UNIX The first true multitasking, multiuser operating system, developed by Ken Thompson and Dennis Ritchie, from which Linux was originated.

upstart init system The next-generation init daemon and related files used by modern Linux distributions such as Fedora 13.

user When used in the mode of a certain file or directory, the owner of that file or directory.

user account The information regarding a user that is stored in a system database (/etc/passwd and /etc/shadow), which can be used to log in to the system and gain access to system resources.

User Datagram Protocol/Internet Protocol (UDP/IP) A faster but unreliable version of TCP/IP.

User Identifier (UID) A unique number assigned to each user account.

user interface The interface the user sees and uses to interact with the operating system and application programs.

user process A process begun by a user and which runs on a terminal.

`useradd` **command** The command used to add a user account to the system.

user-defined variables The variables that are created by the user and are not used by the system. These variables are typically exported to subshells.

`userdel` **command** The command used to remove a user account from the system.

`usermod` **command** The command used to modify the properties of a user account on the system.

variable An area of memory used to store information. Variables are created from entries in environment files when the shell is first created after login, and are destroyed when the shell is destroyed upon logout.

variable identifier The name of a variable.

Very Secure FTP daemon (vsftpd) The default FTP server program used in modern Linux distributions, including Fedora 13.

VFAT (Virtual File Allocation Table) A nonjournaling filesystem that might be used in Linux.

vgcreate command A command used to create LVM volume groups.

vgdisplay command A command used to view LVM volume groups.

vgextend command A command used to add additional physical volumes to an LVM volume group.

vgscan command A command used to view LVM volume groups.

vi editor A powerful command-line text editor available on most UNIX and Linux systems.

virtual memory An area on a hard disk, known as a swap partition, that can be used to store information that normally resides in physical memory (RAM), if the physical memory is being used excessively.

virtualization software Software that can be used to run multiple OSs simultaneously on the same computer.

vmlinuz-<kernel version> The Linux kernel file.

vmstat command The command used to display memory, CPU, and swap statistics.

vncpasswd command A command used to set a VNC password for a user.

vncviewer command A client utility used to connect to a remote VNC server.

volume group (VG) A group of physical volumes that are used by the LVM.

Web page hit A single HTTP request that is sent from a Web browser to a Web server.

well-known ports Of the 65,535 possible ports, the ports from 0 to 1024 used by common networking services.

which command The command used to locate files that exist within directories listed in the PATH variable.

whois command A command used to obtain information about the organization that maintains a DNS domain.

wide area networks (WANs) The networks in which computers are separated geographically by large distances.

wildcard metacharacters The metacharacters used to match certain characters in a file or directory name; they are often used to specify multiple files.

Winbind A set of software components that allows Linux computers to authenticate against a Microsoft Active Directory database.

window manager The GUI component that is responsible for determining the appearance of the windows drawn on the screen by X Windows.

workstation A computer used to connect to services on a server.

workstation services The services that are used to access shared resources on a network server.

X client The component of X Windows that requests graphics to be drawn from the X server and displays them on the terminal screen.

X Display Manager (xdm) A graphical login screen.

X server The component of X Windows that draws graphics to windows on the terminal screen.

X Windows The core component of the GUI in Linux.

X.Org A common implementation of X Windows used in Linux distributions.

XFree86 A common implementation of X Windows used in Linux distributions.

xvidtune A program used to fine-tune the vsync and hsync video card settings for use in X Windows.

yum (Yellowdog Updater Modified) command A program used to install and upgrade software packages.

zcat command A command used to view the contents of an archive created with compress or gzip to SO.

zless command A command used to view the contents of an archive created with compress or gzip to SO in a page-by-page fashion.

zmore command A command used to view the contents of an archive created with compress or gzip to SO in a page-by-page fashion.

zombie process A process that has finished executing, but whose parent has not yet released its PID; the zombie retains a spot in the kernel's process table.

zone A portion of the Domain Name Space that is administered by one or more DNS servers.

zone transfer The process of copying resource records for a zone from a master to a slave DNS server.

Index